BOLLINGEN SERIES LXXXIX

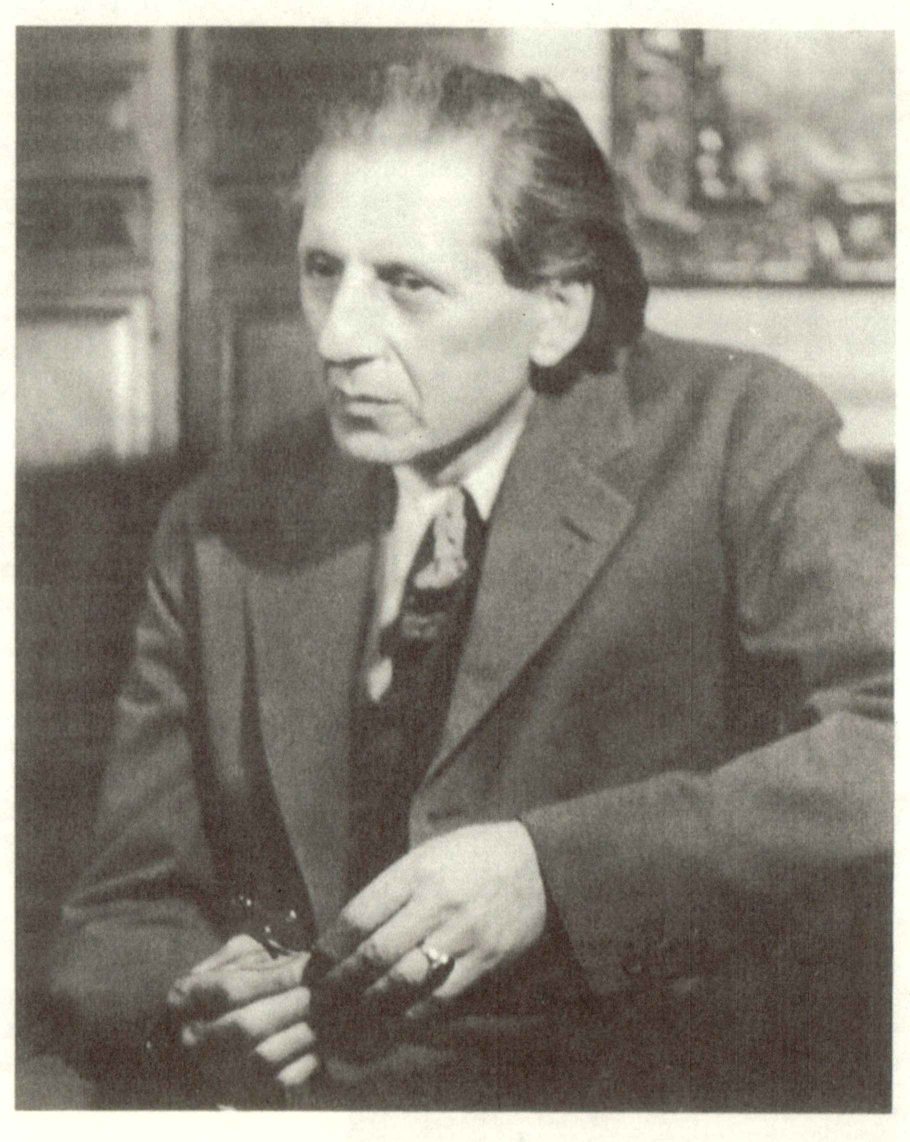

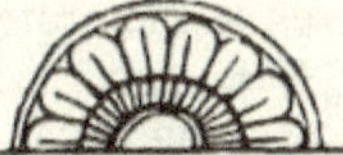

Coomaraswamy

2: SELECTED PAPERS

METAPHYSICS

EDITED BY

Roger Lipsey

BOLLINGEN SERIES LXXXIX

PRINCETON UNIVERSITY PRESS

Princeton and Oxford

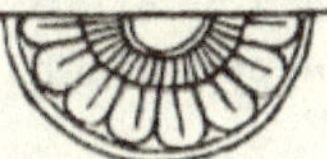

Published by Princeton University Press
41 William Street, Princeton, New Jersey 08540
99 Banbury Road, Oxford OX2 6JX

press.princeton.edu

GPSR Authorized Representative: Easy Access System Europe - Mustamäe tee 50, 10621 Tallinn, Estonia, gpsr.requests@easproject.com

First published in 1977
New cloth, paperback, and e-book Bollingen Recollections editions, 2026

Cloth ISBN 9780691277523
Paperback ISBN 9780691277530
ISBN (e-book) 9780691277516

This was previously published as part of a three-volume work that was eighty-ninth in a series sponsored by Bollingen Foundation

The Library of Congress has cataloged a prior edition of this book as follows:

Coomaraswamy, Ananda Kentish, 1877–1947.
Coomaraswamy.

(Bollingen series; 89)
Includes index.
CONTENTS: V.1. Selected papers, traditional art, and symbolism.—V.2. Selected papers, metaphysics.—V.3. His life and work.

I. Art—Addresses, essays, lectures. I. Lipsey, Roger, 1942– II. Series.
N7445.2.C68 1977 700'.8 76–4II58
ISBN 0-691-09932-4 (V. 2)

Frontispiece photograph by Doña Luisa Coomaraswamy
This book has been composed in Linotype Granjon

Editor's Note

The fifty-six essays in these volumes have been chosen from among many hundred.[1] Without exception, they were written in the period 1932–1947, corresponding to Coomaraswamy's tenure as a Research Fellow at the Museum of Fine Arts, Boston, a position that gave him time for the speculation and scriptural research to which he was particularly drawn in later years. These years were indisputably Coomaraswamy's high period, by which he must and would wish to be judged; his correspondence and conversation corroborate this point. Articles dealing with specific works of art have in general been excluded from these volumes because, although Coomaraswamy continued in this period to write detailed accounts of museum objects, his more characteristic work lay elsewhere. To the best of my knowledge, all the essays have been out of print for many years or were never previously published. After a gap of more than twenty-five years, it is a privilege to present the series of essays at the end of Volume 2 which, although unpublished in Coomaraswamy's lifetime, bear the stamp of finished work. Finally, regarding the selection, it must be mentioned that these volumes do not exhaust the reserve of essays of special merit.

Coomaraswamy's addenda to the essays have been a matter of interest to scholars and friends. He kept desk copies of his published works and added notes to them over the years, doubtless with a view to an edition of collected writings enriched by retrospective insight. After his death in the late summer of 1947, his widow, Doña Luisa (who had served for many years as his daily assistant), determined to incorporate these addenda into the essays. Inasmuch as her husband had already established a working relationship with Bollingen Foundation—he had, in particular, aided Joseph Campbell in the preparation of several posthumous

[1] A bibliography of Coomaraswamy's writings in the period 1900–1942 is published in *Ars Islamica* IX (1942). Currently on press, *A Working Bibliography of Ananda K. Coomaraswamy*, ed. R. P. Coomaraswamy (London: Books From India, Ltd.), is considerably more complete and includes data on late and posthumous publications. Inasmuch as Mr. James Crouch (Melbourne, Australia) has well underway an exhaustive new bibliography of Coomaraswamy's writings, we have decided against including a nominally complete bibliography in the *Selected Papers*. The first installment of Mr. Crouch's work has already appeared: "Ananda Coomaraswamy in Ceylon: A Bibliography," *The Ceylon Journal of Social and Historical Sciences*, N. S. III, No. 2 (1973), 54–66.

publications of the great Indologist Heinrich Zimmer—Mrs. Coomaraswamy successfully applied for a Bollingen Fellowship to carry on this work. For many years, with the help of research assistants recruited from the Harvard University community, near which she lived, she transcribed and incorporated the addenda, meticulously verified references, and filled out bibliographical data where necessary. In due course the editors of Bollingen Series made a place in the program for a publication of selected writings.

Mrs. Coomaraswamy's death in 1971 left the project still incomplete and requiring redirection. Her patient work had brought many treasures to light from the mine of the addenda, but the time had come for refining and selection, a task which devotion to her late husband rendered unpleasant and perhaps impossible, rather as surgeons refuse to operate upon members of their own family. In reformulating the editorial task, I found it appropriate to include no addenda other than those which are genuinely finished paragraphs or clear references; with regret, I eschewed a great many addenda that cannot be taken to be more than raw material for revisions, tending to encumber the essays like barnacles rather than speed them on their way. This policy makes the essays less rich in addenda than was expected by scholars and friends close to the project. With few exceptions, addenda have been placed in footnotes, and in all cases they have been enclosed in brackets [ ] to distinguish them from the text as Coomaraswamy published it. (Editorial notes are also given in brackets, with the designation ED.)

A list of abbreviations, short titles, and editions customarily used by Coomaraswamy is included in the front matter of each volume; readers will find this list indispensable at first but should gradually discover, as did Coomaraswamy, that the abbreviations are convenient and easily recalled. Coomaraswamy's own writings are cited by title and date; further information is available in a short list of cited works at the front of each volume. Punctuation and spelling throughout the papers have been altered where necessary for the sake of uniformity.

While preparing these papers for publication, editor and copy-editors alike have found occasional errors in the enormous mass of references made by Coomaraswamy to literary and scriptural tradition. Such errors as have escaped us will generally do no more harm to the reader than to lead him, for example, to a paragraph in Plato's writings immediately adjacent to the passage that Coomaraswamy wished to cite. Coomaraswamy also, on occasion, refined the translation of passages in standard sources such as the Loeb Classical Library, but neglected to notify the reader of his interventions. Furthermore, he worked from memory more often than one might imagine. Called to the dock on this issue of accuracy by his friend Walter Shewring, Coomaraswamy replied in a letter:

> I am more than appreciative of your corrections. I can only say I am conscious of fault in these matters. It is no excuse to say that checking references and citations is to me a wearisome task. I am sometimes oppressed by the amount of work to be done, and try to do too much too fast. . . . In certain cases I have not been able to see proofs. . . .
>
> One word about the errors. I would like to avoid them altogether, of course. But one cannot take part in the struggle for truth without getting hurt. There is a kind of "perfectionism" which leads some scholars to publish nothing, because they know that nothing can be perfect. I don't respect this. Nor do I care for any aspersions that may reflect upon me personally. It is only "for the good of the work to be done" that one must be as careful as possible to protect oneself. . . . I am so occupied with the task that I rarely have leisure to enjoy a moment of personal realisation. It is a sort of feeling that the harvest is ripe and the time is short. However, I am well aware that all *haste* is none the less an error. I expect to improve.[2]

Recognizing the existence of this problem from the very beginning of my work, and reflecting upon the example of Doña Luisa Coomaraswamy, who worked perhaps too many years to perfect in the letter texts that already approached perfection of spirit, I decided not to verify every reference but rather to let Coomaraswamy bear the responsibility for his occasional errors as he bears responsibility for his frequent grandeur.

THE *Selected Papers* of Amanda K. Coomaraswamy owes a great deal to its friends. Professional and moral support have been provided from the beginning by William McGuire and Carol Orr of Princeton University Press. Herbert S. Bailey, Jr., the director of the Press, has been a persistent friend throughout the complex task. Ruth Spiegel did her initial copy-editing with extraordinary care. Wallace Brockway, Joseph Campbell, Mircea Eliade, I. B. Horner, and Stella Kramrisch have

[2] Letter to Walter Shewring, 4 March 1936, from the collection of Coomaraswamy's papers and books bequeathed to Bollingen Foundation by Doña Luisa Coomaraswamy and now in Princeton University Library.

all contributed their mature judgment regarding both selection and editing. Lynda Beck, Alice Levi, and Carole Radcliffe have been invaluable research assistants. The Indologists Carole Meadow, Svatantra Kumar Pidara, and Kenneth J. Storey have reviewed Sanskrit and Pāli, and Lois Hinckley, Kathleen Komar, and Pamela Long have helped with translations and various bibliographic problems. James Crouch and S. Durai Raja Singam have shared their extensive knowledge of Coomaraswamy's writings.

Preparation of the index required the help of many individuals: Ann Suter compiled the Greek index and also reviewed Greek in the essays; Kenneth J. Storey compiled the Sanskrit index; and a team of some twelve students in the University of Texas, Austin, joined me for the final stages of assembling the general index. I hesitate to list twelve names, but I want very much to thank these participants.

Special acknowledgment must be made to Kurt Kleinman, who set the type for these volumes with such rigor and patience; he gives meaning to Coomaraswamy's cherished aphorism: "Every man is a special kind of artist." Eleanor Weisgerber and her staff in the proofroom of the Press completed an exceedingly difficult task as if it were all in a day's work. Margaret Case, who took over the task of copy-editing at an early stage, thereafter shared every problem as a colleague and friend.

Dr. Rama P. Coomaraswamy and his wife, Bernadette, have helped in countless ways.

R.L.

Contents of Volume 2

List of Abbreviations and Short Titles

A	*The Book of the Gradual Sayings* (*Aṅguttara-Nikāya*), ed. F. L. Woodward and E. M. Hare, 5 vols., London, 1932–1939 (PTS).
AĀ	*Aitareya Āraṇyaka*, ed. A. B. Keith, Oxford, 1909.
AB	(= *Aitareya Brāhmaṇa*). *Rigveda Brahmanas: The Aitareya and Kauṣītaki Brāhmaṇas of the Rigveda*, ed. A. B. Keith, Cambridge, Mass., 1920 (HOS XXV).
Abhidharmakośa	*L'Abhidharmakośa de Vasubandhu*, tr. Louis de la Vallée-Poussin, 6 vols., Paris, 1923–1931.
Abhinaya Darpaṇa	*The Mirror of Gesture: Being the Abhinaya Darpaṇa of Nandikeśvara*, ed. A. K. Coomaraswamy, with Gopala Kristnaya Duggirala, Cambridge, Mass., 1917.
Aeschylus, *Fr.*	In Nauck (see below).
Ait. Up.	(= *Aitareya Upaniṣad*). In *The Thirteen Principal Upanishads*, ed. R. E. Hume, 2nd ed., rev., London, 1931.
Angelus Silesius	(Johann Scheffler) *Cherubinischer Wandersmann*, new ed., Munich, 1949. *The Cherubinic Wanderer*, selections tr. W. R. Trask, New York, 1953.
Anugītā	*The Bhagavadgîtâ, with the Sanatsugâtîya, and the Anugîtâ*, ed. Kâshinâth Trimbak Telang, Oxford, 1882 (SBE VIII).
Apuleius	*The Golden Ass*, tr. W. Adlington, revised by S. Gaselee (LCL).
Aquinas	1. *Sancti Thomae Aquinatis, doctoris angelici, Opera omnia ad fidem optimarum editionum accurato recognita.* 25 vols. Parma, 1852–1872. 2. See also *Sum. Theol.* below.
Aristotle	1. *De anima*, tr. W. S. Hett (LCL). 2. *The Metaphysics*, tr. Hugh Tredennick (LCL). 3. *The Nichomachean Ethics*, tr. H. Rackham (LCL). 4. *The Physics*, tr. Francis M. Cornford (LCL). 5. *The Poetics*, tr. W. Hamilton Fyfe (LCL).
Arthaśāstra	*Kauṭilya's Arthaśāstra*, ed. R. Shamasastry, 2nd ed., Mysore, 1923.

Āryabhata	*Āryabhaṭīya*, tr. Walter Eugene Clark, Chicago, 1930.
'Aṭṭār, Farīdu'd-Dīn	1. Farid ud-Din Attar, *The Conference of the Birds* (Mantiq ut-Tair), tr. C. S. Nott from the French of Garçin de Tassy, London, 1954. 2. *Mantic Uttair, ou le langage des oiseaux*, tr. Garçin de Tassy, Paris, 1863. 3. *Salámán and Absál, . . . with a Bird's-Eye View of Faríd-Uddín Attar's Bird-Parliament*, by Edward Fitzgerald, Boston, 1899.
Atthasālinī	*The Expositor (Atthasālinī): Buddhaghosa's Commentary on the Dhammasangaṇi*, ed. P. Maung Tin and C.A.F. Rhys Davids, 2 vols., London, 1920–1921 (PTS).
AV	1. *Atharva Veda*, ed. W. D. Whitney and C. R. Lanman, Cambridge, Mass., 1905 (HOS VII, VIII). 2. *The Hymns of the Atharva-Veda*, ed. R.T.H. Griffith, 2 vols., 2nd ed., Benares, 1916–1917.
Avicenna	*Metaphysices compendium*, Rome, 1926.
Avencebrol	(Solomon Ibn Gabirol) *Fons Vitae*, see *Fountain of Life*, tr. Alfred B. Jacob, Philadelphia, 1954.
BAHA	*Bulletin de l'Office Internationale des Instituts d'Archéologie et d'Histoire d'Art.*
Baudhāyana Dh. Sū	*Das Baudhāyana-Dharmasūtra*, ed. Eugen Hultzsch, Leipzig, 1922.
BD	*The Bṛhad Devatā of Śaunaka*, ed. A. A. Macdonell, Cambridge, Mass., 1904 (HOS VI).
BÉFEO	*Bulletin de l'École Française d'Extrême-Orient* (Hanoi).
BG	*The Bhagavad Gītā*, ed. Swami Nikhilananda, New York, 1944.
Boethius	*The Theological Tractates and the Consolation of Philosophy*, ed. H. F. Stewart and E. K. Rand (LCL).
Bokhāri	Muhammad ibn-Ismā al-Bukhari. *Arabica and Islamica*, tr. V. Wayriffe, London, 1940.
BrSBh	(= *Brahma Sūtra Bhāṣya*) *The Vedânta-Sûtras with the Commentary by Saṇkarâkârya*, ed. G. Thibaut, 2 vols., Oxford, 1890–1896 (SBE 34, 38).
BSOS	*Bulletin of the School of Oriental and African Studies*

BU — (= *Bṛhadāraṇyaka Upaniṣad*) In *The Thirteen Principal Upanishads*, ed. R. E. Hume, 2nd ed., London, 1931.

Chuang-tzu — *Chuang Tzu: Mystic, Moralist, and Social Reformer*, ed. H. A. Giles, London, 1889.

Cicero —
1. *Academica*, tr. H. Rackham (LCL).
2. *Brutus*, tr. G. L. Hendrickson (LCL).
3. *De natura deorum*, tr. H. Rackham (LCL).
4. *De officiis*, tr. Walter Miller (LCL).
5. *Pro Publio Quinctio*, tr. John Henry Freese (LCL).
6. *Tusculan Disputations*, tr. J. E. King (LCL).

Claudian, *Stilicho* — *On Stilicho's Consulship*, tr. Maurice Platnauer, London and Cambridge, Mass., 1956.

Clement —
1. *Miscellanies*, tr. F.J.A. Hart and J. B. Mayor, London, 1902.
2. *The Clementine Homilies*, Ante-Nicene Christian Library, vol. XVII, Edinburgh, 1870.

Cloud of Unknowing — *A Book of Contemplation the Which is Called the Cloud of Unknowing in the Which a Soul is Oned with God*, anon., ed. E. Underhill, London, 1912.

Coptic Gnostic Treatise — *A Coptic Gnostic Treatise Contained in the Codex Brucianus*, ed. Charlotte A. Baynes, Cambridge, 1933.

CU — (= *Chāndogya Upaniṣad*) In *The Thirteen Principal Upanishads*, ed. R. E. Hume, 2nd ed., London, 1931.

D — (= *Dīgha-Nikāya*) *Dialogues of the Buddha*, ed. T. W. and C.A.F. Rhys Davids, 3 vols., London, 1899–1921 (PTS).

DA — (= *Dīgha-Nikāya Atthakathā*) *The Sumaṅgalavilāsinī: Buddhaghosa's Commentary on the Dīgha Nikāya*, ed. T. W. Rhys Davids and J. Estlin Carpenter (vol. I), and W. Stede (vols. II and III), London, 1886–1932 (PTS).

Damascene — St. John of Damascus. See Migne, PG, Vols. 94–96.

Dante —
1. *Convito* (1529); facsimile edition, Rome, 1932. *Dante and his Convito: A Study with Translations*, W. M. Rossetti, London, 1910.
2. *Dantis Alighieri Epistolae: The Letters of Dante*, ed. P. Toynbee, Oxford, 1966.
3. *The Divine Comedy of Dante Alighieri*, tr. Charles Eliot Norton, 3 vols., Boston and New

	York, 1895–1897. (This is AKC's preferred edition, but he had a dictionary of Dante's Italian and may have done translations on his own in addition to using Norton; he also used the Temple Classics edition.)
Daśarūpa	*The Daśarūpa: a Treatise on Hindu Dramaturgy*, tr. G.C.O. Haas, New York, 1912.
Dh	*The Dhammapada*, ed. S. Radhakrishnan, London, 1950.
DhA	(= *Dhammapada Atthakathā*) *Dhammapada Commentary*, ed. H. C. Norman, 4 vols., 1906–1914 (PTS).
Dionysius	1. *De coelesti hierarchia*, see *La Hiérarchie céleste*, ed. G. Heil and M. de Gandillac, Paris, 1958 (*Sources chrétiennes* LVIII). 2. *De divinis nominibus* and *De mystica theologia*, see *The Divine Names* and *The Mystical Theology*, ed. C. E. Rolt, London, 1920. 3. Epistles, see *Saint Denys L'Aréopagite, Oeuvres*, ed. Mgr. Darboy, Paris, 1932.
Divyāvadāna	*Divyāvadāna*, ed. E. B. Cowell and R. A. Neil, Cambridge, 1886.
Dpv	*Dipavamsa*, ed. H. Oldenberg, London, 1879.
Epiphanius	*Epiphanius* (*Ancoratus und Panarion*), ed. K. Holl, Leipzig, 1915–1933.
Erigena	John Scotus Erigena. See Migne, PL, Vol. 122.
Euripides	1. *Euripides*, tr. A. S. Way (LCL). 2. *Fragments* in Nauck.
Garbha Up.	(= *Garbha Upaniṣad*) In *Thirty Minor Upanishads*, tr. K. Nārāyanasvāmi, Madras, 1914.
Gāruḍa Purāṇa	1. *The Garuda Puranam*, tr. M. N. Dutt, Calcutta, 1908. 2. *The Gāruḍa Purāṇa*, tr. Ernest Wood and S.U. Subrahmanyam, Allahabad, 1911 (SBH IX).
GB	*Gopatha Brāhmaṇa*, ed. R. Mitra and H. Vidyābushana, Calcutta, 1872 (Sanskrit only).
Grassmann	H. G. Grassmann, *Wörterbuch zum Rig-Veda*, Leipzig, 1873 (cf. also *Rig-Veda; übersetzt und mit kritischen und erläuternden Anmerkungen versehen*, 2 vols., Leipzig, 1876–1877).
Greek Anthology	*The Greek Anthology*, tr. W. R. Paton (LCL).
Harivaṃṣa	*Harivamsha*, ed. M. N. Dutt, Calcutta, 1897 (prose English translation).

Haṃsa Up. — (= *Haṃsa Upaniṣad*) In *Thirty Minor Upanishads*, tr. K. Nārāyaṇasvāmi, Madras, 1914.

Heracleitus, *Fr.* — *Heracliti Ephesi Reliquiae*, ed. Ingram Bywater, Oxford, 1877 (see modern editions by G. S. Kirk and Philip Wheelwright; Coomaraswamy numbers Fragments according to Bywater).

Hermes — *Hermetica: The Ancient Greek and Latin Writings which Contain Religious or Philosophic Teachings Ascribed to Hermes Trismegistus*, ed. W. Scott, 4 vols., 1924–1936.

Hesiod — *Theogony* and *Works and Days*, tr. Hugh G. Evelyn-White (LCL).

Hippocrates — *Works*, tr. W.H.S. Jones (LCL).

HJAS — *Harvard Journal of Asiatic Studies.*

Homer — *The Iliad* and *The Odyssey*, tr. A. T. Murray (LCL).

Homeric Hymns — *Homeric Hymns*, tr. Hugh G. Evelyn-White (LCL).

Horace — *Epistula ad Pisones* (= *Ars Poetica*), tr. H. Rushton Fairclough (LCL).

HOS — Harvard Oriental Series.

IPEK — *Jahrbuch für prähistorische und ethnographische Kunst.*

Īśā Up. — (= *Īśā*, or *Īśavāsya, Upaniṣad*) In *The Thirteen Principal Upanishads*, ed. R. E. Hume, 2nd ed., London, 1931.

Itiv — (= *Itivuttaka*) *The Minor Anthologies of the Pali Canon, Part II: Udāna: Verses of Uplift, and Itivuttaka: As It Was Said*, ed. F. L. Woodward, London, 1935 (PTS).

J — *The Jātaka, or Stories of the Buddha's Former Births*, ed. E. B. Cowell, 6 vols., Cambridge, 1895–1907.

Jacob Boehme —
1. *Signatura rerum*, see *The Signature of All Things, and Other Writings*, new ed., London, 1969 (includes *Of the Supersensual Life* and *The Way from Darkness to True Illumination*).
2. *Six Theosophic Points, and Other Writings*, ed. J. R. Earle, Ann Arbor, 1958.
3. *The Way to Christ*, new ed., London, 1964.

Jāmī — *Lawā'ih, A Treatise on Sufism*, ed. E. H. Whinfield and M. M. Kazvīnī, London, 1906.

JAOS — *Journal of the American Oriental Society.*

JB	1. *The Jaiminīya-Brāhmana of the Samveda*, ed. R. Vira and L. Chandra, Nagpur, 1954 (Sanskrit). 2. *Das Jaiminīya Brāhmaṇa in Auswahl*, text and German translation by W. Caland, Amsterdam, 1919.
JHS	*Journal of Hellenic Studies.*
JISOA	*Journal of the Indian Society of Oriental Art.*
Jan van Ruysbroeck	*The Adornment of the Spiritual Marriage; The Sparkling Stone; The Book of Supreme Truth*, tr. C. A. Wynschenk, ed. Evelyn Underhill, London, 1914.
JRAS	*Journal of the Royal Asiatic Society.*
JUB	(= *Jaiminīya Upaniṣad Brāhmaṇa*) *The Jaiminīya or Talavakāra Upaniṣad Brāhmaṇa*, ed. H. Oertel, *Journal of the American Oriental Society*, XVI (1896), 79–260.
Kauṣ. Up.	(= *Kauṣītaki Upaniṣad*) In *The Thirteen Principal Upanishads*, ed. R. E. Hume, 2nd ed., London, 1931.
KB	*Kauṣītaki Brāhmaṇa. Rigveda Brahmanas: The Aitareya and Kauṣītaki Brāhmaṇas of the Rigveda*, ed. A. B. Keith, Cambridge, Mass., 1920 (HOS XXV).
Kena Up.	(= *Kena Upaniṣad*) In *The Thirteen Principal Upanishads*, ed. R. E. Hume, 2nd ed., London, 1931.
KhA	(= *Khuddakapāṭha*) *The Minor Readings, The First Book of the Minor Collection* (*Khuddakanikāya*), ed. Bhikkhu Ñāṇamoli, London, 1960 (PTS).
Kindred Sayings	See S
KSS	(= *Kathā-Sarit-Sāgara*) *Kathāsaritsāgara*, ed. C. H. Tawney, Calcutta, 1880–1887; 2nd ed., 1924.
KU	1. (= *Kaṭha Upaniṣad*) In *The Thirteen Principal Upanishads*, ed. R. E. Hume, 2nd ed., London, 1931. 2. *Kaṭha Upaniṣad*, ed. Joseph N. Rawson, Oxford, 1934.
Lalita Vistara	*Lalita Vistara*, ed. S. Lefmann, 2 vols., Halle, 1902–1908.
Laṅkâvatāra Sūtra	*Laṅkâvatāra Sūtra*, ed. Bunyiu Nanjio, Kyoto, 1923.
LCL	Loeb Classical Library.
Lucian	*De Syria Dea*, tr. A. M. Harmon (LCL).

M — (= *Majjhima-Nikāya*) *The Middle Length Sayings (Majjhima-Nikāya)*, ed. I. B. Horner, 3 vols., London, 1954–1959 (PTS).

Mahavamsa — See Mhv.

Maṇḍ. Up. — (= *Maṇḍūkya Upaniṣad*) In *The Thirteen Principal Upanishads*, ed. R. E. Hume, 2nd ed., London, 1931.

Mantiqu't-Tair — See 'Aṭṭar, Faridu'd-Dīn.

Mānasāra — *Architecture of Mānasāra*, tr. Prasanna Kumar Acharya, London, 1933.

Mañjuśrīmūlakalpa — *Mañjuśrī: An Imperial History of India in a Sanskrit Text*, ed. Ven. Rāhula Sāṇkṛtyāyana, Lahore, 1934.

Manu — (= *Mānava Dharmaśāstra*) *The Laws of Manu*, ed. G. Bühler, Oxford, 1886 (SBE XXV).

Marcus Aurelius — *Marcus Aurelius*, tr. C. R. Haines (LCL).

Markaṇḍeya Purāṇa — *Markaṇḍeya Purāṇa*, ed. J. Woodroffe, London, 1913.

Mathnawī — *The Mathnawí of Jalálu'ddín Rúmí*, ed. R. A. Nicholson, 8 vols., Leiden and London, 1925–1940.

Mbh —
1. *Mahābhārata. The Mahabharata of Krishna-Dwaipayana Vyasa*, ed. P. C. Roy, Calcutta, 1893–1894.
2. *Mahābhārata*, ed. Vishnu S. Sukthankar, Poona, 1933– [24 vols. to date].

Meister Eckhart —
1. *Meister Eckhart*, ed. F. Pfeiffer, 4th ed., Göttingen, 1924 (mediaeval German text).
2. *Meister Eckhart*, ed. C. de B. Evans, 2 vols., London, 1924–1931 (English).

MFA Bulletin — *Bulletin of the Museum of Fine Arts*, Boston.

Mhv — *The Mahāvaṃsa, or The Great Chronicle of Ceylon*, ed. W. Geiger, London, 1908 (PTS).

Migne — Jacques Paul Migne, *Patrologiae cursus completus*
1. [*P. G.*] *Series Graeca*, Paris, 1857–1866, 161 vols.
2. [*P. L.*] *Series Latina*, Paris, 1844–1880, 221 vols.

Mil — (= *Milinda Pañho*) *The Questions of King Milinda*, ed. T. W. Rhys Davids, 2 vols., Oxford, 1890 (SBE XXXV, XXXVI).

Mīmaṃsā Nyāya Prakaśa — *The Mīmamsā Nyāya Prakaśa of Āpadeva*, ed. F. Edgerton, New Haven, 1929.

MU — (= *Maitri Upaniṣad*) In *The Thirteen Principal Upanishads*, ed. R. E. Hume, 2nd ed., London, 1931.

Muṇḍ. Up.	(= *Muṇḍaka Upaniṣad*) In *The Thirteen Principal Upanishads*, ed. R. E. Hume, 2nd ed., London, 1931.
Mv	(= *Mahāvagga*) *Vinaya Texts*, ed. T. W. Rhys Davids and H. Oldenberg, 2 vols., Oxford, 1881–1882 (SBE XIII, XVII).
Nārāyaṇa Up.	(= *Nārāyaṇa Upaniṣad*) In *Thirty Minor Upanishads*, ed. K. N. Aiyar, Madras, 1914.
Nāṭya Śāstra	*The Nāṭya Śāstra* of Bharata, ed. M. Ramakrishna Kavi, Baroda, 1926 (Sanskrit).
Nauck	August Nauck, *Tragicorum Graecorum Fragmenta*, Leipzig, 1856.
NIA	*New Indian Antiquary*.
Nicholas of Cusa	(= Nicolaus Cusanus) 1. (*De visione Dei*) *The Vision of God*, ed. E. G. Salter, London, 1928. 2. *De filiatione Dei*, in *Schriften des Nikolaus von Cues*, Leipzig, 1936–, Vol. II.
Nirukta	*The Nighaṇṭu and Nirukta of Yāska*, ed. L. Sarup, Oxford, 1921.
Origen	*Writings of Origen*, tr. Frederick Cromble, 2 vols., Edinburgh, 1869.
Ovid	1. *Fasti*, tr. Sir James George Frazer (LCL). 2. *Metamorphoses*, tr. Frank Justus Miller (LCL).
OZ	*Ostasiatische Zeitschrift*.
Pañcadaśi	*Pañchadaśi, A Poem on Vedānta Philosophy*, ed. & tr. Arthur Venis, in *Pandit*, V–VIII (1883–1886).
Pañcatantra	*The Panchatantra Reconstructed*, ed. Franklin Edgerton, New Haven, 1924. American Oriental Series, III.
Pāṇini	*The Ashtādhyāyi of Pāṇini*, ed. S. C. Vasu, 8 vols., Allahabad, 1891–1898.
Parāśara	*The Parāśara Dharma Samhitā, or, Parāśara Smṛiti*, ed. Pandit Vāman Śāstrī Islāmapurkar, 2 vols., Bombay, 1893–1906.
Pausanias	*Pausanias*, tr. W.H.S. Jones (LCL).
PGS	*Pâraskara-gṛhya-sūtras*, tr. H. Oldenberg, Oxford, 1886.
Philo	1. Complete works published in LCL; Vols. I–X, ed. F. H. Colson; *Supplements* I, II, ed. R. Marcus. All works cited by full title with exception of: a) *Aet.* (*On the Eternity of the World*, vol. IX); b) *Congr.* (*On the Preliminary Studies*, vol.

	IV); c) *Deterius* (*The Worse Attacks the Better*, vol. II); d) *Heres*. (*Who is the Heir*, vol. IV); e) *Immut*. (*On the Unchangeableness of God*, vol. III).
Philostratus, *Vit. Ap.*	Flavius Philostratus, *The Life and Times of Apollonius of Tyana*, tr. Charles P. Ellis, Stanford, 1923.
Pindar	*The Odes of Pindar*, tr. Richard Lattimore, Chicago, 1947.
Pistis Sophia	1. *Pistis Sophia, A Gnostic Miscellany*, ed. & tr. G.R.S. Mead, London, rev. ed., 1921; 1947. 2. *Pistis Sophia*, ed. J. H. Petermann, Berlin, 1851.
Plato	*The Collected Dialogues of Plato, including the Letters*, ed. Edith Hamilton and Huntington Cairns, Princeton, 1961 (Bollingen Series LXXI).
Plotinus	*Plotinus, The Enneads*, tr. Stephen MacKenna. 3rd ed. rev. by B. S. Page, London, 1962.
Plutarch	1. *Moralia*, tr. Frank Cole Babbitt and others; includes *De genio Socratis* (LCL). 2. *Pericles*, in *Lives*, tr. Bernadotte Perrin (LCL).
PMLA	*Publications of the Modern Language Association.*
Praśna Up.	(= *Praśna Upaniṣad*) In *The Thirteen Principal Upanishads*, ed. R. E. Hume, 2nd ed., London, 1931.
Prema Sāgara	*Prema-Sāgara*, ed. and tr. Edward B. Eastwick, Westminster, 1897.
PTS	Pali Text Society Translation Series.
Pythagoras	*Golden Verses*, see *Les Vers d'or pythagoriciens*, ed. P. C. van der Horst, Leyden, 1932.
PugA	*Puggala-paññatti-atthakatha*, ed. G. Lansberg and C.A.F. Rhys Davids, London, 1914 (Pāli).
Pūrva Mīmāṃsā Sūtras	*The Pūrva Mīmāṃsā Sūtras* of Jaimini, ed. M. Ganganatha Jha, Allahabad, 1916 (SBH X).
Quintilian	*Institutio Oratoria*, tr. H. E. Butler (LCL).
Rāmāyaṇa	*The Rāmāyaṇa*, ed. M. N. Dutt, Calcutta, 1891–1894.
Rūmī, *Dīvān*	*Selected Poems from the Dīvanī Shamsi Tabrīz*, ed. R. A. Nicholson, Cambridge, 1898.
RV	*The Hymns of the Ṛgveda*, ed. R.T.H. Griffith, 2 vols., 4th ed., Benares, 1963.
S	*The Book of the Kindred Sayings* (*Saṃyutta-Nikāya*), ed. C.A.F. Rhys Davids and F. L. Woodward, 5 vols., London, 1917–1930 (PTS).

ŚA	*Śāṅkhāyana Āraṇyaka*, ed. A. B. Keith, London, 1908.
Sa'dī	(Muslih-al-Dīn) *The Bustān of Sadi*, ed. A. H. Edwards, London, 1911.
Ṣaḍva. Brāhmaṇa	(= *Ṣaḍvinśa Brāhmaṇa*) *Daivatabramhana and Shadbingshabramhana of the Samveda with the Commentary of Sayanacharya*, ed. Pandit J. Vidyasagara, Calcutta, 1881.
Sāhitya Darpaṇa	*The Mirror of Composition, A Treatise on Poetical Criticism, being an English Translation of the Sāhitya-Darpana of Viśwanatha Kaviraja*, ed. J. R. Ballantyne and P. D. Mitra, Calcutta, 1875 (reprinted, Benares, 1956).
Śakuntala	*Abhijñāna-Śakuntala* of Kalidāsa, ed. M. B. Emeneau, Berkeley, 1962.
Sanatsujātiya	*The Bhagavadgîtâ, with the Sanatsugâtîya, and the Anugîtâ*, ed. K. T. Telang, Oxford, 1882 (SBE VIII).
Śatapatha Brāhmaṇa	See ŚB.
Sāyaṇa	*Rg Veda Samhitā, with Sayana's Commentary*, ed. S. Pradhan, Calcutta, 1933.
ŚB	*Śatapatha Brāhmaṇa*, ed. J. Eggeling, 5 vols., Oxford, 1882–1900 (SBE XII, XXVI, XLI, XLII, XLIV).
SBB	The Sacred Books of the Buddhists, London.
SBE	The Sacred Books of the East, Oxford.
SBH	The Sacred Books of the Hindus, Allahabad.
Scott	See Hermes.
Sextus Empiricus	*Sextus Empiricus*, tr. R. G. Bury (LCL).
Shams-i-Tabriz	See Rūmī, *Dīvān*.
Siddhāntamuktāvalī	1. *The Vedānta Siddhāntamuktāvalī of Prakāśananda*, tr. Arthur Venis, in *The Pandit*, Benares, 1890. 2. Tr. J. R. Ballantyne, Calcutta, 1851.
Sikandar Nāma	Nizam al-Dīn Abu Muhammad Niẓamī, *Sikandar Nāma e bara*, tr. H. Wilberforce, Clarke, London, 1881.
Śilparatna	*The Śilparatna* by Śrī Kumāra, ed. Mahāmahopādyāya T. Ganapati Sāstri, Trivandrum, 1922–1929.
Sn	*The Sutta-Nipāta*, ed. V. Fausböll, Oxford, 1881 (SBE X).

SnA	*Sutta-Nipāta Atthakathā*, ed. H. Smith, 2 vols., London, 1916–1917 (PTS).
SP	*The Saddharma Puṇḍarīka, or the Lotus of the True Law*, ed. H. Kern, Oxford, 1909 (SBE XXI).
Śrī Sūkta	*The Purusha Sukta*, Aiyar, Madras, 1898.
St. Augustine	1. *The City of God against the Pagans*, tr. William M. Green (LCL). 2. *A Select Library of the Nicene and Post-Nicene Fathers of the Christian Church*, ed. Philip Schaff, New York, 1886–1890, vols. I–VIII, *Collected Works of St. Augustine* (in English tr.).
St. Bernard	St. Bernard of Clairvaux, *Opera omnia* in Migne, *Series latina*, vols. 182–185 (1854–1855).
St. Bonaventura	1. *The Works of Bonaventure, Cardinal, Seraphic Doctor, and Saint*, tr. José de Vinck, Paterson, N.J., 1966– (in progress); Vol. III, *Opuscula, Second Series*, 1966, includes "On Retracing the Arts to Theology" (*De reductione artium ad theologiam*). 2. *Doctoris Seraphici S. Bonaventurae S. R. E. Episcopi Cardinalis opera omnia* . . . , Florence, 1883–1902, 10 vols.; vols. I–IV, *Sententiarum Petri Lombardi* (abbreviated *I Sent.*, etc.).
St. Clement	See Clement.
St. Cyril of Jerusalem	*A Select Library of Nicene and Post-Nicene Fathers*, 2nd ser. ed. Philip Schaff and Henry Wace, New York, 1894. Vol. VII.
St. Jerome	*S. Eusebii Hieronymi opera omnia*, in Migne, *Series latina*, vols. 22–30.
St. John of the Cross	*The Complete Works of Saint John of the Cross, Doctor of the Church*, ed. and tr. E. Allison Peers, Weathampstead, 1974.
Sukhāvatī Vyūha	*Buddhist Texts from Japan*, ed. F. Max Müller and Bunyiu Nanjic, Oxford, 1881 (*Anecdota oxoniensia, Aryan Series* I).
Śukranītisāra	*The Sukranīti of Śukrācārya*, ed. B. K. Sarkar, Allahabad, 1914 (SBH XII).
Sum. Theol.	*The Summa Theologica of St. Thomas Aquinas.* Literally translated by Fathers of the English Dominican Province. London, 1913–1942, 22 vols. Also in Parma ed., 1864; see Aquinas.

Suparṇādhyāya	*Die Suparṇasage*, ed. J. Charpentier, Uppsala, 1922 (Sanskrit text, German translation, commentary).
Suśruta	*The Suśruta-Saṃhita*, tr. Udoy Chand Dutt and Aughorechunder Chattopadhya, 3 fasc., Calcutta, 1883–1891.
Svātma-nirūpaṇa	*Select Works of Sri Sankaracharya*, tr. S. Venkataramanan, Madras, 1911 (includes *Svātma-nirūpaṇa*).
Śvet. Up.	(= *Śvetāsvatara Upaniṣad*) In *The Thirteen Principal Upanishads*, ed. R. E. Hume, 2nd ed., London, 1931.
TA	*The Taittirīya Araṇyaka of the Black Yajur Veda (with the Commentary of Sayaṇacharya)*, ed. R. Mitra, Calcutta, 1872 (Sanskrit).
Taittirīya Pratiśākhya	*The Tâittirîya Prâtiçâkhya, with its Commentary, the Tribhâshyaratna*, ed. W. D. Whitney, JAOS, IX (1871), 1–469.
Tao Te Ching	Arthur Waley, *The Way and Its Power*, London, 1934.
TB	*The Taittirīya Brāhmaṇa of the Black Yajur Veda, with the Commentary of Sayaṇa Archaryya*, ed. R. Mitra, 3 vols., Calcutta, 1859–1890 (Sanskrit).
Tertullian	*The Writings of Q.S.F. Tertullianus*, tr. S. Thelwall, *et al.*, 3 vols., Edinburgh, 1869–1870.
Therīgāthā *Theragāthā*	1. *Psalms of the Early Buddhists*, I. *Psalms of the Sisters*, II. *Psalms of the Brethren*, tr. C. A. F. Rhys Davids, 4th ed., London, 1964 (PTS). 2. *The Thera- and Therī-gāthā*, ed. H. Oldenburg, London, 1883 (PTS).
TS	*Taittirīya Saṃhitā: The Veda of the Black Yajur School*, ed. A. B. Keith, Cambridge, Mass., 1914 (HOS XVIII, XIX).
TU	(= *Taittirīya Upaniṣad*) In *The Thirteen Principal Upanishads*, ed. R. E. Hume, 2nd ed., London, 1931.
Ud	(= *Udāna*) *The Minor Anthologies of the Pali Canon, Part II: Udāna: Verses of Uplift, and Itivuttaka: As It Was Said*, ed. F. L. Woodward, London, 1948 (PTS).
UdA	(= *Udāna Atthakathā*) *Paramattha-Dīpanī Udānaṭṭhakathā (Udāna Commentary) of Dhammapālâcariya*, ed. F. L. Woodward, London, 1926 (PTS).

Uvāsaga Dasão	*Uvāsaga Dasão*, ed. N. A. Gore, Poona, 1953.
VbhA	(= *Vibhanga Atthakathā*) Buddhaghosa, *Sammoha-vinodanī Abhidhamma-piṭake Vibhangattakatha*, ed. A. P. Buddhadatta Thero, London, 1923 (PTS)
Vikramorvaśī	*The Vikramorvasiya of Kalidasa*, tr. and ed. Charu Deva Shastri, Lahore, 1929.
Vin	(= *Vinaya Piṭaka*) *The Book of the Discipline* (*Vinaya Piṭaka*), ed. I. B. Horner, 5 vols., London, 1938–1952 (PTS).
Vis	*The Visuddhi Magga of Buddhaghosa*, ed. C.A.F. Rhys Davids, London, 1920–1921 (PTS).
Viṣṇudharmottara	*The Vishṇudharmottara*, ed. S. Kramrisch, 2nd ed., Calcutta, 1928.
Viṣṇu Purāṇa	*The Vishnu Purana: A System of Hindu Mythology and Tradition*, ed. H. H. Wilson, London, 1864–1877.
VS	*Vājasaneyi Saṃhitā: The White Yajur Veda*, ed. R.T.H. Griffith, 2nd ed., Benares, 1927.
Witelo	Clemens Baeumker, *Witelo, ein Philosoph und Naturforscher des XIII. Jahrhunderts* (with text of his *Liber de intelligentiis*), Münster, 1908.
Xenophon	1. *Memorabilia*, tr. E. C. Marchant (LCL). 2. *Oeconomicus*, tr. E. C. Marchant (LCL).
ZDMG	*Zeitschrift der deutschen morgenländischen Gesellschaft.*
Zohar	*The Zohar*, ed. H. Sperling and M. Simon, 5 vols., London, 1931–1934.

List of Works by A. K. Coomaraswamy Cited in These Volumes

"Angel and Titan: An Essay in Vedic Ontology," JAOS, LV (1935), 373–419.

"Chāyā," JAOS, LV (1935), 278–83.

The Darker Side of Dawn, *Smithsonian Miscellaneous Collections*, XCIV (1935), 18 pp.

"Dīpak Rāga," *Yearbook of Oriental Art and Culture*, II (1924–1925), 29–30.

"Early Indian Architecture: I. Cities and City Gates, etc.; II. Bodhigaras," *Eastern Art*, II (1930), 208–35, 45 figs. "III. Palaces," *Eastern Art*, III (1931), 181–217, 84 figs.

"An Early Passage on Indian Painting," *Eastern Art*, III (1931), 218–19.

"Eckstein," *Speculum*, XIV (1939), 66–72.

Elements of Buddhist Iconography. Foreword by Walter E. Clark. Cambridge, Mass., 1935, 95 pp., 15 pls.

Figures of Speech or Figures of Thought. London, 1946. 256 pp.

"Gradation and Evolution: I," *Isis*, XXXV (1944), 15–16.

"Gradation and Evolution: II," *Isis*, XXXVIII (1947), 87–94.

Hinduism and Buddhism. New York, 1943, 86 pp.

"The Iconography of Dürer's 'Knots' and Leonardo's 'Concatenation,'" *Art Quarterly*, VII (1944), 109–28, 18 figs.

The Indian Craftsman. Foreword by C. R. Ashbee. London, 1909. 130 pp.

Mediaeval Sinhalese Art. Broad Campden, 1908. 340 pp., 55 pls. (425 copies).

A New Approach to the Vedas: An Essay in Translation and Exegesis. London, 1933. 116 + ix pp.

"Nirmāna-kāya," JRAS (1938), pp. 81–84.

"A Note on the Aśvamedha," *Archiv Orientalni*, VII (1936), 306–17.

"Notes on the Kaṭha Upaniṣad," NIA, I (1938), 43–56, 83–108, 199–213.

"On Being in One's Right Mind," *Review of Religion*, VII (1942), 32–40.

"The Pilgrim's Way," *Journal of the Bihar and Orissa Research Society*, XXIII (1937), 452–71.

"Prāṇa-citi," JRAS (1943), pp. 105–109.

"The Reinterpretation of Buddhism," NIA, II (1939), 575–90.

"Sir Gawain and the Green Knight: Indra and Namuci," *Speculum*, XIX (1944), 104–25.

"Some Sources of Buddhist Iconography," in *B. C. Law Volume*, Poona, 1945, pp. 469–76.

Spiritual Authority and Temporal Power in the Indian Theory of Government. New Haven, 1942. 87 pp., 1 pl.

"Spiritual Paternity and the 'Puppet-Complex,'" *Psychiatry*, VIII (1945), 287–97.

"The Sun-kiss," JAOS, LX (1940), 46–67.

"The Symbolism of Archery," *Ars Islamica*, X (1943), 104–19.

"The Technique and Theory of Indian Painting," *Technical Studies*, III (1934), 59–89, 2 figs.

Time and Eternity. Artibus Asiae Monograph Series, suppl. no. 8, Ascona, Switzerland, 1947, 140 pp.

The Transformation of Nature in Art. Cambridge, Mass., 1934 (2nd ed., 1935), 245 pp.

"Uṣṇīṣa and Chatra: Turban and Umbrella," *Poona Orientalist*, III (1938), 1–19.

Why Exhibit Works of Art? London, 1943, 148 pp. Reprinted under the title *Christian and Oriental Philosophy of Art*, New York, 1956.

"The Yakṣa of the Vedas and Upaniṣads," *Quarterly Journal of the Mythic Society*, XXVIII (1938), 231–40.

Yakṣas [I], Smithsonian Miscellaneous Collections, LXXX:6 (1928), 43 pp., 23 pls.

Yakṣas, II, Smithsonian Institution Publication 3059 (1931), 84 pp., 50 pls.

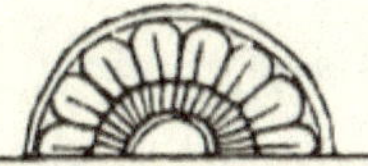

INTRODUCTORY ESSAYS

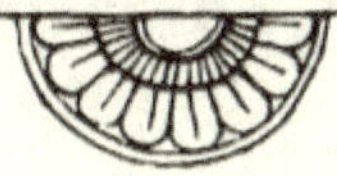

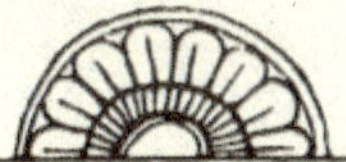

The Vedānta and Western Tradition

These are really the thoughts of all men in all ages and lands, they are not original with me.

Walt Whitman

I

There have been teachers such as Orpheus, Hermes, Buddha, Lao-tzu and Christ, the historicity of whose human existence is doubtful, and to whom there may be accorded the higher dignity of a mythical reality. Śaṇkara, like Plotinus, Augustine, or Eckhart, was certainly a man among men, though we know comparatively little about his life. He was of south Indian Brahman birth, flourished in the first half of the ninth century A.D., and founded a monastic order which still survives. He became a *saṃnyāsin*, or "truly poor man," at the age of eight, as the disciple of a certain Govinda and of Govinda's own teacher Gauḍapāda, the author of a treatise on the Upaniṣads in which their essential doctrine of the non-duality of the divine Being was set forth. Śaṇkara journeyed to Benares and wrote the famous commentary on the *Brahma Sūtra* there in his twelfth year; the commentaries on the Upaniṣads and *Bhagavad Gītā* were written later. Most of the great sage's life was spent wandering about India, teaching and taking part in controversies. He is understood to have died between the ages of thirty and forty. Such wanderings and disputations as his have always been characteristically Indian institutions; in his days, as now, Sanskrit was the lingua franca of learned men, just as for centuries Latin was the lingua franca of Western countries, and free public debate was so generally recognized that halls erected for the accommodation of peripatetic teachers and disputants were at almost every court.

The traditional metaphysics with which the name of Śaṇkara is con-

[Originally an address given before the Radcliffe College chapter of the Phi Beta Kappa Society, the text in its present form was published in *The American Scholar*, VIII (1939).—ED.]

nected is known either as the Vedānta, a term which occurs in the Upaniṣads and means the "Vedas' ends," both as "latter part" and as "ultimate significance"; or as Ātmavidyā, the doctrine of the knowledge of the true "self" or "spiritual essence"; or as Advaita, "Nonduality," a term which, while it denies duality, makes no affirmations about the nature of unity and must not be taken to imply anything like our monisms or pantheisms. A gnosis (*jñāna*) is taught in this metaphysics.

Śaṇkara was not in any sense the founder, discoverer, or promulgator of a new religion or philosophy; his great work as an expositor consisted in a demonstration of the unity and consistency of Vedic doctrine and in an explanation of its apparent contradictions by a correlation of different formulations with the points of view implied in them. In particular, and exactly as in European Scholasticism, he distinguished between the two complementary approaches to God, which are those of the affirmative and negative theology. In the way of affirmation, or relative knowledge, qualities are predicated in the Supreme Identity by way of excellence, while in the way of negation all qualities are abstracted. The famous "No, no" of the Upaniṣads, which forms the basis of Śaṇkara's method, as it did of the Buddha's, depends upon a recognition of the truth—expressed by Dante among many others—that there are things which are beyond the reach of discursive thought and which cannot be understood except by denying things of them.

Śaṇkara's style is one of great originality and power as well as subtlety. I shall cite from his commentary on the *Bhagavad Gītā* a passage that has the further advantage of introducing us at once to the central problem of the Vedānta—that of the discrimination of what is really, and not merely according to our way of thinking, "myself." "How is it," Śaṇkara says, "that there are professors who like ordinary men maintain that 'I am so-and-so' and 'This is mine'? Listen: it is because their so-called learning consists in thinking of the body as their 'self.'" In the Commentary on the *Brahma Sūtra* he enunciates in only four Sanskrit words what has remained in Indian metaphysics from first to last the consistent doctrine of the immanent Spirit within you as the only knower, agent, and transmigrant.

The metaphysical literature underlying Śaṇkara's expositions consists essentially of the Four Vedas together with the Brāhmaṇas and their Upaniṣads, all regarded as revealed, eternal, datable (as to their recension, in any case) before 500 B.C., together with the *Bhagavad Gītā* and *Brahma Sūtra* (datable before the beginning of the Christian era). Of these books, the Vedas are liturgical, the Brāhmaṇas are explanatory of the ritual, and the Upaniṣads are devoted to the Brahma-doctrine or *Theologia Mystica*, which is taken for granted in the liturgy and ritual. The *Brahma Sūtra* is a greatly condensed compendium of Upaniṣad doctrine, and the *Bhagavad Gītā* is an exposition adapted to the understanding of those whose primary business has to do with the active rather than the contemplative life.

For many reasons, which I shall try to explain, it will be far more difficult to expound the Vedānta than it would be to expound the personal views of a modern "thinker," or even such a thinker as Plato or Aristotle. Neither the modern English vernacular nor modern philosophical or psychological jargon provides us with an adequate vocabulary, nor does modern education provide us with the ideological background which would be essential for easy communication. I shall have to make use of a purely symbolic, abstract, and technical language, as if I were speaking in terms of higher mathematics; you may recall that Emile Mâle speaks of Christian symbolism as a "calculus." There is this advantage: the matter to be communicated and the symbols to be employed are no more peculiarly Indian than peculiarly Greek or Islamic, Egyptian or Christian.

Metaphysics, in general, resorts to visual symbols (crosses and circles, for example) and above all to the symbolism of light and of the sun—than which, as Dante says, "no object of sense in the whole world is more worthy to be made a type of God." But I shall also have to use such technical terms as essence and substance, potentiality and act, spiration and despiration, exemplary likeness, aeviternity, form and accident. Metempsychosis must be distinguished from transmigration and both from "reincarnation." We shall have to distinguish soul from spirit. Before we can know when, if ever, it is proper to render a given Sanskrit word by our word "soul" (*anima, psyche*), we must have known in what manifold senses the word "soul" has been employed in the European tradition; what kind of souls can be "saved"; what kind of soul Christ requires us to "hate" if we would be his disciples; what kind of soul Eckhart refers to when he says that the soul must "put itself to death." We must know what Philo means by the "soul of the soul"; and we must ask how we can think of animals as "soulless," notwithstanding that the word "animal" means quite literally "ensouled." We must distinguish essence from existence. And I may have to coin such a word as "nowever" to express the full and original meanings of such words as "suddenly," "immediately" and "presently."

The sacred literature of India is available to most of us only in translations made by scholars trained in linguistics rather than in metaphysics; and it has been expounded and explained—or as I should rather say, explained away—mainly by scholars provided with the assumptions of the naturalist and anthropologist, scholars whose intellectual capacities have been so much inhibited by their own powers of observation that they can no longer distinguish the reality from the appearance, the Supernal Sun of metaphysics from the physical sun of their own experience. Apart from these, Indian literature has either been studied and explained by Christian propagandists whose main concern has been to demonstrate the falsity and absurdity of the doctrines involved, or by theosophists by whom the doctrines have been caricatured with the best intentions and perhaps even worse results.

The educated man of today is, moreover, completely out of touch with those European modes of thought and those intellectual aspects of the Christian doctrine which are nearest those of the Vedic traditions. A knowledge of modern Christianity will be of little use because the fundamental sentimentality of our times has diminished what was once an intellectual doctrine to a mere morality that can hardly be distinguished from a pragmatic humanism. A European can hardly be said to be adequately prepared for the study of the Vedānta unless he has acquired some knowledge and understanding of at least Plato, Philo, Hermes, Plotinus, the Gospels (especially John), Dionysius, and finally Eckhart who, with the possible exception of Dante, can be regarded from an Indian point of view as the greatest of all Europeans.

The Vedānta is not a "philosophy" in the current sense of the word, but only as the word is used in the phrase Philosophia Perennis, and only if we have in mind the Hermetic "philosophy" or that "Wisdom" by whom Boethius was consoled. Modern philosophies are closed systems, employing the method of dialectics, and taking for granted that opposites are mutually exclusive. In modern philosophy things are either so or not so; in eternal philosophy this depends upon our point of view. Metaphysics is not a system, but a consistent doctrine; it is not merely concerned with conditioned and quantitative experience, but with universal possibility. It therefore considers possibilities that may be neither possibilities of manifestation nor in any sense formal, as well as ensembles of possibility that can be realized in a given world. The ultimate reality of metaphysics is a Supreme Identity in which the opposition of all contraries, even of being and not-being, is resolved; its "worlds" and "gods" are levels of reference and symbolic entities which are neither places nor individuals but states of being realizable within you.

Philosophers have personal theories about the nature of the world; our "philosophical discipline" is primarily a study of the history of these opinions and of their historical connections. We encourage the budding philosopher to have opinions of his own on the chance that they may represent an improvement on previous theories. We do not envisage, as does the Philosophia Perennis, the possibility of knowing the Truth once and for all; still less do we set before us as our goal to become this truth.

The metaphysical "philosophy" is called "perennial" because of its eternity, universality, and immutability; it is Augustine's "Wisdom uncreate, the same now as it ever was and ever will be"; the religion which, as he also says, only came to be called "Christianity" after the coming of Christ. What was revealed in the beginning contains implicitly the whole truth; and so long as the tradition is transmitted without deviation, so long, in other words, as the chain of teachers and disciples remains unbroken, neither inconsistency nor error is possible. On the other hand, an understanding of the doctrine must be perpetually renewed; it is not a matter of words. That the doctrine has no history by no means excludes the possibility, or even the necessity, for a perpetual explicitation of its formulae, an adaptation of the rites originally practiced, and an application of its principles to the arts and sciences. The more humanity declines from its first self-sufficiency, the more the necessity for such an application arises. Of these explicitations and adaptations a history is possible. Thus a distinction is drawn between what was "heard" at the outset and what has been "remembered."

A deviation or heresy is only possible when the essential teaching has been in some respect misunderstood or perverted. To say, for example, that "I am a pantheist" is merely to confess that "I am not a metaphysician," just as to say that "two and two make five" would be to confess "I am not a mathematician." Within the tradition itself there cannot be any contradictory or mutually exclusive theories or dogmas. For example, what are called the "six systems of Indian philosophy" (a phrase in which only the words "six" and "Indian" are justified) are not mutually contradictory and exclusive theories. The so-called "systems" are no more or less orthodox than mathematics, chemistry, and botany which, though separate disciplines more or less scientific amongst themselves, are not anything but branches of one "science." India, indeed, makes use of the term "branches" to denote what the Indologist misunderstands to be "sects." It is precisely because there are no "sects" within the fold of Brahmanical orthodoxy that an intolerance in the European sense has been virtually unknown in Indian history—and for the same reason, it is just as easy for me to think in terms of the Hermetic philosophy as in terms of Vedānta. There must be "branches" because nothing can be known except in the mode of the knower; however strongly we may realize that all roads lead to one Sun, it is equally evident that each man must choose that road which starts from the point at which he finds himself at the moment of setting out. For the same reasons, Hinduism has never been a missionary faith. It may be true that the metaphysical tradition has been better and more fully preserved in India than in Europe. If so, it only means that the Christian can learn from the Vedānta how to understand his own "way" better.

The philosopher expects to prove his points. For the metaphysician it suffices to show that a supposedly false doctrine involves a contradiction of first principles. For example, a philosopher who argues for an immortality of the soul endeavors to discover proofs of the survival of personality; for the metaphysician it suffices to remember that "the first beginning must be the same as the last end"—from which it follows that a soul, understood to have been created in time, cannot but end in time. The metaphysician can no more be convinced by any so-called "proof of the survival of personality" than a physicist could be convinced of the possibility of a perpetual motion machine by any so-called proof. Furthermore, metaphysics deals for the most part with matters which cannot be publicly proved, but can only be demonstrated, i.e., made intelligible by analogy, and which even when verified in personal experience can only be stated in terms of symbol and myth. At the same time, faith is made relatively easy by the infallible logic of the texts themselves—which is their beauty and their attractive power. Let us remember the Christian definition of faith: "assent to a credible proposition." One must believe in order to understand, and understand in order to believe. These are not successive, however, but simultaneous acts of the mind. In other words, there can be no knowledge of anything to which the will refuses its consent, or love of anything that has not been known.

Metaphysics differs still further from philosophy in having a purely practical purpose. It is no more a pursuit of truth for truth's sake than are the related arts a pursuit of art for art's sake, or related conduct the pursuit of morality for the sake of morality. There is indeed a quest, but the seeker already knows, so far as this can be stated in words, what it is that he is in search of; the quest is achieved only when he himself has become the object of his search. Neither verbal knowledge nor a merely formal assent nor impeccable conduct is of any more than indispensable dispositive value—means to an end.

Taken in their materiality, as "literature," the texts and symbols are inevitably misunderstood by those who are not themselves in quest. Without exception, the metaphysical terms and symbols are the technical terms of the chase. They are never literary ornaments, and as Malinowski has so well said in another connection, "Technical language, in matters of practical pursuit, acquires its meaning only through personal participation in this type of pursuit." That is why, the Indian feels, the Vedantic texts have been only verbally and grammatically and never really understood by European scholars, whose methods of study are avowedly objective and noncommittal. The Vedānta can be known only to the extent that it has been lived. The Indian, therefore, cannot trust a teacher whose doctrine is not directly reflected in his very being. Here is something very far removed from the modern European concept of scholarship.

We must add, for the sake of those who entertain romantic notions of the "mysterious East," that the Vedānta has nothing to do with magic or with the exercise of occult powers. It is true that the efficacy of magical procedure and the actuality of occult powers are taken for granted in India. But the magic is regarded as an applied science of the basest kind; and while occult powers, such as that of operation "at a distance," are incidentally acquired in the course of contemplative practice, the use of them—unless under the most exceptional circumstances—is regarded as a dangerous deviation from the path.

Nor is the Vedānta a kind of psychology or Yoga a sort of therapeutics except quite accidentally. Physical and moral health are prerequisites to spiritual progress. A psychological analysis is employed only to break down our fond belief in the unity and immateriality of the "soul," and with a view to a better distinguishing of the spirit from what is not the spirit but only a temporary psycho-physical manifestation of one of the most limited of its modalities. Whoever, like Jung, insists upon translating the essentials of Indian or Chinese metaphysics into a psychology is merely distorting the meaning of the texts. Modern psychology has, from an Indian point of view, about the same values that attach to spiritualism and magic and other "superstitions." Finally, I must point out that the metaphysics, the Vedānta, is not a form of mysticism, except in the sense that with Dionysius we can speak of a Theologia Mystica. What is ordinarily meant by "mysticism" involves a passive receptivity—"we must be able to let things happen in the psyche" is Jung's way of putting it (and in this statement he proclaims himself a "mystic"). But metaphysics repudiates the psyche altogether. The words of Christ, that "No man can be my disciple who hateth not his own soul," have been voiced again and again by every Indian guru; and so far from involving passivity, contemplative practice involves an activity that is commonly compared to the blazing of a fire at a temperature so high as to show neither flickering nor smoke. The pilgrim is called a "toiler," and the characteristic refrain of the pilgrim song is "keep on going, keep on going." The "Way" of the Vedantist is above all an activity.

II

The Vedānta takes for granted an omniscience independent of any source of knowledge external to itself, and a beatitude independent of any external source of pleasure. In saying "That art thou," the Vedānta affirms that man is possessed of, and is himself, "that one thing which when it is known, all things are known" and "for the sake of which alone all things are dear." It affirms that man is unaware of this hidden treasure within himself because he has inherited an ignorance that inheres in the very nature of the psycho-physical vehicle which he mistakenly identifies with himself. The purpose of all teaching is to dissipate this ignorance; when the darkness has been pierced nothing remains but the Gnosis of the Light. The technique of education is, therefore, always formally destructive and iconoclastic; it is not the conveyance of information but the education of a latent knowledge.

The "great dictum" of the Upaniṣads is, "That art thou." "That" is here, of course, Ātman or Spirit, Sanctus Spiritus, Greek *pneuma*, Arabic *rūh*, Hebrew *ruah*, Egyptian *Amon*, Chinese *ch'i*; Ātman is spiritual essence, impartite whether transcendent or immanent; and however many and various the directions to which it may extend or from which it may withdraw, it is unmoved mover in both intransitive and transitive senses. It lends itself to all modalities of being but never itself becomes anyone or anything. That than which all else is a vexation—That art thou. "That," in other words, is the Brahman, or God in the general sense of Logos or Being, considered as the universal source of all Being—expanding, manifesting and productive, font of all things, all of which are "in" him as the finite in the infinite, though not a "part" of him, since the infinite has no parts.

For the most part, I shall use the word Ātman hereafter. While this Ātman, as that which blows and enlightens, is primarily "Spirit," because it is this divine Eros that is the quickening essence in all things and thus their real being, the word Ātman is also used reflexively to mean "self"—either "oneself" in whatever sense, however gross, the notion may be entertained, or with reference to the spiritual self or person (which is the only knowing subject and essence of all things, and must be distinguished from the affected and contingent "I" that is a compound of the body and of all that we mean by "soul" when we speak of a "psychology"). Two very different "selves" are thus involved, and it has been the custom of translators, accordingly, to render Ātman as "self," printed either with a small or with a capital s according to the context. The same distinction is drawn, for example, by St. Bernard between what is my "property" (*proprium*) and what is my very being (*esse*). An alternative Indian formulation distinguishes the "knower of the field"—viz. the Spirit as the only knowing subject in all things and the same in all—from the "field," or body-and-soul as defined above (taken together with the pastures of the senses and embracing therefore all things that can be considered objectively). The Ātman or Brahman itself cannot be thus considered: "How couldst thou know the knower of knowing?"—or in other words, how can the first cause of all things be one of them?

The Ātman is impartite, but it is apparently divided and identified into variety by the differing forms of its vehicles, mouse or man, just as space within a jar is apparently signate and distinguishable from space without it. In this sense it can be said that "he is one as he is in himself but many as he is in his children," and that "participating himself, he fills these worlds." But this is only in the sense that light fills space while it remains itself without discontinuity; the distinction of things from one another thus depending not on differences in the light but on differences in reflecting power. When the jar is shattered, when the vessel of life is unmade, we realize that what was apparently delimited had no boundaries and that "life" was a meaning not to be confused with "living." To say that the Ātman is thus at once participated and impartible, "undivided amongst divided things," without local position and at the same time everywhere, is another way of stating what we are more familiar with as the doctrine of Total Presence.

At the same time, every one of these apparent definitions of the Spirit represents the actuality in time of one of its indefinitely numerous possibilities of formal manifestation. The existence of the apparition begins at birth and ends at death; it can never be repeated. Nothing of Śaṇkara survives but a bequest. Therefore though we can speak of him as still a living power in the world, the man has become a memory. On the other hand, for the gnostic Spirit, the Knower of the field, the Knower of all births, there can never at any time cease to be an immediate knowledge of each and every one of its modalities, a knowledge without before or after (relative to the appearance or disappearance of Śaṇkara from the field of our experience). It follows that where knowledge and being, nature and essence are one and the same, Śaṇkara's being has no beginning and can never cease. In other words, there is a sense in which we can properly speak of "my spirit" and "my person" as well as of "the Spirit" and "the Person," notwithstanding that Spirit and Person are a perfectly simple substance without composition. I shall return to the meaning of "immortality" later, but for the present I want to use what has just been said to explain what was meant by a nonsectarian distinction of points of view. For, whereas the Western student of "philosophy" thinks of Sāṃkhya and Vedānta as two incompatible "systems," because the former is concerned with the liberation of a plurality of Persons and the latter with the liberty of an inconnumerable Person, no such antinomy is apparent to the Hindu. This can be explained by pointing out that in the Christian texts, "Ye are all one in Christ Jesus" and "Whoever is joined unto the Lord is one spirit," the plurals "ye" and "whoever" represent the Sāṃkhya and the singular "one" the Vedānta point of view.

The validity of our consciousness of being, apart from any question of being So-and-so by name or by registrable characters, is accordingly taken for granted. This must not be confused with the argument, "Cogito ergo sum." That "I" feel or "I" think is no proof that "I" am; for we can say with the Vedantist and Buddhist that this is merely a conceit, that "feelings are felt" and "thoughts are thought," and that all this is a part of the "field" of which the spirit is the surveyor, just as we look at a picture which is in one sense a part of us though we are not in any sense a part of it. The question is posed accordingly: "Who art thou?" "What is that self to which we should resort?" We recognize that "self" can have more than one meaning when we speak of an "internal conflict"; when we say that "the spirit is willing but the flesh is weak"; or when we say, with the *Bhagavad Gītā*, that "the Spirit is at war with whatever is not the Spirit."

Am "I" the spirit or the flesh? (We must always remember that in metaphysics the "flesh" includes all the aesthetic and recognitive faculties of the "soul.") We may be asked to consider our reflection in a mirror, and may understand that there we see "ourself"; if we are somewhat less naive, we may be asked to consider the image of the psyche as reflected in the mirror of the mind and may understand that this is what "I" am; or if still better advised, we may come to understand that we are none of these things—that they exist because we are, rather than that we exist inasmuch as they are. The Vedānta affirms that "I" in my essence am as little, or only as much, affected by all these things as an author-playwright is affected by the sight of what is suffered or enjoyed by those who move on the stage—the stage, in this case, of "life" (in other words, the "field" or "pasture" as distinguished from its aquiline surveyor, the Universal Man). The whole problem of man's last end, liberation, beatitude, or deification is accordingly one of finding "oneself" no longer in "this man" but in the Universal Man, the *forma humanitatis*, who is independent of all orders of time and has neither beginning nor end.

Conceive that the "field" is the round or circus of the world, that the throne of the Spectator, the Universal Man, is central and elevated, and that his aquiline glance at all times embraces the whole of the field (equally before and after the enactment of any particular event) in such a manner that from his point of view all events are always going on. We are to transfer our consciousness of being, from our position in the field where the games are going on, to the pavilion in which the Spectator, on whom the whole performance depends, is seated at ease.

Conceive that the right lines of vision by which the Spectator is linked to each separated performer, and along which each performer might look upward (inward) to the Spectator if only his powers of vision sufficed, are lines of force, or the strings by which the puppet-master moves the puppets for himself (who is the whole audience). Each of the performing puppets is convinced of its own independent existence and of itself as one amongst others, which it sees in its own immediate environment and which it distinguishes by name, appearance, and behavior. The Spectator does not, and cannot, see the performers as they see themselves, imperfectly, but he knows the being of each one of them as it really is—that is to say, not merely as effective in a given local position, but simultaneously at every point along the line of visual force by which the puppet is connected with himself, and primarily at that point at which all lines converge and where the being of all things coincides with being in itself. There the being of the puppet subsists as an eternal reason in the eternal intellect—otherwise called the Supernal Sun, the Light of lights, Spirit and Truth.

Suppose now that the Spectator goes to sleep: when he closes his eyes the universe disappears, to reappear only when he opens them again. The opening of eyes ("Let there be light") is called in religion the act of creation, but in metaphysics it is called manifestation, utterance, or spiration (to shine, to utter, and to blow being one and the same thing *in divinis*); the closing of eyes is called in religion the "end of the world," but in metaphysics it is called concealment, silence, or despiration. For us, then, there is an alternation or evolution and involution. But for the central Spectator there is no succession of events. He is always awake and always asleep; unlike the sailor who sometimes sits and thinks and sometimes does not think, our Spectator sits and thinks, and does not think, nowever.

A picture has been drawn of the cosmos and its overseeing "Eye." I have only omitted to say that the field is divided by concentric fences which may conveniently, although not necessarily, be thought of as twenty-one in number. The Spectator is thus at the twenty-first remove from the outermost fence by which our present environment is defined. Each player's or groundling's performance is confined to the possibilities that are represented by the space between two fences. There he is born and there he dies. Let us consider this born being, So-and-so, as he is in himself and as he believes himself to be—"an animal, reasoning and mortal; that I know, and that I confess myself to be," as Boethius expresses it. So-and-so does not conceive that he can move to and fro in time as he will, but knows that he is getting older every day, whether he likes it or not. On the other hand, he does conceive that in some other respects he can do what he likes, so far as this is not prevented by his environment—for example, by a stone wall, or a policeman, or contemporary *mores*. He does not realize that this environment of which he is a part, and from which he cannot except himself, is a causally determined environment; that it does what it does because of what has been done. He does not realize that he is what he is and does what he does because others before him have been what they were and have done what they did, and all this without any conceivable beginning. He is quite literally a creature of circumstances, an automaton, whose behavior could have been foreseen and wholly explained by an adequate knowledge of past causes, now represented by the nature of things—his own nature included. This is the well-known doctrine of *karma*, a doctrine of inherent fatality, which is stated as follows by the

Bhagavad Gītā, xviii.20, "Bound by the working (*karma*) of a nature that is born in thee and is thine own, even that which thou desirest not to do thou doest willy-nilly." So-and-so is nothing but one link in a causal chain of which we cannot imagine a beginning or an end. There is nothing here that the most pronounced determinist can disagree with. The metaphysician—who is not, like the determinist, a "nothing-morist" (*nāstika*) —merely points out at this stage that only the working of life, the manner of its perpetuation, can thus be causally explained; that the existence of a chain of causes presumes the logically prior possibility of this existence—in other words, presumes a first cause which cannot be thought of as one amongst other mediate causes, whether in place or time.

To return to our automaton, let us consider what takes place at its death. The composite being is unmade into the cosmos; there is nothing whatever that can survive as a consciousness of being So-and-so. The elements of the psycho-physical entity are broken up and handed on to others as a bequest. This is, indeed, a process that has been going on throughout our So-and-so's life, and one that can be most clearly followed in propagation, repeatedly described in the Indian tradition as the "rebirth of the father in and as the son." So-and-so lives in his direct and indirect descendants. This is the so-called Indian doctrine of "reincarnation"; it is the same as the Greek doctrine of metasomatosis and metempsychosis; it is the Christian doctrine of our preexistence in Adam "according to bodily substance and seminal virtue"; and it is the modern doctrine of the "recurrence of ancestral characters." Only the fact of such a transmission of psycho-physical characters can make intelligible what is called in religion our inheritance of original sin, in metaphysics our inheritance of ignorance, and by the philosopher our congenital capacity for knowing in terms of subject and object. It is only when we are convinced that nothing happens by chance that the idea of a Providence becomes intelligible.

Need I say that this is not a doctrine of reincarnation? Need I say that no doctrine of reincarnation, according to which the very being and person of a man who has once lived on earth and is now deceased will be reborn of another terrestrial mother, has ever been taught in India, even in Buddhism—or for that matter in the Neoplatonic or any other orthodox tradition? As definitely in the Brāhmaṇas as in the Old Testament, it is stated that those who have once departed from this world have departed forever, and are not to be seen again amongst the living. From the Indian as from the Platonic point of view, all change is a dying. We die and are reborn daily and hourly, and death "when the time comes" is only a special case.

I do not say that a belief in reincarnation has never been entertained in India. I do say that such a belief can only have resulted from a popular misinterpretation of the symbolic language of the texts; that the belief of modern scholars and theosophists is the result of an equally naive and uninformed interpretation of texts. If you ask how such a mistake could have arisen I shall ask you to consider the following statements of Saints Augustine and Thomas Aquinas: that we were in Adam "according to bodily substance and seminal virtue"; "the human body preexisted in the previous works in their causal virtues"; "God does not govern the world directly, but also by means of mediate causes, and were this not so, the world would have been deprived of the perfection of causality"; "As a mother is pregnant with the unborn offspring, so the world itself is pregnant with the causes of unborn things"; "Fate lies in the created causes themselves." If these had been texts extracted from the Upaniṣads or Buddhism, would you not have seen in them not merely what is really there, the doctrine of *karma*, but also a doctrine of "reincarnation"?

By "reincarnation" we mean a rebirth here of the very being and person of the deceased. We affirm that this is an impossibility, for good and sufficient metaphysical reasons. The main consideration is this: that inasmuch as the cosmos embraces an indefinite range of possibilities, all of which must be realized in an equally indefinite duration, the present universe will have run its course when all its potentialities have been reduced to act—just as each human life has run its course when all its possibilities have been exhausted. The end of an aeviternity will have been reached without any room for any repetition of events or any recurrence of past conditions. Temporal succession implies a succession of different things. History repeats itself in types, but cannot repeat itself in any particular. We can speak of a "migration" of "genes" and call this a rebirth of types, but this reincarnation of So-and-so's character must be distinguished from the "transmigration" of So-and-so's veritable person.

Such are the life and death of the reasoning and mortal animal So-and-so. But when Boethius confesses that he is just this animal, Wisdom replies that this man, So-and-so, has forgotten who he is. It is at this point that we part company with the "nothing-morist," or "materialist" and "sentimentalist" (I bracket these two words because "matter" is what is "sensed"). Bear in mind the Christian definition of man as "body, soul and spirit." The Vedānta asserts that the only veritable being of the man is spiritual, and that this being of his is not "in" So-and-so or in any "part" of him but is only reflected in him. It asserts, in other words, that this being is not in the plane of or in any way limited by So-and-so's field, but extends from this field to its center, regardless of the fences that it penetrates. What takes place at death, then, over and above the unmaking of So-and-so, is a withdrawal of the spirit from the phenomenal vehicle of which it had been the "life." We speak, accordingly, with strictest accuracy when we refer to death as a "giving up of the ghost" or say that So-and-so "expires." I need, I feel sure, remind you only in parenthesis that this "ghost" is not a spirit in the Spiritualist's sense, not a "surviving personality," but a purely intellectual principle such as ideas are made of; "ghost" is "spirit" in the sense that the Holy Ghost is Sanctus Spiritus. So then, at death, the dust returns to dust and the spirit to its source.

It follows that the death of So-and-so involves two possibilities, which are approximately those implied by the familiar expressions "saved" or "lost." Either So-and-so's consciousness of being has been self-centered and must perish with himself, or it has been centered in the spirit and departs with it. It is the spirit, as the Vedantic texts express it, that "remains over" when body and soul are unmade. We begin to see now what is meant by the great commandment, "Know thyself." Supposing that our consciousness of being has been centered in the spirit, we can say that the more completely we have already "become what we are," or "awakened," before the dissolution of the body, the nearer to the center of the field will be our next appearance or "rebirth." Our consciousness of being goes nowhere at death where it is not already.

Later on we shall consider the case of one whose consciousness of being has already awakened beyond the last of our twenty-one fences or levels of reference and for whom there remains only a twenty-second passage. For the present let us consider only the first step. If we have taken this step before we die—if we have been to some degree living "in the spirit" and not merely as reasoning animals—we shall, when the body and soul are unmade into the cosmos, have crossed over the first of the fences or circumferences that lie between ourselves and the central Spectator of all things, the Supernal Sun, Spirit and Truth. We shall have come into being in a new environment where, for example, there may still be a duration but not in our present sense a passage of time. We shall not have taken with us any of the psycho-physical apparatus in which a sensitive memory could inhere. Only the "intellectual virtues" survive. This is not the survival of a "personality" (that was a property bequeathed when we departed); it is the continued being of the very person of So-and-so, no longer encumbered by the grossest of So-and-so's former definitions. We shall have crossed over without interruption of consciousness of being.

In this way, by a succession of deaths and rebirths, all of the fences may be crossed. The pathway that we follow will be that of the spiritual ray or radius that links us with the central Sun. It is the only bridge that spans the river of life dividing the hither from the farther shore. The word "bridge" is used advisedly, for this is the "causeway sharper than a razor's edge," the Cinvat bridge of the Avesta, the "brig of dread," familiar to the folklorist, which none but a solar hero can pass; it is a far-flung bridge of light and consubstantial with its source. The Veda expresses it "Himself the Bridge"—a description corresponding to the Christian "I am the Way." You will have divined already that the passage of this bridge constitutes, by stages that are defined by its points of intersection with our twenty-one circumferences, what is properly called a transmigration or progressive regeneration. Every step of this way has been marked by a death to a former "self" and a consequent and immediate "rebirth" as "another man." I must interpolate here that this exposition has inevitably been oversimplified. Two directions of motion, one circumferential and determinate, the other centripetal and free, have been distinguished; but I have not made it clear that their resultant can be properly indicated only by a spiral.

But the time has come to break down the spatial and temporal materialism of our picture of the cosmos and of man's pilgrimage from its circumference to its center and heart. All of the states of being, all of the So-and-sos that we have thought of as coming into being on superimposed levels of reference, are within you, awaiting recognition: all of the deaths and rebirths involved are supernatural—that is, not "against Nature" but extrinsic to the particular possibilities of the given state of being from which the transmigration is thought of as taking place. Nor is any time element involved. Rather, since temporal vicissitudes play no part in the life of the spirit, the journey can be made in part or in its entirety, whether before the event of natural death, at death, or thereafter. The Spectator's pavilion is the Kingdom of Heaven that is within you, viz. in the "heart" (in all Oriental and ancient traditions not only the seat of the will but of the pure intellect, the place where the marriage of Heaven and Earth is consummated); it is there only that the Spectator can himself be seen by the contemplative—whose glance is inverted, and who thus retraces the path of the Ray that links the eye without to the Eye within, the breath of life with the Gale of the Spirit.

We can now, perhaps, better understand all that is meant by the poignant words of the Vedic requiem, "The Sun receive thine eye, the Gale thy spirit," and can recognize their equivalent in "Into thy hands I com-mend my spirit," or in Eckhart's "Eye wherewith I see God, that is the same eye wherewith God sees in me; my eye and God's eye, that is one eye and one vision and one knowing and one love," or St. Paul's "shall be one spirit." The traditional texts are emphatic. We find, for example, in the Upaniṣads the statement that whoever worships, thinking of the deity as other than himself, is little better than an animal. This attitude is reflected in the proverbial saying, "To worship God you must have become God"—which is also the meaning of the words, to "worship in spirit and in truth." We are brought back to the great saying, "That art thou," and have now a better idea, though a far from perfect understanding (because the last step remains to be taken), of what "That" may be. We can now see how traditional doctrines (distinguishing the outer from the inner, the worldly from the other-worldly man, the automaton from the immortal spirit), while they admit and even insist upon the fact that So-and-so is nothing but a link in an endless causal chain, can nevertheless affirm that the chains can be broken and death defeated without respect to time: that this may happen, therefore, as well here and now as at the moment of departure or after death.

We have not even yet, however, reached what is from the point of view of metaphysics defined as man's last end. In speaking of an end of the road, we have so far thought only of a crossing of all the twenty-one barriers and of a final vision of the Supernal Sun, the Truth itself; of reaching the Spectator's very pavilion; of being in heaven face to face with the manifested Eye. This is, in fact, the conception of man's last end as envisaged by religion. It is an aeviternal beatitude reached at the "Top of the Tree," at the "Summit of contingent being"; it is a salvation from all the temporal vicissitudes of the field that has been left behind us. But it is a heaven in which each one of the saved is still one amongst others, and other than the Sun of Men and Light of lights himself (these are Vedic as well as Christian expressions); a heaven that, like the Greek Elysium, is apart from time but not without duration; a resting place but not a final home (as it was not our ultimate source, which was in the nonbeing of the Godhead). It remains for us to pass through the Sun and reach the Empyrean "home" of the Father. "No man cometh to the Father save *through* me." We have passed through the opened doorways of initiation and contemplation; we have moved, through a process of a progressive self-naughting, from the outermost to the innermost court of our being, and can see no way by which to continue—although we know that behind this image of the Truth, by which we have been enlightened, there is a somewhat that is not in any likeness, and although we know that behind this face of God that shines upon the world there is another and more awful side of him that is not man-regarding but altogether self-intent—an aspect that neither knows nor loves anything whatever external to itself. It is our own conception of Truth and Goodness that prevents our seeing Him who is neither good nor true in any sense of ours. The only way on lies directly *through* all that we had thought we had begun to understand: if we are to find our way in, the image of "ourselves" that we still entertain—in however exalted a manner—and that of the Truth and Goodness that we have "imagined" *per excellentiam*, must be shattered by one and the same blow. "It is more necessary that the soul lose God than that she lose creatures . . . the soul honors God most in being quit of God . . . it remains for her to be somewhat that he is not . . . to die to all the activity denoted by the divine nature if she is to enter the divine nature where God is altogether idle . . . she forfeits her very self, and going her own way, seeks God no more" (Eckhart). In other words, we must be one with the Spectator, both when his eyes are open and when they are shut. If we are not, what will become of us when he sleeps? All that we have learned through the affirmative theology must be complemented and fulfilled by an Unknowing, the Docta Ignorantia of Christian theologians, Eckhart's *Agnosia*. It is for this reason that such men as Śaṇkara and Dionysius have so strongly insisted upon the *via remotionis*, and not because a positive concept of Truth or Goodness was any less dear to them than it could be to us. Śaṇkara's personal practice, indeed, is said to have been devotional—even while he prayed for pardon because he had worshipped God by name, who has no name. For such as these there was literally nothing dear that they were not ready to leave.

Let us enunciate the Christian doctrine first in order the better to understand the Indian. The words of Christ are these: that "I am the door; by me if any man enter in, he shall be saved, and shall pass in and out." It is not enough to have reached the door; we must be admitted. But there is a price of admission. "He that would save his soul, let him lose it." Of man's two selves, the two Ātmans of our Indian texts, the self that was known by name as So-and-so must have put itself to death if the other is to be freed of all encumbrances—is to be "free as the Godhead in its nonexistence."

In the Vedantic texts it is likewise the Sun of men and Light of lights that is called the doorway of the worlds and the keeper of the gate. Whoever has come thus far is put to the test. He is told in the first place that he may enter according to the balance of good or evil he may have done. If he understands he will answer, "Thou canst not ask me that; thou knowest that whatever 'I' may have done was not of 'my' doing, but of thine." This is the Truth; and it is beyond the power of the Guardian of the Gate, who is himself the Truth, to deny himself. Or he may be asked the question, "Who art thou?" If he answers by his own or by a family name he is literally dragged away by the factors of time; but if he answers, "I am the Light, thyself, and come to thee as such," the Keeper responds with the words of welcome, "Who thou art, that am I; and who I am, thou art; come in." It should be clear, indeed, that there can be no return to God of anyone who still is anyone, for as our texts express it, "He has not come from anywhere or become anyone."

In the same way, Eckhart, basing his words on the logos, "If any man hate not father and mother, . . . yea and his own soul also, he cannot be my disciple," says that "so long as thou knowest who thy father and thy mother have been in time, thou art not dead with the real death"; and in the same way, Rūmī, Eckhart's peer in Islam, attributes to the Keeper of the Gate the words, "Whoever enters saying 'I am so and so,' I smite in the face." We cannot, in fact, offer any better definition of the Vedic scriptures than St. Paul's "The word of God is quick and powerful, and sharper than any two-edged sword, extending even unto the sundering of soul from spirit": "Quid est ergo, quod debet homo inquirere in hac vita? Hoc est ut sciat ipsum." "Si ignoras te, egredere!"

The last and most difficult problem arises when we ask: what is the state of the being that has thus been freed from itself and has returned to its source? It is more than obvious that a psychological explanation is out of the question. It is, in fact, just at this point that we can best confess with our texts, "He who is most sure that he understands, most assuredly misunderstands." What can be said of the Brahman—that "He is, by that alone can He be apprehended"—can as well be said of whoever has become the Brahman. It cannot be said *what* this is, because it is not any "what." A being who is "freed in this life" (Rūmī's "dead man walking") is "in the world, but not of it."

We can, nevertheless, approach the problem through a consideration of the terms in which the Perfected are spoken of. They are called either Rays of the Sun, or Blasts of the Spirit, or Movers-at-Will. It is also said that they are fitted for embodiment in the manifested worlds: that is to say, fitted to participate in the life of the Spirit, whether it moves or remains at rest. It is a Spirit which bloweth as it will. All of these expressions correspond to Christ's "shall pass in and out, and shall find pasture." Or we can compare it with the pawn in a game of chess. When the pawn has crossed over from the hither to the farther side it is transformed. It becomes a minister and is called a mover-at-will, even in the vernacular. Dead to its former self, it is no longer confined to particular motions or positions, but can go in and out, at will, from the place where its transformation was effected. And this freedom to move at will is another aspect of the state of the Perfected, but a thing beyond the conception of those who are still mere pawns. It may be observed, too, that the ertswhile pawn, ever in danger of an inevitable death on its journey across the board, is at liberty after its transformation either to sacrifice itself or to escape from danger. In strictly Indian terms, its former motion was a crossing, its regenerate motion a descent.

The question of "annihilation," so solemnly discussed by Western scholars, does not arise. The word has no meaning in metaphysics, which knows only of the nonduality of permutation and sameness, multiplicity and unity. Whatever has been an eternal reason or idea or name of an individual manifestation can never cease to be such; the content of eternity cannot be changed. Therefore, as the *Bhagavad Gītā* expresses it, "Never have I not been, and never hast thou not been."

The relation, in identity, of the "That" and the "thou" in the logos "That art thou" is stated in the Vedānta either by such designations as "Ray of the Sun" (implying filiation), or in the formula *bhedābheda* (of which the literal meaning is "distinction without difference"). The relation is expressed by the simile of lovers, so closely embraced that there is no longer any consciousness of "a within or a without," and by the corresponding Vaiṣṇava equation, "each is both." It can be seen also in Plato's conception of the unification of the inner and the outer man; in the Christian doctrine of membership in the mystical body of Christ; in St. Paul's "whoever is joined unto the Lord is one spirit"; and in Eckhart's admirable formula "fused but not confused."

I have endeavored to make it clear that Śaṇkara's so-called "philosophy" is not an "enquiry" but an "explicitation"; that ultimate Truth is not, for the Vedantist, or for any traditionalist, a something that remains to be discovered but a something that remains to be understood by Everyman, who must do the work for himself. I have accordingly tried to explain just what it was that Śaṇkara understood in such texts as *Atharva Veda* x.8.44: "Without any want, contemplative, immortal, self-originated, sufficed with a quintessence, lacking in naught whatever: he who knoweth that constant, ageless, and ever-youthful Spirit, knoweth indeed him-Self, and feareth not to die."

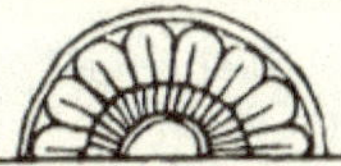

Who Is "Satan" and Where Is "Hell"?

He that doeth sin is of the Devil
I John 3:8

That in this day and age, when "for most people religion has become an archaic and impossible refuge,"[1] men no longer take either God or Satan seriously, arises from the fact that they have come to think of both alike only objectively, only as persons external to themselves and for whose existence no adequate proof can be found. The same, of course, applies to the notions of their respective realms, heaven and hell, thought of as times and places neither now nor here.

We have, in fact, ourselves postponed the "kingdom of heaven on earth" by thinking of it as a material Utopia to be realized, we fondly hope, by means of one or more five-year plans, overlooking the fact that the concept of an endless progress is that of a pursuit "in which thou must sweat eternally,"[2]—a phrase suggestive less of heaven than of hell. What this really means is that we have chosen to substitute a present hell for a future heaven we shall never know.

The doctrine to be faced, however, is that "the kingdom of heaven is within you," here and now, and that, as Jacob Boehme, amongst others, so often said, "heaven and hell are everywhere, being universally extended. . . . Thou art accordingly in heaven or hell. . . . The soul hath heaven or hell within itself,"[3] and cannot be said to "go to" either when the body dies. Here, perhaps, the solution of the problem of Satan may be sought.

It has been recognized that the notion of a Satanic "person," the chief of many "fallen angels," presents some difficulties: even in religion, that

[This essay was first published in the *Review of Religion*, XI (1947).—ED.]

[1] Margaret Marshall in *The Nation*, February 2, 1946.

[2] Jacob Boehme, *De incarnatione Verbi*, II.5.18.

[3] Jacob Boehme, "Of Heaven and Hell," pp. 259, 260.

of a Manichean "dualism" emerges; at the same time, if it be maintained that anything whatever is not God, God's infinity is thereby circumscribed and limited. Is "he," Satan, then a person, or merely a "personification," i.e., a postulated personality?[4] Who is "he," and where? Is he a serpent or a dragon, or has he horns and a poisonous tail? Can he be redeemed and regenerated, as Origen and the Muslims have believed? All these problems hang together.

However the ultimate truth of "dualism" may be repudiated, a kind of dualism is logically unavoidable for all practical purposes, because any world in time and space, or that could be described in words or by mathematical symbols, must be one of contraries, both quantitative and qualitative, for example, long and short, good and evil; and even if it could be otherwise, a world without these opposites would be one from which all possibility of choice, and of procedure from potentiality to act, would be excluded, not a world that could be inhabited by human beings such as we. For anyone who holds that "God made the world," the question, Why did He permit the existence in it of any evil, or that of the Evil One in whom all evil is personified, is altogether meaningless; one might as well enquire why He did not make a world without dimensions or one without temporal succession.

Our whole metaphysical tradition, Christian and other, maintains that "there are two in us,"[5] this man and the Man in this man; and that this is so is still a part and parcel of our spoken language in which, for example, the expression "self-control" implies that there is one that controls and another subject to control, for we know that "nothing acts upon itself,"[6]

[4] "Person cannot be affirmed . . . of living things . . . bereft of intellect and reason . . . but we say there is a person of a man, of God, of an Angel" (Boethius, *Contra Evtychen* II). On this basis, Satan, who remains an angel even in hell, can be called a Person, or indeed, Persons, since his name is "Legion: for we are many"; but as a fallen being, "out of his right mind," in reality a Person only potentially. Much the same could be said of the soul, viz. that there is a Person of the soul, but hardly that the soul, as it is in itself, is a Person. Satan and the soul, both alike invisible, are only "known," or rather "inferred," from behavior, which is just what "personality" implies: "personality, that is the hypothetical unity that one postulates to account for the doings of people" (H. S. Sullivan, "Introduction to the Study of Interpersonal Relations," *Psychiatry*, I, 1938).

[5] Plato, *Republic* 439DE, 604B; Philo, *Deterius* 82; St. Thomas Aquinas, *Sum. Theol.* II-II.26.4; St. Paul, II Cor. 4:16; and in general, as the doctrine is briefly stated by Goethe: "Zwei Seelen wohnen ach, in meiner Brust, die eine will sich von der andern trennen" (*Faust*, I, 759). Similarly in the Vedānta, Buddhism, Islam, and in China.

[6] *Nil agit in seipsum*: axiomatic in Platonic, Christian, and Indian philosophy: "the same thing can never do or suffer opposites in the same respect or in relation

though we forget it when we talk about "self-government."[7] Of these two "selves," outer and inner man, psycho-physical "personality" and very Person, the human composite of body, soul, and spirit is built up. Of these two, on the one hand body-and-soul (or -mind), and on the other, spirit, one is mutable and mortal, the other constant and immortal; one "becomes," the other "is," and the existence of the one that is not, but becomes, is precisely a "personification" or "postulation," since we cannot say of anything that never remains the same that "it *is*." And however necessary it may be to say "I" and "mine" for the practical purposes of everyday life, our Ego in fact is nothing but a name for what is really only a sequence of observed behaviors.[8]

Body, soul, and spirit: can one or other of these be equated with the Devil? Not the body, certainly, for the body in itself is neither good nor evil, but only an instrument or means to good or evil. Nor the Spirit—intellect, synteresis, conscience, Agathos Daimon—for this is, by hypothesis, man's best and most divine part, in itself incapable of error, and our only means of participation in the life and the perfection that is God himself. There remains only the "soul"; that soul which all must "hate" who would be Christ's disciples and which, as St. Paul reminds us, the Word of God like a two-edged sword "severs from the spirit"; a soul which St. Paul must have "lost" to be able to say truly that "I live, yet not I, but Christ in me," announcing, like Manṣūr, his own theosis.

Of the two in us, one the "spark" of Intellect or Spirit, and the other, Feeling or Mentality, subject to persuasion, it is obvious that the latter is the "tempter," or more truly "temptress." There is in each of us, in this man and that woman alike, an *anima* and *animus*, relatively feminine and masculine;[9] and, as Adam rightly said, "the woman gave, and I did eat";

---

to the same thing at the same time," Plato, *Republic* 436B; "strictly speaking, no one imposes a law upon his own actions," *Sum. Theol.* I.93.5; "because of the antinomy involved in the notion of acting upon oneself" (*svātmani ca kriyāvirodhāt*), Śaṅkara on BG II.17.

[7] "Art thou free of self? then art thou 'Self-governed'" (*selbes gewaltic* = Skr. *svarāṭ*), Meister Eckhart, Pfeiffer ed., p. 598.

[8] "How can that which is never in the same state 'be' anything?" (Plato, *Cratylus*, 439E; *Theatetus*, 152D; *Symposium*, 207D, etc.). "'Ego' has no real meaning, because it is perceived only for an instant," i.e., does not last for even so long as two consecutive moments (*naivāham-arthaḥ kṣanikatva-darśanāt*; *Vivekacūḍāmani of Śrī Śaṅkarāchārya*, 293, Swami Madhavananda, tr., Almora, 3rd ed., 1932).

[9] It is unfortunate that, in modern psychology, an originally lucid terminology and distinction has been confused by an equation of the "soul-image" with "the *anima* in man, the *animus* in woman." The terms are even more misused by

also, be it noted, the "serpent," by whom the woman herself was first beguiled, wears, in art, a woman's face. But to avoid all possibility of misunderstanding here, it must be emphasized that all this has nothing whatever to do with a supposed inferiority of women or superiority of men: in this functional and psychological sense any given woman may be "manly" (heroic) or any given man "effeminate" (cowardly).[10]

One knows, of course, that "soul," like "self," is an ambiguous term, and that, in some contexts, it may denote the Spirit or "Soul *of* the soul," or "Self *of* the self," both of which are expressions in common use. But we are speaking here of the mutable "soul" as distinguished from the "spirit," and should not overlook to what extent this *nefesh*, the *anima* after which the human and other "animals" are so called, is constantly disparaged in the Bible,[11] as is the corresponding *nafs* in Islam. This soul is the self to be "denied" (the Greek original meaning "utterly reject,"

Father M. C. D'Arcy in his *Mind and Heart of Love* (London, 1946), ch. 7. Traditionally, *anima* and *animus* are the "soul" and the "spirit" equally in any man or any woman; so William of Thierry (cf. note 22 below) speaks of *animus vel spiritus*. This usage goes back to Cicero, e.g., *Tusculan Disputations* I.22.52, "neque nos corpora sumus . . . cum igitur: Nosce te dicit, hoc dicit, Nosce animum tuum," and v.13.38, "humanus . . . animus decerptus [est] ex mente divina"; and Lucius Accius (*fr.* 296), "sapimus animo, fruimur anima; sine animo, anima est debilis."

[10] In all traditions, not excepting the Buddhist, this man and this woman are both equally capable of "fighting the good fight."

[11] Cf. D. B. Macdonald, *The Hebrew Philosophical Genius* (Princeton, 1934), p. 139, "the lower, physical nature, the appetites, the psyche of St. Paul . . . 'self,' but always with that lower meaning behind it"; Thomas Sheldon Green, *Greek-English Lexikon of the New Testament* (New York and London, 1879), s.v. ψυχικός ("governed by the sensuous nature subject to appetite and passion"); "anima . . . cujus vel pulchritudo virtus, vel deformitas vitium est . . . mutabilis est" (St. Augustine, *De gen. ad litt.* 7.6.9, and *Ep.* 166.2.3).

On the other hand, the "Soul" or "Self," as printed with the capital, is Jung's "Self . . . around which it [the Ego] revolves, very much as the earth rotates about the sun . . . [its] superordinated subject" (*Two Essays on Analytical Psychology*, London, 1928, p. 268); not *a* being, but the inconnumerable and indefinable "Being of all beings."

We are never told that the mutable soul is immortal in the same timeless way that God is immortal, but only that it is immortal "in a certain way of its own" (*secundum quemdam modum suum*, St. Augustine, *Ep.* 166.2.3). If we ask, *Quomodo?* seeing that the soul is in time, the answer must be, "in one way only, viz. by continuing to become; since thus it can always leave behind it a new and other nature to take the place of the old" (Plato, *Symposium* 207D). It is only God, who is the Soul of the soul, that we can speak of as immortal absolutely (1 Tim. 6:16). It is incorrect to call the soul "immortal" indiscriminately, just as it is incorrect to call any man a genius; man has an immortal Soul, as he has a Genius, but the soul can only be immortalized by returning to its source, that is to say, by dying to itself and living to its Self; just as a man becomes a genius only when he is no longer "himself."

with ontological rather than a merely ethical application), the soul that must be "lost" if "it" is to be saved; and which, as Meister Eckhart and the Sūfīs so often say, must "put itself to death," or, as the Hindus and Buddhists say, must be "conquered" or "tamed," for "that is not my Self." This soul, subject to persuasion, and distracted by its likes and dislikes, this "mind" that we mean when we speak of having been "minded to do this or that," is "that which thou callest 'I' or 'myself,' " and which Jacob Boehme thus distinguishes from the I that *is*, when he says, with reference to his own illuminations, that "not I, the I that I am, knows these things, but God in me." We cannot treat the doctrine of the Ego at length, but will only say that, as for Meister Eckhart and the Sūfīs, "Ego, the word I, is proper to none but God in his sameness," and that "I" can only rightly be attributed to Him and to the one who, being "joined unto the Lord, is one spirit."

That the soul herself, our "I" or "self" itself, should be the Devil—whom we call the "enemy," "adversary," "tempter," "dragon,"—never by a personal name[12]—may seem startling, but it is very far from being a novel proposition. As we go on, it will be found that an equation of the soul with Satan has often been enunciated, and that it provides us with an almost perfect solution of all the problems that the latter's "personality" poses. Both are "real" enough for all pragmatic purposes here, in the active life where "evil" must be contended with, and the dualism of the contraries cannot be evaded; but they are no more "principles," no more really real, than the darkness that is nothing but the privation of light.

No one will deny that the battleground on which the psychomachy must be fought out to a finish is within you, or that, where Christ fights, there also must his enemy, the Antichrist, be found. Neither will anyone, "superstition" apart, be likely to pretend that the Temptations of St. Anthony, as depicted in art, can be regarded otherwise than as "projections" of interior tensions. In the same way that Picasso's "Guernica" is the mirror of Europe's disintegrated soul, "the hell of modern existence," the Devil's horns and sting are an image of the most evil beast in man himself. Often enough it has been said by the "Never-enough honoured Auncients," as well as by modern authors, that "man is his own worst enemy." On the other hand, the best gift for which a man might pray is to be "at peace with himself";[13] and, indeed, for so long as he is not at peace with Him-

[12] Even the Hebrew *Sāṭān*, "opponent," is not a personal name.

[13] *Contest of Homer and Hesiod* [Oxford Classical Texts, ed. Allen, Vol. 5—ED.], 165, where the expression *εὔνουν εἶναι ἑαυτῷ* = *μετανοεῖν* ("repentance," i.e., "coming to be in one's right mind"), the opposite of *παρανοεῖν*.

self,[14] he can hardly be at peace with anybody else, but will "project" his own disorders, making of "the enemy"—for example, Germany, or Russia, or the Jews—his "devil." "From whence come wars and fightings among you? Come they not hence, even from your lusts (pleasure, or desires, Skr. *kāmāḥ*) that contend in your members?" (James 4:1).

As Jung so penetratingly observes: "When the fate of Europe carried it into a four years war of stupendous horror—a war that no one wanted—hardly anyone asked who had caused the war and its continuation."[15] The answer would have been unwelcome: it was "I"—your "I" and mine. For, in the words of another modern psychologist, E. E. Hadley, "the tragedy of this delusion of individuality is that it leads to isolation, fear, paranoid suspicion, and wholly unnecessary hatreds."[16]

All this has always been familiar to the theologians, in whose writings Satan is so often referred to simply as "the enemy." For example, William Law: "You are under the power of no other enemy, are held in no other captivity, and want no other deliverance but from the power of your own earthly self. This is the one murderer of the divine life within you. It is your own Cain that murders your own Abel,"[17] and "self is the root, the tree, and the branches of all the evils of our fallen state . . . Satan, or which is the same thing, self-exaltation. . . . This is that full-born natural self that must be pulled out of the heart and *totally denied*, or there can be no disciple of Christ." If, indeed, "the kingdom of heaven is within you," then also the "war in heaven" will be there, until Satan has been overcome, that is, until the Man in this man is "master of himself," *selbes gewaltic*, ἐγκρατὴς ἑαυτοῦ.

For the *Theologia Germanica* (chs. 3, 22, 49), it was the Devil's "'I, Me, and Mine' that were the cause of his fall. . . . For the self, the I, the me and the like, all belong to the Evil Spirit, and therefore it is that he is an Evil Spirit. Behold one or two words can utter all that has been said by these many words: 'Be simply and wholly bereft of self.'" For "there is

[14] The Self we mean when we tell a man who is misbehaving to "be yourself" (ἐν σαυτῷ γενοῦ, Sophocles, *Philoctetes* 950), for "all is intolerable when any man forsakes his proper Self, to do what fits him not" (*ibid.* 902–903).

[15] C. G. Jung, *The Integration of Personality* (New York, 1935), p. 274.

[16] E. E. Hadley, in *Psychiatry* V (1942), 133; citing also H. S. Sullivan, *op. cit.*, pp. 121–134; "emphasized individuality of each of us, 'myself.' Here we have the very mother of illusions, the ever pregnant source of preconceptions that invalidate almost all our efforts to understand other people."

[17] William Law, *The Spirit of Love, and an Address to the Clergy*, cited in Stephen Hobhouse, *William Law and Eighteenth Century Quakerism* (London, 1927), pp. 156, 219, 220.

nothing else in hell, but self-will; and if there were no self-will, there would be no devil and no hell." So, too, Jacob Boehme: "this vile self-hood possesses the world and worldly things; and dwells also in itself, which is dwelling in hell"; and Angelus Silesius:

> Nichts anders stürzet dich in Höllenschlund hinein
> Als dass verhasste Wort (merk's wohl!): das Mein und Dein.[18]

Hence the resolve, expressed in a Shaker hymn:

> But now from my forehead I'll quickly erase
> The stamp of the Devil's great "I."[19]

Citations of this kind could be indefinitely multiplied, all to the effect that of all evil beasts, "the most evil beast we carry in our bosom,"[20] our most godless and despicable part" and "multifarious beast," which our "Inner Man," like a lion tamer, must keep under his control or else will have to follow where it leads.[21]

Even more explicit sayings can be cited from Sūfī sources, where the soul (*nafs*) is distinguished from the intellect or spirit (*aql, rūḥ*) as the Psyche is distinguished from the Pneuma by Philo and in the New Testament, and as *anima* from *animus* by William of Thierry.[22] For the encyclopaedic *Kashfu'l Maḥjūb*, the soul is the "tempter," and the type of hell in this world.[23] Al-Ghazālī, perhaps the greatest of the Muslim theologians, calls the soul "the greatest of your enemies"; and more than that could hardly be said of Satan himself. Abū Sā'īd asks: "What is evil, and what is the worst evil?" and answers, "Evil is 'thou,' and the worst evil 'thou' if thou knowest it not"; he, therefore, called himself a "Nobody," refusing, like the Buddha, to identify himself with any nameable "personality."[24]

[18] Angelus Silesius, *Der Cherubinische Wandersmann*, v.238.

[19] E. D. Andrews, *The Gift to be Simple* (New York, 1940), p. 18; cf. p. 79, "That great big I, I'll mortify."

[20] Jacob Boehme, *De incarnatione Verbi*, 1.13.13.

[21] Plato, *Republic* 588c ff., where the whole soul is compared to such a composite animal as the Chimaera, Scylla, or Cerberus. In some respects the Sphinx might have been an even better comparison. In any case, the human, leonine, and ophidian parts of these creatures correspond to the three parts of the soul, in which "the human in us, or rather our divine part" should prevail; of which Hercules leading Cerberus would be a good illustration.

[22] William of Thierry, *The Golden Epistle of Abbot William of St. Thierry to the Carthusians of Mont Dieu*, tr. Walter Shewring (London, 1930) §§50, 51.

[23] *Kashf al-Mahjūb*, tr. R. A. Nicholson (*Gibb Memorial Series* XVII), p. 199; cf. p. 9, "the greatest of all veils between God and man."

[24] For Abū Sā'īd see R. A. Nicholson, *Studies in Islamic Mysticism* (Cambridge, 1921), p. 53.

Jalālu'd Dīn Rūmī, in his *Mathnawī*, repeats that man's greatest enemy is himself: "This soul," he says, "is hell," and he bids us "slay the soul." "The soul and Shaitān are both one being, but take two forms; essentially one from the first, he became the enemy and envier of Adam"; and, in the same way, "the Angel (Spirit) and the Intellect, Adam's helpers, are of one origin but assume two forms." The Ego holds its head high: "decapitation means, to slay the soul and quench its fire in the Holy War" (*jihād*); and well for him who wins this battle, for "whoever is at war with himself for God's sake, . . . his light opposing his darkness, the sun of his spirit shall never set."[25]

> 'Tis the fight which Christ,
> With his internal Love and Light,
> Maintains within man's nature, to dispel
> God's Anger, Satan, Sin, and Death, and Hell;
> The human Self, or Serpent, to devour,
> And raise an Angel from it by His Pow'r.
>
> John Byrom

"Spark of the soul . . . image of God, that there is ever in all wise at war with all that is not godly . . . and is called the Synteresis"[26] (Meister Eckhart, Pfeiffer ed., p. 113). "We know that the Law is of the Spirit . . . but I see another law in my members, warring against the Law of the Intellect, and bringing me into captivity. . . . With the Intellect I myself serve the Law of God; but with the flesh the law of sin. . . . Submit yourselves therefore to God: resist the Devil."[27] And similarly in other Scriptures, notably the *Bhagavad Gītā* (vi.5, 6): "Lift up the self by the Self, let not self sit back. For, verily, the Self is both the friend and the foe of the self; the friend of one whose self has been conquered by the Self, but to one whose self hath not (been overcome), the Self at war, forsooth, acts as an enemy"; and the Buddhist *Dhammapada* (103, 160, 380), where "the Self is the Lord of the self" and one should "by the Self incite the

[25] Citations are from *Mathnawī* i.2617; ii.2525; iii.374, 2738, 3193, 4053 (*nafs va shaitān har dū ek īn būd'and*); cf. ii.2272 ff., v.2919, 2939. The fundamental kinship of Satan and the Ego is apparent in their common claim to independent being; and "association" (of others with the God who only *is*) amounts, from the Islamic point of view, to polytheism (*ibid.* iv.2675–77).

[26] On the meaning of the "Synteresis," etymologically an equivalent of Skr. *saṃtāraka*, "one who helps to cross over," see O. Renz, "Die Synteresis nach dem Hl. Thomas von Aquin," *Beiträge zur Geschichte der Philosophie des Mittelalters*, X (Münster, 1911).

[27] Rom. 7:14–23; James 4:7.

self, and by the Self gentle self" (as a horse is "broken in" by a skilled trainer), and "one who has conquered self is the best of all champions." (Cf. Philostratus, *Vit. Ap.*, I.13: "Just as we break in skittish and unruly horses by stroking and patting them.")

At the same time, it must not be forgotten that the Psychomachy is also a "battle of love," and that Christ—to whom "ye should be married . . . that we should bring fruit unto God" (Rom. 7:3, 4)—already loved the unregenerate soul "in all her baseness and foulness,"[28] or that it is of her that Donne says: "Nor ever chaste, except *Thou* ravish me." It was for nothing but "to go and fetch his Lady, whom his Father had eternally given him to wife, and to restore her to her former high estate that the Son proceeded out of the Most High" (Meister Eckhart).[29] The Deity's lance or thunderbolt is, at the same time, his yard, with which he pierces his mortal Bride. The story of the thunder-smitten Semele reminds us that the Theotokos, in the last analysis Psyche, has ever been of Lunar, never herself of Solar stock; and all this is the sum and substance of every "solar myth," the theme of the *Liebesgeschichte des Himmels* and of the *Drachenkämpfe.*

"Heaven and earth: let them be wed again."[30] Their marriage, consummated in the heart, is the *Hieros Gamos, Daivam Mithunam*,[31] and those in whom it has been perfected are no longer anyone, but as He is "who never became anyone."[32] Plotinus' words: "Love is of the very nature of the Psyche, and hence the constant yoking of Eros with the Psyches in the pictures and the myths"[33] might as well have been said of half the world's fairy-tales, and especially of the Indian "pictures and myths" of Śrī Krishna and the Milkmaids, of which the Indian commentators rightly deny the historicity, asserting that all these are things that come to pass in all men's experience. Such, indeed, are "the *erōtika* (Skr. *śṛṇgāra*) into which, it seems that you, O Socrates, should be initiated," as Diotima says, and which in fact he so deeply respected.[34]

But, this is not only a matter of Grace; the soul's salvation depends also on her submission, her willing surrender; it is prevented for so long as she resists. It is her pride (*māna, abhimāna*; οἴημα, οἴησις; self-opinion, overweening), the Satanic conviction of her own independence (*asmimāna, ahaṃkāra, cogito ergo sum*), her evil rather than herself, that must

[28] St. Bonaventura, *Dominica prima post octavum epiphaniae*, 2.2. For the whole theme, see also Coomaraswamy, "On the Loathly Bride" [in Vol. I of this edition—ED.].

[29] Pfeiffer ed., p. 288.
[30] RV X.24.5.
[31] ŚB X.5.2.12.
[32] KU II.18.
[33] *Enneads* VI.9.9.
[34] Plato, *Symposium* 210A.

be killed; this pride she calls her "self-respect," and would "rather die" than be divested of it. But the death that she at last, despite herself, desires, is no destruction but a transformation. Marriage is an initiatory death and integration (*nirvāṇa, saṃskāra,* τέλος).[35] "Der Drache und die Jungfrau sind natürlich identisch";[36] the "Fier Baiser" transforms the dragon; the mermaid loses her ophidian tail; the girl is no more when the woman has been "made"; from the nymph the winged soul emerges.[37] And so "through Thee an Iblis may become again one of the Cherubim."[38]

And what follows when the lower and the higher forms of the soul have been united? This has nowhere been better described than in the *Aitareya Āraṇyaka* (II.3.7): "This Self gives itself to that self, and that self to this Self; they become one another; with the one form he (in whom this marriage has been consummated) is unified with yonder world, and with the other united to this world"; the *Bṛhadāraṇyaka Upaniṣad* (IV.3.23): "Embraced by the Prescient Self, he knows neither a within nor a without. Verily, that is his form in which his desire is obtained, in which the Self is his desire, and in which no more desires or grieves." "Amor ipse non quiescit, nisi in amato, quod fit, cum obtinet ipsum possessione plenaria";[39] "Jam perfectam animam . . . gloriosam sibi sponsam Pater conglutinat."[40] Indeed:

> Dafern der Teufel könnt aus seiner Seinheit gehn,
> So sähest du ihn stracks in Gottes Throne stehn.[41]

So, then, the Agathos and Kakos Daimons, Fair and Foul selves, Christ and Antichrist, both inhabit us, and their opposition is within us. Heaven and Hell are the divided images of Love and Wrath *in divinis,* where the Light and the Darkness are undivided, and the Lamb and the Lion lie down together. In the beginning, as all traditions testify, heaven and earth were one and together; essence and nature are one in God, and it remains for every man to put them together again within himself.

[35] *Nirvāṇa,* J. 1.60; *saṃskāra,* Manu II.67; τέλος, H. G. Liddell and R. Scott, *A Greek-English Lexicon,* 8th ed., Oxford, 1897, s.v. VI.2.

[36] E. Siecke, *Drachenkämpfe* (Leipzig, 1907), p. 14.

[37] For the Fier Baiser see the references in Coomaraswamy, "On the Loathly Bride." For the marriage, Meister Eckhart (Pfeiffer ed., p. 407) and Omikron, *Letters from Paulos,* New York, 1920, *passim.*

[38] Rūmī, *Mathnawī* IV.3496.

[39] Jean de Castel, *De adhaerendo Deo,* C. 12.

[40] St. Bernard, *De grad. humilitatis,* VII.21.

[41] Angelus Silesius, I.143. Cf. *Theologia Germanica,* ch. XVI: "If the evil Spirit himself could come into true obedience, he would become an angel [of light] again, and all his sin and wickedness would be blotted out."

All these are our answers. Satan is not a real and single Person, but a severally postulated personality, a "Legion." Each of these personalities is capable of redemption (*apokatastasis*), and can, if it will, become again what it was before it "fell"—Lucifer, Phosphorus, Hēlēl, Scintilla, the Morning Star, a Ray of the Supernal Sun; because the Spark, however it may seem to be smothered, is an Asbestos that cannot be extinguished, even in hell. But, in the sense that a redemption of all beings cannot be thought of as taking place at any one time, and inasmuch as there will be devilish souls in need of redemption throughout all time, Satan must be thought of as being damned for ever, meaning by "damned," self-excluded from the vision of God and the knowledge of Truth.

The problem with which we started has been largely solved, but it still remains to accomplish the harder tasks of an actual "self-naughting" and consequent "Self-realization" to which the answers point, and for which theology is only a partial preparation. Satan and the Ego are not really entities, but concepts postulated and valid only for present, provisional, and practical purposes; both are composite photographs, as it were of X_1, X_2, X_3. It has often been said that the Devil's most ingenious device is to persuade us that his existence is a mere "superstition." In fact, however, nothing can be more dangerous than to deny his existence, which is as real, although no more so, as our own; we dare not deny Satan until we have denied ourselves, as everyone must who would follow Him who said and did nothing "of himself." "What is Love? the sea of non-existence";[42] and "whoever enters there, saying 'It is I,' I [God], smite him in the face";[43] "What is Love? thou shalt know when *thou* becomest *Me*."[44]

[42] *Mathnawī* III.4723.

[43] Rūmī, *Dīvān*, Ode XXVIII. "None has knowledge of each who enters that he is So-and-so or So-and-so," *ibid*., p. 61.

[44] *Mathnawī* II, Introduction.

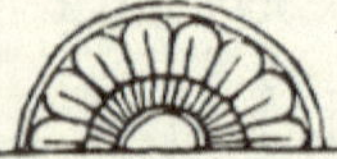

Śrī Ramakrishna and Religious Tolerance

"They call Him by a multitude of names, Who is but One"; "A single Fire that burns on many altars"; "Even as He sheweth, so is He named"; these are affirmations taken from the sacrificial hymns of the *Ṛg Veda.* "As He is approached, so He becomes"; "It is because of His great abundance—or because He can be so variously participated in—that they call Him by so many names." By way of comment, we cite St. Thomas Aquinas, "The many aspects of these names are not empty and vain, for there corresponds to all of them one single reality represented by them in a manifold and imperfect manner" (*Sum. Theol.* 1.13.4 and 2). Nothing, perhaps, so strangely impresses or bewilders a Christian student of Saint Ramakrishna's life as the fact that this Hindu of the Hindus, without in any way repudiating his Hinduism, but for the moment forgetting it, about 1866 completely surrendered himself to the Islamic way, repeated the name of Allah, wore the costume, and ate the food of a Muslim. This self-surrender to what we should call in India the waters of another current of the single river of truth resulted only in a direct experience of the beatific vision, not less authentic than before. Seven years later, Ramakrishna in the same way proved experimentally the truth of Christianity. He was now for a time completely absorbed in the idea of Christ, and had no room for any other thought. You might have supposed him a convert. What really resulted was that he could now affirm on the basis of personal experience, "I have also practiced all religions, Hinduism, Islam, Christianity, and I have also followed the paths of the different Hindu sects. . . . The lake has many shores. At one the Hindu draws water in a pitcher, and calls it *jala*, at another the Muslim in leather bottles, and calls it *pāni*, at a third the Christian finds what he calls 'water.' "

[Originally a lecture given in New York, March 1936, for the centenary of the birth of Śrī Ramakrishna, this text was published in *Prabuddha Bharata*, XLI (1936), and in French by *Études traditionelles,* XLI (1936).—ED.]

Such an understanding may be rare, but is absolutely normal in the East: as the *Bhagavad Gītā* expresses it, "There is no deity that I am not, and in case any man be truly the worshipper of any deity whatever, it is I that am the cause of his devotion and its fruit. . . . However men approach Me, even so do I welcome them, for the path men take from every side is Mine." Similarly the *Bhaktamāla* (cf. G. A. Grierson, ed., London, 1909): "No one is ignorant of the doctrines of his own religion. . . . Therefore let every man, so far as in him lieth, help the reading of the Scriptures, whether those of his own church, or those of another." And similarly also in Islām, "My heart has become capable of every form . . . it is a convent for Christian monks, a temple for idols, the place of pilgrimage at Mecca, the tables of the Torah, the book of the Koran: I follow the religion of Love, whichever way His camels take."

Such an understanding is rarer still, and one may say abnormal to the Western type of humanity. If the modern Christian does not quite endorse the conduct of Charlemagne's heroes at Saragossa—"The synagogues they enter and the mosques, whose every wall with mallet and axes they shatter: they break in pieces small the idols . . . the heathen folk in crowds to the font baptismal are driven, to take Christ's yoke upon them. . . . Thus out of heathen darkness have five-score thousand been redeemed, and be now true Christians," it is at least quite certain that for every man that has died by religious persecution in India, ten thousand have died in Europe, and equally certain that the activity of Christian missions still quite frankly endorses a program of conversion by force—the force of money, not indeed paid out in cash, but expended on education and medical aid bestowed with ulterior motives. "Force," as Lafcadio Hearn once wrote, "the principal instrument of Christian propagandism in the past, is still the force behind our missions." No greater offenders are to be found than missionaries against the commandment, "Thou shalt not bear false witness against thy neighbour." I do not, however, at all wish to dwell upon this point of view, but rather to point out that although religious tolerance in Europe has never, as in Asia, been founded upon the belief that all religions are true, but rather founded on a growing indifference to all religious doctrines, an intellectual basis for a willing tolerance of other forms of belief is by no means wanting in Christianity. John, indeed, speaks of the "True Light that lighteth every man." Even St. Thomas admits that some of the Gentiles who lived before Christ's temporal birth may have been saved. For as Clement of Alexandria had long since said, "There was always a natural manifestation of the one Almighty God, amongst all right-thinking men." Eckhart speaks of "One of our most ancient philosophers who found the truth long, long before God's birth, ere ever there was Christian faith at all as it is now," and again much more boldly, "He to whom God is different in one thing from another and to whom God is dearer in one thing than another, that man is a barbarian, still in the wilds, a child."

Note that "Merlyn made the round table in tokenying of the roundenes of the world for by the round table is the world sygnefyed by ryghte. For all the world crysten and hethen repayren unto the round table . . . (that) by them which should be felawes of the round table the truth of the Sancgreal should be well knowen." (Malory, *Morte Darthur,* XIV.2). The truth is with Blake when he says, "The religions of all nations are derived from each nation's different reception of the poetic genius[1] which is everywhere called the spirit of prophecy. . . . As all men are alike (though infinitely various), so all religions, and as all similars have one source." The Vedic and Christian traditions are never tired of employing "Truth," "Being," and "Beauty," as preeminently fitting, essential names of God. Now we are well aware that in this human world there cannot be a conceptual knowledge or expression of truth except in some way; just as there can be no perceptible beauty except of some kind. What is true in all truths, or what is beautiful in all beauties, cannot itself be any one of these truths or beauties. As Dionysius says, "If anyone in seeing God understood what he saw, he saw not God himself, but one of those things that are His." Belief in Revelation or Audition does not mean that the very words in which the truth is expressed in any case contain the truth, but rather that they point to it, for as St. Thomas says, "Everything has truth of nature according to the *degree* in which it imitates the knowledge of God"; "our intellect considers God *according to* the mode derived from creatures"; and finally, "the thing known is in the knower *according* to the mode of the knower." All concepts of God, even the most nearly adequate, are thus man-made; as we say in India, "He takes the forms that are imagined by His worshippers." Very surely He is not to be thought of as confined by or fully expressed by any of these forms, Who is Himself the single form of every form, and transcendent with respect to each and every form; it is from this point of view that many a Christian teacher has affirmed that "Nothing true can be said of God." The value of concepts, of any expression verbal or visible, *per verbum in intellectu conceptum*, is one of use; the concept is of value not as a thing in itself,

[1] Vedic *kavitva*.

but as dispositive to an essential vision, *not* in any likeness. The beauty of the formula, the verbal or visual icon, poignant as it may be in Christian gospel or Vedic liturgy, is not an end in itself but, referred to him who uses it, is an invitation. The purpose of any art, and no less of that highest art of theology, in which all other arts, whether literary or plastic, subsist *per excellentiam*, is to teach, to delight, and above all to move (Augustine's *docere, delectare, movere*). An exclusive attachment to any one dogma, any one group of verbal or visual symbols, however pertinent, is an act of idolatry; the Truth itself is inexpressible.

If the image is His whose image it is, the colors and the art are ours. Whoever claims that his own manner of understanding and statement is the only true one is moved not by the vision of God, but by spiritual pride. Such a believer, as Ibn 'Arabī says, "praises none but himself, for his God is made by himself, and to praise the work is to praise the maker of it: its excellence or imperfection belongs to the maker. For this reason he blames the beliefs of others, which he would not do if he were just. . . . If he understood the saying of Junayd, 'The color of the water is the color of the vessel containing it,' he would not interfere with others, but would perceive God in every form and every belief. He has opinion, not knowledge: therefore God said, 'I am in my servant's opinion of Me,' that is, 'I do not manifest myself to him save in the form of his belief.' God is absolute or unrestricted as He pleases; and the God of religious belief is subject to limitations, for He is the God who is contained in the heart of His servant." The Oriental Gnostic has no fault to find with any Catholic doctrine; judged by Vedic standards, one can say that Christianity is true and lovely, true so far as any formulation can be true, lovely in so far as any thing, as distinguished from One who is no thing, can be lovely.

Moreover, it can be positively affirmed that every notable Christian doctrine is also explicitly propounded in every other dialect of the primordial tradition: I refer to such doctrines as those of the eternal and temporal births, that of the single essence and two natures, that of the Father's impassibility, that of the significance of sacrifice, that of transubstantiation, that of the nature of the distinction between the contemplative and active lives and of both from the life of pleasure, that of eternity from aeviternity and time, and so forth. Literally hundreds of texts could be cited from Christian and Islamic, Vedic, Taoist, and other scriptures and their patristic expositions, in close and sometimes literally verbal agreement. To cite a trio of instances at random, whereas Damascene has to say that "He Who Is, is the principal of all names applied to God," in the *Kaṭha Upani-*

ṣad we have "He is, by that alone is He to be apprehended": whereas St. Thomas says, "These things are said to be under the sun which are generated and corrupted," the *Śatapatha Brāhmaṇa* affirms that "Everything under the sun is in the power of death"; and whereas Dionysius speaks of That "which not to see or know is really to see and know," the *Jaiminīya Upaniṣad Brāhmaṇa* has it that "The thought of God is his by whom it is unthought, or if he thinks the thought he does not understand." All traditional teaching employs side by side the *via affirmativa* and the *via remotionis*, and in this sense is in agreement with Boethius that "Faith is a mean between contrary heresies." Sin is defined by the Thomist and in India in one and the same way as a "departure from the order to the end." All tradition is agreed that the last end of man is happiness.

On the other hand, while there can be only one metaphysics, there must be not merely a variety of religions, but a hierarchy of religions, in which the truth is more or less adequately expressed, according to the intellectual capacities of those whose religions they are. Nor do I mean to deny that there can be heterodox doctrines, properly to be condemned as heresies, but only that any and every belief is a heresy if it be regarded as the truth, and not merely as a signpost of the truth. Pantheism, for example, is equally a heresy from Christian, Islamic, and Hindu points of view; a confusion of things as they are in themselves with things as they are in God, of the essence of the participant with the participated Essence, is an egregious error, and yet not so great an error as to assume that the being of things as they are in themselves is altogether their own being. The distinction of essence from nature of the Sāṃkhya system is true from a certain point of view, and yet false when regarded from the standpoint of a higher synthesis, as in the Vedānta, and similarly in Christianity, where from one point of view essence and nature are the universe apart, and yet in the simplicity of the First Cause are one impartite substance.

It is perfectly legitimate to feel that a given religion is more adequately true than another; to hold, for example, that Catholicism is more adequately true than Protestantism, or Hinduism than Buddhism. Real distinctions can be drawn: Christianity maintains, for example, that metaphysics, though the highest of the other sciences, is inferior to the sacred science of theology; Hinduism is primarily metaphysical, and only secondarily religious, hence the controversies as to the true significance of "deification," and hence it is that however much a Hindu may find himself in enthusiastic agreement with the angelic and celestial doctors (Thomas and Bonaventura), he is more at home with certain giants of Christian thought whose orthodoxy is suspect, I mean Eriugena, Eckhart, Boehme, Blake, and more at home with Plotinus than with the representatives of exoteric Christian orthodoxy; more at home with St. John than with St. James, more in sympathy with Christian Platonism than with Christian Aristotelianism, scarcely at all in sympathy with Protestant theologies, and far more in sympathy with Qabbalistic interpretations of Genesis and Exodus than with any historical approach. So that we do not for a moment mean to maintain the impropriety of all dogmatic controversy. We must bear in mind that even within the framework of a presumably homogeneous faith it is taken for granted that one and the same truths must be presented in various ways suited to the audience, and that this is not a matter of contradictory statement, but of "convenient means." What we do maintain is that all paths converge; that the Wayfarer, having already trodden a given path, will under all normal circumstances sooner reach that point at which all progress ends—"On reaching God, all progress ends"—than if he retrace his steps and start afresh.

What we must not forget is that no one can finally pronounce upon the truth of a given religion who has not lived it, as Ramakrishna lived both Christianity and Islām, as well as Hinduism; and that once convinced that only one's own truth is true, "It is," as Professor C. A. Briggs of Drew University lately remarked, "the easiest thing imaginable to take the concepts of other faiths, abstract them from their contexts, and demolish them." For example, how easily the Islamic definition of Christianity as a polytheistic religion could be deduced from the considered statement of St. Thomas, that "We do not say *the only God*, because deity is common to several" (*Sum. Theol.* 1.31.2c). In the same way, a pantheistic definition of Christianity could easily be deduced from St. Thomas's "A thing has being by participation. . . . We must consider . . . the emanation of all being from the universal cause, which is God" (*Sum. Theol.* 1.44.1 *ad* 1 and 45 1c).

What is then, in the last analysis, the value of comparative religion? Certainly not to convince us that one mode of belief is the preparation for another, or to lead to a decision as to which is "best." One might as well regard ancient or exotic styles of art as preparations for and aspirations towards one's own. Nor can the value of this discipline be thought of as one conducing to the development of a single universally acceptable syncretic faith embodying all that is "best" in every faith; such a "faith" as this would be a mechanical and lifeless monstrosity, by no means a stream of living water, but a sort of religious Esperanto. Comparative religion can demonstrate that all religions spring from a common source; are, as Jeremias says, the "dialects of a single spiritual speech." We cannot, therefore, take the formulae of one religion and insert them in another without incongruity. One can recognize that many formulae are identical in different religions; confront, for example, St. Thomas, "Creation, which is the emanation of all being from the not-being, which is no thing" (*Sum. Theol.* I.45.1c) with the Vedic "Being is engendered from nonbeing" (*asatah sad ajāyata*, RV x.72.3), and such comparisons can be validly employed (even by the most orthodox) as what St. Thomas calls "extrinsic and probable proofs" of the validity of a given dogma.

But of greater value than this is the clarification that results when the formulae of one tradition are collated with those of another. For, as we have already seen, every tradition is necessarily a partial representation of the truth intended by tradition universally considered; in each tradition something is suppressed, or reserved, or obscure which in another may be found more extensively, more logically, or more brilliantly developed. What then is clear and full in one tradition can be used to develop the meaning of what may be hardly more than alluded to in another. Or even if in one tradition a given doctrine has been definitely named, a realization of the significance of this definition may lead to the recognition and correlation of a whole series of affirmations in another tradition, in all of which the same doctrine is implicit, but which had previously been overlooked in their relation to one another. It is thus a great advantage to be able to make use of the expression *Vedic exemplarism*; or conversely, to speak of Christian *yoga* immediately brings out the analogy between St. Bernard's *consideratio, contemplatio*, and *raptus* with Sanskrit *dhāraṇā*, *dhyāna*, and *samādhi*.

To many Christians, no doubt, Śrī Ramakrishna's primary attachment to the cult of the Great Mother gives offense. Nothing is, indeed, more usual than to consider that Christianity, whether for better or worse, adheres to purely masculine interpretations of divine being; the Christian speaks of a Father, but not of a Mother in Heaven, whereas in India the ancient love of the Magna Mater maintains itself at the present day on equal terms with that of the Propator. And yet the doctrine of the maternity of the divine nature is repeatedly, however reservedly, affirmed in Christian theology, fundamentally in that of the "two natures," more explicitly in that of the temporal *and* eternal nativities, and in that of the Generation of the Son as a vital operation from conjoint principles—"Processio Verbi in divinis dicitur generatio . . . quae est operatio vitae . . . et propter hoc proprie dicitur genitum et Filius" (*Sum. Theol.* I.27.2; cf. I.98.2c, "In every act of generation there is an active and a passive principle."). It is inasmuch as "eternal filiation does not depend on a temporal mother" (*ibid.* III.35.5 *ad* 2) that Eckhart can speak of the "act of fecundation latent in eternity," and say that "it is God who has the treasure and the bride in Him," that the "Godhead wantons with the Word," and that "His birth in *Mary ghostly* was to God better pleasing than His nativity of her in the flesh." One sees that when St. Thomas speaks of "that Nature by which the Father begets" (*Sum. Theol.* I.41.5), the reference is really to the Magna Mater, the Vedic Aditi, not to mention other names of the One Madonna, and sees what is really meant by the otherwise obscure assertion that notwithstanding primary matter "recedes from likeness to God, yet . . . it *retains* a certain likeness to the divine being" (*ibid.* I.14.11 *ad* 3). Natura Naturata indeed "retains" a certain likeness to "Natura Naturans, Creatrix, Deus": Mother Earth to Mother Nature, Mary in the flesh to Mary ghostly. One need only consider Genesis 1:27, "To the image of God He created him; male and female He created them," in connection with Galatians 3:28, "according to the image of Him that created him, where there is neither male nor female," to realize that whereas Essence and Nature *in divinis* are one simple substance without composition, the very fact that the conjoint principles can be separately exemplified is proof that the Supreme Identity can be truly spoken of either as Father or as Mother, or as Father-Mother, just as in the Vedas the Divine "Parents" are indifferently "Fathers" (*pitarā*) or "Mothers" (*mātarā*), or as "That One, spirated, despirated" (*tad ekam ānīt avātam*, RV x.129.2, where no gender is implied; cf. Eckhart's "Where these two abysms hang, equally spirated, despirated, there is the Supreme Being").

Thus we may go so far as to assert on behalf of a true "comparative religion," that however a religion may be self-sufficient if it be followed to the very end to which it is directed, there can hardly be supposed a way so plain that it could not here and there be better illuminated by other lights than that of the pilgrim's private lantern, the light of any lantern being only a refraction of the Light of lights. A diversity of routes is not merely appropriate to a diversity of travelers, who are neither all alike, nor start from one and the same point, but may be of incalculable aid to any traveler who can rightly read the map; for where all roads converge, there can be none of them that does not help to clarify the true position of the center of the maze, "short of which we are still in a duality." Hence we say that the very implications of the phrase "religious tolerance" are to be avoided: diversity of faith is not a matter for unwilling "toleration," but of divine appointment. And this will hold good even if we sincerely believe that other faiths are inferior to our own, and in this sense relatively "evil": for as Augustine says, "The admirable beauty of the universe is made up of all things. In which even what is called evil, well-ordered and in its place, is the eminent commendation of what is good" (*Enchiridion* XIII), whom St. Thomas quotes with approval, adding that "The universe, the present creation being supposed, cannot be better, because of the most beautiful order given to things by God" (*Sum. Theol.* I.48.1 and I.25.6 *ad* 3). As Augustine also says, "There is no evil in things, but only in the sinner's misuse of them" (*De doctrina christiana* III.12). As to the sinner's "misuse," who can assure us of that, with respect to which it has been said, "Judge not, that ye be not judged"?

In the matter of direction towards the Kingdom of Heaven "within you,"[2] the modern world is far more lacking in the will to seek, than likely to be led astray by false direction. From the Satanic point of view there could hardly be imagined a better activity than to be engaged in the "conversion of the heathen" from one to another body of dogmas: that, surely, was not what was meant by the injunction, "Go thou and preach the Kingdom of God"—or was He mistaken, when He said, "The Kingdom of Heaven is within you"?

[2] Sanskrit *hṛdayākāśe, antarbhūtasya khe.*

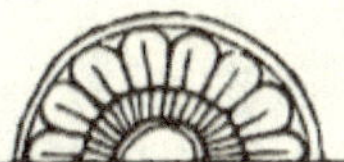

The "E" at Delphi

The essential procedures of initiatory rites, by which the death of an old man and the rebirth of a new man are effected, and the conditions of access to *penetralia*, are alike all over the world. Firmicus Maternus, *De errore profanarum religionum* (ch. XVIII), dealing with these subjects,[1] reminds us that there are right answers to the right questions (*habent enim propria signa propria responsa*), and that the right answer (*proprium responsum*) is made by the initiand (*homo moriturus*) precisely as the proof of his right to be admitted (*ut possit admitti*). A typical example of such a *signum* and of the wrong and right answers can be cited from the *Jaiminīya Upaniṣad Brāhmaṇa*, III.14.1–5. When the deceased reaches the Sundoor the question is asked, "Who art thou?" If he answers by his own or by a family name[2] he is dragged away by the factors of time. He should respond, "Who I am (is) the Light thou (art) (*ko'ham asmi suvas tvam*).

[This note was first published in the *Review of Religion*, VI (1941).—ED.]

[1] For Firmicus Maternus, see G. van der Leeuw, "The ΣΥΜΒΟΛΑ in Firmicus Maternus," in *Egyptian Religion*, I (1933).

[2] "Names are fetters" (AĀ II.1.6). God has no personal or family name (BU III.8.8), nor ever becomes anyone (KU II.18), and it follows that there can be no return to God, no *deificatio* (for which, in Cusa's words, an *ablatio omnis alteritatis et diversitatis* is indispensable) for anyone who still is someone. The initiate is nameless, is not himself but Agni (KB VII.2.3), cf. Gal. 2:20, *vivo autem jam non ego, sed Christus in me*. God is a Sea, "*nostra pace: ella è quel mare, al qual tutto si move*" (*Paradiso* III.85, 86); and as the names of the rivers are lost in the sea, so are our names and likenesses lost when we reach Him (A IV.198, Praśna Up. VI.5). "Also sich wandelt der tropfe in daz mer" (Eckhart, Pfeiffer ed., p. 314), cf. Rūmī, "that your drop may become the sea," and "None has knowledge of each who enters, that he is 'So-and-so' " (Odes XII and XV in *Dīvān*), and Lao-tzu, *Tao Te Ching* XXXII, "To Tao all under heaven will come as streams flow into a great river or sea." ["He that finds (God) becomes lost (in Him): like a torrent he is absorbed in the Ocean" (*Mathnawī* VI.4052).] And so, according to the inscription cited by V. Magnien, *Les Mystères d'Éleusis* (Paris, 1938), p. 334, "Pour mon nom, ne cherche pas qui je suis: le rite mystique l'emmena en s'en allant vers la mer empourprée."

See also Coomaraswamy, "*Ākiṃcaññā*: Self-Naughting" [in this vol.—ED.], and "*Svayamātṛṇṇā: Janua Coeli*" [in Vol. I of this edition—ED.].

As such have I come to thee, the heavenly Light." He (Prajāpati, the Sun) replies, "Who thou art, that same am I; who I am, that same art thou. Enter in." Of numerous parallels that might be cited, perhaps the most striking is Rūmī's myth of the man who knocked at his friend's door and was asked "Who art thou?" He answered "I." "Begone," said his friend. After a year's separation and tribulation he came and knocked again, and to the same question replied, " 'Tis thou art at the door," and received the reply, "Since thou art I, come in, O myself."[3]

Now there can be no question that the entrance to the temple of Apollo at Delphi was literally a Sundoor, a way into the house or temple of the Sun. The superscription, "Know thyself" (*γνῶθι σεαυτόν*) demands a knowledge of the answer to the question, "Who art thou?"[4] and may be said, in the veiled language of the mysteries, to ask this very question. The injunction, as Plutarch says,[5] is addressed by the God to all who approach him; and the famous "E" he takes to be their right answer. If now, as he also suggests, "E" stands for EI, and if we take from his various interpretations the meanings (1) the Sun (Apollo) and (2) "thou art,"

[3] *Mathnawī* I.3056–3065; cf. Song of Songs 1:8, "Si ignoras te, egredere."

[4] That the inscription actually puts this question is explicit in Xenophon, *Memorabilia* IV.2.24, where Socrates asks Euthydemus, "Did you heed it, and try to consider who you were?" (*ὅστις εἴης*).

[5] *Moralia* 384D ff. ("The 'E' at Delphi"). It is likewise assumed in Plato (*Charmides* 164D) that the injunction "Know thyself" is not "a piece of advice" but "the God's salutation (*πρόσρησις*) to those who enter," and that the words are spoken by the God to those who are entering his temple, "otherwise than as men speak" and "very enigmatically" (*αἰνιγματωδέστερον*); i.e., "non in doctis humanae sapientiae verbis, sed in doctrina Spiritus" (1 Cor. 2:13).

The words "Know thyself" are "enigmatic," it would appear, only because they can be taken to refer to a knowledge of either one of man's two souls or selves, the bodily and mortal or the incorporeal and immortal, so often spoken of by Plato and in the Vedic philosophy. In Xenophon, *Memorabilia* IV.2.24 (cf. III.9.6), Socrates speaks of "self-knowledge" as the knowledge of one's own powers and limitations [cf. Philo, *De specialibus legibus* I.44 and Plutarch, *Moralia* 394C]; but this is in conversation with a conceited man who thinks he already knows himself "who" he is, "Euthydemus" by name. But in *Alcibiades* I.130E ff., Socrates says that "he who orders, 'Know thyself,' bids us know the soul," and goes on to say that one who knows only what is of the body "knows the things that are his but not himself" (*τὰ αὑτοῦ ἀλλ' οὐχ αὑτὸν*); cf. BU 1.5.15.

As a parallel to these distinctions may be cited Plutarch's ridicule of those who cannot distinguish Apollo from the Sun (*Moralia* 393D, 400CD), passages that echo *Laws* 898D, where Plato says that "that body of Helios is seen by all, his soul by none," and recall AV x.8.14: "Him (the Sun) all men see, not all know with the mind."

and assume that both these meanings are contained in the one enigmatic syllable, we have the *signum*, "Who art thou (at the door)?" and the *responsum*, "The Sun thou art (am I)." It is certain that no other true answer could have been given by anyone "qualified to go in unto union with the Sun."[6]

[6] JUB 1.6.1.

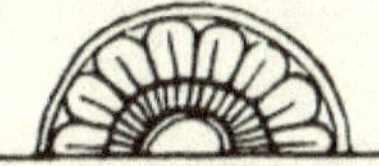

THE MAJOR ESSAYS

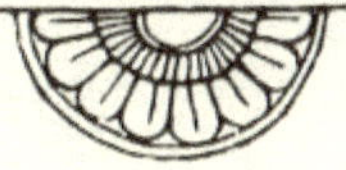

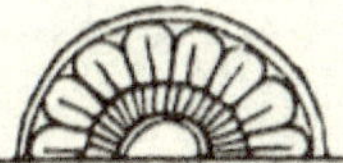

Recollection, Indian and Platonic

Punar ehi vācas pate devena manasā saha
Vasoḥ pate ni ramaya mayy evāstu mayi śrutam

AV I.I.2[1]

Cathedram habet in caelo qui intus corda docet.
St. Augustine, *In epist. Joannis ad Parthos*

My Lord embraces all things in His knowledge; will you not remember?

Koran VI.80, tr. A. J. Arberry

In the following article, the doctrine that what we call "learning" is really a "remembering" and that our "knowledge" is by participation in the Omniscience of an immanent spiritual principle will be traced in Indian and Platonic texts. This corresponds, in the same Perennial Philosophy, to the doctrine that the beautiful is such by a participation in Beauty, and all being a participation of Being absolutely.

The omniscience of the immanent spiritual principle, *intellectus vel spiritus*, is the logical correlative of its timeless omnipresence. It is only from this point of view that the concept of a Providence (*prajñā, πρόνοια, προμήθεια*) becomes intelligible. The Providential Self (*prajñātman*) does not arbitrarily decree our "Fate" but is the witness of its operation: our Fate is merely the temporal extension of its free and instant act of being. It is only because we think of Providence as a foreknowledge of the

[This study was first published as Supplement No. 3 to the *Journal of the American Oriental Society*, LXIV (1944). The abstract that prefaced the article has been retained.—ED.]

[1] AV I.I.2: "Come thou again, O Lord of Speech, with the divine mind, infix it, O Lord of Weal, in me, yea in me let thy lore abide." Cf. AV I.I.4, *sam śrutena gamemahi*, "May we be familiar with thy lore," where *sam gam* corresponds to *anubhū* in other contexts. Cf. also AĀ II.2.7, *Āvir āvir me edhi . . . mā śrutam me pra hāsīt*, "Do thou (Ātman, Brahma) be revealed to me, may thy lore not forsake me" (Keith's rendering).

St. Augustine: "His throne is in heaven who teaches from within the heart." Cf. BU III.9.23, "the support of Truth is in the heart."

future that we are confused; as if we asked, What was God thinking in a time *before* time was! Actually, Providential knowledge is no more of a future than of a past, but only of a *now*. Experience of duration is incompatible with omniscience, of which the empirical self is therefore incapable.

On the other hand, to the extent that we are able to identify ourselves with the Providential Self itself—*Γνῶθι σεαυτόν*, That *art* thou—we rise above the sequences of Fate, becoming their spectator rather than their victim. Thus the doctrine that all knowledge is by participation is inseparably connected with the possibility of Liberation (*mokṣa*, λύσις) from the pairs of opposites, of which past and future, here and there, are the pertinent instances in the present context. As Nicholas of Cusa has expressed it, the wall of the Paradise in which God dwells is made up of these contraries, and the strait way in, guarded by the highest spirit of Reason, lies between them. In other words, our Way lies through the now and nowhere of which empirical experience is impossible, though the fact of Memory assures us that the Way is open to Comprehensors of the Truth.

THE Gāyatrī (RV III.62.10) invokes Savitṛ to "impel our intellections" (*dhiyo yo naḥ pracodayāt*), or better, "our speculations."[2] AĀ II.3.5 tells us that "the self that is in speech (*vāc*)[3] is incomplete, since one intuits (erlebt, *anubhavati*)[4] when impelled to thought (*manase*) by the Breath (*prāṇena*), not when impelled by speech."[5] "Breath" is to be understood here in its highest sense, common in the *Aitareya Āraṇyaka*, that of Brahma and immanent solar Self, and as in BU II.5.19, *ayam ātmā brahma*

[2] MU VI.10 explains *dhiyaḥ* by *buddhayaḥ*; the *dhīra* is "contemplative" rather than merely "wise." With *pracodayāt*, cf. MU II.6 *pratibodhanāya* and *pracodayitṛ*.

[3] The powers of the soul are called "selves" in CU VIII.8.12.4 ff. and Kauṣ. Up. IV.20. That is to say, "the self of speech" means the man considered as a speaker. In this sense, man has as many selves as he has powers.

[4] *Anubhū* (cf. "*gleichkommen*" and *accognoscere*) is literally "to come to be along with," or "adapted or conformed to, or identified with" the object of knowledge, whether in the epistemological or the erotic (JUB I.54.7) sense; cf. *adaequatio rei et intellectus*. [Cf. *anu . . . vid* in RV IV.27.1 = σύνεσις as defined in *Cratylus* 412.] We have tried to suggest this content by using the word "intuit," and sometimes "experience" (with implied "immediacy"), reserving "know" for *jñā*.

[5] This hardly differs from Keith's version. On Manas (and Vāc), cf. Coomaraswamy, "On Being in One's Right Mind," 1942, p. 11; and CU VIII.12.5, "Now he who knows, 'Let me think this'—that is the Self (*ātman*, Spirit). The Mind is his 'divine eye' (*daiva cakṣus*); he, verily, with that divine eye, the Mind, beholds these objects of desire, and is content." Mind is the "prior" and the "overlord" of the other powers of the soul (ŚB X.5.3.7, XIV.3.2.3).

sarvānubhūḥ, "this Self, Brahma, experient of all."[6] The sense is, then, that it is not by what we are told, but by the indwelling Spirit, that we know and understand the thing to which words can only refer us; that which is audibly or otherwise sensed does not in itself inform us, but merely provides the occasion and opportunity to re-cognize the matter to which the external signs have referred us.

While these texts unmistakably present us with the notions of illumination and inspiration, we should not propose to deduce from them alone a fully developed theory of "Recollection" (*smara, smṛti; sati*) without further support; we cite them first by way of introduction to other texts treating directly of Memory.

The doctrine is simply stated in CU VII.26.1: "Memory is from the Self, or Spirit" (*ātmataḥ smaraḥ*). For "the Self knows everything" (*sarvam ātmā jānīte*, MU VI.7), "this Great Being is just a recognition-mass" (*vijñānaghana*, BU II.4.12), or "precognition-mass" (*prajñāna-ghana*, BU IV.5.13, cf. Māṇḍ. Up. 5). Brahma, Self, is "intuitive of everything" (*sarvānubhūḥ*, BU II.2.19) because, as Śaṇkara says, it is the "Self of all" (*sarvātman*); He, indeed, is "the *only* seer, hearer, thinker, knower, and fructuary in us" (BU III.8.11, IV.5.15; cf. AĀ III.2.4) and therefore, because of His timeless omnipresence, *must* be omniscient. Memory is a participation of His awareness who never himself "remembers" anything, because he never forgets. "Memory," as Plotinus says, "is for those who have forgotten."[7]

CU VII.13.1 echoes and expands AĀ II.3.5 as cited above: "Memory (*smara*) is more than Space (*ākāśa*, the medium of hearing). Accordingly, even were many men assembled, not being possessed of Memory, neither would they hear any one at all, nor think (*man*), nor recognize (*vijñā*), but if possessed of Memory, they would hear and think and recognize. By Memory, assuredly, one recognizes (*vijānāti*) children, recognizes cattle. Revere Memory."

The power-of-the-soul that remembers is the Mind (*manas* = νοῦς),[8] undistracted by the working of the powers of perception and action. "There, in 'clairvoyant-sleep' (*svapne*)[9] that divinity intuits (*anubhavati*)

[6] *Sarvānubhūḥ* states rather the basis than the bare fact of omniscience. The Self is necessarily "omniscient" because it is "the only seer, hearer, thinker, etc." in us (BU III.4.2, III.7.23, etc.). The empirical self is its instrument.

[7] *Enneads* IV.4.7.

[8] Cf. MU VI.34.6–9.

[9] *Svapna* here, as often elsewhere, is not ordinary sleep or dreaming, but a state of contemplation (*dhyāna*). The "divinity" is the "Recognitive Person" (*vijñānamaya puruṣa*) of BU II.1.17, 18, "who is said to be 'asleep' (*svapiti*) when he controls the

Greatness. Whatever has been seen (*dṛṣṭam*), he proximately sees (*anupaśyati*), whatever has been heard, he proximately hears (*anuśruṇoti*). Whatever has been and has not been seen, whatever has been heard and has not been heard, intuitively known or unknown (*anubhūtam, ananubhūtam*), good or evil (*sat, asat*),[10] whatever has been directly experienced (*pratyanubhūtam*) in any land or airt, again and again he directly experiences; he sees it all, he sees it all" (Praśna Up. IV.5); or, as the Commentator understands the conclusion, "being himself the all, he sees it all," in accordance with the principle of the identity of knowing and being enunciated in verse 11, where the Comprehensor of the Self "knowing all, becomes all." In the foregoing context, Śaṇkara interprets, rightly I think, "seen and not seen" as referring to "what has been seen in this birth and what has been seen in another birth":[11] the meaning of this

---

powers of perception and action. Resuming the recognitive power (*vijñānam ādāya*), he rests in the heart. . . . When he 'sleeps,' these worlds are his. . . . Controlling the powers of perception and action, he drives around in his own person (lit. 'body') as he will." As in BU V.3.7, where this Person "as it were contemplates (*dhyāyatīva*), as it were disports, for when he is 'asleep' (*svapno bhūtvā*) he transcends this world and the forms of death."

In this technical sense, "sleep" and "dreaming" are not the sleep of fatigue but the act of imagination. And this is quite universal. For example, "I will pour out my spirit upon all flesh . . . your old men shall dream dreams, your young men shall see visions" (Joel 2:28); "my thoughts had soared high aloft, while my bodily senses had been put under restraint by sleep—yet not such sleep as that of men weighed down by fullness of food or by bodily weariness—[and] methought there came to me a Being . . . the Mind of the Sovereignty . . . [who said] 'Keep in mind all that you desire to learn, and I will teach you,'" (Hermes, *Lib.* I.1; in I.28 he refers to the sleep of fatigue as "irrational sleep"); "Me bi-fel a ferly . . . I slumberde in a slepyng . . . þenne gon I meeten a meruelous sweune . . . I beo-heold. . . ." (*Piers the Plowman*, Prologue). *Mathnawī* IV.3067 contrasts the sleep of the vulgar with that of the elect; the latter "has nothing in common with the sleep of ignorance (*ḵhwab-i-ghaflat*) in which most people pass their conscious lives" (Nicholson's note on *Mathnawī* II.31, cf. I.388–393; also BG II.69 [and M I.260]). Life is an "awakening" from nonexistence; "sleep" is an awakening from life.

> *What availeth me to sleep and wake?*
> *If to sleep unsleeping the way is seen,*
> *Ah,* then *I see it availeth me.*
>
> Tayumānavar (P. Arunachalam, "Luminous Sleep," reprinted from the *Westminster Review*, Colombo, 1903).

[10] Lit. "aught and naught," and here "good and evil" rather than "real and unreal"; cf. *puṇyam ca pāpam ca* in BU IV.3.5 and *sadasat* in MU III.1.

[11] "God enjoys eternalwise the contingency of things. . . . The knower being that which is known" (Meister Eckhart, Evans ed., I, 391, 394). "The mind of the Sage at rest becomes the mirror of the universe" (*Chuang-tzū*, p. 158).

will become clearer when we deal with *jātavedas* and *jātissaro* and if we bear in mind that though he speaks of former births, the Lord is for him "the only transmigrant."[12]

The subject of Memory is discussed in Mil 78–80. It is first shown that it is not by thinking (*citta*) but by Memory (*sati* = *smṛti*) that we remember; for we are not without intelligence even when what was done long ago has been forgotten (*pamuṭṭham* = *pramṛṣṭam*). It is then asked, "Does Memory arise (*appajjati*) always as an over-knowledge state (*sabbā . . . abhijānantā*)[13] or is Memory factitious (*kaṭumikā* = *kṛtimā*), and answered that "Memory occurs as an over-knowledge state, and is also factitious," i.e., it may be either spontaneous or artificially stimulated.[14] The king rejoins, "That amounts to saying that all Memory is over-knowing, never factitious." Nāgasena replies, "In that case, craftsmen would have no need of workshops or schools of art or science, and masters would be useless; which is not true." So the king asks, "In how many ways does Memory arise?" Nāgasena answers, "Sixteen."[15] These are really only two ways, either by over-knowing without means (*abhijānato*), or by

[12] See Coomaraswamy, "On the One and Only Transmigrant" [in this volume—ED.].

[13] *Abhi* in *abhijñā* intensifies *jñā*, to know (γιγνώσκω, νοέω, *kennen*, cunning): to remember is something more than simply to perceive; cf. Meister Eckhart's "I can see a rose in winter when no rose is there." Hence, while *abhijñā* can mean just "remember" or "understand" (Pāṇini III.2.112, *abhijānāsi* = *smarasi, budhyase*; Mil 77, *abhijānāsi*, "Did you ever remember?"), in Pāli Buddhism generally the sense of the marvellous predominates, and *abhiññā* = *abhijānanā* is usually the supernatural knowledge or omniscience of a Buddha, an *iddhi* acquired by contemplative discipline and which he or other Arhats can "intuit" (*anubhū*) at will. In this sense *abhiññā* includes the six powers of levitation (motion at will through the air), clairaudience, thought-reading, knowledge of one's own and of other people's former births, and assurance that liberation has been attained (D III.281, based on many other contexts, PTS Dictionary, s.v.). It is noteworthy that "over-knowing" and "liberation" coincide, reminding one of Meister Eckhart's "Not till the soul knows all that there is to be known can she pass over to the unknown good."

Abhijñā does not appear in the Upaniṣads; in BG it is always only used of "knowing" Krishna—certainly an "over-knowing" and not an empirical experience. [Alternatively, one "remembers" Krishna, BG VIII.5.]

[14] The *Milindapañha* categories are not quite the same as those of the previously cited texts, in which *abhijñā* does not appear. But it is made very clear that all learning is really *re*-cognition, i.e., re-collection.

[15] I.e., one *abhijānato* and the rest *kaṭumikā*. This must have something to do with the well-known doctrine of the "sixteen parts" of which the "Self" is the sixteenth (BU I.5.15) and that part "with which you now understand (*anubhavasi*) the Vedas" (CU VI.7.6). [Cf. *The Gospel of Sri Ramakrishna*, tr. Swami Nikhilananda, New York, 1942, p. 367.] On the number "16," cf. E.J.H. MacKay, *Chanhu-Daro Excavations (1935–1936)*, pp. 240–241 (*American Oriental Series*, Vol. 20, 1943).

external stimulation (*kaṭumikā*), the total of sixteen being made up by a subdivision of the second category according to the nature of the means. Thus Memory occurs by over-knowledge simply when such as Ānanda or others who are "birth-rememberers" (*jātissarā*)[16] remember a birth (*jātiṃ saranti*): it occurs factitiously when those who are naturally forgetful (*muṭṭha-ssatiko = mṛṣṭa-*)[17] are constrained or stimulated to remember by another person (or thing), e.g., when one recognizes a relative by likeness, or cattle by their brands,[18] or reads letters or numbers, or consults a book, or intuitively (*anubhūtato*), as when one remembers what has already been seen or heard (without being "reminded" of it). Memory, in any case, is a latent power.

Thus what we think we "learn," but really "remember," implies that in intuition directly, and in learning indirectly, we are really drawing upon or, as the older texts would express it, "milking" an innate prescience (*prajñāna = πρόνοια, προμήθεια*). In D I.19–22 we are told that the gods fall from heaven only when their "memory fails, and they are of confused memory" (*sati mussati, satiyā sammosā*); those whose mind remains

[16] This refers to the supernormal faculty of remembering past "habitations," as possessed by a Buddha or other Arhat, and is to be distinguished from the memory of a former habitation by an ordinary brother, whose memory of the past is included in the list of factitious rememberings because means are employed to evoke it. The supernormal power is exercised at will by a Buddha and extends to the recollection of any birth whatever, however remote; the brother who is not yet an Arhat can only, by a step-by-step procedure, recover the memory of one or more births, but no more (Vis 411): in the first case the all-seeing view is, as it were, from the center of a circle, whence all "moments" within or upon the circumference can be seen at a glance; the second case is that of a being whose range is naturally confined to motion along the circumference itself (i.e., in time, so far as memories are concerned), who cannot *see* forward or backward immediately but can only predict by inference or recover the past by successive steps—he can look inward by analogy, but has neither foresight nor hindsight nor insight, unless suprarationally and by inspiration. The Buddha has "prior knowledge of the ultimate beginning (*agaññam . . . pajānāmi*), and more than that" (D III.28); his range is infinite (*anantagocaram*, Dh 179); but it is as the Buddha, the Wake, not as this man Gotama, now waking and now sleeping, that he is thus omniscient (*sabbaññu = sarvajñā*), and similarly in the case of others. This amounts to saying that Buddha = Paramātman.

[17] TS VII.6.10.4, *madya*, is glossed by *vismṛtyonmatta*, "oblivious," "in a state of amnesia." Sn 815, *mussati*, is explained by *nassati*, "perishes" (SnA 536); and *parimussati* is *paribāhiro hoti*, i.e., "wholly forgets" is to be "alienated" (Vis 44). I infer that amnesia was a known malady, and further that *all* forgetfulness was thought of as a madness of the same kind, only the Buddha and other Arhats being perfectly sane.

[18] Cf. CU VII.13.1, "recognize cattle," cited above. On cattle brands see Pohath-Kehelpannala in *Ceylon National Review*, I (1907), 334, and John Abbott, *The Keys of Power* (New York, 1932), p. 140, and figs. 19–21 and 52.

uncorrupted, and do not forget, are "steadfast, immutable, eternal, of a nature that knows no change, and will remain so for ever and ever"; and such, likewise, is the liberated (*vimutto*) Buddha's prescience (*pajānanā*), or foreknowing, "on which, however, he lays no stress" (*taṃ ca pajānanaṃ na parāmasati*).[19] It is significant, in the first place, that what is thus said of the Buddha is, as so often happens, only a paraphrase of what has already been said of Agni, who "does not forget the prior nor the latter word, but is not vainglorious by reason of his counsel" (*na mṛṣyate prathamaṃ nāparaṃ vaco'sya kratvā sacate apradṛpidaḥ*, RV 1.145.2).[20] And secondly, that for Plato also it is precisely a *failure to remember* that drags down from the heights the soul that has walked with God (*θεῷ ξυνοπαδός* = *brahmacārī*) and had some vision of the truths,[21] but cannot retain it (*Phaedrus* 248c, cf. Plotinus, IV.4.7 ff.).[22]

[19] I.e., *na parāmṛśati*, and rendered by Rhys Davids, "he is not puffed up"; in a similar context, D III.28, *na paramāsāmi* (cf. M I.433 for this word) is rendered by "I do not pervert it"—"I am not attached to it" might be better. That these are the right connotations seems to follow from the Vedic parallel cited above. It will be because his prescience is "of far more than that" (*tato ca uttaratataritaram pajānāmi*, M I.433 and D III.28), rather than because such knowledge is not essential to liberation (M I.277), that it is not overvalued; there are other than cosmic possibilities.

On the distinctions of gnosis amongst the gods in the Brahma worlds, cf. A IV.74 ff.: some are content with its beatitudes, others are prescient (*pajānanti*) of an absolute liberation.

[20] Suggestive of Agni's epithet *satya-vāc*, "whose word is truth," RV III.26.9, VII.2.3; cf. Pāli *sacca-vācā, sacca-vādin*. "The flower and fruit of speech is truth" (AĀ II.2.6 [or "meaning," *Nirukta* 1.10]). *Prathamam nāparam* may well mean "eternal" rather than "earlier and latter"; cf. BU II.5.19, *apūrvam anaparam* = *Paradiso*, XXIX.20, *nè prima nè poscia*.

Agni, *krátvā . . . ápradṛpitah*, contrasts with the Indra of BD 7.54, *svena vīryena darpitah*, until he is reawakened by Saptagu-Bṛhaspati = Agni and comes to himself again. The Sacerdotium is not intoxicated by knowledge, but the Regnum may be intoxicated by power.

[21] Few retain an adequate memory of them (*Phaedrus* 250A).

[22] The gods do not sometimes forget and sometimes remember—"such memory is for those who have lost it." The omniscience of Zeus does not depend on observation, but on the innate gnosis of his own unlimited life. Cf. Ibn 'Aṭā, "Openly the heart's eye then beholds him, and doth scorn remembrance, as a burden hardly to be borne," quoted by Abū Bakr, *Kitāb al Ta'arruf*, ch. 47 [cf. *Paradiso* XXIX.79 ff.]. For Aristotle, too, the Divine Mind "does not remember," as does the perishable mind, which is reminded by its sense perceptions (*De anima* 3.5). "In the heart one knows the truth, in the heart alone, forsooth, is truth established" (BU III.9.23); the soul's recognition of the visions stored up in her is the process of "remembering" (*Enneads* IV.7.10, 12). When everything has been remembered, once and for all, then there is no more remembering as a process, but only an immemorial knowledge. The disparagement of memory will not, then, be misunderstood; one might say

No less striking is the fact that *mosā, musā* (*mṛṣā*), "false," is regularly opposed to *saccam* (*satyam*), "true"; and since this *musā, mṛṣā* derives from *mussati, mṛṣ*, to "ignore," "forget," "overlook," it is clear that "not-true" coincides with "forgotten." In the same way, although conversely, λήθη is "oblivion," "forgetting," and ἀληθεια "truth," or literally "not-forgetting." Accordingly, ὁ ἀληθῶς οὐρανός (*Phaedo* 109E) is not merely "true, or real, heaven" but also "heaven where there is no forgetting," and where, by the same token, the gods "never learn" because there is nothing ever absent from their ken (Plotinus, IV.4.7); in the same way Plato's τὸ ἀληθείας πεδίον is not merely "plain of truth" but also "land of no forgetting," and the opposite of Aristophanes' τὸ λήθης πεδίον, "land of oblivion" (*The Frogs*, 186). *Lethe*, too, is one of Discord's deadly brood (Hesiod, *Theogony* 227), and still for Shakespeare means "death"; so that the "land of *not*-forgetting" is also the "land of immortality." In the sense that we are what we know, and that to be and to know are the same (τὸ γὰρ αὐτὸ νοεῖν ἐστιν τε καὶ εἶναι),[23] recollection is life itself, and forgetfulness a lethal draught.

So far, it is clearly implied that Memory is a kind of latent knowledge,[24]

---

that, like "consciousness" in the Buddhist parable of the Raft, remembering is "good for crossing over, but not an activity to be clung to." To remember is a virtue in those who have forgotten, but the perfected never lose their vision of the truth and have no need to recall it (*Phaedrus* 249CD, cf. Proclus as discussed in n. 25).

Sister M. P. Garvey, *St. Augustine, Christian or Neo-Platonist* (Milwaukee, Wis., 1939), (p. 107, confuses memory with remember*ing*, as one might being with becoming. Memory, taken absolutely, coincides with omniscience and is not a procedure; but remember*ing* is learn*ing* and would be a contradiction in one whose memory never fails. This is, in fact, Philo's distinction of memory (μνήμνη) from recollection (ἀνάμνησις), the latter being a *means* of escape (ἐκ λήθης), but evidently needless as such on the part of one whose memory has never lapsed (*Legum allegoriae* III.91–93). This distinction, if I am not mistaken, is that of *smara* from *smarana*, the former denoting love as well as memory, and the latter the act of remembering, which implies a desiring or seeking rather than a loving.

[23] Hermann Diels, ed., *Die Fragmente der Vorsokratiker* (Berlin, 1903), fr. 18B 5. Cf. MU VI.34.3, *yac cittas tanmayo bhavati*, "What is one's thought, that he becomes," and St. Augustine, *Confessions* XIII.11, "esse, nosse, velle . . . in his tribus . . . et una vita mens et una essentia."

[24] "A fund of omniscience exists eternally in our heart" (*Mahāvairocanā-bhisambodhi*, cited by R. Tajima from the *Taisho* (Tripitaka, XVIII, 38c.20). This "fund" corresponds to the *Ālayavijñāna* ("Hoard of Discernment"), which is to be distinguished from all specific (singular) discernments, and identified with the "Compendious Providence" (*vijñāna-ghana, prajñāna-ghana*) of the Upaniṣads, and with the form of God's knowledge in Christian theology, where his knowledge of himself is his knowledge of all things. [Cf. *Enneads*, IV.7.10,12, on the "eternal science" latent within you.]

which may be either self-revealing or revived by an appropriate external sign, for example, when we are "taught," or more truly "re-minded." There is a clear distinction of mere perception from recognition, whether or not evoked by the percept. Memory is a re-covery or re-experiencing (*pratyanubhū*, Praśna Up. IV.5), and it may be observed that the other supernatural powers (*iddhi*) which can be experienced at will by the Arhat are similarly called "recoveries" (*pāṭihāra*, $\sqrt{}$*prati-hṛ*). It is evidently not, then, the outer, aesthetic self, but an inner and immanent power, higher than that of the senses, that remembers or foreknows (*prajñā*), by a "fore" knowledge that is rather "prior" with respect to all empirical means of knowing than merely "fore" with respect to future events—*unde non* prae*videntia sed* pro*videntia potius dicitur* (Boethius, *De consolatione philosophiae* v.6.69, 70). That which remembers, or rather which is always aware of all things, must be a principle always present to (*anubhū*) all things, and therefore itself unaffected by the duration in which these events succeed one another.[25] We are thus reduced to a Providence (*prajñā*, *πρόνοια*)[26] or Providential Self or Spirit (*prajñātman*) as the ultimate source on which all Memory draws, and with which

[25] "He knows, but it is not by means of anything other than himself that he knows," BU IV.5.15, etc. This is essentially also the Christian doctrine about the divine manner of knowing, cf. St. Thomas, *Sum. Theol.* I.14. [note Euripides, *Helen*, 1015–1017.]

Cf. *Phaedrus* 247E ff., "Knowledge, but not such knowledge as has a beginning and varies as it is associated with (*ἐν . . . οὖσα* = *anubhavati*) the things we now call realities, but that has its being in the reality that *is*." The soul that can always hold this vision remains inviolable; but even of those who have seen it, "few are possessed of a consistent memory."

"Every God has an undivided knowledge of things divided and a timeless knowledge of things temporal; he knows the contingent without contingency, the mutable immutably, and in general all things in a higher mode than belongs to their station" (Proclus, *Elements of Theology* 124, cf. E. R. Dodds' ed., Oxford [reprinted 1963], p. 226). The gods of Proclus are, of course, the angels of Dionysius the Areopagite and of Christian theology in general.

[26] To employ the word "Providence" correctly, it must always be remembered that the foreknowing principle is that which gives being, and only indirectly a manner of being. It is much rather Fate (the operation of mediate causes, *karma*) that "allots" or "provides *for*" the being of things *as* they are, than Providence, which is the timeless *witness* of this operation. The divine foreknowing is not, as such, a transitive act, but the act of being, prior to all becomings, of which it knows because it is the only real subject in them all.

Thus in Dodds' Proclus, *Elements of Theology*, p. 126, "for which it (Providence) provides" should read "of which it is provident." Fate inheres in time, Providence is *ex tempore*, and these are as much to be distinguished as are mediate causes from a first cause. [Cicero, *De natura Deorum* II.xxix, confuses prudence and providence! St. Thomas, *Sum. Theol.* I.23.2: "Providence is not anything in the things provided for; but a type in the mind of the provider"—therefore, not fate.

whoever attains to the same uninterrupted omniscience must be identified, as in Praśna Up. IV.10.

We have already seen that there is such an omniscient Self, the fount of Memory (CU VII.26.1, MU VI.7; cf. 1 Cor. 2:11), and it is repeatedly affirmed that this immortal, spiritual, fore-knowing solar Self of all beings, whose presence is undivided in things divided (BG XIII.15, 16),[27] is our real Self, to be distinguished from the contingent Ego, an apparently unanimous (except in cases of schizophrenia) aggregate of powers of perception and action which are "only the names of *His* acts" (BU I.4.7, MU II.6d, etc.). The providential principle, in other words, is the immanent Spirit, the Knower of the field, apart from whom on the one hand no birth could take place (BG XIII, etc.), and apart from whom, as only seer, hearer, thinker, etc. in us (BU III.7.23, etc.), neither experience nor memory could be conceived.[28] We see also that the verification of the words, "That art thou," must involve at the same time liberation and omniscience.

The connection of omniscience with birth implied above is significant. *Jātissaro*, cited above from Mil 78, in fact immediately suggests the older epithet Jātavedas, Agni's because "he knows all births" (*viśvā veda janimā*, RV VI.15.13; *jātānāṃ veda*, AB II.39), and the term *jātavidyā*, knowledge of births, or genealogy.[29] It is because *Tanū-napāt* (Agni-Prajāpati) becomes the immanent Breaths or Powers of the Soul (cf. ŚB I.8.3.2; TS II.1.1.3, 4; JUB IV.2.6; MU II.6a, b, etc.) and is thus "his offspring's witness" (*prajānām upadraṣṭā*; cf. JB III.261, *agnir jajñe . . . aupadraṣṭryāya*) that the gods through him "know the mind of man" (ŚB III.4.2.5–7).[30] How should He "who faces all ways" (*viśvatomukha*, RV I.97.6) and is "of many births" (*bhūri-janmā*, RV X.5.1), he who is the "universal life" (*viśvāyu*, RV I.27.3, and *passim*) or "mover of universal life" (RV VIII.43.25), and who assumes all forms (*viśvarūpa*, RV III.38.4), not be also the "All-knower" (*viśvavit*, RV III.29.7; *viśvavedās*, RV III.20.4, and *passim*)?

[27] As in Dionysius, *De divinibus nominibus* XII.11.

[28] Cf. Heb. 4:13. The recollected and regenerated man is "*renewed in knowledge* after the image of him who created him" (Col. 3:10).

[29] For the Knower of Births *in divinis* this will mean the "genealogy" of all things always; in the case of the human priest, his mortal analogue, who *vadati jātavidyām* (RV X.71.11), the genealogy will have to do with a particular line of descent (*santāna*).

[30] The all-seeing Sun and the myriads of the solar "rays" or "eyes" [feet or hands] that become the immanent Breath and the Breaths, our interior powers of which the sense organs are the instruments (JUB I.28; MU VI.8, etc.) are precisely "die göttlicher Späher, die der Menschen Thaten erschauen" (Grassmann), RV *passim*.

Agni, Jātavedās, is the Breath (AB II.39, ŚB II.2.2.15): "those of whose births he knows, they verily come to be (*bhavanti*), but of those whose births he knoweth not, how might they exist?" (AB II.39); "in that it is the Breath that mounts (quickens) the emitted semen and knows it, therefore He knows whatever is born" (ŚB IX.5.1.68). Being omniprogenitive, the Spirit is omnipresent; and being omnipresent, necessarily omniscient.

This immanent Breath (or "Life") is, moreover, Vāmadeva (AĀ II.2.1), who says of himself, "Being now[31] in the womb (*garbhe nu san*) I have known all the births of the gods" (RV IV.27.1; AĀ II.5); "thus spake Vāmadeva, lying in the womb" (*garbhe . . . sayānaḥ*, AĀ II.5).[32] As Agni, etc., engendered in all things in motion or at rest (*garbhaś ca sthātāṃ garbhaś carathām*), the Only Transmigrant[33] knows the operations of the gods and the births of men, and is besought to ward (*ni pāhi*) their births (RV I.70.1–3); as Gandharva[34] Soma-guardian "he wards (*pāti*) the generations of the gods" (RV IX.83.4), and as the All-seeing (*viśvam abhi caṣṭe*, RV VII.61.1), the Self of all that is in motion or at rest (RV I.115.1) and our true Father (JUB III.10.4), he is, as aforesaid, the "Knower of births" (RV I.50.1). As Krishna, "Self abiding in all beings" (*aham ātmā . . . sarva-bhūtāśaya-sthitaḥ*, BG X.20; cf. Heb. 4:12, 13) he knows all their births (*janmāni . . . tāny ahaṃ veda sarvāṇi*, BG IV.5).

This is not a knowledge of successive events, but of all at once—"Dove s'appunta ogni ubi ed ogni quando . . . chè nè prima nè poscia procedette" (*Paradiso* XXIX.11, 20; Śvet. Up. I.2). The Person of whom all things are born, the Lord of Immortality (*amṛtatvasyeśānaḥ*), "when he rises up on food"[35] (*yad annenāti rohati*) becomes "all this, both what hath been

[31] Vedic *nu*, like *sakṛt*, "once for all," "nowever." Similarly the gnomic aorist, "I have known."

[32] As in BU II.5.18, *puriśaya*; *pura*, as in Plato πόλις, being "body," and *śaya* or *śayāna* etymologically *civis*. Paul Deussen (*Sechzig Upanishads des Veda*, Leipzig, 1897, p. 606) has pointed out that the doctrine of a knowledge within the womb that is lost at birth, enunciated in Garbha Up. 3.4, corresponds to the Platonic doctrine that all "learning" is really recollection; cf. the Hebrew sources cited on pp. 63–64. [Similarly, Udayana's view in the 10th-century *Kusumāñjali*; see A. B. Keith, *Indian Logic and Atomism* (Oxford, 1921), pp. 31, 269 (he calls the view "quaint").]

[33] See Coomaraswamy, "On the One and Only Transmigrant" [in this volume—ED.].

[34] The progenitive solar deity, as in M I.265,266, *gandhabbo*, apart from whom the union of human parents is sterile.

[35] When he "comes eating and drinking" (Luke 7:34). "That Golden Person in the Sun . . . is even He who dwells within the lotus of the heart and eats food" (MU VI.1). "Food" in this context is not, of course, merely "solid food," but whatever fuel feeds the fires of life, whether physical or mental.

and what shall be" (RV x.90.2, cf. 1.25.10–12; Śvet. Up. III.15).[36] "That God (Ātman and Brahma of the preceding verses), indeed, fills all quarters of the Sky, aforetime was he born, and he is within the womb. He alone hath been born, will be born. He standeth toward men, facing all ways" (Śvet. Up. II.16). "Other than past and future . . . Lord of what hath been and shall be, he alone is today and tomorrow" (KU I.14, IV.13). That Great Being is All-knowing, just because All things originate in him (Śaṇkarācārya on BrSBh I.1.3, BU II.4.10). *In divinis,* Brahma is the lightning flash, which reveals all things instantaneously; and within you, "that which comes to mind, and by which it instantly remembers" (*upasmaraty abhīkṣnam,* JUB IV.21.4, 5 = Kena Up. IV.4.5). [Cf. Plato, *Epistle* VIII, 341D, "sometimes this knowledge does blaze forth with a most instantaneous flash. . . ."]

There has thus been clearly established, in the Indian sources, a logical connection of Omniscience, an unbroken Memory of all things, with temporal and spatial omnipresence.[37] Only from this point of view can the notion of a "Providence" be made intelligible, the divine life being uneventful, not in the sense that it knows nothing of what we call events, but inasmuch as all of the events of what are for us past and future times are present to it *now*, and not in a succession. It is just at this point that we can most advantageously turn to consider the similar Platonic doctrine "that we do not learn, and that what we call learning is recollection" (ὅτι οὐ μανθάνομεν, ἀλλὰ ἥν καλοῦμεν μάθησιν ἀνάμνησίς ἐστι), and that there is "no teaching, but only recollection" (ὅς οὔ φημι διδαχὴν

[36] There is a significant doctrine of past (*bhūtam*) and future (*bhavyam*). Past is to future as Sky, Day, Sun, Sacerdotium (*brahma*), Reality (*satyam*), and Certainty are to Earth, Night, Moon, Regnum (*kṣatra*), Unreality (*anṛtam*), and Uncertainty (AV II.15; ŚB II.3.1.25). These are progenitive pairs, respectively m. and f., differentiated here but coincident *in divinis.* Man is generated (*prajāyate*) and increases from the clash or conjugation (*maithunam*) of real and unreal (AĀ II.3.6); or as we might put it, man is the child of past and future. It is our uninterrupted genesis that separates these contraries; their reunion taking place only upon condition of our ceasing to become, so as to be what we are ("That art thou"), now, *sub specie aeternitatis.*

[37] It is, of course, "only as it were with a part of himself" (BG XV.7) that the Supreme Identity of Being and Nonbeing can be thought of as Omnipresent, Omniform, Omniscient. For Omniscience can be only of the possibilities and actuality of manifestation: of what remains (*ucchiṣṭam,* AV XI.7, etc.) there can be neither science nor omniscience, and it is from this point of view that, as Erigena justly remarks, "God does not know *what* he is, because he is not any what" (cf. Buddhist *ākimcaññā*). It is only his possibilities of manifestation that become "whats" of which there can be science or omniscience.

εἶναι ἀλλ' ἀνάμνησιν, *Meno* 81E, 82A; cf. *Phaedrus* 278A).[38] Taking for granted Plato's repeated distinction of mortal and immortal "souls" that dwell together in us,[39] and assuming further that the immortal is not an individual but a universal principle "participated in" by the individual, not as a thing divided up but as one of which we can know—and be—according to the measure of our ability to "know our selves,"[40] we proceed to cite the main text, that of *Meno* 81CD.

"Seeing, then, that Soul [θεός of *Laws* 897B] is immortal and has been born many times, and has beheld all things both in this world and in Hades, she has learnt all things, without exception; so that it is no wonder that she should be able to remember all that she knew before[41] about virtue

[38] It is in accordance with this doctrine that Plato takes it for granted that the function of works of art is to *remind us* of the eternal realities (*Phaedo* 74 ff., *Phaedrus* 278A); cf. MU VI.34, *fin.*, where for those who do not sacrifice, or know, or contemplate, "the *remembrance* (*smaranā*, [*docta ignorantia*]) of the heavenly abode of Brahma (i.e., *brahmaloka*) is obstructed." "It is the unknown, methinks, that thou shouldst remember" (*atha nu mīmāṃsyam eva te manye 'viditam*, JUB IV.19.1). In the iconography of Śiva, the demon on whom he tramples is called "the person of amnesia" (*apasmāra puruṣa*).

[39] *Timaeus* 69D, 90AC, *Republic* 430, 604B; the Immortal Soul being the "real Self" of *Laws* 959B. That this Soul has never become anyone is clear from *Meno* 81B, where the hieratic doctrine is cited, that "the Soul of Man is immortal, and at one time reaches an end, which is called 'dying,' and is 'born again,' but is never slain." This is almost identical with BU IV.4.5,6, BG II.13 and 17–26, Plato's ἀπόλλυσθαι δ' οὐδέποτε corresponding to *na hanyate hayamāne śarīre* and ὁ δὴ ἀποθνήσκειν καλοῦσι to *nityam vā mṛtam*. In the same way *Phaedo* 83BC, "the Self of (all) beings" (αὐτὸ τῶν ὄντων) and "Soul of every man" (ψυχὴ παντὸς ἀνθρώπου, Fowler's version, preferable to Jowett's "every soul of man"), corresponds to the "Self of all beings" (*sarveṣam bhūtānām ātmā, BU* I.4.16) of the Upaniṣads. Cf. *Phaedrus* 246B, πᾶσα ἡ ψυχὴ παντός, and 249E; and Hermes, *Lib.* X.7, ψυχὴ τοῦ παντός. Particular attention may also be called to *Phaedo* 77A, where we are told, not that "our souls existed before we were born," but that "the soul of us (ἡμῶν ἡ ψυχή) existed before we were born." There is a parallel in the Buddhist *Vinaya*, I.23 (i.e., Mv I.14, cf. Vis 393), where the Buddha asks a group of young men who are searching for a missing woman, "Which were the better for you, to go seeking the woman, or to go seeking the Self"; he does not say "your selves." In both cases the reference is to the unique principle of many individuals. [Cf. Boehme, *Signatura rerum* IX.65.]

[40] "Philosophy . . . admonishing the soul to collect and assemble herself in her Self, and to throw in nothing but her Self, that she may know her Self itself, the Self of (all) beings" (*Phaedo* 83B). Cf. Coomaraswamy, "The 'E' at Delphi" [in this volume—ED.], and *Hinduism and Buddhism*, 1943, pp. 15–18, 58.

[41] The doctrine of Recollection recurs in the Koran (VI.80), and permeates Rūmī's *Mathnawī* (see Anamnesis in Nicholson's subject index). *Mathnawī* IV.3632–3635 runs, "What wonder, then, if the spirit does not remember its ancient abodes, which have been its dwelling place and birthplace aforetime, since this world, like sleep,

and other things. And since all Nature is congeneric, there is no reason why we should not, by remembering but one single thing[42]—which is what we call 'learning'—discover all the others, if we are brave and faint not in the enquiry; for it seems that to enquire and to learn are wholly a matter of remembering."[43] The same doctrine is discussed in *Phaedo*

---

is covering it over as clouds cover the stars? Especially as it has trodden so many cities, and the dust has not yet been swept from its perceptive faculty, nor has it made ardent efforts that its heart should become pure and behold the past; that its heart should put forth its head from the aperture of the mystery and should see the beginning and the end with open eye." The wording is suggestive of Indian rather than Platonic derivation. The connected doctrine that God is the real agent and man only his instrument, as expressed, for example, in the *Manṭiqu'ṭ-Ṭair*,

> All you have been, and seen, and done, and thought,
> Not *you*, but *I*, have seen and been and wrought

is equally Indian (JUB I.5.2, MU III.2, BG III.27, etc.) and Neo-Platonic (Philo, *De opificio mundi* 78, etc.).

[42] Cf. *Timaeus* 50AB, and CU VI.1.4, "That teaching (*ādeśam*) whereby what has not been heard of becomes heard of, what has not been thought of becomes thought of, what has not been known becomes known of. . . . Just as by one piece of clay everything made of clay may be known of, the modification being only a matter of naming, and the reality (*satyam*) just clay." Cf. BU IV.5.6. [Socrates claims to know everything always by means of his soul, *Euthydemus* 295 ff.]

[43] "Virtue" (ἀρετή) is the subject under discussion. The Dialogue does not decide what "virtue" is; it is neither natural nor taught, nor is it prudence (φρόνησις), but a thing "that comes to us by a divine dispensation (*Meno* 98E, 99E ff.). It is a thing to be *remembered*, which remembrance is properly called "learning" (μάθησις, cf. μαθητής, disciple, *śrāvaka*): whence it follows that ignorance, or rather "want of learning" (ἀμαθία, cf. Pāli *assutavā putthujanā* = profane οἱ πολλοί), the ignorance that is so disgraceful (*Apology* 29B, *Phaedrus* 277E), is really "forgetfulness"; cf. Skr. *aśruta*, "untaught," and *aśruti*, "oblivion." For Hermes, "the soul's vice is ignorance (ἀγνωσία) and her virtue (ἀρετή) gnosis" (*Lib.* x.8.9, cf. 13.7B); and that, I think, is just what Socrates means to imply, namely, that virtue is a function of self-knowledge (Skr. *ātmajñāna*), and can be theirs only who "know themselves."

The traditional "ignorance" has nothing, of course, to do with what we call "illiteracy." The exaggerated value that we attach to "literature" as such would have been, indeed, for Plato, in itself an evidence of "ignorance" (*Phaedrus* 275, 278); [cf. *Laws* 689, "only those should govern who are masters of themselves, not those who are merely literate or otherwise expert"]. Ignorance is "subjection to pleasure," or what amounts to the same thing, "subjection to oneself" (τὸ ἥττω εἶναι αὑτοῦ, *Protagoras* 357E, 358C; cf. *Republic* 430E ff.); ignorance is of what is just and what unjust (*Phaedrus* 277E); nothing is worse than to think one knows what one does not know (*Apology* 29B). It is the Self that should be known (Γνῶθι σεαυτόν): for when the Self is seen, is heard, thought of and known, this All is known (BU IV.5.6). Whereas to put our trust in the written characters, which are not a part of our Self, is a hindrance to that recollection that is in and of the Self (*Phaedrus* 275A).

72E ff., and 75E, where "we must necessarily have learned in some prior time what we now remember. But this is impossible if the Soul in us had not existed anywhere before being born in this human nature; and so by this consideration it appears again that the Soul is immortal"; as in *Meno* 86AB, "if in us the truth of all things be the Soul, then Soul must be 'immortal' for it knows things of which we could not have acquired knowledge in this life and 'must have had this learning through all time' (ὅτι τὸν πάντα χρόνον)"[44] [cf. πρὸς τὸν ξύμπαντα χρόνον, *Timaeus* 36E]. Following *Meno* 81, Socrates goes on to give a practical demonstration by educing from rather than communicating to a pupil, knowledge which he did not appear to possess; and this seems to show that all true education is rather a destruction of ignorance[45] than the gift of a knowledge, a view that is in close agreement with what is called in India the "self-manifestation" nature (*sva-prakāśatva*) of the intellectual principle.

Plato's Immortal Soul, "the most lordly and divine part of us" (*Timaeus* 90AB), can be only the immanent Daimon, "that vulgar fellow, who cares for nothing but the truth" (*Hippias major* 286D). It is Philo's "Soul of the soul"; the Sanctus Spiritus as distinguished from the (mortal) "soul" (Heb. 4:12) and "source of all that is true, by whomsoever it has been said" (St. Ambrose on 1 Cor. 12:3, cited by St. Thomas Aquinas, *Sum. Theol.* I-II.109.1); the Scholastic Speculum Aeternum[46] and Synteresis,[47] Dante's Amor (*Purgatorio* XXIX.52–54), and our own "conscience" (E.E. "inwyt") in the original and fullest sense of the word; and the Immortal Self, the source of Memory, of the Vedānta.

We meet the doctrine of recollection also in Hebrew contexts. In the Talmud (*Nidda* 30B) and Zohar (*Wayyiqra, Aharei Mot*), we are told that all human souls have a full knowledge of the Torah, etc. (see n. 32),

[44] Here again "soul" in the singular, "we" plural. But elsewhere we find (immortal) "souls" in the plural (*Phaedo* 76). Both uses are consistent with the view that all souls are facets of one Soul, which I think was Plato's belief, as it was certainly that of Plotinus and Hermes.

[45] Not that ignorance is "real" (in which case it could not be "destroyed"), but as darkness (privation of light) it is removed by illumination. Pāli texts often employ this illustration: when the Buddha has *cleared* up some problem by his *argu*ment, "it is just as if a lamp were brought into a dark room."

[46] "Wherein those who gaze behold all things, and better than elsewhere" (St. Bonaventura, *I Sent.* d.35, a unic., q. 1, fund. 3, "sicut dicit Augustinus"); "as a clear mirror sees all things in one image" (Meister Eckhart, Evans ed., I, 253).

[47] Cf. O. Renz, "Die Synteresis nach dem Hl. Thomas von Aquin," in *Beiträge zur Geschichte der Philosophie des Mittelalters*, X (Münster, 1911).

and retain all their knowledge until they come down to earth and are born. Manasseh ben Israel (seventeenth century) saw here the equivalent of Plato's doctrine of Recollection, for it must follow that whatever is learnt after birth can only amount to a recovery of this knowledge; and so Elimelech of Lizensk (eighteenth century) says, "By relearning the Torah later on for its own sake he (the child) succeeds in grasping the truth as it was originally implanted in him."[48] The implied eternity of "the Torah that created all the worlds and is the means by which these are sustained" (Zohar, *Beha 'Alotheka*) is like that of the Veda, of the origin of which nothing more can be said than that "the Lord" (Īśvara = Kyrios, Demiourgos), at the beginning of each world-aeon, "remembers" (*smṛtvā*) it and promulgates it, and there is no ground for supposing that it was composed by any other standard (Āpadeva).[49] Again, the doctrine of Recollection is explicit in Meister Eckhart, who says: "If I knew my Self as intimately as I ought, I should have perfect knowledge of all creatures," for "the soul is capable of knowing all things in her highest power," viz. "as a clear mirror sees all things in one image," and so "not until she

[48] For a fuller discussion of this material see J. Finkel, "A Psychoanalytic Prefiguration in Hasidic Literature," *Eidenu*, New York, 1942. Finkel justly observes that Elimelech's "Unconscious" is not psychological but transcendental. Cf. n. 33. [Eleazar of Worms (d. 1223–1232) held that a guardian angel causes forgetfulness at birth because if it is remembered, the contradiction of the course of the world with its knowledge would drive it to madness (G. G. Scholem, *Major Trends in Jewish Mysticism*, Jerusalem, 1941 [New York, 1954], p. 92).]

[49] *Mimamsā Nyāya Prakāśa* 6; late, but a restatement of the oldest *Pūrva Mīmāṃsā* doctrine; [cf. *Pūrva Mimāṃsā Sūtras* 1.1.5 and BrSBh 1.3.28]. The similar doctrine that the Koran is "uncreated" is fundamental to Islam.

Not to have studied (*adhī*) or understood (*vijñā*) the Veda ("wit," as in Wycliffe's version of Rom. 11:34) is utter ignorance (ŚA XIV). Since the dictionary meanings of *adhī* (lit. "go to") are to "study" or "remember," and of *smṛ*, to "remember" or "teach," all this amounts to saying that to learn is to remember. Closely related to this are the well-known Indian pedagogic principles of oral instruction and learning by heart, which are, again, in agreement with Plato (*Phaedrus* 275A, 278A). To have to "look up" a text implies that although we have been once reminded, we have again forgotten, and are no less ignorant than before. We only really *know* what we can always quote. Hence the preference for oral instruction, which *must* be remembered, if we are to possess it. Under these conditions, as also in many "primitive" civilizations, culture is independent of literacy, which last Plato called "a device for forgetting." Cf. Coomaraswamy, "The Bugbear of Literacy," 1944.

The further argument of the *Pūrva Mimāmsā*, that words participate in eternity because they have a meaning, is entirely comprehensible from the Platonic, Aristotelian, and Scholastic doctrine that knowledge can be only of the immutable, and not of any things in flux, singulars, or accidentals, which never retain their identity from one moment to another. In other words, perception and knowledge, facts and realities, are very different things.

knows all that there is to be known does she (the soul) cross over to the Unknown Good."[50] The doctrine survives in Blake's "Is the Holy Ghost any other than an intellectual fountain?"

We need not attempt to follow up the history of the doctrine in any greater detail. Our main object has been to call attention both to the importance and to the universality of the doctrine of Recollection, and to bring out that it is only one of the many consistent features of a philosophy that is essentially the same in Plato and in the Vedānta.[51]

[50] Evans ed., I, 324, 253, 359, 385.

[51] The virtual identity of Indian and Socratic-Platonic philosophy is of far greater significance than the problem as more often discussed in connection with Plotinus. There we are dealing, not with "influences," but—just as in the case of the roots and idioms of the languages, Greek and Sanskrit themselves—with cognate doctrines and myths, many of which are as much Sumerian as they are Greek or Indian. The Philosophia Perennis antedates the whole historical period within which "influences" can be predicated.

For example, it is not by a borrowing but only by a long inheritance that we can explain the occurrence of the "cutting reed" and "clashing rock" forms of the "active door" (Janua Coeli) in Greece on the one hand and in Navajo and Eskimo, Mexican and South American, and Chinese and Indian mythology, on the other. Cf. R. Guénon, *Introduction to the Study of the Hindu Doctrines*, tr. Marco Pallis (London, 1945), p. 50. All mythology involves a corresponding philosophy; and if there is only one mythology, as there is only one "Perennial Philosophy," then that "the myth is not my own, I had it from my mother" (Euripides) points to a spiritual unity of the human race already predetermined long before the discovery of metals. It may be really true that, as Alfred Jeremias said, the various cultures of mankind are no more than the *dialects* of one and the same spiritual language. For this point of view, as now entertained by a large school of anthropologists, for whom the concept of one "High God" antedates even the development of animism, cf. Father Wilhelm Schmidt, *Der Ursprung der Gottesidee* (Münster, 1912–1939); *The Origin and Growth of Religion*, tr. H. J. Rose (New York, 1931); and *High Gods in North America* (Oxford, 1933). [Fundamentally, it is held in common that *philosophy* is both a way of life and a means of escape from the wheel, whereby the soul returns to its own.]

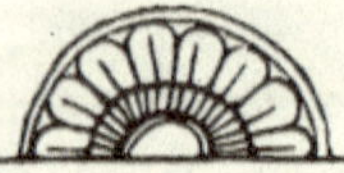

On the One and Only Transmigrant

Man is born once; I have been born many times.
Rūmī

Bei Gotte werden nur die Götter angenommen.
Angelus Silesius

Liberation is for the Gods, *not for men.*
Gebhard-Lestrange

Ātmety evopāsīta, atra hy ete sarva ekam bhavanti
BU 1.4.7

N'atthi koci satto yo imamha kaya anyam kayam sankamati
Mil 72, cf. 46.

I

Śaṇkarācārya's dictum, "Verily, there is no other transmigrant but the Lord" (*satyaṃ, neśvarād anyaḥ saṃsārī*, BrSBh 1.1.5),[1] startling as it may appear to be at first sight, for it denies the reincarnation of individual essences, is amply supported by the older, and even the oldest texts, and is by no means an exclusively Indian doctrine. For it is not an individual soul that Plato means when he says: "The soul of man is immortal, and at one time comes to an end, which is called dying away, and at another is born again, but never perishes . . . and having been born many times has acquired the knowledge of all and everything";[2] or that Plotinus means when he says: "There is really nothing strange in that reduction

[This study was published in supplement No. 3 to the *Journal of the American Oriental Society*, 1944.—ED.]

[1] Cf. T.A.G. Rao, *Elements of Hindu Iconography*, II (Madras, 1914–1916), p. 405, "When Īśvara absorbs in himself, he is known as the Puruṣa, and as Saṃsārī when he has manifested himself." Cf. n. 66.

[2] *Meno* 81BC, where this is cited as the doctrine of learned priests and priestesses, and is approved by Socrates. Of the same sort is Agni's omniscience as Jātavedas, "Knower of Births," and the Buddha's, whose *abhiññā* extends to all "former abodes." He who is "where every where and every when is focused" (Dante) cannot but have knowledge of every thing.

(of all selves) to One; though it may be asked, How can there be only One, the same in many, entering into all, but never itself divided up";[3] or by Hermes who says that "He who does all these things is One," and speaks of Him as "bodiless and having many bodies, or rather present in all bodies."[4]

The "Lord" of whom Śaṇkarācārya speaks is, of course, the Supreme and Solar Self, Ātman, Brahma, Indra, "of all beings Overlord, of all beings King," whose omniformity is timeless and whose omnipresence enables us to understand that He must be omniscient (*sarvānubhūḥ*, BU II.5.15, 19, cf. IV.4.22 and AĀ XIII); Death, the Person in the Sun, Indra and Breath of Life, "One as he is Person there, and many as he is in his children here," and at whose departure "we" die (ŚB X.5.2.13, 16); the Solar Self of all that is in motion or at rest (RV I.115.1); our Immortal Self and Inner Controller "other than whom there is no seer, hearer, thinker or knower" (BU III.7.23, III.8.11); the solar Indra of whom it is said that whoever speaks, hears, thinks, etc., does so by his ray (JUB I.28, 29); Brahma, of whom it is said that our powers "are merely the names of *his* acts" (BU I.4.7, cf. I.5.21); the Self, from whom all action stems (BU I.6.3; BG III.15); the Self that knows everything (MU VI.7).[5]

Whether as Sūrya, Savitṛ, Ātman, Brahma, Agni, Prajāpati, Indra, Vāyu or *madhyama* Prāṇa—*yādṛg eva dadṛśe tādṛg ucyate* (RV V.44.6)[6]—this Lord, from within the heart here,[7] is our mover, driver and actuator (*īri-*

[3] Plotinus, IV.9.4, 5 (condensed); cf. I.1, *passim*. In our Self, the spiritual Self of all beings, all these selves and their doings are one simple act of being; hence it is not the separated selves and acts, but rather the Real Agent that one should seek to know (BU I.4.7, Kauṣ. Up. III.8, Hermes, *Lib.* XI.2.12A). "Thou hast seen the kettles of thought a-boiling; consider also the fire!" (*Mathnawī* V.2902).

[4] Hermes, *Lib.* V.10A (cf. BU I.5.21), and XI.2.12A (cf. KU II.22).

[5] In "Recollection, Indian and Platonic" [the preceding essay in this volume—ED.], we have shown that timeless omnipresence and providential omniscience are interdependent and inseparable notions. The related thesis of the present article is that the omnipresent omniscient is "the only transmigrant," and that in the last analysis this "transmigration" is nothing but his knowledge of himself expressed in terms of a duration. If there were really "others," or any discontinuity within the unity, each "other" or "part" would not be omnipresent to the rest, and the concept of an omniscience would be inconceivable.

[6] "He is given names that correspond exactly to the forms in which He is apprehended." Cf. "All names are names of Him, who has no name, for that he is their common Father," Hermes, *Lib.* V.10A.

[7] "Who takes up his stand in every heart" (*hṛdi sarvasya adhitiṣṭhan*, BG XIII.17); "Questi nei cor mortali è permotore, questi la terra in se stringe ed aduna," Dante, *Paradiso* I.116—*stringe*, as in ŚB VIII.7.3.10, etc.

taḥ,[8] *codayitṛ,*[9] *kārayitṛ*[10]) and whole source of the evanescent consciousness (*cetana* = *saṃjñāna*)[11] that begins with our birth and ends with our death (MU II.6D, III.3).[12] We do nothing of ourselves and are merely his vehicles, and instruments (as for Philo, *passim*).

This "higher" (*para*) Brahma is that "One, the Great Self, who takes up his stand in womb after womb (*yo yoniṃ yonim adhitiṣṭhati*[13] *ekaḥ . . . mahātmā*) . . . as the omniform Lord of the Breaths (*viśvarūpaḥ* . . .

[8] Cf. the "potter's wheel"; cf. Muṇḍ. Up. II.2.6; BU II.5.15; Plotinus, VI.5.5; Isa. 64:8, etc.

[9] Of the "chariot," cf. RV VI.75.6; KU III.3 ff.; J VI.252; Plato, *Laws* 898C, "Soul is the driver of all things." In MU II.6, the driver's "reins" or "rays" (*raśmayaḥ*) are the intelligential powers (*buddhīndriyāṇi*) by which the equine powers of sensation (*karmendriyāṇi*) are governed. Similarly, Hermes, *Lib.* X.22B, "The energies of God are, as it were, His rays," and XVI.7, "His reins are (His rays)." Cf. Boethius, *De consolatione philosophiae* IV.11, "Hic regum sceptrum dominus tenet, Orbisque habenas temperat, Et volucrem currum stabilis regit, Rerum coruscus arbiter"; *Mathnawī* I.3268, 3273, 3575–3576. "Under the theory of presence by powers, souls are described as rays" (Plotinus, VI.4.3). This is "the living doctrine that ascribes to God the totality of all powers," and to be distinguished from "the pierced and cloven doctrine that is conscious of a man's own mind at work" (Philo, *Legum allegoriae*, I.93, 94).

[10] Of the "elemental self" (*bhūtātman*) as "agent" (*kartṛ*) of the Inner Man. "He is blind indeed who sees only the active self" (*kartāram ātmānam kevala tu yaḥ paśyati . . . na sa paśyati*, BG XVIII.16), whereas "He sees indeed, who sees the Overlord who is the same in all beings, imperishable in those that perish . . . the Overself who, although present in the body, neither acts nor is contaminated by action" (*na karoti na lipyate*, BG XIII.27, 31).

[11] "The dead know not anything" (Eccl. 9:5). *Na pretya saṃjñāsti* (BU II.4.12); *saññā, bhikkhave, loke lokadhammo*, S III.140, cf. Sn 779, 1071, and M I.260. The Self is indestructible (BU IV.5.14; BG IV.13), but "consciousness" in terms of subject and object is a contingency, and loses its meaning "where everything has become just the Self" (BU II.4.14), "actively Itself when it is not intelligizing" (Plotinus, IV.4.2).

[12] "Spirit (*rūḥ*), concealing its glory and pinions and plumes, says to the body, 'O dunghill, who art *thou*? Through *my* beams (cf. n. 9) thou hast come to life for a day or two. . . .' The beams of the spirit are speech and eye and ear" (*Mathnawī* I.3267–3273).

[13] The body being the domain or garden (*ārāma*, BU IV.3.14) or platform (*adhiṣṭhānam*, CU VIII.12.1) of the unseen, incorporeal, and impassible Self. *Adhiṣṭhā* (sometimes *avasthā, āruh*) is regularly employed in connection with the "mounting" of the psycho-physical vehicle (*ratha*) by the Spirit (*ātman*), e.g., AV X.8.1, (Brahma) *śarvam . . . adhitiṣṭhati*; AĀ III.3.8.5B, *prāna adhitiṣṭhati* (*devaratham*); KU II.22, *śarīreṣv avasthitam . . . ātmānam*; BG XIII.17, *hṛdi . . . adhitiṣṭhan*. At the same time *adhiṣṭhā* implies administration, management, as in Praśna Up. III.D: similarly *anuṣṭhā* in KU V.1.

prāṇādhipaḥ)[14] he wanders about (*saṃcarati* = *saṃsarati*)[15] by his own actions, the fruition of which he enjoys (*upabhoktṛ*),[16] and, being associated with conceptuality and the notion 'I am,' is known as the 'lower' (*apara*). . . . Neither male nor female nor neuter, whatever body he as-

[14] Not, as understood by Deussen and Hume, the "individual soul," which is not a "Lord" but a compound of the Breaths or Beings that are the subjects (*svāh*) of the Great Being or Breath from which they arise and into which they return (JUB IV.7; MU III.3, *bhūtagana*). It would be an antinomy to describe the composite individual soul, subject to persuasion, as a sovereign power. "The Lord of the Breaths," who is "the Leader of the Breaths and of the body" (*prāṇaśarīranetṛ*, Muṇḍ. Up. II.2.8) is much rather *the* Being and Breath that is "Lord of all (*prāṇáh . . . bhūtáḥ sárvasyeśvaráh*, AV XI.4.1.10)," the "Lord of the gods (powers of the soul) who enters the womb and is 'born again' (*yonim aiti sa u jāyate punah, sa devānām adhipatir babhūva*," AV XIII.2.25) or "Lord of Beings" (*bhūtānām adhipatiḥ*, AV IV.8.1; TS VI.1.11.4; MU V.2), i.e., the imperial Breath on whose behalf the "other Breaths" function as ministers (Praśna Up. III.4), and the Brahma whom all things hail as king (BU IV.3.37). The "Lord of the Breaths" (*prāṇādhipah*) is *the* Breath whose superiority to all the other Breaths (*prāṇāh* = *devāh, bhūtāni*) is again and again insisted upon in the contests of the Breaths for supremacy (Brāhmaṇas and Upaniṣads, *passim*), and other than the subjected elemental self (*bhūtātman*) that is a host of beings (*bhūtagana*, MU III.3). The Lord of the Breaths, "neither male nor female," is the Breath thus described in AĀ II.3.8.5, in whom all the gods (Breaths or powers of the soul) are unified (AĀ II; Kauṣ. Up. III.3; cf. BU I.4.7), the Breath that mounts the bodily vehicle and is regularly identified with the Sun, Brahma, Ātman, Vāmadeva, Indra, etc. This Lord of the Breaths is likewise the Inner Person (*antahpuruṣa* = *antarātman* of Śvet. Up. III.13; KU V.9–13, VI.17) who wanders (*carati*) from body to body unovercome by the fruits of the actions that determine the aughty or naughty wombs in which the elemental self alone suffers (MU III.1–3).

When at death this Self recollects itself (BU IV.4.3, VI.1.13, etc.)—ὅμως εἰς ἓν ἀνατρέχει ἀποστάντος τοῦ σώματος (Plotinus IV.9.2)—then "we" are no more (BU II.4.12, IV.4.3; CU VIII.9.1, etc.), "we who in our junction with our bodies are composites and have qualities shall not exist, but shall be brought into the regeneration by which, becoming joined to immaterial things, we shall become incomposite and without qualities" (Philo, *De cherubim* 113 ff.; cf. Plato, *Phaedo* 78c ff.).

[15] Cf. nn. 26, 40.

[16] *Upabhoktṛ* = *bhoktṛ* in KU III.4 (Ātman) and MU II.6 (Prajāpati). This fruition does not necessarily involve a subjection: insofar as it remains a spectator (*abhi cākaśīti*, RV I.164.20; *prekṣada*, MU II.7; Pāli *upekhaka*), or in other words disinterestedly enjoys only the flavor of life (*akāmo . . . rasena tṛptah*, AV X.8.44), the governing and immortal Self of the self, or Inner Self (*amṛto 'syātmā, antarātman*), remains immune (KU V.13; MU III.2, etc.). As Experient (*bhoktṛ*) this immanent Person (*puruṣo 'ntasthah*) is himself without qualities (*nirguna*), while the elemental self (*bhūtātman*) with its three qualities (*triguṇa*)—i.e., the individual soul—is his "food" (*annam*, MU VI.10). The contemplative Experient is both the Giver-of-being and a Mighty Lord (*bhoktā ca prabhur eva ca . . . bhoktā mahesvarah*, BG IX.24, 13, 22); the All-soul that "suffers no hurt whatever by furnishing the body with the power to existence" (Plotinus, IV.8.2; cf. KU V.1 and BG XIII.32).

sumes, therewith he is connected (*yujyate*):[17] through the delusions of concept, touch, and sight, there is birth and growth of the Self by the rain of food and drink;[18] the embodied Self (*dehī*)[19] assumes functional forms in their stations in regular order (*karmāṇugāny anukrameṇa dehī sthāneṣu rūpāṇy abhisampadyate*)[20] . . . and because of conjunction with

---

For, as Meister Eckhart says, "With the love with which God leaves Himself, He loves all creatures, not as creatures but more: creatures as God. . . . God tastes (Skr. *bhuñkte*) himself in all things. . . . Men as creatures taste as all creatures in measures and quantities, as wine and bread and meat. But my inner man tastes not as a creature, but more: as a gift of God. But my innermost man does not taste it as a gift of God, but more: as eternity" (Pfeiffer ed., 180).

[17] *Yujyate*, like *samyoga* below, as in BG I.26, where every birth is said to depend upon a "connection" or "yoking" (*samyoga*) of the Knower of the Field with the Field. Conversely, *asamyoga*, "liberation," "unyoking," MU VI.21.

[18] "The nourishment of 'sense-perception' which he (the author of Gen. 2:5) figuratively calls 'rain'" (Philo, *Legum allegoriae*, I.48). Here with reference to the falcon-brought Soma, and the "Shower of Wealth (*vasor dhārā*)." "Touch," because "all experience is contact-born" (BG V.21); cf. Coomaraswamy, "Note on the Stickfast Motif," 1944.

[19] The embodied Self (*dehī*) of BG II.18 ff., and quick or vibrant (*vipaścit*) Self of KU II.18, 19, that never becomes anyone, but passes over from body to body, and is not slain when the body is slain, unborn though it can be thought of as continually born and continually dying. This is precisely the doctrine of the immortal Soul, which Plato cites as that of learned priests and priestesses: "They say that the soul of man is immortal, and at one time ends, which they call 'dying away,' and at another is born again, but never perishes" (*Meno* 81AB). The embodied Self (*dehī, paramātmā . . . śarīrasthaḥ*) is to be distinguished from the elemental self (*bhūtātman, bhūtagaṇa*, MU III.2, 3). The former is the unperishing (*avinaśyat*) Self of CU VIII.5.3 and BG XIII.27, the latter arises out of the elements and perishes (*vinaśyati*) with them (BU II.4.12).

[20] These words describe the entry of the Self into any one body and its extension therein in the form of the Intelligences (Breaths, powers of the soul) that work through the doors of the senses, as in MU II.6, etc. *Karmānugāni*, "corresponding to the variety of actions to be performed," as in BU I.5.21, "'I am going to speak,' began the Voice," etc. The powers of speaking, seeing, thinking, etc., "are just the names of His acts" (BU I.4.7)—not "ours" (BG III.27). "Stupefied by the notion of an 'I that acts,' the self believes that 'I am the actor'"; similarly, countless Buddhists texts; cf. Philo, *Legum allegoriae*, I.78, "I deem nothing so shameful as to suppose that 'I' know and 'I' perceive. My own intellect the author of its own intelligizing, how could that be?" *Anukramena*, like *yathāyatanam* in Kauṣ. Up. III.3 and Ait. Up. II.3, and *yathākramena* in MU VI.26, "As rays from Sun, so from him (immanent Brahma, Fire of Life) his Breaths and the rest come forth continually here in the world in due order (*tasya prāṇādayo vai punar eva tasmād abhyuccarantīha yathākramena*)." *Sthānesu*, "in their places," as in Praśna Up. III.2, *sthānam. Rūpāṇi*, "forms," i.e., "Prajāpati's breath-forms" (*prāṇarūpā*, Sāyaṇa on RV X.90.16, and as in BU I.5.21, where the Breaths are the "forms" of the median Breath and called after him; similarly in Praśna Up. II.12).

the qualities, both his own and of action, he seems to be 'another'" (*teṣāṃ saṃyogahetur aparo*[21] *'pi dṛṣṭaḥ*, Śvet. Up. v.1–13, condensed).

This transmigrating "Lord of the Breaths" is the Breath (*prāṇa*), "the most excellent (*vasiṣṭha*, BU vi.1, 14),"[22] Brahma, Prajāpati, he who divides himself five- and manifold to support and sustain the body, to awaken his children, to fill these worlds (Praśna Up. ii.3; MU ii.6, vi.26), remaining nevertheless undivided in things divided (BG xiii.16, xviii.20). To him as Prajāpati it is said, "'Tis thou, thyself, that art counterborn (*pratijāyase*),[23] to thee all thy children (*prajāḥ* = *raśmayah*, *prāṇāh*, *devāḥ*, *bhūtāni*) bring tribute (*baliṃ haranti*),[24] O Breath" (Praśna Up.

[21] *Apara*, "lower" or "other" as in MU iii.2 (Ātman), and to be contrasted with *para* (Brahma) in verse 1 = *para* (Ātman) of Praśna Up. iv.7. For the "one essence and two natures" of Brahma see BU ii.3, Praśna Up. v.2, MU vi.3, 22, 23 and vii.11.8, *dvaitībhāva*). This is the doctrine of Hermes, viz. that to say that "God is both One and All does not mean that the One is two, but that the two are One" (*Lib.* xvi.3). Similarly Plotinus, iv.4.10, "The ordering-and-governing-principle (τὸ κοσμοῦν = Plato, *Phaedo* 97c, ὁ διακοσμῶν τε καὶ παντῶν αἴτιος) is twofold, one that we call Demiurge and one the Soul of All (τοῦ παντὸς ψυχή): we speak of Zeus sometimes as Demiurge (Creator) and sometimes as the Leader of all (ἡγεμὼν τοῦ παντός)"; which is as much as to say that we speak of Varuṇa sometimes as such and sometimes as Mitra or Savitṛ (*netṛ*, RV v.50.1 = *prāṇaśarīranetṛ*, Muṇḍ. Up. ii.2.8 = *ātmano 'tmā netāmṛtākhyah*, MU vi.7), of Brahma as *parāpara*, *dvirūpa* and *dvaitībhāva*, of Agni as Indrāgnī, and of Prajāpati as *parimitāparimita*, *niruktāniruhta*, etc., in the same way imputing two contrasted natures to one and same essence. And just as in one of these natures the deity is immortal and impassible and in the other mortal and passible, so in the one he is without needs and in the other has ends to be attained. At the same time, in him these are not two, but one simple essence; the distinction is "logical but not real." So Nicholas of Cusa speaks of the "wall of Paradise" that conceals God from our sight as constituted of the "coincidence of opposites" and of its gate as guarded by "the highest spirit of reason, who bars the way until he has been overcome" (*De visione Dei* ix, xi)—as in JUB i.5.

[22] Implying Agni who as the "Fire of Life" is the "Breath of Life," cf. Heracleitus, fr. 20, and Coomaraswamy, "Measures of Fire" [in this volume—ED.].

[23] BU ii.1.8 *pratirūpo 'smāj jāyase*; cf. Śvet. Up. ii.16, v.11. The Self is the Father of the Breath and consubstantial (MU vi.1); like the human father and son, in accordance with the normal doctrine that the father himself is reborn in his progeny (RV v.4.10, vi.70.3; BD vii.50; AB vii.13; AĀ ii.5; BG iv.7, 8, etc.), the only Indian doctrine of rebirth on earth. It is a character that is thus reborn; it is in his "other self" that the father departs at death; and we are often reminded (ŚB *passim*) that the dead have departed "once for all." The heredity of vocation is connected with the traditional (for it is not only Indian) doctrine of progenitive rebirth. In the same way *in divinis*, the Father is reborn as the Son; cf. the Christian *Alma redemptoris Mater . . . tu quae genuisti tuum sanctum genitorem*.

[24] Cf. AV x.7.38, 39, x.8.15, xi.4.19; ŚB vi.1.1.7; JUB iv.23.7, iv.24.1–7; BU vi.1.13; Kauṣ. Up. ii.1. The various names by which the recipient and the tributaries are referred to in these contexts all imply the Breath and the Breaths, i.e., God and gods under various aspects. Hence "All these gods are *in* me" (JUB i.14.2; ŚB ii.3.2.3;

II.7). By this Prajāpati this body of ours is set up in possession of consciousness (*cetanāvat*), he as its driver passing on from body to body (*pratiśarīreṣu carati*), unovercome by the bright and dark fruit of his acts, or rather those acts of which he, as our Inner Man (*antaḥ puruṣa*),[25] is the actuator (*kārayitṛ*) and spectator (*prekṣaka*) rather than the doer (MU II.6–III.3). This Prajāpati is likewise "the divine Breath who, whether or not transmigrating (*saṃcaraṇś cāsaṃcaraṇś ca*),[26] is neither injured nor distressed, and whom all beings serve," and with respect to whom it is further said that "however his children may suffer, that pertains to them alone, good only goes to him, evil does not reach the gods" (BU I.5.20).

Thus this One, spoken of by many names, is everywhere born and reborn. "Unseen, Prajāpati moves in the womb (*carati garbhe antaḥ*) and is multifariously born" (*bahudhā vi jāyate*, AV X.8.13, cf. Muṇḍ. Up. II.2.6); "The Person expires[27] and suspires in the womb, and then is he

---

AĀ II.1.5, etc.). The *prajā* of AV XI.4.19 (like Praśna Up. II.7) are not "human beings" (Whitney), but the "rays" by which "we" are ensouled and energized (JUB I.28, 29), the Viśvedevāḥ (TS IV.3.1.26). These rays are withdrawn at our death (BU V.5.2; AĀ III.2.4, etc.), viz. when Death himself, the Breath, withdraws his "feet" from our heart and "we" are cut off (ŚB X.5.2.13); for the Breaths cannot live without him (BU VI.1.13 = CU V.1.12). It is true that we are children of the Sun in the sense that our life depends upon him who is our real Father (JUB III.10.4; ŚB VII.3.2.12, etc.), but we are naturally sons of our own fathers, and until we have acquired a second self or Self, born of the sacrifice (JB I.17, etc., cf. John 3:3) we do not "really become the immortal children of Prajāpati" (ŚB V.2.1.11, 14), his natural sons (ŚB IX.3.3.14), or himself (ŚB IV.6.1.5). "That art thou" is always true, but only potentially for us, for so long as we are "this man, So-and-so." We are ensouled and quickened by the rays of the Sun, the Breaths, the All-Gods, but it can only be said of the perfected that they *are* those rays of the Sun (ŚB I.9.3.10, cf. RV I.109.7), his sons (JUB II.9.10).

[25] The *puruṣo 'ntasthaḥ* of MU VI.10; *puruṣaḥ sarvāsu pūrṣu puriśayaḥ* of BU II.5.18; *sarveṣām bhūteṣāṃ antahpurusaḥ* of AĀ III.2.4, described as the unseen seer, etc., and as "unbowed" (*anata*), i.e., *anabhibhūta* as in MU II.7; Vāmadeva *garbhe . . . śayānah* of AĀ II.5; Agni *a yaḥ puram narminīm adīdet . . . śatatmā* of RV I.149.3. For the distinction of this Inner Man from our outer man (the elemental self, *bhūtātman*) cf. II Cor. 4:16, "Is qui foris est noster homo corrumpitur tamen is qui intus est renovatur de die in diem," like MU III.2. Undoubtedly John 1:14 should be understood to read "And the Word was made flesh, and dwelt *in* us" (ἐν ἡμῖν) rather than "amongst us," by which "amongst" the Incarnation would be considered only historically.

[26] I.e., whether immanent or transcendent; whether he "wanders in the Field, together with his acts (*kṣetre saṃcarati . . . svakarmabhiḥ*, Śvet. Up. V.3, 7)," or remains aloof.

[27] The descent into the blind darkness of the womb, into hell (*niraya*, MU III.4); from which one comes into being again, being saved from that first death by the

born again when thou, O Breath, givest life" (AV xi.4.14, cf. JUB iii.8.10–ix.1); "Thou alone, O Sun, art born about the whole world" (*eko viśvam pari bhūma jāyase*, AV xiii.2.3);[28] "One God indwelling the mind, of old was he born and is even now in the womb" (AV x.8.28 = JUB iii.10.12). Similar texts could be cited at greater length, but it will suffice for the present to observe the emphasis laid upon the fact that it is always *One* that is diversely and recurrently born: He, that is, who is "undivided in, though *as it were* divided by his presence in divided beings" (BG xiii.16 and xviii.20), being "One as he is in himself, and many as he is in his children" (ŚB x.5.2.16), who are not Beings independently, but Beings by participation.[29]

All this is also the oldest Saṃhitā doctrine, where it is the Sun or Fire that enters into the womb and transmigrates:[30] thus RV x.72.9, where Aditi "bears Mārtāṇḍa unto repeated birth and death (*prajāyai mṛtyave tvat punaḥ*)"; viii.43.9, "Thou, O Agni, being in the womb, art born again (*garbhe san jāyase punaḥ*)"; x.5.1, where Agni is "of many births (*bhūri-janmā*)"; iii.1.20, where as Jātavedas he is "set down in birth after birth (*janmañ-janman nihitaḥ*)," i.e., as Sāyaṇa adds, "in all these human beings." As Jātavedas he is omniscient of births (i.70.1, i.189.1, vi.15.3), and necessarily so because, as ŚB ix.5.1.68 paraphrases, "he finds birth again and again (*jātaṃ jātaṃ vindate*)." In the same way "filling the (three) light-realms of this,[31] the mobile and immobile, he cometh manifoldly into being, the Sire in these wombs" (*purutrā yad abhavat, sūr ahaibhyo garbhebhyaḥ*, RV i.146.1, 5), "yet in one semblance manifold, as giver-of-being to all thy people[32] (*viśo viśvā anu prabhuḥ*, RV viii.11.8)."

Sun (JUB iii.9.1, iii.10.4). Cf. St. Bernard, *prius morimur nascituri* (*De grad. humilitatis* 30). AV *apānati* = JUB *mriyate*.

[28] Who as the sacrificial Person "was poured out upon the earth from East to West" (*aty aricyata paścād bhūmin atho puraḥ*, RV x.90.5).

[29] "Et inspexi cetera infra te, et vidi nec omnino esse nec omnino non esse: esse quidem, quoniam abs te sunt, non esse autem, quoniam id quod es non sunt" (St. Augustine, *Confessions* vii.11). This "is and is not" is essentially the Buddhist doctrine of *satto*, "existence."

[30] Throughout the present article and elsewhere we are careful to distinguish transmigration from reincarnation; the former implying a transition from one state of being to another, the latter to the transmission or renewal of a former state of being. Cf. n. 23, and Coomaraswamy, "Measures of Fire."

[31] I.e., as Prajāpati divides himself to fill these worlds.

[32] *Viśaḥ*, i.e., Viśvedevāḥ, Maruts, *prāṇaḥ, prāṇāgnayaḥ* directly and hence to prāṇinaḥ, "living beings," indirectly. *Viśvaṃ tvayā dhārayate jāyamānam . . . prajās*

It need not be demonstrated here that the Saṃhitās do not know of a "reincarnation" (individual rebirth on earth) since it is generally accepted that even the Brāhmaṇas know nothing of such a doctrine (cf. the Keith edition of AĀ, Introduction, p. 44)—except, of course, in the normal progenitive sense of rebirth in one's offspring (RV v.4.10, vi.70.3; AB vii.13; AĀ ii.5). Our concern is rather to point out that the Veda speaks both of transmigration and of a one and only transmigrant, and distinguishes "liberation" from "coming back again" (*vimucaṃ nāvṛtam punaḥ*, RV v.46.1). Our argument is that the expressions *punarmṛtyu* and *punarjanma* which occur already in RV and the Brāhmaṇas do not in the later scriptures acquire the new meanings of "dying again" (elsewhere) and "being born again" (here) that are generally read into them. In the majority of cases the references of "repeated death" and "repeated birth" are to this present life or "becoming," as in AB viii.25, *sarvam āyur eti, na punar mriyate*, and ŚB v.4.1.1, *sarvān . . . mṛtyūn atimucyate*, where it is the relative immortality of not dying prematurely that is involved, and there is no question of never dying at all. In "becoming" (*bhava*, *γένεσις*) we die and are reborn every day and night, and in this sense "day and night are recurrent deaths" (*punarmṛtyū . . . yad ahorātre*, JB i.11). *Punarmṛtyu* is not some *one* other death to be dreaded as ending a future existence but, together with *punarbhava* or *janma*, the condition of *any* form or type of contingent existence; and it is from this process, this wheel of becoming (*bhavacakra*, ὁ τροχός τῆς γενέσεως in James 3:6) here or hereafter, and not from any one death only, that liberation is sought.[33]

We have so far considered the Transmigrant, Parijman, only as the Great Catalyst who remains unaffected by the actions he empowers. The Supreme Lord and Self who is seated one and the same in all beings' hearts (BG x.20, xiii.27), the citizen in every "city" (BU ii.5.18; Philo,

tatra yatra viśvā 'mṛto 'si, MU vi.9. "La circular natura, ch'è sugello alla cera mortal, fa ben sua arte, ma non distingue l'un dall' altro ostello," Dante, *Paradiso* viii.127–129 (ostello = *nivāsa*, esp. in the Pāli Buddhist expression *pubbenivāsan anussarati*). "One Divine Life, mov'd, shin'd, sounded in and thro' all," Peter Sterry (V. de Sola Pinto, *Peter Sterry, Platonist and Puritan*, Cambridge, 1934, p. 161).

[33] Cf. Coomaraswamy, *Spiritual Authority and Temporal Power*, 1942, n. 35. On James 3:6, cf. R. Eisler, "Orphisch-Dionysische Mysterien-Gedanken in der christlichen Antike," in *Vorträge der Bib. Warburg* II (1922–1923), 86 ff.; P. Deussen, *Vier philosophische Texte des Mahābhāratam* (Leipzig, 1906), 272 ff.; Plato, *Sophist* 248A, *Timaeus* 29C (contrast γένεσις and οὐσία); and O. Kern, *Orphicorum fragmenta*, fr. 32 (1922), κύκλου δ' ἐξέπταν βαρυπενθέος ἀργαλέοιο.

De cherubim 121), participating in action not because of any need on his part but only sacrificially and to maintain the world process (BG III.9, 22), wherein as it were disporting (BrSBh II.1.32, 33)[34] he remains undivided amongst divided beings and indestructible amongst the destructible (BG XIII.16, 27). So long as he (Makha, the Sacrifice) is One, they cannot overcome him (TA V.1.3); but as One he cannot bring his creatures to life, and must divide himself (MU XII.6). We are repeatedly told, indeed, that he, Prajāpati, "desired (*akāmayat*)" to be many, and so, as it seems to us, it is not quite disinterestedly[35] but "with ends not yet attained and with a view to enjoying the objects of the senses" that he sets us agoing (MU II.6d). But this is a dangerous enterprise, for being their experient, he is carried away by the flood of the qualities of the primary matter (*prakṛtair guṇaiḥ*) with which he operates;[36] and as the corporeal (*śarīra*) elemental self (*bhūtāt-*

[34] Cf. Coomaraswamy, "Līlā," 1941, and "Play and Seriousness," 1942 [both in this volume—ED.]. Cf. Dante, *Purgatorio* XXVIII.95, 96:

> Per sua diffalta in pianto ed in affanno
> cambiò onesto riso e dolce gioco

and *Mathnawī* I.1787, 1788:

> Thou didst contrive this "I" and "we" in order that
> Thou mightest play the game of worship with Thyself,
> That all "I"s and "thou"s should become one life.

When, as in MU II.6–III.2, we speak of Him as having ends still to be attained, we also conceive that *He* is caught in the net, and that *He* is liberated again, and this is the truth in terms of human thinking. But like all else that pertains to the *via affirmativa*, this is a truth to be finally denied. For the *viae*, see MU IV.6.

[35] Whenever we explain the existence of the world not directly by God's being, or by His knowledge of Himself, but as a consequence of His Will, i.e., "of expression," as here, or when it is said that "Prajāpati desired (*akāmayat*), May I be many" (Brāhmaṇas, *passim*), we are speaking metaphorically as if He really had ends to be attained, as is explicit in MU II.6, and, just as in dividing effect from cause, we impose our duration upon His eternity. More truly, "There is nothing whatever that I might obtain that I am not already possessed of" (*na . . . me kimcana anavāptam avāptavyam*, BG III.22): "Non per aver a sè di bene acquisto, ch'esser non può" (Dante, *Paradiso* XXIX.13, 14).

So Pentheus conceives that Dionysius can be bound; but He declares that "Of himself the Daimon shall release me when I will," and later, that "I myself myself did save, full easily and painlessly" (Euripides, *Bacchae* 498, 613). The "Daimon" is, of course, "himself."

[36] Just as the Man (ἄνθρωπος), Son of the Father, is seduced by the reflection of the divine beauty in the mirror of Nature, and loving it becomes involved in it (Hermes, *Lib.* I.14, 15; TS V.3.2.1; AB III.33; PB VII.8.1). The "flood of qualities by which the soul is swept away" (*guṇaughair uhyamānaḥ*) corresponds to Plato's "river of sensations" (*Timaeus* 43B); to the "crossing over" (διαπορεία = *taraṇa*)

man),[37] knowing subject over against ostensibly external objects of perception, and composite of all desires (*sarvakāma-maya*),[38] he is bemused and does not see the bountiful Giver-of-being and Actuator within him,[39] "but conceives that 'this is I' and 'that is mine,' and therewith binds himself by himself like a bird in the net (*jāleneva khacaraḥ*)[40] and so wanders around (*paribhramati* = *saṃsarati, saṃcarati*) in wombs both aughty and

---

of which there is a reference in *Epinomis* 894E; and to Philo's river of the objects of sense that swamps and drowns the soul under the flood of the passions until "Jacob" (νοῦς) crosses it (*Legum allegoriae* III.18 and *De gigantibus* XIII). Cf. St. Augustine's *cum transierit anima nostra aquas, quae sunt sine substantia* (*Confessions* XIII.7).

[37] As in CU VIII.12.1, cited above.

[38] "The Person of desires composite" (*kāmamayam evāyam puruṣam*), BU IV.4.5.

[39] Apart from whom the soul is bound "because of its enjoyment" (*bhokṛtvāt*, Śvet. Up. I.8), deadly for those who conceive that the experience is their own.

[40] "A little Bird ty'd by the Leg with a String, often flutters and tries to raise itself. . . . Thus a Soul fixt in a *Self-principle* . . . is snatched down by that String of *Self*, which ties it to the Ground," Peter Sterry (de Sola Pinto, *Peter Sterry*, p. 169). "Tomb'd in my self: my self my grave. . . . My self even to my self a slave" (Phineas Fletcher)—"the prisoner himself being the main occasion of his own imprisonment" (Plato, *Phaedo* 83A, cf. *Mathnawī*, I.154).

The net (or spider's web, Śvet. Up. VI.10; Muṇḍ. Up. I.7; KB XIX.3, etc.) that he himself has spread (*ya eko jālavān*, Śvet. Up. III.1), the one and only net that he manywise transforms and "in which field he wanders" (*samcarati*, Śvet. Up. V.3, 7, i.e., *samsarati*, "transmigrates" rather than Deussen's "wieder entzieht" or Hume's "draws it together").

Insofar as the Only Transmigrant is overcome by the notions "This is I" and "Those are others," the Bird is conceptually one of many, and no longer "the One Controller of the created many" (Śvet. Up. VI.13), and we, who are preeminently subject to these delusions, speak of the liberation of a plurality of individuals, e.g., "Many are the essences that are bound by wanting, like a bird in the net (*icchābaddhā puthusattā pāsena sakuni yathā, ti*" (S I.44).

That "A being is a flux, action is its passing over" (*satto samsāram āpādi, kammam tassa parāyanam*, S I.38, cf. *sadasad yonim āpadyate*, MU III.2) taken together with Mil 72, "There is no particular essence (*n'atthi koci satto*) that reincarnates (*imamhā kāyā aññam kāyam sankamati*)," means that there is no constant individuality that treads the round; as how might there be, when even today our personality is "other" than it was yesterday (S II.95, 96)? It is not a life, but the fire of life that is transmitted (BrSBh IV.4.15; Mil 71; cf. Heracleitus, fr. 20). The Comprehensor of the Buddha's teaching will not ask himself either What was "I"? or What shall "I" become? (S II.26, 27).

Khacara is almost literally "skylark"; *kha* is anagogically Brahman as unlimited "Space" (*ākāśa, quintessentia*), or τόπος, as in Bruce Codex, C. A. Baynes, tr., *A Coptic Gnostic Treatise* (Cambridge, 1933), p. 3. Cf. BU V.1; CU I.9, III.12.7–9, IV.10.4, VII.12, VIII.1.14; and Coomaraswamy, "*Kha* and Other Words Denoting 'Zero,' in Connection with the Indian Metaphysics of Space" [in this volume—ED.].

naughty (*sadasat*),[41] overcome by the fruits of actions and by the pairs of opposites" (MU III.2, VI.10).[42]

There is, indeed, a corrective (*pratividhi*) for this elemental self, viz. in the study and mastery of the wisdom of the Vedas and in the fulfilment of one's own duty (*svadharma*)[43] in its regular stages (*āśrama*, MU IV.3). "By the knowledge of Brahman, by ardor (*tapas*) and contemplation (*cintā* = *dhyāna*) he getteth everlasting bliss, yea, when this 'man in the cart' (*rathitaḥ*)[44] is liberated from those things with which he was filled up[45] and by which he was overcome, then he attains to conjunction with the Spirit (*ātman eva sāyujam upaiti*, MU IV.4)," i.e., "being very Brahma enters into Brahma (*brahmaiva san brahmāpyeti*, BU IV.4.6),"[46] and thus "authentically Brahma-become, abides (*brahmabhūtena attanā viharati*, A II.211)." That is Nicholas of Cusa's *deificatio,* for which the *sine qua non* is an *ablatio omnis alteritatis et diversitatis*.[47]

41 "For the movement of the Kosmos varies the birth of things, and gives them this or that quality; it fouls with evil the births of some and purifies with good the births of others" (Hermes, *Lib.* 9.5).

Asat as "evil," here and elsewhere, corresponds exactly to English "naughty," in accordance with the principle *ens et bonum convertuntur*.

42 Conversely, "liberated from the pairs of opposites" (BG XV.5, cf. VII.27), and "becoming a bird, the sacrificer goes to the world of heaven" (PB V.3.5, cf. XIV.1.13). With this whole context, cf. Plotinus, *Enneads* I.1, especially I.1.12.

43 As in BG III.35, XVIII.41–48. This is the *τὸ ἑαυτοῦ πράττειν, κατὰ φύσιν* that Plato makes his type of justice.

44 Apparently pp. of *rath*, not otherwise known as a verb, and signifying "embodied" (KU III.3 *viddhi śarīram ratham*; MU II.3 *śakaṭam ivācetanam idam śarīram*). That to "be carted about" is a traditional punishment and disgrace involving loss of honor and legal rights is metaphysically significant, and corresponds to the subjection of the free spirit to the body and senses; while conversely, it is a royal procession when the spirit drives the vehicle to a destination that it itself wills (as in BU IV.2.1). On the Royal Road, cf. Philo, *De posteritate Caini* CI, and on how one strays, *Legum allegoriae*, IV.79 ff.

The ignominy (like that of crucifixion) is one to which the Solar Hero may have to condescend in his pursuit of the imprisoned Psyche; and Lancelot's "hesitation" in the *Chevalier de la charrette* corresponds to Agni's reluctance to become the charioteer of the Sacrifice (RV X.51), the Buddha's hesitation to "turn the wheel," and Christ's "May this cup be taken from me."

45 *Yaiḥ paripūrṇaḥ*, as in CU IV.10.3 *vyādhibhiḥ paripūrṇo 'smi*, "I am filled up with diseases." For "the body fills us up with loves and passions and all kinds of images and folly, so that, as they say, it verily and really prevents our ever understanding anything" (Plato, *Phaedo* 66C); from which plethora we ought to purify ourselves as far as possible "until the God himself delivers us" (*Phaedo* 67A).

46 *Qui autem adhaeret Domino, unus spiritus est*, 1 Cor. 6:17.

47 "If you cannot equate yourself with God, you cannot know Him; for like is known by like" (Hermes, *Lib.* XI.2.20B).

Otherwise stated, Prajāpati "desires (*kam, man*)" to become many, to "express (*sṛj*)" his children, and having done so is spilled and falls down unstrung (Brāhmaṇas, *passim*). It is "with love (*preṇā*)" that he enters into them, and then he cannot come together (*sambhū*) again, whole and complete, except by the sacrificial operation (TS v.5.2.1); he cannot from his disjointed parts put himself together (*saṃhan*), and can only be healed through the sacrificial operations of the gods (ŚB 1.6.3.36, etc.). It is sufficiently well known, and needs no demonstration here, that the final purpose of this operation in which the sacrificer symbolically sacrifices himself is to build up together again, whole and complete, both the sacrificer and the divided deity at one and the same time. It is evident that the possibility of such a simultaneous regeneration rests upon the theoretical identity of the sacrificer's real being with that of the immanent deity, postulated in the dictum, "That art thou." To sacrifice our self is to liberate the God within us.

In still another way we can illustrate the thesis by referring to those texts in which the immanent deity is spoken of as a "citizen" of the body politic in which he is, as it were, confined, and from which he also liberates himself when he remembers himself and we forget our selves. That the human body is called a "city of God (*puraṃ . . . brahmanaḥ*, AV x.2.28; *brahmapura, passim*)" is well known;[48] and he who as a bird (*pakṣī bhūtvā*) becomes a citizen in all these cities (*sarvāsu pūrṣu puriśayaḥ*) is hermeneutically *puruṣa* (BU II.5.18). The Solar Man or Person who thus inhabits us and is the Friend of All is also the beloved Vāmadeva, the Breath (*prāṇa*), "who set himself in the midst of all that is (*sa yad idaṃ sarvaṃ madhyato*[49] *dadhe*) . . . and protected all that is from evil"[50] (AĀ II.2.1); and being in the womb (*garbhe . . . san*) is the knower of all the births of the gods (Breaths, Intelligences, powers of the soul) who serve him (RV IV.27.1; KU V.3, etc.). He says of himself that "although a hundred cities[51] held me fast,[52] forth I sped with falcon speed" (RV

[48] Just as also for Plato, man is a "body politic" (πόλις = *pur*). [Cf. Coomaraswamy, "What is Civilization?" 1946—ED.]

[49] The immanent Breath is repeatedly referred to as "median" (*madhyama*), i.e., with respect to the Breaths, by whom it is surrounded and served. As in Philo, *Legum allegoriae* I.51, where "God extends the power that is from him by means of the median breath (διὰ τοῦ μέσου πνεύματος) until it reaches the subject," on which it stamps the powers that are within the scope of its understanding, thus (*ibid.*, 50) ensouling what was soulless.

[50] As in BU I.3.7 ff.

[51] Probably the hundred years of a man's life, during which time the Breath shines upon him (AĀ II.5.1). When he departs, we die (ŚB x.5.2.13, etc.), for "as a mighty

posing that the "land leech" of verse 3 is an individual and definitely characterized "soul" that passes over from one body to another. Rather, it is the undivided and never individualized Self that having now re-collected itself (*ātmānam upasaṃharati*, cf. BG II.58), and free from the "ignorance" of the body (with which it no longer identifies itself), transmigrates; this re-collected Self is the Brahma that takes on every form and quality of existence, both good and evil,[65] according to its desires and activities (verse 5); if it is still attached (*saktaḥ*), still desirous (*kāmayamānaḥ*), this Self (*ayam*, i.e., *ayam ātmā*) returns (*punar aiti*) from that world to this world, but if without desire (*akāma-yamānaḥ*), if it loves only itself (*ātmakāmaḥ*, cf. IV.3.21), then "being very Brahma, it enters into Brahma (*brahmaiva san brahmāpyeti*)," then "the mortal becomes the immortal" (verses 6, 7). The meaning of these passages is distorted, and given a reincarnationist sense, by all those translators (e.g., Hume and Swāmi Mādhavānanda) who translate *ayam* of verse 6 by "he" or "the man," overlooking that this *ayam* is nothing but the *ayam ātmā brahma* of the preceding verse.[66] The distinction is not of one "man" from another, but of the two forms of Brahma-Prajāpati, "mortal and immortal,"[67] desirous and undesirous, circumscribed and uncircumscribed, etc. (ŚB IV.7.5.2; BU II.3; MU VI.36, etc.), and of the "two minds, pure and impure" (MU VI.34.6), from one another.[68] If we were in any doubt on this point, it is made very clear by the words of BU IV.3.35–38, "Here

[65] As in MU VII.11.8 *carati . . . satyānṛtopabhogārthāh dvaitībhāvo mahātmānaḥ*, "The Great Self, having two natures, proceeds (moves, circulates, transmigrates) with intent to experience both the true and the false."

[66] On the interpretation of this *ayam*, cf. Śaṅkarācārya on BU I.4.10, "One must not think that the word 'Brahma' here means 'a man who will become Brahma,' for that would involve an antinomy. . . . If the objection be made that from BU III.2.13 *punyena karmanā bhavati* 'by good deed one becomes good,' . . . it follows that there must be a transmigrating self other than and distinguishable from the Supreme (*parasmād vilakṣaṇo 'nyah samsārī*), . . . we say, No . . . for one thing cannot 'become' another." It can only become what it is. Γνῶθι σεαυτόν; *Werde was du bist.*

[67] RV I.164.38 *amartya martyenā sayoniḥ*. On these two selves (Plato's mortal and immortal souls that dwell together in us) see Coomaraswamy, *Spiritual Authority and Temporal Power*, 1942, pp. 72 ff.

[68] Pure, "by disconnection with desire," impure "by contamination with desire." The pure Mind is the *daivam manas* of BU I.5.19, identified with Brahma in BU IV.1.6 (*mano vai samrāṭ paramam brahma*) and with Prajāpati in TS VI.6.10.1, ŚB IX.4.1.12, and *passim*. This is Plato's unchangeable Mind "in which only the Gods and but few men participate," as distinguished from irrational Opinion, subject to persuasion (*Timaeus* 51DE). Cf. Coomaraswamy, "On Being in One's Right Mind," 1942.

comes Brahma!", that it is not an individual but God himself that comes and goes when "we" are born or die.

It would be an antinomy to apply to myself—this man, So-and-so—or to any other someone amongst others the words, "That art thou," or to think of myself, *le moi*, as the "I" of Swāmi Nirbhyānanda's

> I am the bird caught in the net of illusion,
> I am he who bows down the head
> And the One to whom he bows:
> I alone exist, there is neither seeker nor sought.[69]
> When at last I realized Unity, then I knew what
> had been unknown,
> That I had always been in union with Thee.[70]

When the soul-bird at last escapes from the net of the fowler (Psalms 124:7) and finds its King, then the apparent distinction of immanent from transcendent being dissolves in the light of day, and it hears and speaks with a voice that is at once its own and its King's, saying

> I was the Sin that from Myself rebell'd:
> I the remorse that tow'rd Myself compell'd . . .
> Pilgrim, Pilgrimage and Road
> Was but Myself toward Myself: and Your
> Arrival but Myself at my own door.[71]

II

It has been, we think, sufficiently shown that the scriptures of the Vedānta, from the *Ṛg Veda* to the *Bhagavad Gītā*, know of but One Transmigrant. Such a doctrine follows, indeed, inevitably from the word Advaita. The argument, "Brahma is only metaphorically called a 'life' (*jīva*, living being) on account of his connection with accidental conditions, the actual existence of any one such 'life' lasting for only so long as He continues to

[69] "The eternal procession is the revelation of Himself to Himself. The knower being that which is known" (Meister Eckhart, Evans ed., I, 394). "It knew Itself, that 'I am Brahma,' therewith It became the All" (BU 1.4.10).

[70] I know these lines only from H. P. Shastri, *Indian Mystic Verse* (London, 1941).

[71] Faridu'd-Dīn 'Aṭṭār, *Mantiqu't-Tair*; cf. Rūmī, *Mathnawī*, 1.3056–3065, and JUB III.14.1–5.

be bound by any one set of accidents" (Śaṇkarācārya on BrSBh III.2.10), is only an expansion of the implications of the logos, "That art thou."

We have also indicated more briefly the *ὁμολογία* of the Indian and Platonic traditions, and have alluded to the Islamic parallels: rather to make the doctrine more comprehensible than to imply any derivation. From the same point of view we have still to refer to the Judaic and Christian doctrines. In the Old Testament we find that when we die and give up the ghost, "Then shall the dust return to the dust as it was: and the spirit (*ruaḥ*) shall return to God who gave it" (Eccl. 12:7). Of this, D. B. Macdonald remarks, the Preacher "is heartily glad, for it means a final escape for man."[72] To be "glad" of this can be thought of only for one who has known *who* he is and in *which* self he hopes to go hence. For the Jews, who did not anticipate a "personal immortality," the soul (*nefeṣ*) always implies "the lower, physical nature, the appetites, the psyche of St. Paul"[73]—all that in Buddhist terms "is not my Self"—and they must therefore have believed, as Philo assuredly did, in a "soul of the soul," the *πνεῦμα* of St. Paul.[74]

[72] *Hebrew Philosophical Genius*, Princeton and Oxford, 1936, p. 136.

[73] *Ibid.*, p. 139. So in Islam, e.g., Rūmī, *Mathnawī*, I.1375 ff., "This carnal self (*nafs*) is Hell, and Hell is a Dragon. . . . To God (alone) belongs this foot (the power) to kill it"; I.3274, "When the Soul of the soul (*jān-ī-jān* = God, I.1781) withdraws from the soul, the soul becomes even as the soulless body, know this"; cf. JUB IV.26, "Mind is a hell, speech is a hell, sight is a hell," etc. The internal conflict of Reason (*'aql* = *νοῦς*) with the carnal soul (*nafs*) is compared to that of a man and woman living together in one house (*ibid.*, I.2616 ff.). As Jahangir said in his memoirs apropos of Gosain Jadrūp, Tasawwuf and Vedānta are the same. As R. A. Nicholson (on *Mathnawī* I.2812) puts it, the Sūfī doctrine is that "God is the essence of all existences . . . [while] everything in the world of contingency is separated from the Absolute [only] by individualization. The prophets were sent to unite the particulars with the Universal."

[74] With reference to the doctrine elsewhere, A. H. Gebhard-Lestrange states very correctly that "the transmigration of souls is generally misinterpreted as the passing of a soul from one person to another. . . . What actually takes place is that the Individual[ized] God-Soul incarnates again and again until It attains the aim of incarnating as a Seeker who will go upon the Quest and eventually lose individuality and become one with the freed God-Soul" (*The Tradition of Silence in Myth and Legend*, Boston, 1940, p. 63). Notable repudiations of reincarnationist interpretation will be found in *Hierocles on the Golden Verses of Pythagoras*, tr. N. Rowe (London, 1906), v.53; in Hermes, *Lib.* x.19–22; and in Marsilio Ficino, who held, in the words of Kristeller, that "wherever Plato seems to speak of a transmigration of the human soul into other natural species, we must understand by it the different forms and habits of human life" (Paul O. Kristeller, *The Philosophy of Marsilio Ficino*, New York, 1943, p. 118). Cf. Eisler, "Orphisch-Dionysische Mysterien-Gedanken," p. 295.

In Christianity there is a doctrine of *karma* (the operation of mediate causes) and of a fate that lies in the created causes themselves, but no doctrine of reincarnation. No stronger abjections of the "soul" are anywhere to be found than are met with in the Christian Gospels. "No man can be my disciple who hateth not . . . his own soul" (*ἑαυτοῦ ψυχήν*, Luke 14:26); that soul which "he who hateth in this world shall keep it unto life eternal" (John 12:25), but which "whoever seeks to save, shall lose" (Luke 9:25). Compared with the Disposer (*conditor* = *saṃdhātṛ*), other beings "are neither beautiful, nor good, nor are at all" (*nec sunt*, St. Augustine, *Confessions* XI.4). The central doctrine has to do with the "descent" (*avataraṇa*) of a Soter whose eternal birth was "before Abraham" and "through whom all things were made." This One himself declares that "no man hath ascended up to heaven, but he that came down from heaven, even the Son of Man which is in heaven" (John 3:13); and says, moreover, "Whither I go, *ye* cannot come" (John 8:21), and that "If any man would follow me, let him deny himself" (Mark 8:24).[75]

"The word of God is quick and powerful, and sharper than any two-edged sword, piercing even to the dividing asunder of soul (ψυχή) from spirit (πνεῦμα, Heb. 4:12)." When St. Paul, who distinguishes the Inner and the Outer Man (II Cor. 4:16; Eph. 3:16), says of himself, "I live, yet *not I*, but Christ in me" (Gal. 2:20)[76] he has denied himself, has lost his soul to save it and knows "in whom, when he departs hence, he will be departing"; what survives (*atiśiṣyate*) will not be "this man," Paul, but—the Savior himself. In Sūfī terms, "St. Paul" is "a dead man walking."[77]

When the Savior's visible presence is withdrawn he is represented *in*

[75] "Man should strive for this, that he turn his thoughts away from himself and all creatures and know no father but God alone" (Meister Eckhart, Pfeiffer ed., p. 421). Much more is implied than a merely ethical "self-denial." On our two selves, cf. also Jacob Boehme, *Signatura rerum* IX.65.

[76] In the same sense St. Paul writes to his disciples, "For ye are dead, and your life is hid with Christ in God . . . who is our life" (Col. 3:3, 4).

For a discussion of the implications of St. Paul's words see É. Mersch, *The Whole Christ*, tr. John R. Kelly (London, 1949), II.274 ff. (1936). Thus for Cajetan they mean that Christ is the sole thinker, seer, actor, etc. in "Paul." Barthélemy of Medina maintained that whatever good works "we" do are really done by Christ in us as sole agent.

[77] Like Abū Bakr; see Rūmī, *Mathnawī* VI.747–749. In this sense the saying, "Die before ye die," is attributed to Muḥammad.

us by the Counsellor (παράκλητος),[78] "Even the Spirit of Truth (τὸ πνεῦμα τῆς ἀληθείας) . . . which is the Holy Ghost, whom the Father will send in my name, he shall teach you all things, . . . He will lead you into all truth" (John 14:17, 26; 16:13). In him we cannot but see Plato's immanent Δαίμων and Ἡγεμών,[79] "who cares for nothing but the truth" and whom God has given to each one of us "to dwell along with him and *in* him" (*Hippias major* 288D, *Timaeus* 90AB); St. Augustine's Ingenium, the scholastic Synteresis, Dante's Amor, and our Inwyt or Conscience in its fullest (and not merely ethical) significance.

"His world is the World-indeed,[80] whose Self, the All-maker, All-doer, who indwells this abysmal bodily-composite, has been found and is awakened (*yasyānuvittaḥ pratibuddha ātmā*)[81] . . . the Lord of what hath been and shall be. . . . Desiring him only for their World, the Travellers (*pravrājin*) abandon this world" (BU IV.4.13, 15, 22)—"lest the Last Judgment come and find me unannihilate, and I be seiz'd and bound and given into the hands of my own selfhood" (William Blake).

Only, indeed, if we recognize that Christ and not "I" is our real Self and the only experient in every living being can we understand the words, "I was an hungered . . . I was thirsty . . . Inasmuch as ye have done it unto one of the least of these my brethren, ye have done it unto me" (Matt. 26:35 ff.). It is from this point of view that Meister Eckhart speaks of the man who knows himself as "seeing thy Self in everyone, and everyone in thee" (Evans ed., II, 132), as the *Bhagavad Gītā* speaks of the unified man as "everywhere seeing the same Lord universally hypostasized, the Self established in all beings and all beings in the Self" (VI.29 with XIII.28). Were it not that whatever we do to "others" is thus really done to our Self that is also their Self, there would be no metaphysical basis for any doing to "others" as we would be done by; the principle is implicit in the rule and only more explicit elsewhere. The command to "hate" our relatives (Luke 14:26) must be understood

[78] *Cathedram habet in caelo qui intus corda docet* (St. Augustine, *In epist. Joannis ad Parthos*). *Omne verum, a quocumque dicatur, est a spiritu sancto* (St. Ambrose on I Cor. 13:3). *Dhiyo yo naḥ pracodayāt* (RV III.62.10) . . . *yo buddhyantastho dhyāyīha* (MU VI.34).

[79] *Ātmano 'tmā netā 'mṛtah*, MU VI.7. *Viśvo devasya* (*savitur*) *netur marto vurīta sakhyam*, RV V.50.1.

[80] "World" (*loka*) here absolutely (as in BU I.4.15–17, I.5.17; CU I.9.3; MU VI.24; ŚB I.8.1.31, etc., where the contingent and real worlds are contrasted); the Kingdom of Heaven, "within you" (BU III.9.17, 25).

[81] *Pratibuddha* agreeing with *ātmā*, not with *yasya*. Cf. BD VII.57 (n. 85).

from the same point of view: "others" are no more valid objects of love than "I" am; it is not as "our" relatives or neighbors that they are to be loved, but as our Self (*ātmanas tu kāmāya*, BU II.4.5);[82] just as it is only himself that God loves in us, so it is God we ought to love in one another.

Upon this immanent Spirit of Truth, the Divine Eros, our very life depends, until we "give up the ghost"—the Holy Ghost. "It is the Spirit that quickeneth; the flesh avails nothing" (John 6:63). "The power of the soul, which is in the semen through the Spirit enclosed therein, fashions the body" (*Sum. Theol.* III.32.11).[83] This is the "Sower (*ὁ σπείρων*) went forth to sow. . . . Some fell upon stony places. . . . But other fell into good ground. . . . The field is the world" (Matt. 13:3–9, 37)—*sadasad yonim āpadyate* (MU III.2).[84] And is this Divine Eros, the "Knower of the Field" (BG XIII), any other than the Prodigal Son "who was dead, and is alive again; and was lost, and is found"—dead for so long as he had forgotten who he was, and alive again "when he came to himself"[85] (Luke 15:11 ff.)?

It has been said, "Ye crucify him daily" (cf. Heb. 6:6), and so assuredly does every man who is convinced that "I am" or "I do" and therewith divides up this One conceptually into many independent and possible beings.[86] Of all the conclusions to be drawn from the doctrine of the One

---

[82] So "a man, out of charity, ought to love himself more than he loves any other person . . . more than his neighbor" (*Sum. Theol.* II-II.26.4). Cf. BU II.4.1–9 (mutual love is not of one another as such, but of the immanent spiritual Self); Hermes, *Lib.* IV.6B; Aristotle, *Nichomachean Ethics* IX.8; and Marsilio Ficino, originator of the term "Platonic love," importing that "true love between two persons is by nature a common love for God" (Kristeller, *The Philosophy of Marsilio Ficino*, pp. 279, 287).

[83] "He who, dwelling in the semen, yet is other than the semen, unseen Seer, unthought Thinker . . . Inner Controller" (BU III.7.23), "who grasps and erects the flesh" (Kauṣ. Up. III.3). "Say not 'from semen'" (BU III.9.28.5), for "without the Breath semen is not effused, or if it be, it will decay, and not produce" (AĀ III.2.2).

[84] Cf. Plato, *Timaeus* 41 and 69, where God, the Maker and Father, instructs the gods, his sons, as subservient causes, to bring together the mortal part of creatures, but "as for that immortal part, which we call the Divine Guide (*Θεῖον . . . ἡγεμονοῦν*), that part I will deliver unto you when I have sown it (*σπείρας . . . ἐγὼ παραδώσω*)."

[85] "Came to himself," *εἰς ἑαυτὸν δὲ ἐλθών*. Sāyaṇa on RV IV.27.1, *ātmānam jānan*; BD VII.57, *tatah sa buddhvā ātmānam*; Sāyana on BU I.4.10, *nanu smarasy ātmānam*.

[86] RV X.90.11, *katidhā vy akalpayan*, "How manyfold did they divide him?"; conversely AB I.18, *na vai na ittham vihrto'nnam bhaviṣyati, hantemam yajñam sambharāma*, "It will not suffice for our food that we have dismembered the Sacrifice, come, let us gather him together again."

and Only Transmigrant, the most poignant is this, that whereas He is the bird caught in the net, the Ram caught in the thicket, the sacrificial Victim and our Savior, he cannot save *us* except and unless we, by the sacrifice and denial of our self, also save *Him*.[87]

[87] As is also implied in the Christian doctrine of the Mystical Body of Christ. Cf. St. Augustine, "When we all sing, it is that One Man who sings in us" (*In Ps.* 136); in praying, we should not say "we" but "I," because although it is actually a multitude that speaks severally, really "it is that One Man who speaks, who is distributed throughout the world" (*In Ps.* 122); and so, "If, on the one hand, we die in him and in him are resurrected, he on the other hand dies and is resurrected in us" (*Epist.* 140).

The Doctrine of the Mystical Body of Christ is represented in Buddhism by that of the Buddha, Dhamma and Saṃgha. It is in the Saṃgha (√*saṃhan*) that the distributed Buddha-nature is reintegrated; in this communion those separated members are reunited, which Prajāpati "could not put together again" (*na śaśāka saṃhātum*, ŚB 1.6.3.36) otherwise than by means of the Sacrifice in which the sacrificer (identified with the oblation) and the Sacrifice are jointly regenerated.

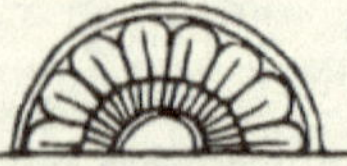

Ākiṃcañña: Self-Naughting[1]

Vivo autem, jam non ego Gal. 2:20

Eyā diz solte du sêle scheiden von allem dem, daz iht ist.
Eckhart, Pfeiffer ed., p. 525

Her umbe sol der mensche geflizzen sīn, daz er sich entbilde sīn selbes unt allen crēatūre nock keinen vater wizze denne got alleine. . . . Dis ist allen menschen fremde . . . ich wolde, das irz befunden hētet mit lebenne.
Eckhart, Pfeiffer ed., pp. 421, 464

When thou standest still from the thinking of self, and the willing of self
Jacob Boehme, *Dialogues on the Supersensual Life*

An egomania occasioned the fall of Lucifer, who would be "like the most High" (Isa. 14:14), thinking, "Who is like me in Heaven or Earth?" (*Tabārī* XXIV), and desiring to deify himself (Augustine, *Quaestiones veteris et novi testamenti* CXIII), not in the way discussed below by an abnegation of selfhood, but, as St. Thomas Aquinas says, "by the virtue of his own nature" and "of his own power" (*Sum. Theol.* I.63.3c). We are all to a greater or less extent egomaniacs, and to the same extent followers of Satan. Acts 5:36 refers to a certain Theudas as "boasting himself to be somebody."

In the vernacular, when a man is presumptuous, we ask him, "Who do you think you are?" and when we refer to someone's insignificance, we call him a "nobody" or, in earlier English, a "nithing." In this worldly sense it is a good thing to be "someone" and a misfortune to be "nobody," and from this point of view we think well of "ambition" (*iti-bhavābhava taṇhā*). To be "someone" is to have a name and lineage (*nāma-gotta*) or, at least, to have a place or rank in the world, some distinction that makes us recognizable and conspicuous. Our modern civilization is essentially individualistic and self-assertive, even our educational systems being more

[This essay was first published in the *New Indian Antiquary*, III (1940).—ED.]

[1] As the title implies, this study is mainly based on Christian and Buddhist sources.

and more designed to foster "self-expression" and "self-realization"; and if we are at all concerned about what happens after death, it is in terms of the survival of our treasured "personality"[2] with all its attachments and memories.

On the other hand, in the words of Eckhart, "Holy scripture cries aloud for freedom from self." In this unanimous and universal teaching, which affirms an absolute liberty and autonomy, spatial and temporal, attainable as well here and now as anywhere else, this treasured "personality" of ours is at once a prison and a fallacy, from which only the Truth shall set you free:[3] a prison, because all definition limits that which is defined, and a fallacy because in this ever-changing composite and corruptible psychophysical "personality" it is impossible to grasp a constant, and impossible therefore to recognize any authentic or "real" substance. Insofar as man is merely a "reasoning and mortal animal," tradition is in agreement with the modern determinist in affirming that "this man," So-and-so (*yoyamāyasmā evaṃ nāmo evaṃ gotto*, S III.25) has neither free will[4]

[2] We write "personality" because we are using the word here in its vulgar sense and not in the stricter and technical sense in which the veritable "person" is distinguished from the phenomenal "individual," e.g., in AĀ II.3.2 and Boethius, *Contra Evtychen* II.

[3] The doctrine is one of escape and the pursuit of happiness. It will not be confused with what has been called escapism. Escapism is an essentially selfish activity, failure to "face the music" (as when one "drowns one's sorrows in drink"), and the choice of easier paths; escapism is a symptom of disappointment and is cynical rather than mature. We need hardly say that to "wish one had never been born" is the antithesis of the perfect sorrow that may be occasioned by the sense of a continued existence: we are born in order to die, but this death is not one that can be attained by suicide or by suffering death at the hands of others; it is not of ourselves or others, but only of God that it can be said in the words of St. John of the Cross, "and, slaying, dost from death to life translate."

At the same time, the true way of "escape" is more strenuous by far than the life that is escaped (hence the designation of the religious in India as a "Toiler," *śramaṇa*), and it is the degree of a man's maturity (in Skr. the extent to which he is *pakva*, "pukka," and no longer *āma*, "raw") that is the measure of the possibility of his escape and consequent beatitude.

"The minds of some are set on Union (*yoga*), the minds of others on comfort (*kṣema*)" (TS II.5.11.5; cf. KU II.1–4).

[4] The denial of freedom in "this man," the individual, is explicit in Sn 350, "It does not belong to the many-folk to do what they will (*na kāmakāro hi puthujjanānam*)." Cf. "Ye cannot do the things that ye would" (Gal. 5:17). This denial is made in a very striking manner in Vin I.13–14 and S III.66–67, where for the usual formula according to which the body and mentality are *anattā*, not I, nor mine, the proof is offered that this body, sensibility, etc., cannot be "mine," cannot be "I," for if these were myself, or mine, they would never be sick, since in this case one could say, "Let my body, sensibility, etc., be thus, or not-thus," nothing being really

nor any element of immortality. How little validity attaches to this man's conviction of freedom will appear if we reflect that while we speak of "doing what we like," we never speak of "being when we like," and that to conceive of a spatial liberty that is not also a temporal liberty involves a contradiction. Tradition, however, departs from science by replying to the man who confesses himself to be only a reasoning and mortal animal that he has "forgotten who he is" (Boethius, *De consolatione philosophiae*, prose VI), requires of him to "Know thyself,"[5] and warns him "If thou knowest not thyself, begone" (*si ignoras te, egredere*, Song of Solomon, 1:8). Tradition, in other words, affirms the validity of our consciousness of being but distinguishes it from the So-and-so that we think we are. The validity of our consciousness of being is not established in metaphysics (as it is in philosophy) by the fact of thought or knowledge; on the contrary, our veritable being is distinguished from the operations of discursive thought and empirical knowing, which are simply the causally determined workings of the "reasoning and mortal animal," which are to be regarded *yathābhūtam*, not as affects but only as effects in which we (in our veritable being) are not really, but only supposedly, involved.

---

ours except to the extent that we have it altogether in our power, nor anything variable any part of an identity such as the notion of a "very person" (*satpuruṣa*) intends. A further consideration is this, that if the becoming (*bhāva*) of the finite individual were not absolutely determined by "fate," "mediate causes," or "*ḳarma*" (the terms are synonymous), the idea of an omniscient providence (*prajñā, paññā*, knowledge of things not derived from the things themselves) would be unintelligible. In this connection we may remark that we are not, of course, concerned to prove dialectically any doctrine whatever, but only to exhibit its consistency and therewith its intelligibility. This consistency of the Philosophia Perennis is indeed good ground for "faith" (i.e., confidence, as distinguished from mere belief), but as this "philosophy" is neither a "system" nor a "philosophy," it cannot be argued for or against.

[5] E.g., Avencebrol, *Fons vitae* 1.2, "quid est ergo, quod debet homo inquierere in hac vita? . . . hoc est ut sciat se ipsum." Cf. Jacob Boehme, *De signatura rerum* 1.1. The reader will not confuse the "science of self" (*ātmavidyā*) here with that intended by the psychologist, whether ancient or modern; as remarked by Edmond Vansteenberghe, the γνῶθι σεαυτόν with which Nicholas of Cusa opens his *De docta ignorantia* "n'est plus le 'Connais-toi toi-même' du psychologue Socrate, c'est le 'Sois maître de toi' (= Dh 160, 380, *attā hi attano nātho*) des moralistes stoïciens" (*Autour de la docte ignorance*, Münster, 1915, p. 42). In the same way, the only *raison d'être* of "Buddhist psychology" is not "scientific," but to break down the illusion of self. The modern psychologist's only concern and curiosity are with the all-too-human self, that very self which even in its highest and least suspected extensions is still a prison. Traditional metaphysics has nothing in common with this psychology, which restricts itself to "what can be psychically experienced" (Jung's own definition).

Tradition, then, differs from the "nothing-morist" (Skr. *nāstika*, Pāli *natthika*) in affirming a spiritual nature that is not in any wise, but immeasurable, inconnumerable, infinite, and inaccessible to observation, and of which, therefore, empirical science can neither affirm nor deny the reality. It is to this "spirit"[6] (Gk. *πνεῦμα*, Skr. *ātman*, Pāli *attā*, Arabic *rūḥ*, etc.) as distinguished from body and soul—i.e., whatever is phenomenal and formal (Gk. *σῶμα* and *ψυχή*, Skr. and Pāli *nāma-rūpa*, and *savijñana-kāya, saviññāṇa-kāya*, "name and appearance," the "body with its consciousness")—that tradition attributes with perfect consistency an absolute liberty, spatial and temporal. Our sense of free will is as valid in itself as our sense of being, and as invalid as our sense of being So-and-so. There *is* a free will, a will, that is, unconstrained by anything external to its own nature; but it is only "ours" to the extent that we have abandoned all that we mean in common sense by "ourselves" and our "own" willing. Only *His* service is perfect freedom. "Fate lies in the created causes themselves" (*Sum. Theol.* I.116.2); "Whatever departeth farthest from the First Mind is involved more deeply in the meshes of Fate [i.e., *karma*, the ineluctable operation of "mediate causes"]; and everything is so much freer from Fate by how much it draweth nigh to the pivot of all things. And if it sticketh to the constancy of the Supernal Mind, that needs not move, it is superior to the necessity of Fate" (Boethius, *De consolatione philosophiae*, prose IV). This freedom of the Unmoved Mover ("that which, itself at rest, outgoeth them that run," Īśā Up. IV) from any *necessitas coactionis* is that of the spirit that bloweth where and as it will (*ὅπου θέλει πνεῖ*, John 3:8; *carati yathā vaśam*, RV X.168.4).[7] To possess it, one must have been "born again . . . of the Spirit" (John 3:7–8) and thus "in the spirit" (St. Paul, *passim*), one must have "found and awakened to the Spirit[8] (*yasyānuvittaḥ pratibuddha ātmā*, BU IV.4.13)," must be in *excessus*

[6] The phenomena of this "spirit" (the realizations of its possibilities of manifestation under given conditions) are all phenomena whatever, among which those called "spiritualistic" have no privileged rank; on the contrary, "a mouse is miracle enough. . . ."

[7] RV X.168.3–4, John 3:7–8, and *Gylfaginning* 18 present remarkable parallels [cf. *Edda Snorra Sturlusonar með Skáldatali*, ed. Guðni Jónsson (Reykjavik, 1935).—ED.].

[8] "He who sees, thinks and discriminates this Spirit, whose pleasure and play are with the Spirit, whose dalliance is with the Spirit [as in BU IV.3.21, "All creation is female to God"] and whose joy is in the Spirit, he becomes autonomous (*svarāj*), he becomes a Mover-at-will (*kāmācārin*) in every world; but the worlds of him whose knowledge is otherwise than this are corruptible, he does not become a Mover-at-will in any world" (CU VII.25.2). The conception of motion-at-will is developed in many texts, from RV IX.113.9, "Make me undying there where motion

("gone out of" oneself, one's senses), in *samādhi* (etymologically and semantically "synthesis"), unified (*eko bhūtaḥ*, cf. *ekodi-bhāva*), or in other words "dead" in the sense that "the kingdom of God is for none but the thoroughly dead" (Eckhart), and in the sense that Rūmī speaks of a "dead man walking" (*Mathnawī* VI.742–755), or again that of initiatory death as the prelude to a regeneration. There is not, of course, any necessary connection between liberation and physical death:[9] a man can as well be liberated "now in the time of this life" (*diṭṭhe va dhamme parinibbuto, jīvan mukta*) as at any other time, all depending only upon his remembering "who he is," and this is the same as to forget oneself, to "hate one's own life" (psyche, "soul," or "self," Luke 14:26), *deficere a se tota* and *a semetipsa liquescere* (St. Bernard),[10] the "death of the soul" (Eckhart),

is at will" (*yatrānukāmam caranam . . . mām amṛtaṃ kṛdhi*), onwards. The Christian equivalent can be found in John 3:8 and 10:9 ("shall go in and out, and find pasture," as in TU III.10.5, "he goes up and down these worlds, eating what he will and assuming what aspect he will").

Motion-at-will is a necessary consequence of filiation or deification, the Spirit moving "as it will" in virtue of its omni- and total presence and because "he that is joined unto the Lord is one Spirit" (1 Cor. 6:17), all possession of "powers" (*ṛddhi, iddhi*, such as flying through the air or walking on the water) being gifts of the Spirit and depending upon a more or less *ablatio omnis alteritatis et diversitatis* (Nicholas of Cusa). In other words, our freedom and beatitude are the less the more we are still "ourselves," *un tel*. The "miracle" is never an "impossibility," but only so according to our way of thinking: performance is always the demonstration of a possibility. It is not opposites (as "possible" and "impossible"), but contraries—for example, rest and motion—both of which are "possibles," that are reconciled *in divinis*. "Primitive" languages retain the stamp of this polarity in words which may mean either of two contrary things (cf. Freud on Abel, "Gegensinn der Urwort" in *Jahrbuch für psychoanalytische und psychopathologische Forschungen*, II 1910, and Betty Heimann, "The Polarity of the Infinite," JISOA, V, 1937).

It may be added that because of the identity of the immanent and transcendent Spirit (1 Cor. 6:17; "That art thou" of the Upaniṣads, etc.), we make no real distinction in the present article between "my spirit" (the "ghost" that we "give up" at death) and "the Spirit" (the Holy Ghost), although sometimes writing "spirit" with reference to the immanent essence (*antarātman*) and "Spirit" with reference to the transcendent essence (*paramātman*). So far as a distinction can be made, it is "logical but not real" (*secundum rationem, non secundum rem*).

[9] "Then shall the dust return to the earth as it was: and the spirit shall return unto God who gave it" (Eccl. 12:7). Our sense of being may be "in the spirit" or "in the dust," and so either "saved or lost." It is well for him "who has been of strength to awaken before the body is unstrung" (KU VI.4).

[10] For St. Bernard, see Étienne Gilson, *La Théologie mystique de Saint Bernard* (Paris, 1934), ch. 5. How close to Indian formulation St. Bernard comes appears in his distinction of *proprium* from *esse* (*mama* from *attā*) and in Rousselet's summary (*ibid.*, p. 150, n. 2) "Cela revient à dire qu'on ne peut pleinement posséder Dieu sans pleinement se posséder soi-même," at the same time that (*ibid.*, p. 152, n. 1)

"nothing else than that the spirit goeth out of itself, out of time, and entereth into a pure nothingness" (Johannes Tauler), becoming thus "free as the Godhead in its non-existence" (Eckhart); to have said "Thy will be done, not mine" or, in other words, to have been perfected in "Islām."[11]

Man has thus two selves, lives or "souls," one physical, instinctive, and mortal, the other spiritual and not in any way conditioned by time or space, but of which the life is a Now "where every where and every when is focused" (*Paradiso* XXIX.12), and "apart from what has been or shall be" (KU II.14), that "*now* that stands still" of which we as temporal beings, knowing only a past and future, can have no empirical experience. Liberation is not a matter only of shaking off the physical body—oneself is not so easily evaded—but, as Indian texts express it, of shaking off all bodies, mental or psychic as well as physical. "The word of God is quick and powerful, and sharper than any two-edged sword, piercing even to the dividing asunder of soul (ψυχή) and spirit (πνεῦμα)" (Heb. 4:12). It is between these two that our choice lies: between ourselves as we are in ourselves and to others, and ourselves as we are in God—not forgetting that, as Eckhart says, "Any flea as it is in God is higher than the highest of the angels as he is in himself." Of these two "selves" the psychophysical

"Il n'y a plus de *suum*, l'être s'est vidé de lui-même," as in ŚB III.8.1.2–3, where the initiated sacrificer is "as if emptied out of himself" (*riricāna ivātmā bhavati*) in order to enter into possession of his "whole self" (*sarvātmānam*), or as in A I.249, where the man who "has brought into full being body, will and foreknowing (*bhāvita-kāyo, -citto, -pañño*—i.e., whole self) is not emptied out (*aparitto* = *apra-rikta*) but the Great Spiritual-Self of which the way is beyond all measure (*mahattā appamāṇa vihārī*)."

[11] As far as possible this clear distinction of "Soul" (ψυχή, *anima, nafs, vedanā*, etc.) from "spirit" (πνεῦμα, *spiritus, rūḥ, ātman*, etc.) is maintained in the present article; cf. Origen, cited by Eckhart (Pfeiffer ed., p. 531) "dīn geist ist dīr niht genomen: die krefte dīner sèle sint dir genomen" ("It is not thy spirit, but the powers of thy soul [= *indriyāṇi*] that art taken from thee"). It must also be recognized, however, that in the European tradition the word "soul" is used in many senses (for example, "animal" is literally "ensouled," *anima* here as *spiraculum vitae*; cf. Skr. *prāṇa-bhṛt*) and that in one of these senses (which is strictly that of Philo's "soul of the soul," *Heres* LV; cf. Augustine, *De duabis animabis contra Manicheos*) "soul" means "spirit." In what sense "soul" is or is not to be taken to mean "spirit" is discussed by William of Thierry in the *Golden Epistle*, I. (p. 87 in Walter Shewring's English version, London, 1930). In the same way, *ātman* may refer to the psychophysical "self" or to the spiritual self; from the latter point of view, the psychophysical self is *anattā*, "not spiritual"!

It is because both "soul" and "spirit" are selves, although of very different orders, that an equivocation is inevitable. The use of the words in their context has always to be very carefully considered; the proper sense can always be made out.

and spiritual, one is the "life" (ψυχή) to be rejected and the other the "life" that is thereby saved (Luke 17:33 and Matt. 16:25), and of these again the former is that "life" (ψυχή) which "he who hateth . . . in this world shall keep it unto life eternal" (John 12:25) and which a man *must* hate, "if he would be my disciple" (Luke 14:26). It is assuredly all that is meant by *psyche* in our "psychology" that is in this way *le moi haïssable*; all of us, in fact, that is subject to affects or affections or wants of any sort, or entertains "opinions of his own."[12]

The unknown author of the *Cloud of Unknowing* is therefore altogether in order when he says so poignantly (ch. 44) that "All men have matter of sorrow: but most specially he feeleth matter of sorrow, that wotteth and feeleth that he is. . . . And whoso never felt this sorrow, he may make sorrow: for why, he never yet felt perfect sorrow.[13] This sorrow, when it is had . . . maketh a soul able to receive that joy, the which reeveth from a man all witting and feeling of his being." And so also William Blake, when he says, "I would go down unto Annihilation and Eternal Death, lest the Last Judgment come and find me Unannihilate, and I be seiz'd and giv'n into the hands of my own Selfhood."[14] In the same way St. Paul, *vivo, autem jam non ego: vivit vero in me Christus* (Gal. 2:20) [and Rūmī, "He has died to self and become living through the Lord" (*Mathnawī* III.3364)].

[12] Cf. the citation from Jacob Boehme at the head of this article. It is comparatively easy for us to admit that a "self-willing" is egotistical; it is far more difficult but equally indispensable to realize that a "self-thinking"—i.e., "thinking for oneself" or "having opinions of one's own"—is as much an error or "sin," defined as "any departure from the order to the end," as any wilfulness can be. A good case of "thinking for oneself" is what is called the "free examination of scripture"; here, as was remarked by David MacIver, "the number of possible objections to a point of doctrine is equal to the number of ways of misunderstanding it, and therefore infinite."

[13] *Vairāgya*, "dis-gust," as distinguished from *āśa bhanga*, "disappointment": *nekkhamana-sita* as distinguished from *geha-sita* in S IV.232 and in Mil 76. Cf. κατὰ θεὸν λύπη as distinguished from τοῦ κόσμου λύπη in I Cor. 7:10.

[14] As remarked by St. Thomas Aquinas (*Sum. Theol.* I.63.3), "no creature can attain a higher grade of nature without ceasing to exist," which self-denial is a thing "against the natural desire." It is not of its "own" will that the creature can desire its own "annihilation" or "death" [cf. Meister Eckhart, Evans ed., I, 274]. But our consciousness of being (as distinguished from any conceit of being So-and-so or Such-and-such) is precisely *not* the "creature"; it is another will in me than "mine," the lover of another (S IV.158) self than "mine" that "longs intensely for the Great Self" (*mahattam abhikkhankatā*, A II.21)—i.e., for Itself. This does not pertain to *our* self-love, but God's, who is in all things self-intent and loves no one but himself. ["Thus we understand how a life perishes. . . . If it will not give itself up to death, then it cannot attain any other world" (Boehme, *Sex puncta* V.10).]

We are sometimes shocked by the Buddhist disparagement of natural affections and family ties [cf. MU vi.28, "If to son and wife and family he is attached—for such a one, no, never at all!"]. But it is not the Christian who can thus recoil, for no man can be Christ's disciple "and hate not his father, and mother, and wife, and children, and brethren, and sisters," as well as himself (Luke 14:26 [cf. Plato, *Phaedo* 68A]). These uncompromising words, from one who endorsed the command to honor father and mother and who equated contempt with murder, show clearly enough that it is not an ethical doctrine of unselfishness or altruism that we are dealing with but a purely metaphysical doctrine of the transcending of individuation. It is in the same sense that he exclaims, "Who is my mother, or my brethren?" (Mark 3:33, etc.), and accordingly that Meister Eckhart warns, "As long as thou still knowest who thy father and thy mother have been in time, thou art not dead with the real death" (Pfeiffer ed., p. 462).

There can be no return of the prodigal, no "turning in" (*nivṛtti*), except of same to same. "Whoever serves a God, of whom he thinks that 'He is one and I another,' is an ignoramus" (BU i.4.10); "If then you do not make yourself equal to God, you cannot apprehend God: for like is known by like" (Hermes, *Lib.* xi.2.20b). The question is asked of the one who comes home, "Who art thou?" and if he answers by his own or a family name, he is dragged away by the factors of time on the threshold of success (JUB iii.14.1–2):[15] ". . . that ill-fated soul is dragged back again, reverses its course, and having failed to know itself, lives in bondage to un-

[15] The traveler, at the end of life's journey (not necessarily on his deathbed), knocks at the Sundoor (as in JUB, etc.), which is the door of the house of Death (as in KU) and that of Yama's paradise (as in RV), and would be received as a guest or, as expressed in Pāli, *amata-dvāram āhacca tiṭṭhati* (S ii.43). Admission, however, depends upon anonymity, with all its implications of "being in the spirit" (*ātmany etya mukha ādatte*, "going in the spirit, the gate accepts him," JUB iii.33.8). There can be no doubt that the same mythical and profound eschatology underlies the Homeric legend of Ulysses and Polyphemus. The latter is assuredly Death. (His one eye corresponds to Śiva's third; that it is blinded and thus "closed" means that the world illumined by sun and moon, the *two* eyes of the gods, is to persist for Ulysses and his companions. It must be an initiatory, not a final death that is overcome, as is also suggested by the "cave".) His land which yields crops untilled is a Paradise, like Yama's or Varuṇa's; Ulysses would be his guest. The story, as told by Homer (and Euripides), has become an adventure rather than a myth, but it remains that the hero who overcomes Death is the one man who when he is asked, "Who art thou?" answers, "No one"; and it is noteworthy that in the Euripides version, when the blinded Cyclops cries out, "Where is Nobody?" the chorus answers, "Nowhere, O Cyclops." It would be hard to say whether Homer still "understood his material"; it may be taken for granted that Euripides did not.

couth and miserable bodies. The fault of this soul is its ignorance"[16] (Hermes, *Lib.* x.8a). He should answer, "Who I am is the light Thou art. What heavenly light Thou art, as such I come to Thee," and answering thus is welcomed accordingly, "Who thou art, that am I; and who I am, art thou. Come in" (JUB III.14.3–4). To the question, "Who is at the door?" he answers, "*Thou* art at the door," and is welcomed with the words, "Come in, O myself" (Rūmī, *Mathnawī* I.3062–3). It is not as *un tel* that he can be received—"Whoever enters, saying 'I am So-and-so,' I smite him in the face" (*Shams-i-Tabrīz*); as in Song of Solomon 1:7, *si ignoras te, . . . egredere.*

"He that is joined unto the Lord is one spirit" (1 Cor. 6:17). But this Spirit (*ātman*), Brahman, God, the "What?" of JUB III.14, "hath not come anywhence nor become anyone" (KU II.18). The Imperishable has neither personal nor family name (BU III.8.8, *Mādhyaṃdina* text) nor any caste (Muṇḍ. Up. I.1.6); "God himself does not know what he is, because he is not any what"[17] (Erivgena); the Buddha is "neither priest nor prince nor husbandman nor any one at all (*koci no'mhi*). . . . I wander in the world a veritable naught (*akiṃcana*). . . . Useless to ask my kin" (*gottam*, Sn 455–456).[18]

[16] Cf. Dh 243 where, after a list of "faults," we have: "the supreme fault is ignorance" (*savijjā paramam malam*).

[17] The deiformed soul in which an *ablatio omnis alteritatis et diversitatis* has been effected (Nicholas of Cusa) is therefore beyond our speechways (*vādapatha*, Sn 1076); "unknown to herself or any creature, she knows well that she is, but she does not know what she is" (Meister Eckhart, Pfeiffer ed., p. 537).

[18] In the same way, the famous ode XXXI of *Shams-i-Tabrīz* [Rūmī, *Dīvān*], ". . . I know not myself . . . ; I am not of Adam nor of Eve . . . ; my place is the Placeless, my trace is the Traceless; nor body nor life, since I am of the life of the Beloved" (*na tan nāsad na jān nāsad, ki man az jān jānān-am*). Nicholson comments: "'I am nought' means 'God is all.'" From the Indian point of view, the "Beloved" is, of course, "the Spirit, which is also one's own spiritual essence"—"For one who has attained, there is none dearer than the Spirit" or "than the Self" (*na piyataram attanā*, S I.75; cf. BU I.4.8, *tad etat preyah putrāt . . . yād ayam ātmā . . . ātmānam eva priyam upāsīta*; BU II.4; BU IV.5; CU VII.25; [Muṇḍ. Up. II.2.1 ff.]; etc.). With "traceless" compare Dh 179, *tam buddham anantagocaram padam, kena padena nessatha*, "that Buddha, whose pasture is without end, the footless [or trackless], by what track can you find him out?" (This is complementary to the usual doctrine of the *vestigium pedis*, according to which the intelligible Buddha [or Agni] can be tracked by his spoor, *pādā* or *padāni*.) Cf. Coomaraswamy, *Elements of Buddhist Iconography*, 1935, nn. 145 ff. "A Tathāgata, I say, is actually (*dhamme*) beyond our ken" (*ananuvejjo*, M I.140 [similarly *anupalabbhī yamāno*, S III.112]); and in the same way of Arhats "there is no demonstration" (*vaṭṭam tesam natthi paññāpanāya*; S 141): "Him neither gods nor men can see" (*tam ce hi nādakkhum*, S I.23). The last is spoken in the Buddha's physical presence and corresponds to the

Having drawn the outlines of the universal doctrine of self-naughting and of self-sacrifice or devotion in the most literal sense of the words, we propose to devote the remainder of our demonstration to its specifically Buddhist formulation in terms of *ākiṃcaññāyatana*, "the Station of No-what-ness," or, more freely, "the Cell of Self-naughting." "When it is realized that 'There is no aught' (*n'atthi kiṃci*), that is 'Emancipation of the Will'[19] (*ceto-vimutti*) in the 'Station of No-what-ness'" (S IV.296 and M I.297; cf. D II.112). The exact meaning of "There is naught"—i.e.,

---

well-known text of the *Vajracchedikā Sūtra*, "Those who see me in the body (*rūpena*) or think of me in words, they do not see me at all, their way of thinking is mistaken; the Blessed Ones are to be seen only in the Body of the Law, the Buddha can only be rightly understood as the principle of the Law, assuredly not by any means." Cf. St. Thomas Aquinas, "Therefore if anyone in seeing God conceives something in his mind, this is not God, but one of God's effects" (*Sum. Theol.* III.92.1 *ad* 4); "We have no means for considering what God is, but rather how He is not" (I.3.1). [Cf. Hermes, *Lib.* XIII.3, οὐκ ὀφθαλμοῖς τοιούτοις θεωροῦμαι, ὦ τέκνον. "The new man, being incorporeal, can be seen only with 'the eyes of the mind.'" Cf. JUB IV.19 and *The Doctrine of the Sūfis*, A. J. Arberry, tr. (Cambridge, 1935), p. 34.]

[19] *Ceto-vimutti* (often rendered "heart's release") in contrasted with *paññā-vimutti*, "intellectual emancipation," *ceto* and *paññā* denoting both the means or way of liberation and the respect in which liberation is obtained. The texts often speak of a "being free in both departments" *ubhato-bhāga-vimutti*, as well as of other types of liberation, and it is evident that the two ways, which are those of the will and the intellect, converge and ultimately coincide. A II.36, *ceto-vasipatto hoti vitakka-pathesu*, "He is a past master of the will in matters of choice [or 'matters of counsel']," brings out very clearly the conative connotations of *ceto*, which are evident also for *cetas* in AV VI.116.3. S III.60 defines *saṅkhārā* as *saṃcetanā*, rendered by Rhys Davids "seats of will." It is clear, then, that the connection of *ceto-vimutti* with *ākiṃcañña* is intrinsic, since it is just to the extent that one ceases to feel that one is anyone and to the extent that one loses all sense of *proprium* (*mama*) that self-willing and self-thinking must cease. It is just because *ceto* implies both willing *and* thinking that it is difficult to represent it by a single English word; however, it is in just the same way that English "to have a mind to" is the same as "to wish to" or "to want to" and so, too, that Skr. *man*, to "think," and *kam*, to "wish" or "want," are virtually synonymous in many contexts. *Paññā* is not, of course, "thought" in this sense, but much rather "speculation" in the strict sense of this word (*āditye mahat . . . ādarśe pratirūpaḥ* Kauṣ. Up. IV.2. with very many Christian and other parallels—e.g., *Sum. Theol.* I.12.9c, "All things are seen in God as in an intelligible mirror," i.e., the *speculum aeternum*). It is asked in M I.437, how is it that some are liberated in one way and some in the other, the Buddha replying that it depends upon "a difference in faculties" (*indriya-vemattatam*). The difference is, in fact, typically that of the royal from the sacerdotal, Kṣatriya from Brāhman character; because of this difference a *bhakti-mārga* and *karma-mārga* are stressed in the *Bhagavad Gītā* and a *jñāna-mārga* in the Upaniṣads. The two ways of *ceto-vimutti* (in *Itivuttaka* 27, identified with *mettā*, "charity") and *paññā-vimutti* correspond to and are essentially the same as the *bhakti-mārga* and *jñāna-mārga* of Brahmanical texts.

"naught of mine"[20]—is brought out in A II.177: "The Brāhman[21] speaks the truth and no lie when he says 'I am naught of an anyone anywhere, and therein there is naught of mine anywhere soever'" (*nāhaṃ kvacani kassaci kiṃcanaṃ, tasmiṃ na ca mama kvacani katthaci kiṃcanam n'atthi*; also in M II.263–264),[22] the text continuing, "Therewith he has no conceit of being 'a Toiler' (*samaṇa*) or 'a Brahman,' nor conceit that 'I am better than' or 'I am equal to' or 'inferior to' (anyone). Moreover, by a full comprehension of this truth, he reaches the goal of veritable 'naughting' (*ākiṃcaññam yeva paṭipadam*)." What is neither "I" nor "mine" is above all body, sensibility, volitional conformations, and empirical consciousness (i.e., the psychophysical self), and to have rejected these is "for your best good and beatitude" (S III.33; the chapter is entitled *Natumhāka*, "What Is Not 'Yours'"). Accordingly, "Behold the Arhats' beatitude! No wanting can be found in them: excised the thought 'I am' (*asmi*);[23] delusion's net is rent. . . . Unmoving, unoriginated . . . Brahma-

[20] It will be seen that the Arhat or Brāhman who has attained to self-naughting and confesses accordingly *n'atthi* or *n'atthi kimci* might have been called a *natthika* or *natthikavādi* ("denier"). If he is never in fact so called (but, rather, *śūnyavādī*), it is because these were designations current in a very different sense, with reference namely to the "materialist" or "skeptic" who denies that there is another world or hereafter (as in M I.402–403) or takes the extreme view (*natthitā*) that there is absolutely nothing in common between the individual that acts and the individual that experiences the results of the acts (S II.17). We propose to discuss this other "denier" upon another occasion.

[21] Pāli Buddhism not only equates *brahma-bhūta* with *buddha*, *brahma-cakka* with *dhamma-cakka*, etc., but (where there is no polemic involved) maintains the old and familiar distinction of the Brāhman by birth (*brahma-bandhu*) from the Brāhman as Comprehensor (*brahma-vit*), in the latter sense equating Brāhman with Arhat.

[22] *Netti* 183 (cited in a note on A I.203) explains *kimcana* here by *rāga-dosa-moha*—i.e., ethically—and this is true in the sense that when self is let go, there remains no ground for any "selfish" passion; *kimcana* is the "somewhat" of the man who still feels that he is "somebody" and accordingly the ground in which interest, ill-will, and delusion can flourish.

In all respects equivalent to *n'atthi* (Skr. *nāsti*) is Persian *nēst* in *Shams-i-Tabrīz* (T 139.12a, cited by Nicholson, p. 233), "Be thou naught (*nēst shū*), naughted of self, for there is no crime more heinous than thine existence."

[23] This does not imply that the Arhat "is not," but excludes from an ineffable essence the process of thought. From this point of view, *cogito ergo sum* is altogether without validity; what I call "my" thinking is by no means my Self. The Arhat does not wonder whether he is, what he is, or how he is, has been, or will be (S II.26, Sn 774). "He does not worry about what is unreal" (*asatti na paritassati*, M I.136); he is self-synthesized (*ajjhattam susamāhito, passim*), and in this state of synthesis (*samādhi*), though he is unaware of anything, "yet there is awareness in him" (S V.74; cf. BU IV.3.28–30). The Buddha neither teaches that *nibbāna* is a "nothingness" nor that the Arhat "comes to naught": "There *is* (*atthi*) an unborn, unbecome, un-

become . . . true 'Persons' (*sappurisā*), natural sons of the Wake. . . . That heart-wood of the Brahma-life is their eternal reason; unshaken in whatever plight, released from 'still becoming' (*punabbhava*), on ground of 'dompted [-self]' they stand, they in the world have won their battle. . . . They roar the 'Lion's Roar.' Incomparable are the Wake (*arahanta*, S III.83–84, 159)." There is no question of a post-mortem "annihilation" here, then, but of "Persons" triumphant here and now; their unconditionality will not be changed by death, which is not an event for those who have "died before they die" (Rūmī), not an event for the *jīvan-mukta*, the veritable *dīkṣita* for whom the funeral rites have already been performed and for whom his relatives have already mourned (JUB III.7.9). Of these it is only the manifestation in terms of "name and appearance" (*nāma-rūpa*) that comes to an end (as all things must that have had a beginning), so that after death they will be sought for in vain by Devas or men in this world or any other (S I.123, D I.46, etc.), just as one might seek in vain for a God any*where*, of whom it is asked "Whence did he come to be?" (*kuta ā babhūva*, RV X.168.3), "In what quarter is He or in what?" (TS V.4.3.4) and "Who knows where He is?" (KU II.25): Thou "canst not tell whence it cometh, and whither it goeth: so is every one that is born of the Spirit" (John 3:8). In spite of this, however, it must be remarked that the attainment of infinity is not a destruction of finite possibility, for the deceased Comprehensor, being a Mover-at-will (*kāmācārin*), can always therefore reappear if, when, where, and as he will. Examples of this "resurrection" may be cited in JUB III.29–30 (where the *noli me tangere* offers a notable parallel to the Christian resurrection), and in the *Parosahassa Jātaka* (No. 99), where a Bodhisattva is asked on his deathbed, "What good has he gotten?," and he answers: "There is naught" (*n'atthi kiṃci*), which is misunderstood by his disciples to

created, uncompounded, and were there not, there would be no way out here of this born, become, created and compounded existence" (Ud 80); a Tathāgata (see Coomaraswamy, "Some Pāli Words" [in this volume—ED.]) whose " 'I am' has been cast off" (*asmimāno pahīno*) is not "destroyed"—"It is in the very presence of such a Tathāgata that I call him 'past finding out' (*ananuvejjo*), and yet there are some who naughtily, vainly, falsely, and contrary to what is the fact (*asatā tucchā musā abhūtena*) charge that the Tathāgata is a misleader (*venayika*; cf. *dunnaya*, heresy) who propounds the cutting off, destruction, and ceasing to be of essences. That is just what I am not, and what I do not propound. The stoppage (*nirodha*) that I have reached, both of old and now, is nothing but the stoppage of Grief (*dukkhassa*—i.e., of that which is *anattā*, not I nor mine)," M I.139–140. (The coincidence of *anattā* with *dukkha* corresponds exactly to the *eṣa ta ātmā sarvāntaraḥ ato'nyad artam* of BU III.4.2.)

mean that he had gotten "no good" by his holy life. But when the conversation is reported to his chief disciple, who had not been present, he says "You have not understood the meaning of the Master's words. What the Master said was that he had attained to the 'Station of No-what-ness' (*ākiṃcaññāyatana*)."[24] And thereupon the deceased Master reappears from the Brahma-world to confirm the chief disciple's explanation.[25]

The man self-naughted is a happy man; not so those still conscious of their human ties. "Look you, how they are blest, these 'Nobodies,' yea these Comprehensors who are 'men of naught': and see how hindered he for whom there is an 'aught,' the man whose mind is tied up with 'other men'" (Ud 14).[26] For "to have known the forthcoming of not being 'anyone' (*ākiṃcaññā-sambhavaṃ ñātvā*) . . . *that* is 'gnosis' (*etaṃ ñānam*, Sn 1115)"; this is the Way, "Perceiving that there is 'No-what-ness' (*ākiṃcaññam*) . . . convinced that 'There is not' (*n'atthi*—i.e., 'naught mine,' as above), so cross the flood" (Sn 1070). And this is not an easy matter: "Hard to perceive what's false (*anattam*; here probably = *anṛtam*),[27] nor is it easy to perceive the truth (*saccam* = *satyam*); he knows,

[24] It is worthy of note that Ālāra Kālāma's doctrine and realization extended to the experience of *ākimcaññāyatana* (M I.165).

[25] Again a sufficient proof that even in "late" Hinayāna Buddhism to have become "no one" was by no means the same as to have been "annihilated." The Buddhist position is in no way inconsistent with the "never have I not been and never hast thou not been . . . nor ever shall not be" of BG II.12. It should be observed that the resurrections of JUB III.29–30 and the *Jātaka* as cited above are wholly "in order" and have nothing in common with the phenomenon of spiritualism. It is as much a Buddhist as a Brāhmanical commonplace that "the dead are not seen again amongst the living," as asked in the *Jātaka*; cf. CU VIII.13–14.

[26] In context the reference is to a man who steals for his wife. The contrasted terms are *akimcana*, "man of naught," and *sakimcana*, "man of aught," the man, that is, who "has" what he calls "his" individuality, which individuality in this case "expresses itself" in an act of partiality. This "man of aught" is hindered by the notions of "himself" and of "his" wife, the "tie" being as between these two selves, subjective and objective; insofar as he does not "hate" both himself and his wife, he is not the Buddha's disciple but is troubled and gets into trouble. In all these contexts it must be remembered that it is a question of the *summum bonum* and man's last end, and not of the "good of society," which is not a final end. The man's first duty is to work out his own salvation (Dh 166). Abandonment of self and of all ties is not only literally "un-self-ish," but it is also both better and kinder to point out the way to happiness by following it than to be "sympathetic"—i.e., to "suffer with"—those who will not "seek peace, and ensue it."

[27] The PTS editor, Paul Steinthal, reads *anattam*, but ms A, admittedly the best manuscript, has *anatam*, which is the form that would be assumed by *anṛtam* in Pāli (cf. *amṛtam*, *amatam*). A commentary has *anatam*, but apparently in the sense of the "not-bent," hence *nibbāna*, and it must be with this in view that Woodward trans-

whose wanting has been smitten through, who sees that 'There is naught' " (*n'atthi kiṃcanam*, Ud 80); "who hath overpast becoming or not becoming in any way" (*iti-bhavābhavam*, all relativity, Ud 20).[28]

It will be seen that anonymity is an essential aspect of *ākiṃcaññā*. All initiations (*dīkṣā*) and, likewise, Buddhist ordination (*pabbajana*), which as in monasticism elsewhere is a kind of initiation,[29] involve at the outset a self-denial.[30] This is explicit in Ud 55, where "Just as rivers lose their

---

lates "infinite." But it is almost impossible to doubt that what we have is the familiar antithesis of *anṛtam* to *satyam*. The uncertainty of the reading nevertheless expresses a sort of *double entendre*; that which is *anattā*, "not what I really am" (*na me so attā*, *passim*) but "devoid of any spiritual-essence" (S IV.54) and "naught-y" (*asat*, M I.136), is equally from the Brahmanical point of view at the same time "false" and "human" as distinguished from what is "true" and "non-human"—i.e., divine—as is explicit in VS I.5 and ŚB I.9.3.23 (cf. AB VII.24), where the sacrificer (always in the last analysis the sacrificer of himself) when initiated and during the performance of the rite "has entered from the untruth (*anṛtam*) into the truth (*satyam*)" and when at the close of the operation he formally desecrates himself, but does not like to say plainly the converse of this and so says instead, "Now I am he that I actually (empirically) am," So-and-so.

[28] "It is the Spirit in thee, O man, that knows which is the true and which the false (*attā te purisa jānāti saccam vā yadi vā musā*)—the 'fair self' (*kalyānam . . . attānam*) . . . or the 'foul' (*pāpam attānam*)" (A I.149), in other words the "great self" (*mahattā*) or the "petty" (*app'ātumo*) of A I.249, the "Self that is Lord of self" or the "self whose Lord is the Self" of Dh 380. The false view is to see "self in not-self" (*anattani . . . attā*, A II.42, etc.)—i.e., in the empirical subject or its percepts (S III.130, etc.). It is "well for him that knows himself" (*atta-saññato*, S I.106; *attaññū*, D III.252), "whose light is the Spirit" (*atta-dīpa*, D II.100), the "self-lover" (*attakāmo*, S I.75, etc.), "inwardly self-synthesized" (*ajjhatam susamāhito*, A II.31, etc.), "in whom the Spirit has been fully brought to birth" (*bhāvitattā*, *passim*). "Go seek your Self" (*attānam gaveseyyātha*, Vin I.23; *attānam gavesitum*, Vis 393). "Quicken thy Self" (*coday'attānam*, Dh 379), for "self is the Lord of self" (Vis 380).

[29] The initiate is "nameless" in KB VII.2–3 and speaks of none by name; he is not himself, but Agni. In ŚB III.8.1.2, he is "emptied of self." Buddhist ordination (*pabbajana* from the point of view of the ordained, *pabbajana* from that of the ordainer, who during the Buddha's lifetime is the Buddha himself) has many of the characteristics of, and is sometimes called, an initiation (S I.226; Commentary [= ŚA I.346] explains *cira-dikkhita*, "long since initiated," by *cira-pabbajita* "long since ordained"; cf. J V.138). In *Jātakamāla* X.32, a Bodhisattva is *dīkṣita*.

The primary senses of *pabbajati* are to "wander, travel," and "be in exile," and so, to become a fellow in the "Companionship" (*sangha*) of Mendicant Travelers (*bhikkhu*, *pabbājaka*), a true Wayfarer; cf. Coomaraswamy, "The Pilgrim's Way," and "The Pilgrim's Way, A Buddhist Recension," 1938 (article in two parts); the Traveler is bound for a world's End that is within himself.

[30] The ethical aspect of this self-denial is a dispositive means to the end of self-naughting and self-realization, not an end in itself. *Tapas*, whether Brahmanical

former name and lineage (*purimāni nāma-gottāni*) when they reach the sea, and are accounted just as 'the great sea,' so men of the four castes (*brāhmaṇa khattiyā vessā suddā*), when they 'as-wanderers-are-ordained' (*pabbajitvā*), discard their former names and lineage, and are reckoned only to be 'Toilers, Sons of the Sakyan.'" It is thus that the "exile" (*pabbājaka*) sets to work to "de-form himself of himself," as Eckhart expresses it (*daz er sich entbilde sin selbes*) or, in other words, to "transform" himself.

The anonymity which we have described above as a doctrinally inculcated principle is by no means only a monastic ideal, but has far-reaching repercussions in traditional societies, where our distinctions of sacred from profane (distinctions that are, in the last analysis, the signature of an internal conflict too rarely resolved) can hardly be found. It reappears, for example, in the sphere of art. We have discussed elsewhere "The Traditional Conception of Ideal Portraiture"[31] (citing, for example, the *Pratimānāṭaka* III.5, where Bharata, though he exclaims at the artists' skill, is unable to recognize the effigies of his own parents), and we may point out here that there is a corresponding anonymity of the artist himself, not only in the field of the so-called "folk arts" but equally in a more sophisticated environment. Thus, as H. Swarzenski has remarked, "It is in the very nature of Mediaeval Art that extremely few names of artists have been transmitted to us . . . the entire mania of connecting the few names preserved by tradition[32] with well-known masterpieces, . . . all this is characteristic of the nineteenth century's cult of individualism, based upon ideals of the Renaissance."[33] Dh 74 exclaims, "May it be known to religious and profane that 'This was my work' . . . that is an

---

or Buddhist, is never a "penance," but in its disciplinary aspect a part of that training by means of which the petty self is subjected and assimilated to the Great Self or, in a familiar symbolism, by which the steeds are brought under the driver's control, apart from which the man is "at war with himself" (S I.71–72, like BG VI.5–6); and in its intrinsic character, a radiance, reflecting his "Who glows (*tapati*) yonder."

[31] Cf. Coomaraswamy, *Why Exhibit Works of Art?* 1943, ch. 7.

[32] "History," rather than "tradition" in our stricter sense.

[33] *Journal of the Walters Art Gallery*, I (1938), 55. Cf. Josef Strzygowski, "the artist in Viking times is not to be thought of as an individual, as would be the case today. . . . It is a creative art" (*Early Church Art in Northern Europe*, New York, 1928, pp. 159–160); and with respect to this distinction of "individual" from "creative" art, "I do nothing of myself" (John 8:28), and, "I take note, and even as He dictates within me, I set it forth" (Dante, *Purgatorio* XXIV.52). ["No pronouncement of a prophet is ever his own," Philo, *De specialibus legibus* IV.49; cf. IV.192.] Better to be an amanuensis of the Spirit than to "think for oneself"!

infantile thought."[34] DhA I.270 relates the story of thirty-three youths who are building a "rest hall" at four crossroads, and it is explicit that "The names of the thirty-three comrades did not appear," but only that of Sudhammā, the donor of the roofplate (the keystone of the dome).[35] One is irresistibly reminded of the "Millennial Law" of the Shakers that "No one should write or print his name on any article of manufacture, that others may hereafter know the work of his hands."[36] And all this has not only to do with the body of the work and its aesthetic surfaces; it has just as much to do with its "weight" (*gravitas*) or essence (*ātman*). The notion of a possible property in ideas is altogether alien to the Philosophia Perennis, of which we are speaking. It is of ideas and the inventive power that we can properly say, if we are thinking in terms of the psycho-

[34] The words of the original could mean either my "work" or my "doing," *kamma* covering both things made and things done. The same ambiguity, or rather ambivalence, is present in the corresponding text of BG III.27, "One whose self is confounded by the concept of an 'I' imagines that 'I am the doer,'" and V.8, where the Comprehensor does not think of "himself as the doer of anything," the word for "doer," *kartr*, meaning equally "maker" or "creator"; cf. JUB I.5.2, "Thou (God) art the doer," and IV.12.2, "I (God) am the doer" (or "maker"). Like BG, as cited above, is Ud 70, "Those who give ear to the notion 'I am the doer' (*ahaṃkāra*), or are captivated by the notion 'another is the doer' (*paraṃkāra*), do not understand this matter, they have not seen the point."

We need hardly remind the reader that this is a metaphysical position and must not be confused with the *akiriyāvāda* heresy—namely that of the man in Ud 45 who is represented as saying, "even while acting, 'It is not I that am agent' (*yo c'āpi katvā na karomī'ti c'āha*)." "I," "this man," *un tel*, have no right to evade "my" responsibility in this way, by maintaining that it does not matter what I do, because it is not really I that am doing it. It is only when the nonentity of this "I" [which is not "mine" (Dh 62) but an assumption], has been *verified* (*sacchikatvā*) that 'I,' in the sense of I John 3:9, being "born of God, . . . cannot sin," or that of Gal. 5:18, am "not under the law."

[35] In early Indian art, the names of the donors are constantly met, those of artists almost never. The donor's name is recorded because he wishes to "acquire merit" for what he has done; the artist is not, as such, in this specifically moral sense acquiring merit, but on the one hand earning his wages and on the other working for the good of the work to be done, neither of these points of view implying any wish for fame.

[36] Edward and Faith Andrews, *Shaker Furniture* (New Haven, 1937), p. 44. In all these connections, however, it is the spirit rather than the letter that matters. In the same community, for example, furniture could not be owned "as private property, or individual interest" and yet might be marked with a person's initials "for purposes of distinction." And it was, in just the same way, in order for a Buddhist monk to say, "I" or "mine," when convenient (S I.14). In the same way an artist's signature need not be an advertisement but can be, like a hallmark, a simple guarantee of quality and acceptance of responsibility.

physical ego, that this is not "mine" or—if the self has been naughted, so that, to use the Brāhmaṇa phrase, we have "come into our own"—that these gifts of the Spirit are truly "mine," since it is the Synteresis, the Divine Eros, inwit, "in-genium," immanent spirit, daimon, and not the natural individual that is the ground of the inventive power, and it is precisely this inwit, this intellectual light, and not our own "mentality" of which it is said that "That art thou."

In conclusion, the student must not be misled by such terms as self-naughting, nonbeing, or any other of the phrases of the negative theology. Nonbeing, for example, in such an expression as Eckhart's "nonexistence of the Godhead," is that transcendent aspect of the Supreme Identity which is not, indeed, being, but that to which all being, even God's, can be reduced, as to its principle; it is that of God's which is not susceptible of manifestation, of which, therefore, we cannot speak in terms that are applicable only to states of manifestation, yet without which God would be only a "pantheon," a "pantheistic" deity, rather than "all this" *and* "more than this," "within" *and* "without." In the same way, it must be realized that of one assimilated to God by self-naughting and therefore no longer anyone, we have no longer any human means or speechway (*vādapatha*) to say what he is, but only to say that he is not such or such. It would be even more untrue to say that he is not than that he is; he is simply inaccessible to analysis. Even a theoretical grasp of metaphysics is impossible until we have learned that there are "things which our intellect cannot behold . . . we cannot understand what they are except by denying things of them" (Dante, *Convito* III.15) and that these very things are the greater part of man's last end. If, for example, the Arhat no longer desires, it is not because he is in human language "apathetic," but because all desires are possessed, and pursuit has no longer any meaning; if the Arhat no longer "moves," it is not as a stone lies still but because he no longer needs any means of locomotion in order to be anywhere; if he is not curious about empirical truths, whether "this is so" or "not so," it is not because he does not know but because he does not know as we know in these terms. For example, he does not think in terms of past or future, but only is now. If he is "idle," from our point of view who still have "things to do," it is because he is "all in act" (*kṛtakṛtyaḥ, katakaraṇīyo*), with an activity independent of time.

But if we cannot know him, it does not follow that he cannot know or manifest himself to us. Just as in this life, while in *samādhi*, he is inaccessible and for all practical purposes dead, but on emerging from this synthesis and "returning to his senses" can conveniently make use of such expressions as "I" or "mine" for practical and contingent purposes without attainder of his freedom (S I.14), so after death, by which he is not changed, a resurrection is always possible in any guise (he "shall go in and out, and find pasture," John 10:9, with many Indian parallels—e.g., TU III.5, "he goes up and down these worlds, eating what he desires and assuming what aspect he will"). This possibility by no means excludes that of reappearance in that very (dis-)guise by which he had been known in the world as So-and-so. Examples of such resurrection can be cited not only in the case of Jesus, but in that of Uccaiśśravas Kaupayeya (JUB III.29–30), in that of the Boddhisattva of the *Parosahassa Jātaka*, and in that of the former Buddha Prabhūtaratna. Such a resurrection, indeed, is only one of innumerable "powers" (*iddhi*), such as those of walking on the water, flying through the air, or disappearing from sight, which are possessed by one who is no longer "in himself" but "in the spirit," and inevitably possessed precisely because they are the powers of the Spirit with which he is "one" (1 Cor. 6:17):[37] which powers (as listed, for example, in S II.212 ff., A I.255 ff., and S V.254 ff.) are precisely the "greater works" of John 14:12, "the works that I do shall he do also; and greater works than these shall he do." There can, indeed, be no question for those who know the "facts" that insofar as the *yogin* is what the designation implies, "joined unto the Lord," these "powers" are at his command; he is only too well aware, however, that to make of these powers an end in themselves would be to fail of the real end.

It will be seen that in speaking of those who have done what was to be done, we have been describing those who have become "perfect, even as your Father in Heaven is perfect." There will be many to say that even if all this holds good for the all-abandoner, it can have no meaning for "me," and it is true that it cannot have its full meaning for "me" who, *en étant un tel*, am insusceptible of deification and therefore incapable of

[37] This unification is to be understood in the same way that the "eternal reasons" are one with the intellect that entertains them and yet distinguishable among themselves, so as to be *in posse* to project their images upon the walls of our cave. Filiation or theosis by an *ablatio omnis alteritatis et diversitatis* can be expressed in terms of "glorification" as a becoming consciously a ray of the Light of lights: the relation of a ray, although of light throughout its course, is that of identity with its source at one end and separate recognizability at the other, where its effect is observed as color. In no better way than by this adequate symbol, made use of in all traditions, can we express or suggest the meaning of Eckhart's "fused but not confused" or Indian *bhedābhedha*, "distinction without difference."

reaching God. Few or none of "us" are yet qualified to abandon ourselves. As far as there is a Way, it can be trodden step by step. There is an intellectual preparation, which not merely prepares the way to a verification (*sacchikiriyā*) but is indispensable to it. As long as we love "our" selves and conceive of a "self-denial" only in terms of "altruism," or cling to the idea of a "personal" immortality for our or other selves, we are standing still. But a long stride has been taken if at least we have learned to accept the idea of the naughting of self as a good, however contrary it may be to our "natural" desire, however *allen menschen fremde* (Eckhart). For if the spirit be thus willing, the time will come when the "flesh," whether in this or any other ensemble of possibilities forming a "world," will be no longer weak. The doctrine of self-naughting is therefore addressed to *all*, in measure of their capacity, and by no means only to those who have already formally abandoned name and lineage. It is not the saint, but the sinner, that is called to repent of his existence.

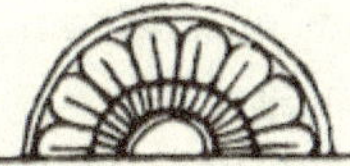

Ātmayajña: Self-Sacrifice

Svasti vaḥ pārāya tamasa parastāt
Muṇḍaka Upaniṣad, II.2.6[1]

When a man vows to Almighty God all that he has, all his life, all his knowledge, it is a holocaust.
St. Gregory, XX Homily on Ezekiel

Just as Christianity turns upon and in its rites repeats and commemorates a Sacrifice, so the liturgical texts of the *Ṛg Veda* cannot be considered apart from the rites to which they apply, and so are these rites themselves a mimesis of what was done by the First Sacrificers who found in the Sacrifice their Way from privation to plenty, darkness to light, and death to immortality.

The Vedic Sacrifice is always performed for the Sacrificer's benefit, both here and hereafter.[2] The immediate benefits accruing to the Sacrificer are that he may live out the full term of his life (the relative immortality of "not dying" prematurely) and may be multiplied in his children and in his possessions; the Sacrifice ensuring the perpetual circulation of the "Stream of Wealth" (*vasor dhārā*),[3] the food of the gods reaching them in the smoke of the burnt offering, and our food in return descending from heaven in the rain and thus through plants and cattle to ourselves, so that neither the Sacrificer nor his people shall die of want. On the other hand, the ultimate benefit secured to the Sacrificer who thus lives out his life on earth and in good form is that of deification and an absolute

[This essay was first published in the *Harvard Journal of Asiatic Studies*, VI (1942). —ED.]

[1] "Welfare to ye in crossing over to the farther shore of darkness!"

[2] "For the winning of both worlds," TS VI.6.4.1; "that 'life's best' that has been appointed by the gods to men for this time being and hereafter," Plato, *Timaeus* 90D.

[3] TS V.4.8.1, V.7.3.2, 3; ŚB V.4.1.16, VII.3.1.30, IX.3.2, etc.; MU VI.37, BG III.10 ff. The *vasor dhārā* is represented iconographically in the Cakravartin compositions at Jaggayapeta, cf. James Burgess, *Buddhist Stûpas of Amarâvatî and Jaggayapeṭa* (London 1887), pl. LV, fig. 3, etc.

immortality. These distinctions of temporal from eternal goods correspond to that which is sharply drawn in the Brāhmaṇas between a mere performance or patronage of the rites and a comprehension of them, the mere participant securing only the immediate, and the Comprehensor (*evaṃvit*, *vidvān*, *viduḥ*) both ends of the operation (*karma*, *vrata*). This is likewise the well-known distinction of the *karma kāṇḍa* and *karma mārga* from the *jñāna kāṇḍa* and *mārga*—a division of *viae*[4] that is ultimately resolved when the whole of life is sacrificially interpreted and lived accordingly.

To know Indra as he is in himself is the *summum bonum* (Kauṣ. Up. III.1, cf. AĀ II.2.3); and already RV VIII.70.3 points out that "none attaineth Him by works or sacrifices" (*na . . . karmaṇā . . . na yajñaiḥ* [cf. ŚB X.5.4.16]). If it is not by any mere activity nor by any ritual means, it is clear that it can only be by an understanding or verification of what is done that he can be found. Here, then, we propose to ask not what is enacted outwardly, but what is accomplished inwardly by the understanding sacrificer.

The Brāhmaṇas abound with evidence that the victim is a representation of the sacrificer himself, or as the texts express it, *is* the sacrificer himself. In accordance with the universal rule that initiation (*dīkṣā*) is a death and a rebirth, it is explicit that "the initiate is the oblation" (*havir vai dīkṣitaḥ*, TS VI.1.4.5; cf. AB II.3), "the victim (*paśu*) substantially (*nidānena*) the sacrificer himself" (AB II.11).[5] This was to be expected, for it is repeatedly emphasized that "We [the sacrificers here and now] must do what was done by the gods [the original sacrificers] in the beginning." It is, in fact, himself that the god offers up, as may be seen in the prayers "O Agni, sacrifice thine own body" (*yajasva tanvaṃ tava svām*, RV VI.11.2; cf. I.142.11, *avasṛja upa tmanā*), and "sacrifice thyself, augmenting thy body" (*svayaṃ yajasva tanvaṃ vṛdhānaḥ*, RV X.81.5), ["Worship thyself, O God" (*yajasva tanvaṃ*, RV X.7.6, VI.11.2)]. To sacrifice and to be sacrificed are essentially the same: "For the gods' sake he chose death, for his offspring's [the same 'gods'] sake chose not im-

[4] The *locus classicus* for the *viae, affimativa* and *remotionis*, is MU IV.6. These are also the *śaikṣa* and *aśaikṣa* paths, of those who are and are no longer under the law. Those who attempt to take the latter before the first has been followed to its end are certain to lose their way.

[5] Cf. TS VI.1.5.4, ŚB I.2.3.5 with Eggeling's note (SBE, Vol. 12, p. 49) and ŚB III.3.4.21.

mortality: they made Bṛhaspati the sacrifice, Yama gave up (*arirecīt*,[6] poured or emptied out) his own dear body" (RV x.13.4). [So in ŚB i.6.3.21, "Me (Soma) shall they offer up to all of you." Prajāpati at his own sacrifice "gave himself up to the gods" (ŚB xi.1.8.2 ff.; the sacrificer "gives himself up to the gods, even as Prajāpati gave himself up to the gods . . . for the (Sacrifice) becomes an oblation to the gods"; cf. ŚB viii.6.1.10.] And so it is "by the Sacrifice that the gods offered up the Sacrifice" (*yajñena yajñam ayajanta devaḥ*, RV x.90.16): we shall see presently why, and how correctly, Sāyaṇa says in commenting on the last passage that "the gods" are "Prajāpati's breath-forms" (*prāṇarūpā*; see n. 56).

The sacrificer's offering up of himself is ritually enacted in various ways. The *prastara*, for example, which represents the sacrificer, is thrown into the Fire, and he only saves himself from an actual immolation by an invocation of the Fire itself (ŚB i.9.2.17, cf. iii.4.3.22): one who ritually approaches either the household or the sacrificial Fire does so reflecting that "that Fire knows that he has come to surrender himself to me" (*paridāṃ me*, ŚB ii.4.1.11, cf. ix.2.1.17, ix.2.3.15, 17, ix.4.4.3, AB ii.3), and if, indeed, "he did not expressly make this renunciation of himself (*ātmanaḥ paridāṃ na vadeta*), the Fire would deprive him of it" (ŚB ix.5.1.53).[7]

Otherwise stated, "the Sacrificer casts himself in the form of seed[8] (represented by grains of sand[9]) into the household Fire (*ātmānaṃ . . . retobhūtaṃ siñcati*, ŚB vii.2.1.6) to ensure his rebirth here on earth, and

[6] $\sqrt{ric}$ is to "pour out" or "flood," and with *ati-*, to "overflow," the passive "to be emptied out over" having often the same value. A superabundance in the source and deficiency in the recipient are implied, hence *ūnātiriktau* = minus and plus, *pudendum muliebre et membrum virile* (cf. Caland on PB xix.3.9). To be "spent, or emptied out, as it were" (*riricāna iva*, PB iv.10.1 and *passim*) follows emission: only "as it were," however, *in divinis*, because "the Single Season is never emptied out (*nātiricyate*, AV viii.9.26)." In RV x.90.5, the sacrificial Person "is poured out over, i.e., overflows the Earth from East to West" (*atyaricyata paścād bhūmin atho puraḥ*); cf. JUB i.54.7, *atyaricyata*, and i.57.5, *ubhayato vācā atyaricyata.*

[7] *Qui enim voluerit animam suam salvam facere, perdet eam*, Mark 8:35.

[8] Just as also, in being initiated, the sacrificer had been made to pass through all the stages of insemination, embryonic development in the womb, and birth; see AB i.3, where we have *saretasam . . . kṛtvā* "having made him possessed of seed," the seed from which he will arise as a new man (cf. Eckhart's "He who sees *me*, sees *my child*").

[9] The Kuṣāna coins, notably Kaniṣka's, on which the king is shown standing left with his right hand over a small altar, are probably representations of this ritual action, and as much as to say that the king has performed the Rājasūya sacrifice and is, if not a god, in any case a ruler by divine sanction.

into the sacrificial altar with a view to his rebirth in heaven,[10] employing verses containing the verb *āpyai*, "to grow,"[11] and referring to Soma, for "Soma being the Breath" (*prāṇaḥ*), he thus introduces Breath into the effused seed and so quickens it (ŚB VII.3.1.12, 45, 46); the verses (VS XII.112, 113) concluding "growing, O Soma, unto immortality, gain thou thy highest glory in the Sky," i.e., that of the Moon (ŚB III.4.3.13).

This introduces us to "Soma," of whom we shall have much to say. For he too, King Soma, is the victim: Agni the eater, Soma the food here below, the Sun the eater, the Moon his food and oblation above (ŚB XI.1.6.19, X.6.2.1–4, and *passim*). We cannot pursue this relationship here at full length except to say that "when eater and food (*adya* = *puroḍāśa*, sacrificial cake) unite (*ubhayaṃ samāgacchati*), it is called the eater, not the food" (ŚB X.6.2.1), i.e., there is an assimilation in both senses of the word; that this assimilation is also the marriage effected on the night before the new moon's rising (*amāvāsya*, "cohabitation,"[12] *Pāṇini* III.1.122) when she enters into (*praviśati*) him (JUB I.33.6); that the

[10] Sexual intercourse, ritually understood, is a kind of Soma sacrifice (BU VI.2.13, VI.4.3). The household Fire is identified with the wife, of whom one is born again here; the sacrificial Fire is the divine womb into which one pours (*siñcati*) himself, and from which a solar rebirth ensues. The Comprehensor of this doctrine, making the Burnt Offering (*agnihotra*), has therefore two selves, two inheritances, human and divine; but one who offers, not understanding, has but one self, one inheritance, viz. the human (JUB I.17.18). "That which is born of the flesh is flesh; and that which is born of the Spirit is spirit" (John 3:6). With the sowing of one self as seed into the Fire and the quickening of this seed by the Breath, cf. Rom. 6:4 ff.: "We are buried with him [Christ] by baptism unto death . . . planted together . . . our old man is crucified with him, that the body of sin might be destroyed. For he that is 'dead' is freed from sin. Now if we be dead with Christ we believe that we shall also live with him."

[11] At the full moon offering there are references to the slaying of Vṛtra (the moon, ŚB I.6.4.18), "because Indra smote Vṛtra with the full moon offering. In that they have references to waxing at the new moon offering, it is because then the moon passes away (*kṣapaṃ . . . gacchati*) and verily thus does he cause it to grow and wax" (KB III.5).

[12] Sun and Moon, Breath and Substance, are a progenitive pair (Praśna Up. I.4.5, cf. Plutarch, *Moralia* 368D). Their marriage is probably implied in RV LXXXV.18, 19 (cf. A. A. Macdonell and A. B. Keith, *Vedic Index of Names and Subjects*, London, 1912, s.v. *candra*), and by the word *amāvāsya* itself. For comparative material cf. Ernest Siecke, *Die Liebesgeschichte des Himmels*, Strasbourg, 1892. Love and Death are one person. There are inseparable connections between initiation, marriage, and death, and alimentary assimilation; the word "marriage" itself seems to contain *mer* (Skr. *mṛ* to die, cf. *maryah*, marriageable youth); and very many of the words used in our texts with respect to the unification of the many in the one imply both death and marriage, e.g., *api-i, eko bhū, sambhū, saṃgam, saṃdhā*; cf. τελέω to be perfected, be married, die.

Sun and Moon are the divine and human worlds, Oṃ and Vāc (JUB III.13, 14), [i.e., Self and self, *le soi* and *le moi*]; and again, that the Sun is Indra, the Moon Vṛtra, whom he swallows on that night before the new moon appears (ŚB I.6.4.18, 19). It appears, indeed, from a correlation of this passage with ŚB II.4.4.17–19, that Vṛtra is the solar Indra's bride—cf. RV X.85.29, where the Sun's bride, who enters into him (*viśati patim*), is originally ophidian, acquiring feet only on her marriage (as in the marriage of a mermaid to a human); and that there are more ways than one of "killing" a dragon. All this expresses the relationship of the Breath to the "elemental self," Eros to Psyche, the "Spirit" to the "soul," and is paralleled in Meister Eckhart's "The soul, in hot pursuit of God, becomes absorbed in Him . . . just as the sun will swallow up and put out the dawn" (Evans ed., I, 292; cf. Dante, *Paradiso* XXVII.136–138), who is herself a "snake" (*apād*) in the beginning (RV I.152.3, VI.59.6).[13]

Into the details of the Soma Sacrifice (an indispensable part of the Agnihotra, oblation to Agni, burnt-offering), we need not enter here, except to remind ourselves that the shoots (*aṃśu*) of the Soma plant, or any plant that represents Soma and of which the stems or fruits are used, are "pressed" (*suta*)—i.e., crushed and ground—and that the strained and purified juice is offered in the Fire, and also partaken of by the priests and the sacrificer. There is a real analogy of the Soma mill to the wine-press, and of Soma juice to the "pure blood of the grape" (Deut. 32:14), and of the rite to the "drink offering" of the wine in the Fire (Lev. 23:13), *noster deus consumens* (Deut. 4:24), and of the slaying of Soma to the killing of the grain when it is threshed and ground. Ac-

[13] Cf. Coomaraswamy, "Two Passages in Dante's *Paradiso*" and "The Rape of a Nāgī" [both in the present volumes—ED.].

[From another point of view, the coition (*samāgamana*) of the Sun (Mitra) and Moon (Varuṇa) on the night of their dwelling together (*amāvāsya*), called a marriage of the full and waning moons, the (full) moon being identified with Varuṇa and the waning moon identified with Mitra (see ŚB II.4.4.17–19): precisely because the waning moon is assimilated by the Sun, and that which is eaten is called by the name of the eater (ŚB X.6.2.1, with specific reference to the Sun and Moon). This is the same thing as the solar Indra's swallowing up the lunar Vṛtra on "the night of dwelling together" (cf. KB III.5); Vṛtra is therefore to be seen as Indra's wife—"Potentiality hath gotten feet (i.e., shed her ophidian nature) and as a wife *jāyā* with her Lord" (RV X.85.29). In erotic parlance, to be "slain" and to be *in gloria* are one and the same thing. Now we see just what it is that the "hero" failed to do in the story of the Lady of the Land in The Earthly Paradise. And we see again that marriage is an assimilation of hostile principles, and that to be assimilated is to die. It is precisely in all these senses that the soul (which must as Eckhart says, "put itself to death") is to be thought of as the Bride of Christ. Can we wonder that Vincent of Beauvais spoke of Christ's *ferocitas*?]

cording to Plutarch (*Moralia* 353), the Egyptians thought of wine as "the blood of those who had once battled against the gods, and from whom when they had fallen and had been mingled with the earth, they believed vines to have sprung."

As to this last, "barley stalks are Soma stems" (ŚB xii.7.3.13); "barley is Varuṇa" (ŚB xiii.3.8.5),[14] as was Soma tied up before his pressing (TS vi.1.11.2, 5); and brandy (*surā*, fermented liquor prepared from rice and barley) is one of the substances that can be made to be Soma by rites of transubstantiation (ŚB xii.7.3.11). The grains contain the sacrificial essence (*medha*) that had been in Man (*puruṣa*, cf. RV x.90), from which it passed to the horse, etc., and finally into the earth, whence it is regained by digging (cultivation). The grain is threshed, husked, winnowed, and ground. In the kneading and cooking the sacrificial cake (*puroḍasa*) acquires the animal qualities of hair, skin, flesh, bone, and marrow, and "the Man whom they had offered up becomes a mock-man" (*kiṃpuruṣa*).[15] The cake becomes the sacrificial animal, and contains the sacrificial essence of the former animal victims. It can hardly be doubted that, like our "gingerbread men," the cake was made in the shape of a man.[16] The whole procedure is expressly equated with the sacrifice of a living victim; the threshing and grinding are, like the slaying of Vṛtra

[14] For the inauspiciousness of Varuṇa's uncultivated barley ("wild oats") cf. KB v.3 (those who eat of it are Varuṇa's prisoners); RV vii.18.5–10 (the *yavasa* of the unherded kine), and *per contra* the Aryan barley that the liberated kine enjoy, x.27.8.

The agricultural symbolism survives in our word "culture." The rocky ground of the soul must be opened up if it is to yield fruit; and this is a matter of spade-work and sweat. Cf. Philo, *Legum allegoriae*, 1.48 (on Gen. 2:4, 5), Mind as the laborer in the field of sense perception.

[15] Analogous to the mock man (*kimpuruṣa, anaddha-puruṣa*) made "in the place of a man" (Sāyaṇa, *puruṣasthāne*), and no doubt in human form, to represent the chthonic (*purīṣya*) Agni (ŚB vi.3.1.24, 3.3.4, 4.4.14) and "heaped up for to be the sacrificial essence, to be food" (*ciyamāna . . . medhāyety annāyeti*, ŚB vii.5.2.32). The untamed soul is indeed a *kimpuruṣa*, a mockery of the real Man.

[16] The shape of the sacrificial cake may depend on the context. In ŚB iii.8.3.1, the *puroḍāsa* is certainly a round cake, representing a man's head, or rather face, and the Sun's disk; seven other cakes, representing the "seven breaths" (ears, eyes, nostrils, and mouth) are arranged about it to complete it. As these "breaths" are also "glories" (*śriyah*), this is made the basis of the hermeneutic etymology of "head" (*śiras*). Cf. Philo, *De opificio mundi*, 1.29 (κεφαλή . . . ἑπτά χρῆται, δυσὶν ὀφθαλμοῖς, etc.) and 1.33 (πρόσωπον, ἔνθα τῶν αἰσθήσεων ὁ τόπος, etc.) cf. 1.51 (ἐν προσώπῳ τὰς αἰσθήσεις ἐδημιούργει). Philo says that the divine power is infused "by means of the median breath" (διὰ τοῦ μέσου πνεύματος); this median breath is precisely the *madhyamah prāṇah* and *madhye vāmana* of the Āraṇyakas and Upaniṣads.

and Soma, sins requiring expiation; the flour that has been "killed" by the mortar and pestle and millstones is ritually quickened in order that the gods may be given the "living food"[17] they require (ŚB I.1.4.6–I.2.3.9 and AB II.8, 9). ["Verily, living he goes to the gods" (TS V.6.6.4); cf. Rom. 12:1, "present your bodies a living sacrifice."] The traces of the passion of the "Vegetation Spirit" survive in popular[18] agricultural rites all over the world, and notably in the words of the song "John Barleycorn," whose awns, like those of the rice in AB II.9, are his "beard," the mark of his manhood, and who, although they treat him so "barbarously," springs up again.

The polarity of Soma is like Agni's. The Soma when bought and tied up (in the form of a man, to represent the sacrificer himself, ŚB III.3.2.18) is of Varuṇa's nature, and must be made to be a Friend (Mitra) with the words, "Come unto us as the Friend (Mitra) creating firm friendships for pacification" (*śāntyai*, TS VI.1.11, 1.2.7).[19] It must never be forgotten that "Soma was Vṛtra" (ŚB III.4.3.13, III.9.4.2, IV.4.3.4), and it needs no proof here that Vṛtra = Ahi, Pāpman, etc. Accordingly, "Even as Ahi from his inveterated skin, so [from the bruised shoots] streams the yellow rain, prancing like a horse" (RV IX.86.44), "even as Makha thou, Soma, goest prancing to the filter" (RV IX.20.7).[20] "The Sun, indeed, is Indra, and that Moon none but Vṛtra, and on the new-moon night he,

[17] On the "living food" of the gods, cf. Coomaraswamy, "The Sun-kiss," 1941, p. 55, n. 26.

[18] It may be noted that *lokyam* in AB II.9 is *not* "the people's" (Keith), but "conducive to the sacrificer's world," i.e., the "world" (*lokah*) of ŚB X.5.2.12, X.5.4.16; KB VIII.3; BU I.4.15, I.5.17; MU VI.24, etc., i.e., the world of the Self, world of the gods, Brahmaloka, heaven.

Popular agricultural rites are no more, generally speaking, of popular origin than are the narrative forms of folklore. It is a mistake to suppose that scripture ever makes use of "old folklore ideas pressed into its service" (Keith, AĀ, p. 251, n. 5). On the contrary, as Professor Mircea Eliade has very justly observed, "La mémoire collective conserve . . . des symboles archaïques d'essence purement métaphysique. . . . La mémoire populaire conserve surtout les symboles qui se rapportent à des 'théories' même si ces théories ne sont plus comprises" ("Les Livres populaires dans la littérature roumaine," in *Zalmoxis*, II, 1939, p. 78). Cf. Coomaraswamy, "Primitive Mentality" [in Vol. I of this edition—ED.].

[19] See Appendix I.

[20] It is the general rule that the Ādityas have been originally Serpents, and have vanquished Death by the sloughing of their inveterated skins (PB XXV.14.4). Cf. the procession (*udāsarpaṇī*) of the *sarparṣir mantrakṛtah . . . āśiviṣaḥ* Arbuda in AB VI.1; it is curious that just as Soma is strangled with a turban (*uṣṇīṣa*), ŚB III.2.18, so Arbuda (whose glance is baleful) is blindfolded with a turban in AB. On Soma's "prancing" or "playing" (*krīḍā*) cf. Coomaraswamy, "Līlā," 1941 [in this volume—ED.].

Indra, completely destroys him, leaving nothing remaining; when the Sun devours (*grasitvā*) him,[21] he sucks him dry and spits him out (*taṃ nidhīrya nirasyati*); and having been sucked out (*dhītaḥ*), he grows again (*sa punar āpyāyate*); and whoever is a Comprehensor of this [myth or doctrine] in the same way overcomes all Evil (*pāpman*), leaving naught of it remaining" (ŚB I.6.4.13, 19, 20; cf. TS II.5.2.4, 5, JUB I.33.6 [and *vṛtram ahim . . . āvayat*, RV X.113.8]). The stone, in fact, with which Soma is pressed and slain, is identified with the Sun (Āditya Vivasvant, ŚB III.9.4, 8), what is enacted here corresponding to what is done there. And as *in divinis* (*adhidevatam*) and in the ritual mimesis, so "within you" (*adhyātmam*): the powers of the soul (sight, hearing, etc.) that are Brahma's immanent forms are called his "swallow" or "sink" (*giri*); and conversely the Comprehensor of this himself "swallows" or "sinks" (*girati*) the hateful, evil foe (*dviṣantaṃ pāpmānaṃ bhrātṛvyam* = Vṛtra),[22] and "becomes with Self" (*bhavaty ātmanā*), and like Brahma "one whose evil foe is as refuse" (*parāsya*, a thing to be cast out, spat out, rejected or refused, AĀ II.1.8); the cycle is reversed and completed when in sleep (or in *samādhi* or at death) the Breath (*prāṇaḥ*, immanent deity, Sun, Brahma) itself "swallows up" (*jagāra*) the "four great selves,"[23] viz. these same powers of sight, hearing etc. (JUB III.2).

So also in terms of the animal sacrifice offered to Agnīṣomau, who, when they have been united, jointly "overcome the Sacrificer," who is born in debt to Death (ŚB III.6.2.16) and is only redeemed by the actual victim, "or rather [i.e., more truly], they say: 'Unto Agnīṣomau Indra

[21] As Bṛhaspati "eats" (*ādat*) Vala, RV X.68.6. Cf. n. 72.

[22] When Indra casts his bolt "at the evil hateful foe" (*pāpmane dviṣate bhrātṛvyāya*), it is "Vṛtra the Evil One" (*vṛtram pāpmānam*) that he smites (ŚB IV.3.3.5): "brotherhood" expressing "enemy" because the Asuras are the "elder brothers" of the Devas (*jyeṣṭha*, "elder," from √*jya*, to "oppress." We have argued elsewhere (*Spiritual Authority and Temporal Power in the Indian Theory of Government*, 1942, n. 22) that throughout the sacrificial texts the "Enemy" is primarily Vṛtra, Pāpman, Mṛtyu (Buddhist Māra, Pāpivant), and that any application of the formulae to other and human enemies is always secondary; that it is only when the King has overcome his own Devil that he is empowered to overcome other devilish rebels. Keith is clearly right in saying that a magical application of the rites is foreign to the *Ṛg Veda*, but as certainly wrong in saying that "the sacrifice in the Brāhmaṇas is a piece of magic pure and simple" (*Religion and Philosophy of the Veda and Upanishads*, London, 1925, p. 454).

[23] The breaths or powers of the soul are so many "selves" or "persons" (the seeing man, the hearing man, etc.), but act unanimously as the man himself, for or against his real Self, the Breath, their Head and Leader (AĀ II.3.5, 6, III.2.1; JUB IV.7.4; CU VIII.12.4 ff.; Kauṣ. Up. III.2, 8, IV.20), source and last end.

slew Vṛtra'" (TS VI.1.11.5;[24] similarly ŚB III.3.4.21). Thus "ransoming Self by self" (KB XIII.3),[25] "by self he enters into Self" (VS XXXII.11). The like holds good in terms of the supplementary sacrifice of the Cake (*puroḍāsa*), which contains the sacrificial property (*medha*) that was originally in the human victim (ŚB I.1.4.8, 9, III.8.3.1–3).

Or rather, it is not Soma himself, but only his evil (*pāpman*) that is slain (ŚB III.9.4.17, 18).[26] For "Soma is the Regnum" (*kṣatra*, ŚB V.3.5.8); and it is precisely that he may be enthroned, and rule indeed, that he is "slain" (ŚB III.3.2.6). The guilt from which Soma is cleansed is that he oppressed Bṛhaspati, his Purohita, or that he was even capable of thinking of such a thing (ŚB IV.1.2.4); his passion is an assimilation to and a marital reunion with the Sacerdotum. The whole pattern underlies and is reflected in the rites of royal initiation (*rājasūya* = *varuṇa-sava*)—"This man is *your* king, Soma the king of us Brāhmans" (VS X.18). The prince dies that the king may be born of him; there remains no evil, nothing of his Varuṇya nature in the king; it is not himself but his evil that is killed. The beating with sticks (ŚB V.4.4.7) may be compared to the pressing of Soma and to the threshing of grain by which it is separated from the husks. As Indra slew Vṛtra, so the king overcomes his own hateful, evil foe (ŚB V.2.3.7).

In the beginning, Indra overcomes Vṛtra for the sake of Agni and Soma, whom he has swallowed; in the Sacrifice Agni and Soma overcome

[24] Not as Keith renders it (against the Commentary) "*by* Agni and Soma," but *for* them because they are in Vṛtra, from whom they can escape only when Indra makes him yawn (TS II.5.2.3, 4), only when "Indra forced the Engulfer to disgorge, compelled the panting Dānava" (*jigartim indro apajagurānah prati śvasantam dānavam han*, RV V.29.4; cf. VIII.21.11, *śvasantam*, and note √*śvas*, *śus*, in "Śuṣṇa"). Vṛtra is the Sacrifice; it is in the same way that Indra and Agni are brought forth from the Person, the Sacrifice, in RV X.90.13, and that "as from a fire laid with damp fuel . . . so from this great being (*bhūta*, viz. *ātman*) were the Vedas, worlds and all things breathed forth" (*niśvasitam*, BU IV.5.11, MU VI.32; cf. JUB I.47.3, "The All, that is his breathing forth"). Beyond all question the "Great Being" from whom all these things are breathed out is the Vṛtra from whose mouth (when Indra made him yawn) "went forth all gods, all sciences, all glory, all food, all weal," leaving him drained (ŚB I.6.3.15.16); just as Śeṣa (*yad aśiṣyata*, see Appendix 2) = Ātman, so here also Ātman, Mahābhūta = Vṛtra. For just as "Him being One they call by many names" (RV I.164.46, etc.), so the one Urmythos (*bhāvavṛtta*, Genesis) has been told and retold in many ways, and that not only in India, but all over the world where "*in den verschiedenen Kulturen findet man die Dialekte der einen Geistessprache*" (Alfred Jeremias, *Altorientalische Geisteskultur*, Berlin, 1929, foreword).

[25] Cf. Lev. 1:4.

[26] "That the body of sin might be destroyed," Rom. 6:6.

the sacrificer, or rather what in him is of Vṛtra's nature, and so the circle is completed. Thus: Tvaṣṭṛ cast the residue (*yad aśiṣyata*)[27] of the Soma upon his sacrificial Fire, saying, "Wax great as Indra's foe." Then, "whether it was what was falling (*pravaṇam*, lit. 'on the slope')[28] or what was on the Fire (*adhy agneḥ*), that coming into being (*sa sambhavan*, i.e., as Vṛtra) overcame (*abhisamabhavat*) Agni and Soma," and then Vṛtra "waxed" and, as his name implies, "enveloped (*avṛṇot*)" these worlds (TS II.4.12, cf. II.5.2). Whereas in the Sacrifice "they bring forward the Soma (juice), and when he is established in Agni [the *regnum* in the *sacerdotum*], they coexisting (*sambhavantau*) overcome (*abhisambhavataḥ*) the sacrificer[29] [represented by the victim, TS VI.6.9.2, etc.]. Now the initiate (*dīkṣitaḥ*) has been hitherto holding himself in readiness to serve as the sacrificial essence; but (*eva*) in that Agni and Soma receive a victim, that is his redemption. . . . Or, rather [i.e., more truly] they say: 'Indra smote Vṛtra for Agni and Soma.' Inasmuch as the sacrificer offers up a victim to Agni and Soma, it verily becomes 'his Vṛtra-slayer'" (*vārtraghna evāsya sa*, TS VI.1.11.6). The Comprehensor who offers the full and new moon offering does so *with* Indra (TS II.5.4.1); as Indra repelled Vṛtra, the Evil One, by the new moon offering, so does the sacrificer (ŚB VI.2.2.19). "Agni, the Lord of the operation, makes him who has slain his Vṛtra to operate [sacrifice] for a year; thereafter he may sacrifice at will" (TS II.5.4.5). "At will," for when the purpose of the Sacrifice has been accomplished, there is nothing more that

[27] *Yad aśiṣyata* = *śeṣa*, see Appendix 2.

[28] Cf. RV IX.17.1, *pra nimnena*, Sāyaṇa *pravaṇena*.

[29] "The initiate enters the jaws of Agnīṣomau; in that on the fast day he offers a victim to them, this is a redemption of himself" (KB X.3). Similarly, ŚB III.3.4.21 and III.6.3.19, where "the initiated is the oblation offered to the gods" (*havir vā'eṣa devānām bhavati*), i.e., their food, and must redeem himself from Soma, that is to say from Varuṇa's noose (*ibid.*, 20) or curse (III.3.2.2), for Soma was Varunya—in other words, from the jaws of Death into which the sacrificer would be swallowed up at every stage of the sacrifice if he did not in one way or another redeem himself. The Soma sacrifice is a "mysterious rite" (*gambhīram adhvaram*, ŚB III.9.4.5 *adhvara*, lit. "not-a-slaying," "no doubt referring to the nature of the sacrifice, in which the victim is slain but revivified, and the sacrificer would die were he not redeemed). "Such, indeed, are the forests and ravines of the sacrifice (*yajñāranyāni yajña-kṣatrāni* [? for *khātrānī*]) . . . and if any enter into them ignorantly, then hunger and thirst, ill-doers and devils harass them . . but if Comprehensors enter into them, they pass on from one task to another, as from one stream to another, from one refuge to another, and obtain well-being, the world of heaven" (ŚB XII.2.3.12); "dangerous are the ways between heaven and earth" (ŚB II.3.4.37); "the sacrifice is razor-edged, and swiftly he (who sacrifices) becometh holy or he perishes" (*puṇyo vā bhavati pra vā mīyate*, TS II.5.5.6).

must be done; such an one is now a *kāmācārin*, he is no longer under the law but delivered from the law of obedience to that of liberty, and to him it can be safely said, *Lo mai piacere omai prende per duce*. The Buddha no longer makes burnt offering (as he had done in former states of being), he does what he likes (*kāmakāro*, Sn 350) just because he has overcome and dispossessed *his* Vṛtra.

The word *giri* (AĀ II.1.8), rendered above by "swallow" (n.), lends itself to a far-reaching exegesis. Keith translates it by "hiding place" (of Brahma), and in a note says very rightly that "it is called *giri*, because *prāṇa* is swallowed up and hidden by the other senses."[30] In a note on AĀ II.2.1, he adds, "The sun and *prāṇa* are as usual identified, the one being the *adhidaivatam*, the other the *adhyātman* representation. The former attracts the vision, the latter impels the body."[31] It is, in fact, within us that the deity is "hidden" (*guhā nihitam*, *passim*), there that the Vedic *ṛṣayaḥ* sought him by his tracks, there in the heart that the "hidden Sun" (*sūryaṃ gūḷham*, RV V.40.6, etc.) is to be "found." "For this in ourself is hidden (*guhādhyātmam*), these deities (the breaths); but manifest *in divinis*" (*āvir adhidaivatam*, AĀ I.3.3), speech being "manifest" as Agni, vision as the Sun, etc. (AĀ II.1.5, etc.). These are the "two forms of Brahma, the formed (*mūrta*, i.e., visible) and the unformed (*amūrta*) . . . presented (*sat*) and immanent (*tya*),"[32] respectively the visible Sun disk and the eye, and the unseen Persons in the disk and in the eye (BU II.3).

[30] The "other senses" (sight, hearing, etc.) identified with the *giri* of Brahma are extensions or sendings (*prahitāḥ*, AĀ II.1.5 = *hitāḥ*, Upaniṣads *passim*, *guhāśayā nihitāḥ* in Muṇḍ. Up. II.1.8, *prativihitāḥ* in Kauṣ. Up. III.5, and as the *iṣṭāni* of the Ṛṣis are *vihitāni*, RV I.164.15, and the Maruts *hitāḥ* in I.166.3) of the central Breath (*prāṇaḥ*) or Spirit (*ātman*) from which they originate and to which they return. Hence his name of "Gṛtsamada": *gṛtsa*, "greedy," because as *prāṇaḥ* he breathes in, and as *madaḥ*, "pleasure," he breathes out these powers (AĀ II.2.1). That is, God is swallowed up in us when he proceeds, and we in him when he recedes.

[31] "The Sun's body is seen by everyone, its soul by no one. And the same is true of the soul of any other body . . . embracing all the senses of the body, but only knowable by the mind. . . . Soul (as charioteer) drives the Sun about . . . (and) moves us about in all ways," Plato, *Laws* 898D–899A; cf. AV X.8.14, "Him all see with the eye, not all know with the mind"; and for the "chariot" (bodily vehicle), MU II.6, etc.

[32] *Tya* is not "yonder" (Hume); it is the manifested God, the visible Sun that is "yonder"; *tya*, as the following verses show, refers to the transcendent principle that is invisibly in the Sun and within you. Cf. *tyasya* = *mama* in BU I.3.24.

With *giri* (√*gir*, "swallow") compare *gṛha* (√*grah*, "grasp"); both imply enclosures, resorts, a being within something. At the same time, *giri* is "mountain"; and *garta* (from the same root) both "seat" and "grave" (one can be "swallowed up" in either). The semantics is paralleled in Ger. *Berg*, "mountain," and its cognates Eng. *barrow*, (1) "hill" and (2) "burial mound," *burgh*, "town," *borough*, and finally *bury*; cf. Skr. *stūpa*, (1) "top," "height," and (2) burial mound. *We* are then, the "mountain" in which God is "buried," just as a church or a *stūpa*, and the world itself, are His tomb and the "cave"[33] into which He descends for our awakening (MU II.6, *pratibodhanāya*; cf. AV XI.4.15,

[33] Cf. Plato's "cave," and the "cavernous" quality of early traditional architecture, floor, space, and roof corresponding to earth, air, and sky equally in a cavern and in a chamber; cf. *guhā*, "cave," "hiding place," and "hut." Brahma is indeed *guhyam* (KU V.6), the spirit *nihito guhāyam* (KU II.20), "hidden" in us, as a "cave-dweller."

That God is "buried" in us underlies the Vedic metaphor of digging for hidden treasure, and that of mining in MU VI.29. The powers of the soul (τῆς ψυχῆς δυνάμεις, which Hermes calls δαίμονες, *Lib.* XVI.14 ff.) are "elementals" (*bhūtāḥ*), and their concern is with the "elements" (*bhūtāni*) or "ores" (*dhātavaḥ*). *Bhūtāḥ*, "beings," are likewise elves, sprites (spirits), fairies, or dwarfs, who may be either good or evil; it is not without reason that these beings, the Sidhe for example, are so often thought of as living in "fairy mounds"—or when the "little people" are thought of as dwarfs or gnomes, then in mountains. The head and leader of these psychic *Bergleute*, thought of as dwarfs, is himself the immanent Dwarf, Vāmadeva, Vāmana, the "Dwarf enthroned in the midst whom all the gods serve (*madhye vāmanam āsīnam viśve devā upāsate*, KU V.3); the "gods," in accordance with Śaṅkara's inevitable explanation, being the powers of the soul ("vision, etc.," i.e., the "breaths"), bringing tribute (*balim upaharantaḥ*) to their head, the "Other One" of verse 5, who is beyond all question the median "Breath," as is explicit in AĀ II.2.1. Thus the dwarfs and gnomes of the European tradition, digging for treasure in the mountains, are the projected images and trace in folklore of our own elemental powers. In one of our best known *Märchen*, the formulation is very precise: it is the natural function of the "seven dwarfs" to serve and protect Snow White, who is herself Psyche; Snow White is poisoned by the "fruit of the tree," and that this is the tree of good and evil is clear from the fact that the apple is parti-poisonous and parti-wholesome (the fruit of the tree is wholesome for those who eat to live, but deadly for those who live to eat; cf. ŚB II.4.2.1–6). Of themselves the dwarfs can protect but cannot heal her; this is done by the solar hero, a "Prince Charming" (i.e., in the full sense of the word, "enchanting": the solar Hero is the master of enchantment—blessed are those whom this magician enchants), and it is only when the tasted apple falls from her lips that she awakens from her deadly sleep.

In an alternative symbolism, the cave becomes a laboratory and the workers alchemists seeking for the philosopher's stone; or a smithy in which ores are refined and beaten into shape—"as a goldsmith taking a piece of gold draws out of it (*tanute*, √*tan*, also to sacrifice and to propagate) another, newer and fairer form, so the Spirit . . ." (BU IV.4.4).

jinvasyatha). What all this leads to, bearing in mind that both the Maruts and Soma shoots are equated with the "breaths" (ŚB IX.3.1.7, AB III.16, and TS VI.4.4.4), is the probability that *giri* in the *Ṛg Veda*, although translatable by "mountain," is really rather "cave" (*guhā*) than "mountain," and *giriṣṭha* "in the mountain" rather than upon it, and tantamount to *ātmastha* (KU V.12, MU III.2), notably in RV VIII.94.12, where the Marut host is *giriṣṭha*, and IX.85.12 and V.43.4 where Soma and Soma juice (*rasa*) are *giriṣṭha*. Just the same is implied in RV V.85.2, where Varuṇa is said to have put "Counsel in hearts, Agni in the waters, the Sun in the sky, and Soma in the rock" (*adrau*, Sāyaṇa *parvate*).[34] "The

[34] In this context *adrau* is, like the other words *hṛtsu*, etc., a locative of place *in*: in TS VI.1.11, where the text is cited, Keith renders rightly "in the hill." In the same way Soma is "shut up in the rock" (*aśnāpinaddham*, RV X.68.8); and in JUB IV.5.2, *aśnasu somo rājā* is rendered rightly by Oertel "in the stones King Soma." In ŚB III.4.3.13 and III.9.4.2, we are reminded that "Soma was Vṛtra" (= Ahi, described in RV I.32.2 as "having his lair in the mountain," *parvate śiśrayānam*, i.e., in a cave; one recalls that dragons always live in caves, and not on mountaintops), and we are told that "Soma's body ('body' is that *in* which the subject lives) was the mountains and the rocks (*tasyaitaccharīram yad giriyo yad aśmānas*), thence is born that plant called 'Uśānā' (*tad eṣośānā nāmauṣad hir jāyate*), . . . which they collect thence and press" (*tām etad āhṛtyābhiṣunvanti*). We naturally think of plants as growing on mountains, and so they do; but things are *born* from what *contained* them, plants are *in* the earth before they spring up. Sāyaṇa's commentary, moreover, makes it clear that by "mountains" are to be understood "beings" (*soma-śarīra-bhūteṣu . . . atas tām eva girāv utpannām . . . abhiṣunvanti*), i.e., the Soma = *bhūtātman*, as in MU VI.10, cited below; and that the plant that is actually collected is "not really Soma" (*na sākṣāt somam*), but only ritually made to be Soma. Thus Vṛtra (= Vala) is the rock that Indra smites and from which Indra (or Bṛhaspati or both) releases cattle, streams, and all those things that had been covered up and hidden away (*vṛtam = verbergt, verhüllt*, "hilled") in the beginning.

Not only then is *giri* (mountain) to be connected with *gir* to "swallow" (not *gir* to "sing"), but there can be no doubt that Indian hermeneutists connected *aśman* (and doubtless *aśna*) with *aś*, to "eat"; e.g., Mahidhara glosses VS XVII.1 *aśman* by *aśnātīty, aśma*; *he aśman, sarvabhakṣaka agne*. In AV XVIII.4.54 *aśmānnānam adhipatyam jiyāma*, Whitney renders *aśman* by "stone" but Böhtlingk and Roth by "*Esser*." The hermeneutist might in the same way derive *adri* from *ad*, to "eat." I by no means assert that all these hermeneia are etymologically valid; what they nevertheless point to is that early man (the troglodyte) thought of a mountain as a place to live not *on*, but *in*, and as a depository of treasure—a manner of thinking that survives in the concept of the "house" which is not that of a solid mass but that of a "dome" (*dama*) in which things are housed and hidden, and in which, indeed, the owner himself is "swallowed" up when he enters its doorway (*mukham = ostium*), disappearing when he "goes home" (*astam gacchati*) and reappearing when he comes out of doors (*prādur bhavati*). We are such "houses."

Soma oblation . . . is incorporeal" (AB II.14). No wonder that "of him the Brāhmans understand by 'Soma' none ever tastes, none tastes who dwells on earth" (RV x.85.3, 4).

Soma's death is his procession; he is slain in the same sense that every initiand, *homo moriturus*, dies, to be born again. "A man is unborn insofar as he does not sacrifice" (JUB III.14.8), to sacrifice is to be born (KB xv.3), Vṛtra's slaughter is Indra's birth (as Mahendra, ŚB I.6.4.21). The Sacrificer, participating in Soma's passion, is born again of the sacrificial Fire in the sense that "except a man be born again . . ." and "Except a corn of wheat fall into the ground and die . . ." (John 3:3 and 12:24).

We observed that Yama "gave up," or much more literally, "emptied out" (*arirecīt*) his body. In the same way the Person, the One whom the gods make manifold, is said to have been poured out completely, or have been "all emptied out" (*aty aricyata*, RV x.90.5, Sāyaṇa *atirikto'bhūt*); it is often stated that Prajāpati, desiring to be many, and emanating offspring (*prajā sṛṣṭvā*), was emptied out (*riricānaḥ*, ŚB III.9.1.2, and *passim*). In the same way, Vṛtra, in whom the streams had been covered up (RV VII.100.7), and from whom Indra and Viṣṇu win "that by which he is these worlds" (TS II.4.12), is like a leather bottle "drained" (*niṣpītaḥ*)[35] of his contents (ŚB I.6.3.16); just as, conversely, in "sleep" these same powers are "drunk in" (*āpītā bhavanti*) by the Breath (ŚB x.5.2.14–15). That all This (Universe) was in Vṛtra is the very *raison d'être* of the Sacrifice (ŚB v.5.5.1).

All this is reflected in the ritual, as if in a mirror, inversely. Whereas Prajāpati divides himself, pours out his offspring, makes himself many and enters into us in whom he is swallowed up and hidden, so in his turn the sacrificer "draws in (*uddhṛtya*, $\sqrt{}$ *hṛ*) these breaths with Oṃ, and sacrifices them in the Fire without evil" (MU VI.26). As Prajāpati "emanated offspring, and thought himself emptied out" (*riricāno'manyata*), so "the sacrificer as it were emanates offspring and is thereupon emptied out as it were" (*riricāna iva*, TS VI.6.5.1): "With his whole mind, his whole self (*sarveṇevātmanā*), indeed, the initiate (*dīkṣitaḥ*) assembles

[35] As the powers of the soul are "drunk in" (*āpītāḥ*) in ŚB x.5.2.12, when they "enter into" (*apiyanti*, Kauṣ. Up. III.3, etc.) the Breath in "sleep," in *samādhi*, or at death.

The roots *apī* (go in to), *āpī* (drink in), *āp* (possess), *āpyai* (swell) must be very carefully distinguished in all texts having to do with the procession and recession of the powers of the soul; in AV x.8.5, Whitney's Index is certainly wrong in reading *āpitvam*, Lanmann right in reading *apitvam*.

(*sambharati*) and would collect (*saṃ ca jihīrṣati*, √ *hṛ*) the Sacrifice; his self, as it were, is emptied out" (*riricāna ivātmā bhavati*, ŚB III.8.1.2, KB x.3). That the sacrificer thus "collects" (*saṃharati*, √ *hṛ*) himself is the active equivalent on his part of what is done to him by the Spiritual Self itself at death (or in sleep, or in *samādhi*) "when the breaths (*prāṇāḥ*, i.e., *indriyāṇi*, τῆς ψυχῆς δυνάμεις) unite with it (*abhisamāyanti*) and it, taking complete possession of those measures of fire[36] (*etā tejo-mātrāḥ samabhyādadāno*') descends into the heart (*hṛdayam evānvakrāmati*)[37] . . . (and thus) striking down the body, dispelling its ignorance, collects itself (*ātmānaṃ saṃharati*) in order to pass on" (BU IV.4.1, 3);[38] the equivalent on his part of what is done by the departing Breath (*prāṇaḥ*) when it "extracts" (*saṃvṛh*, BU VI.1.13) or "impresses" (*saṃkhid*, CU V.1.2, i.e., "levies") the breaths, as a horse might tear out the pegs by which it is tethered.

This takes place in any case when "the dust returns to the dust as it was: and the spirit unto God who gave it" (Eccl. 12:7).[39] The burning question for us is, "In whom, when I go forth, shall I be going forth? On whose ground shall I be standing?" (Praśna Up. VI.3).[40] Shall I *be collected* or shall I *collect myself*? Shall I be passively repossessed or actively self-possessed? "Whoever departs from this world, not having seen his very own world (*svaṃ lokam adṛṣṭvā*),[41] he unaware of it no more

[36] The breaths or "sense powers" are "fires." Cf. Coomaraswamy, "Measures of Fire" [in this volume—ED.].

[37] As in ŚB x.5.2, where the ἱερὸς γάμος of Indra and Indrāṇī is consummated in the heart. Indrāṇī (Psyche) is the sum of the *indriyāṇi*, as Śacī is the person of Indra's *śacīh*, Śrī the person of many *śriyah*, and in Buddhist contexts Sudhammā = *sudhammā*, cf. Victoria, properly n. pl. of *victor*, but as a person f.

[38] In this whole context (BU IV.4.1–7), it is especially important to bear in mind that He who is the only seer, only hearer, only thinker, only comprehensor in us (BU III.7.23), He who wanders from womb to womb (AV x.8.13), the charioteer who sets us agoing (MU II.6, etc.), is by the same token the only transmigrant; as Śaṅkara puts it, "Of a truth, the Lord is the only transmigrant" (*satyam, neśvarād anyah saṃsārin*, BrSBh I.1.5). Neither in the Brahmanical nor in the Pāli Buddhist texts can any doctrine of the "reincarnation" of an individual be found, except in the sense that a man is reborn in his children.

[39] "The spirit (*akh*) is for heaven, the body (*khet*) for the earth" (K. H. Sethe, "Saqqarah Pyramid Texts," in Margaret A. Murray, *Saqqara Mastabas*, London, 1905, 474): to become this *akh*, or *ka*, at death, is to become a God, an Immortal (A. Moret, *The Nile and Egyptian Civilization*, London, 1927, pp. 169, 182, 183).

[40] Cf. the answers in CU III.14.4, Kauṣ. Up. II.14, and Praśna Up. IV.7, and cf. AV x.8.44. The resurrection is the "birth out of doubt" of ŚB II.2.4.9, and accordingly to faith, JUB III.11.7.

[41] See n. 18, first paragraph.

profits than one might from the Vedas unrecited or a deed undone" (BU I.4.15); whereas, "One who knows that contemplative, ageless, youthful Self has nothing to fear from death" (AV X.8.44).

The relationship of the breaths to the Breath, like that of the Maruts (identified with the breaths in ŚB IX.3.1.7, etc.), is that of subjects (*viśaḥ, svāḥ*) to their king or duke. They are, accordingly, his legitimate "food," he lives *on* them. They are, in fact, his "divisions." As he (Bhagavan), distributing his powers, divides himself (*ātmānaṃ vibhajya, passim*) in them, so are they his devoted supporters (*bhaktāḥ*) in that it is theirs to "support" him, in every sense of the word, but especially inasmuch as it is theirs to render him his "share" (*bhāgam*). This feudal relationship is repeatedly stated in the words "We are thine and thou art ours" (RV VIII.92.32, BU IV.4.37, etc.; cf. Plato, *Laws* 904B). That they "feed" him is constantly stated in the phrase, "they bring him tribute" (*baliṃ haranti* or *bharanti*).[42] In BU VI.1.3, when the superiority of the Breath has been acknowledged, he, addressing the breaths, says, "In that case, pay me tribute" (*me baliṃ kuruta*); each, accordingly, makes acknowledgment that its particular function is not its own, but his; in the case of speech (*vāc*), for example, "That wherein I am the 'worthiest' (f.) (*yad vā ahaṃ vasiṣṭhāsmi*), that 'worthiest' (m.) art thou" (*tvaṃ tad vasiṣṭho'si*).[43] They,

[42] AV X.7.39, *yasmai devāḥ sadā baliṃ haranti*; X.8.15, *mahadyakṣaṃ* (Brahma) . . . *tasmai baliṃ rāṣṭrabhṛto bharanti*; XI.4.19, *prajā imā balim harān*; Kauṣ. Up. II.1, *ayācamānāya* (without his asking) *balim haranti*; JUB IV.23.7, *balim hareyuḥ*; MU VI.18, *pratyāhāra* (= later *devāhāra, amṛta*), as in BG II.58, *yadā samharati indriyānīndriyārthebhyaḥ*.

In the same way, ritually, *bali* offerings are made at Yakṣa shrines, and politically subjects offer tribute.

If the king "plunders" his subjects' cattle (*pecunia*!) it is because what seems to be theirs is really his; just as God plunders us, all of whose great possessions are borrowed from Him (PB XXI.1.1). Therefore "Render unto Caesar the things that are Caesar's and unto God the things that are God's." It is for Caesar as for God to redistribute the "food." The reciprocal relations of the powers of the soul to the Spirit in the individual microcosm and the circulation of money (*pecunia*!) in the political microcosm correspond to that of the "shower of wealth" (*vasor dharā*) in the macrocosm. It is not by demanding tribute and service, but by failing to expend his revenues for his people's good, that a king becomes ungodly, a Vṛtra rather than an Indra.

[43] Vasiṣṭha, the primal Brahman of RV VII.33.11, is regularly Agni; who "abides in beings as speech (*vāc*) in the speaker" (AV II.1.4) and is *in divinis* what speech is in us, just as the Sun is *in divinis* what the power of vision is in us (*passim*). Hence she is Vasiṣṭhā to him as Vasiṣṭha. These traditional correspondences underlie the connection between the tongues of fire and the speaking with tongues in Acts 2:3; see Coomaraswamy, "*Līlā*" [in this volume—ED.].

in other words, ***contribute*** offerings to him that are in reality his ***attributes*** (*ābharaṇa*); they acknowledge that they are "only the names of his acts" (BU I.4.7, cf. I.5.21, I.6.3; BG III.15, etc.).

In TS II.4.12.5, 6 and ŚB I.6.3.17, Vṛtra enters into Indra by agreement. The fire is, indeed, the consumer of food both for gods and men (JUB IV.11.5–7). Or rather, that part of the bisected Vṛtra which was of Soma's nature becomes the Moon, and that part of him which was Asurya (i.e., the ophidian part, the tail) became the belly, "to kindle (*indhīya*) him" and "for his enjoyment (*bhogāya*)," and is in men the tyrannical appetite to which these creatures (*imāḥ prajāḥ*, sc. *prāṇāḥ*, sensitive powers of which the individual is a host) pay tribute (*baliṃ haranti*) whenever they are hungry. So men say that "Vṛtra is within us"; and the Comprehensor of this doctrine, that Vṛtra is the consumer, slays man's enemy, privation or hunger. As to this, one recalls on the one hand that the bowels are of a serpentine aspect and, as it were, headless; and on the other that for Plato, and traditionally, the bowels are the seat of the emotions and appetites.[44] We must, of course, beware of understanding "food" in any restricted sense; in all our texts, "food" is whatever can be desired, whatever nourishes our existence, whatever feeds the fires of life; there are foods for the eye and foods for the mind, and so forth. Vṛtra's fire is the source of our ***voluptas*** when we seek in works of art nothing but an "aesthetic" experience, and of our ***turpis curiositas*** when we "thirst for knowledge" for its own sake. Of the "two birds," one eats, the other oversees but does not eat (RV I.164.20, Muṇḍ. Up. III.1.1, etc.).

Hence, in the significant verses of MU VI.34, "As fire deprived of fuel (*nirindhaḥ*)[45] is extinguished in its own hearth (*svayonāv upaśāmyate*), so when its emotions[46] have been killed (*vṛtti-kṣayāt*) the will is extinguished in its own seat (*cittaṃ svayonāv upaśāmyate*). It is from the love of Truth (*satyakāmatas*) that the mind (*manas*) is extinguished in its own seat; false are the actions and the wantings that haunt (*karmavaśānugāḥ*) one bemused by the objects of the sensitive powers (*indriyārtha-vimūḍhasya*). Transmigration (*saṃsāra*) is nothing but our willing

[44] Hence the necessity for a purgation, katharsis, *śuddha karana*, of the mind (*manas, kratu*, νοῦς) in order to eliminate these waste products.

[45] To have extinguished the fire of life by withholding its fuel becomes a common Buddhist metaphor. In this broader sense, fasting and continence mean far more than mere abstention from concrete foods or sexual acts.

[46] For *citta-vṛtti* I believe that "emotions" is a more accurate rendering than is Woods' "fluctuations." Note that *vṛtti* assimilates the *aśuddham kāmasamparkaṃ manas* (MU VI.34) to the Vṛtra of ŚB I.6.3.9, so called because he was "on the move" (*avartayat*).

(*cittam eva*); purge it (*śodhayet*) carefully, for 'As is one's willing, so one comes to be' (*yac cittas tanmayo bhavati*).[47] . . . The mind is said to be twofold, clean and unclean (*śuddhaṃ cāśuddham eva*); unclean by connection with wanting (*kāma*), clean when dissevered from wanting. . . . 'The mind, indeed, is for human beings (*manuṣyāṇām*) the means alike of bondage and of freedom, of bondage, when attached to objects (*viṣaya*), and of release (*mokṣa*) when detached therefrom.'" And "Hence, for those who do not perform the Agnihotra (do not make burnt-offering), who do not edify the Fire, who do not know and do not contemplate, the recollection of Brahma's empyrean abode is obstructed. So the Fire is to be served with offerings, to be edified, lauded, and contemplated."[48]

[47] Cf. AĀ II.1.3, *karma kṛtam ayam puruṣo brahmaṇo, lokaḥ*, "this Person is what he does, he is the Brahma-world"; BU IV.4.5, *yathākārī yathā cārī tathā bhavati . . . sa yathākāmo bhavati . . . tad abhisampadyate*, "As he (this Person) acts, as he conducts himself, so he becomes; what he wants . . . that he attains"; Plato, *Laws* 904C, "Such as are the trend of our desires and the nature of our souls, just such each of us becomes"; and similarly for Hermes, whose δαίμονες are the innate tendencies or powers and the nature or "fate" of the soul, "the being of a daimon consists in his working" (δαίμονος γὰρ οὐσία ἐνέργεια, *Lib.* XVI.14); a man cannot be and yet be doing nothing, God himself *is* what he does (*Lib.* XI.2.12b, 13a). At the same time, the *act* of being is one of self-knowledge (BU I.4.10); and so "to know and to be are the same" (τὸ γὰρ αὐτὸ νοεῖν ἐστίν τε καὶ εἶναι, Hermann Diels, *Fragmente der Vorsokratiker*, Berlin, 1903, 18B5).

[48] Cf. Muṇḍ. Up. I.2.3. The supposed opposition of the Upaniṣads to the observance of rites is largely a figment of the imagination; and similarly in Buddhism, where the Buddha says that so long as the Vajjians observe their ancient customs "and honor (*sakkaronti*, lit. 'verify'), esteem (*garukaronti*, lit. 'treat as weighty'), respect (*mānenti*) and serve (*pūjenti*) the Vajjian (Yakkha-) shrines within or without the city, and do not withhold the tribute (*balim no parihāpenti*) formerly given and duly rendered, . . . so long may they be expected not to decline, but to prosper" (D II.75).

It is only for those already liberated and already in a "state of grace" that observances are unnecessary, though they may still remain convenient. What is always necessary to liberation is to understand and be fully aware of what one is doing.

"All rites are *rites de passage*. . . . Rite opens the portals through which none may pass but the dead. . . . At each of the crises which usher in the successive phases of great lives, the vital tide rises and falls, first at its ebb in the mystical (*sic*) state of ritual death, then at the moment of annihilation, suddenly at flood, inflowing miraculously to a higher level of life" (Andrew Rugg Gunn, *Osiris and Odin*, London, 1940, pp. 152, 153). For, as Meister Eckhart has said, "He who would be what he ought to be must stop being what he is."

"He is a truly poor man (*sannyāsī*), he is a harnessed man (*yogī*) who does what ought to be done (*kāryam karma karoti*), regardless of consequences; not such is one who kindles no sacred fire and performs no rites" (BG VI.1).

In other words, the appetitive soul, the greedy mind, is the Sacrifice; we, as we are in ourselves, seeking ends of our own, are the appropriate burnt-offering: "The chariot of the gods (i.e., the body born of the Sacrifice) is yoked for the world of heaven, but that of man for wherever his purpose (*artha*) is fixed; the chariot of the gods is the Fire" (TS v.4.10.1, cf. AĀ II.3.8 *fin.*). We see why it is always assumed that the Sacrifice, even of an animal, is a voluntary one; there could be no inner meaning of an unwilling victim.[49] We see what is really accomplished by the heroic Indra (who, be it remembered, is an immanent deity, as the "Person in the right eye," and so *our* real Person) when he "crushes, rends and cuts to pieces Vṛtra's seat (*yoni*) and lair (*āsaya*),[50] and it becomes this offering," and so recovers the Vedas (ŚB v.5.5.4–6). Now as we have already seen, the sacrificer is the oblation (*havis*). He is identified with the *prastara*, which is anointed with the words, "May they (the gods) eat, licking the anointed bird" (VS II.16—"licking," because Agni is their mouth, his flames their tongues), thus "making it a bird and to fly up from the world of men to the world of the gods"; the *prastara* is like "any other corpse," except that it is to be touched with the fingers only, not with sticks (ŚB I.8.3.13–23). The sacrificer's "death" is at the same time his salvation; for the Self is his reward:[51] "They who take part in a

[49] See further above and Appendix I.

[50] "Seat" or "womb," as in MU VI.34.1, 2, cited above; and "lair" (*āśaya*), hardly to be distinguished from "womb" (cf. Pāli *abbuda* = *arbuda*, as "foetus"), that in which the sense powers are *guhāśaya nihitāḥ*, Muṇḍ. Up. II.1.8. It is inasmuch as Varuṇa "lies" (*āśaye*) in them that Varuṇa, like Agni who makes them his seat, knows all the births of the gods, i.e., their births as the powers of the soul and all their workings (RV VIII.41.7). In RV I.32.7, that dissevered Vṛtra's lair is in many places (*purutrā vṛtro aśayad vyāstaḥ*) suggests the Agni of III.55.4 (*vibhṛtaḥ purutrā śaye*): cf. "I am the Spirit, my station in the lair (*āśaya*) of all beings. . . . Ananta am I of snakes" (BG x.20, 29). The cavern (*guhā*) from which the streams and all other living principles are released can be equated with the "bellies of the mountains" in RV I.32.1 and I.54.10. Cf. Isa. 51:1, "Look unto the rock whence ye are hewn, and to the hole of the pit whence ye are digged."

The "Person in the right eye" is regularly equated with "the Person in the Sun," of whom it is said that "He who is yonder, yonder Person in the Sun, I myself am he" (MU VI.35). It is only to my real Self, this "inward Person" (*antaḥ puruṣa*), that the words "That art thou" can be applied; not to "this man" who still knows in the worldly sense who he is, by name and family descent.

[51] Cf. JUB III.11.3, *yad dīkṣate . . . dakṣiṇām abhijāyate*. Any reception of material gifts by Brāhmans participating in a sacrificial session (*sattra*) is condemned in the strongest possible terms (TS VII.2.10.2). Guerdons (*dakṣiṇā*) may and ought to be given only when the priests are sacrificing on behalf of others than themselves (ŚB IV.3.4.5), just as a Christian priest saying a Mass on another's behalf properly receives a fee.

sacrificial session (*sattra*) go to the world of heavenly light. They kindle (vivify) themselves with the initiations and cook (mature) themselves with the sacrificial seances. With two they cut off their hair (except the topknot), with two their skin, with two their blood, with two their flesh, with two their bones, with two their marrow. In the sacrificial session the Self is the guerdon (*ātma-dakṣiṇam*); verily receiving the Self as their guerdon, they go to the world of heaven. They cut off the topknot at last for success (*ṛddhyai*), thinking, 'More quickly may we attain to the world of heaven'" (TS vii.4.9, cf. PB iv.9.19–22, ŚB i.8.3.16–19).[52]

The mortal, psychophysical self (*ātman*) that the sacrificer immolates, whether as above ritually, or when he actually dies and is made an oblation (*āhuti*, AB ii.4; ŚB ii.2.4.8, xii.5.2.13; BU vi.2.14, 15, etc.) in the Fire (the sacrificial rite prefiguring his final resurrection from the Fire), while it acts as a unity (AĀ iii.2.1, JUB iv.7.4, Kauṣ. Up. iii.2, 8) is not one member (cf. 1 Cor. 12:12 ff.) but a compound (*saṃhata*, *saṃdeha*, *sambhūti*, *σύγκριμα*, etc.), or "host of elemental beings" (*bhūtagaṇa*), called "elemental self" (*bhūtātman*) and, as such, distinguished (as in Plato) from "its immortal Self" (*amṛto'syātmā*, *ψυχή ψυχῆs*), the impassible and un-affected Inner Man (*antaḥpuruṣaḥ* = *prajñātman*, solar Self; cf. MU iii.2, 3). In view of what has already been said of the Soma sacrifice, a symbolic self-immolation, it will not now surprise us to find that this passible "elemental self" is identified with Soma (*soma saṃjño'yam bhūtātmā*, MU vi.10). Not, of course, the Soma that "*was* Vṛtra," or Varuṇya, but the Soma that still is Vṛtra, or Varuṇya; not Soma the Friend (*mitra*) but Soma the Titan (*asura*, ŚB xii.6.1.10, 11); not Soma the immortal, but the Soma that is to be pressed and slain and from whom the immortal extract is to be separated out. In MU vi.10 we are, accordingly, further reminded that Soma is the food and Fire the eater [it is with this Fire and not with the Soma that the Sacrificer identifies his Self], and that the Comprehensor of the equation Soma = *bhūtātman* is a truly poor man (*sannyāsī*), a harnessed man (*yogī*), and a "self-sacrificer" (*ātmayājī*), i.e., "one who himself officiates as his own sacrificial priest, as distinguished from the *devayājī*, for whom the sacrifice is

[52] All this corresponds to the removal of the *annamaya* and other "sheaths" (*koṣa*) of Brahma, to the "shaking off of bodies" (JUB i.15.5, iii.30.2, etc.), essential because "no one becomes immortal with the body" (ŚB x.4.3.9). It is symbolized also in the Vaiṣṇava *vastra-haraṇa*. Love reminds us that "across my threshold naked all must pass." This is Philo's "noble nudity" (*ἀρίστη γύμνωσις*, *Legum allegoriae* i.77).

performed by another, notably by the god (Agni, *devayaj*, ŚB *passim*)[53] as missal priest: the Sacrificer's immolation of himself, the "elemental self," is his "self-sacrifice" (*ātmayajña*).

In the same way we shall now be able to understand how in MU vi.35 the powers of the soul are equated with Soma shoots: here "of the Fire that is hidden within the Sky it is but a little measure that is the Water of Life (*amṛtam*) in the midst of the Sun, of which the growing shoots (*āpyay-aṅkurāḥ*)[54] are Soma or the Breaths (*soma prāṇā vā*)." The equation of the breaths with Soma shoots is even more explicit in TS vi.4.4.4, *prāṇā vā aṃśavaḥ*, "the breaths are Soma shoots." Now we have seen that "Soma was Vṛtra," and that he emerges from these shoots "as the Serpent from his skin"; the powers of the soul, the collective soul itself are, then, Vṛtra's "seat and lair" from which the offering (*iṣṭi*) is extracted (ŚB v.5.5.1, 6, cited above). The real Soma sacrifice is the bruising of these shoots, the breaths, the elemental self or soul: "One withdraws (*uddhṛtya*) these breaths (from their objects)[55] and sacrifices them in the Fire" (*prāṇān . . . agnau juhoti*, MU vi.26); "the (immanent) deities[56] are the breaths, mind-born and mind-yoked, in them one

[53] Cf. RV i.142.11, *devān yakṣi, vanaspate*.

[54] This is my own reading of the text, avoiding all emendation.

[55] As in MU vi.19, BG ii.58, iv.27, etc. and in all contemplative practice leading to synthesis (*samādhi*). Cf. Psalms 51:16, 17, "Thou delightest not in burnt offering. The sacrifices of God are a broken spirit."

[56] "All these deities are in me" (JUB i.14.2); "they make their home in me" (ŚB ii.3.2.3); they are neither in heaven nor on earth, but in breathing creatures, i.e., living beings (*prāṇinaḥ*, VS xvii.14). Strictly speaking, Prajāpati's children (his "breath forms" as Sāyaṇa calls them, cf. BU i.5.21 where it is after him Prajāpati, the Breath, and as his forms, *rūpāṇi*, that the powers of the soul are called "breaths") are gods and titans, competing in these worlds for possession of them; the sense organs of speech, scent, hearing, vision, and thought sang for the gods all fruition (*bhogān*) and for themselves whatever was beautiful (*kalyāṇam*), until the titans infected them with evil—that is, whatever is done by any of them informally (*apratirūpam*). Only the Breath remained immune to this infection, and he translates (*atyavahat*) the senses, striking off their evil, their mortality, so that each becomes its macrocosmic equivalent, speech becoming Agni, smell Vāyu, vision the Sun, hearing the Quarters of heaven, mind the Moon. The Breath then shares out the nourishment that it sings for itself (the Breath is the organ-blower, the breaths the Maruts that move in the bodily organ-"pipes, *nāḍyaḥ*," into which they have been "put, *hitāḥ*"), playing the part of host to the breaths that take up their places round about him as a regiment of the "King's Own (*svāḥ*)" that at the same time forms his bodyguard and is fed by him. The Breath is identified with (Agni-) Bṛhaspati-Brahmaṇaspati, i.e., the Spiritual Power in which the Temporal Power inheres (BU i.3, cf. JUB ii.8). It is in this sense that the gods were originally

sacrifices metaphysically" (*prāṇā vai devā, manojātā manoyujas, teṣu parokṣaṃ juhoti*, TS vi.1.4.5, cf. JUB 1.40.3).[57]

"Mind-born and mind-yoked": in the ever-recurrent simile of the chariot,[58] i.e., the bodily vehicle in which the solar spiritual Self takes up its stand as a passenger for so long as the chariot lasts, the sense organs are the steeds and the reins are held by the directing mind (*manas*, νοῦς) on behalf of the passenger; "Savitṛ yokes the gods (*devāḥ* = *prāṇāḥ*) with mind, he impels them (*yuktvāya manasā devān . . . savitā prasuvati tān*, TS iv.1.1)." When the horses willingly obey the rein, the chariot conducts the passenger to his proper destination; but if they pursue their own ends, the natural objects of the senses, and the mind yields to them, the journey ends in disaster (it must be remembered that the mind is "twofold," bound by the senses or independent of them, MU iv.34, cf. Philo, *Legum allegoriae* 1.93). The man whose senses are under control, or "yoked" (*yuktāḥ*, *yujaḥ*), i.e., the yogī, can say accordingly "I yoke myself, like an understanding horse (*svayam ayuji hayo na vidvān*, RV v.46.1)"; which is only another way of referring to those who "offer up all the workings of the senses and the breaths in the Fire of the *yoga* of self-control, kindled by gnosis" (BG iv.27).

It is now also clear why we are told in RV x.85.3–4 that though "they fancy when they crush the plant that they are drinking very Soma;

---

mortal (TS vii.4.2.1, ŚB ii.2.2.8, etc.), and only by Agni's counsels, or by the sacrifice, or by making the *brahma* their own, attained their present dignity (*arahatta*), immortality (*amṛtatva*), and victory (*jiti*), RV vi.7.4, x.63.4, ŚB iii.4.3.15, xi.2.3.6, etc.

[57] That is to say that when the sacrificer, in whom these powers are immanent, ceasing to use them for improper (*apratirūpa*) ends, i.e., the pursuit of pleasure, returns himself with the immanent deities to their source, then "he" becomes an immortal. It is not his personality but his Person that then survives after death, when "we who, in our junction with our bodies are mixtures and have qualities, shall not exist, but shall be brought into the rebirth, by which, becoming joined to incorporeal things, [we] shall become unmixed and without qualities" (Philo, *De cherubim*, 113 ff.). The TS passage sums up in a few words the whole thesis of "self-sacrifice," i.e., the sacrifice of oneself by oneself to one's Self, "this self's immortal Self" (MU iii.2). Whoever will not make this sacrifice is "damned": "Whosoever hath not [possessed his Self], from him shall be taken away even that [self] he hath," Matt. 13:12.

[58] The symbol of the chariot is employed by Plato and the Platonists in exactly the same way. To exhibit the collation in full would require a separate article, but we may point out that the notion of a *yoking* of the senses is conspicuous in Hermes, *Asclepius* 1.5 ff.

yet of him the Brāhmans understand by 'Soma' none ever tastes, none tastes who dwells on earth."[59] The extracted juice is not immediately, not really Soma (Sāyaṇa, *na ca sa sākṣāt somaḥ*). The drinking of Soma, in other words, is a rite of transubstantiation; "it is metaphysically (*parokṣam*) that the Kṣatriya obtains the Soma drinking, it is not immediately (*pratyakṣam* = *sākṣat*) partaken of by him . . . (but only) through the High Priest (*purodhas*), through the initiation (*dīkṣā*), and the ancestral invocation" (*pravara*, implying "apostolic succession"), AB VII.31; cf. ŚB III.6.2.9, where the Soma pressing stones are Initiation (*dikṣā*) and Ardor (*tapas*); "they collect (*āhṛtya*) the plant *uśānā* and press it, and by means of the initiation (*dīkśā*) and the seances (*upasads*, sacrificial sittings-in), by the Tānūnaptra (-covenant) and the 'making to grow' (*āpyāyana*), they make it to be 'Soma'" (ŚB III.4.3.13); "by Faith, the daughter of Sūryā, he makes it (*surā*, brandy, properly the drink of the Asuras and loathsome to Brāhmans) to be Soma juice" (ŚB XII.7.3.11); that which was taken away from Namuci (Vṛtra) by the Aśvins is now drunk as Soma (ŚB XII.8.1.3–5), the "Supreme Offering" (VS XIX.2, ŚB XII.8.2.12).

Such is the significance of what is called the "Subjective Interior Burnt-offering" (*ādhyātmikam āntaram agnihotraḥ*), of which ŚA X.1 ff. affirms that "if one sacrifices, knowing not *this* Agnihotra, it is for him as though he pushed aside the coals and made oblation in the ashes."

The assumption of the Fire is described in ŚB II.2.2.8–20, of which the following is a summary. The gods (*devāḥ*) and titans (*asurāḥ*) were both the children of Prajāpati, both alike devoid-of-any-spiritual-Self (*anātmanaḥ*) and consequently mortal: only Agni was immortal. Both parties set up their sacrificial Fires. The titans performed their rite externally (profanely); but "the gods then set up that Fire in their inward self (*enam . . . antarātman ādadhata*), and having done so became immortal and invincible and overcame their mortal and vincible foes." In the same way now the sacrificer sets up the sacrificial Fire within himself. As to this Fire thus kindled within him he thinks, "herein will I

[59] An explicit warning that the Elixir of Life is not a physical medicine of any kind; it is no more than the *fons vitae* to be found outside ourselves. Cf. AB II.14, ". . . the Soma oblation is one of ambrosia. These oblations are incorporeal (i.e., invisible and intangible); it is with those oblations that are incorporeal that the sacrificer wins immortality."

sacrifice, here do the good work." Nothing can come between him and *this* Fire;[60] "Surely, as long as I live, that Fire that has been set up in my inward self does not die down in me." He feeds that flame who utters right (*satyam*), and more and more becomes his own fiery force (*tejas*); he quenches it who utters wrong (*anṛtam*),[61] and less and less becomes his fiery force. Its service is just "right."

Accordingly, "being about to edify Agni (build up the Fire-altar) the sacrificer apprehends him in himself (*ātmann agniṃ gṛhṇīte*); for it is from himself that he brings him to birth (*ātmano . . . adhijāyate*, ŚB VII.4.1.1)." The true Agnihotra is, in fact, not a rite to be merely performed at fixed seasons, but within you daily,[62] after the primordial pattern of the thirty-six thousand Arka-Fires that were of mental substance and mentally edified by the first sacrificers: "mentally (*manasā*)[63] were they edified, mentally were the cups of Soma drawn, mentally they chanted. . . . These

[60] Cf. AB VII.12, where if anything passes between the sacrificer and his ritual fires he may ignore it, because his fires "have been set up within himself (*ātmany asya hitā bhavanti*)."

[61] For *satyam* (*ṛtam*) and *anṛtam* our words "truth" and "untruth" have a too definitely ethical and empirical significance to be entirely adequate; just as our word "sin" is too ethical to represent what is implied by Sanskrit and Greek terms meaning "incorrect," or more literally, "missing the mark." Properly speaking, "sin," as defined by St. Thomas Aquinas, is "*any* departure from the order to the end," and not merely moral error. *Satyam* and *anṛtam* are nearer to "correct" (*integer*) and "incorrect." In the same way, virtue (*kauśalam*, Pāli *kusalam*), like wisdom (σοφία), is radically "skill"; and the beautiful (*kalyāna*, καλός) not what we like, but whatever is appropriate or "in good form (*pratirūpa*)," as opposed to what is ugly, improper, or more literally "informal (*apratirūpa*)"; nor are these merely "aesthetic" values, for *kalyāna* and *kauśala*, *kusala*, are both opposed to *pāpa*, "evil" or "foul," as in Scholastic philosophy *pulcher* is opposed to *turpis*, whether as "ugly" or as "disgraceful." Only what is correct is effective; and hence the great emphasis laid on the correct, i.e., beautiful, performance of the sacrificial rites, and the necessity for expiation in the case of any error (Brāhmaṇas, *passim*). Whenever the conduct of life is sacramentally envisaged, this perfectionism is carried over into every possible field of doing or making: in the single concept of skill, "prudence" and "art" coincide. "Skilful performance is Yoga (*yogaḥ karmasu kauśalam*, BG II.50)."

[62] Similarly AĀ II.3.8 (the 36,000 days of a man's life), and KU IV.8 (*dive diva iḍyo . . . haviṣmadbhir manuṣyebhir agniḥ*, "The Fire should be served every day with human oblations"). In this sense human sacrifice is essential to salvation.

[63] *Manasā*, "with the mind as instrument" or "mentally," occurs some 80 or more times in RV, frequently in connection with the Sacrifice—e.g., I.172.2, *stomo . . . hṛdā taṣṭau manasā*; II.40.3, *ratham . . . manasā yujyamānam* (cf. V.46.1, *svayam ayuji*); VII.64.4, *gartaṃ manasā takṣat*; VII.67.1, *haviṣmata manasā yajñiyena*; similarly VI.16.4, *havir hṛdā taṣṭam*. We have no reason to suppose that the Sacrifice had ever been a merely mechanical operation.

Fires, indeed, are knowledge-built (*vidyācita eva*); and for the Comprehensor thereof all beings (*sarvāṇi bhūtāni*, all the powers of the soul) build up these Fires, even while he is asleep." And so "by knowledge (*vidyayā*) they ascend to where desires have migrated (*parāgatāḥ*); it is not by guerdons (*dakṣiṇābhiḥ*) nor by ignorant ardour (*avidvaṃsaḥ tapasvinaḥ*) . . . but only to Comprehensors that that world belongs" (ŚB x.5.4.16). This last passage states explicitly what is clearly implied by RV VIII.70.3, cited above.

A distinction is thus clearly drawn between mere performance and the understanding of what is done, performance as such and performance as the support of contemplation; and between an objective performance on stated occasions and a subjective and incessant performance. The first of these distinctions is made again in ŚB x.4.2.31, "Whosoever as a Comprehensor performs this sacred work, or even one who is a Comprehensor (but does not actually perform the rites), puts together again this (divided) Prajāpati, whole and complete" (and therewith at the same time reintegrates himself); and again in ŚB XIII.1.3.22, where the distinction is drawn between those who are merely "seated at a sacrificial session" (*sattrasadaḥ*) and those who are "seated in reality" (*satisadaḥ*), only those who thus sacrifice in truth being "seated amongst the very gods" (*satīsu devatāsu sīdantaḥ*).

The *satisad* is the same as the Ātmayājī referred to above, namely one who is his own priest. The *ātmayājī* is "one who knows, 'this (new) body of mine hath been integrated (*saṃskriyata*), hath been superimposed (*upadhīyate*) by that body (of the Sacrifice)': and even as Ahi from his skin, so does he free himself from this mortal body, from the evil (*pāpmanas*, i.e., from Vṛtra), and as an offering (*āhuti*),[64] as one composed of the Three Vedas, so he passes on to the world of heavenly light. But the Devayājī (for whom another officiates), who merely knows that 'I am sacrificing this (victim) to the gods, I am serving the gods,' is like an inferior who brings tribute to (*baliṃ haret*) a superior . . . he does not win so much of a world" (ŚB XI.2.6.13, 14).[65] The distinction

[64] "Having come into being from Agni, the womb of the gods (cf. JB I.17) from the oblation, with a body of gold (= light, immortality) he proceeds to the world of heavenly light" (AB II.14); and similarly in ŚB XII.2.2.5–6, and many contexts.

[65] Cf. JUB I.14.1, "He should not be one whose gods are far away. Verily, it is insofar as he approaches the gods with himself (*ātmanā devān upāste*, i.e., is an *ātmayājī*) that become gods for him"; and BU I.4.10, "So whoever approaches a deity as being other, thinking 'He is one, and I another,' does not comprehend; he

is of active and passive *viae*, of "salvation" from "liberation." The Ātmayājī is "one who sacrifices in himself" (*ātmann eva yajati*, MU VII.9). "Seeing the Self[66] impartially in all beings and all beings in the Self, the Ātmayājī obtains autonomy" (*svarājyam*, *Mānavadharmaśāstra* XII.91; cf. CU VIII.1.1–6, BG VI.29).

The foregoing interpretation of the Sacrifice as an exhaustive series of symbolic acts to be treated as supports of contemplation (*dhiyālamba*) reflects a traditional assumption that every practice (πρᾶξις) implies and involves a corresponding theory (θεωρία). The observation of ŚB IX.5.1.42 that the building of the Fire (-altar) includes "all kinds of works" (*viśvā karmāṇi*) assimilates the sacrificer to the archetypal sacrificer, Indra, who is preeminently the "All-worker" (*viśvakarmā*). It is just because the Sacrifice, if it is to be correctly performed (and this is quite indispensable), demands the skilled cooperation of all kinds of artists, that it necessarily determines the form of the whole social structure. And this means that in a completely traditional society there is no real distinction of sacred from profane operations; rather, as the late A. M. Hocart expressed it, "chaque occupation est un sacerdoce";[67] and it is a consequence that in such societies, "the needs of the body and the soul are satisfied together."[68] In view of this, it will not surprise us to find what in any investigation of the "caste system" must never be overlooked, namely, that the primary application and reference of the verb *kṛ* (*creo*, κραίνω), to do or make, and the noun *karma*, action or making, is to sacrificial operation (cf. Grassmann, s.vv., *insbesondere, opfern, Opferwerk*; and Lat. *operari* = *sacra facere*). It will be as true of every agent as it is for the king that whatever he does of himself, unsupported by any spiritual reason, will be to all intents and purposes "a thing not done" (*akṛtam*). What might otherwise seem to our secular eyes a revolutionary principle, viz. that the true Sacrifice ("making sacred," ἱεροποία) is to be performed daily and hourly in each and every one of our func-

---

is a mere victim for them." Similarly Meister Eckhart, "Some there are so simple as to think of God as if He dwelt *there*, and of themselves as being *here*. It is not so, God and I are one" (Pfeiffer ed., p. 206).

[66] The solar Self of RV I.115.1 and AV X.8.44.

[67] *Les Castes*, Paris, 1938, p. 27.

[68] R. R. Schmidt, *Dawn of the Human Mind*, London, 1936, p. 167. That manufacture should serve the needs of body and soul at one and the same time was also Plato's demand; and wherever there is not this intention, man is attempting to live an atrophied existence, by "bread alone."

tionings—*teṣu parokṣaṃ juhoti*, TS vi.1.4.5—is really implicit in the concept of action (*karma*) itself; it is, in fact, only *inaction*, what is *not* done, that can be thought of as unholy, and this is explicit in the sinister meaning of the word *kṛtyā*, "potentiality" personified; the perfect man is "one who has done what there is to do" (*kṛtakṛtyaḥ*), the Arhat *kataṃ karaṇiyam*. The sacrificial interpretation of the whole of life itself, the *karma mārga* doctrine of the *Bhagavad Gītā*, is implicit in texts already cited, and explicit in many others, e.g., JUB iv.2, where the man is the Sacrifice, and his breaths, the powers of the soul, acting as Vasus, Rudras, and Ādityas, carry out the morning, midday, and evening pressings (i.e., the Soma sacrifice) during his first 24, second 44, and last 48 years of a life of 116 years. Similarly CU iii.16, followed by iii.17, where privation is equated with initiation, enjoyments with the sacrificial sessions and chantings, the virtues with the guerdons, generation with regeneration, and death with the last ritual ablution. In the same way in the "thousand years" operation of the all-emanating (*viśvasṛjaḥ*) deities, "Death is the slayer" (*śamitṛ*, PB xxv.18.4), who *dispatches* the resurrected victim to the gods.[69]

In Kauṣ. Up. ii.5, in Hume's version appropriately entitled "A person's entire life symbolically a Soma-sacrifice," it is affirmed with respect to the Interior Burnt-offering (*āntaram agnihotra*) that our very breathings in and out (*prāṇāpānau*: the two primary breaths or lives, which include and represent all those of sight, hearing, thought, and speech, etc., AĀ ii.3.3) "are two endless ambrosial oblations (*nante amṛtāhutī*) that whether waking or sleeping one offers up (*juhoti*) continuously and without a break; and whatever other oblations there are, have an end (*antavatyas tāḥ*), for they amount to no more than activity as such (*karmmamayo hi bhavanti*). And verily the Comprehensors thereof in former time abstained from making actual burnt offerings (*agnihotraṃ na juhuvāṃ cakruḥ*)." It is from the same point of view that the Buddha, who found and followed the ancient Way of the former Fully Awakened (S ii.106, etc.) and expressly denies that he taught a doctrine of his own invention (M i.77), pronounces: "I pile no wood for altar fires; I kindle a flame within me (*ajjhatam* = *adhyātmikam*), the heart the hearth, the flame thereon the dominated self" (*attā sudantā*, S i.169; i.e., *saccena danto*, S i.168 = *satyena dantaḥ*). We have seen already that one who has slain his Vṛtra, i.e., dominated self, and is thus a true autocrat (*sva-*

[69] On the "happy dispatch," cf. Appendix 1.

rāj), is liberated from the law according to which the Sacrifice is factually performed (TS II.5.4.5); and in the same way in AĀ III.2.6, the Kāvaṣeyas who (as in Kauṣ. Up. II.5, cf. BG IV.29) sacrifice the incoming breath when they speak and the outgoing breath when they remain silent, ask: "To what end should we recite the Veda (cf. BG II.46), to what end should we sacrifice externally)?"[70]

In the sacrificial interpretation of life, acts of all kinds are reduced to their paradigms and archetypes, and so referred to Him from whom all action stems; when the "notion that I am the doer" (*ahaṃkāra, karto'ham asmīti*) has been overcome, and acts are no longer "ours," when we are no longer any one (*vivo autem, jam non ego sed Christus in me*, Gal. 2:20), then we are no longer "under the law," and what is done can no more affect our essence than it can His whose organs we are. It is in this sense only, and not by vainly trying to do nothing, that the causal chain of fate (*karma* with its *phalāni*) can be "broken"; not by any miraculous interference with the operation of mediate causes, but because "we" are no longer part and parcel of them. The reference of all activities to their archetypes (essentially a *reductio artium ad theologiam*) is what we ought to mean when we speak of "rationalizing" our conduct; if we cannot give a true account (ratio, λόγος) of ourselves and our doings it will mean that our actions have been "as you like it (*vṛthā*)," reckless (*asaṃkhyānam*) and informal (*apratirūpam*) rather than to the point (*sādhu*) and in good form (*pratirūpam*).[71]

For one who has completely realized the sacrificial implications of every action, one who is leading not a life of his own in this world but a transubstantiated life, there are no compulsory forms. This must not be understood to mean that he must adopt the role of a nonconformist, a "must" that would be altogether incompatible with the concept of "freedom." If, in the last analysis, the Sacrifice is a mental operation even for the *Ṛg Veda*, where the ritual acts are mentally performed (*manasā, passim*) but it is not to be inferred that there is no manual procedure, it is also true that an emphasis on the ultimate inwardness of the Burnt-offering by no

[70] It is, no doubt, in their character as nonsacrificers that the Kāvaṣeyas of RV VII.18.2 are enemies of Indra, whose very *raison de devenir* is sacrificial operation. They have, by their repudiation of the divine activity and imitation of the divine idleness, become again Asuras, and are no longer the loyal subjects of the king of this world.

[71] Cf. notes 56 and 61. Right offering is whatever is neither excessive nor defective in the Sacrifice (ŚB XI.2.3.9).

means necessarily involves a disparagement of the physical acts that are the supports of contemplation. The priority of the contemplative does not destroy the real validity of the active life, just as in art the primacy of the free and imaginative *actus primus* does not remove the utility of the manual *actus secundus*. In the *karma mārga*, *karma* retains, as we have seen, its sacrificial implications. A mere and ignorant performance of the rites had always been regarded as insufficient (*na karmaṇā . . . na yajñaiḥ*, RV VIII.70.3). If the *karma* of the *Bhagavad Gītā* is essentially (*svabhāvaniyatam*, XVIII.47 = κατὰ φύσιν) a work to which one is called by one's own nature or nativity, this had been equally true in the Vedic period when the sacrificial operation involved "all kinds of works" and the acts of the carpenter, doctor, fletcher, and priest had all been regarded as ritual "operations (*vratāni*)." And so as BG IV.15, reminding us of several contexts cited above, affirms and enjoins, "Understanding this, the sacrificial work was performed even by the ancients desirous of liberation (*kṛtaṃ karma pūrvair api mumukṣubhiḥ*); so do thou do work (*kuru karma*) even as by the ancients of old it was done." It is true that, as the Vedānta consistently maintains, man's last end is unattainable by any means, whether sacrificial or moral, but it is never forgotten that means are dispositive to that end: "This Spiritual Self is not to be taken hold of (*labhyaḥ*) by the weak, nor in arrogance, nor by ardor without its countersign (of poverty); but he who being a Comprehensor labors (*yatate*) with these means (*upāya*), that Self dwells in Brahma-home" (Muṇḍ. Up. III.2.4).

We have seen that the conquest of Ahi-Vṛtra, the slaying and eating[72] of the Dragon, is nothing but the domination of the self by the Self; and that the Burnt-offering is the symbol and should be the fact of this conquest. "He who makes the Burnt-offering (*agnihotram*) tears up the snare of greed, cuts down delusion and disparages anger" (MU VI.38); and so, "transcending the elemental powers and their objects . . . he whose bowstring is his solitary life[73] and whose arrow is his lack of the conceit

[72] The eucharistic meal is of extreme importance in the Sacrifice. The essential and only indispensable part of the victim is the heart, for this is the mind, the life-breath and the "very self" of the victim; it is basted with *ghī* on a spit, and so made to be that living food of which the gods partake. In the Edda, Sigurd understands the language of birds ("angels," cf. René Guénon, "*La Langue des oiseaux*," *Voile d'Isis*, XXXVI, 1931) when he tastes of Fafnir's heart.

[73] The *parivrājaka's* quest (a Grail quest, like that of the Vedic *ṛṣayaḥ*) is strictly analogous to that of the knight errant and to that of the solar hero in our fairy tales. There must be no looking back (ŚB XII.5.2.15).

of self-existence,[74] fells the keeper of the first of Brahma's palace-gates, whose crown is delusion . . . and who slays all these beings with the arrow of wishful thinking," and may enter Brahma's palace, whence he can look down upon the revolving wheel as may the charioteer upon the turning wheels of his vehicle; "but for one who is smitten and enflamed by darkness and passion, a body-dweller attached to son or wife or kindred, no, never at all!" (Kauṣ. Up. 1.4 and MU VI.28).[75] This "keeper" is assuredly the Dragon on the Hero's path and the Guardian of the Tree of Life; in other words, the Death that every Solar Hero must overcome. We hope to show elsewhere that Indra's defeat of Ahi-Vṛtra and the Bodhisatta's conquest of Māra are relations of one and the same universal mythos. Here we have only proposed to emphasize that the Dragon, or Giant—by whatever name, whether we call him Ahi, Vṛtra, Soma, Prajāpati or Puruṣa, or Osiris or Dionysos or Ymir—is always himself the Sacrifice, the sacrificial victim; and that the Sacrificer, whether divine or human, is always himself this victim, or else has made no real sacrifice.

In sacrificing himself in the beginning, the Solar Hero, having been single, makes himself—or is made to be—many for the sake of those into whom he must enter if they are to find their Way "from darkness to light, death to immortality" (BU 1.3.28). He divides himself, and "Except ye eat the flesh of the Son of man, and drink his blood, ye have no life in you" (John 6:53); and as we have seen, he is swallowed up in us, like a buried treasure. In this cosmic crucifixion the Sacrifice is "extended"; and insofar as we think and act in terms of the pairs of opposites, think of him in the noumenal and phenomenal aspect under which he enters into the world (ŚB XI.2.3.4, 5), we "crucify him daily." If his sacrifice is an act of grace, and it is because of his love (*preṇā*) for his offspring that he enters into them (TS V.5.2.1) in whom as only Saṃsārin (BrSBh 1.1.5) he submits to repeated deaths (JUB III.11.1 ff., cf. RV X.72.9), it is, on the other hand, a murder that is committed by whoever, human or divine, sacrifices another; the slaying and dismem-

[74] Cf. Mund. Up. II.2.3, where the arrow is oneself, Brahma the target. ["Such a blind shot with the sharp dart of longing love may never fail of the prick, which is God," *Epistle of Discretion*, by the author of the *Cloud of Unknowing* (cf. Edmund Gardner, ed., *The Cell of Self-knowledge*, London, 1910, for text of the Epistle).]

[75] "If any man come to me, and hate not his father and mother, and wife, and children, and brethren, and sisters, yea, and his own life (ψυχή, soul) also, he cannot be my disciple" (Luke 14:26).

berment of Vṛtra is, in fact, on Indra's part an original sin (*kilbiṣa*) because of which he is often excluded from the Soma drinking, and for which atonement must be made (TS II.5.3.6, AB VII.31, KB XV.3; cf. ŚB I.2.3, III.9.4.17, XII.6.1.40, etc.).[76]

"We" are aggregates of the functional powers that are the offspring (*prajāḥ*) of Prajāpati (Brahma, Ātman, Prāṇa, Sun) and the names of his acts; it is the universal Self that operates in each of our many selves, seeing, thinking, etc., into which it is divided; it is this Self that collects itself when we die, and that passes on to other habitations, the nature of which is predetermined by its own former activities. Whether or not "we" survive this passage will depend upon whether our consciousness of being—not to be confused with our "waking" powers of perception, of which nothing survives the transition[77]—is in him, or in "ourselves." It remains, however, for this Wanderer, and for us if we have known him and not merely ourselves, to "collect himself" once and for all and to return from this round of becomings to himself; having been many, he must again become one; having died again and again, he must be resurrected once and for all. The second phase of the Sacrifice, then, and from our present position in the manifold the most essential part of it, consists in the putting together (*saṃdhā*) again of what had been dismembered, and the building up (*saṃskṛ*) of another and unitary Self that shall be our Self when this present self is no more. This unification and "coming into one's own" is at once a death, a rebirth, an assimilation, and a marriage.

We must not, however, suppose that "we" are the heroes of this cosmic drama: there is but One Hero. It is the God that "fetters himself by himself like a bird in the net" laid by the huntsman Death, and the God that breaks out of the snare,[78] or, otherwise stated, crosses over the torrent of life and death to its further shore by the bridge that is made of his own Spirit, or as one climbing reaches the top of the tree to rest on his eyrie or soar at will. He, and not this man So-and-so, is my Self, and it is not by any acts of "mine," but only by knowing Him (in the sense that knowing and being are one), by knowing Who we are that "we"

[76] Just as in the slaying of Soma, Mitra does a "cruel deed" (TS VI.4.8.1).

[77] "After death there is no consciousness" (*na pretya saṃjñāsti*, BU II.4.12): "the dead know not anything" (Eccl. 9:5).

[78] "Liberation is for the Gods, *not for man*" (A. H. Gebhard-L'Estrange, *The Tradition of Silence in Myth and Legend*, Boston, 1940, p. 7). In the Philosophia Perennis, this is as strictly orthodox as Śaṅkara's "Verily, there is no other transmigrant than the Lord" (BrSBh I.1.5).

can be set free. That is why all traditions have insisted upon the primary necessity of self-knowledge: not in the modern psychologist's sense, but in that of the question "Which self?" that of the oracle "Know thyself," and that of the words *Si ignoras te, egredere*. "By the Self one findeth manhood, by comprehension findeth immortality; great is the destruction if one hath not found Him here and now! (*ātmanā vindate vīryaṃ, vidyayā vindate'mṛtam . . . na ced ihā'vedīn mahatī vinaṣṭiḥ*, JUB IV.19.4, 5)." "With himself he indwells the Self, who is a Comprehensor thereof" (*saṃviśaty ātmanātmānaṃ ya evaṃ veda*, VS XXXII.11). "What thou, Agni, art, that may I be!" (TS I.5.7.6).

Appendix 1: On Peace

"What is the best thing of all for a man,
that he may ask from the gods?"
"That he may be always at peace with himself."
Contest of Homer and Hesiod, 320.

Soma's "pacification" is his *quietus* as a Varuṇya principle. Cf. TS II.1.9.2, where by means of Mitra the priest "pacifies" (*śamayati*) Varuṇa, and thus frees the sacrificer from Varuṇa's noose; and TS V.5.10.5, where the dangerous deities might suck in (*dhyāyeyuḥ*) the sacrificer and he "appeases" (*śamayati*) them with the oblations. The ritual slayer is a *śamitṛ*, one who gives the quietus (RV V.43.4, ŚB III.8.3.4, etc.). In the same way, the sacrifice of the Christian victim is for atonement, to make peace with the angry Father. And while appeasement implies a satisfaction or gratification of the person appeased, it must never be overlooked that peace (*śānti*) can never be made with an enemy; in one way or another he must be put to death as an enemy (although "it is his evil, not himself that they slay") before he can be made a friend of. So when the will is pacified (*upaśāmyate*, MU VI.34) it is "stilled," and when the psychophysical self is "conquered and pacified (*jita . . . praśāntaḥ*, BG VI.7)" by the Supreme Self, it has been sacrificed. Desire cannot survive the attainment of its object; only the "dead" who do not desire, because their desire is realized, are at peace, and hence the frequent association of the words *akāma* (without desire) and *āptakāma* (with desire attained), e.g., BU IV.3.21 and IV.4.6.

There is similarly in Lat. *pax* a sinister significance (well seen in the case of imperalistic wars of "pacification"); the connections of the word are with *pangere*, *paciscor*, and Skr. *pāśa*, "fetter," esp. of Death. Eng. dispatch (esp. in the sense to "kill") contains the same root; the victim's is a "happy dispatch" precisely because he is released or unleashed from the fetter or penalty imposed by the Law. A treaty of peace is a thing *imposed* (primary sense of *pangere*) on an enemy: it is only insofar as the enemy, presumed a rebel (the war being just and the victory that of right rather than might, as is assumed in all traditional ordeals including those of single or other combat), repents and willingly submits to the bonds into which he enters, that the "peace" is really an "agreement," the *śānti* a *saṃjñāna*, and that is why the "consent" of the sacrificial victim is always secured; cf. ŚB xiii.2.8.2, where that "they make it consent (*saṃjñāpayanti*) means that they kill the victim." In this case the "enemy" is really resurrected as a "friend"; or in other words, it is not himself but his evil that is "killed."

There is thus a kind of peace (which I have elsewhere called "internecine") that can be only too easily understood; but also another "that passeth all understanding." It is only the peace by agreement that is real and that can endure; and it is for this reason that Gandhi would rather see the English relinquish, i.e., sacrifice, their hold on India of their own free will than see them compelled to do so by force. The same applies to the holy war of the Spirit with the carnal soul; if there is to be "unity in the bond of peace" (Eph. 4:3), the soul must have "put *itself* to death," and not simply have been suppressed by *force majeure* of violent asceticism and penances. And similarly in the case of the "war of the sexes," which is only a special case of war of the Spirit with the Soul.

Appendix 2: Śesa, Ananta, Anantaram

TS ii.4.12, *yad aśiṣyata* = RV i.28.9, *ucchiṣṭam*, not the "dregs" of Soma, but what is "left" when the Soma has been extracted from the now dry twigs or husks. In this inexhaustible *ucchiṣṭam* (as in Vṛtra) all things are contained (AV xi.7), "everything is synthesized within it (*ucchiṣṭe . . . viśvam antaḥ samāhitam*, AV xi.7.1)"; "plenum is That (Brahma), plenum This (All), when plenum is out-turned (*udacyate*) from plenum, (e.g., This All from Vṛtra) plenum remains" (*avaśiṣyate*, BU v.5), ". . . yea, That may we know today whence This was poured out" (*uto tad adya vidhyāma yatas tat parisicyate*, AV x.8.29; Whitney's "that . . . whence that" for *tad . . . yatas tat* betrays the literal and the logical sense). Brahma, in other words, is infinite (*anantaram*), the *brahma-yoni* inexhaustible.

Yad aśiṣyata = Śeṣa, i.e., Ananta, the World Serpent, the Swallower in whom all possibilities whatever are latent and from whom all possibilities of manifestation are extracted; and this endless (*ananta*) circle is precisely that of Midgardsworm (*Gylfiginning*, 46–48) [see *Edda Snorra Sturlusonar með Skáldatali*, ed. Guðni Jónsson (Reykjavik, 1935)—ED.], that of "der Schlange, die sich in den eigenen Schwanz beisst, [und die] stellt den Äon dar" (Alfred Jeremias, *Der Antichrist in Geschichte und Gegenwart*, Leipzig, 1930, p. 5), that of Agni "footless and headless, hiding both his ends (*apād aśīrṣā guhamāno antā*) when first born in the region's ground (*budhne rajasaḥ*, i.e., as Ahi Budhnya), from his womb (*asya yonau*, RV IV.1.11; cf. x.79.2, *guhā śiro nihitaṃ ṛdhag akṣī*)," Prajāpati "sightless, headless, recumbent (*apaśyam amukhaṃ śayānam*, JUB III.38)," Vṛtra-Kumāra "handles and footless (*ahastam . . . apādam*, RV x.30.8)." In the same way Brahma "was the one and only Endless (*eko'nantaḥ*, MU VI.17)," Brahma has no ends (*anto nāsti yad brahma*, TS VII.3.1.4), "footless he came into being erst (*apād agre samabhavat*, AV x.8.21),"[79] "as an Asura (*so'gre asurābhavat*)": he (Akṣara) is a "blind (-worm) and deaf (-adder) having no interval (*acakṣuṣkam aśrotram . . . anantaram*, BU III.8.8)"; "both blind and deaf, without hands or feet (*acakṣuḥśrotraṃ tad apāṇy apādaṃ . . . bhūtayonim*, Muṇḍ. Up. I.2.6)"; the "endless (*anantam*)" Chant is like a necklace "of which the ends come together (*samantam*)," a serpent constricting its coils (*bhogān samāhṛtya*, meaning also "assembling its enjoyments"), and the Year,[80]

[79] Cf. "Inasmuch as he came into being footless (*apād*), he (Vṛtra) was the Serpent (Ahi)," ŚB I.6.3.9. The Commentary on AV IV.6.1 equates the prime-born Brahma, who drank the Soma and made its poison harmless, with Takṣaka (Śeṣa).

AV IV.6.3 makes Garutman the first drinker of the poison. This Garutman is probably that one of the two Suparṇā of RV I.164.20 that eats of the fruit of the tree; there may be a real connection of *viṣa*, poison, and *viṣaya*, object of perception. In any case these legends are perhaps the prototypes for the Puranic myth of Śiva's drinking of the poison produced at the Churning of the Ocean.

[80] Cf. AV x.8.12, "Ending, indeed, but endless inasmuch as his (Brahma-Prajāpati's) ends are united," or "finite, indeed, but infinite because of confinity (*anantam . . . antavac cā samante*); these two (ends, confines) the Keeper of the Vault, comprehending what hath been and shall be (*bhūtam uta bhavyam*) thereof, goes on distinguishing (*carati vicinvan*)." This is the "entering in of time from

"endless" because its two ends, Winter and Spring, are united (*saṃdhataḥ*, JUB I.35.7 ff.). The Buddha is "footless (*apadam*, Dh 179)," like Māra (A IV.434, M I.180).

"What is the beginning, that is the end" (Keith), or rather "He who is the coming forth is also the returning (*yo hy eva prabhavaḥ sa evāpyayaḥ*, AĀ III.2.6; cf. KU VI.11, Maṇḍ. Up. 6, and BG XVIII.16)." "His before and after are the same" (*yad asya pūrvam aparam tad asya*, AB III.43); in other words, "He is fontal and inflowing" (Eckhart), his departure when we end is "the flight of the alone to the alone" (Plotinus). And accordingly "That" is what remains there (*atra pariśiṣyate*) when the body-dweller (*dehinaḥ*, not my "soul" but my Self) is untied and liberated from the body (KU V.4); what then remains over (*atiśiṣyate*) is the immortal Self (*ātman*, CU VIII.1.4–5). As it is in and as this Self that the Comprehensor is reborn from the pyre, the "transcendent residue (*atiśeṣa*)" is the analogue there of the "residue (*śeṣa*)" that he leaves behind him *here* to inherit the character from which, as *brahmavit* and *brahmabhūta*, he has now been released from mortal manifestation to immortal essence without distinction of *apara* from *para brahma*. Therefore the Serpent (*nāga*) is the interpretation (*nirvacanam*) of the "religious whose issues have ceased (*khīṇāsava bhikkhu*, M I.142–45)": as is Brahma *akṣara*. "The last step to fare without feet"; "in me is no I and no we, I am naught, without head without feet" (Rūmī, *Dīvān*, pp. 137, 295). Thus "we are brought face to face with the astounding fact [less astounding, perhaps, in view of what has been said above] that Zeus, father of gods and men, is figured by his worshippers as a snake," and the correlative fact that "all over Greece the dead hero was worshipped in snake form and addressed by euphemistic titles akin to that of Meilichios" (Jane Harrison, *Prolegomena to the Study of the Greek Religion*, Cambridge, 1922, pp. 18, 20, 325 ff.).[81] God is the undying, or rather ever renascent Serpent, with whom every Solar Hero must do battle, and to whom in turn the Hero is assimilated when he tastes of the great antagonist's flesh and blood. We take this opportunity to call attention to the Story of King Karade in the "Alsatian Parzival,"[82] a legend

the halls of the outer heaven," the bisection or decapitation of Makha-Vṛtra, the "act of creation," and the first act of the Sacrifice of which the last end is to reunite the "head" with the "body."

[81] The "beards" of the Greek snakes perhaps represent the "spectacle marks" of a cobra.

[82] Cf. E. K. Heller, "The Story of the Sorcerer's Serpent," *Speculum*, XV (1940), 338 ff., and literature there cited.

that recalls in more than one detail the Indian versions of the enmities of Indra and Vṛtra. In the Karade story, the sorcerer Elyafres, who himself performs the Green Knight's feat, allowing himself to be decapitated and later reappearing uninjured, is the Queen's lover and the natural father of the King's supposed son Karados. Elyafres has been decapitated by Karados, and when he reappears at the end of a year to return blow for blow, in place of any physical blow he reveals to Karados his true paternity. Karados, however, takes the side of his legal father. The Queen then persuades Elyafres to create a serpent, to be the destroyer of Karados, just as Vṛtra is created to be Indra's mortal enemy, with the same result in both cases, the intended victor becoming either directly or indirectly itself the sufferer. The serpent winds itself about Karados' arm, and cannot be undone. Karados is only saved by his betrothed, Guingenier, and her brother; Guingenier exposes her breast to the serpent's gaze, and when it extends itself towards her, the brother cuts it to pieces. We shall not attempt to analyze the whole of this most interesting myth here, but point out that the sorcerer Elyafres corresponds to Tvaṣṭṛ, the Māyin; Karados to Indra, who is Tvaṣṭṛ's son and enemy as Karados is Elyafres'; the serpent to Ahi-Vṛtra; and that the motif of the coils corresponds to the event as related in TS v.4.5.4, where Vṛtra "ties up Indra in sixteen coils (*soḍaśabhir bhogair asinät*)." From these coils Indra can only be freed by Agni, who burns them. In the Indian mythology, Agni is Indra's brother; in the Karade story, it is not, indeed, the hero's brother, but it is his brother-in-law that destroys the serpent.

Appendix 3: Nakula: Ὀφιομάχης

In AV vi.139.6, we find a love charm, "as the mongoose, having cut to pieces a snake, puts it together again, so do thou, herb of virility, put together again what of love was cut to pieces (*yathā naku̧lo vichidya saṃdadhāti ahim punaḥ, eva . . .*)." The mongoose is, indeed, a killer of snakes, an *ahihan*, but it has not been recorded by naturalists that it can put them together again. Perhaps we should have said, "as the Mongoose, having cut Ahi (-Vṛtra) to pieces, puts him together again." In order to solve this riddle, we shall go far afield before returning to it.

In Lev. 11:22, the word *ḥargal*, one of four creatures presumed to be insects and permitted to be used as food, is rendered in the Revised

Version by "beetle" and in the Septuagint by ὀφιομάχης, lit. "snake-fighter." Philo (*De opificio mundi* 1.39) says that "this is an animal (ἑρπετόν)[83] having legs above its feet, with which it springs from the ground and lifts itself into the air like a grasshopper." This is a fair description of the behavior of a mongoose or ichneumon in the presence of a snake, and is also justified by the derivation of *ḥargal* from √ *ḥarag*, to leap suddenly; that is what a mongoose does when struck at by a snake, thus avoiding the blow; in any case the Hebrews did not eat beetles, but might eat quadrupeds "which have legs above their feet, to leap withal upon the earth" (Lev. 11:21), i.e., having legs long enough to do so, and there is nothing in the text of vv.21, 22 to show that all four of the creatures listed in v.22 must have been insects. However, we shall not say anything more about *ḥargal*, as it is sufficient for our purpose that it is rendered in the Septuagint, which Philo follows, by ὀφιομάχης, and in the Vulgate by *ophiomachus*.

According to Hesychius, ὀφιομάχης is ἰχνεύμων, and also a kind of wingless locust. This ambiguity can be explained by the fact that there is an "ichneumon fly," a kind of wasp, doubtless so called because it lays its eggs in caterpillars and so kills them,[84] and hence might be called a "snake killer" if we bear in mind that snakes are traditionally "worms." But such wasps are neither edible nor wingless, and there can be no doubt that our ὀφιομάχης is an ichneumon, i.e., the Egyptian mongoose, *Herpes ichneumon*, an animal that "tracks" (as the word ἰχνεύμων implies)[85]

[83] The rendering of ἑρπετόν by "reptile" (Colson and Whitaker in LCL) is impossible. Philo cannot have meant this, as he would have known very well that the Hebrews did not eat reptiles; the original sense of ἑρπετόν, despite the etymology, identical with that of "serpent," is merely that of "quadruped" as distinguished from "biped" (H. G. Liddell and R. Scott, *A Greek-English Lexicon*), and it is certainly in this sense that Philo used the word.

[84] The Indians were aware of this, and though they did not quite understand what actually takes place in nature, used the simile, "as the worm becomes the wasp" (losing its own nature and taking on that of its slayer), as an exemplum of deification, of what takes place when the liberated self *devo bhūtvā devān apyeti* (BU IV.1.2); this θέωσις implying, in the words of Nicolas of Cusa, an *ablatio omnis alteritatis et diversitatis*.

[85] Skr. *mṛg* and Gk. ἰχνεύω are used alike in the Vedic texts and by Plato with reference to the "tracking" of the Hidden Light or the Truth.

Lat. *calcatrix* = cockatrice is also properly the "Tracker" (if not rather "Treader"), and according to Webster "originally an ichneumon" but also a "water snake," sometimes confused with the crocodile but an enemy of crocodiles. The heraldic Cockatrice or Basilisk, a winged Griffin, with a serpent's tail, is sometimes thought of as an asp, sometimes as a bird. The Hebrew *tsefar* (Isa. 11:8, Vulgate *regulus*) seems to have been a bird, and as enemy of reptiles must be thought

crocodiles and eats their eggs, and also kills and eats snakes (as the word ὀφιομάχης implies). Plutarch, *Moralia* 380F, quite rightly says that the Egyptians "revered" (ἐτίμησαν) the ichneumon. For as Adolf Erman tells us, in an account of the divine animals of Egypt, "amongst these is the ichneumon rat into which Atum (the Sun god) changed himself when fighting against Apophis" (*Die Religion der Ägypter*, Berlin and Leipzig, 1934, p. 46), i.e., Apophis-Seth, the Egyptian Serpent or Dragon god, the constant enemy of the Sun, in a word the "Egyptian Vṛtra." Thus Daressy, discussing an inscription on the statue of the Pharoah "Zedher le Sauveur" (4th century B.C.), reads "Iusāāt, the eye of Rā, became an animal of 46 cubits in order to combat Āpap in his fury . . . ," the text proceeding to say that he may be invoked in cases of snake poisoning (*Annales du Service des Antiquités de l'Egypte*, XVIII, 116, 117). Sethe takes up the matter again in "Atum als Ichneumon" in *Aegyptische Sprache und Altertumskunde*, LXIII (1928), 50: "Re' changed himself into a '*d* animal of 46 ells, to slay the serpent Apophis as he raged." He further cites and illustrates a sculptured representation of the Egyptian mongoose, bearing the inscription "Atum, the guardian God of Heliopolis," and concludes that the ichneumon and the Sun god "share a common name ('*nd*) because they are both victors in the dangerous battle with the snake." A more detailed account of "Das Ichneumon in der ägyptischen Religion und Kunst" is given by Günther Roeder in *Egyptian Religion*, IV (1936): in several statuettes of the erect type, the Sun and Uraeus are represented on the ichneumon's head.

Can we assume that the Indian mongoose (*nakula*) had also been a symbol and type of the solar Indra as Ahihan? We have no direct evidence for this, beyond the implications of AV VI.139.5 already cited. But there is rather cogent indirect evidence in the fact that the female mongoose (*nakulī*), equated with the tongue, was certainly a type of the feminine principle in the cosmos, namely, Vāc (Sarasvatī, Earth, etc.). In RV I.126.6, Svanaya (whom Indra has aided, probably the Sun) says that "She who is clasped and clipt, who like the she-mongoose (*kaśikā*, Sāyaṇa *nakulī*) conceals herself (*jaṅgahe*), she moistened gives me the

of as a Sunbird, perhaps a vulture, which actually tramples on its ophidian prey. The heraldic Cockatrice, with its combination of avian and ophidian characters, should be a type of the Supreme Identity of the two contrasted principles, divine and titanic, which can only be characterized as "good and evil" when they are in opposition, i.e., in the world with its "pairs of opposites," which opposites are, properly speaking contraries rather than contradictories.

hundred joys of rutting"; she, who in her reply calls herself Romaśā (hairy) and says that she is fleeced like a Gandharan ewe, is, according to Sāyaṇa, "Bṛhaspati's daughter." She must be, in fact, the "tongue" (*juhu*, i.e., Vāc), Bṛhaspati's wife in RV x.109.5 and the she-mongoose of AĀ iii.2.5, "the mistress of all speech, shut in by the two lips, enclosed by the teeth (*oṣṭā apinaddhā nakulī dantaiḥ parivṛtā sarvasyai vāca īśā-nā*)," *apinaddhā* and *parivṛtā* corresponding to *āgadhitā* and *parigadhitā* in i.126.6 and explaining *jaṅgahe* (middle intensive from √*gah*, "sich verstecken").[86] The point of all this is that *nakulī* being Vāc, etc., her masculine counterpart must have been thought of as *nakula*, the male mongoose, and may have been so spoken of in some lost text (as in the case of other pairs with corresponding names, such as Sūrya, Sūryā; Vaśa, Vaśī; Rukma, Rukmā; Mahiṣa, Mahiṣī, etc.). The "mongoose" (m.) would thus have been a type (*rūpa*) of Indrābṛhaspatī or of either Bṛhaspati or Indra as "snake-fighter." Bṛhaspati and Indra are preeminently sacrificers. And what is the essential in the Sacrifice? In the first place, to divide, and in the second to reunite. He being One, becomes or is made into Many, and being Many becomes again or is put together again as One. The breaking of bread is a division of Christ's body made in order that we may be "all builded together in him." God is One as He is in Himself, but Many as He is in His children (ŚB x.5.2.16). Prajāpati's "joints are unstrung" by the emanation of his children, and "he, whose joints were unstrung, could not put them together again (*sa visrastaiḥ parvabhiḥ na śaśāka saṃhātum*, ŚB i.6.3.36 = *prajāḥ . . . tābhy-aḥ punaḥ sambhavituṃ nāśaknoti*, TS v.5.2.1)";[87] the final purpose of the Sacrifice is to put him together again and it is this that is done in the Sacrifice by himself (*sa chandobhir ātmānaṃ samadadhāt*,[88] AĀ iii.2.6, etc.) or by the gods or any sacrificer, who reintegrate themselves with him at one and the same time (ŚB *passim*). Prajāpati is, of course, the Year (*saṃvatsara*, *passim*); as such, his partition is the distinction of times from the principle of Time; his "joints (*parvāṇi*)" are the junc-

[86] Other interpretations of *jaṅgahe* are possible and even plausible. Our purpose has been to show that *nakulī* is, in fact, a type of the feminine half of the divine syzygy, *nakula* by implication a type of the male half. If *nakula* can be equated with Indra as Ahihan, as is intrinsically plausible, this would also serve to explain Kubera's *nakula* as his purse, the inexhaustible source of his wealth, Indra being always the great dispenser.

[87] Having fettered himself by himself, like a bird in the net, MU ii.2, vi.30.

[88] Becoming thus again *samāhita*, "in *samādhi*," converse of *hita*, *prahita*, *prativihita*, *nihita*, etc.

tions of day and night, of the two halves of the month, and of the seasons (e.g., Winter and Spring, see Appendix 2 for the "united ends of the endless Year"), ŚB I.6.3.35, 36. In the same way Ahi-Vṛtra, whom Indra cuts up into "joints (*parvāṇi*, RV IV.19.3, VIII.6.13, VIII.7.23, etc.)" was originally "jointless" or "inarticulate[89] (*aparvaḥ*, RV IV.19.3)," i.e., "endless (*anantaḥ*)." In the same way, Indra divides Magha-Vala (RV III.34.10, TB II.6.13.1), i.e., Makha (the Sacrifice, PB VII.5.6, and *saumya*, cf. RV IX.20.7 *makho na . . . soma*) "whom so long as he was One the Many could not overcome" (TA V.1.3).

We have already seen that the Indian texts interpret the slaying of Ahi-Vṛtra metaphysically and identify Vṛtra with the aesthetic, passible, emotional "elemental self" that is seated in the "bowels." I cannot cite Egyptian texts to the same effect, but there can be no doubt that for the Egyptians the conflict of the Sun with Apophis-Seth was one of light against darkness, good against evil. For the Hebrews, the Serpent who persuaded the mother of all mankind to eat of the fruit of the tree is certainly the type of evil and the enemy above all others; while "the word [*nefeṣ* = *anima*] translated 'soul' so often in our English version meant . . . for all Hebrews, the lower, physical nature, the appetites, the psyche of Paul. It was used also to express 'self,' but always with that lower meaning behind it" (D. B. Macdonald, *The Hebrew Philosophical Genius*, Princeton, 1934, p. 139, cf. p. 99).[90] The serpent is explicitly this "soul" for Philo and Plutarch. Philo says that "the snake-fighter (ὀφιομάχης) is, I think, nothing but a symbolic representation of self-control (ἐγκράτεια), waging a fight that never ends and a truceless war against incontinence and pleasure. . . . For if serpentlike pleasure is a thing unnourishing and injurious, sanity, the nature that is at war with pleasure,

[89] "Inarticulate," here "continuous," "undivided"; but also just as in another sense the silent (*aśabda*) Brahma is inarticulate (*anirukta*, etc.), and the expressive (*śabda*) Brahma articulate (*nirukta*, etc.).

[90] It is one of the chief defects of this interesting book that the author speaks of "Plato's *psyche*" as if this had been one single and altogether divine principle (pp. 99, 139). Plato, in fact, always speaks of two souls, appetitive and rational, the former corresponding to Hebrew *nefeṣ* and St. Paul's *psyche*, and the latter to Hebrew *ruaḥ* and St. Paul's *pneuma* (as also to the Indian *śarīra* and *aśarīra ātman*, *bhūtātman* and *antaḥ puruṣa*). Macdonald does not see that inasmuch as the Hebrew could "speak with himself and reason with himself" (p. 139), this involves two "selves," as was demonstrated once for all by Plato (*Republic* 430EF, 436B, 604B, etc.), these two being *nefeṣ* and *ruaḥ*. The latter, which comes from God and is reabsorbed in him (of which Ecclesiastes "is heartily glad, for it means a final escape for man" [p. 128], i.e., if he knows *who* he is and in *which* self he will be departing at death) is the "one and only Saṃsārin" of the Vedānta.

must be most nutritious and a saving power. . . . Therefore set up mind (*γνώμη*), the snake-fighter, against it, and contend to the last in this noblest contest" (*Legum allegoriae* I.39, 85, 86); and Plutarch that "Typhon (Seth) is that part of the soul which is passible and titanic (*παθητικὸν καὶ τιτανικόν*) irrational (*ἄλογον*) and forward, and of the bodily part the perishable, diseased and disordered, as is shown in abnormal seasons and temperatures, and by eclipses of the sun and disappearances of the moon, eruptions as it were and lawless acts on the part of Typhon . . . whose name signifies 'restraint' or 'hindrance'" (*Moralia* 371 B.C.).[91] In Christianity, the "Serpent" is still the "Tempter."

The Indians *may* have thought that the mongoose not only bit to pieces the snake but also put it together again, somewhat as the weasel of folklore is supposed to revive its dead mate by means of a life-giving herb. It may be, and probably is, with an "herb of virility" that the mongoose of AV 139.6 puts the "snake" together again and so "heals (*bheṣajati*)" it as they "heal" the divided Year in ŚB I.6.3.35, 36; and we can even say that the Ahi identified with the "soul" (the "double-tongued" Aditi-Vāc of ŚB III.2.4.16) *is* the "mate" of the Nakula identified with the divine Eros who, assuredly, "puts together again whatever of love is divided." But bearing in mind that supernatural no more means unnatural than superessential means nonessential, we say that it is not as natural history but as myth that the acts of the mongoose are to be understood. The *nakula-ὀφιομάχης* is a type or exemplum of the divine or human sacrificer; the snake "a symbol of magic healing."[92]

[91] "Self-government" (*svarāj*), i.e., "inward government of the worse by the naturally better part" of us (Plato, *Republic* 431AB, etc.).

[92] Cf. Grimm, *Märchen*, 16, "Die drei Schlangenblätter," and the snake that Asklepios was, which later survives coiled about his staff.

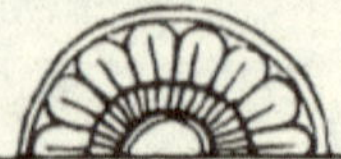

Līlā

The late Sanskrit word *līlā*, as is well known, describes any kind of playing, and may be compared in meaning to Gr. *παιδιά*. Here we shall be chiefly concerned with the reference of *līlā* to the divine manifestation and activity thought of as a "sport," "playing," or "dalliance."

In such a conception there is nothing strange or uniquely Indian. Meister Eckhart, for example, says: "There has always been this play going on in the Father-nature . . . from the Father's embrace of his own nature there comes this eternal playing of the Son.[1] This play was played eternally before all creatures. . . . The playing of the twain is the Holy Ghost in whom they both disport themselves and he disports himself in both. Sport and players are the same" (Evans ed., p. 148); Boehme adds "not that this joy first began with the creation, no, for it was from eternity. . . . The creation is the same sport out of himself" (*Signatura rerum* XVI.2–3).

That Plato thought of the divine activity as a game is shown by his calling us God's "toys"—"and as regards the best in us, that is what we really are";[2] whence he goes on to say that we ought to dance accordingly,

[This article was first published in the *Journal of the American Oriental Society*, XLI (1941).—ED.]

[1] Cf. BU IV.1.6, where the beatitude (*ānanda*) of Brahma is explained by the fact that "by means of his Intellect (*manas*) he consorts with the Woman," i.e., Vāc. The divine beatitude is occasioned, so to say, by the eternal reunion of essence and nature *in divinis*; "that same mystery of the eternal generation, in which there has been an eternal perfection" (Jacob Boehme, *Signatura rerum* XVI.1).

[2] We are the "pieces" that the Draughts-player moves, not arbitrarily, but in accordance with our own deserts; "a wondrous easy task" because, although He is the author of our being, we ourselves are responsible for being *what* we are, and all that the game requires is to move each piece into a better or worse position in accordance with its own character (*Laws* 904, cf. Heracleitus, fr. 79). This is essentially an enunciation of the law of *karma* and the doctrine that "Fate lies in the created causes themselves." [On God's game of chess, cf. Rūmī, *Dīvān*, Ode x, "How happy the king that is mated to thy rook," and *Mathnawī* I.600, II.2645, 3213, IV.1555, on the ball in the polo-field, which only moves as it ought "when it is made to dance by the King's hand."

D. B. Macdonald, on the basis of Prov. 8:30, 31, remarks that the Hebrews "came to think of man as part of an animated toy spread before the eyes of Jehovah and obeying only that one golden cord of the Law by which the puppet is suspended from above,[3] and so pass through life not taking human affairs to heart but "playing at the finest games"; not as those playboys play whose lives are devoted to sports, but being "otherwise minded" than those whose acts are motivated by their own interest or pleasure (*Laws*

---

giving Him joy" (*The Hebrew Philosophical Genius*, Princeton, 1936, pp. 50, 134, 136).]

[3] Cf. BU III.7.1, where (to combine the text and Sāyaṇa's commentary): "Do you know that Thread by which, and that Inner Controller by which and by whom, this world and the other and all beings are strung together and controlled from within, so that they move like a puppet, performing their respective functions?" That Plato knew of a "thread-spirit" (*sūtrātman*) doctrine is implied in the passage cited from the *Laws* and confirmed by the fact that in *Theaetetus* 153 he connects the golden cord of *Iliad* VIII.18 ff. with the Sun, to whom all things are bound by it, just as in ŚB VI.7.1.17; cf. AV X.8.39 and BG VII.7. [We cannot treat the doctrine of the "golden cord" at full length here, but may point out that the thought of *Iliad* VIII.23 ἐρύσαιμι (bearing in mind that in this verb, notably in middle and passive forms, the sense of "draw" can hardly be separated from that of "rescue") underlies John 12:32 πάντας ἑλκύσω πρὸς ἐμαυτόν, Hermes, *Lib.* XVI.5 εἰς αὑτόν τὰ πάντα ἕλκων and XVI.7 ἀναδήσας εἰς ἑαυτόν, and Dante, *Paradiso* I.117, "Questi la terra in sè stringe ed aduna."]

The two notable Buddhist references to the human puppet (S I.134, *Therīgāthā* II.390 ff.) ignore the Puppeteer, their only purpose being to show that the puppet is a composite and evanescent product of causal concatenation, not to be regarded as one's Self. Rūmī apostrophises, "O ridiculous puppet, that leapest out of thy hole (box), as if to say 'I am the lord of the land,' how long wilt thou leap? Abase thyself, or they will bend thee, like a bow" (Rūmī, *Dīvān*, Ode XXXVI); ridiculous, because "Whoso hath not escaped from (self-)will, no will hath he" (*ibid.*, Ode XIII). Here "they" refers to the contrary pulls of the affections, instincts, likes, and dislikes by which the animal man, by no means self-moving, "is dragged this way or that," to good or evil as the case may be (Plato, *Laws* 644D, echoed in Hermes, *Lib.* XVI.14). Cf. Aristotle, *De anima* III.10 (433a), "Appetite produces unaccountable (παρὰ τὸν λογισμόν) movement: for ἐπιθυμία is a kind of appetite, and reason (νοῦς) is never wrong."

We, in fact, resent the mechanistic interpretation of our individuality only because we identify our being with the "little self" of the puppet, and not with that of the Great Self of the Puppeteer. Man, *Per sua diffalta . . . ed in affanno cambiò onesto riso e dolce gioco* (Dante, *Purgatorio* XXVIII.95, 96)! What is really meant to be God's toy and dance accordingly is to have made His will our own; to play with him on the stage rather than for ourselves; and at the same time to share his point of view who looks on from above, or from the stalls, or from the sidelines (according to the metaphor); to have become no longer the victims, but the spectators of our own fate.

[D. B. Macdonald, *Hebrew Philosophical Genius*, p. 135, observes that "the puppets are self-conscious and have a certain choice as to which cord they will allow to draw them." The choice lies between the life of instinct and the "reasonable" (κατὰ λόγον) life; but in saying this we must remember that when Plato says "guided by Reason" he means "doing the will of God" and not a merely common *sense* or pragmatic "behavior"; *we* mean by "reason" what *he* calls "opinion."]

644, 803, 804). Plato's otherwise-minded "philosopher" who, having made the ascent and seen the light, returns to the Cave to take part in the life of the world (*Republic* VII) is really an *avatāra* ("one who has gone down again"), one who could say with Krishna: "There is naught in the Three Worlds I have need to do, nor anything I have not gotten that I might get, yet I participate in action. . . . Just as the ignorant, being attached to actions, act, even so should the Comprehensor, being unattached, also act, with a view to the maintenance of order in the world" (BG III.22–25).[4] It is in the same connection of ideas that the word *līlā* appears for the first time in the *Brahma Sūtra*, II.1.32, 33, *na prayojanatvāt, lokavat tu līlākaivalyam*, "Brahma's creative activity is not under taken by way of any need on his part, but simply by way of sport, in the common sense of the word."[5]

The emphasis is, we realize, always upon the idea of a "pure" activity that can properly be described as "playful" because the game is played, not as "work" is ordinarily performed, with a view to secure some end essential to the worker's well-being, but exuberantly; the worker works for what he needs, the player plays because of what he is. The work is

[4] To complete the parallel, it should be borne in mind that "one's own norm, the work appointed by one's own nature" (*svadharma . . . svabhāvaniyatam karma*, BG XVIII.47) corresponds exactly to that "doing of what it is by nature one's own to do (τὸ ἑαυτοῦ πράττειν, κατὰ φύσιν)" that Plato makes his type of "justice," and also terms "sanity" (*Republic* 433, *Charmides* 161, etc.).

[5] Whereas Plutarch (*Moralia* 393EF) was rather shocked by the notion of God's playfulness implied in *Iliad* XV.355–366, where Phoebus Apollo bridges a moat and casts down a wall, and we are told that this was child's play for him to do. He thinks irreverent to say that "the God indulges in this game (παιδιά) constantly, molding (πλάττων) the world that does not (yet) exist and undoing (ἀπολύων) it again when it has come into being. For on the contrary, insofar as he is in some way present in the world, by this his presence does he bind together (συνδεῖ) its substance and prevail over its corporal weakness, which tends towards corruption." Plutarch did not see that these works of creation, preservation, and destruction are of the very essence of the divine operation; the life of any one creature, and finally of the world itself, lasting only for so long as He remains with it and until "the Spirit returns to God who gave it."

[In this citation from Plutarch συνδεῖ refers to the σύνδεσμος by which all things are strung together within themselves and also connected with the Sun, as the limbs of a puppet are strung together and attached to the manipulator's hand. We cannot deal here with this aspect of the thread-spirit doctrine, except to refer to the "straight line like a pillar extended from above throughout Heaven and Earth," of which Plato says that this was the "fastening of Heaven" (σύνδεσμον τοῦ οὐρανοῦ, *Republic* 616c), and to point out that this shaft of "light" that "comprises-and-controls the whole revolving circuit" (cf. Rūmī, *Mathnawī* V.2345) is the traditional Axis Mundi (Skr. *skambha*), properly described as a shaft of light.]

laborious, the playing hard; the work exhausting, but the game a recreation. The best and most God-like way of living is to "play the game." And before we relinquish these general considerations, it should be realized that in traditional societies all those actual games and performances that we now regard as merely secular "sports" and "shows" are, strictly speaking, rites, to be participated in only by initiates; and that under these conditions proficiency (*kauśalam*) is never a merely physical skill, but also a "wisdom" (*σοφία*, of which the basic sense is precisely "expertise"). And so extremes meet, work becoming play, and play work; to live accordingly is to have seen "action in inaction, and inaction in action" (BG IV.18), to have risen above the battle, and so to remain unaffected by the consequences of action (BU IV.4.23, Īśā. Up. 5, BG V.7, etc.), the actions being no longer "mine" but the Lord's (JUB I.5.2, BG III.15, etc.), to whom they "do not cling" (KU V.11, MU III.2, BG IV.14, etc.).

The notion of a divine "playing" occurs repeatedly in the *Ṛg Veda*. Out of twenty-eight occurrences of *krīḷ*, to "play" (in various senses), and related adjectives, we cite IX.20.7 *krīḍur makho na maṇhayuḥ*, "disporting, like a liberal chief, thou goest, Soma," IX.86.44 where "Soma, even as Ahi, creeping forward from his inveterated skin, flows like a prancing (*krīḷan*) steed,"[6] X.3.5, where Agni's flames are the "playful ones" (*krīḷumat*), and X.79.6 where, with respect to his dual operation, *ab intra* and *ab extra*, unmanifested and evident, Agni is described as "not playing, and playing" (*akrīḷan krīḷan*). It is obvious that Agni is thought of as "playful" inasmuch as he "flares up and dies down" (*uc ca hṛṣyati ni ca hṛṣyati*, AB III. 4), and that the designation of his tongues as the "flickerers" (*lelāyamānāḥ*) in Muṇḍ. Up. I.2.4 corresponds to their designation as the "playful ones" in RV X.3.5. At the same time Agni is constantly spoken of as "licking" (*rih, lih*) whatever he loves or devours; for example, "Agni licks at (*pari . . . rihan*) his mother's mantle (of forest trees) and . . . is ever licking (*rerihat sadā*, RV I.140.9)," and "as with his tongue he moves, he continually licks (*rerihyate*) his mother" (X.4.4).

The idea of a divine play or dalliance is fully represented in the Upaniṣads and the *Bhagavad Gītā*, but the word *līlā* does not occur, and *krīḍ* appears only in CU VIII.12, where the incorporeal Spirit (*aśarīra ātman*) is thought of as "laughing, playing (*krīḍan*) and taking its pleasure," and MU V.1, where "the Universal Spirit (*viśvātman*), Universal Creator,

[6] Agni's flames are compared to mettled horses in RV IV.6.5.

Universal Enjoyer, Universal Life" is also "the Universal Lord of sport and pleasure" (*viśvakrīḍāratiprabhuḥ*)[7] in which he participates without being moved, being at peace with himself (*śāntātman*).

It is clear from what has been cited above that we might as legitimately speak of a Soma-*krīḍā* or Agni-*krīḍā* or Ātma-*krīḍā* or Brahma-*līlā* as we do of a Buddha-*līḷhā* or Kṛṣṇa-*līlā*. The expression Buddha-*līḷhā* occurs in the Jātakas,[8] e.g., 1.54, where it is said by the gods that "it will be given to us to behold the Bodhisatta's (Gautama Buddha's) infinite Buddha-*līḷhā* and to hear his word." The rendering of *līḷhā* here and in the PTS Dictionary by "grace" is far too weak; the grace of the Buddha's virtuosity (*kusalam*) is certainly implied, but the direct reference is to his "wonderful works"; the Buddha's *līḷhā* is, like Brahma's *līlā*, the manifestation of himself in act. Elsewhere in the Jātakas we find the word *līlā*, in the expression *līlā-vilāsa* (J v.5 and 157); *līlā-aravinda* occurs in *Vimānavatthu Atthakatha* 43 [E. R. Gooneratne, ed., London, 1886 (PTS)]. If, now, we had only the word *līḷhā* to consider, the derivation from *lih* (*rih*) to "lick"[9] would suffice to confirm our view that it was the "playing" of Agni's flames that from the beginning afforded a natural support for the notion of a divine "playing." But while we have not the slightest doubt as regards the connection of ideas, it would be impossible to derive the equivalent *līlā* from the same root. *Līlā* must be connected with *lēlay*, "to flare" or "flicker" or "flame," a stem that is like *līlā* itself post-Vedic; and this can hardly be anything but a reduplicated form of *lī*, to "cling." A semantic development from "cling" to "play" would not be inconceivable if we stress the erotic senses of the Sanskrit words. On the other hand, as the St. Petersburg Dictionary says, *līlā* has often been regarded as a corruption of *krīḍā*. We shall only suggest that the root is actually *lī*, but that the form of the word *līlā* may have been assimilated to that of the equivalent *krīḍā*.

This brief discussion will leave us free to consider the very interesting uses of the verb *lelāy*. We have already cited *lelāyamānāḥ* qualifying Agni's "tongues." In Muṇḍ. Up. 1.2.2, *yadā lelāyate hy arciḥ* is "as soon as the point of flame burns upward." A natural development is found in

[7] This is virtually identical with BU iv.3.13, where we are also reminded that "men behold his pleasuring (*ārāmam*), but see not Him."

[8] I cannot trace the DhA references given by the PTS Dictionary.

[9] The PTS Dictionary makes *lih* mean "polish," but this is at the most a derivative sense; the primary meanings are to "lick," and in this sense "kiss."

Śvet. Up. III.18, *haṃso lelāyate bahiḥ*, "outwardly hovers the Gander," i.e., the Lord (*prabhuḥ*), the Person, Spirit (*ātman*), Brahma as Sun-bird; this "hovering" being evidently another way of referring to the Gander's "enjoyments" described in BU IV.3.12–14. In the same context (BU IV.3.7), this Spirit, Person, and Intellectual Light of the Heart, as he moves to and from that world and this, remaining himself ever the same, is said to seem now to contemplate, and now to hover or visibly shimmer or burn (*dhyāyatī 'va lelāyatī 'va*), to be "asleep" or to be "awake." It is, then, of the motion and effects of Fire, Light, and Spirit that *lelāy* can be predicated.

We must deal next with a series of texts in which the Sun, or solar Indra, or Sāman, or Urgītha identified with the Sun or Fire, is said to flame aloft or overhead. In JUB I.45.1–6, the solar Indra "born here again as a Ṛṣi, a maker of incantations (*mantrakṛt*), for the keeping (*guptyāi*) of the Vedas,"[10] when he comes as the Udgītha "ascends from here to the world of heavenly light (*ita evordhvas svar udeti*) and burns overhead (*upari mūrdhno lelāyati*); and one should know that 'Indra hath come.'"[11] In the same way in JUB I.51.3, the Sāman, having been expressed (*sṛṣṭam*) as the Son of Sky and Earth, "came forward there and stood flaming" (*lelāyad atiṣṭhat*). Again, in JUB I.55, where the Sun ("He who burns yonder") has been born of Being and Nonbeing, Sāman and Ṛc, etc., it is said that "He burns aloft (*upariṣṭāt* = *upari mūrdhnas*), the Sāman set above." But at first "he was unstable, it seemed (*adhruva iva*), he did not flame, it seemed (*alelāyad iva*), he did not burn aloft" (*nordhvo 'tapat*).[12] Only when made firm by the gods did he burn upwards, hitherward and crosswise (i.e., shine from the center in the six directions, being himself the "seventh and best ray"). What is said in JUB I.45.4–6, cited above, is repeated with reference to the "Breath" (*prāṇa*), identified with the solar Herdsman of RV I.164.31, cf. AĀ

[10] It will be understood that Agni and Indra are just as much "resonances" as "lights," and that the "licking" of Agni's flames is also their "crackling" or "singing." The Sun himself "sings" as much as he "shines," and this finds expression in the verb *arc*, meaning either to "sing" or to "shine," or perhaps rather both in one (*verbum et lux convertuntur*); cf. Coomaraswamy, "The Sun-Kiss," 1940, n. 12.

[11] *Āgamana* is literally "advent": cf. "Tathāgatha."

[12] *Alelāyat* I take to be an example of the negative verb, which the sense requires in the present context. [Otherwise, "only flickered, and did not glow"; cf. TS V.6.4.2 and VII.3.10.4, "did not shine."] With *na . . . atapat*, cf. ŚB IV.6.6.5, where also "at first the Sun did not shine" (*na ha vā eṣo'gre tatāpa*).

II.1.6; the Breath, accordingly, *upari mūrdhno lelāyati* (JUB III.37.7). In JUB II.4.1, this same "Breath" is called the controlling flame-pointed Udgītha" (*vaśī dīptāgra udgītho yat prāṇaḥ*), and II.4.3, "Verily, 'flame-pointed' becomes his renown who is a Comprehensor thereof."[13]

Now it appears that while *in divinis* (*adhidevatam*) "overhead" will mean "in the sky," with reference to a given person here below (*adhyātmam*) it will mean *just* overhead. We find accordingly in the *Lalita Vistara* (I, p. 3) that when the Buddha is in *samādhi* "a Ray, called the 'Ornament of the Light of Gnosis' (*jñānālokālaṇkāraṃ nāma raśmiḥ*), proceeding from the opening in the cranial protuberance (*uṣṇīṣavivarāntarāt*),[14] plays above his head" (*upariṣṭān mūrdhnaḥ . . . cacāra*). This is manifestly the iconographic prescription underlying the representation of a flame that is made to rise from the top of the head in so many of the later Buddha figures. The *Saddharma Puṇḍarīka* [tr. H. Kern, Oxford, 1884] (text p. 467) asks: "By reason of what gnosis (*jñāna*) is it that the Tathāgatha's cranial protuberance (*mūrdhnyuṣṇīṣa*) shines (*vibhāti*)?" The answer to this is given partly above, and more generally in BG XIV.11: "When there is gnosis, light shines forth (*prakāśa upajāyate jñānaṃ yadā*) from the orifices of the body, then be it known that 'Being has matured'" (*vṛddhaṃ sattvam*), i.e., that the man *has* "become what he is" [cf. St. Thomas Aquinas, "Bodily refulgence is *natural* in a glorified body . . . but miraculous in a natural body," *Sum. Theol.* III.45.2c]. Before going on to the last step we must make allusion to another well-known context in which a flame appears "overhead." Dīpak Rāga is famed as a melody that is literally an illumination and that may consume the singer in its flame; in the Hindī text it is said that "Dīpak disports (*kēli karata* = *krīḍati*), Dīpak is a king, who displays the fullness of beauty, and upon whose head there shines a flickering flame (*bigala bijotī mastaka ujiyārī*)."[15] Now, bearing in mind that the Sanctus Spiritus is the "intellectual light," Meister Eckhart's "fünkelîn

[13] Cf. Plato, *Symposium* 197A, where those whom Love inspires are "beacon lights."

[14] It is unnecessary to discuss here whether *uṣṇīṣa* already means (as we have assumed) "cranial protuberance," or still means "turban." In either case it is from the top of the head that the light proceeds. A close parallel to the wording in J VI.376, where the deity of the royal umbrella emerges from an opening in its finial (*chattapiṇḍikavivarato nikkhamitvā*). We have already pointed out that *piṇḍika* corresponds to *uṣṇīṣa* as "cranial protuberance" (cf. Coomaraswamy, "Some Pāli Words," s.v. *Piṇḍaka* [in this volume—ED.]).

[15] See Coomaraswamy, "Dīpak Rāga," 1924–1925, p. 29. In some representations of this Rāga the singer stands in a pool of water for greater safety. For Dīpak Rāga see also Sheikh Chilli, *Folk-tales of Hindustan* (Allahabad, 1913), pp. 118, 125.

der sêle," and that Fire is the principle of Speech,[16] a remarkable parallel to some of the foregoing contexts can be cited from Acts 2:3–4, where the Spirit appears to the Apostles in the form of "cloven tongues of fire and it sat upon each of them. And they . . . began to speak with other tongues, as the Spirit gave them utterance."

We have been able to trace, accordingly, not only the continuity and universality of the notion of the divine activity thought of as a kind of game and dalliance, but also to recognize in the "play" of a flickering flame or vibrant light the adequate symbol of this epiphany of the Spirit.

[16] ["Fire, becoming speech, occupied the mouth" (*agnir vāg bhutvā mukham praviśat*, AĀ II.4.2), "abiding in beings as Speech in the speaker" (AV II.1.4). It is true that all the powers of the soul (*prāṇaḥ*) are "measures of fire," nevertheless, whenever the correspondences are particularized, Speech corresponds to Fire, Vision to the Sun, etc. (e.g. ŚB X.3.3.8).]

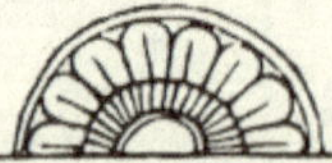

Play and Seriousness

Dr. Kurt Riezler's valuable discussion under this heading in the *Journal of Philosophy*, XXXVIII (1941), 505–517, and my own "*Līlā*," deal with complementary aspects of the notion of playful activity; the points of view converge and meet in the citation from Heracleitus made by both authors [see p. 148n—ED.].

Dr. Riezler's interest lies mainly in the distinction of (mere) play from (real) seriousness; mine in the indistinction of play and work on a higher level of reference. In the sense that the divine part of us, our real Self, or "Soul of the soul" is the impassible spectator of the fates that are undergone by its psychophysical vehicles (MU II.7, III.2, etc.), it is clearly not "interested" or involved in these fates, and does not take them seriously; just as any other playgoer does not take the fates of the stage characters seriously, or if he does can hardly be said to be looking on at the play, but is involved in it. It is surely with reference to this best part of us, with which we identify ourselves if we "know who we are," that Plato says more than once that "human affairs ought not to be taken very seriously" (*μεγάλης μὲν σπουδῆς οὐκ ἄξια*, *Laws* 803BC, cf. *Apology* 23A), and that we are asked to "take no thought for the morrow" (Matt. 6:34).

We must not confuse such a lack of "interest" with what we mean by "apathy" and the inertia that we suppose must be the consequence of such an ataraxia. All that "apathy" really implies is, of course, an independence of pleasure-pain motivation; it does not exclude the notion of an activity *κατὰ φύσιν*, but only that of an activity compelled by conditions not of our own choosing. Apathy is spiritual equipoise and a freedom from sentimentality. We are still aware that a disinterested statesman will make a better ruler than one who has "interests" of his own to be furthered; "tyranny is monarchy ruling in the interest of the monarch" (Aristotle, *Politics* III.5). The good actor is one for whom "the

[First published in *Journal of Philosophy*, XXXIX (1942), 550–52.—ED.]

play's the thing," not one who sees in it an opportunity to exhibit himself. The physician calls in another medical man to operate on a member of his family, just because the stranger will be less "interested" in the fate of his wife or child and therefore better able to play his game with death. "It is contrary to the nature of the arts to seek the good of anything but their object" (Plato, *Republic* 342BC).

Games are insignificant to us. But that is abnormal; and if we are to consider play and seriousness from a more universally human point of view we must remember that "games"—and this covers the whole circus of athletic contests, acrobatic and theatrical performances, jugglery, chess, gambling, and most of the organized games of children and the folk, all in fact that is not merely the artless gamboling of lambs[1]—are not "merely" physical exercises, spectacles, or amusements, or merely of hygienic or aesthetic value, but metaphysically significant. Plato asks, "Are we to live always at play? and if so, at what sort of games?" and answers, "such as sacrifices, chanting, and dancing, by which we can win the favor of the gods and overcome our foes" (*Laws* 803DE). *Ludus* underlies our word "ludicrous"; but in the Latin Dictionary (Harper) we find "Ludi, *public games, plays, spectacles, shows, exhibitions*, which were given in honor of the gods, etc."

Although, then, in a game there is nothing to be gained except "the pleasure that perfects the operation," and the understanding of what is properly a rite, we do not therefore play carelessly, but rather as if our life depended upon victory. Play implies order; of a man who ignores the rules (as he may be tempted to do if the result is to him the matter of primary importance) we say that he is "not playing the game"; if we are so much in earnest, so much "interested" in the stakes, as to "hit below the belt," that is not duelling, but nearer to attempted murder. It is true that by not cheating we may lose: but the whole point of the game is that we are not playing only to win, but playing a part, determined by our own nature, and that our only concern is to play well, regardless of the result, which we can not foresee. "Mastery is of action only, not of its fruits; so neither let the fruit of action be thy motive, nor hesitate to act" (BG II.47). "Battles are lost in the same spirit in which they are won" (Whitman); victory depends on many factors beyond

[1] Cf. Otto Ranke, *Art and Artist*, New York, 1932, ch. 10, "Game and Destiny," and Coomaraswamy, "The Symbolism of Archery," 1943.

our control, and we ought not to be concerned about what we are not responsible for.

The activity of God is called a "game" precisely because it is assumed that *he* has no ends of his own to serve; it is in the same sense that our life can be "played," and that insofar as the best part of us is in it, but not of it, our life becomes a game. At this point we no longer distinguish play from work.

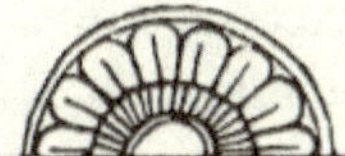

Measures of Fire

The Fire is the principle of every life.
Jacob Boehme, *Signatura rerum* XIV.29

In a recent thesis,[1] Dr. William C. Kirk has fulfilled his immediate purpose, which was to discover, as far as that is possible, what was actually said by Heracleitus on Fire. We do not propose to review this brochure, which is fully documented and well constructed. It is rather the restricted purpose of historical scholarship itself that we wish to criticize. We must, indeed, know what has been said: but of what use will such knowledge be to us, unless we consider the meaning of what was said and can apply this meaning to our own experience? Here Dr. Kirk has little more to say than is contained in the significant words, "Heracleitus is one of the Greek philosophers who sought to explain the whole universe in terms of some one basic entity. . . . After his time, to be sure, fire decreased in importance, and men ceased to look for one principle[2] that would explain all phenomena." This is a confession that men have fallen to the level of that empiricism of which Plato was so contemptuous, and to that of those Greeks whom Plutarch ridiculed because they could no longer distinguish Apollo from Helios, the reality (τὸ ὄν) from the phenomenon, "so much has their sense perception (αἰσθήσις) perverted their power of discrimination (διάνοια)."[3] It is, however, only partially true that "the importance of fire has decreased," and only some men have abandoned the search for "one principle."

Dr. Kirk sees that Heracleitus must have had forerunners, but scarcely

[This essay was first published in *O Instituto*, C (1942), Coimbra, Portugal.—ED.]

[1] *Fire in the Cosmological Speculations of Heracleitus* (Minneapolis, 1940).

[2] "One principle" . . . "that One by which, when it is known, all things are known" (BU II.4.5).

[3] Plutarch, *Moralia* 393D, 400CD. Cf. Plato, *Laws* 898D, "The body of Helios is seen by all, his soul by none," and AV X.8.14, "Him (the Sun) all men see, not all know with the mind." "Apollo" is Philo's ὁ νοητὸς ἥλιος. [Note Victor Magnien, *Les Mystères d'Éleusis* (Paris, 1929), p. 143.]

realizes that he may not have been a philosopher in the modern sense, but rather one in the highest ancient sense, according to which the veritable teacher is one who understands and transmits a doctrine of immemorial antiquity and anonymous divine origin.[4] He does say that Heracleitus speaks as one who propounds an obvious and generally accepted truth, not as one who argues for a personal opinion. What remains of Heracleitus is, indeed, unquestionably "orthodox," i.e., in accordance with the Philosophia Perennis (et Universalis), of which the teachings are always and everywhere the same.

The conception of a transcendent and universal Fire, of which our fires are only pale reflections, survives in the words "empyrean" and "ether"; the latter word derives from *αἴθω*, to "kindle" (Skr. *indh*) and it is, incidentally, not without interest that Blake's "tiger burning bright" echoes the *αἴθωνες θῆρες* of the Greeks, who thus referred to the horse, the lion, and the eagle; the *Ṛg Veda* (II.34.5) speaks of "blazing (*indhanvan* = *αἴθων*) kine." For Aeschylus, *Ζεὺς ἐστιν αἰθήρ* (*Fr.* 65A; cf. Virgil, *Georgics* II.325); in the Old Testament (Deut. 4:24) and for St. Paul (Heb. 12:29), *Noster Deus ignis* (*πῦρ*) *consumens est*; and the epiphany of the Spirit is as "tongues of fire" (Acts 2:3, 4).[5] Agni (*ignis*, Fire) is one of the principal, and perhaps the chief of the names of God in the *Ṛg Veda*. Indra is "metaphysically Indha" (*αἴθων*), a "Kindler," for he "kindles" (*inddha*) the Breaths or Spirations (*prāṇāḥ*, ŚB VI.1.1.2).[6] The solar Gander (*haṃsa*), "on seeing whom one sees the All," is a "blazing Fire" (*tejas-endham*, MU VI.35), and spoken of as "flaming" (*lelāyati*, BU IV.3.7), like Agni's tongues (*lalāyamānāḥ* in Muṇḍ. Up. I.2.4). The Buddha, who can be regarded as a humanized type of Agni or Indrāg-

[4] The Buddha, for example, proclaims that he "has followed the ancient path" (S II.106), and says that "Whoever pretends that I preach a doctrine wrought by my own reasoning and argumentation shall be cast out" (M I.77); ["the Source of a hundred streams (*bhūtānāṃ garbham*)," RV III.26.9].

[5] The connection of the tongues of *fire* and the *speaking* with tongues is not fortuitous, but depends on the doctrine that Fire (Agni) is the principle of Speech (Vāc); to which she is reduced when freed from her natural mortality (BU I.3.8, etc.; for the mortality of all the functional powers, cf. JUB IV.19); Agni, like Plato's *δαίμων*, "cares for nothing but the Truth," being *satyavācah* (RV III.26.9, VII.2.3). Cf. ŚB X.3.3.1, "What becomes of one who knows that Fire? He becomes eloquent, speech does not fail him." See René Guénon, "Le Don des langues," *Études traditionnelles*, XLIV (1939). [The *Ṛṣis* (Sages) are described as sacrificers and singers "born hither again for the keeping of the Vedas" (JUB I.45.2).]

[6] [For Indra-Agni as twins see RV VI.59.2, X.8.7. For the fullest account of the *Ṛṣis* as "Breaths," the *maruts* as "Storms," see ŚB VI.1.1.6 and JUB I.45.1–6; IV.12.6.]

nī,[7] is "a master of the element of fire" (*tejo-dhātum-kusalo*, Vin I.25) which he can assume at will, and he is represented iconographically not only as a Tree but also as a Pillar of Fire.[8] Meister Eckhart can still speak of "the motionless heaven, called fire or the empyrean" and say that the nectar (*die züezekeit* = ambrosia, *amṛta*, "honey," "water of life") is withheld from all who do not reach "that fiery heavenly intelligence."[9]

Let us now consider the Indian doctrine of "Measures of Fire." I use capitals here and in the many contexts where it is the God, and not the natural phenomenon in which He manifests Himself, that is referred to.[10] We must first explain that while Skr. *agni* is literally *ignis*, "fire," the word *tejas*, which we shall have to cite repeatedly, is strictly speaking not so much the fire itself as an, or the most, essential quality of "fire," whether as deity or natural phenomenon. *Tejas* (√ *tij*, to be sharp, cf. στίζω, στίγμα, *di-stinguo*, *in-stig-o*, stick, stake, stitch), is, as nearly as possible, what Jacob Boehme calls the "sharpness of the fire-flash" (*Three Principles* XIV.69). In RV VI.3.5, Agni is said to whet his *tejas* like a point of iron. The corresponding adjective *tigma* commonly qualifies *śocis*, "flame," and Agni himself is *tigma-śocis*, "of sharp flame." The word *tejas* is usually and rightly, however, translated by "fire"[11] or "fiery energy," the essential quality standing for the essence, the characteristic act for the agent; just as the Blast (*vāyu*) of the Spirit (*ātman*) is nothing but the Spirit itself in terms of its characteristic activity. At the same

[7] Indrāgnī, like Mitrāvaruṇau, is the *mixta persona* of the Sacerdotum (Agni being the *brahma*) and the Regnum (Indra, the *kṣatra*) *in divinis*. Thus "Indra is Agni as Supreme Overlord," Sāyaṇa on RV V.3.2, cf. V.3.1; also AB III.4, IV.22, and BD I.68. Names are given according to the aspect under which God is considered (RV V.44.6); [*brahma sat kṣatrām ucyate*, "even as he seemeth so he is called," AV X.2.23].

[8] Cf. Coomaraswamy, *Elements of Buddhist Iconography*, 1935, Pl. II; also Exod. 13:21.

[9] Meister Eckhart, Pfeiffer ed., pp. 214 ff.

[10] The customary designation of the early Greek and Indian philosophies as "naturalistic" is a betrayal of the truth ["physical" in Greek had not this meaning.] A philosophical "development" from naturalism to abstraction, coincident with an aesthetic development from abstraction to naturalism, would have been strange indeed. It is we, for whom "such knowledge as is not empirical is meaningless," who fail to distinguish the adequate natural symbol from its reference, we who see the pointing finger rather than the moon itself.

[11] Cf. J. Ph. Vogel, "Het Sanskrit Woord Tejas (= Gloed, Vuur) in de Beteekenis van Magische Kracht," *Med. d.k.ak.v. Wetenschappen, afd. Letterkunde*, Deel 70, Serie B, No. 4 (1930).

time it must be understood that neither *agni* nor *tejas* imply a heat as distinguished from a light; *tejas*, for example, is not merely a "sharpness" but also a "brilliance" as of lightning, hence the correlation "Fire and what can be illuminated" (*tejaś ca vidyotayitavyaṃ ca*, Praśna Up. IV.8[12]). In *Fr.* 77 Heracleitus himself substitutes *φάος* for the *πῦρ* of *Fr.* 20, the verbs remaining unchanged. Since we have made him our starting point, and since it would be awkward to repeat Boehme's "sharpness of the fire-flash," we shall adhere to the customary rendering of *tejas* by "fire" or "Fire."

Now, "Of the Fire (*tejas*) that is hidden within the Sky,[13] it is but a little measure (*aṃśa-mātram*) that (glows) in the midst of the Sun, in the eye and in fire. That (Fire) is Brahma, Immortal.[14] . . . It is but a little measure (*aṃśa-mātram*) of that Fire that is the ambrosia (*amṛtam*) in the midst of the Sun, whose growing shoots (*āpayanṅkurāḥ*) are Soma and the Breaths" (*prāṇāḥ*, MU VI.35).[15] And so, indeed, just as sparks

[12] "It is as the Breath (*prāṇā*) that Agni shines" (*dīpyate*, JUB IV.12.6); "I am the flash in what is luminous (*tejas . . . vibhāva vasau*) . . . the splendor of the splendid" (*tejas tejasvīnām*, BG VII.9, 10). [Agni is the *tejas* wherewith they slew Vṛtra (ŚB II.5.4.3, 8), Agni is the *tejas* of the Sacrifice (ŚB V.3.5.7–8) and the immortal in the mortal (AV XII.2.33).]

[13] I.e., is ὑπερουράνιος (cf. Plato, *Phaedrus* 247C); beyond the Sky (*uttaraṃ divah*, AV X.7.3; *parena divam*, Ait. Up. I.2; *pare-ardhe*, RV I.164.10); in the empyrean as distinguished from the celestial or Olympian paradise.

[14] The immortal, fiery (*tejomayam*) Brahma, the Spirit (*ātman*) of BU II.5.1 ff.; [see Coomaraswamy, "The Sun-kiss," 1940, especially n. 15.]

[15] The functional powers are called Spirations, Lives, or Breaths after the central Spiration, Life, or Breath of which they are participations and on which they depend (BU I.5.21, CU V.1.15); and "Indra's energies" (*indriyāni*) with reference to Indra, identified with the central Breath; and by other names, e.g. "Elemental Beings" (*bhūtāni*) with reference to the "Great Being" (*mahābhūtah*) from which their being stems. The passible Ego or "Elemental Self" (*bhūtātman*, MU III.2) is accordingly a "host of beings" (*bhūtagana*, MU III.3) and, in fact, the "Marut host" (*marudgana*), for "the Maruts are the Breaths" (AB III.16), as they are also "Fires" (*agnayah*, RV III.26.4). The true relation of these Breaths or Storms (our "stormy passions") to their Head is that of subjects to a king, loyal unto death; but if they are allowed to run wild in pursuit of their natural objects, serving themselves and not their king, "we" are distracted by this body of fallen Angels within us. Self-integration is a matter of orientation. That is, in brief, "Indian psychology."

The assimilation of the Breaths to (Soma-) shoots, implied in our text, is of very great significance for the exegesis of the Soma-sacrifice, but needs more space than can be devoted to it here.

The Commentators read *apyayanṅkurāḥ* and emend to *apyanṅkurāḥ*, i.e., *api anṅkurāh*. In order to avoid any emendation we have assumed a reading *āpyayanṅkurāh*, i.e., *āpyai-anṅkurāh*, which is not impossible and gives an appropriate meaning; cf. ŚB VII.3.1.45 [and AĀ I.4.1].

disperse in all directons from a blazing fire, so from this Prescient Spirit (*prajñātman*, the ultimate and solar Self) the Breaths and other substances disperse to their stations" (BU II.1.3, Kauṣ. Up. III.3, IV.20, Muṇḍ. Up. II.1.1, MU VI.26, 31, with negligible variants), and it is from this point of view that Brahma is compared to a "sparkling fiery wheel" (MU VI.24). Now "these functional powers (*indriyāṇi* = *prāṇāḥ*) are of the Spirit (*ātmakāni*), it is the Spirit (*ātman*) that proceeds (in them) and that controls them" (MU VI.31);[16] they are the solar rays or reins[17] (*raśmayaḥ*) by which the Only Seer and Thinker sees, hears, thinks and eats within us (MU II.6, VI.31, BU III.7.23, JUB I.29, 30, etc.), being accordingly the "Only Saṃsārin" (BrSBh I.1.5). Thus these active powers of speech, vision, thought, etc. "are only the names of His acts," of the forces that he puts forth and again absorbs (BU I.4.7, I.5.21, I.6.3, etc.). In their operation in ourselves all these Breaths or Lives act together, so that we are able to refer to, see, hear, and think of one and the same object simultaneously (Kauṣ. Up. III.2; cf. 1 Cor. 12:14 ff.).

Now He, the Spirit (*ātman*), Brahma, Prajāpati, the Immortal, who in us assumes the appearances (*rūpāṇi*) of speech, vision, mind, etc. (these being, as we have seen, the names of His acts, not "ours"), is himself "of the substance of fire" (*tejo-mayam*, BU II.5.1–15); he "divides himself" (*ātmānaṃ vibhajya*) to quicken his children (MU II.6), himself remaining "undivided amongst the divisions" (BG XVIII.20).[18] Again, the act of "creation," or rather "expression" (*sṛṣṭiḥ*), is typically thought of as a "determination" or "measuring out" (*nirmāṇam*),[19] the Measurer who is himself the measure of all things remaining "unmeasured amongst the measured" (AV X.7.39). It follows from this that His divisions, the

[16] ["In me I take first Agni" (TS V.7.9); "let the fires of the sacred hearths (*ātmā*) again officiate just here in their respective stations (*yathāsthāma*)" (AV VII.67). *Indriyāgnayaḥ* are the senses sacrificed into the fire of restraint, i.e., *teṣu parokṣam juhoti*, the individual's Internal Agnihotra (BG IV.26, 27); "when the Comprehensor controls the mind and the Breath has put the objects of the senses in their place" (MU VI.19); also, "the fires (*tejas*) of the senses wear away. . . . Thine alone is the chariot, the dance and the chant" (KU I.26).]

[17] The metaphor of the chariot, common to Plato and our Indian sources, is here involved. In MU II.6, Prajāpati is the driver of the bodily vehicle, controlling the steed (the sensitive powers) by the "rays" or "reins" (*raśmayaḥ*) that extend from his station in the heart to the objects of sense perception; cf. Plato, *Laws* 898c, *ψυχὴ μὲν ἐστιν ἡ περιάγουσα ἡμῖν πάντα*, and Hermes, *Lib.* X.22, *καὶ τοῦ μὲν θεοῦ καθάπερ ἀκτῖνες αἱ ἐνέργειαι*, and XVI.7, *εἰσί δὲ καὶ ἡνίαι* (*ἑαυτοῦ ἀκτῖνες*).

[18] Cf. Plotinus, IV.1.1.

[19] Cf. Coomaraswamy, "*Nirmāna-kāya*," 1938, citing RV III.29.11, etc., where Agni is "measured out."

aforesaid faculties (or "intelligencies," *jñānāni*, KU VI.10, MU VI.30; *prajñā-mātrāḥ*, Kauṣ. Up. III.8; *buddhīndriyāṇi*, MU II.6)[20] must be "Measures (*mātrāḥ*)[21] of Fire." It is, in fact, as "Fires" (*agnayaḥ*, ŚB X.3.3.1 ff.), as the "Fires of the Breaths" (*prāṇāgnayaḥ*, Praśna Up. IV.3) and as "Measures of Fire" (*tejo-mātrāḥ*, BU IV.4.1, Praśna Up. IV.8) that these active hypostases of the Spirit are actually referred to.

We have shown, then, that the elementals of the active life are "Measures of Fire," and that being mortal in themselves they proceed from and again return to the immortal fiery Breath of the Total Presence within us. It is just this Indian and universal doctrine that Heracleitus (*Fr.* 20) enunciates: "*κόσμον τόνδε τὸν αὐτὸν ἁπάντων οὔτε τις θεῶν οὔτε ἀνθρώπων ἐποίησεν, ἀλλ' ἦν ἀεὶ καὶ ἔστιν καὶ ἔσται· πῦρ ἀείζωον, ἁπτόμενον μέτρα καὶ ἀποσβεννύμενον μέτρα.*" "That Kosmos, the identity of all things, no one of gods or men hath ever wrought, but it ever was, and is and ever shall be everliving Fire, in measures being kindled and in measures dying out."[22]

Very many others of Heracleitus' dicta are in the same way enunciations of doctrines that are both Indian and universal.[23] That "The Thunderbolt (*κεραυνός* = *vajra*) governs all things" (*Fr.* 28), for example, states the doctrine of the Axis Mundi.[24] In drawing parallels, it has been very far from my intention to suggest that the philosophies of Hera-

[20] The Breaths as "Intelligencies" are the "gods within you" of JUB I.14.1, 2, and the "angels" of Christian theology; their Duke (*netṛ*), *rex angelorum, devānāṃ rājā*, Indra (Vāyu).

[21] *Mātrā* (like *μέτρον*) is etymologically "matter," not in the sense of "that which is solid," but in the proper sense of "that which is quantitative" and has a position in the world (*loka-locus*). Whatever is thus in the world can be named and perceived (*nāma-rūpa*) and is accessible to a physical and statistical science; the unmeasured being the proper domain of metaphysics.

[22] "That Kosmos" evidently being the *νοητὸς κόσμος* = *νοητὸς ἥλιος*, the "uncreated Brahma-world" of CU VIII.13.1, the "world-picture" ("painted by the Spirit on the canvas of the Spirit," Śaṅkarācārya. *Ātmanirūpaṇam* 95); the pattern of the sensible world. "It knows only itself, that 'I am Brahma'; thereby it becomes the All" (BU I.4.10). "Sicut erat in principio, est nunc et semper erit," because for Brahma there is neither past nor future but only the eternal now.

[23] So that, as Heracleitus also says (*Fr.* 77), *ἄνθρωπος ὅκως ἐν εὐφρόνῃ φάος, ἅπτεται ἀποσβέννυται* "Man, like a light in the night, is kindled and extinguished." (*ἀπο*)*σβέννυμι* is to be despirated; of wind, to die down; of fire, to go out; of passion, to be stilled. These are precisely the senses of Skr. *nirvā*, Pāli *nibbāyati* (also to be finished, be perfected). The *samādhi* of the Breaths is their *nirvāṇa* and their *τελευτή*.

[24] Skr. *skambha, sthūṇa, yūpa*, etc., Christian *stauros*, Islamic *qutb*, etc.

cleitus or Plato are derived from Indian or other Oriental sources.[25] No culture, people, or age can lay claim to any private property in the Philosophia Perennis. All that I have tried to show is that the axioms of this philosophy, by whomsoever enunciated, can often be explained and clarified or emphasized by a correlation with the parallel texts of other traditions. And finally, I can only say of Heracleitus, with Socrates, that "What I understand of him is excellent, and what I do not [yet] understand is also excellent."

[25] For example, it does not seem to be necessary to derive the "negative theology" of Plotinus from Indian sources, as Emile Bréhier wishes to do (*La Philosophie de Plotin*, Paris, 1928, pp. 107–133). It is quite true that a negative theology is fully developed in the Indian sources and that in MU VI.30 both *viae*, *affirmativa* and *negativa*, are commended and are to be followed in their logical sequence. But it would be far simpler to think of Plotinus as dependent on such Platonic sources as *Phaedrus* 247C, "The region above the sky was never worthily sung by any earthly poet, nor will it ever be . . . For the colorless, formless and intangible . . . ," and *Epistle* VII, 341D, where Plato says that the subject of his most serious study (i.e., the ultimate nature of deity) "does not at all admit of verbal expression like other studies."

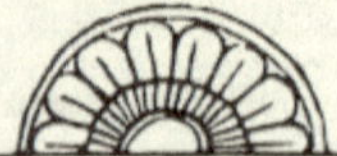

Vedic "Monotheism"

> One only Fire is kindled manifold, one only Sun is present to one and all, one only Dawn illuminates this all: that which is only One becomes this all.
>
> *Rg Veda* VIII.58.2

Modern scholarship for the most part postulates only a gradual development in Indian metaphysics of a notion of a single principle, of which principle the several gods (*devāḥ*, *viśve devāḥ*, etc.) are, as it were, the powers, operative aspects, or personified attributes. But as Yāska expresses it, "It is because of His great divisibility (*mahā-bhāgyāt*) that they apply many names to Him, one after another. . . . The other gods (*devāḥ*) come to be (*bhavanti*) submembers (*pratyangāni*) of the One Spirit (*ēkasyātmanaḥ*) . . . their becoming is a birth from one another, they are of one another's nature; they originate in function (*karma*);[1] the Spirit is their origin . . . Spirit (*ātman*) is the whole of what a God is" (*Nirukta* VII.4). Similarly, BD I.70–74: "Because of the magnitude of the Spirit (*mahātmyāt*) a diversity of names is given (*vidhīyatē*) . . .[2] ac-

[This essay was first published in the *Dr. S. Krishnaswami Aiyangar Commemoration Volume* (Madras, 1936), and revised for the *Journal of Indian History*, XV (1936). The second version, with the author's further revisions and addenda, is printed here.—ED.]

[1] It is, in fact, *Viśvakarmā*, the Doer of All Things, that gives their "names," that is to say, their individual being, to the gods, and is therefore called *dēvānām nāmadhāh*, X.82.3. [The functions are "merely the names of Brahma's acts," BU I.4.7; "all functionings arise from the Spirit," *ibid.* I.6.3; "all action stems from Brahma," BG III.5; cf. Meister Eckhart, Evans ed., II, 175].

[2] [Almost verbally identical with Jan van Ruysbroeck, "because of his incomprehensible nobility and sublimity, which we cannot rightly name nor wholly express, we give Him all these names," *Adornment of the Spiritual Marriage*, XXV. "For I deem it impossible that He who is the maker of the universe in all its greatness, the Father or Master of all things, can be named by a single name; I hold that He is nameless, or rather, that all names are names of Him. For He in his unity is all things; so that we must either call all things by his name, or call him by the name of all things," Hermes, *Asclepius* III.20A.

"He alone has the spirit of Christ who has changed his forms and his names

cording to the distribution of their spheres (*sthānavibhāgēna*). It is inasmuch as they are 'differentiations,' 'presences' (*vibhūtiḥ*),[3] that the names are innumerable. But the shapers (*kavayaḥ*) in their incantations (*mantrēṣu*) say that the godhoods (*dēvatās*) have a common source; they are called by different names according to the spheres in which they are established.[4] Some say that they are participants therein (*tad bhaktāḥ*), and that such is their derivation; but as regards the aforesaid Trinity of world-rulers, it is well understood that the whole of their participation (*bhaktiḥ*) is in the Spirit (*ātman*)."[5]

---

from the beginning of the world and so reappeared again and again in the world" (Clement, *Clementine Homilies* III.20, cf. BG IV.8, *sambhavāmi yuge yuge*). "Each angelical prince is a property out of the voice of God, and bears the great name of 'God'" (Jacob Boehme, *Signatura rerum* XVI.5). Cf. JUB III.1, where the Gale of the Spirit (*vāyu*) is called "the one entire godhood" (*eka . . . kṛtsnā devatā*), the rest are "semigodhoods."]

[3] ["The Gale is omnipresent (*vāyur ākāśam anuvibhavati*)," JUB IV.12.10; and so, as Krishna says, "There is no end to my divine presences" (*nānto'sti mama divyānām vibhūtīnām*, BG X.40). It is to these "presences" or "powers" that the many names are given.]

[4] [Cf. PB XX.15.2–2 where the spheres of action of Agni, Vāyu and Āditya are called their "lots" or "shares" (*bhaktiḥ*).]

[5] An ontology of this kind is not properly to be called pantheistic or monistic. This would only be legitimate if, when the essence has been analyzed into its many aspects, there were no remainder; on the contrary, the whole of Indian scripture, beginning with the *Ṛg Veda*, consistently affirms that what remains exceeds the whole of that which suffices to fill up these worlds, and that the source remains unaffected by whatever is produced from it or returned to it at the beginning or end of an aeon. The view that all this is a theophany does not mean that *all* of Him is seen; on the contrary, "only a quarter," so to speak, of his abundance (RV X.90.3, cf. MU VI.35, BG X.42) suffices to fill up the worlds of time and space, however far they may extend, however long they may endure.

Cf. Whitby in the preface to the English version of René Guénon, *L'Homme et son devenir selon le vêdanta* (Paris, 1925): "It is to be hoped that this book will give the *coup de grâce* to the absurd and well-nigh unaccountable prejudice which persistently depreciates the *Vêdic* doctrine on account of its alleged 'pantheism.' This parrot-cry . . ."; and Lacombe, in the preface to René Grousset, *Les Philosophies indiennes* (Paris, 1931) "Il ne faut pas conclure, à notre avis, que le Vedānta soit panthéiste, ou même moniste, surtout au sens que ces mots ont chez nous. Il se nomme lui-même *advaita*, non-dualiste. Sa préoccupation d'assurer la transcendance de Brahman non moins que son immanence, de maintenir l'intériorité de son Gloire, est manifesté. Position irréductible . . ."; and Coomaraswamy, *A New Approach to the Vedas: An Essay in Translation and Exegesis*, 1933, p. 42.

It may be added that similar objection can be made to the word "Monotheism" in the title of the present essay. *Tad ekam* in RV X.129.2 is much rather "Supreme Identity" than "only God." It is as "only God," with aspects as many as the points of view from which He is regarded, that "That One" becomes intelligible; but

The foregoing passages illustrate the normal method of theology in any discussion *de divinis nominibus*, when a recognition of the various operations of a single principle gives rise to the superficial appearance of a polytheism. In Christianity, for example, "we do not say the *only God*, for deity is common to several" (*Sum. Theol.* I.31.2c); still, "To create beings belongs to God according to His own being, that is His essence, which is common to the three Persons. Hence to create is not peculiar to any one Person, but is common to the whole Trinity" (*Sum. Theol.* I.45.6c); and it is well understood that "Although the names of God have one common reference, still because the reference is made under many and different aspects, these names are not synonymous. . . . The many aspects of these names are not empty and vain, for there corresponds to all of them one single reality represented by them in a manifold and imperfect manner" (*Sum. Theol.* I.13.a *ad* 2).[6] [Cf. Sāyaṇa on ŚB I.6.1.20: Prajāpati is inexplicit because He is essentially all the gods and hence it cannot be said of Him that "He is this or that" (*ayam asāviti*) but only that "He is." And also Hermes Trismegistos: "Are we to say that it is right that the name of 'God' (*θεός*, *deva*) should be assigned to Him, or that of Maker (*ποιητής*, *kāvya*) or that of Father (*πατέρ*, *pitṛ*, Prajāpati)? Nay, all three names are His; He is rightly named 'God' by reason of His power, and 'Maker' by reason of the work He does, and Father by reason of His goodness," *Lib.* XIV.4.] In the same way, Plotinus: "This life of the ensouled stars is one identical thing, since they are one in the All-Soul, so that their very spatial movement is pivoted upon identity and resolves itself into a movement not spatial but vital," *Enneads* IV.4.8.

That these conceptions of the identity of the First Principle with all its powers are current in the Brāhmaṇas and the *Atharva Veda* is well

---

what That One may be in itself can only be expressed in terms of negation, for example, "without duality." See Erwin Goodenough, *An Introduction to Philo Judaeus* (New Haven, 1940), p. 105.

[6] [In "dividing Himself (*ātmānam vibhajya*) to fill these worlds" (MU VI.26, etc.), He remains "undivided in these divisions" (*avibhakta vibhakteṣu*, BG XVIII.20, cf. XIII.16), "unmeasured, i.e., im-material, amongst the measured" (*vimite'mita*, AV X.7.39; *amātra*, BU III.8.8, etc.); the immanent gods, the Spirations (*prāṇāḥ*), are "measures of Fire" (*tejo-mātrāḥ*, BU IV.4.1), viz. "the ever-lasting Fire, in measures being kindled and in measures dying out" (Heracleitus, *Fr.* 30). "In other words, there are not in Him many existences, but only one sole existence, and his various names and attributes are merely his modes and aspects" (Jāmī, *Lawā'ih* XV).]

known. There may be cited, for example, ŚB x.5.2.16, "As to this they say, 'Is then Death one or many?' One should answer, 'One and many.' For, inasmuch as He is That (Person in the Sun), He is one; and inasmuch as He is multiply distributed (*bahudhā vyāviṣṭiḥ*) in His children, He is many," to be read together with verse 20: "As He is approached, even such He becomes (*yathōpāsate tad ēva bhavati*)";[7] and AV viii.9.26, "One Bull, one Prophet, one Home, a single Ordinance, one simplex Yakṣa in His ground, one Season that is never emptied out"; and AV i.12.1, where Agni is described as "One energy whose procession is threefold (*ekam ojas tredhā vicakrame*)."

It is more often overlooked that the same point of view is so explicitly and repeatedly affirmed in the *Ṛg Veda* as to leave no room for any misunderstanding. A full discussion of the Vedic formulation of the problem of the one and the many would require an extended study of Vedic exemplarism (see Coomaraswamy, "Vedic Exemplarism" [in the present volume—ED.]), but we may call attention to the expression *viśvam ēkam*, "integral multiplicity," in RV iii.54.8. All that we propose now is to assemble some of the most conspicuous of the Vedic texts in which the identity of the one and the many is categorically affirmed; adding that, even were none of these explicit statements available, the law expressed in them could have been independently deduced from an analysis of the functions attributed to the various powers, for although these functions are characteristic of particular deities, they are never entirely peculiar to any one of them.[8]

[7] [E.g., AB iii.4, "In that one resorts to (*upāsate*) Him as one to be made a friend of (*mitrakṛtyaiva*), that is his form as the Friend (*mitra*)." In the *Kailāyamalai*, Śiva is addressed as "Thou that take the forms imagined by thy worshippers" (see *Ceylon National Review*, January 1907, p. 285).]

[8] Max Müller invented the term "henotheism" to describe this method, which he apparently imagined to have been peculiar to the Vedas. Christianity, as a matter of fact, is "henotheistic" in so far as it affirms that whatever is done by one of the Persons is done by all, and *vice versa*. A fully developed "henotheism" is even more characteristic of Stoicism and of Philo, cf. Émile Bréhier, *Les Idées philosophiques et religieuses de Philon d'Alexandrie* (Paris, 1925), pp. 112, 113: "La conception de dieux myrionymes, d'un dieu unique auquel sous ses différentes formes s'adressent les prières des initiés était familière au stoïcisme . . . de même que dans les hymnes orphiques, la toutepuissance de chaque Dieu n'empêche pas leur hiérarchie, de même ici [that is, according to Philo] les êtres sont classés bién souvent hiérarchiquement comme s'il s'agissait d'êtres distincts." [And Plotinus, v.8.9, "He and all have one existence, while each again is distinct. It is distinction by state without interval: there is no outward form to set one here and another there and to prevent any from being an entire identity; yet there is no sharing of parts from one to another. Nor

Familiar passages, often dismissed as "late," include RV I.164.46: "The priests refer in many different ways (*bahudhā vadanti*) to That that is but one, they call Him Agni, Yama, Mātariśvān: they call Him Indra, Mitra, Varuṇa, Agni, who is the heavenly eagle (*suparṇa*) Garutmān"; RV x.114.5, "Ecstatic shapers (*viprāḥ kavayaḥ*) conceive of Him in many ways (*bahidhā kalpayanti*) the eagle that is one"; and x.90.11, where, after the First Sacrificers have divided up (*vyadadhuḥ*) the Person, the question is posed in *brahmōdaya* fashion, "How many-fold did they think Him out?" (*katidhā vyakalpayan*).[9] It is precisely this goal (*artham*) of being made to dwell in many places (*bahudhā niviṣṭa*) that Agni dreads, as He lingers in the darkness (*tamasi kṣeṣi*, x.51.4–5), although, in fact, even while He proceeds He still remains within (*anu agraṃ carati kṣeti budhnaḥ*, III.55.7 = *kṛṣṇe budhne*, IV.17.14 = *vṛṣabhasya nīḷe*, IV.1.12, etc.). As Eckhart expresses it, "the Son remains within as essence and goes forth as person . . . the divine nature steps forth into relation of otherness, other but not another, for this distinction is rational, not real." "To the Shapers He is manifested as the Sun of men" (*āvir . . . abhavat sūryō nṛn*, RV I.146.4).[10] Cf. Plotinus, v.8.9, "He who is the one God . . . what place can be named to which He does not reach?"

Equally explicit, however, are the statements scattered through the other books. In particular, He is often said to have two different forms, according to His being in the Day or Night, and this is "as He wills" (*yathā vaśam*, RV III.48.4, VII.101.3; cf. x.168.4 and AV VI.72.1). When this is expressed as "Now He becometh sterile (*starīr u tvad bhavati*) now begets (*sūte u*)," VII.101.3, the latter expression, like His designation as *sūḥ* in I.146.5, is as much as to say *savitā bhavati*, "He becomes Savitṛ." Cf. III.55.19 and x.10.5, where Tvaṣṭṛ and Savitṛ are identified by ap-

---

is each of these divine wholes a power in fragment . . . the divine is one all-power." The second passage might have been written of the Christian Trinity.] Here also, then, we meet with that superficial appearance of polytheism by which the apologist of some other religion than that under discussion is so conveniently deceived, the Muslim for example, when he calls the Christian doctrine of the Trinity "polytheistic."

[9] Vāc, the Magna Mater, is similarly "divided" by the gods, and made to occupy multifarious stations (*mā devā vyadadhuh purutrā bhūristhātrām bhūryā-veśayantim*, RV x.125.3). It is made abundantly clear throughout that the divine unity is essential, the multiplicity conceptual.

[10] John 1:4, *et vita erat lux hominum*. [The Spiritual Sun (of RV I.115.1, etc.) is the "Light of lights" (*jyotiṣām jyotis*, RV I.113.1, BU IV.4.16, etc.); "The bright Light of lights is what the knowers of the Spirit (*ātma-vidah*) know," Muṇḍ. Up. II.2.10); the "Father of lights" (James 1:17).]

position. In RV III.20.3 and VIII.93.17, Agni and Indra are called polynominal (*bhūrīṇi-nāma, puru-nāma*) and in II.1, Agni is addressed by the names of nearly all the powers, and there are countless passages in which Indra is a designation of the Sun. In VIII.11.8, Agni is "to be seen in many different places, or aspects" [cf. I.79.5 and VI.10.2, Agni *purvanīkaḥ*.] Although His semblance is the same in many places (*purutrā hi saḍṛṇn asi*, VIII.11.8, I.94.7), yet His becoming is manifold (*purutrā . . . abhavat* I.146.5), and He is given many names, for "Even as He showeth, so is He called" (*yādṛg ēva dadṛśē tādṛg ucyatē*, V.44.6),[11] of which ŚB X.5.2.20, cited above, is hardly more than a paraphrase. RV I.146.5, cited above, is based on innumerable texts scattered throughout the *Ṛg Veda*, e.g., III.5.4 and 9, where Agni is identified with Mitra, Varuṇa, and Mātariśvān; in IV.42.3, Varuṇa identifies Himself with Indra and Tvaṣṭṛ; similarly in V.3.1–2, Agni is identified with Mitra, Varuṇa, and Indra. Nor is this a matter of mere suggestion; the particular points of view from which the different names are appropriate is carefully stated.

[In the same way, if Agni as the Sun is the "face" or "point" (*anīkā*) of the gods (RV I.115.1, VII.88.2, etc.), and at the same time logically "many-faced" (*pūrvanīkaḥ*), "this does not put something real in the eternal God, but only something according to our way of thinking" (*Sum. Theol.* III.35.5c), for "Men in their sacrificial worship have imposed upon Thee, Agni, the many faces" (*bhūrīṇi hi tve dadhire anīkâgne devasya yājnavo janāsaḥ*, RV III.19.4). The "faces" or "points" of the solar Agni are in fact his "rays," those very rays by which the Spiritual Sun supports the being of all things, but by which the solar Gateway is concealed (JUB I.3.6), he who would enter in praying, accordingly, that the rays may be dispersed (Īśā Up. 15, etc.). Otherwise expressed, Agni is the Tree of Life (*vanaspati*, *passim*), "The 'other Fires' are thy branches" (RV I.59.1): "all other Agnis stem from thee, O Agni"; "All these deities are forms of Agni" (AB III.4).[12]]

[11] As in *Sum. Theol.* I.13.1 *ad* 3, "Pronomina vero demonstrativa dicuntur de Deo, secundum quod faciunt demonstrationem ad id quod intelligitur, non ad id quod sentitur. Secundum enim quod a nobis intelligitur, secundum hoc sub demonstrationem cadit."

[12] E.g., AV XIII.3.13, "This Agni becomes Varuṇa in the evening; in the morning he becomes Mitra," etc.; JUB III.21.1–2, where the Gale (Vāyu) blows from the five quarters—east, south, west, north, and above—respectively as Indra, Īśāna, Varuṇa, Soma, and Prajāpati; JUB IV.5.1, where Agni, "Varuṇa's messenger," becomes Savitṛ at Dawn, Indra Vaikuṇṭha at noon, Yama at night; J IV.137, "Sujampati in heaven proclaimed, as Maghavā on earth is named."

In many cases the verb *bhū*, to "become," as it occurs in the *Brāhmaṇa* and *Nirukta* texts already cited, is employed in the *Ṛg Veda* to denote in the same sense the passing over from one name and function to another. For example, RV III.5.4, "Agni becometh (*bhavati*) Mitra when enkindled, Mitra the priest; and Varuṇa becometh Jātavēdas"; cf. IV.42.3, "I, Varuṇa, am Indra," and V.3.1–2, "Thou, Agni, art Varuṇa at birth, (*bhuvo varuṇo yad ṛtāya veṣi*, X.8.5), becomest (*bhavasi*) Mitra when enkindled. In thee, O Son of Strength, abide the Universal Gods; Indra art thou to the mortal worshipper. With respect to maidens thou becomest Aryaman, and as Svadhāvan bearest a secret name" (*nāma . . . guhyam*), probably as Trita of I.163.3, "Trita art thou by the interior operation (*asi . . . tritoguhyēna vratēna*)." Again, RV III.29.11, "As Titan Germ he hight Tanūnapāt,[13] when born abroad is Narasāṇsa, when fashioned in the Mother he becometh Mātariśvān, the Gale of the Spiritus in its course" (*tānunapāt ucyate garbha āsuro narasāṇso bhavati yad viyāyate mātariśvā yad amimīta mātari vātasya sargo* [*garbha*] *abhavat sarīmaṇi*, cf. III.5.9). That Spiritus is indeed Varuṇa's own Essence (*ātma te vāta*, VII.87.2), and the breath of Vāc (X.125.8), a gale whose form is never seen, but is the Essence (*ātmā*) of all the gods, moving as it listeth (X.168.4).

To the foregoing passages, in which the diversified effects of what is really a single operation are considered, may be added RV VI.47.18, "He is the counterform of every form, it is that form of His that we should look upon; Indra, by virtue of His magic powers proceeds as multiform" (*rūpaṃ rūpam pratirūpam babhūva tad asya rūpaṃ cakṣaṇāya, indrō māyābhiḥ purūrūpa īyatē*), a passage closely corresponding to Eckhart's "single form that is the form of many different things," resuming the scholastic doctrine of exemplarism. And whereas in X.5.1 Agni alone is *ṛtupati*, in RV VI.9.5, "The Several Gods with one common mind and common will unerring move upon the single season" (*ekaṃ ṛtum*, cf. *ēka ṛtu* in AV VIII.9.26, cited above), closely corresponding to *Sum. Theol.* III.32, I *ad* 3, where what is done by one of the Persons of the Trinity is said to be done by all, "because there is one nature and one will."

ŚB VIII.7.3.10, "Yonder Sun strings these worlds upon his Spirit as upon

[13] The name Tanūnapāt, "Grandson of Himself," formulates the well-known doctrine that "Agni is kindled by Agni" (RV I.12.6, VIII.43.14), according to which in ritual the new Gārhapatya must be lit from the old. Cf. *Sum. Theol.* III.32A *ad* I, "the taking itself (i.e., the assumption of human nature, taking birth) is attributed to the Son," i.e., it is the Son's own (αὐτογενής) act as well as that of the other Persons.

a thread," BG vii.7, "All this is threaded upon me," and x.20, "I am the Spirit seated in the heart of all beings," merely repeat the thought of RV i.115.1, "The Sun is the Spirit (*ātman*) of all that is moving or at rest." In x.121.2, Hiraṇyagarbha (Agni, Prajāpati), is called the "giver of Spirit," (*ātmadā*), and it is in this sense that Agni in i.149.3, is "of hundred-fold Essence" (*śatātmā* [cf. *bhūri nāma vandamāno dadhāti*, v.3.10]. In x.51.7 Agni is called upon to give the gods their "share" (*bhāgam*); that is his particular function as priest.

It is thus clear enough that the *Nirukta* and the *Bṛhad Dēvatā* are fully justified in saying that the gods are participants (*bhakta*) in the divine Essence or spiration; even the phraseology of the Vedic *mantras* is retained by the expositors. The reference to "participation" leads us to the consideration of Vedic Bhaga, later *Bhagavān*. Bhaga is not a personal name, but rather a general designation of the active power in any of his aspects, as the "Free Giver" or "Sharer-out," who makes his *bhaktas* to participate in his riches. These riches can be only the aspects of his Essence, for assuredly we cannot think of deity as possessing anything more than what He himself is; "Sharing out himself, He fills these worlds full" (*ātmānaṃ vibhajya pūrayati imān lōkān*). This last is indeed an Upaniṣadic text (MU vi.26), but the concept is Vedic. Bhaga is, in fact, referred to by apposition as the "Dispenser" (*vibhaktṛ*, RV v.46.6); and *bhāga* is "share" or "dispensation," as in ii.17.7, addressed to Indra, "I pray thee, Bhaga . . . measure out, bring forward, give me that share (*bhāgam*) whereby the body is empowered (*māmaḥ*)," where *bhāgam* = *amṛtasya bhāgam*, in i.164.21; cf. also viii.99.3, "Depending upon him, as upon the Sun, the Several (*viśve*, sc. *devaḥ*) have participated in what is Indra's"; i.68.2, where in a laud addressed to Agni, the Several (*viśve*, sc. *devāḥ*) are said to "participate in thy deity" (*bhajanta dēvatvam*); vii.81.2 has the prayer at dawn, "May we be associated in participation" (*sam bhaktēna gamemahi*). From these passages it is sufficiently plain that *bhāga* and *vibhaktṛ* are the dispenser or giver, who bestows himself or his substance; *sambhāja*, the participant who shares in the gift; *bhāga*, *bhakṣa*, and *bhakta* the share that is given or received. While these are Vedic expressions, *bhakti*, the act of distribution, or making to partake of what is given, and *bhakta* as the synonym of *vibhaktṛ*, the giver, occur only later.

The vexed problem of the "origin of the *bhakti* movement" need never, perhaps, have been posed, if renderings such as these had been retained in the translation of later texts, especially that of *Bhagavad Gītā*. *Bhakta* in the *Ṛg Veda* may be either the share of "treasure" obtained by the sacrificer from the deity (IV.1.10, *ratnaṃ devabhaktam*, etc.), or, conversely, the share that is given or appointed to the deities by the sacrificer (I.91.1, *pitaro . . . dēveṣu ratnam abhajanta dhīrāḥ*), [and typically by Agni as sacrificial priest (*hotṛ*), "Convey thou graciously unto the gods their share (*bhāgam*) of the oblation" (X.51.7): *Ita missa est*!]. In the latter case the sacrificer or sacrificial priest is the *vibhaktṛ*, and the substitution of *bhakta* for the Vedic *vibhaktṛ* introduces no new conception.

Bhakti implies devotion, because all giving presupposes love: it does not follow that *bhakti* should be translated by "love." It is true that the *bhakti-mārga* is also the *prēma-mārga*, the passive "Way of Love," as distinguished from the *jñāna-mārga*, the active "Way of Gnosis"; but that the expressions *bhakti-mārga* and *prēma-mārga* have a common reference does not make them synonymous (expressions are only "synonymous" when they refer to the same thing *under the same aspect*). It can hardly be denied that the *pitaraḥ* who in RV I.91.1, *abhijanta*, were *bhaktas* in the later sense, or that theirs was a *bhakti-mārga*. We should render *bhakti-mārga* "Way of Dedication" or "Way of Devotion" rather than "Way of Love." It is true in the same way that "participation" implies "love," and *vice versa*, since a love that does not participate in the beloved is by no means "love," but rather "desire." Love and participation are nevertheless logically differentiated conceptions, each of which plays its own part in the definition of the devotional act; and when the two expressions are confused in an equivocal rendering, not only are these shades of meaning lost, but at the same time the evidence of the continuity of Vedic with later thought is concealed, and an unreal problem is evoked.

We then wish to express ourselves as in full agreement with the views of Franklin Edgerton, who concluded that "everything contained in at least the older Upaniṣads, with almost no exceptions, is not new to the Upaniṣads, but can be found set forth, or at least *very* clearly foreshadowed, in the older Vedic texts,"[14] and those of Maurice Bloomfield, who argued "that *mantra* and *brāhmaṇa* are for the least part chronological distinctions; that they represent two modes of literary activity, and two modes of literary speech, which are largely contemporaneous. . . . Both forms existed together, for aught we know, from the earliest times; only the redaction of the *mantra* collections seems on the whole to have preceded the redaction of the *Brāhmaṇas*. . . . The hymns of the *Ṛg Veda*,

[14] JAOS, XXXVI (1917), 197.

like those of the other three Vedas, were liturgical from the very start. This means that they form only a fragment . . . late texts and commentaries may contain the correct explanation";[15] Bloomfield also, with reference to the oldest parts of the *Ṛg Veda*, calls it "the last precipitate, with a long and tangled past behind it of a literary activity of great and indefinite length."[16]

We are in agreement with Alfred Jeremias, when he says in the Foreword to his *Altorientalische Geisteskultur* (Berlin, 1929): "Die Menschenheitsbildung ist ein einheitliches Ganzes, und in den verschiedenen Kulturen findet man die Dialekte der einen Geistessprache"; with Carl Anders Scharbau (*Die Idee der Schöpfung in der vedischen Literatur*, Stuttgart, 1932), "die Tiefe und Grösse der theologischen Erkenntnis des Ṛgvedas keineswegs hinter der des Vedānta zurücksteht";[17] and finally with Sāyaṇa, that none of the Vedic references are historical.

It is precisely the fact that the Vedic incantations are liturgical that makes it unreasonable to expect from them a systematic exposition of the philosophy they take for granted; if we consider the *mantras* by themselves, it is as if we had to deduce the Scholastic philosophy only from the libretto of the Mass. Not that this would be impossible, but that we should be accused of reading into the Mass meanings that could not possibly have been present to the mentality prevailing in the "Dark Ages," of yielding, as Professor Keith expresses it (who cannot himself be accused of any such weakness), to "our natural desire . . . to find reason prevailing in a barbarous age." In fact, however, the *mantras* and the Latin hymns alike are so closely wrought, their symbolism is employed with such mathematical exactitude (Emile Mâle speaks of Christian symbolism as a "calculus"), that we cannot possibly suppose that their authors did not understand their own words; it is *we* who misunderstand, if we insist on reading algebra as though it were arithmetic. All that we can learn from literary history is that the doctrines which are taken for granted in the *mantras* were not, perhaps, published until after a certain amount of linguistic change had already taken place; we may find some new words, but we do not meet with new ideas. It is our own fault if we cannot see that Mitrāvaruṇau, of whom the latter is "the immortal brother of the mortal" former, are none other than the *apara* and the *para* Brahman to whom the Upaniṣads refer as mortal and immortal respectively.

[15] JAOS, XV (1893), 144.

[16] JAOS, XXIX (1908), 288.

[17] P. 168, n. 166.

Just as, in relation to the Babylonian liturgies, there must also have existed a "wisdom literature . . . not written to be repeated in temples,"[18] and as it must be assumed that there existed the concept of a "single God . . . [whose] various aspects were not yet considered separate deities in the Sumero-Accadian pantheon,"[19] so in the case of the Vedic liturgies, where the occurrence of the concepts of a "One, that is equally spirated, despirated" (*ānīt avātam*, x.129.2), and of Agni as "being and non-being in one" (*sadasat*, x.5.7) cannot be called surprising. We see then in the Brāhmaṇas, Upaniṣads, *Bhagavad Gītā*, and even in Buddhism, nothing but an ultimate recension and publication of what had always been taught, whether to initiates or in those circles the existence of which is implied by the *brahmōdaya* form of many hymns, and by such Brāhmans as that one who in RV x.71.11 is referred to as expounding the lore of the genesis (*vadati jāta-vidyām*), and whom we may assume to have been, like Agni himself, a "comprehensor of the generations of all things (*viśvā vēda janimā*, vi.15.13; cf. iv.27.1)."

[18] Stephen Herbert Langdon, *Tammuz and Ishtar* (Oxford, 1914), p. 11.

[19] Henri Frankfort, *Iraq Excavations of the Oriental Institute, 1932/1933* (Chicago, 1934), I, 47.

[*Addendum*: Meister Eckhart, Evans ed., II, 153, "Were there an hundred Persons in the Godhead, the man who sees distinctions apart from time and number would apprehend no more than one."]

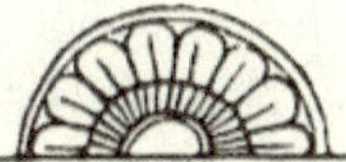

Vedic Exemplarism

God is the cause of all things by His knowledge.
St. Thomas, *Sum. Theol.* (Suppl.) III.88.3.

The doctrine of Exemplarism is bound up with that of forms or ideas, and has to do with the intelligible relation that subsists as between the forms, ideas, similitudes, or eternal reasons of things (*nāma*, "name" or "noumenon" = *forma*) and the things themselves in their accidental and contingent aspects (*rūpa*, "phenomenon" = *figura*). This is as much as to say that Exemplarism, in the last analysis, is the traditional doctrine of the relation, cognitive and causal, between the one and the many: the nature of which relation is implied in Vedic Sanskrit by the expressions *viśvam ekam* (RV III.54.8), "the many that are one, the one that is manifold" (= Plotinus, "integral multiplicity"), *viśvaṃ satyam* (RV II.24.12), "the manifold truth," and *viśvaṃ . . . garbham* (RV X.121.7), "the germ of all," and more fully enunciated in ŚB X.5.2.16, "As to this they say, 'Is He then one or many?' One should answer, 'One and many.' For inasmuch as He is That, He is one; and inasmuch as He is multiply distributed (*bahudhā vyaviṣṭiḥ*) in his children, He is many,"[1] i.e., as the

[This essay was first published in the *Harvard Journal of Asiatic Studies*, I (1936). —ED.]

[1] "He," in the original, "Death" (*mṛtyu*); "That," i.e., "the Person in the Sun." In order not to complicate the present exposition by a discussion *de divinis nominibus*, the pronoun has generally been substituted for the name of deity actually employed in the passages cited. I have discussed the use of essential names in my "Vedic 'Monotheism'" [in the present volume—ED.]. The general principle is as follows: deity is everywhere of one and the same form (RV VIII.11.8, *purutrā hi sadṛṇn asi*; I.94.7, *yo viśvatah supratīkah sadṛṇn asi*), i.e., is perfectly simple but has many names, the application of which inheres not in Him, but in the percipient; "Even as He seems, so is He named" (*yādṛg eva dadṛśe tādṛg ucyate*, RV V.44.6); ["He Himself is all the gods," BU II.5.19;] "As He is approached, so He becomes (*yathopāsate tad eva bhavati*, ŚB X.5.2.20), for example, "Indra art Thou to the mortal worshipper" (RV V.3.1), "Thou art Varuṇa at birth, becomest Mitra when kindled" (RV III.5.4 and V.3.1).

"Person in the mirror (*ādarśe puruṣaḥ*), Who is born in his children in a likeness" (*pratirūpaḥ . . . prajāyāmājāyata*, Kauṣ. Up. IV.11).[2]

The doctrine in these respects cannot be better demonstrated than by means of a diagram consisting of two concentric circles, with their common center and two or more radii, or by the corresponding Vedic symbol of a wheel (*cakra*) with its felly, hub, and spokes. Such a diagram or symbol represents the universe in cross section, the circles any two levels of reference or "worlds" (*loka*), or more specifically, the individual and intellectual, or human and angelic (*adhyātma* and *adhidaivata*) levels of reference. The whole world, or universe (*viśvam*), thus represented corresponds to the ensemble of all possibilities of manifestation, whether informal, formal, or sensible; a world (*loka* = *locus*) is a given ensemble of possibilities, a given modality. The infinite ocean of all possibility, whether of manifestation or nonmanifestation, is represented by the blank surface of the paper which at the same time interpenetrates and transcends the indefinite extension of the finite universe represented by the diagram; this unlimited surface is unaffected by the extension or abstraction of the diagram, which has no position. Each radius, spoke, or ray represents the whole being of an individual consciousness, its intersection with any circumference the operation of this consciousness at that level of reference; each such point of intersection forming the center of a minor "world," which must be thought of as a smaller circle struck about its own center, on the inner surface of the sphere of which the diagram is a cross section, in a plane, that is, at right angles to the radius or ray that connects the unique center with the point in question.

The unique center is, like the whole diagram, without position in its ambient, "position" having a meaning only upon or within the circumference; and just as this ambient is unaffected by the presumption of a center with or without its dependent radii, so the properties of the unique center once assumed are unaffected by the extension or subtraction of radii. And as the indefinitely numerous points which constitute the surface of

[2] [*Anurūpah*, conformable by name; *pratirūpa*, corresponding form, JUB I.27 cf. RV VI.47.18; *ādarśe pratirūpah*, "I worship the Being in the mirror . . . I also worship His reflection," Kauṣ. Up. IV.11; *tvam eva pratijāyase*, "Thou alone art counter born (reborn, born in a likeness)," Praśna Up. II.7. "All mirrors in the universe, I ween, display Thy image with its radiant sheen," Jāmī, *Lawā'ih*, 26; *apratirūpah* is foul, deformed, *pāpam*, evil, improper, BU I.3.4; *na . . . patirūpam*, "unseemly," "not in good form," A I.148.

Monier-Williams gives *pratimā*, masc. creator, fem. likeness; cf. Augustine, *De spiritu et littera* 37, "This likeness begins now to be formed again in us"; and *Paradiso* XXVI.106, XXIX.142 ff., for "mirror."]

indefinitely numerous concentric spheres represent the points of view of individual knowing subjects, so the unique point from which all radii proceed and to which all converge represents an omniscient, supra-individual consciousness, metaphysically the First Principle, theologically God in his intelligible aspect, that of the Supernal Sun, or Light; while what we have called the ambient, at once immanent and transcendent, represents the Godhead or Divine Darkness. Strictly speaking, the diagram should have been drawn not in black on white, but in gold against a black ground, and it is thus in fact that the Vedic *jyotiratha*, "the chariot of light" (= Biblical "chariot of fire"), and its wheels are conceived.

In such a diagram, it is obvious that for every point on the outer circumference there is a corresponding and analogous point on the inner circumference, with only this difference, that on the inner circumference the "points" are more closely packed. If the circumference of the inner circle be reduced, the same condition holds good. In such reduction, there can be no moment at which the "points" of which the circumference (or spherical surface represented by it) is composed can be thought of as annihilated; we can only continue to think of them as more and more densely packed, and finally coinciding in a unity without composition. In other words, all of the radii, all individual principles, and in their total extension, are represented at their common center *in principio*, in an inconnumerable principle (*tattva*), which is at the same time an altogether simple substance (*dharma*) and possessed of a multifarious nature (*svabhāva*); a single point, and yet for each radius its own and private starting point. In just this sense, "The notions of all created things (*ḳāvyā* = *ḳaviḳarmāṇi*) inhere in Him, who is as it were the hub within the wheel (*caḳre nābhir iva śritā*, RV VIII.41.6);[3] "In Him are all beings,

[3] Similarly, RV x.82.6, "Inherent in the nave(l) of the Unborn, in which insist the several worlds as one" (*ajasya nābhau adhi eḳam arpitam yasmin viśvāni bhuvanāni tasthuḥ*); or *aja* may be rendered by "Goat," the reference being to the Sun as Viśvakarma, the "All-maker," in either case.

As to the rendering of *ḳāvya* by "notions of all created things": Vedic *ḳavi* is "poet" in the sense of the original Greek ποιητής, that is, Philo's sense, and as the word is applied to God in the New Testament. It is as "creator" that the term *ḳavi* is used of the Sun, Agni, and others in the *Rg Veda*; while *ḳāvya*, cited above from VIII.41.6, is not as in the later rhetoric merely a "poem," but "whatever is made by a *ḳavi*," whether by way of generation or art. If the word *ḳāvyā* in the sense of "poem" also implies a diction, expression, and utterance, this corresponds to the Scholastic equation of *rationes* with λόγοι (St. Bonaventura, *83 Quaestiones*, q.46, n. 2).

If the Vedic *ḳavayaḥ* are in a certain sense the authors of the *sūḳtas*, it is rather as finders or inventors (in the etymological sense of *in-venio*, dis-cover) than as

and the eye that oversees; intellect (*manas*), spiration (*prāṇaḥ*), and noumenon (*nāma*) coincident (*samāhitam*, 'being in *samādhi*'); in him when he comes forth all his children enjoy (*nandanti*) (the fulfilment of their ends or purposes, by which their will to life is determined);[4] sent by him, and born of him, it is in him that all this universe is stablished," AV xix.53.6–9; and in the same way as the Person, or Man, He is called the "resort of all phenomena" (*rūpāṇy eva yasyāyatanaṃ . . . puruṣam*, BU iii.9.16).

This inherence in the central consciousness is accordingly the means of a "unified density of cognition" (*ekībhūta prajñāna-ghana*, Maṇḍ. Up. 5), a "cognitive pleroma" (*kṛtsnaḥ prajñāna-ghana*, BU iv.5.13); "He knows the whole speculatively" (*viśvaṃ sa veda varuṇo yathā dhiyā*,[5] RV x.11.1), and *ab intra*, "being provident, even before birth, of all the generations of the Angels" (*garbhe nu sann anveṣāṃ avedam ahaṃ de-*

composers; theirs is the "prophetic" faculty; and the *sūktas* themselves are of quickening efficacy; all of which is far removed from conceptions of authorship and "literature" nowadays current. It is as *kavi* that the Sun "wears the forms of all things in their kind" (*viśva rūpāṇi prati muñcate*, RV v.81.2), that is, "frees his comrades from the curse" (*amuñcat nir avadyāt*, RV iii.31.8), from the bonds of Varuṇa (*varuṇyāt*, RV x.92.14), i.e., from the fetter of Death (*bandhanāt mṛtyor*, RV vii.59.12); and because, by the mere act of shining, the Supernal Sun thus releases all things from darkness to light, from potentiality to act, he is called, as Pūṣan, the "Son of liberation" (*vimuco napāt*, RV i.42.1 and *passim*).

[4] AV xix.53.7, *kālena sarvā nandanty āgatena*, translated above, reflects RV x.71.10, *sarve nandanti . . . āgatena . . . sakhyā*, Kāla ("Time," the "Year") replacing Sakhi (the "Comrade," sc. Varuṇa, cf. God as the "Friend" in Sūfī parlance). This variant is omitted in Bloomfield's *Concordance*.

[5] Sāyaṇa's paraphrase is admirable: *dhiyā* is *ātmānurūpayā prajñayā*, "by his foresight (providence) in his own likeness." *Dhi* = *dhyāna* = *contemplatio*. The *dhi* or *dhyāna* of Varuṇa corresponds to the *ādarśa-jñāna* or "mirror-knowledge" of the *jñāna-dharmakāya*, which in Mahāyāna Buddhism is also a "knowledge of sameness" (*samatā-jñāna*), e.g., in the *Abhisamayalaṃkāra* (Obermiller, in *Acta Orientalia*, IX), and a simultaneous act; cf. *Laṅkāvatāra Sūtra* ii.115, "Just as waves arise in the sea simultaneously (*yugapatkāle*), as things are seen simultaneously in a mirror or in dream, so is the mind in its own pasture" (*cittam svagocare* [= *svayonau* in MU vi.34, where *cittam svayonau upaśāmyate*]). I do not agree with Suzuki that this verse is out of place in its context; the idea is that just as when a breeze springs up, the dawn wind of creation for example, the whole surface of the waters is covered by ripples, which arise all together and not one by one or one after another here and there, so in the world-picture the mind sees all things at one and the same time (*yugapatkāle*); while *svagocare*, "in its own pasture," does not mean "in its own sense-fields," but the contrary of this, being equivalent to *svastha-cittaḥ*, *svastha-buddhiḥ*, *anāyasa-cittaḥ*, and such expressions employed in connection with *dhyāna*.

vānāṃ janimāni viśvā, RV IV.27.1);[6] in other words, His knowledge of things is not derived from them objectively and *post factum*, but from their prior likeness in the mirror of His own intellect. Just as the physical sun enjoys a bird's-eye view of this whole earth in its orbit, so the Supernal Sun "surveys the whole" (*viśvam . . . abhicaṣṭe*, RV I.164.44), being the eye or *Aussichtspunkt* (*adhyakṣa*) of Varuṇa or of the Angels collectively (*vāṃ cakṣur . . . sūryaś . . . abhi yo viśvā bhuvanāni caṣṭe*, RV VII.61.1; cf. I.115.1, X.37.1, X.129.7; VS XIII.45, etc.), just as, in the Avesta, the Sun (*hvare* = *svar* = *sūrya*) is Ahura Mazda's eye, and in Buddhism, the Buddha is still the "eye in the world" (*cakkhuṃ loke*). What this eye sees in the eternal mirror is the "world-picture"; "The Primal Spirant (*paramātman*) sees the world-picture (*jagac-citra*, lit. the 'picture of what moves') painted by itself upon a canvas that is nothing but itself, and takes a great delight therein" (Śaṇkarācārya, *Svātmanirūpaṇa* 95); "sees all things at once in their diversity and in coincidence" (*abhi vi paśyati* and *abhi saṃpaśyati*, RV III.62.9, X.187.4; cf. VS XXXII.8, *saṃ ca vi ca eti*; and BG VI.29–30).

Taken in and by itself, this First Spirant, without composition (*advaita*), and at rest (*śayāna*), is the "living conjoint principle" of St. Thomas (*Sum. Theol.* I.27.2c), the unity of the "cohabitant parents" (*sakṣitā ubhā . . . mātarā*, RV I.140.3, *parikṣitā pitarā*, III.7.1, etc.) who are innumerably named, but typically "Intellect" (*manas*) and "Word (*vāc*),[7] whose conjunction effects what Eckhart calls "the act of fecundation latent in eternity." But this unintelligible unity of the Father (-Mother)[8] belongs entirely to the darkness of the "common nest" or

[6] It is as *viśvā veda janimāni* that Agni is called Jātavedas, "comprehensor of the genesis of things," RV *passim*, and as such that he is identified with Varuṇa, *ab intra* (III.5.4), being indeed the "comprehensor of Varuṇa" (IV.1.4); and this "lore of genesis" (*jātavidyā*) which the Brahman knows in X.71.11 is the same thing as the "hidden names of the Angels" (*devānām guhyā nāmāni*, V.5.10), as will be evident when we turn to the further discussion of *nāma*. This divine providence or wisdom is also spoken of as "counsel" (*kratu*, often, like *māyā* and *śacī*, met with in pl. and then equivalent to "powers"), e.g., IV.12.1, "Thou art a Comprehensor by thy counsel, Jātavedas (*tava kratvā jātavedas cikitvān*)."

[7] Manas and Vāc as conjoint pair occur in the *Rg Veda*, *Brāhmanas*, and *Upaniṣads*, *passim*. Vāc is *verbum*, and as in Italian, feminine (*la parola*). Cf. Eckhart, "The Father wantons with the Word"; "From the Father's embrace of his own nature (= *svabhāva*, *prakṛti*, Vāc, Sāvitrī, Sūryā, etc.) comes the eternal playing (= *nitya līlā*) of the Son."

[8] AV VIII.9.10, "Who knoweth the *mithunatva* of Virāj?"; cf. JUB I.54, "They (dual) becoming Virāj (s.) engendered (yonder Sun) (*tau virāḍ bhūtvā prājanayatām*)" [cf. *purutrā . . . abhavat*, RV I.146.5; *pururūpa īyate*, VI.47.18; and AV II.1.3].

"matrix" wherein all things come to be of one and the same ilk (*yatra viśvaṃ bhuvaty ekanīḍam*, Nārāyaṇa Up. 3, cf. RV IV.10.1 *khila*, and VS XXXII.8; *sarve asmin devā ekavṛto bhavanti*, AV XIII.4.20).

Thus, while the divine intellect and the ideas or forms or eternal reasons apparent to it are one simply *secundum rem*, the latter are at the same time manifold *secondum rationem intelligendi sive dicendi* (St. Bonaventura, *I Sent.* d.35, a. unic., q.3, concl.). As Plotinus expresses it (IV.4.1) "The Highest, as a self-contained unity, has no outgoing effect.[9] . . . But the unity of the power is such as to allow of its being multiple to another principle, to which it is all things."

What is represented in our diagram already presumes the diremption (*dvedhā*, BU I.4.3) of those that had been closely embraced (*saṃpariṣvaktau, ibid.*), that is, of knower and known, subject and object, essence and nature, Heaven and Earth, as indicated by the remotion of the circumference from the center. This diremption and divine procession (*krama = dvitva, Taittirīya Pratiśākhya* XXI.16)[10] is coincident with the birth of the Son (Indrāgnī), of Light (*jyotis*), of the Sun, "Savitṛ the creator, who wears the visible forms of all things" (*viśvā rūpāṇi prati muñcate kaviḥ . . . savitā*, RV V.81.2); "by the separation of the prior, the latter came forth" (*prathamāḥ . . . kṛntatrād eṣām uparā udāyan*, RV X.27.23). In other words, the act of being implied by the words "I am *that* I am," "I am Brahman,"[11] although entirely one of self-intention, becomes from an external point of view the act of creation, which is at the same time a

[9] "Having no outgoing effect," Skr. *aviśvaminva.*

[10] Conversely, "There is no procession of one in *samādhi*" (*kramo nāsti samāhite, Laṅkāvatāra Sūtra* II.117). *Samādhi* corresponds to *raptus* or *excessus* in Christian *yoga*, but metaphysically a con-centration must be distinguished from a religious *ecstasy* in the etymological sense of the latter word, viz. that of a going *outside* oneself.

[11] "It knew, indeed, itself, that 'I am Brahman,' thereby it became the All" (BU I.4.10). This does not, of course, represent an empirical consideration of one's own mentality as object, but is the pure act of being, where to be and to know are the same thing; it in no way contradicts Erigena's magnificent words, "God does not know *what* He himself is, for He is not any what; and this ignorance surpasses all knowledge."

BU I.4.10, "It became the All" (*sa idaṃ sarvaṃ bhavati*), corresponds to RV VIII.58.2, "One only Fire is kindled manifold, one only Sun is present to one and all, one only Dawn illuminates this All; that which is only One becomes this All (*ekaṃ vā idaṃ vi babhūva sarvam*)," and is echoed also in connection with the Buddha, S II.212, "I being One become many, and being many become One (*eko pi bahudhā homi, bahudhā pi hutvā eko homi*)." Cf. also MU VI.26 and KU V.12, "Who maketh His single form to be manifold" (*ekaṃ rūpaṃ bahudhā yaḥ karoti*).

generation (*prajanana*) and an intellectual (*mānasa*) creation *per artem* (*taṣṭa*) and *ex voluntate* (*yathā vaśaṃ*, *ḳāmya*); for the Son "in whom were created all things" (Col. 1:16) is also their form and exemplar, the whole occasion of their existence,[12] and it is, accordingly, that species and beauty are appropriated to the Son, whom as being the Word, i.e., as concept, Augustine calls the "art" of God.[13]

The Son or Sun is thus the "single form that is the form of very different things" (Eckhart, resuming in these words the whole doctrine)[14] all of which are in his likeness, as he is in theirs—but with this very important distinction necessitated by the inconnumerability of the unique center, that while the likeness in the thing depends upon the archetype, the latter in no way depends upon the thing, but is logically antecedent: "The model of all that is, preexistent, He knows all generations (*satahsatah pratimānaṃ purobhur viśvā veda janimā*), He smites the Dragon; shining (or 'sounding') forth (*pra . . . arcan*) from Heaven our Leader, cattle-fain, as Comrade frees his comrades from the curse" (*amuñcat nir avadyāt*, RV III.31.8; *pratijūti-varpasaḥ*, III.60.1; *ekaṃ rupaṃ bahudhā yaḥ karoti*, KU V.12).[15] The terms "exemplar" and "image," which imply in strictness "model" and "copy," can, however, be used equivocally, and for this reason a distinction is made between the archetype as *imago imaginans* and the

[12] "Exemplar means *raison d'être*" (*exemplar rationem producentis dicit*, St. Bonaventura, *I Sent.*, d.31, p.II, a.1, q.1 *ad* 3); "Idea is the likeness of a thing, by which it is known and produced" (*ibid.*, d.35, a. unic., q.1, fund.2); "Exemplar implies idea, word, art, and reason (*idea, verbum, ars, et ratio*); idea, with respect to the act of foresight; word, with respect to the act of statement; art, with respect to the act of making; and reason, with respect to the act of completing, because it adds the intention of the end in view. And because all these are one and the same in God, one is often said in place of another" (*Breviloquium*, p.1, c.8). From these definitions the reader will be enabled to judge of the propriety of the employment of the terms in translation.

[13] See *Sum. Theol.* I.39.7; the artist, accordingly, whether human or divine, works "by a word conceived in his intellect" (*per verbum in intellectu conceptum*, *ibid.*, I.45.6c). Cf. St. Bonaventura, "Agens per intellectum producit per formas, quae non sunt aliquid rei, sed idea in mente sicut artifex producit arcam" (*II Sent.*, d.1, p.1, a.1, q.1 *ad* 3, 4): "et quia multa sunt cognita, et unum cognoscens, ideo ideae sunt plures, et ars tantum una" (*ibid.*, I.35, a. unic., q.3 *ad* 2).

[14] Cf. St. Bonaventura, "Quia vero (exemplar in Deo) infinitum et immensum, ideo extra omne genus. Et hinc est, quod existens unum potest esse similitudo expressiva [= *sṛjyamāna*] multorum" (*Breviloquium*, p.1, c.8).

[15] Here the divine providence is directly connected with the act of creation (conquest of the dragon, and release of individual potentialities from the darkness, duress, and deformity or evil of the antenatal tomb, to light and operation). "Cattle" in the *Ṛg Veda* are unrealized potentialities of every kind, of which the proceeding principles desire to take effective possession.

imitation as *imago imaginata* (St. Bonaventura, *I Sent.*, d.31, p.11, a.1, q.1, concl.). A corresponding ambiguity is met with in Sanskrit, where the distinction must be made according to the context. As *imago imaginans*, the deity is called "primordial omniform" (*agriyaṃ viśvarūpam*, RV I.13.10), "the likeness of all things" (*viśvasya pratimānam*, RV II.12.9; cf. III.31.8, cited above), "the omniform likeness of a thousand" (*sahasrasya pratimāṃ viśvarūpam*, VS XIII.41), "the counterpart of Earth" (*pratimānaṃ pṛthivyāḥ*, RV I.52.13), "for every figure He hath been the form (*rūpaṃ rūpaṃ pratirūpo babhūva*), that is his likeness that we should regard (*tad asya rūpaṃ praticakṣanāya*), it is by His magic powers (*māyābhiḥ*) that He proceeds in a plurality of aspects" (*pururūpa īyate*, RV VI.47.18). If it be asked, "What was the model, what the starting point?" (*kā . . . pratimā nidānaṃ kim*, RV X.130.3), the answer is, the sacrificial victim; for this image and this likeness by which the Father proceeds is the sacrifice—"yielding himself up to the Angels, he expressed a likeness of himself, to wit, the sacrifice, hence one says, 'Prajāpati is the sacrifice' " (*ātmanaḥ pratimānam asṛjata, yad yajñām, tasmād āhuḥ prajāpatir yajñaḥ*, ŚB XI.1.8.3), cf. "Manu is the sacrifice, the standard (*pramitiḥ*), our Sire," RV X.100.5; where the relation of the one and the many is again involved, for the Father remains impassible, although in a consubstantial likeness (that of the "Year," *ibid.* XI.1.6.13) sacrificially divisible. But while in these passages there can be no doubt of the priority of the pattern (*pratimāna*, *pratimā*, *pratirūpa*), *pratirūpa* in *Kauṣitaki Upaniṣad* cited below is no less surely *imago imaginata*; and although He is the model of all things, no one of them can be called His like, "There is no likeness (*pratimānam*) of him amongst those born or to be born" (RV IV.18.4.12; cf. BU IV.1.6).[16]

The exemplary image, form, or idea is then a likeness in the prior sense of imitable prototype; in fact, "It is inasmuch as God knows His essence as being imitable by this or that creature, that He knows it as the particular reason and idea of that creature" (*Sum. Theol.* I.15.2c).[17] An assimilation such as this need not imply a likeness of nature or mode; indeed, *minima assimilatio sufficit ad rationem exemplaris* (St. Bonaventura, *I Sent.*, d.36, a.3, q.2 fund.). For example, if "He shines upon this world in the aspect of Person" (*puruṣa-rūpeṇa*, AĀ II.2.1), if man is "made in the image and

[16] "No likeness," i.e., no *similitudo univocationis sive participationis* (St. Bonaventura, *I Sent.*, d.35, a. unic., q.1, concl.); *non est similitudo per unius naturae participationem* (*ibid.*, d.34, a. unic., q.4 *ad* 1).

[17] "Idea non nominat tantum essentiam, sed essentiam imitabilem," St. Bonaventura, *I Sent.*, d.36, q.2, a.2 *ad* 1.

likeness of God," it does not follow that God as He is in Himself is just like or of the same kind as a man, but only that the form or idea of man is present to his consciousness and being, and, be it noted, there on equal terms with an amoeba. And it is in the same way that the human artist embodies the single form entertained in his intellect in other natures such as those of stone or pigment; the *imago imaginans* here as before being the formal cause of the becoming of the *imago imaginata*; as is implied in the dictum *ars imitatur naturam in sua operatione*, where *natura* is "Natura Naturans, Creatrix, Deus."

In Kauṣ. Up. IV.2, "The macrocosm in the Sun, the likeness in the mirror" (*āditye mahat . . . ādarśe pratirūpaḥ*), *pratirūpa* is evidently *imago imaginata*. It is, in fact, as a reflection or projection and, as we shall see, expressively (*sṛjyamāna*) that the eternal reasons or ideas (*nāmāni*) are represented in their contingent aspects (*rūpaṇi*); a formulation that implies the traditional doctrine of the correspondence of macrocosm and microcosm, as enunciated, for example, in AB VIII.2, "Yonder world is in the likeness of (*anurūpa*) this world, this world in the likeness of that," a condition that is clearly exhibited in our diagram by the correspondence of circle with circle, point for point. In what manner the ideas are causal with respect to all their contingent aspects will be apparent when we recall that the central consciousness is always thought of as a Light or Sound, of which the contingent forms on any circumference are projections, reflections, expressions, or echoes thrown, as it were, upon the wall of Plato's cave, or upon the screen of a theater, with only this difference, that the pattern or lantern slide which corresponds to the "form" or "idea" of the picture actually seen is not merely close to the source of light, but intrinsic to the light itself, so that we meet on the one hand with such expressions as "formal light" (Ulrich of Strassburg) and "image-bearing light" (Eckhart), and on the other such as VS v.35, "Thou art the omniform light" (*jyotir asi viśvarūpam*).[18] "He lent their light to other lights" (*adadhāj jyotiṣu jyotir antaḥ*, RV x.54.6), "Ye, Agnīṣomau,

[18] In Scholastic philosophy, the nature of the divine exemplarism is constantly illustrated by means of the likeness of light, e.g., "which although it is numerically one, nevertheless expresses many and different kinds of color" (St. Bonaventura, *I Sent.*, d.35, a. unic., q.2 *ad* 2); "Exemplary cause, just as physical light is one in kind, which is nonetheless that of the beauty that is in all colors, which the more light they have the more beautiful they are, and of which the diversity is occasioned by the diversity of the surfaces that receive the light" (Ulrich of Strassburg); see Coomaraswamy, "The Mediaeval Theory of Beauty" [in Vol. I of this edition—ED.]; cf. Dante, *Paradiso* XXXIII.82–90, "One simple Light, that in its depths encloses, as in a single volume, all that is scattered on the pages of the universe."

found the single light for many"; and in the building of the fire altar, the brick laid down "for progeny" and representing Agni is called the "manifold light" (*viśvajyotis*, ŚB VIII.4.2.25–26).

A subtle problem arises here. For what is meant by the assertion that "The Spirant is interminable, omniform, and yet no doer of anything" (*anantaś cātmā viśvarūpo hy akartā*, Śvet. Up. I.9), or, as Eckhart expresses it, by the apparent contradiction of the statements that "He works willy nilly" and "there no work is done at all"? In view of this, that all the personal powers may be described as reaching out to all things (*viśvaminva*, RV *passim*, cf. II.5.2, where Agni *viśvam invati*), what is meant by the assertion, "At the back of yonder heaven,[19] what they chant is an omniscient word compelling nothing" (*mantrayante divo amuṣya pṛṣṭhe viśvavidaṃ vācam aviśvaminvam*, RV I.164.10, cf. 45), and why is the chariot of the Sun, although by nature directed everywhere (*viṣūvṛtam*), also described as having no effect on anything (*aviśvaminvam*, RV II.40.3)? These questions have an important bearing on the problems of destiny and free will. As follows: the centrifugal procession of individual potentialities depends upon the central unity essentially; their becoming, life, or spiration depends entirely upon the being and spiration of the Primal Spirant, in this sense, that the very existence of individual radii or rays becomes unthinkable if we abstract the central luminous point;[20] and this dependence is constantly asserted, for example, in the designation of Agni as "all-supporting" (*viśvambhara*).

On the other hand, it is not the single form of all potentialities, making arbitrary dispositions ("Heaven gives no orders"), but the specific[21] form

[19] I.e., "In the world beyond the falcon," JB III.268, "there the Sun does not shine" (Muṇḍ. Up. II.2, 10 and KU V.15); in the divine darkness (*tamas, passim*); "Things belonging to the state of glory are not under the sun" (*Sum. Theol.*, III.91.1), "One escapes altogether through the midst of the Sun" (JUB I.3); "No man cometh to the Father save through me" (John 14:6), who as the Sun is the "gateway of the worlds" (*lokadvāra*, CU VIII.6.6).

[20] In this case, that of *pralaya* absolutely, all things are returned to the condition of potentiality, and even the first assumption in Godhead, that of light or being, has not been made. The individual is then "drowned," losing "name and aspect," and, if a Comprehensor, is completely enlarged from all necessity without residual elements of existence; or if not wholly and consciously perfected, must await the opportunities of manifestation and experience in a succeeding aeon, when the dawning of another day again effects the Harrowing of Hell.

[21] Form, idea, reason, species, truth, virtue, and beauty, although not synonymous, are interchangeable terms in Scholastic exemplarism, because one at their source. Species, however, in this sense, does not imply a group within a genus, but what

of each potentiality that determines each thing's individual mode or character, and gives to it its "proper likeness" (*sva-rūpam*). In other words, God or Being is the common cause of the becoming of all things, but not immediately of the distinctions between them, which distinctions are determined by "the varying works inherent in the respective personalities" (Śaṇkarācārya, on *Vedānta Sūtra* II.1, 32, 35); they are born according to the measure of their understanding (*yathā-prajñam*, AĀ II.3.2); or, as more commonly implied in the *Ṛg Veda*, according to their several ends or purposes (*anta*, *artha*); "they live dependent on (*upajīvanti*) their such-and-such desired ends" (*yaṃ yam antam abhikāmaḥ*, CU VIII.2.10). So it is said, "Now run ye forth your several ways" (*pra nūnaṃ dhāvatā pṛthak*, RV VIII.100.7).[22] "In fine," as Plotinus expresses it (IV.3.13 and 15), "the law is given in the entities upon whom it falls; these bear it about with them. Let but the moment arrive, and what it decrees will be brought to act by those beings in whom it resides; they fulfil it because they contain it; it prevails because it is within them; it becomes like a heavy burden, and sets up in them a painful longing to enter the realm to which they are bidden from within," and thus "all diversity of condition in the lower spheres is determined by the descendant beings themselves."[23]

A doctrine of this kind, which makes each creature the source and bearer, not of its own being but of its own destiny (and this is what one means by "free will," although this is in reality a state of bondage, viz. to the idiosyncracy of the individual will), is common to all tradition, and has been everywhere expressed in almost the same way: for example, "It is manifest that fate is in the created causes themselves" (*Sum. Theol.*, I.116.2); "God's being is bestowed on all creatures alike, only each receives it according to its receptivity" (Johannes Tauler, *The Following of Christ*, tr. J. K. Morrell, London, n.d., §154, p. 135); "As is the harmony, so also is the sound or tone of the eternal voice therein; in the holy, holy, in the perverse, perverse" (Jacob Boehme, *Signatura rerum* XVI.6–7); "formal light . . . of which the diversity is occasioned by the diversity of the sur-

---

is individually specific, and similarly as regards goodness (or perfection) and beauty, things being good or beautiful in their kind (and there is only one of each kind), and not indefinitely.

[22] In this connection may be noted KU IV.14, "Just as water rained upon a lofty peak runs here and there (*vidhāvati*), so one who sees the principles in multiplicity (*dharmāny pṛthak paśyan*) pursues after them (*anudhāvati*)."

[23] "According to their receptive powers," Dionysius, *De divinis nominibus* IV.1.

faces that receive the light" (Ulrich of Strassburg; see Plotinus, IV.4.8); for, as Macrobius says, *unus fulgor illuminat, et in universis appareat in multis speculis* (*Somnium Scipionis* I.14). We find this point of view also in Islam: the creative utterance, *kun*, "Be," causes or permits the positive existence of individuals, but in another sense (that of mode), they are causes of themselves "because He only wills what they have it in them to become" (Ibnu'l 'Arabī, as cited by R. A. Nicholson, *Studies in Islamic Mysticism*, Cambridge, 1921, p. 151).

That we do what we must is a matter of contingent necessity (*necessitas coactionis*), altogether distinct from the infallible necessity (*necessitas infallibilitatis*) with which He who acts "willingly but not from will" (Eckhart), "does what must be done" (*cakriḥ . . . yat kariṣyam*, RV VII.20.1, cf. I.165.9 and VI.9.3), viz. "those things which God must will of necessity" (*Sum. Theol.* I.45.2c); the individual is then only freed (*mukta*) to the extent that the private will to which he is in bondage consents to His who wills all things alike, a condition implied in RV V.46.1, his condition "who hath what he will, for whom the Spirit is his will, who doth not will" (*āpta-kāmam ātma-kāmam akāmam*, BU IV.3.21); as Boethius expresses it, "The nearer a thing is to the First Mind, the less it is involved in the chain of fate." It is because these considerations can hardly be made intelligible without reference to the concept of the relation of the one and the many, proper to Exemplarism, that we have thought it proper to refer to the matter in the present connection.

As to our rendering of *ātman*: in the citation from Tauler, above, "being" or "essence" corresponds to *ātman* as the *suppositum* of accidents and *sine qua non* of all modality (*-maya*). We have experimented elsewhere with a rendering of *ātman* by "essence," but propose in future to adhere to a more strictly etymological equivalent, more especially inasmuch as the *ātman* doctrine in the *Ṛg Veda* must be considered in connection with X.129.2, *ānīd avātam*, equivalent to "at the same time *ātmya* and *anātmya*," or "equally spirated, despirated." The word *ātman*, derived from *an* or *vā*, to "breathe" or "blow," is, in fact, more literally "spirit," spirant, or spiration, and hence "life."[24] This Spirit or Gale (*ātman*, *prāṇa*,

[24] The translation of *ātman* as "Self" is unsatisfactory in any case, and mainly for two reasons: (1) that it introduces an altogether unfamiliar terminology, one that lends itself to misunderstandings connected with the connotation "selfishness," and (2) that the reflexive use of *ātman*, which underlies the rendering "Self," hardly occurs in the *Rg Veda*. *Ātman* is "spirit," as this word is used, for example, in the trilogy, "body, soul, and spirit (*rūpa, nāma, ātman*)."

vāta, or *vāyu*) is, as may be understood from what has been said above, the only property that can be shared and is thus apparently divided, as Being amongst beings, the breath of life in breathing things; cf. BD I.73, "Spiration (*ātman*) is said to be the only participation (*bhaktiḥ*) that can be attributed to the three great Lords of the World" (the functional Trinity). In RV I.115.1, "The Sun, as being the spirant (*ātman*) in all that is mobile or immobile, hath filled Midhome and Heaven and Earth" (the "Three Worlds," the Universe); in X.121.2, "The Golden Germ (*hiraṇyagarbha*, Agni, the Sun, Prajāpati) is the bestower of spiration" (*ātmadā*); Agni in this sense is "a hundred-fold spirant (*śatātmā*, RV I.149.3)," that is, he has innumerable lives or hypostases, as many, in fact, as there are living things (*antar āyuṣi*, RV IV.58.11), to each of which he is a total presence (as can be clearly seen in our diagram), although as we have seen, each is but a participant (*bhakta*) of his life, for though "all is offered, the recipient is able to take only so much" (Plotinus, VI.4.3).[25] In JUB III.2–3, "Spiration (*ātman*) both of Angels and mortals, Spiritus (*ātman*) arisen from the sea, and which is yonder Sun"[26] may be read in connection with ŚB VIII.7.3.10, "Yonder Sun connects (*samāvayate*)[27] these worlds by a thread (*sūtre*),[28] and what that thread is is the Gale" (*vāyuh*); cf. *ibid.* II.3.3.7, "it is by His rays (*raśmibhiḥ*) that all creatures are endowed with their spirations (*prāṇeṣu abhihitāḥ*), and so it is that the rays extend downwards to these spirations." These texts recall RV I.115.1, cited above, and III.29.11, "formed in the Mother, He is Mātariśvan (= Vāyu, Spiritus) and becomes the draught of the Gale in its course" (*vātasya sargaḥ*); cf. VII.87.2, "The Gale that is thy breath (*ātmā te vātaḥ*) thunders through the Firmament . . . and in these spheres of Earth and lofty Heaven are all those stations dear to thee." In RV X.168.4, "This Angel, the spiration of the Angels (*ātmā devānām*), Germ of the World (*bhuvanasya garbha* = *Hiraṇyagarbha*) moves as He will (*yathā*

[25] "All beings are not their own being, but beings by participation" (*Sum. Theol.* I.44.1c); "Creation is the emanation of all being from the Universal Being" (*ibid.* I.45.4 *ad* 1); [but (*ibid.* I.45.1c), "Creation is the emanation of all being from the Nonbeing, which is nothing." Also, "To create is to make something out of nothing"; and I.45.4 *ad* 3, "Creation is the creation of Being, and not only of matter." Cf. BU II.1.20 and CU VI.10.2, "All creatures have come forth from *sat*."]

[26] Cf. *ibid.* III.32, where the Angel's omniformity (*sarvam rūpam*) is illustrated by the five *exemplata*, "and what his single form is, is the Spirit (*tad etad ekam eva rūpam prāna eva*)."

[27] *Samavāga* is "perpetual co-inherence," and in the symbolism based on weaving is illustrated by the relation of thread to the cloth.

[28] The doctrine of the "thread-breath" (*sūtrātman*) recurs in BG VII.7, cf. X.21.

vaśam),[29] His sound (*ghoṣā*)[30] is heard but never his likeness (*rūpam*), so let us offer with oblation to the Gale (*vātāya*)."

Similarly in later texts: "For that sharing out his spiration, or himself (*ātmānaṃ vibhajya*, cf. *bhakti* in BD I.73), He fills these worlds, it is said that as indeed sparks from fire and as light rays from the sun, so from Him in the course of his procession (*yathā kramaṇena*) the spirations and other powers of perception (*prāṇādayaḥ*) go forth again and again" (*abhyuccaranti punaḥpunar*, MU VI.26). Much later: "That (viz. the principle, *tattva*, called Sadāśiva, the 'Eternal Śiva') becomes by inversion (*viparyayeṇa*)[31] and in the splendor of its practical power (*kriyā-*

[29] "The wind bloweth as it listeth," etc. (John 3:8). Cf. Prose Edda, *Gylfi* 18, "He is so strong that he rears great seas, but strong though he be, yet may he not be seen, therefore is he surely wonderfully shapen"; and Rūmī, *Dīvān*, "Foamed the sea (*āb*, Skr. *ap*), and at every foam-fleck, something took figure and something was bodied forth" (Ode 19); "The Spirit of God moved upon the face of the waters" (Genesis).

[30] *Ghoṣā* is to be noted here, as the "voice" of the Gale. This Ghoṣā is the mother of Hiraṇyahasta, Savitṛ, the Sun, and one with Vadhrimatī and Vāc: cf. RV I.116.13 and VI.62.7, where the Aśvins hear the call of Ghoṣā, the soughing of the dawn-wind (*vasarhā vātaḥ*, RV I.122.3) of creation, the breath of Vāc, "Whose breathing is the Gale, whenas I take in hand to shape the several worlds" (*vāta iva pravāmi*, etc., RV X.125.8).

[31] "By inversion" or "by revolution" (*viparyayena*) involves the notions of the "face" and "back" of God—the Janus symbolism—and is reminiscent of RV IV.1.2, "Do thou, Agni, turn round thy brother Varuṇa (*bhrātaram varuṇam agne a vavṛtsva*)," and thus, indeed, "the kingdom is reversed" (*paryāvart rāṣṭram*, RV X.124.4), dominion passing from the "Father" or "Elder Brother" to the "Son" or "Younger Brother" (both relations as well as that of consubstantiality are predicated of Varuṇa and Agni in the *Rg Veda*).

It is the "rotation" of this central principle, "the axle-point on which the aeviternal substances depend" (*āṇim na rathyam amṛtādhi tasthuḥ*, RV I.35.6)—Dante's "il punto dello stelo al cui la prima rota va dintorno"—that initiates the revolution of the Wheel of the Year, "mounted whereupon the Angels move round all the worlds" (KB XX.1). It must not, however, be overlooked that the "rotation" of a point means nothing *secundum rem*; the unique center, though the prime mover, is by no means the *primum mobile*, but in itself immoveable. It is only when the radii are projected and circles struck, that is, when diremption of essence and nature has taken place, that we are given the two *points d'appui* indispensable for leverage and local motion, and only from an exterior point of view that we can speak of a rotation of the axle-point, or distinguish "face" and "back" in the Supreme Identity (*tad ekam*): it is the felly, not the axle-point, that actually turns, impelled by the will to life in individual principles. That is why at the same time that the Supreme Identity is spoken of as turning from interior (*guhya*) to exterior (*āvis*) operation (*vrata*) at will (*yathā vaśam*), the *Rg Veda* also treats of the separation of Heaven and Earth, that is to say of creation, as being effected by the several desirous principles, whose co-creative activity—the *śakty-aujjvalaye*, cf. *ujjvalati* in MU vi.26) the form of the universal demiurge of things in their manifested likeness (*vyaktākara-viśvānusaṃdhātṛ-rūpam*), and this is the principle called 'Lord'" (*īśvara-tattvam*, *Mahārtha-mañjarī* xv, Commentary);[32] virtually identical with the formulation of Philo, according to whom "two powers are first distinguished (σχίζονται) from the Logos, viz. a poetic, according to which the artist ordains all things and which is called God; and the royal power of Him called the Lord, by which He controls all things."[33]

From all of the foregoing passages it is evident that as in Scholastic and Neoplatonic, so also in the Vedic tradition, it is a formal light that is the cause of the being and becoming of all things (as light, the cause of their being, as formal the cause of their becoming); the fontal raying of this primal light seeming to be an actual expression or emanation (*sṛṣṭi*) and local motion (*caraṇam*, *gati*), although really this Agni, even while "He proceedeth foremost, still remains in his ground" (*anvagraṃ carati kṣeti budhnaḥ*, RV iii.55.7), "While yet abiding in the Germ, He is repeatedly born" (RV viii.43.9); cf. Plotinus (iv.3.13), "abiding intact above, while giving downwards," and Eckhart, "The Son remains within as Essence

operation of "mediate causes"—is brought forward in the first and subsequent sacrifices, by which the unitary principle is intellectually contracted and identified, as, for example, in x.114.5, "By their wordings they made him logically manifold who is but One," and x.90.11 and 14, "They subdivided the Person . . . thought out the worlds," and thus in fact by their thousand years' session "expressed everything" (*viśvam asṛjata*, PB xxv.18.2). It is just because of the distinction of these two points of view (*secundum rem* and *secundum rationem intelligendi sive dicendi*) that one can ask in *brahmodaya*, as in RV x.129.7, whether, indeed, the world was expressed from within or determined from without.

The ontology of RV x.90.14, *lokān akalpayan*, and x.114.5, *bahudhā kalpayanti*, is preserved in *Laṅkāvatāra Sūtra* iii.77, "The being of the three worlds is conceptual (*vikalpa-mātram*), without external validity (*bāhyamartham na vidyate*); it is as a concept that it is seen pictorially (*vikalpam dṛśyate citram*)."

[32] Kashmir Series XI (Bombay, 1918), 44; *rūpam* is here *imago imaginans*. Other instances of the persistence of the exemplarist concept in later literature may be cited in the *Kādambarī* (Parab's ed., Bombay, 1928, p. 10), where King Śudraka is compared to God, "whose abundance (*vasatā*, cf. Vedic Vasu, Vasiṣṭha) displays the likeness of every form" (*prakaṭita-viśvarūpākṛteh*), and in *Śakuntalā* ii.9, where the heroine is so beautiful that she seems to have been "intellectually created by Brahmā" (*manasā kṛtā vidhinā*), to be, that is, rather a divine idea than a mundane actuality.

[33] Émile Bréhier, *Les Idées philosophiques et religieuses de Philon d'Alexandrie* (Paris, 1925), p. 113. "Two powers," i.e., spiritual and temporal, *brahma* and *kṣatra*.

and goes forth as Person . . . other, but not another, for this distinction is logical (Skr. *vikalpam*), not real (Skr. *satyam*)."

As Plotinus expresses it (VI.4.3), "Under the theory of procession by powers,[34] souls are described as rays."[35] In other words, the animating (*jinva*, *codana*, *sava*) principle is both a living and a vocal power, and the light of the world. Āyu, "Life," and Viśvāyu, "Universal Life," are constant epithets of Agni, who is "the one life of the Angels" (*asur ekaṃ devānām*, RV X.121.7) and "the only guardian of being" (*bhūtasya . . . patir ekaḥ*, *ibid.* 1), and manifests himself as Light (*jyotis*, *bhāna*, *arka*, etc.), whether of the Fire-flash or the Supernal Sun; *brahmaṇa vācaḥ parama vyoma*, TS VII.4.18. As in John 1:1–3, "In principio erat verbum, et verbum erat apud Deum, et Deum erat verbum . . . Omnia per ipsum facta sunt . . . Quod factum est in ipso vita erat; et vita erat lux hominum."[36]

This equivalence of life, light, and sound must be taken into account when we consider the causal relationship of Vedic *nāma*, "name" or "noumenon," to *rūpa*, "phenomenon" or "figure," which is that of exemplary cause to *exemplatum*; for while *nāma* involves the concept primarily of thought or sound, *rūpa* involves the concept primarily of vision. Not that light and sound are strictly speaking synonymous (for though they refer to one and the same thing, they do so under different

[34] "Powers," in Skr. *śaci*, *śakti*, *svadhā*, *vibhūti*, *kṣatra*, etc. "It is the manifestation of their (the devas') powers that their names are various" (BD 1.71).

[35] Cf. MU VI.26, as cited above. In Christian iconography, in representations of the Annunciation, the Spirit (dove) moves on the path of a ray that extends from the Supernal Sun to the Virgin, while in representations of the Nativity a similar ray (which is in fact coincident with the axis of the universe, the trunk of the Tree of Life, Gnostic σταυρός, and the "one foot" of the Sun) connects the Bambino with the Sun. Even in the case of ordinary conceptions the Spirit is the animating power, *Sum. Theol.* III, q.32, a.1, agreeing with KB III.3, "It is spiration (*prāna*), verily the conscious Spirit (*prajñātman*) that grasps and quickens the flesh."

[36] According to a variant text (cf. Augustine, *Confessions* VII.9), "quod factum est, in eo vita est, et vita erat lux hominum," i.e., "There is life in what was made, and this life was the light of men." See also René Guénon, "Verbum, Lux, et Vita," *Le Voile d'Isis*, XXXIX (1934), 173, and P. Mus, "Le Buddha paré," *BÉFEO*, XXVIII (1928), 236, n. 4, "la voix et la lumière . . . deux manifestations connexes d'une même nature transcendente." It may be noted that in RV X.168.4, cited above, one and the same verb *śṛṇvire*, "is heard," is employed in connection with both sound and appearance; while alternatively in 1.164.44, one and the same verb *dadṛśe*, "seen," is similarly employed. ["La parole est vie, elle possède toute vie, elle est toute vie" (Willem Caland and Victor Henry, *L'Agniṣṭoma* (Paris, 1906–1907), I, 232, quoting *Aśvalāyanaśrautasūtra* V.9.1).]

aspects), but that the utterance *fiat lux* and the manifestation *lux erat* by no means imply a temporal succession of events; the utterance (*vyāhṛti*) of names and the appearance of the worlds is simultaneous, and, strictly speaking, eternal.[37] Thus we find in JUB III.33 that "The Sun is sound; therefore they say of the Sun, 'He proceeds resounding'" (*ya ādityassvara eva saḥ, tasmād etam ādityam āhus, svara etīti*): the humming of the world wheel is the music of the spheres. It is, in fact, hardly possible to distinguish the roots *svar*, to "shine" (whence *sūrya*, "sun"), and *svṛ*, to "sound" or "resound" (whence *svara*, "musical note") and also in some contexts to "shine." The like applies in the case of root *arc*, which means either to "shine" or to "intone," and to its derivatives such as *arka*, which may mean either "sheen" or "hymn." There is also a close connection, and was probably an original coincidence, of the roots *bhā* to "shine" and *bhan* to "speak." Even in English we still speak of "bright" ideas and "brilliant" sayings.

The shining of the Supernal Sun is then as much an "utterance" as a "raying"; he, indeed, "speaks" (*mitro . . . bhruvāṇaḥ*, RV III.59.1; VII.36.2; I.92.6), and what he has to say is "that great and hidden name (*nāma guhyam*) of multiple effect (*puruspṛk*), whereby thou dost produce all that has come to be or shall become" (RV X.55.2) ("The Father spoke himself and all creatures in the Word, to all creatures in the Son," Eckhart). The name or form of the thing is thus prior—prior, that is, in hierarchy rather than in time—to the thing itself, and is its *raison d'être*, whether as pattern or as name; and it is accordingly as an expression (*sṛṣṭi*) or utterance (*vyāhṛti*) that the thing itself is manifested or evoked; "in the beginning this universe was unuttered" (*avyāhṛti*, MU VI.6).

In the concluding paragraphs of the present essay we shall accordingly assemble certain of the Vedic texts in which the doctrine is explicit or implicit that the utterance of a name is of creative efficacy. For example, "He by the names of the four (seasons) has set in motion his ninety coursers, as a rounded wheel" (RV I.155.6), viz. the Wheel of the Year, as made up of four ninety-day seasons; it is "by those four titan names immaculate (*asuryāṇi nāmādābhyāni . . . yebhiḥ*), that He well knows, that thou, Indra, hast performed all thy mighty deed" (*karmāṇi cakartha*,

[37] That is to say "now"; that "now" of which a temporal experience is impossible, being only of a past and a future, and where becoming never stops to be. We have discussed elsewhere (*The Rg Veda as Land-Náma-Bók*, 1935) the proposition enunciated by Sāyaṇa and others that the Veda deals only with what is eternal (*nityam*), and shall return to the subject.

RV x.54.4; cf. III.38.4, x.73.8); it is after these hidden names that the maker of all things names, that is, creates, the Angels, being *devānāṃ nāmadhāḥ*, RV x.82.3; it is by recourse to Agni that these Angels "get for themselves those names by which they are worshipped sacrificially, and thus contrive their own well-born embodiment" (*nāmāni . . . dadhire yajñiyāny, asūdayanta tanvaḥ sujātāḥ*, RV I.72.3);[38] it is inasmuch as he "knows the distant hidden names (*apīcyā veda nāmāni guhyā*) that Varuṇa propagates the multiplicity of notions of created things (*kāvyā puru . . . puṣyati*), even as Heaven (i.e., the Sun) propagates their aspect (*rūpam*),"[39] which "notions of created things" (*kāvyā* = *kavikarmāṇi*, see n. 4) "inhere in him as hub within the wheel" (RV VIII.41.5 and 6). The productive activity of the co-creative principles is similarly nominative (*nāmadheyaṃ dadhānāḥ*, RV x.71.1);[40] "What was the bovine virtue (*sakmyaṃ goḥ*, cf. *śagmyena*, III.31.1) of the Bull and Cow,

[38] Here the sequence of ideas corresponds to that implied in the Scholastic dictum, "the soul is the form of the body."

[39] As in RV v.81.2, where the Sun *viśva rūpāni prati muñcate*; "He illumines (*bhāsayati*) these worlds . . . incarnadines (*rañjayati*) existences here" (MU VI.7); "This supremely pure splendor of the impartible essence illumines all things at once . . . the patent of his power, resplendent in luminous detail" (Eckhart).

[40] Cf. CU VI.1.4, "Modification is a matter of wording, a giving of names to things" (*vācārambhaṇaṃ vikāro nāmadheyam*, reminiscent also of RV x.125.8, where the Word, Vāc, speaks of herself as *ārambhamāṇā bhuvanāni*; *ārambha* has been defined as evocation, "mental initiation of action"). It is on the basis of the magical efficacy of enunciation that the employment of words of power in ritual depends: for example, PB VI.9.5, "By saying 'born' (*jātam iti*), he brings to birth (*jījanat*)," and *ibid.* VI.10.3, "In saying 'lives' he puts life into them that live." Cf. *Laṅkāvatāra Sūtra*, VI, p. 228, "When names are enunciated, there is the manifestation of appearance (*nimittābhivyañjakam*), there is concept (*vikalpaḥ*)."

The doctrine of ideas, inseparable from that of exemplarism, recurs in traditional teachings at all times. As remarked by E. Gilson, "Le mot *idée* remonte à Platon, mais la chose elle-même existait avant lui, puisqu'elle est éternelle. On doit d'ailleurs supposer que d'autres hommes les avaient connues avant lui, de quelque nom ils les aient désignées, car il y eut des sages antérieurement à Platon et en dehors même de la Grèce, et il n'y a pas de sagesse sans la connaissance des idées" (*Introduction a l'étude de Saint Augustin*, Paris, 1929, p. 257). The doctrine, for example, appears already in the Sumero-Babylonian conception of creation as a *term*inology or de*term*ination, for "the Babylonians regarded the name of a thing as its reality . . . to name a thing practically means in their theology to determine its essence" (Stephen Langdon, *Sumerian Epic*, Philadelphia, 1915, pp. 39–40, cf. *idem, Semitic Mythology*, Boston, 1931, pp. 91, 289). In the Clementine Homilies, in connection with the doctrine of the True Prophet, similar to the Indian "Eternal Avatar," we find with reference to Adam's calling of things by their names, "He himself, being the only true prophet, fittingly gave names to each animal, according to the merits of its nature, as having made it."

that they measured out by names (*ā nāmabhiḥ mamire*), making a manifested image in it" (*ni . . . mamire rūpam asmin*, RV III.38.7), "Then verily they recollected (*amanvat*) the distant name (*nāma . . . apīcyam*, admirably rendered by Griffith's 'essential form') of Tvaṣṭṛ's Cow within the mansion of the Moon" (RV I.84.15), "When he (the Sun) upstood, all things him adorned; who moves self-luminous, indued in glory; that is the Bull's, the Titan's mighty form, it is the Omniform who takes his stand upon his aeviternities" (*mahat tad vṛṣṇo asurasya nāmā, ā viśvarūpo amṛtāni tasthau*, RV III.38.4, where Viśvarūpa must be Tvaṣṭṛ, and *amṛtāni*, pl., contrasts with an implied *anantatva* in or as which the Asura lies recumbent, *ante principium*); "The Son (the Sun) in Heaven's light determines the Father-Mother's third hidden name" (*dadhāti putraḥ pitror apīcyaṃ nāma tṛtīyam adhi rocane divaḥ*, IX.75.2, where *dadhāti . . . nāma* is the same as to be *nāmādhāḥ* in X.82.3, as cited above); and all this is at the same time a creative recollection in the Platonic sense, as in RV X.63.8, where the Viśve Devāḥ are "mindful of all that is mobile or immobile" (*viśvasya sthātur jagataś ca mantavaḥ*). It is "by wordings" (*vacobhiḥ*) that they "think Him out as manifold who is but One"[41] (RV X.114.5); that He, indeed, appears at all depends upon the ritual incantation, "And sundry sang, they brought to mind the Great Chant, whereby they made the Sun to shine"[42] (*arcanta eke mahi sāma manvata*, etc., RV VIII.29.10); "by an angelic utterance they opened up the cattle fold" (*vacasādaivyena*, etc., RV IV.1.15).[43]

[41] That this is possible depends on His Protean nature, who is "omniform" (*viśvarūpa*, *passim*), and is "man-made" in the sense that He assumes the forms that are imagined by His worshippers.

[42] "For that God is God he gets from creatures. . . . Before creatures were, God was not God" (Eckhart).

[43] Intellect being identical with its noumenal content, the intellectual creation so often referred to in Vedic tradition is essentially the same thing as a creation by the utterance of a name or names. The intellectual creation is typically *per artem*, as for example in RV I.20.2, "they wrought by intellect" (*tatakṣur manasā*), where √*takṣ* implies the use of an axe on wood, viz. that "wood from which they fashioned Heaven and Earth," RV X.31.7. The intellectual operation is, moreover, strictly speaking a conception; what is formulated in the "heart" by the application of *manas* to *vāc* is literally a generation and a vital operation; as in BU I.5.7, "The Father is *manas* (intellect), the Mother *vāc* (Word), the Child *prāṇa* (life)." [The new born Kumāra (Agni) demands a name, for it is "by name that evil is smitten away," i.e., by name that there is procedure from potentiality to act, ŚB VI.1.3.8–9.] In RV X.71.2 there may be noted the expression *manasā vācam akrata*; *manasā kṛ* being parallel to *haste* or *panau kṛ*, to "marry," where *kṛ*, to "make," has a value comparable to that of "make" in the modern erotic vernacular. Cf. *Sum. Theol.* I.45.6c, where the artist is said to operate by a word conceived in his

The "names" or noumena of things are, moreover, everlasting, and in this respect unlike the things themselves in their contingent manifestation: "When a man dies, what does not go out of him is his name (*nāma*; similarly BU III.1.9, *manas*), that is endless (*ananta*), and inasmuch as what is endless is the Several Angels, thereby he wins accordingly the endless world (*anantaṃ lokam*)," BU III.2.12; in other words, his name is "written in the Book of Life." From the point of view of the desirous principles, *in potentia* but eager to be in act, the possession of a "name" and corresponding entity is naturally the great desideratum,[44] and what they most fear is to be "robbed of their names"; cf. RV v.44.4, "Krivi in the forest steals away their names (*krivir nāmāni pravaṇe muṣāyati*)."

On the other hand, it must not be overlooked that individuation and identification are specific limitations, implying the possession of only a particular ensemble of possibilities to the exclusion of all others. "Speech (*vāc*) is the cord, and names (*nāmāni*) the knots whereby all things are bound" (AĀ II.1.6). Liberation (*mukti*), then, as distinguished from salvation, is something other than a perpetual and ideal being still oneself and, as it were, a part of the world picture; liberation in the fullest sense of the word is a liberation not merely from phenomenal becoming, but from any noumenal determination whatever.[45] The cycle that must for the Wayfarer begin with the audition or the finding of a name, must for the Comprehensor end in silence, where no names are spoken, none is named, and none remembered. There knowledge-of, which would imply division, is lost in the coincidence of knower and known, "as a man locked in the embrace of a dear bride knows naught of a within or a without" (BU IV.3.21); There "none has knowledge of each who enters, that he is so-and-so or so-and-so" (Rūmī); the prayer of the soul is an-

---

intellect (*per verbum in intellectu conceptum*), that is, like the Father and Divine Architect, *per artem* and *ex voluntate*, both with knowledge and with will; the consciousness of the artist being in either case a conjoint principle, and the "work" (*karma*) the artist's child.

[44] Hence the distress of the Devas at Agni's hesitation in RV x.51, and their corresponding fear when the Buddha, who is the same as Agni *uṣarbudh*, hesitates to set in motion the Wheel of Order, by which the Way is to be opened for them to proceed.

[45] "Released from form or aspect (*nāmarūpad-vimuktah*), the Comprehensor reaches thus the heavenly Person beyond the yon, knowing the ultimate Brahman, he indeed becomes the Brahman" (Muṇḍ. Up. III.2.8–9; [*padam gacchanty anāmayam*, BG II.51]).

swered, "Lord, my welfare lies in thy never calling me to mind" (Eckhart). If what of the Supreme Identity is manifestable appears to us to be contrasted into variety and individualized, the doctrine of Exemplarism, common to both the Eastern and the Western forms of a common tradition, exhibits the relation of this apparent multiplicity to the unity on which it hangs, and apart from which its being would be a pure nonentity; and furthermore, inasmuch as the last end must be the same as the first beginning, the way is pointed out that leads again from multiplicity to unity, from the semblance to reality. As in AĀ II.3.8.3, 4, "The Makers, laying aside the Yes and No, what's 'blunt' and what is veiled of speech,[46] have found their quest; they that were held in bond by names are now beatified in that which was revealed; they now rejoice in what had been revealed by name, in that in which the host of Angels cometh to be one; putting away all evil by this spiritual power, the Comprehensor reaches Paradise."[47]

[46] I.e., abandoning all dialectic; cf. BU III.5, "laying aside both innocence and learning, then is he a Silent Sage." *Krūra* and *ulbaniṣnu*, rendered tentatively by "blunt" and "veiled," seem to imply *pratyakṣam* and *parokṣam*—all that is formal, no longer significant for one to whom the content of all form is immediately present.

[47] The text is difficult, but there can be no doubt that Keith correctly explains that it means "they rose above mere names to the unity of *brahman* or *prāna*." Cf. *khila* (= *niḍa*), RV IV.10.1, and *yatra viśvam bhuvaty ekanīḍam*, "Where all abides in one nest," Nārāyaṇa Up. 3, previously cited.

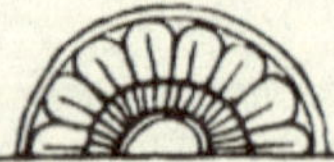

The Vedic Doctrine of "Silence"

Then only will you see it, when you cannot speak of it; for the knowledge of it is deep silence, and suppression of the senses. Hermes, *Lib.* X.5

The general significance of "silence" in connection with rites, myths, and mysteries has been admirably discussed by René Guénon in *Études traditionelles*.[1] Here we propose to cite other, more specific details from the Vedic tradition. It must be premised that the Supreme Identity (*tad ekam*) is not merely in itself "without duality" (*advaita*), but when considered from another and external point of view is an identity of many different things. By this we do not mean only that a first unitary principle transcends the reciprocally related pairs of opposites (*dvandvau*) that can be distinguished on any level of reference as contraries or known as contradictories; but rather that the Supreme Identity, undetermined even by a first assumption of unity, subsumes in its infinity the whole of what can be implied or represented by the notions of the infinite and the finite, of which the former includes the latter, without reciprocity.[2] On the other hand, the finite cannot be excluded or isolated from or denied to the infinite, since an independent finite would be in itself a limitation of the infinite by hypothesis. The Supreme Identity is, therefore, inevitably repre-

[This essay was published in *Indian Culture*, III (1937).—ED.]

[1] René Guénon, "Organisations initiatiques et sociétés secrètes," and "Du Secret initiatique," *Le Voile d'Isis* (1934), pp. 349 and 429; "Mythes, mystères et symboles," *Le Voile d'Isis* (1935), p. 385. Since 1936 *Le Voile d'Isis* has been published as *Études traditionelles*.

[2] "The Infinite (*aditiḥ*) is Mother, Sire, and Son, whatever hath been born, and the principle of birth, etc." (RV I.89.10); "Nothing is changed in the immovable Infinite (*ananta*) by the emanation or the withdrawals of worlds" (Bhāskara, *Bījaganita* [Benares, 1927], repeating the thought of AV x.8.29 and BU v.1, that "Though plenum (*pūrnam*) be taken from plenum, plenum yet remains."). The inclusion of the finite in the Infinite is expressly formulated in AĀ II.3.8, "A is Brahman, the ego (*aham*) is within it."

On the relation of unity to multiplicity see Coomaraswamy, "Vedic Exemplarism" [in the present volume—ED.].

sented in our thought under two aspects, both of which are essential to the formation of any concept of totality *secundum rem*. So we find it said of Mitrāvaruṇau (*apara* and *para* Brahman, God and Godhead) that from one and the same seat they behold "the finite and the infinite" (*aditiṃ ditiṃ ca*, RV I.62.8); where, of course, it must be borne in mind that *in divinis* to "see" is the same as to "know" and to "be." Or in like manner, but substituting the notion of spiration for that of manifestation, it can be said that "That One is equally spirated, despirated" (*tad ekam ānīd avātam*, RV X.129.2); or is at the same time "Being and Nonbeing" (*sadasat*, RV X.5.7).[3]

The same conception, expressed in terms of utterance and silence, is clearly formulated in RV II.43.3, "Whether, O Bird, thou utterest weal aloud, or sittest silent (*tūṣṇīm*), think on us with favor."[4] And similarly in the ritual, we find that rites are performed either with or without enunciated formulae, and that lauds are offered either vocally or silently; for which the texts also provide an adequate explanation. Here it must be premised that the primary purpose of the Vedic Sacrifice (*yajña*) is to effect a reintegration of the deity conceived of as spent and disintegrated by the act of creation, and at the same time that of the sacrificer himself, whose person, considered in its individual aspect, is evidently incomplete. The mode of reintegration is by means of initiation (*dīkṣa*) and symbols (*pratika, ākṛti*), whether natural, constructed, enacted, or vocalized; the sacrificer is expected to identify himself with the sacrifice itself and thus with the deity whose primordial self-sacrifice it represents, "the observance of the rule thereof being the same as it was at the crea-

[3] The "distinct operations" (*vivrata*), interior and exterior (*tira* or *guhya*, and *āvis*), of the Supreme Identity are represented by many other pairs, e.g., order and disorder (cosmos and chaos), life and death, light and darkness, sight and blindness, waking and sleep, potency and impotence, motion and rest, time and eternity, etc. It may be observed that all of the negative terms represent privations or evils if considered empirically, but absence of limitation, and good, when considered anagogically—the negative concept including the positive, as cause includes effect. [This is further illustrated by the two natures, *niruktāniruktа*, mortal and immortal, like Mitrāvaruṇau in RV I.164.38, the two Brahmans in BU II.3.1, Prajāpati in ŚB X.1.3.2.]

[4] Cf. RV X.27.21, "Beyond what is heard here, there is another sound" (*śrava id ena paro anyad asti*); I.164.10, "At the back of yonder Heaven the gods incant an omniscient word without outgoing effect" (*mantrayante . . . viśvavidam vācam aviśvaminvam*); JUB III.7–9, where the initiate (*dīkṣitah*, regarded as one dead to the world) is said to utter a "nonhuman" word (*amānuṣīm vācam*) or "brahmadictum" (*brahmavādyam*). Nothing but an echo of the veritable Word can be heard or understood by human ears.

tion." A clear distinction is drawn between those who may be merely "present" and those who "really" participate in the ritual acts which are performed on their behalf.

As already stated, there are certain acts that are performed with a vocal accompaniment and others silently. For example, in ŚB VII.2.2.13–14 and 2.3.3, in connection with the preparation of the Fire-altar, certain furrows are ploughed and certain libations made with an accompaniment of spoken words, and others silently—"Silently (*tūṣṇīm*), for what is silent is undeclared (*aniruktam*), and what is undeclared is everything (*sarvam*). . . . This Agni (Fire) is Prajāpati, and Prajāpati is both declared (*niruktaḥ*) and undeclared, bounded (*parimitaḥ*) and unbounded. Now whatever he does with spoken formulae (*yajuṣā*), thereby he integrates (*saṃskaroti*) that form of his which is declared and bounded; and whatever he does silently, thereby he integrates that form of his which is undeclared and unbounded. Verily, whoever as a comprehensor thereof does thus, he integrates the whole totality (*sarvam kṛtsnam*) of Prajāpati; the *ab extra* forms (*bāhyāni rūpāṇi*) are declared, the *ab intra* forms (*antarāṇi rūpāṇi*) are undeclared." An almost identical passage appears in ŚB XIV.1.2.18; and in VI.4.1.6 there is another reference to the performance of a rite in silence: "He spreads the black antelope skin silently, for it is the Sacrifice, the Sacrifice is Prajāpati, and Prajāpati is undeclared."

In TS III.1.9, the first libations are drawn off silently (*upāṇśu*), the latter with noise (*upabdim*), and "thus one bestows upon the deities the glory that is theirs, and upon men the glory that is theirs, and becomes divinely glorious amongst the deities and humanly glorious amongst men."

In AB II.31–32, the Devas, unable to overcome the Asuras, are said to have "seen" the "silent laud" (*tūṣṇīm śaṇsam apaśyam*), and this the Asuras could not follow. This "silent laud" is identified with what are called the "eyes of the *soma*-pressings, by means of which the Comprehensor reaches the Light-world." There is a reference to "these Eyes of *soma,* by which eyes of contemplation (*dhī*) and intellect (*manas*) we behold the Golden" (*hiraṇyam*, RV I.139.2, to wit, Hiraṇyagarbham, the Sun, the Truth, Prajāpati, as in X.121). It may be observed in this connection that, like the wine of other traditions, the *soma* partaken of is not the very elixir (*rasa*, *amṛta*) of life, but a symbolic liquor—"Of what the Brāhmans understand by '*soma*,' none ever tastes, none tastes who dwells on earth" (RV X.85.3–4): it is "by means of the priest, the initiation, and the invocation" that the temporal power partakes of the semblance of the spiritual power (*brahmaṇo rūpam*), AB VII.31.[5] Here the distinction between the *soma* actually and the *soma* theoretically partaken of is analogous to that between the spoken words of the ritual and that which cannot be expressed in words, and similarly analogous to the distinction between the visible representation and the "picture that is not in the colors" (*Laṅkāvatāra Sūtra* II.118).

The well-known orison in RV X.189, addressed to the Serpent Queen (*sarparājñī*) who is at once the Dawn, Earth, and Bride of the Sun, is also known as the "mental chant" (*mānasa stotra*), evidently because it is, as explained in TS VII.3.1, "chanted mentally" (*manasā*[6] *stuvate*), and this just because it is within the power of the intellect (*manas*) not merely to encompass this (*imām*, i.e., the finite universe) in a single moment, but also to transcend it, not only to contain (*paryāptum*) but also to environ (*paribhavitum*) it. And in this way, by means of what has previously been enunciated vocally (*vācā*) and what is afterwards enunciated mentally, "both (worlds) are possessed and obtained." Precisely the same is implied in ŚB II.1.4.29, where it is said that whatever has not been obtained by the preceding rites is now obtained by means of the Sarparājñī verses, recited, as is evidently taken for granted, mentally and silently; and thus the whole (*sarvam*) is possessed. Similarly in KB XIV.1, where the two first parts of the Ājya are the "silent murmur" (*tūṣṇīm-japaḥ*) and the "silent laud" (*tūṣṇīṃ-śaṇsa*), "He recites inaudibly, for the attainment of all desires," it being understood, of course, that the vocalized chant pertains to the attainment only of temporal goods.

It may be noted, too, that the correspondence of the spoken words to the exterior and those unspoken to the interior forms of deity, cited above, is in perfect agreement with the formulation of AB I.27, where when the *soma* has been bought from the Gandharvas (types of Eros, armed with bows and arrows, who are the guardians of Soma, *ab intra*)

[5] AĀ II.3.7, "By means of the form of Yonder-one one has being in this world" (*amuno rūpeṇēmaṃ lokam ābhavati*); the converse, "by means of this (human) form one is wholly reborn in that world" is stated here, and also in II.3.2 where a "person" (*puruṣa*) is distinguished from the animal (*paśu*) in that he "by the mortal seeks the immortal, that is his perfection." For example, in AB VII.31, cited above, it is by means of the *nyagrodha* shoots that the representative of the temporal power partakes of *soma* metaphysically (*parokṣeṇa*). This doctrine of "transubstantiation" is similarly enunciated in ŚB XII.7.3.11, "By faith he makes the *surā* to be *soma*," cf. ŚB XII.8.1.5 and XII.8.2.2. See also Coomaraswamy, "Angel and Titan: An Essay in Vedic Ontology," 1935, p. 382, n. 12.

[6] Hence Manasā Devī, the modern Bengali designation of the Serpent Goddess.

at the price of the Word (*vāc*, fem., called here "the Great Naked One" —the Nude Goddess—and represented in the rite by a virgin heifer), it is prescribed that the recitative is to be performed in silence (*upāṇśu*) until she has been redeemed from them, that is to say, so long as she remains "within."

In BU III.6, where there is a dialogue on Brahman, the position is finally reached where the questioner is told that Brahman is "a divinity about which further questions cannot be asked," and at this the questioner "holds her peace" (*upararāma*). This is, of course, in perfect agreement with the employment of the *via remotionis* in the same texts, where it is said that the Brahman is "No, No" (*neti, neti*), and also with the traditional text quoted by Śaṇkara on *Vedānta Sūtras* III.2.17, where Bāhva, questioned regarding the nature of Brahman, remains silent (*tūṣṇīm*), only exclaiming when the question is repeated for the third time, "I teach you indeed, but you do not understand: this Brahman is silence." Precisely the same significance attaches to the Buddha's refusal to analyze the state of *nirvāṇa*. [Cf. *avadyam*, "the unspeakable," *from* which the proceeding principles are liberated by the manifested light, RV *passim*.] In BG x.38, Krishna speaks of himself as "the silence of the hidden ones (*mauna guhyāṇām*), and the gnosis of the Gnostics" (*jñanaṃ jñanavatām*); where *mauna* corresponds to the familiar *muni*, "silent sage." This is not, of course, to say that He does not also "speak," but that his speaking is simply the manifestation, and not an affection, of the Silence; as BU III.5 also reminds us, the supreme state is one that transcends the distinction of utterance from silence—"Without respect to utterance or silence (*amaunaṃ ca maunaṃ nirvidya*), then is he indeed a Brāhman." When it is asked further, "By what means does one thus become a Brāhman?" the questioner is told, "By that means by which one does become a Brāhman," which is as much as to say, by a way that can be found but cannot be charted. The secret of initiation remains inviolable by its very nature; it cannot be betrayed because it cannot be expressed—it is inexplicable (*aniruktam*), but the inexplicable is everything, at the same time all that can and all that cannot be expressed.

It will be seen from the citations above that the Brāhmaṇa texts and the rites to which they refer are not only absolutely self-consistent but in complete agreement with the values implied in the text of RV II.43.3; the explanations are, indeed, of universal validity, and could be applied as well to the Orationes Secretae of the Christian Mass (which is also a sacrifice) as to the unvoiced repetition of the Indian Yajus-formulae.[7] The consistency affords at the same time an excellent illustration of the general principle that what is to be found in the Brāhmaṇas and Upaniṣads represents nothing new in principle, but only an expansion of what is taken for granted and more "eminently" enunciated in the "older" liturgical texts themselves. Those who assume that quite "new doctrines" are taught in the Brāhmaṇas and Upaniṣads are simply placing unnecessary difficulties in the way of their own understanding of the Saṃhitās.

It will be advantageous also to consider the derivation and form of the word *tūṣṇīm*. This indeclinable form, generally adverbial ("silently") but sometimes to be rendered adjectivally or as a noun, is really the accusative of a supposedly lost *tuṣṇa*, fem. *tuṣṇī*, corresponding in meaning to Greek σιγή, and derived from √*tuṣ*, meaning to be satisfied, contented, and at rest, in the sense that motion comes to rest in the attainment of its object, and indeed as speech comes to rest in silence when all has been said that can be said. The word *tūṣṇīm* occurs as a real accusative (W. Caland, "*tūṣṇīm* is equal to *vācaṃyamaḥ*")—for to speak of "contemplating silently" would involve a tautology—in PB vii.6.1, where Prajāpati, desiring to proceed from the state of unity to that of multiplicity (*bahu syām*), expressed himself with the words "May I be born" (*prajāyeya*), and "having by intellect contemplated the Silence" (*tūṣṇīm manasā dhyāyat*), therewith "saw" (*ādīdhīt*) that the Germ (*garbham*, to wit, Agni or Indra, who as the Bṛhat becomes the "eldest son") lay hidden within himself (*antarhitam*), and so proposed to bring it to birth by means of the Word (*vāc*). [Cf. TS ii.5.11.5, *yad-dhi manasā*

[7] It may be added that while, from a religious point of view, silence and fasting and other acts of abstention are acts of penance, from a metaphysical point of view their significance has no longer to do with the mere improvement of the individual as such, but with the realization of supra-individual conditions. The contemplative life as such is superior to the active life as such. It does not follow, however, that the state of the Comprehensor or even that of the Wayfarer should be one of total inaction; this would be an imperfect imitation of the Supreme Identity, where eternal rest and eternal work are one and the same. There is an adequate imitation only when inaction and action are identified, as intended by the *Bhagavad Gītā* and the Taoist *wu wei*; action no longer implies limitation when it is no longer determined by needs or compelled by ends to be attained, but becomes a simple manifestation. In this case, for example, utterance does not exclude, but rather represents silence ["It is just by sound that the nonsound is revealed," MU vi.22]; and it is in just this way that a myth or other adequate symbol, although an "expression" actually, remains a "mystery" essentially. In the same way, every natural function, when referred to the principle it represents, can properly be said to have been renounced even when it is performed.

dhyāyati, where *yad* is equivalent to "unspoken word," "unuttered concept."] *Tūṣṇīm manasā dhyāyat* then corresponds to the more usual *manasā vācam akrata* (RV x.71.2) or *manasāivā vācaṃ mithunaṃ samabhavat* (ŚB vi.1.2.9), with reference to "the act of fecundation latent in eternity," for thus[8] "He (Prajāpati) became pregnant (*garbhin*)[9] and expressed (*asṛjata*) the Several Angels." The birth of the Son is, strictly speaking, not only a conception from the conjoint principles, in the sense of vital operation, but at the same time a conception intellectually, *per verbum in intellectu conceptum*, corresponding to the designation of the Germ (*garbham*, to wit, Hiraṇyagarbha) as a concept (*dīdhitim*) in this sense, RV iii.31.1.

The *Pañcaviṃśa Brāhmaṇa*, cited above, goes on to explain with reference to the intention of "bringing to birth by means of the Word" (*vācā prajanayā*) that Prajāpati "released the Word[10] (*vācaṃ vyaṣrjata*, in other words, effected the separation of Heaven and Earth), and She descended as Rathantara (*vāg rathantaram avapadyata*, where *avapad* is literally to 'step down,') . . . and thence was born the Bṛhat . . . that had lain so long within" (*jyog antar abhūt*); cf. RV x.124.1, "Thou hast lain long enough in the long-darkness" (*jyog eva dīrghaṃ tama āśayiṣṭhāḥ*).[11] That is to say that Aditi, Magna Mater, Night, becomes Aditi, Mother

[8] "Thus," i.e., as St. Augustine expresses it: having thus "made Himself a mother of whom to be born" (*Epiphanius contra quinque haereses*, 5). [See *A Coptic Gnostic Treatise Contained in the Codex Brucianus Ms. 96*, tr. Charlotte Baynes (Cambridge, 1933), xii.10 (p. 48), for Source and Silence.]

[9] Cf. *Epiphanius contra quinque haereses* xxxiv.4, "The Father was in travail," and in folklore, the "couvade."

[10] It is of interest to note the ritual parallel in ŚB iv.6.9.23–24 where, after sitting speechless (*vācamyamaḥ*), the sacrificers are to "release their speech" (*vācam visṛjetan*) according to their desires, e.g., "May we be abundantly supplied with offspring." [Note *tūṣṇīm śansam tira iva vai retāmsi vikryante*, AB ii.39; cf. especially JUB iii.16.]

[11] Dīrghatamas, "Long Darkness," one of the blind "prophets" (*ṛṣi*) of the *Rg Veda*, is, accordingly, the designation of an *ab intra*, occulted form of Agni, whose relation to his younger brother Dīrghaśravas, "Far Cry," is as that of Varuna to his younger brother Mitra or Agni, or, in other words, as of Death (*mṛtyu*) to Life (*āyus*). Of Dīrghaśravas it is also said that he had "long been under resraint and lacking food" (*jyog aparuddho' śayānaḥ*, PB xv.3.25), and all these expressions correspond to what is said of Vṛtra in RV i.32.10, namely, that "Indra's enemy lay in the long darkness (*dīrgham tama aśayat*) beneath the Waters"; the *ab intra* aspect of deity being that of the Dragon or Serpent (*vṛtra, ahi*), the procession of Prajāpati a "creeping forth from the blind darkness" (*andhe tamasi prāsarpat*, PB xvi.1.1), and that of the Serpents generally a "crawling forth" (*ati sarpana*), whereby they become the Suns (PB xxv.15.4). On this serpentine procession see Coomaraswamy, "Angel and Titan," 1935. The procession of Dīrghatamas requires a longer discussion.

Earth, and Dawn, to be represented in the ritual by the altar (*vedi*) that is the birth-place (*yoni*) of Agni: distinction is made between the Word that "was with God and was God" from the Word as Earth Mother, or in other words of "Mary ghostly" from "Mary in the flesh."[12] For, as we know from TS III.1.7 and JB I.145–146, the Bṛhat (the Father brought to birth) corresponds to Heaven,[13] the future (*bhaviṣyat*), the unbounded (*aparimitam*), and to despiration (*apāna*); the Rathantara (the Father's separated nature) corresponds to Earth, the past (*bhūtāt*), the bounded (*parimitam*), and spiration (*prāṇa*).[14] The same assumptions are found in JUB I.53 ff., substituting Sāman and Ṛc for Bṛhat and Rathantara: the Sāman (masc.) representing intellect (*manas*) and despiration (*apāna*), the Ṛc (fem.) the Word (*vāc*) and spiration (*prāṇa*). The Sāman is also *in seipso* "both she (*sā*) and he (*ama*)," and it is as a single luminous power (*virāj*)[15] that the conjoint principles generate

[12] Otherwise represented mythically as the rape of the Word (RV I.130.9, where Indra "steals the Word," *vācam . . . muṣāyati*), or as an analysis of the Word (RV VII.103.6, X.71.3 and 125.3), or again as a measurement or birth of Māyā from Māyā (AV VIII.9.5, "Māyā was born from Māyā," followed by the *Lalita Vistara* XXVII.12, "Inasmuch as her, i.e., the Buddha's mother's, likeness was modeled after that of Māyā, Māyā she was called.").

[13] Agni, although the Son, is the Father himself reborn, and immediately ascends; moreover, "Agni is kindled by Agni" (RV I.12.6). It can be said of him, accordingly, not only that "Being the Father, he became the Son" (AV XIX.53.4) and that He is both "the Father of the gods and their Son" (RV I.69.1, see ŚB VI.1.2.26), but also that "He who heretofore was his own Son now becomes his own Father" (ŚB II.3.3.5), that he is "His Father's father" (RV VI.16.35), at once the Son and Brother of Varuṇa (RV IV.1.2 and X.51.6), and "Own-son" (*tanūnapat, passim*)—this last expression exactly corresponds to the Gnostic "αὐτογενής." It is, then, easy to see how Agni, although a Son of chthonic birth, can in his identity with the Sun be regarded also as the Lover of the Earth Mother; the syzygy Agni-Pṛthivī being then an aspect of the parents Heaven and Earth, Savitṛ-Sāvitrī, and more remotely Mitrāvaruṇau (GB I.32 and JUB IV.27, etc.).

[14] Cf. in AĀ II.3.6 the distinction of spirit (*prāṇa*) from body (*śarīra*), of which the former is hidden (*tira*) and the latter evident (*āvis*), like "a" inherent and "a" expressed: ŚB X.4.3.9, "No one becomes deathless by means of the body, but whether it be by gnosis or by works, only after abandoning the body."

[15] Virāj, from whom all things "milk" their specific virtue or character, is commonly a designation of the Magna Mater, but even when so regarded is a syzygy—"Who knoweth her progenitive duality?" AV VIII.9.10. The terms *virāj* and *aditi*, although both usually feminine, may also have a masculine sense with similar reference to the first principle. To maintain, indeed, that any creative power considered in its creative aspect can be defined as exclusively "male" or exclusively "female" involves a contradiction in terms, all creation whatever being a *co*-gnition and *con*-ception; even in Christianity, the generation of the Son is "a vital operation from a conjoint principle" (*a principio conjuncto, Sum. Theol.* I.27.2), i.e., a principle that is both an essence and a nature—"That nature by which the Father

the Sun, and then immediately depart from one another, this division of essence from nature, Heaven from Earth, or Night from Day being the inevitable condition of all manifestation; it is invariably the coming of the light that separates in time the Parents that are united in eternity. Now *sāman* always has reference to the music, *ṛc* to the articulate wording of the incantations (*ṛc*, *mantra*, *brahma*), so that when words are sung to measured music this represents an analysis and naturing of a heavenly music that in itself is one, and inaudible to human ears.[16] We may say,

---

begets." It is only when it is realized once and for all that the creative power on any level of reference—whether, for example, as God or Man—is always a unity of conjoint principles, that is to say, a syzygy and *mithunatva*, that the propriety can be seen of such expressions as "He (Agni) was born from the Titan's womb (*asurasya jaṭharāt ajāyata*)," RV III.29.14; "Mitra pours the seed in Varuṇa (*retaḥ varuṇo siñcati*)," PB XXV.10.10; "My womb is the Great Brahman, therein I lay the Germ," BG XIV.3, and many similar references to the maternity of a deity referred to by names grammatically masculine or neuter.

[16] Just as in Plotinus, *Enneads* I.6.3, "Harmonies unheard in sound create the harmonies we hear and wake the soul to the one essence in another nature"; and V.9.11, "An earthly representation of the music that there is in the rhythm (= Skr. *chandānsi*) of the ideal world." It is precisely in this sense that the ritual music, like every other part of the Sacrifice, is an imitation of "what was done by the Divinities in the beginning" (ŚB VII.2.1.4 and *passim*), which holds good no less for the Christian Mass or Sacrifice.

It may be observed that in the operation of conjoint principles we necessarily conceive of one as active, the other as passive, and say that one is agent and the other means, or that one gives and the other receives. The apparent conflict with the Christian doctrine, which denies a "passive power" in God (*Sum. Theol.* I.41.4 *ad* 2), is unreal. St. Thomas himself remarks that "in every generation there is an active and a passive principle" (*Sum. Theol.* I.98.2c). The fact is that a distinction of this kind is determined by the necessity of speaking in terms of time and space; whereas *in divinis* action is immediate, and there is no real, but only a logical distinction of agency from means. Savitṛ and Sāvitrī are both equally "wombs" (*yonī*, JUB IV.27). If "One of the perfections acts (*kartā*), the other fosters (*ṛndhan*)," RV III.31.2, and both of these are active operations; it does not mean that either "act" or "fostering" represents possibilities which might or might not have been realized, but merely refers to the co-operation of the conjoint principles, intention and power. There is no distinction of potentiality from act. It is only when the creation has taken place, and concepts of time and space are therefore involved, that we can think of a *puro atto* as divided from *potenza* by the measure of the whole universe (Dante, *Paradiso* XXIX.31–36), of Heaven and Earth as "driving apart" (*te vyadravatām*, JUB I.54), or of "Nature as receding from likeness to God" (*Sum. Theol.* I.14.11). This separation (*viyoga*) is the occasion of cosmic suffering (*traiśoka*, the pain of the Three Worlds that had once been one, PB VIII.1.9, *loka-duhkha*, *Weltschmerz*, KU V.11), and it is no wonder that "When the conjoint pair were parted, the Devas moaned, and said, 'Let them be wed again'" (RV X.24.5); it is, however, only "at the meeting of the ways," "at the worlds' end," that Heaven and Earth "embrace" (JUB I.5, etc.), only "in the heart" that the marriage of Indra and Indrāṇī is really consummated (ŚB X.5.2.11), that

accordingly, that the name "Great Liturgy" (*bṛhad ukthaḥ*, where *ukthaḥ* is from *vāc*, "to speak") applied to Agni, e.g., in RV v.19.3, represents the Son as a *spoken* Word, and *manifested* Logos;[17] and in the same way Indra is "the most excellent incantation" (*jyeṣṭhaś ca mantraḥ*, RV x.50.4).

The spoken Word is a harmony. In KB xxiii.2 and xxiv.1, "Prajāpati is he whose name is not mentioned;[18] this is the symbol of Prajāpati. . . . 'Aloud' in 'Sing aloud, O thou of wide radiance' (Agni) is a symbol

---

is to say, in a silence and darkness that are the same as that "Night that hides the darkness of the conjoint pair" in RV i.123.7, the *Śatapatha Brāhmana* interpreting this condition of unconscious cognition (*samvit*), perfect beatitude (*paramānanda*), and sleep (*svapna*) as an "entering into, or being possessed by, what is one's very own" (*svāpyaya*) [cf. Māṇḍ. Up. ii, *apīti.*].

[17] The Sacrifice in its *liturgical* aspect is a "bringing to birth by means of the Word": one "sings the Sāman on a Ṛc," and this is a procreative coupling (*mithunam*), identical with that of Intellect and Word (*manas* and *vāc*), Sacrifice and Guerdon (*yajña, dakṣinā*, i.e., Prajāpati and Dawn), and literally an in-*formation* of Nature, "for were it not for Intellect, the Word would be incoherent" (ŚB iii.2.4.11), whereas it is in fact the "birthplace of Order." The Rathantara, for example, is a "means of procreation" (*prajananam*, PB vii.7.16, corresponding to *prajananam* as "mistress" *viśpatnī*, the "mother" of Agni in RV iii.29.1); *Sāvitrī* in this sense is identified with the meters (*chandānsi*) and called the "Mother of the Vedas" (*Gopatha Brāhmana* i.33 and 38), which "meters" are commonly referred to as the means *par excellence* of reintegration (*samskarana*, AB vi.27, ŚB vi.5.4.7, etc.), and in her conjunction with Savitṛ presents an analogy with the Gnostic Ecclesia ("Mother Church") and Gnosis as constituting with Man (ἄνθροπως = Prajāpati, Agni, Manu) a syzygy. In this connection also there should be noted the close relationship of the words *mātrā*, *mātṛ*, and *māyā*, "meter," "mother," and "magical-means" or "matrix"; *mā* to "measure" and *nir-mā*, to "measure out" being constantly employed not only in the sense of giving form and definition, but in the closely related sense of creating or giving birth to, notably in RV iii.38.3, iii.53.15, x.5.3, x.125.8, AV viii.9.5, and in the well-known expression *nirmāna-kāya*, denoting precisely the assumed and actually manifested and born "body" of the Buddha.

Sacrifice and birth are inseparable concepts; the *Śatapatha Brāhmana*, indeed, proposes the *hermeneia*, "*yajña*, because '*yañ jayate*.'" Sacrifice is divisive, a "breaking of bread"; the product is articulated and articulate. The Sacrifice is a spreading out, a making a tissue or web of the Truth (*satyam tanavāmahā*, ŚB ix.5.1.18), a metaphor commonly employed elsewhere in connection with the raying of the fontal light, which forms the texture of the worlds. Just as the kindling of Agni is the making perceptible and evident of a hidden light, so the utterance of the chants is the making perceptible of a silent principle of sound. The spoken Word is a revelation of the Silence, that measures the trace of what is in itself immeasurable.

[18] [Prajāpati chooses *aniruktam sāmno . . . svargyam*, the "indistinct (part) of the *sāman* which belongs to heaven," JUB i.52.6; cf. *manasā* "silently," opposed to *vācā*, as in JUB i.58.6; see ŚB iv.6.9.17 and Eggeling's note on *manasā stotra*, also JUB i.40.4.]

of the Bṛhat." In ŚB vi.1.1.15, the triumphant Jubilate of the spoken Word is described as follows: "She (the Earth, *bhūmi*, being *pṛthivī*, 'spread out'), feeling herself altogether complete (*sarvā kṛtsnā*), sang (*agāyat*); and because she 'sang,' therefore she is Gāyatrī. They say too that 'It was Agni, indeed, on her back (*pṛṣṭhe*)[19] who, feeling himself altogether complete, sang; and inasmuch as he sang, therefore he is Gāyatra.' And hence whosoever feels himself altogether complete, either sings or delights in song."

We have thus briefly discussed the divine nativity from certain points of view in order to bring out the correspondences of the Vedic and the Gnostic references to the Silence. In both traditions the authentic and integral powers on every level of reference are syzygies of conjoint principles, male and female; summarizing the Gnostic doctrine of the Aeons (Vedic *amṛtāsaḥ* = *devāḥ*) we may say that *ab intra* and informally these are *βυθός* and *σιγή*, "Abyss," and "Silence," and *ab extra*, formally, *νοῦς* and *ἔννοια* or Sophia, "Intellect," and "Wisdom," and without going into further detail, that *σιγή* corresponds to Vedic *tuṣṇī* and *νοῦς* to *manas*, *σιγή* and Sophia respectively to the hidden and manifested aspects of Aditi-Vāc; and also that the "fall" of the Word (*vāg . . . avapadyata*, cited above), and her purification as Ṛc, Apālā, Sūryā (JUB i.53 ff., RV viii.91 and x.85) correspond to the fall and redemption of Sophia and the Shekinah in the Gnostic and Qabbalistic traditions, respectively. In what are really more academic rather than more "orthodox" forms of Christianity, the two aspects of the Voice, within and without, are those of "that nature by which the Father begets" and "that nature which recedes from likeness to God, and yet retains a certain likeness to the divine being" (*Sum. Theol.* i.41.5c and i.14.11 *ad* 3), the eternal and the temporal Theotokoi, respectively.

Let us repeat in conclusion that the Supreme Identity is neither merely silent nor merely vocal, but literally a no-what that is at the same time indefinable and partially defined, an unspoken and a spoken Word.

[19] *Pṛṣṭhe*, i.e., either (1) with reference to Agni's being seated on the earthen altar (*vedi*) which is his birthplace (*yoni*), and/or (2) with reference to Agni's being supported by the Pṛṣṭhastotra, of which hymn the Gāyatrī is the mother by Prajāpati, PB vii.8.8.

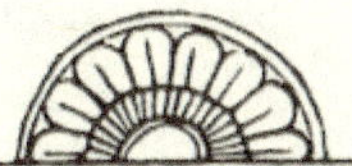

Manas

In the words of ŚB x.5.3.3, Agni should be "intellectually laid and intellectually edified" (*manasaivādhīyanta manasācīyanta*).

"Intellectually laid and intellectually edified": for inasmuch as Agni Himself "performs an intellectual sacrifice" (*manasā yajati*, RV 1.77.2), it is evident that one who would attain to Him as like to like must have done likewise, without which a true "Imitation of Agni" would be impossible. *Manas* in the Saṃhitās and Brāhmaṇas, and sometimes in the Upaniṣads, is the Pure or Possible Intellect, at once a name of God and that in us by which He may be grasped. Thus RV 1.139.2, "We have beheld the Golden-one by these our eyes of contemplation and of intellect" (*apaśyāma hiraṇyaṃ dhībhiś cana manasā svebhir akṣibhiḥ*); RV 1.145.2, "What He [Agni], contemplative, hath as it were grasped by His own intellect" (*sveneva dhīro manasā yad agrabhīt*); RV vi.9.5, "Intellect is the swiftest of birds" (*mano javiṣṭhaṃ patayatsu antas*); RV viii.100.8, "The Eagle cometh with the speed of intellect" (*mano javā ayamāna . . . suparṇaḥ*; cf. Manojavas as a name of Agni, JB 1.50); RV x.11.1, "Varuṇa's knowledge of all things is according to His speculation" (*viśvaṃ sa veda varuṇo yathā dhiyā*); RV x.181.3, "By an intellectual speculation they found the Godward-path" (*avindan manasā dīdhyānā . . . devayānam*); TS ii.5.11.5, "Intellect is virtually Prajāpati" (*mana iva hi prajāpatiḥ*); ŚB x.5.3.1-4, where Intellect (*manas*) is identified with "That which was in the beginning neither Non-being nor Being" (RV x.129.1), and this Intellect emanates the Word (*vācam asṛjata*), a function usually assigned to Prajāpati; BU 1.5.7, "The Father is Intellect (*manas*); The Mother, Word (*vāc*); the Child, Spirit or Life (*prāṇa*)," in agreement with the usual formulation, according to which Intellect and Word, Heaven and Earth, as Knower and Known, are the universal parents of

[This essay was first published in the *A. C. Woolner Commemoration Volume*, ed. Mohammad Shafi (Lahore, 1940).—ED.]

the conceptual universe;[1] and KU IV.11, "He is attainable intellectually" (*manasaivedam āptavyam*).

On the other hand, we meet with such expressions as *pākena manasā*, (RV VII.104.8 and X.114.4), implying the distinction of a "mature" from an "unripened" Intellect; and in such characteristic texts as Kena Up. I.3, "There the intellect does not attain" (*na tatra . . . gacchati manaḥ*), and MU VI.34, "Intellect must be arrested in the heart" (*mano niroddhavyaṃ hṛdi*), as well as wherever the transcendental Person is spoken of as "de-mented" (*amanas, amānasaḥ*),[2] and generally in Buddhism, the Intellect (*manas*) is the Reason or Practical Intellect—that Intellect which in MU VI.30 is described as the seat, not of science, but of opinion and all pros and cons, the term *buddhi* now coming into use as a designation of the speculative as distinguished from the empirical and dialectic Reason.

These apparent contradictions are completely resolved in MU VI.34, where "Intellect is for men a means of bondage or liberation (*kāraṇaṃ bandha-mokṣayoḥ*)" as the case may be—"of bondage if it clings to objects of perception (*viṣayasaṅgi*), and of liberation if not directed towards these objects (*nirviṣayam*)," i.e., if thought, the only basis of the world-

[1] Intellect (*manas, buddhi*) and will (*vaśa, kāma*), being coincident *in divinis* = *adhidevatam*, the divine procession is "conceptual" in both senses of the word; cf. ŚB VI.1.2.9, where Prajāpati *manasā iva vācam mithunam samabhavat, sa garbhy abhavat . . . asṛjata.* The same is explicit in the Scholastic expressions *per verbum in intellectu conceptum* and *per artem et ex voluntate.* Needless to say, the intellectual and artificial processions are the same, procession or creation *per artem* = *taṣṭaiva* being essentially an intellectual operation; cf. RV I.20.2, *vacoyujā tatakṣu manasā*, and similar texts. In other words, while the procession of the Word (act of the Divine Intellect) and the procession of the Spirit (act of the Divine Will), although coincident, are nevertheless logically distinguishable, the procession of the Word and procession *per artem* are not merely coincident but logically indistinguishable, and this, indeed, is sufficiently evident in Christian theory, where Christ is called "the art of God" (Augustine, *De trinitate* VI.10).

[2] In BU III.8.8, the *akṣara brahman* is *amanas*; in Muṇḍ. Up. II.1.2, the despirated Puruṣa not in any likeness, i.e., *para brahman*, is *amanāḥ*; in BU VI.2.15 = CU IV.15.5, 6 and V.10.2, He who acts as Guide on the *devayāna* = *brahmapatha* beyond the Sun is, according to different readings, the "de-mented" or "superhuman" Person (*puruṣo'mānasah* or *'āmnavah*). Inasmuch as those who are thus conducted "nevermore return to this human cycle" (*imam mānavam āvartaṃ nāvartante*), it is clear that both Indian commentators, together with Hume, who follows them, are wrong in reading BU VI.2.15 as *puruṣo mānavaḥ* without *avagraha*; the reading must be here just as in the parallel passages, *puruṣo'mānavah* or *'mānasaḥ*. For it is obvious that it can only be the Superhuman Person who guides on the superhuman trail, Agni Vaidyuta then, rather than Agni Vaiśvānaraḥ; cf. the contrast of "lightning" and "concept"—i.e., of immediate vision with theological formulation—in Kena Up. 29–30.

vortex (*cittaṃ eva hi saṃsāram*), "is brought to rest in its own source (*cittam svayonāv*[3] *upaśāmyate*) by a surcease from fluctuation (*vṛtti-kṣayāt*)." "Intellect is said to be twofold, Pure and Impure" (*mano hi dvividhaṃ, śuddhaṃ cāśuddhaṃ ca*)[4]—impure when there is correlation with desire (*kāmasamparkāt*), pure by remotion of desire; and when the intellect, sentimentality, and distraction having been subtracted, has been brought to a thorough stillness,[5] when one reaches dementation, that is the last step (*layavikṣeparahitaṃ manaḥ kṛtvā suniścalam, yadā yāty amanībhāvaṃ tadā tat paramaṃ padam*), that is, Gnosis and Liberation; all else is but a tale of knots (*etaj jñānaṃ ca mokṣaṃ ca, śeṣānye granthavistarāḥ*).[6]

The quoted passages and whole context show that by *amanībhāva*, "dementation," nothing so crude is meant as a literal annihilation of the

[3] *Svayonau* corresponds to *svagocare* in *Laṅkāvatāra Sūtra* II.115, where the intellect being "in its own pasture, beholds all things at once, as if in a mirror"; cf. Chuang-tzu, "The mind of the sage being brought to rest becomes the mirror of the universe." The opposite of *svayonau* and *svagocare* (= *svastha*) is *viṣaya-gocare* in the expression, "as firmly as the intellect is attached in the pasture of the senses" (*viṣaya-gocare*, also in MU VI.34), *viṣaya-gocara* being further synonymous with *indriya-gocara* in BG XIII.5. D. T. Suzuki entirely misses the point when he renders *Laṅkāvatāra Sūtra* II.115, *sva-gocare*, by "in its own sense-fields"; the meaning really being "in its own pasture"—i.e., when *not* directed toward sense objects. *Vṛtti-kṣaya*, as in *Yoga Sūtra, passim*, "cessation of the fluctuations of the mind-stuff."

[4] As also, of course, in Buddhist formulation, where the mind is either defiled by ignorance or as it is in itself, "immutable, although the cause of mutation"; see, for example, Aśvaghoṣa, *Śraddhotpāda* (*Açvaghosha's Discourse on the Awakening of Faith in the Mahāyāna*, tr. Teitaro Suzuki, Chicago, 1900), p. 79. Cf. the concept of the "two-fold mind," in Erwin Goodenough, *By Light, Light* (New Haven, 1935), p. 385.

[5] Cf. KU VI.10, "That they call the supreme goal, when the five perceptions conjointly with the mind (*manas*) come to a standstill, and intellect (*buddhi*) makes no motion"; also Jacob Boehme, *The Supersensual Life*, p. 227, "But if thou canst, my son, for a while but cease from all thy thinking and willing, then shalt thou hear the unspeakable words of God. . . . When thou standest still from the thinking of self, and the willing of self: when both thy intellect and will are quiet . . . above . . . the outward senses."

[6] *Laya*, from *lī*, "to cling, adhere," is here the act of clinging or attachment to desirable things and tantamount to "stickiness" in the modern vernacular sense; cf. *asneha* in BU III.8.8. *Laya*, therefore, can properly be rendered by "sentimentality" or by "materialism," implying both an infatuation with what we like and a worship of what we know as "fact."

Grantha is "knot" in the psychological sense of "complex," those Gordian knots of the heart that must be cut before the experience of eternity is possible (CU VII.26.2, KU VI.15, Muṇḍ. Up. III.2.9).

intellect, but rather that the last end has been attained when the intellect no longer intelligizes, that is, when there is no longer a distinction of Knower from Known or of Knowledge and Being, but only a Knowledge as Being and a Being as Knowledge; when, as our text expresses it, "Thought and Being are consubstantial" (*yat cittas tanmayo bhavati*). BU IV.3.30 similarly states, "Although he does not know, nevertheless he knows; he does not know but there is no loss on the knower's part, since he is indestructible; it is just that there is no second thing other than and distinct from himself that he might know."[7] Or again, as Aquinas expresses it, "When the Intellect attains to the form of Truth, it does not think, but perfectly contemplates the Truth[8] . . . which means complete identity, because in God the Intellect and the thing understood are altogether the same. . . . God has, of Himself, speculative knowledge only. . . . God does not understand things by an idea existing outside Himself . . . an idea in God is identical with His essence" (*Sum. Theol.* I.34.1 *ad* 2 *et* 3, I.14.16, and I.15.1).

With further reference to *yat cittas tanmayo bhavati*, cited above: the whole verse reads, "The world vortex is merely Thought (*cittam eva hi saṃsāram*), labor then to cleanse it (*śodhayet*); as is the Thought, such is the mode of Being (*yat cittas tanmayo bhavati*); this is the Eternal Mystery (*guhyaṃ . . . sanātanam*)."[9] Much more is evidently intended than merely the "character-making power of Thought" (Hume), for the whole context has to do with a plane of reference where "Thought does

[7] That "he" thus *na vijānāti* is, then, an "Unknowing" that is really perfection of knowing, and altogether unlike the "ignorance" of the agnostic (*avidvān*). Christian parallels could be cited without end. See Erigena's "God does not know what He Himself is, because He is not any what; and this ignorance surpasses all knowledge," and the significant title of the well-known anonymous work, *A Book of Contemplation the Which is Called the Cloud of Unknowing in the Which a Soul Is Oned with God.*

For a further analysis of what is meant by "unconsciousness" (*asaṃjñāna*) post mortem and in "deep sleep," see ŚB X.5.2.11–15 and BU II.1.19, II.4.12–14, and IV.5.13–15. It is an unconsciousness because it is not a consciousness *of* anything, which would be impossible where there is no duality, but so far from being an absence or privation of consciousness, it is a consciousness *as* all that might otherwise be known only conceptually (*saṃkalpitam*), and hence it is described by such expressions as "condensation of discrimination" (*vijñāna-ghana*) and "cognoscent" (*saṃvit*).

[8] Cf. BG VI.25, *ātmasaṃsthaṃ manaḥ kṛtvā na kiṃcid api cintayet.*

[9] Cf. Śvet. Up. VI.22, where there is no question of works, but Gnosis and the Love of God are described as the indispensable and only means of liberation, and "this is the ultimate secret of the Vedānta promulgated in a former aeon" (*vedānte paramaṃ guhyaṃ purākalpe pracoditam*).

not think" and with the attainment of an uncharacterized goal;[10] there is no question of a salvation by merit, but only of liberation by gnosis. Nor could we expect the expression "Eternal Secret" to be applied to anything so obvious as the "character-making power of Thought." This character-making power is, moreover, explicitly dealt with in BU IV.4.5, where the whole reference is to the plane of conduct; thus, "As one acts, as is one's habit, such is his being (*yathākārī yathācārī tathā bhavati*). . . . As one wills (*kāmo bhavati*), so he intends (*kratur bhavati*); as he intends, so he does; and as are his deeds, such is the goal that he attains." In our text, MU VI.34, the reference is likewise to the plane of conduct or active life insofar as Thought has *not* been cleansed: but how is it when Thought *has* been cleansed? We know that this means cleansed of the concept of "I and Mine," "I as a Doer," and of all pairs of opposites, Vice and Virtue included, and as specifically stated in our text (*mano hi . . . śuddham . . . kāmo vivarjitam*), of that very "willing" which in BU IV.4.5 is found to be the ultimate basis of "character."[11] *Yas cittas tanmayo bhavati* has reference, then, to a state of being where "character" has no longer any meaning, and where "identity of Thought and Being" can only mean that the goal of Thought has been attained in a perfect *adaequatio rei et intellectus*; Thinker and Thought *in divinis*, in *samādhi*, being one perfectly simple essence, "characterized" only by "sameness" (*samatā*; cf. Muṇḍ. Up. III.1.3, *paraṃ sāmyam*) or "perfect simplicity" (*ekavṛtatva*) and peace (*śanti*).

"Thither neither sight nor speech nor intellect can go; we neither 'know' it nor can we analyze it, so as to be able to communicate it by instruction" (*anuśiṣyāt*, Kena. Up. I.3). The realization of the corresponding state in which the Intellect does not intelligize, which is called in our text "the Eternal Mystery" and in KU VI.10, "the Supreme Goal" and which "cannot be taught," is the ultimate "secret" of initiation. It must not be supposed that any mere description of the "secret," such as can be found in Scripture (*śruti*) or exegesis, suffices to communicate the secret of "de-mentation" (*amanībhāva*); nor that the secret has ever

[10] Cf. Jāmī, *Lawā'iḥ* 24, "His first characteristic is the lack of all characteristics"; Eckhart, "God's only idiosyncrasy is being."

[11] A further definition of the cleansing of thought is implied in Muṇḍ. Up. III.1.9, "The thought of men is altogether interwoven with the physical functions (*pranaiś cittam sarvam otam prajānām*, tantamount to the Thomist "All our knowledge is derived from the senses"); it is in him whose thought is cleansed (of this contamination) that the Spirit manifests (*yasmin viśuddhe vibhavati eṣa ātmā*)."

been or could be communicated *to* an initiate or betrayed to anyone, or discovered by however much learning. It can only be realized by each one for himself; all that can be effected by initiation is the communication of an impulse and an awakening of latent potentialities; the work must be done by the initiate himself, to whom the words of our text, *prayatnena śodhayet*, are always applicable until the very end of the road (*adhvanaḥ pāram*) has been reached.

We make these remarks only to emphasize that whatever can be said *of* it, the secret remains inviolable, guarded by its own essential incommunicability. It is in this sense only that the Sun, the Truth, in JUB I.5.3, is said to "repel" (*apasedhantī*) the would-be "winner beyond the Sun"[12] (CU II.10.5–6, JUB I.6.1), who must "break through" into the Inexhaustible (Muṇḍ. Up. II.2.2, *tad evākṣaraṃ . . . viddhi*)[13] by his own powers and, as in our text MU VI.34, "by effort" (*prayatnena*). It is not a question of φθόνος ("jealousy") on the part of an Olympian deity or on the part of any human *guru*. Esoteric doctrines are not withheld from anyone soever lest he should understand; on the contrary, and although the words of scripture are inevitably "enigmatic," the doctrine is communicated with all *possible* clarity, and it is for those who have ears to hear, to hear in fact (RV X.71.6, Mark 4:11–12). It is not for interested reasons that the words or other symbols by which the ultimate secret

[12] We cannot undertake here a detailed analysis of the stages of deification but may point out that the "breaking through" (the Sun into what lies beyond the Sun) is Eckhart's "second death of the soul and is far more momentous than the first" (Evans ed., I, 275). The prolongation of the *brahmapatha* beyond the Sun, where neither Sun nor Moon nor Stars give light and the only guidance is that of the superhuman Lightning or immediate vision leading on to the *para brahman*, describable only by the *via remotionis* (*neti, neti*), implies a renunciation even of the Wayfarer's "eternal prototype" (*svarūpa*) in the divine mind, and the last step (*param padam*), by which one mounts upon the very throne of Brahman (Kauṣ. Up. I.5–7)—that is, "knowing Brahman as very Brahman"—is the Wayfarer's last death, who thus as in BU I.2.7, "becoming Death, dies no more deaths, for Death does not die." All this is implied by the superlative *pariṣṭād etasyāi'tasminn amṛte nidadhyāt*, "should commit himself to that Immortality far beyond this (Sun)," JUB I.6.1, and *param ādityāj jayati . . . paro hāsyādityajayāj jayo bhavati*, "wins beyond the Sun, yea, conquers beyond the conquest of the Sun" (CU II.10.5–6).

[13] In connection with the expression "breaking through" (cf. MU VI.30, *dvāraṃ bhitvā*), I take this opportunity to point out that Vedic *vedhas*, commonly rendered by "wise," as if from *vid*, is far more probably "penetrating," from *vyadh*, and tantamount to *vedhin* ("archer") in the sense of Muṇḍ. Up. II.2.2, *tad evākṣaram viddhi*; cf. also BG XI.54, *śakyo hy aham viddhaḥ*. And if, indeed, *vedhas* and *viddhi* are also possible forms of *vid*, no antinomy is involved, inasmuch as it is precisely by gnosis (*jñāna, vidyā*) that the breaking through or hitting of the mark is effected.

is adumbrated "are not to be communicated unless to one who is at peace (*praśānta*) and has perfect devotion (*yasya . . . parā bhaktiḥ*), being, moreover, either one's own son or a disciple" (Śvet. Up. VI.22–23)—and therefore fit for initiation (*dīkṣā*)—but, essentially, because any such communication would be useless in the case of an unqualified auditor, for "what is the use of the texts to one who does not know Him" (*yas tan na veda kiṃṛcā kariṣyati*, RV I.164.39 = Śvet. Up. IV.8); and, accidentally, as a matter of "convenience" because of "those who can only approach the Word in sin" (*ta ete vācam abhipadya pāpayā*, RV X.71.9).[14]

The "secret" of what is meant by "dementation" (*amanībhāva*) being inaccessible to "mere learning" (cf. *paṇḍitaṃ manyamānāḥ . . . mūḍhaḥ*,[15] Muṇḍ. Up. I.2.8; cf. Īśā Up. 9), it is thus by definition inaccessible to "scholarship" in the modern and philological sense of the word, and from this point of view it must be confessed that the greater part of our

[14] Cf. Muṇḍ. Up. III.2.10–11: "The Brahma doctrine may be communicated to such as perform the sacrifice (*kriyāvantaḥ*), who are auditors (*śrotriyāḥ*), who are men of faith (*śraddhayantaḥ*), who take their stand in 'Brahman,' and making an offering of themselves to the Only Prophet (Agni), bearers of coals of fire on their head. . . . But it is not for one to study who does not practice." It may be remarked, incidentally, that rendered into purely Christian terms, *kriyāvantaḥ* would be "regular celebrants of the Mass."

[15] Primarily the Asuras, from whom the Devas are often represented as concealing their procedure, lest these "mortals" should follow them, cf. Genesis 3:22, "lest he put forth his hand, and take also of the tree of life, and eat, and live forever"; and secondly, the "profane," childish, opinionated and unripe multitude (*avidvānsaḥ, mūḍhaḥ, bālāḥ, nāstikāḥ, pṛthagjanāḥ, laukikāḥ*, etc.), cf. Mark 4:11–12, "Unto you it is given to know the mystery of the Kingdom of God: but unto them that were without, all these things are done in parables: that seeing they may see, and not perceive; and hearing they may hear, and not understand; lest at any time they should be converted, and their sins should be forgiven them"; Mark 4:23, "If any man have ears to hear, let him hear"; and Origen, *Contra Celsum* I.7, "That there should be certain doctrines not made known to the multitude . . . is not a peculiarity of Christianity alone."

To resume, it is inherently *impossible* to communicate the highest (anagogic, *pāramārthika*) Truth otherwise than parabolically by means of symbols (verbal, visual, mythical, ritual, dramatic, etc.) and equally *undesirable* to attempt to communicate the highest Truth to anyone or everyone, because the unqualified auditor must inevitably, if he thinks he understands, misunderstand; cf. Kena Up. II.3b, "It is not understood by those who 'understand' It; but only by those who do not 'understand' It." The point of view is unwelcome to a democratic age of pathetic belief in the efficacy of indiscriminate "education," yet even in such an age it is sufficiently evident to what an extent publicity (French, *vulgarisation*) involves a distortion of all but the most elementary *theoria*—the theory of relativity, for example, being really "forbidden" to all those who cannot think in the technical terms of higher mathematics.

"Vedic studies" amounts to nothing more than a "wandering about in ignorance on the part of blind leaders of the blind" (Muṇḍ. Up. I.2.8) and certainly not to such a "comprehension" as is implied by the constantly repeated *ya evaṃ vidvān* of the texts, a comprehension which is either a matter of experience, or no matter. Learning, then, like other "means" (*upāya*), may be dispositive "either to bondage or to liberation," and that this is so is a proposition with which even some Western critics of modern educational aims are in hearty agreement.[16] The last end or "value" depends, as usual, on the final cause; when learning becomes an end in itself, a science for the sake of science, then it amounts to no more than what was called by St. Bernard a "vile curiosity" (*turpis curiositas*). But if the learning is acquired not for its own sake, but as a means to a further end, and thus becomes a "sacrifice of knowledge . . . offered to Me" (*jñāna-yajñam . . . mad arpaṇam*, BG IX.15, 27), it is conducive to the *summum bonum* envisaged by all scripture as man's last end.

We have been led to a discussion of these matters in connection with such hard sayings as "the mind must be arrested" (*mano niroddhavyam*) and "de-mentation" (*amanībhāva*), partly by the occurrence of such expressions as "ultimate secret" in the same context, and more particularly in order to explain just how it is that in spite of the prestige of modern scientific methods and in spite of their general adoption in Indian seats of learning, there remains an unknown and for various reasons largely inarticulate—but far from insignificant—body of opinion according to which, apart from the limited field of editorship and publication, the results obtained by modern Vedic scholarship have been fundamentally nil, precisely because in almost all these studies the heart of the matter has been evaded, either because the "doctrine that escapes beneath the veil of the strange verses" (Dante, *Inferno* IX.61), the "picture that is not in the colors" (*Laṇkāvatāra Sūtra* II.117–118), has exceeded the capacities of the student or translator or, what amounts to the same thing, has not interested him.

It is not without reason, then, that the whole Vedic (and likewise the Christian) tradition has insisted on the necessity of "Faith" (*śraddhā*).

[16] C. G. Jung has indeed attributed the "failure" of Western Orientalism partly to pride and partly to a more or less conscious attitude of aloofness assumed by the scholar, precisely because "a sympathetic understanding might permit contact with an alien spirit to become a serious experience" (Richard Wilhelm and C. G. Jung, *The Secret of the Golden Flower*, 2nd rev. ed., New York, 1962, p. 81). And indeed, there can be no real knowledge of anything from which one holds aloof and cannot love.

We assume the Scholastic definition of *Fides* as a "consent of the intellect to a credible proposition, of which no empirical proof is available."[17] If one has not so much con*fidence* in the texts as to believe that behind the words lies more than can be told in words, if one is not convinced by the technical consistency of the verses that their "authors" could not have spoken thus without themselves possessing a clear understanding and actual experience of what they were speaking *of*, if one does not so far *trust* the texts as to realize that they are not merely fashioned in the literary sense but are strictly speaking "in-formed," how can one pretend to have grasped or aspire to grasp their true intention, Dante's *vera sentenzia*? As the Buddhist texts so often express it, the nominalist's preoccupation with the aesthetic surfaces and neglect of their content can only be compared to the case of the man who, when the moon is pointed out, sees nothing but the pointing finger; we refer to the condition which a modern European writer has so aptly diagnosed as an "intellectual myopia."

The terms of Scripture and Ritual are symbolic (*pratīkavat*); and merely to submit this self-evident proposition is to say that the symbol is not its own meaning but is significant *of* its referent.[18] Under these

[17] This briefly resumes the Thomist definitions. It may be observed that the proposition *Ad fidem duo requiruntur, s. quod credibilia proponantur, et assensus* (*Sum. Theol.* v.111.11 *ad* 1 and 22.6.1c) excludes the ridiculous interpretation *Credo quia incredibilis.* On the other hand, it may be remarked that the euhemeristic interpretations of metaphysical texts, suggested by most modern exegetes, are literally "incredible." The fact is that a majority of modern exegetes have approached their task from the standpoint of the anthropologist rather than that of the metaphysician; in which connection the story related by Eusebius and quoted by H. G. Rawlinson in "India and Greece: A Note," *Indian Arts and Letters*, X (1936) is very pertinent: "Aristoxenus the musician tells the following story about the Indians. One of these men met Socrates at Athens, and asked him what was the scope of his philosophy. 'An enquiry into human phenomena,' replied Socrates. At this the Indian burst out laughing. 'How can a man enquire into human phenomena,' he exclaimed, 'when he is ignorant of divine ones?' "

[18] It will hardly be out of place to remind the philologist or anthropologist who undertakes to explain a myth or traditional text that it has long been the recognized method of exegesis to assume that at least four valid meanings are involved in any scriptural text, according to the level of reference considered; the possible levels being, respectively, the literal, moral, allegorical, and anagogic. If the four levels be reduced to two by treating the three last as collectively "spiritual" meanings, the consequent "literal and spiritual" correspond to Skr. *pratyakṣam* and *parokṣena* or *adhyātman* and *adhidevatam*: the "anagogic" or highest spiritual significance corresponding to Skr. *pāramārthika.* The student, evidently, who deliberately restricts himself to the lowest and most obvious (naturalistic and historical) level of reference cannot expect to achieve a great exegetic success; he may, indeed, succeed

circumstances, would it not be a contradiction in terms for one who can say that "such knowledge as is not empirical is meaningless to us" to claim to have understood the texts, however encyclopedic his knowledge *of* them might be? Must there not be recognized an element of perversity in one who can stigmatize the Brāhmaṇas as "puerile, arid, and inane" and yet propose to study or translate such works?[19] Under such conditions, what other results could have been expected than have been actually attained? To take only one example: the whole doctrine of "reincarnation" and the supposed "history" of the doctrine have been so distorted by a literal interpretation of symbolic terms as to justify a designation of the doctrine thus presented as "puerile," just as the results of the study of Indian mythology by statistical methods may fairly be described as "arid and inane."

We should not like it to be supposed that the foregoing remarks are directed against Western scholars as such or personally. The defects of modern Indian scholarship are of the same sort, and no less glaring. The recent adoption of the naturalistic and the nominalistic point of view by Indian scholars has led, for example, to such absurdities as the belief that the "sky-faring vehicles" (*vimāna*, etc.) of the ancient texts were actually airplanes; we are merely pointing out that such absurdities are no greater than, but of the same sort as, those of Western scholars who have supposed that in the Vedic rescue of Bhujyu from the "sea" there is no more to be seen than the vague reminiscence of the adventure of some man who, once upon a time, fell into the salt sea and was duly rescued, or those who argue that RV v.46.1 represents no more than the case of the royal retainer who follows his leader no matter what befalls—not recognizing that verses of this kind, far from being anecdotal, are general equations or forms of which events as such, whether past or present, can only be regarded as special cases. Our only purpose has been to show that to make of Vedic studies nothing more than "an inquiry into human conduct" (to quote the phrase attributed to Socrates) presupposes a complete misunderstanding of the nature of the texts themselves; and in the present case, that those who propose to investigate

in depicting the myth as he sees it "objectively"—i.e., as something into which he cannot enter, but can only look *at*. But in thus describing a myth according to what is, strictly speaking, his "accidental" knowledge of it, he is really discussing only its "actual shape" and leaving altogether out of account its "essential form."

[19] Quotations in this and the preceding sentence are from the published works of two of the most distinguished Sanskritists.

such terms as *manas* from this all-too-human and exclusively humanistic point of view must necessarily fail to distinguish "dementation" from "insanity" and "unknowing" from "ignorance." We maintain, accordingly, that it is an indispensable condition of true scholarship to "believe in order to understand" (*crede ut intelligas*), and to "understand in order to believe" (*intellige ut credas*), not, indeed, as distinct and consecutive acts of the will and of the intellect, but as the single activity of both. The time has surely come when we must not merely, as heretofore, consider the meanings of particular terms but also reconsider our whole method of approach to the problems involved. We venture to propound that it is precisely the divorce of intellect and will in the supposed interests of objectivity that primarily explains the relative infirmity of the modern approach.

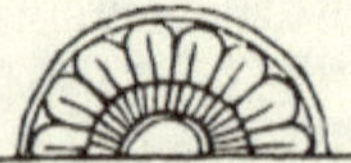

Kha and Other Words Denoting "Zero," in Connection with the Indian Metaphysics of Space

Kha, cf. Greek χᾶος, is generally "cavity"; and in the *Ṛg Veda*, particularly "the hole in the nave of a wheel through which the axle runs" (Monier-Williams). A. N. Singh has shown conclusively that in Indian mathematical usage, current during the earlier centuries of the Christian era, *kha* means "zero";[1] Sūryadeva, commenting on Āryabhaṭa, says that "the *khas* refer to voids (*khāni śūnyā upa lakṣitāni*) . . . thus *khadvinake* means the eighteen places denoted by zeros." Among other words denoting zero are *śūnya*, *ākāśa*, *vyoma*, *antarikṣa*, *nabha*, *ananta*, and *pūrṇa*.[2] We are immediately struck by the fact that the words *śūnya*, "void," and *pūrṇa*, "plenum," should have a common reference; the implication being that all numbers are virtually or potentially present in that which is without number; expressing this as an equation, $0 = x - x$, it is apparent that zero is to number as possibility is to actuality. Again, employment of the term *ananta* with the same reference implies an identification of zero with infinity; the beginning of all series being thus the same as their end. This

[This essay was first published in the *Bulletin of the School of Oriental Studies* (London), VII (1934).—ED.]

[1] *Journal of the United Provinces Historical Society*, VII, 44–45, 62.

[2] It may as well be pointed out here that although "the decimal notation must have been in existence and in common use among the mathematicians long before the idea of applying the place-value principle to a system of word names could have been conceived" (*ibid.*, p. 61), and although a decimal scale has actually been found at Mohenjo Daro (E.J.H. Mackay, "Further Excavations at Mohenjodaro," *Journal of the Royal Society of Arts*, LXXXII, 1934, 222) it is by no means the intention of the present article to present an argument for a *Rg Vedic* knowledge of either the decimal system or the concept of "zero" as such. Our purpose is merely to exhibit the metaphysical and ontological implications of the terms which were later on actually used by Āryabhaṭa and Bhāskara, etc., to designate "zero," "one," and some higher numbers.

last idea, we may observe, is met with already in the earlier metaphysical literature, for example RV IV.1.11, where Agni is described as "hiding both his ends (*guhamāno antā*)"; AB III.43, "the Agniṣṭoma is like a chariot wheel, endless (*ananta*)"; JUB I.35, "the Year is endless (*ananta*), its two ends (*antā*) are Winter and Spring . . . so is the endless chant (*anantaṃ sāman*)." These citations suggest that it may be possible to account for the later mathematicians' selection of technical terms by reference to an earlier usage of the same or like terms in a purely metaphysical context.

Our intention being to demonstrate the native connection of the mathematical terms *kha*, etc., with the same terms as employed in purely metaphysical contexts, it will be necessary to prepare the diagram of a circle or cosmic wheel (*cakra*, *maṇḍala*) and to point out the significance of the relationships of the parts of such a diagram according to universal tradition and more particularly in accordance with the formulation of the *Ṛg Veda*. Take a piece of blank paper of any dimensions, mark a point anywhere upon it, and with this point as center draw two concentric circles of any radii, but one much less than the other; draw any radius from the center to the outer circumference. With exception of the center, which as a point is necessarily without dimension, note that every part of our diagram is merely representative; that is, the number of circles may be indefinitely increased, and the number of radii likewise, each circle thus filled up becoming at last a plane continuum, the extended ground of any given world or state of being; for our purpose we are considering only two such worlds—mythologically speaking, Heaven and Earth, or psychologically, the worlds of subject and object—as forming together the world or cosmos, typical of any particularized world which may be thought of as partial within it. Finally, our diagram may be thought of either as consisting of two concentric circles with their common radii and one common center, or as the diagram of a wheel, with its felly, nave, spokes, and axle-point.

Now in the first place, as a geometrical symbol, that is to say with respect to measure or numeration, our diagram represents the logical relationships of the concepts naught or zero, inconnumerable unity, and indefinite multiplicity; the blank (*śūnya*) surface having no numerical significance; the central point (*indu*, *bindu*) being an inconnumerable unity (inconnumerable, *advaita*, because there cannot be conceived a second center); and either circumference an endless (*ananta*) series of points, which may be thought of as numbers; the totality (*sarvam*) of the numbered, that is to say individual, points representing the sum of a mathematically infinite series extending from one to "infinity," and conceivable as plus or minus according to the direction of procedure. The whole area (*śarīra*) delimited corresponds to place (*déśa*), a revolution of the circles about their center corresponds to time (*kāla*). It will be observed further that any radius connects analogous or corresponding points or numbers on the two circumferences;[3] if, now, we suppose the radius of one or both circles indefinitely reduced, which brings us to the central point as limiting concept (that is also "as it was in the beginning"), it is evident that even this point can be thought of only as a plenum of all the numbers represented on either circumference.[4] On the other hand, this point, at the same time that it represents an inconnumerable unity and, as we have seen, a plenum, must also be thought of as representing, that is, as the symbol of, zero, for two reasons: (1) inasmuch as the concept to which it refers is by definition without place and without dimensions, and therefore nonexistent, and (2) the mathematically infinite series, thought of as both plus and minus according to direction, cancel out where all directions meet in common focus.

So far as I know, Indian literature does not provide a specifically geometrical exegesis exactly corresponding to what is given in the preceding paragraph. What we do find in the metaphysical and religious traditions is a corresponding usage of the symbol of the Wheel (primarily the solar chariot, or a wheel thereof), and it is in this connection that we first meet with some of the most significant of those terms which are later on employed by the mathematicians. In RV I.155.6 and I.164.2, 11, 13, 14, 48; AV X.8.4-7; KB XX.1; JUB I.35; BU I.5.15; Śvet. Up. I.4; Praśna Up. VI.5-6, and like texts, the Year as an everlasting sequence is thought of as an unwasting wheel of life, a revolving wheel of the Angels, in which all things have their being and are manifested in succession; "none of its spokes is last in order" (RV V.85.5). The parts of the wheel are named as follows: *āṇi*, the axle-point within the nave (note that the axle causes revolution, but does not itself revolve); *kha*, *nābhi*, the nave (usually as space within the hub, occasionally as the hub itself); *ara*, spoke, connecting hub and felly; *nemi*, *pavi*, the felly. It should be observed that *nābhi*, from √ *nabh*, to expand, is also "navel"; similarly in anthropomorphic formulation, "navel" corresponds to "space" (MU

[3] The familiar principle "as above, so below" is illustrated here.

[4] The notion of exemplarism is expressed here, with respect to number or mathematical individuality.

vi.6); in the *Ṛg Veda*, the cosmos is constantly thought of as "expanded" (√*pin*) from this chthonic center.

Certain passages indicating the metaphysical significance of the terms *āṇi*, *kha*, and *nābhi* in the *Ṛg Veda* may now be cited. It should be premised that we find here in connection with the constant use of the wheel symbol, and absence of a purely geometrical formulation, the term *āṇi* employed to express ideas later on referred to by the words *indu* or *bindu*.[5] Vedic *āṇi*, being the axle-point within the nave of the wheel, and on which the wheel revolves, corresponds exactly to Dante's "il punta dello stelo al cui la prima rota va dintorno" (*Paradiso* xiii.11–12). The metaphysical significance of the *āṇi* is fully brought out in RV i.35.6, *āṇiṃ na rathyam amṛtā adhi tasthuḥ*, "as on the axle-point of the chariot wheel are actually existent the undying [Angels or intellectual principles]," which also supplies the answer to the well-known problem, "How many Angels can stand on the point of a needle?" More often the nave of the wheel, rather than the axle-point specifically, is treated as its center; nor need this confuse us if we reflect that just as under limiting conditions (indefinite reduction of the radius, or when the central point has been identified but the circle not yet drawn) the center represents the circle, so under similar conditions (metaphysically, *in principio*) the axle-point implies the nave or even the whole wheel—the point without dimension, and a principial space not yet expanded (or as the *Ṛg Veda* would express it, "closed") being the same in reference. The nave then, *kha* or *nābhi*, of the world wheel is regarded as the receptacle and fountain of all order, formative ideas, and goods: for example, ii.28.5, *ṛdhyāma te varuṇa khām ṛtasya*, "may we, O Varuṇa, win thy nave of Law"; viii.41.6, where in Trita Āptya "all oracles (*kāvyā*) are set as is the nave within the wheel (*cakre nābhir iva*)"; iv.28, where Indra opens the closed or hidden naves or rocks (*apihitā . . . khāni* in verse 1, *apihitāni aśnā* in verse 5) and thus releases the Seven Rivers of Life.[6] In v.32.1, where

[5] *Indu* occurs in the *Rg Veda* as "drop" in connection with Soma: in AV vii.109.6 as "point on a die"; and grammatically as the designation of *Anusvāra*. PB vi.9.19–20 is of interest: *indava iva hi pitarah, mana iva*, i.e., "the Patriarchs are as it were drops (*indu* in pl.), as it were the intellectual principle." In RV vi.44.22, Indu is evidently Soma; in vii.54.2, Vāstoṣpati.

[6] The Rivers, of course, represent ensembles of possibility (hence they are often spoken of as "maternal") with respect to a like number of "worlds," or planes of being, as in i.22.16, *pṛthivyā sapta dhāmabhiḥ*. Our terms *kha*, *aśna*, etc., are necessarily employed in the plural when the "creation" is envisaged with respect to the cosmos not as a single "world," but as composed of two, three, or seven originally unmanifested but now to be conceptually distinguished "worlds"; the solar chariot

Indra breaks open the Fountain of Life (*utsam*), this is again an emptying out of the hollows (*khāni*), whereby the fettered floods are released.

According to an alternative formulation, all things are thought of as *ante principium* shut up within, and *in principio* as proceeding from, a common ground, rock, or mountain (*budhna*, *adri*, *parvata*, etc.): this ground, thought of as resting island-like within the undifferentiated sea of universal possibility (x.89.4, where the waters pour *sāgarasya budhnāt*), is merely another aspect of our axle-point (*āṇi*), regarded as the primary assumption toward which the whole potentiality of existence is focused by the primary acts of intellection and will. This means that *a priori* undimensioned space (*kha*, *ākāśa*, etc.) underlies and is the mother of the point, rather than that the latter has an independent origin; and this accords with the logical order of thought, which proceeds from potentiality to actuality, nonbeing to being. This ground or point is, in fact, the "rock of ages" (*aśmany anante*, I.130.3; *adriṃ . . . acyutam*, VI.17.5). Here *ante principium* Agni lies occulted (*guhā santam*, I.141.3, etc.) as Ahi Budhnya, "in the ground of space, concealing both his ends" (*budhne rajaso . . . guhamāno antā*, IV.1.11, where it may be noted that *guhamāno antā* is tantamount to *ananta*, literally "end-less," "in-finite," "eternal"), hence he is called "chthonic" (*nābhir agni pṛthivyā*, I.59.2, etc.), and is born in this ground (*jāyata prathamaḥ . . . budhne*, IV.1.11) and stands erect, Janus-like, at the parting of the ways (*ayor ha skambha . . . pathām visarge*, x.5.6); hence he gets his chthonic steeds and other treasures (*aśvabudhnā*, x.8.3; *budhnyā vasūni*, VII.6.7). It is only when this rock is cleft that the hidden kine are freed, the waters flow (I.62.3, where Bṛhaspati *bhinad adrim* and *vidadgāḥ*; v.41.12, *śṛṇvanty āpaḥ . . . adreḥ*). This is, moreover, a center without place, and hence when the Waters have come forth (that is, when the cosmos has come to be) one asks, as in x.111.8, "where is their beginning (*agram*), where their ground (*budnaḥ*), where now, ye Waters, your innermost center (*madhyam . . . antaḥ*)?"[7]

---

having one, two, three, or seven wheels, accordingly. It is perhaps because the chariot of the Year is more often than not thought of as two-wheeled (Heaven and Earth), and therefore provided with two analogous axle-points, that *āṇi* was not later employed as a verbal symbol of "one."

[7] *Madhya* is "middle" in all senses, and also algebraically "mean." For the metaphysical values, cf. RV *madhye samudre*, and *utsasya madhye* = *sindhūnām upodaye*, as the place of Agni or Varuṇa, and in CU III.11.1, *ekata madhye sthāne*, "single in the midmost station."

Thus metaphysically, in the symbolism of the Wheel, the surface—blank (*śūnya*) in the initial nonbeing (*asat*) of any formulation (*saṃkalpa*)—represents the truly infinite (*aditi*) and maternal possibility of being; the axle-point or nave, exemplary being (*viśvam ekam*, RV III.54.8 = integral omnipresence); the actual construction, a mentally accomplished partition of being into existences; each spoke, the integration of an individual as *nāma-rūpa*, that is, as archetypal inwardly and phenomenal outwardly; the felly, the principle of multiplicity (*viṣamatva*). Or, employing a more theological terminology: the undetermined surface represents the Godhead (*aditi, parabrahman, tamas, apaḥ*); the axle-point or immovable rock, God (*āditya, aparabrahman, īśvara, jyoti*); the circle of the nave, Heaven (*svarga*); any point on the circumference of the nave, an intellectual principle (*nāma, deva*); the felly, Earth with its analogous (*anurūpa*) phenomena (*viśvā rūpāṇi*); the construction of the wheel, the sacrificial act of creation (*karma*,[8] *sṛṣṭi*), its abstraction, the act of dissolution (*laya*). Furthermore, the course (*gati*) of any individual upon the pathway of a spoke is in the beginning centrifugal (*pravṛtta*) and then again centripetal (*nivṛtta*), until the center (*madhya*) is found; and when the center of individual being coincides with the center of the wheel, he is emancipated (*mukta*), the extension of the wheel no longer involving him in local motion, at the same time that its entire circuit now becomes for him one picture (*jagaccitra*)[9] seen in simultaneity, who as "round-about-seer," *paridraṣṭṛ*, now "overlooks everything," *viśvam . . . abhicaṣṭe*, I.164.44.

In order to understand the use of terms for "space" (*kha, ākāśa, antarikṣa, śūnya*, etc.)[10] as verbal symbols of zero (which represents privation of number, and is yet a matrix of number in the sense $0 = x - x$),[11] it must be realized that *ākāśa*, etc., represent primarily a concept not of physical space, but of a purely principial space without dimension, though the matrix of dimension.[12] For example, "all these beings arise out of the

[8] For the construction of the wheel, cf. RV VIII.77.3, *akhidat khe arān iva khedayā*, and the discussion in Coomaraswamy, "Angel and Titan: An Essay in Vedic Ontology," 1935.

[9] Śaṅkarācārya, *Svātmanirūpana* 95.

[10] *Śūnya* does not appear in RV, though *śūnam* occurs in the sense of "privation."

[11] Observe that the dual series of plus and minus numbers represents "pairs of opposites," *dvandvau*.

[12] C. A. Scharbrau, "Transzendenter Raum der Ewigkeit ist der Ākāśa vor allem auch da, wo er als Ausgangspunkt, als Schöpfungsgrund und als Ziel, als A und O

space (*ākāśād samapadyanta*) and return into the space (*ākāśaṃ pratyastaṃ yanti*). For the space is older than they, prior to them, and is their last resort (*parāyaṇam*)," CU I.9.1; "space is the name of the permissive cause of individual-integration (*ākāśo vai nāma nāmarūpayor nirvahitā*)," CU VIII.14; and just as Indra "opens the closed spaces (*apihitā khāni*)," RV IV.28.1, so the Self "awakens this rational [cosmos] from that space (*ākāśāt eṣa khalu idaṃ cetāmātraṃ dobhayati*)," MU VI.17, in other words, *ex nihilo fit*. Furthermore, the locus of this "space" is "within you": "what is the intrinsic aspect of expansion is the supernal fiery energy in the vacance of the inner man (*tat svarūpaṃ nabhasaḥ khe antarbhūtasya yat paraṃ tejaḥ*)," MU VII.11;[13] and this same "space in the heart" (*antarhṛdaya ākāśa*) is the locus (*āyatana, veśma, nīḍa, kośa*, etc.) where are deposited in secret (*guhā nihitaṃ*) all that is ours already or may be ours on any plane (*loka*) of experience (CU VIII.1.1–3). At the same time, in BU V.1, this "ancient space" (*kha*) is identified with Brahman and with the Spirit (*khaṃ brahma, khaṃ purāṇaṃ, vāyuraṃ khaṃ iti*), and this Brahman is at the same time a plenum or pleroma (*pūrṇa*) such that "when plenum is taken from plenum, plenum yet remains."[14]

Here we get precisely that equivalence of *kha* and *pūrṇa*, void and plenum, which was remarked upon as noteworthy in the verbal notation of the mathematicians. The thought, moreover, is almost literally repeated when Bhāskara in the *Bījagaṇita*[15] defines the term *ananta* thus: *ayam ananto rāśiḥ khahara ity ucyate. Asmin vikāraḥ khahare na rāśāvapi praviṣṭeṣvapi niḥsṛteṣu bahuṣvapi syāl layasṛṣṭikāle 'nante 'cyute bhūtagaṇesu yadvat*, that is, "This fraction of which the denominator is zero, is called an infinite quantity. In this quantity consisting of that which has cipher for its divisor, there is no alteration, though many be added or subtracted; just as there is no alteration in the Infinite Immovable (*anante acyute*)[16] at the time of the emanation or resolution of worlds, though hosts of beings are emanated or withdrawn."

---

der Welt angeschaut wird," *Die Idee der Schöpfung in der vedischen Literatur* (Stuttgart, 1932), p. 56; "size which has no size, though the principle of size," Meister Eckhart, Evans ed., I, 114.

[13] *Nabha*, from √ *nabh*, to "expand," etc., as also in *nābhi*, "navel" and "nave." A secondary sense of *nabh* is "to destroy."

[14] This text occurs in almost the same form in AV X.8.29.

[15] Calcutta, 1917, pp. 17–18.

[16] Cf. *aśmany anante* and *adrim acyutam* cited above, with the meaning "rock of Ages."

It may be observed further that while in the *Ṛg Veda* we "do not find the use of names of things to denote numbers, we do find instances of numbers denoting things."[17] In vii.103.1, for example, the number "twelve" denotes the "year"; in x.71.3, "seven" stands for "rivers of life" or "states of being." It is thus merely a converse usage of words when the mathematicians make use of the names of things to denote numbers; to take the most obvious examples, it is just what should be expected, when we find that 1 is expressed by such words as *adi*, *indu*, *abja*, *pṛthvī*; 2 by such as *yama*, *aśvinā*; 3 by such as *agni*, *vaiśvānara*, *haranetra*, *bhuvana*; 4 by *veda*, *diś*, *yuga*, *samudra*, etc.; 5 by *prāṇa*; 6 by *ṛtu*; and so forth. It is not to be understood, of course, that the number-words are all of Vedic origin; many suggest rather an Epic vocabulary, e.g., *pāṇḍava* for 5, while others, such as *netra* for 2, have an obvious and secular source. In certain cases an ambiguity arises, for example, *loka* as representing either 3 or 14, *diś* as representing 4 or 10, but this can be readily understood; in the last-mentioned case, for example, the quarters have been thought of in one and the same cosmology as either four, or if we count up eight quarters and half-quarters, adding the zenith and nadir, as ten. Taken in its entirety as cited by Singh, the numeral vocabulary can hardly antedate the beginning of the Christian era (we find that 10 is represented, among other words, by *avatāra*; and 6 by *rāga*).

If we attempt to account for the forms of the ideograms of numbers in a similar fashion, we shall be on much less certain ground. A few suggestions may nevertheless be made. For example, a picture-writing of the notion "axle-point" could only have been a "point," and of the concept "nave" could only have been a "round O," and both of these signs are employed at the present day to indicate "zero." The upright line that represents "one" may be regarded as a pictogram of the axis that penetrates the naves of the dual wheels, and thus at once unites and separates Heaven and Earth. The Devanāgarī and Arabic signs for "three" correspond to the trident (*triśūla*), which is known to have been from very ancient times a symbol of Agni or Śiva. *A priori* it might be expected that a sign for "four" should be cruciform, following the notion of extension in the directions of the four airts (*diś*); and in fact we find in Saka script that "four" is represented by a sign X, and that the Devanāgarī may well be thought of as a cursive form derived from a like prototype. Even if there be sufficient foundation for such suggestions, it is hardly likely that a detailed interpretation of ideograms of numbers

[17] Singh, p. 56, (as cited in n. 1).

above four could now be deduced. We can only say that the foregoing suggestions as to the nature of numerical ideograms rather support than counter the views of those who seek to derive the origins of symbolism, script, and speech from the concept of the circuit of the year.

It is, however, beyond question that many of the verbal symbols—the case of *kha* for "zero" is conspicuous—used by Indian mathematicians had an earlier currency, that is to say before a development of mathematical science as such, in a more universal, metaphysical context. That a scientific terminology should thus have been formulated on the basis of a metaphysical terminology, and by no means without a full consciousness of what was being done (as the citation from Bhāskara clearly shows), is not only in accordance with all that we know of the natural course of Indian thought, which takes the universal for granted and proceeds to the particular, but also admirably illustrates what from a traditionally orthodox point of view would be regarded as constituting a natural and right relationship of any special science to the metaphysical background of all sciences. One is reminded of words in the *Encyclical* of Pope Leo XIII, dated 1879, on the "Restoration of Christian Philosophy": "Hence, also, the physical sciences, which now are held in so much repute, and everywhere draw to themselves a singular admiration, because of the wonderful discoveries made in them, would not only take no harm from a restoration of the philosophy of the ancients, but would derive great protection from it. For the fruitful exercise and increase of these sciences it is not enough that we consider facts and contemplate Nature. When the facts are well known we must rise higher, and give our thoughts with great care to understanding the nature of corporeal things, as well as to the investigation of the laws which they obey, and of the principles from which spring their order, their unity in variety, and their common likeness in diversity. It is marvelous what power and light and help are given to these investigations by Scholastic philosophy, if it be wisely used . . . there is no contradiction, truly so called, between the certain and proved conclusions of recent physics, and the philosophical principles of the Schools." These words by no means represent a merely Christian apologetic, but rather enunciate a generally valid procedure, in which the theory of the universal acts at the same time with suggestive force and normatively with respect to more specific applications. We may reflect, on the one hand, that the decimal system, with which the concept "zero" is inseparably connected, was developed by Indian scholars[18] who were very surely, as their own words prove, deeply versed in and dependent upon an older and traditional metaphysical interpretation of the meaning of the world; and on the other, that had it not been for its boasted and long-maintained independence of traditional metaphysics (in which the principles, if not the facts, of relativity are explicit),[19] modern scientific thought might have reached much sooner than has actually been the case a scientifically valid formulation and proof of such characteristic notions as those of an expanding universe and the finity of physical space. What has been outlined above with respect to the special science of mathematics represents a principle no less valid in the case of the arts, as could easily be demonstrated at very great length. For example, what is implied by the statement in AB VI.27, that "it is in imitation of the angelic works of art that any work of art such as a garment or chariot is made here,"[20] is actually to be seen in the hieratic arts of every traditional culture, and in the characteristic motifs of the surviving folk arts everywhere. Or in the case of literature: epic (*Volsunga Saga*, *Beowulf*, the Cuchullain and Arthurian cycles, *Mahābhārata*, *Buddhacarita*, etc.) and fairy tale (notably, for example, *Jack and the Beanstalk*) repeat with infinitely varied local coloring the one story of *jātavidyā*, Genesis.[21] The whole point of view can, indeed, be recognized in the Indian classification of traditional literature, in which the treatises (*śāstras*) on auxiliary science such as grammar, astronomy, law,[22] medicine, architecture, etc., are classed as Vedāṇga, "limbs or powers of the Veda," or as Upaveda, "accessory with respect to the Veda"; as

[18] "The place system of the Babylonians . . . fell on fertile soil only among the Hindus. . . . Algebra, which is distinctly Hindu . . . uses the principle of local value" (M. J. Babb, in JAOS, LI, 1931, 52). That the "Arabic" numerals are ultimately of Indian origin is now generally admitted; what their adoption meant for the development of European science need not be emphasized.

[19] Āryabhata, *Āryabhaṭīya* IV.9, "As a man in a boat going forward sees a stationary object moving backward, just so at Lankā a man sees the stationary asterisms moving backward."

[20] See Coomaraswamy, *The Transformation of Nature in Art*, 1934, p. 8 and n. 8.

[21] Cf. Ernest Siecke, *Die Liebesgeschichte des Himmels* (Strassburg, 1892); and Alfred Jeremias, *Handbuch der altorientalischen Geisteskultur* (Berlin, 1929), p. x: "Die Menschheitsbildung ist ein einheitliches Ganzes, und in den verschiedenen Kulturen findet man die Dialekte der einen Geistessprache."

[22] Even the "Machiavellian" *Arthaśāstra* (I.3) proceeds from the principle *svadharmah svargāya ānantyāya ca, tasya atikrame lokah sankarād acchidyeta*, "vocation leads to heaven and aeviternity; in case of a digression from this norm, the world is brought to ruin by confusion."

Guénon expresses it, "toute science apparaissait ainsi comme un prolongement de la doctrine traditionelle elle-même, comme une de ses applications . . . une connaissance inférieure si l'on veut, mais pourtant encore une véritable connaissance," while, *per contra*, "Les fausses synthèses, qui s'efforcent de tirer le supérieur de l'inférieur . . . ne peuvent jamais être qu'hypothétiques. . . . En somme, la science, en méconnaissant les principes et en refusant de s'y rattacher, se prive à la fois de la plus haute garantie qu'elle puisse recevoir et de la plus sûre direction qui puisse lui être donnée . . . elle devient douteuse et chancelante . . . ce sont là des caractères généraux de la pensée proprement moderne; voilà à quel degré d'abaissement intellectuel en est arrivé l'Occident, depuis qu'il est sorti des voies qui sont normales au reste de l'humanité."[23]

[23] René Guénon, *Orient et Occident* (Paris, 1930), extracts from ch. 2.

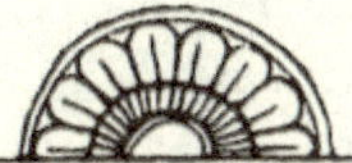

The Tantric Doctrine of Divine Biunity

"You say, then, Trismegistus, that God is of both sexes?"
Hermes, *Asclepius* III.21

All tradition speaks in the last analysis of God as an inconnumerable and perfectly simple Identity, but also of this Supreme Identity as an identity *of* two contrasted principles, distinguishable in all composite things, but coincident without composition in the One who is no thing. The Identity is of Essence and Nature, Being and Nonbeing, God and Godhead—as it were, masculine and feminine. *Natura naturans, Creatrix universalis est Deus.*[1] On the other hand, a division of Essence from Nature, Heaven from Earth, subject from object, is a *sine qua non* of the existence of composite things, all of which are, but in different and particular ways. Nature then "recedes from likeness to God, yet even insofar as it has being in this wise, it retains a certain likeness to the divine being" (*Sum. Theol.* I.14.11 *ad* 3). Henceforth Essence is the Creator and active power, Nature the means of creation and passive recipient of form —"Nature as being that by which the generator generates" (Damascene, *De fide orthodoxa* I.18). Of which the relation of man to woman is a likeness: the relation of marriage is a sacrament and rite because an adequate symbol and reflection of the identification of Essence and Nature *in divinis*.

The notion of a bisexual polarity in Deity suggested above has sometimes been regarded as a peculiarity of the mediaeval Hindu and Buddhist

[First published in French in *Études traditionelles*, XLII (1937), this essay later appeared in its original English version in the *Annals of the Bhandarker Oriental Research Institute*, XIX (1938).—ED.]

[1] *Sum. Theol.*, Turin edition, 1932 ("*nihil obstat*"), *Lexikon* by J. M. Mellinio, p. 22*: cf. references to the text, J. M. Mellinio, *Index Rerum*, s.v. Natura, item 7, *natura dicitur dupliciter*, etc. Throughout the present article, "Nature" stands for *Natura naturans.*

Tantric systems of India, in which it is so clearly enunciated and made the basis of a visual and ritual symbolism:[2] and especially so regarded by those who disparage the use of any sexual symbolism and are therefore unwilling to recognize it elsewhere. Within the limits of the present article it would be impossible to demonstrate the veritable universality of the doctrine of a divine biunity; we shall not, for example, attempt to discuss the Chinese *yin* and *yang*, and shall merely allude to the Gnostic syzygies. What we propose to show as briefly as possible is that a symbolism of this sort permeates not only the older Indian tradition, of which the later Tantrism is, in fact, a perfectly orthodox adaptation, but also the Christian ontology from first to last.

In the Vedic tradition, the Supreme Identity (*tad ekam*) is "at the same time spirant and despirated" (*ānīt avātam*, RV x.129.2), "Being and Nonbeing[3] (*sad-asat*) in the uttermost Empyrean, in the womb of the Infinite" (RV x.5.7). In the same way in Muṇḍ. Up. ii.2.1–2, the supralogical Brahman is "Being and Nonbeing . . . Intellect and Voice" (*sad-asat . . . vāg-manas*). The coincidence of the proximate and ultimate (*apara* and *para*) Brahman in the Upaniṣads is that of Mitrāvaruṇau in the Vedas. The Supreme Identity is equally bipolar whether one thinks of "It" as masculine or feminine: so one asks with respect to the Magna Mater, Natura Naturans Creatrix, the Infinite (*virāj*, *aditi*), "Who knoweth Her progenitive duality?" (*mithunatvam*, AV viii.9.10); and conversely, "He (Brahman) is a womb" (*yoniś ca gīyate*, VS i.4.7.27). But if the conjoint principles are considered in their reciprocity, it is the manifested God that is the masculine and unmanifested Godhead that is the feminine power, as being the inexhaustible reservoir of all possibility, including that of manifestation: it is, then, Mitra that inseminates Varuṇa (PB xxv.10.10), Krishna who "deposits the embryo in the Great Brahman, my womb . . . mine ultimate Nature (*para prakṛti*), the womb of all existence" (BG xiv.3 and vii.5, 6), and "Into the womb of the In-

[2] To what extent "Tantrism" and "Śāktism" are to be identified has been discussed by Glasenapp in OZ, XII (1936), 120–133, where it is concluded that "a starting point for the *Śākta* doctrines is given in the philosophy of 'Speech' (*vāc*) of the Mantra-Śāstras." See also the same author's "Die Entstehung des Vajrayāna," ZDMG, XC (1936), 546–572; Mircea Eliade, *Yoga: Essai sur les origines de la mystique indienne*, Paris and Bucharest, 1936; S. K. Das, *Śakti or Divine Power*, Calcutta, 1934; Coomaraswamy, "*Parāvṛtti* = Transformation, Regeneration, Anagogy," 1933, and "A Note on the Aśvamedha," 1936.

[3] "Nonbeing" must not be understood to mean a nothingness: Nonbeing is predicated of the Infinite *qua* "non-Ens," not *quia* "non Est"; i.e., negatively, but not by way of privation. Cf. G. de Mengel, "La Notion de l'absolu dans diverses formes de la tradition," *Le Voile d'Isis* (June 1929).

finite that Soma puts the embryo" (RV IX.74.5), in accordance with RV X.121.7, "Waters wherein was laid the universal embryo," namely, the "Golden Germ," Hiraṇyagarbha.

Intellect and Voice (*manas* and *vāc*) are One *ab intra*: "The Voice is verily Brahman in the uttermost Empyrean" (TS VII.18e). But "This Brahman is Silence" (Śaṇkarācārya on VS III.2.17). Just as the incantation (*brahman*) is there inaudibly the Brahman, so is the Voice unvoiced; the Intellect is there "de-mented" of itself, the Voice unuttered.[4] It is only when these two are divided, when heaven and earth are pillared apart by the axis of the universe (*skambha*, σταυρός), that Intellect and Voice become the "poles of the Vedas" (*vedasya āṇī*, AĀ II.7), respectively celestial and chthonic, then only that Being and Nonbeing take on an ethical qualification as of Life and Death, Good and Evil, divided from one another as the hither from the farther shore by the width of the universe: it is from a position here below that one prays, "Lead us from Nonbeing to Being, Darkness to Light" (BU 1.3.28). Nonbeing then acquires, indeed, the value *non Est*, inasmuch as it refers to all things under the Sun, of which Augustine says that as compared to God "nec pulchra sunt nec bona sunt nec sunt" (*Confessions* XI.4):[5] the creation and cosmic crucifixion are not merely the necessary means of redemption, but also the very antithesis of the last end, which must be the same as the first beginning. Accordingly, as RV X.24.5 expresses it, "When the conjoint pair were parted, the Devas moaned, and cried 'Let them be wed again'"; and hence the enactment of the marriage in ritual, symbolic of the reunion of Indra and Indrāṇī in the heart, so poignantly described in the analogy of human union in ŚB X.5.2.11-15.

Let us consider now one of the many texts describing the divine procession from interior to exterior operation. In PB VII.6.1-6, "Prajāpati,[6]

[4] RV X.27.1, "Beyond this here, assuredly, there is another sound" (*śrava id ena paro anyad asti*); Plotinus, *Enneads* I.6.3, "Harmonies unheard create the harmonies we hear and wake the soul to the one essence in another nature"—which is the essential function alike of the Vedic and Christian liturgies.

See also MU VI.34, "The mind must be brought to a stop (*mano nirddhavyam*)," with many parallels, Brahmanical and Buddhist; and Meister Eckhart, "The mind must be de-mented. . . . None may attain be he not stripped of all mental matter."

[5] Augustine continues, making a distinction of two kinds of knowledge, empirical and absolute, analogous to the Indian *avidyā* and *vidyā*—"Scientia nostra scientiae tuae comparata ignorantia est." For the unreality of things as they are in themselves, cf. *Acts of Peter* XXXIX, "there is naught else that is save Thee only."

[6] The implications of the name "Prajāpati" and of the designation of "creatures" as *prajā*, literally "progeny," are the same as those of Acts 17:28, "We are the offspring of God."

being One and desiring to be Many, with Intellect looked upon the Silence: what was in Intellect, became the 'Great.' He perceived, 'This embryo of Myself is hidden within Me: I shall bring it to birth by means of the Voice.'[7] He separated off the Voice: She went the way of the Vehicle of Passing-over, so-called because it swiftly 'bringeth over.' Thence the 'Great' was duly born: of which Prajāpati spake that 'This is the greatness of the Great, that it was so long a time within.' The 'Great' was unto Prajāpati even as his eldest Son."

The Son is thus already in the undivided unity of the conjoint principles the Father's image in himself, *per verbum in intellectu conceptum*;[8] and this conception is Eckhart's "act of fecundation latent in eternity." Prajāpati's "contemplation of the Silence" is unmistakably a vital operation: the wording *tūṣṇīm manasā dhyāyat* closely corresponds to that of RV x.71.2, *manasā vācam akrata*, "had intercourse by Intellect with the Voice," and ŚB vi.1.2.9, *sa manasaiva vācam mithunaṃ samabhavat, sa garbhy abhavat*, "He had intercourse by Intellect with Voice, He became pregnant." That Prajāpati divides the Voice from himself (which Voice had been his "Silence"), *vācaṃ vyasṛjata*, corresponds to BU vi.4.2, "He separated the Woman," *striyam asṛjata*—"This Voice is indeed a maiden," *yoṣā vā'yaṃ vāk*, ŚB iii.2.1.19—and to St. Augustine's "I made myself a Mother of whom to be born" (*Contra V Haereses* 5). It is precisely because the Father *himself* takes birth through the Mother that there is a

[7] "What was engendered had been life in Him" (John 1:4, from the Greek and according to the traditional punctuation). That the Vulgate renders ὅ γέγονε by *quod factum est* abstracts from the original meaning the sense of vital operation. Notwithstanding that to generate and to make are the same *in divinis*, the words themselves are not synonymous, inasmuch as they consider the same thing under different aspects. The Latin version suggests what de Gaigneron has called an effort to " 'dénaturer,' pour ne pas scandaliser." The Nicaean Council, however, maintained that the Son was "begotten, not made," and we find accordingly in the credo *genitum non factum*, γεννηθέντα οὐ ποιηθέντα.

[8] Said by St. Thomas with reference to the artist's operation in the likeness of divine creation; the mental concept of the work to be done is literally the artist's child. A similar application occurs in the Indian texts, for example, ŚB iii.2.4.11, "Intellect prevents the Voice . . . were it not for the Intellect, the Voice would speak incoherently"; ŚB iv.6.7.10, "The Voice speaks not but what is contemplated by Intellect"; TS ii.5.11.5, "What he contemplates by Intellect (*yad dhi manasā dhyāyati*), that he utters by the Voice"; cf. RV i.20.2, where the Ṛbhus, the artists of the gods, "wrought by conjoining Intellect with Voice" (*vacoyujā tatakṣur manasā*, where *takṣ* has the sense of working like a carpenter with an axe on wood, in this case that wood of which the world is made). The work of art is always the embodiment of a *conception*. See Coomaraswamy, "The Vedic Doctrine of 'Silence' " [in the present volume—ED.].

coessentiality of the Son with the Father, as in AB vii.13: "Becoming an embryo, he enters the wife, the mother, and being renewed, is born again (*punar . . . jāyate*)." There is a delegation and transmission of the universal Nature in the *genealogia regni Dei* just as there is of a particular human nature in a dynastic succession of functional types; it may be added that a "rebirth" in this sense—"the doer aright is ordinately born in his children," RV vi.70.3; "my children are my coming to be again," JUB iii.27.17; "that he has engendered is his going on again," CU iii.17.3—constitutes all that is, properly speaking, the Indian doctrine of the reincarnation of the individual, as distinguished from that of the transmigration of the Spiritual Person who, when the body dies, "hurries again to a womb," BU iv.3.36—reincarnation and transmigration coinciding only *in divinis*. The separated Voice now assumes a vehicular function, that of the liturgy in its verbal aspect, the Ṛc, elsewhere identified with this world and the Earth. The "Great" (*bṛhat*, implying an indefinite extension in time and space), at first contained as an embryo (*garbha*) within the Unity and now transferred by vital operation to the Mother, in whom it waxes, and of whom it is born, is primarily Agni, the visible and audible Prajāpati,[9] considered here in a liturgical aspect: "He is born from the Titan's loins and shines in the Mother's lap" (RV iii.29.14), the altar-womb of Mother Earth.[10] That the "Great" is said to have lain "great while within" (*jyog antar*) is a form of expression characteristic for Agni, as in RV x.124.1, "a great while hast Thou lain in the long darkness" (*jyog eva dīrghaṃ tama āśayiṣṭāḥ*), and for his cognate Dīrghaśravas as in PB xv.3.25, where the "Far-cry" "was long in exile and in want of food" (*jyog aparuddho' śanāyaḥ* [not yet come "eating and drinking"]).

[9] Agni (or Indra, Sūrya, or Soma) is as much the "Great Liturgy" (*bṛhad uktha*) as, literally, a Fire. Cf. RV v.87.1, where the hymns are described as "born of the Voice" (*vāci-niṣpannā*). We have discussed elsewhere the identity *in divinis* of sound and light. The Son is as much a resonance as luminous and calorific. The Son of God is an utterance; "In the beginning, this world was unuttered" (MU vi.6).

[10] In Christian nativities of the Byzantine type, where there is a broken cave in place of the later and more familiar ruined stable (the significance of both is the same in the last analysis, as is also the case in the Vedic tradition, where the creative act involves the breaking open of a cave which is also a stable of cattle), it is made as clear as possible that the Theotokos is the Earth, Gaia. It is, moreover, with perfect accuracy that Wolfram von Eschenbach sings, "the Earth was Adam's mother . . . yet still was the Earth a maid. . . . Two Men have been born of maidens, and God hath the likeness ta'en of the son of the first Earth-maiden . . . since He willed to be Son of Adam" (*Parzifal*, I, ix.549 ff.).

The worlds are ever impatient for the birth and coming forth by day: "When shall the Child be born?" RV x.95.12.

Another and very informative text is that of BU 1.4.1–4. Here the account of the creation begins with the Spirit (*ātman*) "alone in the aspect of Person (*puruṣa*)." This person in the beginning "was of such sort as are a man and a woman closely embraced (*etāvan āsa yathā strī-pumāṇsau sampariṣvaktau*). He desired a second. He caused that Spiritual-Self of his to fall atwain (*ātmānaṃ dvedhāpātayat*).[11] Thence came into being 'husband and wife.' . . . He had intercourse with Her: thence were human beings engendered (*mānuṣyā ajāyanta*)." In the same way He and She assuming other than human forms begat their like in these animal types.[12]

Thus once more the One becomes Many by an act of generation. Again, the converse operation by which the conceptually separated self is reunited to the ever undivided Self or Spiritual Essence is a "deification" described as a marriage: "This is that form of his that is beyond the meters,[13] that hath smitten away all evil, and that hath no fear. It is as when one is closely embraced (*sampariṣvaktaḥ*, corresponding to *sampariṣvaktau*, above) by a darling bride and knows naught of a within or a without, even so that the (spiritual) Person (of a man) embraced by the prognostic Spirit (*prajñātmanā*)[14] knows naught of a within nor a without. That is his true form, in which his desire is obtained, the Spirit is the whole of his desire, he has no unfulfilled desire, nor any grief" (BU iv.3.21).

[11] As in RV x.27.23, "In the dwelling of the gods had been the first; from their diremption sprang the latter."

[12] RV 1.179.2, *nu patnīr vṛṣabhir jagamyuḥ*; x.5.2, *vṛṣaṇo saṃjagmire . . . arvatībhiḥ*. "Our original nature was by no means the same as it is now. . . . For 'man-woman' (ἀνδρόγυνον) was then a unity in form no less than name," *Symposium* 189E.

[13] *Aticchandā*, usually rendered as "beyond desires," but we think it means, rather, "beyond the meters," which are the means by which he is approached.

[14] *Prajñātman*, the fore-knowing and all-knowing Spirit, whose "true form," transcending all distinction of subject and object, is a "unitary condensation of prior gnosis" (*ekībhūta prajñāna-ghana*, Muṇḍ. Up. v; *kṛtsna prajñāna-ghana*, BU iv.5.13), i.e., a single totality of knowledge not derived from any source external to itself—"the One Word of the Ineffable which is the Gnosis of the Whole" (*Pistis Sophia*, Codex Askew, ed. Petermann, p. 233). *Prajñā* is etymologically and semantically the equivalent of the Gnostic *prognosis* (πρόγνωσις), spoken of in the *Apocryphon of John* as belonging to the male-female Pentad of the Aeons of the Father, and as having been the first gift bestowed by the Invisible One upon the First Man, the Virginal Spirit, the Image of Himself (cited from Schmidt, in Charlotte A. Baynes, *A Coptic Gnostic Treatise*, Cambridge, 1933, pp. 8, 9).

It would scarcely be an exaggeration to say that the whole ontology of the Vedic tradition, alike in the Saṃhitās and in the Brāhmaṇas and Upaniṣads, is expressed rather typically than incidentally in terms of sexual symbolism. We have not by any means exhausted the material, some of which is far more outspoken than are the texts that have been discussed; but we think that enough has been said to demonstrate the perfect orthodoxy of the Tantras in these respects. It remains to consider the divine polarity and bisexuality in Christian scripture and exegesis.

The problem is directly suggested by the doctrine of the two-fold, temporal and eternal, birth of the Son of God. Let us remember that it is impossible to think of these as having been two different events in the divine life, which is intrinsically uneventful. Indeed, as St. Thomas says himself, "On the part of the child there is but one filiation in reality, although there be two in aspect" (*Sum. Theol.* III.35.5 *ad* 3). All this suggests that there must have been an eternal as well as a temporal Madonna.[15] And that is clearly what is implied by Meister Eckhart: "His birth in Mary ghostly was to God better pleasing than his nativity of her in the flesh" (Evans ed., I, 418). If St. Thomas says that "eternal filiation does not depend on a temporal Mother" (*Sum. Theol.* III.35.5 *ad* 2), are we not entitled to add, "but on an eternal Mother"? Who then is Eckhart's "Mary ghostly" but "that divine Nature by which the Father begets" (*Sum. Theol.* I.45.5.6), Natura naturans, Creatrix?

In case it should seem that we are forcing the sense of St. Thomas, let us consider the Thomist doctrine of the divine procession. "The procession of the Word *in divinis* is called a generation.[16] . . . Generation means the

[15] [On the two Aphrodites, one Οὐράνια, the elder daughter of Heaven (Οὐρανός), the other, the younger, daughter of Zeus and Dione, called Πάνδημος (= Vaiśvānara), cf. *Symposium* 180D.]

[16] It may be remarked that it is a cardinal doctrine of Christianity that there is no potentiality or passivity in God, who is all in act. On the other hand, while for St. Thomas "The power of generation belongs to God" (*Sum. Theol.* I.41.5, and as must also be assumed from the general use of γίγνομαι side by side with ποιέω in the Greek New Testament), he says also that "In every act of generation there is an active and a passive principle" (*Sum. Theol.* I.98.2c). A reconciliation can be effected if we consider that the conjoint principles *in divinis* are not two separate beings; just as in the case of the Three Persons, of whom there can be predicated characteristic functions without impugning their co-essentiality. There is no *unrealized* potentiality in God; at the same time His inexhaustible potentiality remains intact without diminution: as in BU V.1, "When plenum is taken from plenum, plenum remains." The conjoint principles *in divinis* are those of a static Essence (*bhūtatā*) and dynamic Power (*śakti*) [Eckhart, Evans ed., p. 276, "Es-

origin of any living thing from a living conjoint principle (*a principio vivente conjuncto*); and this is rightly called 'nativity.' . . . So, then, the procession of the Word *in divinis* is of the nature of a generation. For it proceeds in the manner of an intelligible act, which is a vital operation (*operatio vitae*). . . . Therefore is He rightly called begotten, and Son. Hence also that these things which belong to the generation of living things are used in Scripture to denote the procession of the divine Wisdom; that is to say, by way of conception and birth (*conceptione et partu*); for, as it has been said of the person of the Divine Wisdom, 'When there were no depths, I was brought forth (*concepta*). Before the hills was I brought forth (*parturiebar*)'" (*Sum. Theol.* I.27.2c and *ad* 2, citing Prov. 8:24, 25).

The whole of Proverbs 8 recalls RV x.125. Compare, for instance, "Unto you, O men, I call. . . . Hear; for I will speak of excellent things; and the opening of my lips shall be right things. . . . I am understanding; I have strength. By me kings reign. . . . I love them that love me. . . . The Lord possessed me in the beginning of his way, before his works of old. I was set up from everlasting, from the beginning, or ever the earth was. . . . When he prepared the heavens I was there. . . . I was by him, as one brought up with him: and I was daily his delight, rejoicing always before him, rejoicing in the habitable parts of his earth; and my delights were with the sons of men. . . . All they that hate me love death," with "I wend with the Rudras, Vasus, Ādityas, and several Angels; I am the support of Mitrāvaruṇau, Indrāgnī, and the paired Aśvins. . . . I am the Queen, in whom all goods are garnered, most knowledgeable. . . . Through me all eat the bread of life, whoever sees, or breathes, or hears; though unawares, all these abide in me. Hear ye my faithful saying. I, none but I, utter what is most pleasant, both to

---

sence, so far as it is *active* in the Father, is Nature"; cf. Hermes, *Asclepius* III.21]; when these are actually divided, static and dynamic become active and passive, and this is one of those senses in which it can be said that "Nature recedes from likeness to God," inasmuch as She becomes the *recipient* of form; and then it can be said, with Dante, "cima nel mondo, in che puro atto fu produtto. Pura potenza tenne la parte ima" (*Paradiso* XXIX.32–34), "Summit of the world, where pure act came into being; pure potentiality was in the nether part." [On *Mathnawī* I.2437, "She is a ray of God, she is not your darling: she is creative, you might say she is not created," Wali Muḥammad in his *Sharh-i-Mathnawī* (Lucknow, 1894), p. 156, comments: "for the attributes, *agens* and *patiens*, belong to the essence of the Creator and both are manifested in woman." Note also RV III.31.2, *anyaḥ kartā . . . anya ṛndhan*.]

men and angels: him whom I love I make an Awful-power, Brahman, or Prophet, or Comprehensor. . . . I that am the matrix in the Waters and the Sea, bring forth the Father, [i.e., as the Son] when I originate, being his head. . . . My breath it is, forsooth, that blows the Gale, whenas I take in hand the several worlds to fashion them: so far my sway, I do insist beyond these heaven and this wide earth." In the first of these citations it is Sophia, and in the second Vāc that speaks.[17]

It is sufficiently clear from the text of St. Thomas quoted above that his "conjoint principle" *in divinis* corresponds to the notions of Essence and Nature ("that Nature by which the Father begets," *Sum. Theol.* I.41.5c); and that he identifies this Nature with the "Wisdom" of Proverbs, Dante's Sophia, whom he (Dante) calls "the bride of the Emperor of Heaven, and not bride alone, but sister and most beloved daughter," and of whom he says that "She exists in him in true and perfect fashion as if eternally wedded to him" (*Convito* III.12).[18]

A greater authority can be cited in Gen. 1:25, 26, "And God said, Let us make man in our own image, after our likeness. . . . So God created man in his own image, in the image of God created he him; male and female created he them."[19] The likeness is exemplary. The created form of humanity is not that of this man as distinguished from that of this woman, but that of their common humanity: "He called *their* name Adam," Gen. 5:2. This Man (Adam) is, in fact, a syzygy, until the Deity brings forth the woman out of him, that he may not be alone:[20] "She

[17] [Cf. CU VI.1.4, *vācā ārambhana*, only cause of the variety of appearances; on Hokhmah (= Sophia) as God's "wife" or "daughter," cf. D. Nielsen, "Die altsemitische Muttergötten," ZDMG, XCII (1938), 550.]

[18] Whom also Dante addresses as "Virgin Mother, daughter of thy Son" (*Paradiso* XXXIII.1). A similarly "incestuous" confusion of relationships is met with in the Indian, and even also the Islamic formulations (cf. Coomaraswamy, "The Darker Side of Dawn," 1935, p. 5, and *A New Approach to the Vedas*, 1933, p. 3 and nn. 9 and 10); in other words, the polarity of the conjoint principles is not merely analogous to that of male and female in one particular and marital relation, but in all possible reciprocal relations.

[19] On this passage see the Commentary in the *Zohar* I, 90–92, "the Father said to the Mother by means of the Word" and "the Man of emanation was both male and female, from the side of both Father and Mother."

[20] Observe the parallel in BU I.4, where Prajāpati divides himself, desiring a second, because "for one who is alone there is no delight." Another parallel that may be noted appears in connection with the Biblical description of Eve as having been made from Adam's rib (Gen. 2:21–22), just as in RV X.85.23 the daughter of Manu is called the "rib" (*parśu*), "through whom (under the name of Iḍā or Iḷā) he generated this race of men" (ŚB I.8.1.10). This Iḷā is also a name of the mother of Agni (RV III.29).

shall be called Woman because she was taken out of Man," Gen. 2:23.[21] "In this likeness," then, could never have been said had there not already been an archetype of this polarity in God—that is to say, of course, *in principle*, for we are not speaking of a composition *in divinis*.[22] The Christian doctrine, moreover, like the Indian, envisages an ultimate reunion of the divided principles, there where "there is neither male nor female: for ye are all one [Skr. *ekī-bhūta*] in Christ Jesus" (Gal. 3:28).[23] That is where it is no longer a question of this man or that woman, but only of that Universal Man of whom Boehme says that "this champion or lion is no man or woman, but he is both" (*Signatura Rerum* XI.43).

If it be objected, finally, that all this sexual phraseology is a sort of rhetoric and not to be taken literally, we say that while it is not a matter of rhetoric in any "literary" sense, it is a matter of analogy and symbolism: as is explicit in both passages from the *Bṛhadāraṇyaka Upaniṣad* cited above, it is not a question of a man and a woman in fact, nor of any existence, but of the form of being which is "as if it were (*yathā*) that of a man and woman closely embraced." Our whole intention has been to indicate that an adequate symbolism of this sort has been universally employed in the unanimous and orthodox tradition and, more specifically, within the limits of the present article, to show in what like manner it has been employed in the Hindu and Christian forms of the transmitted revelation.

[21] "All living creatures, having been till then bisexual, were parted asunder, and man with the rest; and so there came to be males on the one part, and likewise females on the other part" (Hermes, *Lib.* I.18).

[22] Cf. the *Apocalypse of John* (cited by Baynes, tr., *A Coptic Gnostic Treatise*, p. 14), "The Three, the Father, the Mother, and the Son, the perfect Power"; and ŚA VII.15, "All that is declared to be One. For the Mother and the Father and the Child are this all."

[23] [Gal. 3:28 is cited by St. Thomas, *Sum. Theol.* I.93.6 *ad* 2, in illustration of his own statement, "the image of God belongs to both sexes, since it is in the mind, wherein is no sexual distinction"; *Omne quod generatur, generatur ex contrario*, *Sum. Theol.* I.46.1 *ad* 3.]

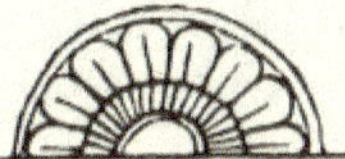

Two Passages in Dante's *Paradiso*

It has now for some time been fully recognized that Islamic analogies are of singular value for an understanding of Dante's *Divina Commedia*, not only in connection with the basic form of the narrative[1] but as regards the methods by which the theses are communicated.[2] And this would hold good, entirely apart from the consideration of any problems of "influence" that might be considered from the more restricted point of view of literary history. It has been justly remarked by H. A. Wolfson that the mediaeval Arabic, Hebrew, and Latin "philosophical literatures were in fact one philosophy expressed in different languages, translatable almost literally into one another."[3] Again, if this is true, it is not merely a result of proximity and influence nor, on the other hand, of a parallel development, but because "Human culture is a unified whole, and in the various cultures one finds the dialects of one spiritual language,"[4] because "a great universal line of metaphysics is evident among all peo-

[This essay was first published in *Speculum*, XI (1936).—ED.]

1 See Miguel Asín y Palacios, *La Escatología musulmana en la Divina Comedia* (Madrid, 1919), and the abridged translation by H. Sunderland, *Islam and the Divine Comedy* (London, 1926).

2 Luigi Valli, *Il Languaggio segreto di Dante e dei "Fedeli d'Amore"* (Rome, 1928); René Guénon, *L'Ésotérisme de Dante* (Paris, 1925); *idem*, "Le Langage secret de Dante et des 'Fidèles d'Amour,'" and "'Fidèles d'Amour' et 'Cours d'Amour,'" *Le Voile d'Isis*, XXXVII (1932), and XXXVIII (1933). Indian and Zoroastrian comparisons have been made in Angelo de Gubernatis, "Dante e l'India," *Giornale della Società Asiatica Italiana*, III (1889), and "Le Type indien de Lucifer chez Dante." *Actes du Xe Congrès des Orientalistes*; and J. J. Modi, *Dante Papers: Viraf, Adamnan, and Dante, and Other Papers* (London, 1914). Many of the problems are bound up with those of the history of the Templars and Rosicrucians.

3 *The Philosophy of Spinoza*, Cambridge, Mass. (1934), I, 10.

4 Alfred Jeremias, *Handbuch der altorientalischen Geisteskultur* (Berlin, 1929), p. x.

ples."[5] Without going too far afield in time or space—and one could go at least as far as Sumeria and China—it will suffice for present purposes to say that what is affirmed by Wolfson for Arabic, Hebrew, and Latin will be of equal validity if Sanskrit is added to the list.

In recent years I have repeatedly drawn attention to the remarkable doctrinal and even verbal equivalents that can be demonstrated in mediaeval Latin and Vedic Indian traditional literature, in respect to which, if borrowing were assumed, priority would have to be allowed to the Vedic side; but borrowing is not assumed. As these equivalences are not likely to be familiar to my present readers, a few will be cited here; and striking as they may be, they are merely samples of countless others of the same sort.

We find it said, for example, in connection with the orthodox doctrine of Christ's two births, eternal and temporal, that "on the part of the child there is but one filiation in reality, though there be two in aspect" (*Sum. Theol.* III.35.5 *ad* 3); cf. "His birth in Mary ghostly was to God better pleasing than his nativity of her in the flesh" (Eckhart, Evans ed., I,418). And inasmuch as Christ's filiation is in any case a "vital operation from a conjoint principle (*a principio conjunctivo*)," and the "eternal filiation does not depend upon a temporal mother" (*Sum. Theol.* I.27.2c and III.35.5 *ad* 2), it follows that Christ is mothered in eternity no less than in time; the mother in eternity, Eckhart's "Mary ghostly," being evidently "that divine nature by which the Father begets" (*Sum. Theol.* I.41.5c), "That nature, to wit, which created all others" (St. Augustine, *De trinitate* XIV.9)—Natura naturans, Creatrix universalis, Deus, inasmuch as essence and nature are one in Him, in the Supreme Identity, who is the unity of the conjoint principles. Finally, inasmuch as the divine life is uneventful, there is evidently but one act of generation, though there be "two in aspect, corresponding to the two relations in the parents, as considered by the intellect" (*Sum. Theol.* III.35.5 *ad* 3). It is, then, Latin Christian doctrine that there is one generation, but two mothers logically distinguishable. The exact equivalent of this, in the fewest possible words, occurs in the *Gopatha Brāhmaṇa* I.33, "two wombs, one act of generation (*dve yonī ekaṃ mithunam*)." This brief text, on the one hand, resumes the familiar Vedic doctrine of the bimotherhood of Agni who is *dvimātā*—as, for example, in RV III.2.2 and 11, "He became the son of two mothers . . . he was quickened in unlike wombs," and RV I.113.1–3, where Night, "when she hath conceived for the Sun's

[5] J. Sauter, "Die altchinesische Metaphysik und ihre Verbundenheit mit der abendländischen," *Archiv für Rechts- und Sozial-philosophie*, XXVIII (1934), 90.

quickening, yields the womb to [her sister] Dawn"—and, on the other, to the derivative dogma of the dual motherhood (or alternatively motherhood and foster motherhood) by which the eternal Avatar is manifested in Vaiṣṇavism, Buddhism, and Jainism, where by a somewhat materialized formulation the divine child is actually transferred from the womb of the spiritual power to that of the temporal power, represented respectively by the queens Devānandā and Tisalā.[6]

In AB III.43, the pattern of the Sacrifice performed in imitation of what was done in the beginning is described as "without beginning or end. . . . That which is its beginning is also its end, that again which is its end is also its beginning, they do not discriminate which is anterior and which posterior," with which may be compared Boethius, *De consolatione philosophiae* I, prose 6, "is it possible that you who know the beginning of all things should not also know their end?"; *Sum. Theol.* I.103.2c, "the end of a thing corresponds to its beginning"; Eckhart (Evans ed., I, 224), "the first beginning is because of the last end"; and Dante, *Paradiso* XXIX.20, 30, *né prima né poscia . . . sanza distinzione in essordire.*

The definition of a personal as distinguished from an animal nature in AĀ II.3.2, viz. "A person (*puruṣa*) is most endowed with understanding, he speaks what has been discriminated, he draws distinctions, he knows the morrow, he knows what is and is not mundane, and by the mortal seeks the immortal," while "as for the other cattle, theirs is a valid perception merely according to hunger and thirst, they do not speak what has been discriminated," etc., is as nearly as possible identical with the classical definition in Boethius, *Contra Evtychen* II: "There is no person of an ox or any other of the animals which dumb and unreasoning live a life of sense alone, but we say there is a person of a man, of God, or an angel . . . there is no person of a man if animal or general."

"'HE WHO IS' is the principal of all names applied to God," says St. John of Damascus (*De fide orthodoxa* I); so in KU VI.13, "He is to be laid hold of as 'HE IS.'" With respect to the "thought of God," which "is not attainable by argument" (KU II.9), that "His is that thought by whom it is unthought, and if he thinks it, then he does not understand" corresponds to Dionysus (*De mystica theologica* I): "Which not to see or know is really to see and know," and *Ep. ad Caium Mon.*: "If anyone seeing God understood what he saw, he saw not God himself, but one of those things that are God's."

In connection with the Immaculate Conception, St. Thomas (*Sum.*

[6] For further parallels, see Coomaraswamy, "The 'Conqueror's Life' in Jaina Painting," JISOA, III (1935), 132.

Theol. III.32.1 *ad* 1) remarks that while in this case the Spiritus entered the material form without means, in normal generation "the power of the soul, which is in the semen, through the Spirit enclosed therein, fashions the body." This corresponds not only to the brief formulation of RV VIII.3.24, "The Spirit is the father's part, raiment of the body (*ātmā pitus tanūr vāsaḥ*)," but more explicitly to JUB III.10.5, "It is inasmuch as the Breath-of-life inhabits the expended seed, that he [who is to be born] takes shape (*yadā hyeva retas siktaṃ prāṇa āviśaty atha tat sambhavati*)," and Kauṣ. Up. III.3, "It is as the Breath (*prāṇa*) that the Intelligizing Spiritus (*prajñātman*) grasps and erects the body."

Sum. Theol. I.45.1c, "Creation, which is the emanation of all being, is from nonbeing, which is nothing (*Creatio, quae est emanatio totius esse, est ex non ente, quod est nihil*)," combined with I.14.8c, "The knowledge of God is the cause of things. For the knowledge of God is to all creatures what the knowledge of the artificer is to things made by his art (*sicut scientia artificis se habet ad artificiata*)" and with the doctrine of the Spirit as the animating power in the act of generation, whether human or divine (see above)—all this is represented in a briefer formulation of the *Ṛg Veda*. Thus RV x.72.2: "The Master of the Spiritual power like as a blacksmith with his bellows welded all these generations of the Angels; in the primal aeon, being was begotten from nonbeing," where "Blacksmith"[7] (*karmāra*, "maker," "workman"), like Tvaṣṭṛ (the "Carpenter,"[8] who in the *Ṛg Veda* "hews by intellect [*manasā takṣati*]," in the sense of the Scholastic *per verbum in intellectu conceptum*, predicated of the artificer in *Sum. Theol.* I.45.6c) and Viśvakarman ("All-maker," later the patron aspect of deity with respect to the crafts and worshiped as such in their lesser mysteries), corresponds to *Deus sicut artifex* in Scholastic imagery; and "welded with his bellows" (*samadhamat*) alludes to the "blast" of the Spirit, the animating Gale (*vāta*, *vāyu*) by which the Son himself is "aroused" (Agni, *vātajūtaḥ*, RV I.65.4, VI.6.3, etc.) and "made to blaze" (*dhamitam*, RV II.24.7), "when Vāta blows upon his flame" (RV IV.7.10), "that Gale, thy Spiritus that thunders through the universe" (*ātmā te vātaḥ*, etc., RV VII.87.2), "Vāyu, spiration of the Angels, whose sound is heard indeed, though his form is never seen" (RV x.168.4).

[7] This image of the Master Blacksmith with his bellows admirably illustrates *Sum. Theol.* I.1.9c: "Spiritual truths are fittingly taught under the likeness of material things."

[8] It is by no means without good and sufficient reasons that Jesus was called the "Son of the carpenter," for, indeed, there is a "wood" of which the world is wrought by the Master Carpenter.

The most general Scholastic definition of sin, of any kind, is as follows, "Sin is a departure from the order to the end" (*Sum. Theol.* II-I.21.1c and 2 *ad* 2), and in connection with the artistic sin, St. Thomas goes on to explain that it is a sin proper to the art "if an artist produce a bad thing, while intending to produce something good; or produce something good, while intending to produce something bad." In KU II.1.1, he who chooses what he likes most (*preyas*) rather than what is most lovely (*śreyas*) is said to "deviate from the end" (*hīyate arthāt*); in ŚB II.1.4.6, if a certain part of the rite is wrongly done, "that would be a sin (*aparāddhi*),[9] just as if one were to do one thing while intending to do another; or if one were to say one thing while intending to say another; or if one were to go one way while intending to go another."

In *Sum. Theol.* I.103.5 *ad* 1: "These things are said to be under the sun which are generated and corrupted according to the sun's movement," and III (Supp.) 91. 1 *ad* 1: "The state of glory is not under the sun." In ŚB II.3.3.7, "He who glows [the Sun] is this Death [an essential name of deity *ab intra*]"; accordingly, all creatures below Him are mortal, but those beyond Him are Angels (or "Gods") who are alive; and X.5.1.4, "Everything hitherward from the Sun is in the grasp of Death (*mṛtyunāptam*)."

There may also be cited a pair of examples of earlier origin on the European side. Matt. 10:16, "*prudentes sicut serpentes, et simplices sicut columbae*," corresponds to RV X.63.4, *ahimāyā anāgasaḥ*. Again, whereas in Gen. 2:21–22 God "took one of his [Adam's] ribs, . . . And the rib which the Lord God had taken from man, made he a woman," and 3:20, "Adam called his wife's name Eve; because she was the mother of all living," so also in the *Ṛg Veda* the name of Manu's daughter is the "Rib" (*parśur ha nāma mānavī*), who under another name, Īḍā, is the mother "through whom he [Manu] generated this race of men" (ŚB I.8.1.10), Manu being in the Hindu tradition the archetype and progenitor of men in the same way as Adam in the Hebrew tradition, the condition of incest in both formulations depending on the "blood relationship" (*jāmitra*) of the original parents.

A single Islamic example may be added. Whereas St. Augustine, *Confessions* VII.11, has, with reference to created things, "A being they have, because they are from Thee: and yet no being, because what Thou art they are not," and *Sum. Theol.*, I.44.1c, "All beings apart from God are not their own being, but beings by participation," we find in Jāmī, *La-*

[9] *Aparāddhi* derives from *aparādh*, defined by Monier-Williams as "to miss one's aim."

wā'iḥ XIII, "Earth lacks true Being, yet depends thereon—Thou art true Being."

Not merely could other doctrinal and verbal parallels of this sort be cited almost *ad infinitum*[10]—e.g., in connection with such matters as Exemplarism,[11] Transubstantiation, and Infallibility—but similar equivalencies could be even more easily demonstrated in the domain of visual symbolism,[12] a mode of communication that even more than verbal symbolism is the characteristic idiom of traditional metaphysics. For example, there has often been brought out the common valency of the Christian rose and Indian lotus as representations of the ground of all manifestation, the support of being when it proceeds or seems to proceed from being to becoming. The case of musical form is the same: "An example of the tenacity with which the music of a cult survives is afforded in the West by Catholic church music which, deriving from Jewish temple singing, stands apart from the quite different art-music of today, like an erratic block. There are similar instances in the East, such as those of the Indian Sāmaveda melodies, and in Japan the singing of the No dramas, which even in the late courtly and profane environment in which we hear it, has preserved its original liturgical significance" (Robert Lachmann, *Musik des Orients*, Breslau, 1929, pp. 9–10). It is, in fact, the case that even the "secular" music of India, where nothing, indeed, can be defined as wholly secular, has preserved that quality of endlessness which is predicated of the liturgical chant in a passage from the *Aitareya Brāhmaṇa* cited above and which is equally recognized in Christian plainsong.

The commonly accepted formula of the existence of a gulf dividing Europe from Asia is thus fallacious in the sense that while there is a division, the dividing line is traceable not between Europe and Asia normatively considered but between mediaeval Europe and Asia, on the one

[10] Single parallels might be referred to "coincidence," which is merely to substitute description for explanation. If, however, we believe with St. Augustine (*De diversis quaestionibus* LXXXIII.24) that "Nothing in the world happens by chance" (a proposition with which the scientist will scarcely quarrel [nor the theologian, for whom "if God did not govern by mediate causes, the world would be deprived of the perfection of causality," St. Thomas]), three explanations, and only three, of repeated and exact "coincidences" are possible: There must have been (1) a borrowing on the part of the later source, (2) a parallel development, or (3) a derivation from a common anterior source.

[11] Cf. Coomaraswamy, "Vedic Exemplarism" [in this volume—ED.].

[12] Cf. J. Baltrusaitis, *Art sumérien, art romain* (Paris, 1934), and Coomaraswamy, "The Tree of Jesse and Oriental Parallels," *Parnassus*, VII (1935).

hand, and modern Europe on the other: in general and in principle, whatever is true for mediaeval Europe will also be found to be true for Asia, and vice versa.

As regards the bearing of all these parallels on the validity of Christian doctrine and exegesis: from the Hindu point of view, the natural consequence of collation will be to evoke the consideration, "Christian doctrine, judged by Vedic standards, is also orthodox." The converse recognition, that "Vedic doctrine, judged by Christian norms, is also orthodox," might be, and *a priori* should be, expected, but given the Christian assumption not only of a knowledge of the truth (which may be freely granted) but also of an exclusive possession of this knowledge (such as Hindus neither claim for themselves nor grant to any others), all that can be predicted for the moment is an acceptance of Vedic data as "extrinsic and probable arguments" (*Sum. Theol.* 1.1.8 *ad* 2), just as St. Thomas himself, in fact, made use of Aristotle, and just as St. Jerome, in discussing the superiority of the virgin to the married estate (*Adversus Jovinianum* 1.42), actually invoked the doctrine of the "Gymnosophists of India, amongst whom the dogma is handed down that Buddha, the head of their teaching, was born of a virgin from her side."

So far as the comparisons that have been so extensively made as between Christianity and Buddhism (in which field St. Jerome seems to have been the pioneer, though the case of Jehoshaphat = Bodhisattva must also be borne in mind), or Neoplatonism and Buddhism, are in question, it must be remembered that although the parallels are real, nevertheless deductions as to derivation or influence are insecurely founded, inasmuch as the Buddhist doctrines are themselves derivative, and Christian and Neoplatonic analogies with pre-Buddhist texts can be presented in greater number and with greater cogency. For instance, all of the details of the Buddha's nativity, not excluding the detail of lateral birth, are, in fact, already traceable in the Vedic nativities of Indra and Agni, respectively types of the temporal and spiritual powers, often combined in the dual Indrāgnī, king-and-priest. We maintain, in other words, the relative independence of the Christian tradition at any one time, whether that of Dionysius or that of Dante, at the same time that we relate all orthodox teaching, of which the Vedic expression itself is merely a late expression, to one common and (as may be added, though this is not essential to the presently restricted argument) ultimately superhuman source. The problems are not essentially, but only accidentally, problems of literary history.

Enough has now been said to indicate the principles involved, and perhaps to convince the reader that it may not be unreasonable to look in Sanskrit as well as in Islamic texts for parallels to or even explanations, but not necessarily sources, of particular idioms of thought employed by Dante, none of whose ideas are novel, though he clothes the traditional teaching in a vernacular form of incomparable splendor, *splendor veritatis*. The two passages chosen for comment are selected not because of their special importance, nor because they can be more easily paralleled than very many others, but as having presented particular difficulties to commentators relying only on European sources. *Paradiso* XXVII.136–138 reads:

> *Così si fa la pelle bianca nera,*
> *nel primo aspetto della bella figlia*
> *di quel ch' apporta mane e lascia sera.*

In P. H. Wicksteed's version: "So blackeneth at the first aspect the white skin of his fair daughter who bringeth morn and leaveth evening." We remark first the parallel in Eckhart, Evans ed., I, 292: "The soul, in hot pursuit of God, becomes absorbed in him, . . . just as the sun will swallow up and put out the dawn"; [and *ibid*., p. 365: "Atoned with her Creator, the soul has lost her name, for she herself does not exist; God has absorbed her into him just as the sunlight swallows up the Dawn till it is gone"]. The *Paradiso* text has been called "a difficult and disputed passage," although in any case it is admittedly the Sun who, in line 138, "bringeth morn and leaveth evening." Eckhart's words already indicate that the "daughter" must be Dawn. It is true that in Classical mythology, Dawn is the sister rather than the daughter of the Sun, but it is just here that the Vedic tradition will be of help. For while Dawn is sometimes there the sister of the Sun or Fire (RV VI.55.5 and X.3.3), she is typically and constantly the daughter, as well as the bride, of the Sun, who is called her "ravisher" (*jāra*). She is, indeed, from the Hindu point of view, the same as Dante's "virgin mother, daughter of thy son" (*Paradiso* XXXIII.1); the Mother of God, of Christ, by whom "all things were made" (John 1:3), "for by him were all things created" (Col. 1:16), and as thus the Mother of all things, one with Eve in the same sense that Christ is one with Adam. It is, indeed, precisely as the Magna Mater, *die eine Madonna* (Jeremias), that Uṣas, Dawn, otherwise known as Sūryā (the Sun "goddess," as distinguished from Sūrya, the Sun "god"), becomes the bride of the Sun in the endless *Liebesgeschichte des Himmels* (E. Siecke).

Vedic references to these events and especially to Dawn's destruction by her lover, the Sun, who follows after her in hot pursuit (the converse of Eckhart's formulation cited above), are innumerable. In the famous hymn of RV x.189, commonly employed as an *oratio secreta*, the Serpent Queen (another of the names of Dawn and Mother Earth) is "She who moves within the luminous spheres, She as his Voice (*vāc*, fem.) is given to the Winged-Sun; when He suspires, then She expires (*'asya prāṇāt apānatī*)."

Dawn's glorious hour is very transient; "A virgin uncontrolled, She cometh forth, foreware of Sun and Sacrifice and Fire" (RV vii.80.2), but no sooner has the Sun caught up with her than He and She shine out together (vii.81.2); no longer shining privately with her own radiance, but clothed with the Sun, She now "shines forth in the bright eye of her Seducer" (i.92.11). It is often Indra as the Sun that is spoken of as "striking down the chariot of Dawn" (x.73.6), who thus becomes Indrāṇī, the Queen of Heaven, but without distinction of King and Queen.

This is, furthermore, a purification, for anterior to her procession, Dawn has been a "footless snake,"[13] ophidian rather than angelic, Night being related to her sister Dawn as Lilith to Eve. It is precisely to this ophidian nature that She dies when She proceeds, her Assumption then following his Ascension. Drawn through the nave of the solar Wheel, She as Apālā ("Unguarded" in the sense "unwedded") is given a sunny skin in place of her old snake skin (viii.91), and made "fit to be fondled" (*saṃśliṣṭikā*; *Śātyāyana Brāhmaṇa* cited by Sāyaṇa). There Heaven and Earth are embraced (*saṃśliṣyataḥ*, JUB i.5)[14]—which is not a "myth" within the current anthropological misunderstanding of the word, but a union (*mithuna*) to be realized "within the heart's void (*hṛdayākāśa*)" by the true Cognostic (*saṃvit*) and is the "supreme beatitude" (*paramo hy eṣa ānandaḥ*, ŚB x.5.2.11), Dante's *piacere eterno* (*Paradiso* xviii.16).

And all this is significant from the point of view of the interpretation of our Dante text, for it has been suggested that the Sun's *bella figlia* is Humanity, the Sun being "father of each mortal life" (*Paradiso* xxii.116) and man "begotten of man and of the Sun" (cf. *De monarchia* i.9 and 6–7). There is no antinomy here, for as we have seen, Dawn and Mother

[13] For a more detailed presentation see Coomaraswamy, "The Darker Side of Dawn," 1935.

[14] This is in William Blake's sense the "Marriage of Heaven and Hell," all the earthly properties by which individuation is determined being "hells," as is explicit in JUB iv.26; cf. S x.5.

Earth, in the same sense as Adam and Eve—i.e., seminally—are all men, Everyman,[15] and Everyman is the Church, the Bride of Christ. To be united with Him, Humanity, the Church, must be transformed—in Vedic language, must shed her serpent skin and put off evil. Just this is described, not only in the story of Apālā, but again in that of the marriage of Sūryā (RV x.85.28–33), where the Bride puts off her scaly *kṛtyā* ("potential") form, evil and inglorious, and in a most felicitous (*sumaṅgalī*) likeness ("fairest of all fair forms," as the *Sāṭyāyana Brāhmaṇa* describes the once reptilian Apālā) "assumes her Lord as doth a Bride" (*ā jāyā viśate patim*, RV x.85.29). And this is said as nearly as possible in the same way by St. Bonaventura of the Marriage of Christ with his Church: "Christ will present his bride, whom he loved in her baseness and all her foulness, glorious with his own glory, without spot or wrinkle" (*Dominica prima post octavum epiphaniae* II.2).

We have presented the tradition as to Dawn in some little detail in order to remind the reader how dangerous it is, in connection with writers of this caliber and with such preoccupations as Dante's and Eckhart's, who are not belle-lettrists,[16] though each is the "father" of a language, to attribute to individual poetic invention or artistry what are really technical formulae and symbols with known connotations. At the very least, our Vedic citations suffice to give a consistent meaning to Dante's and Eckhart's words. Both are always aware of much more than they tell; as Dante himself forewarns the reader, "mirate la dottrina, che s' asconde sotto il velame degli versi strani" (*Inferno* IX.61). It must also be remembered that the illustration of Christian doctrine by means of pagan

[15] It will not be forgotten that from the Scholastic point of view, Humanity is a form that has nothing to do with time; not the humanity of "humanism," but a creative principle informing every man, and according to which he must be judged. Thus, Thierry of Chartres speaks of the *forma humanitatis* which *nunquam perit*, and St. Thomas says that "humanity is taken to mean the formal part of a man" (*Sum. Theol.* I.3.3). ["God assumed manhood and not man" (Meister Eckhart, Pfeiffer ed., p. 250).]

[16] Eckhart, "All happiness to those who have listened to this sermon. Had there been no one here, I must have preached it to the poor-box"; "work as though no one existed, no one lived, no one had ever come upon the earth" (Evans ed., I, 143 and 308). Dante, "The whole work was undertaken not for a speculative but for a practical end . . . the purpose of the whole and of this portion [*Paradiso*] is to remove those who are living in this life from the state of wretchedness and to lead them to the state of blessedness" (*Epistle ad Can. Grande* 15, 16); BG II.47, "Be thy property in works by no means in their fruits," and III.9, "This world is enchained by works, save they be directed to the Sacrifice; so do thy work unto this end, without concern."

symbols was not only from the mediaeval point of view quite legitimate, but even persisted in permitted practice until comparatively modern times, of which an example can be cited in the work of Calderón.[17] It is not unreasonable, then, to suppose that both Eckhart and Dante were acquainted with traditional doctrines—perhaps initiatory and only orally transmitted, or perhaps only not yet traced in extant documents—such as have been cited above apropos of *il somma sol* and *bella figlia.*

Our second passage occurs in *Paradiso* XVIII.110–111:

> *. . . da lui si rammenta*
> *quella virtù ch' è forma per li nidi.*

In Wicksteed's version, supplying only the capital, this is, "from Him cometh to the mind that power that is form unto the nests." It should be hardly necessary to point out that "form" must be taken here, in its usual Scholastic and exemplary sense, to be "essential form" (as when it is said that "the soul is the form of the body") and not in the modern vernacular sense of "actual form" or shape. Now, quite apart from the parallels to be cited below, it may be remarked that nests imply birds, and that both imply trees, and that "birds" is traditionally a designation of the Angels, or intellectual substances, wings denoting independence of local motion, and the "language of birds" that of "angelic communication";[18] or "birds" in a more general way may stand for the quick (in all senses of the word) as distinguished from the inanimate and immobile. From this point of view, which is, in fact, the right one, "nests" will be the habitations of the Angels and other living beings amongst the branches of the Tree of Life, "nest" will signify the phenomenal—bodily or otherwise individually appropriated—environment of the soul, and the "power that is form unto the nests" will be His who made Man in his own image and likeness. Nevertheless, the passage has been regarded as obscure; the comments made by Wicksteed and Oelsner,[19] who ask, "But why *nests*? Are the nests the heavens, nestling one within the other?" etc., are particularly devious, perhaps because in discussing the Jovian M of verses 94–96, although they recognize that the likeness of a bird is intended, they do

[17] Cf. René Allar, "Calderón et l'unité des traditions," *Le Voile d'Isis*, XL (1935), 407 ff.

[18] RV VI.9.5, "Intellect is the swiftest of birds." Cf. René Guénon, "La Langue des oiseaux," *Le Voile d'Isis*, XXXVI (1931), 667 ff.

[19] Temple Classics Edition, *Paradiso*, p. 227.

not realize that it is precisely the likeness of an eagle that is meant—that is, the likeness of God himself, here "exemplified" by Jove—and consequently fail to see that the "nests" are those of beings in that same image.

All that has been said above is explicit in the Vedic tradition, where, moreover, of the two words for "nest," *nīḍa* and *kulāya*, the former at once recalls Dante's *nidi*. The general significance of "nest" is defined in PB xix.15.1: "Nest is offspring, nest is cattle ["great possessions," "realized potentiality"], nest is dwelling." In RV i.164.20–22, there occurs the image of two Eagles who comradely occupy the Tree of Life and are the dual aspect of the Deity, who on the one hand sees all things[20] and on the other eats of the fig;[21] and the image of others perched below, "who chant with ever-open eyes their share of life[22] (*amṛtasya bhāgam animeṣam . . . abhi svaranti*), taste of the honey, and beget their children," but of whom "none can reach the summit of the Tree who knoweth not the Father, the great Herdsman of the Universe."[23] But inasmuch as He whose being is Contemplative (*dhīraḥ*) has also "made his home in me that am made ready here (*mā dhīraḥ pākam atrāviveśa*)," we find him elsewhere spoken of not only as "nestless"[24] (*anīḍaḥ*, RV x.55.5–6, Śvet.

[20] The Sun is Varuṇa's eye, with which He surveys the whole universe (RV, *passim*); none can even wink without His knowledge (RV vii.86.6); He counts the winkings of men's eyes and knows all that man does, thinks, or devises (AV iv.16.2, 5), which knowledge on His part is speculative (*viśvaṃ sa vedo varuṇo yathā dhiyā*, RV x.11.1). Cf. Luke 12:6–7, "Are not five sparrows sold for two farthings, and not one of them is forgotten before God? But even the very hairs of your head are all numbered"; Heb. 4:12–13, "For the word of God . . . *is* a discerner of the thoughts and intents of the heart. Neither is there any creature that is not manifest in His sight"; *Sum. Theol.* i.14.16c and *ad* 2, "God has of Himself a speculative knowledge only . . . [in which] He possesses both speculative and practical knowledge of all other things."

[21] Luke 7:34, "The Son of man is come eating and drinking"; Deut. 4:24, "God is a consuming fire." Agni the Heavenly Steed, the Spiritus, the Winged Sun "Who from here below soared unto Heaven . . . is the greediest of eaters" (RV i.163.6–7). God's "eating" is our Life, for thereby the Spiritus is clothed in flesh, becoming *anna-maya*.

[22] As also RV viii.21.5, "Seated like birds, O Indra, we raise our song to Thee"; cf. *Paradiso* xviii.76–77, "So within the lights the sacred creatures flying sang."

[23] Cf. *Paradiso* x.74, "He who doth not so wing himself that he may fly up there," for which numerous Sanskrit parallels could be adduced—e.g., PB xiv.1.13, "Those who ascend to the top of the Great Tree, how do they fare thereafter? Those who have wings fly off, those without wings fall down," and similarly, JUB iii.13.9.

[24] Matt. 8:20, "the birds of the air have nests; but the Son of man hath not where to lay his head."

Up. v.14), but also as the Swan (*haṃsa*) who by the Breaths of Life protects his "lower seats" (*avaraṃ kulāyam*, BU iv.3.12), whose own "perch is as it were a bird's" (*sadanaṃ yathā veḥ*, RV iii.54.5–6): "nestless" and "nested" corresponding to the nature of the Deity who is "One as he is yonder" and also "manifoldly present in his children" (ŚB x.5.2.16–17), whence he is spoken of as Nṛṣad "Seated in man," Nṛcakṣus, "Having regard for man," and Vaiśvānara, "Common to all men."[25]

The "lower nests," however, are not merely those of the individual substances in the sense explained above, but are at the same time every sacrificial altar, whether concrete or within you,[26] on which the sacred Fire is kindled, and it is in these senses that "the Deity, abandoning his golden throne, hastens to the Falcon's seeming birthplace, the seat by speculation wrought" (*śyeno na yoniṃ sadanaṃ dhiyā kṛtam hiraṇyayam āsadaṃ deva eṣati*, RV ix.71.6), where the Falcon, is as usual, the Fire; the birthplace, as usual, the Altar; the lap of Mother Earth, the Mother's womb; and the aspect of Deity (*deva*) referred to as hastening is that of Soma, sap of the Tree of Life, the "Wine" of life, and willing (*krīḷuḥ*) Sacrifice.[27] We find accordingly an elaborate symbolism of the Altar, which is the "lower throne" of Deity, in this very likeness of a bird's nest, and even that the Altar is completed in such a manner as to be manifestly like a nest, as, for example, in AB i.28, where the Priest, invoking the sacred "Fire and the Angelic Host to be seated first on the birthplace rich in wool" (represented by the "strew," these words being taken from RV vi.15–16), proceeds with the formula "Making an anointed nest for Savitṛ" (the Sun as "Quickener") and, in fact, prepares "as it were a nest with the enclosing sticks of *pītudāru-wood*, bdellium, tufts of wool, and fragrant grasses," and all of this is really a representation of the nest of the Phoenix, in which the life of the Eagle, the Fire, is perpetually renewed.

It remains only to add what is already implied in the words "by speculation wrought" (*dhiyā kṛtam,* cited above, *dhī* in Vedic Sanskrit being

[25] Cf. Coomaraswamy, "Vedic Exemplarism."

[26] On the kindling of Agni "within you," see ŚB vii.4.1.1 and x.5.3.3.

[27] Partaken of by way of transubstantiation: "Men fancy when the plant is pressed, they drink of very Soma, but of Him the Brahmans understand by Soma, nonesoever tastes who dwells on earth" (RV x.85.3–4). "The Nyagrodha is parabolically King Soma; parabolically the temporal power obtains the semblance of the spiritual power, by means of the priest, the initiation, and the invocation as it were" (AB vii.31). The only approach to Him is by way of initiation and ardor (ŚB iii.6.2.10–11); cf. Gen. 3:22, "lest he put forth his hand, and take also of the tree of life, and eat, and live for ever."

used synonymously with *dhyāna* = *contemplatio*), that the kindling of Agni in his lower nests, where until kindled He is merely latent—in other words, the bringing of God to birth who else remains unknown—while it is effected symbolically in the ritual of Sacrifice or Mass, is effected by "him who understands it (*ya evaṃ vidvān*)," the Comprehensor thereof (*evaṃvit*), the Gnostic (*jñānin*), "in the empty space of the heart (*hṛdayākāśe*)," "in the bare room of the inner man (*antar-bhūtasya khe*)"; it is an interior darkness that is illuminated. "No man by works or sacrifices attains to Him who quickeneth for ever" (RV VIII.70.3), but only those in whom a last death of the soul has been effected and who, when they stand before the gates of heaven and face the question, "Who art thou?" are qualified to answer not with any personal or family name, but in the words, "This *who* that I am is the Light, Thyself"—only these are welcomed with the benediction, "*Who* thou art, that am I, and *Who* I am, That art thou: proceed" (JUB III.14), nothing then remaining of the individual, whether as to "name" or "likeness" (*nāma-rūpa*), but only that Spiration (*ātman*) that seemed indeed to have been determined, and participated, but is in fact impartible.[28] One thus freed, entering through the midst of the Sun ("I am the Way . . . no man cometh to the Father, but by Me," John 14:6; "Only by knowing Him does one pass over death, there is no other Way to go there," VS XXXI.18), "the gate through which all things return perfectly free to their supreme felicity" (Eckhart, Evans ed., I, 400), becomes a "Mover-at-will" (*kāmacārin*) whose will, indeed, is no longer his own, but confused with God's. "That is his proper form, who hath his will,[29] the Spirit is his will, he hath no will, nor any want" (BU IV.3.21); "he goes up and down these worlds, eating what he will, and assuming what likeness he will" (TU III.10.5); just as in John 10:9, "I am the door: by Me if any man enter in, he shall be saved, and shall go in and out, and find pasture," and more explicitly again in the *Pistis Sophia*.

We have sketched above a summary outline of the implications of the symbol "nest" in the Vedic Gnostic tradition. It is true that Dante's use

[28] "The fastidious soul can rest her understanding on nothing that has name. She escapes from every name into the nameless nothingness. . . . These are the blessed dead . . . buried and beatified in the Godhead. . . . In this state we are as free as when we were not; free as the Godhead in its non-existence" (Eckhart, Evans ed., I, 373, 381–382). "I would go down unto Annihilation and Eternal Death, lest the Last Judgment come and find me Unannihilate, and I be seiz'd and giv'n into the hands of my own Selfhood" (Blake).

[29] Cf. *Paradiso* XXII.64–65, "Ivi è perfetta, matura ed intera ciascuna disianza."

of the word should have been understood either from other passages (e.g., *Paradiso* XXIII.1–12, where Beatrice herself is compared to a bird that rises from its nest at dawn to greet the sun), or by comparison with Biblical texts such as Matt. 7:20 cited in a footnote above; but at the same time, and just as in connection with the Sun, it may be taken for granted that Dante, whose knowledge of Christian and Pagan symbolism is so extensive and so accurate,[30] was more than well aware of all the technical meanings of the symbols he employs—"technical," because such terms are neither employed by way of ornament, nor are they explicable at will, but belong to the vocabulary of a consistent parabolic language.[31] We think that it has been shown that the references of an exponent of orthodox Christian principles, writing at the end of and, as it were, resuming all the doctrine of the Middle Ages, can actually be clarified by a comparison with those of scriptures that were current half the world away and three millenniums earlier in time; and that this can only be explained on the assumption that all these "alternative formulations of a common doctrine (*dharma-paryāya*)" are "dialects of the one and only language of the spirit," branches of one and the same "universal and unanimous tradition," *sanātana dharma*, Philosophia Perennis, St. Augustine's "Wisdom uncreate, the same now as it ever was, and the same to be for evermore" (*Confessions* IX.10).

[30] Cf., for example, the metaphysically technical description of the Three Worlds in *Paradiso* XXIX.28–36, and the treatment of *il punto* in XIII.11–13, XVII.17–18, and XXVIII.16, 25–26, and 41–42, for all of which the Indian parallels could be adduced: "in punta dello stelo, a cui la prima rota va dintorno. . . . Da quel punto depende il cielo, e tutta la natura" (XIII.11–12 and XXVIII.41–42) corresponding, for example, to RV I.35.6, *āṇim na rathyam amṛtā adhi tasthuḥ*.

[31] Clement, *Miscellanies* VI.15, "Prophecy does not employ figurative forms in the expressions for the sake of beauty of diction"; *Sum. Theol.* I.1.10c, "Whereas in every other science things are signified by words, this science has the property, that the things signified by the words have themselves a signification." Émile Mâle aptly referred to the language of Christian symbolism as a "calculus."

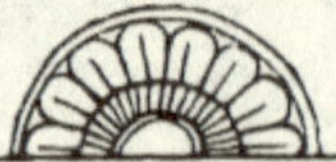

Nirukta = *Hermeneia*

Every student of Vedic literature will be familiar with what are called by modern scholars "folk etymologies." I cite, for example, the *Chāndogya Upaniṣad* (VIII.3.3), "Verily, this Spirit is in the heart[1] (*eṣa ātmā hṛdi*). The hermeneia (*niruktam*) thereof is this: 'This is in the heart' (*hṛdayam*), and that is why the 'heart' is called '*hṛdayam*.' Whoever is a comprehensor of this reaches Heaven every day." Specimens, of course, abound in Yāska—for example, *Nirukta* V.14, "*Puṣkaram* means 'mid-world,' because it 'fosters' (*poṣati*) things that come to be.[2] Water is *puṣkaram* too, because it is a 'means of worship' (*pūjākaram*), and 'to be worshipped' (*pūjayitavyam*). Otherwise, as 'lotus' (*puṣkaram*) the word is of the same origin, being a 'means of adorning' (*vapuṣkaram*); and it is a 'bloom' (*puṣyam*) because it 'blossoms' (*puṣpate*)." Explanations of this kind are commonly dismissed as "etymological triflings" (J. Eggeling), "purely artificial" (A. B. Keith), and "very fanciful" (B. C. Mazumdar), or as "puns." On the other hand, one feels that they cannot be altogether ignored, for as the last-mentioned author says, "There are in many Upaniṣads very fanciful explanations . . . disclosing bad grammar and worse idiom, and yet the grammarians who did not accept them as correct, did not say anything about them";[3] that is, the early Sanskrit grammarians, whose "scientific" abilities have been universally recognized, did not embody these "explanations" in their "grammar," but at the same time never condemned them.

Nirukta is not, in fact, a part of philology in the modern sense; a herme-

[This essay appeared in the *Viśva-Bhāratī Quarterly*, NS II (1936) and concurrently in French in *Études traditionelles*, XLI (1936); the Addendum which concludes the essay was published in each journal the following year.—ED.]

[1] I.e., "within you," in the sense that "The Kingdom of Heaven is within you."

[2] The space between Heaven and Earth, being and not-being, light and darkness, essence and nature, being precisely the locus, opportunity, and "promised land" of all birth and becoming.

[3] B. C. Mazumdar, review of J. N. Rawson, *The Kaṭha Upaniṣad*, in *Indian Culture*, II (1935/1936), 378.

neutic explanation may or may not coincide with the actual pedigree of a word in question. *Nirukta* = *hermeneia* is founded upon a theory of language of which philology and grammar are only departments, one may even say the most humble departments, nor do I say this without a real and genuine respect for those "omniscient impeccable leviathans of science that headlong sound the linguistic ocean to its most horrid depths, and (in the intervals of ramming each other) ply their flukes on such audacious small fry as even on the mere surface will venture within their danger,"[4] and whose advice in matters of verbal genealogy I am always ready to accept. Etymology, an excellent thing in its place, is nevertheless precisely one of those "modern sciences which really represent quite literally 'residues' of the old sciences, no longer understood."[5] In India the traditional science of language is the special domain of the *pūrva-mīmāṃsā*, of which the characteristic is that "It lays stress on the proposition that articulate sounds are eternal,[6] and on the consequent doctrine that the connection of a word with its sense is not due to convention, but is by nature inherent in the word itself." When, however, A. A. Macdonell adds to this excellent characterization that "Owing to its lack of philosophical interest, the system has not as yet much occupied the attention of European scholars,"[7] he only means that the subject is not of interest to himself and his kind; it is implausible that he should have had in mind deliberately to exclude Plato from the category of "philosophers." For not only does Plato employ the hermeneutic method in the *Cratylus*—for example, when he says " 'to have called' (τὸ καλέσαν) things useful is one and the same thing as to speak of 'the beautiful' (τὸ καλόν)"—but throughout this dialogue he is dealing with the problem of the nature of the relation between sounds and meanings, inquiring whether this is an essential or an accidental one. The general conclusion is that the true name of anything is that which has a natural (Skr. *sahaja*) meaning—i.e., is really an "imitation" (μίμησις) of the thing itself in

[4] Standish Hayes O'Grady, *Silva Gadelica* (London and Edinburgh, 1892), II, v.

[5] René Guénon, *La Crise du monde moderne* (Paris, 1927), p. 103.

[6] What is meant by the "eternity of the Veda" is sometimes misunderstood. "Eternal" is "without duration," "not in time" (*akāla*), therefore ever present. The "eternity" of tradition has nothing to do with the "dating" of a given scripture, in a literary sense. As St. Thomas Aquinas expressed it, "Both the Divine Word and the writing of the Book of Life are eternal. But the promulgation cannot be from eternity on the part of the creature that hears or reads" (*Sum. Theol.* II-I.91.1 *ad* 2).

[7] *History of Sanskrit Literature* (London, 1900), p. 400.

terms of sound, just as in painting things are "imitated" in terms of color —but that because of the actual imperfection of vocal imitation, which may be thought of as a matter of inadequate recollection, the formation of words in use has been helped out by art and their meaning partly determined by convention. What is meant by natural meaning can be understood when we find that Socrates and Cratylus are represented as agreeing that "the letter *rho* (Skr. *ṛ*, *r*) is expressive of rapidity, motion, and hardness." Cratylus maintains that "he who knows the names knows also the things expressed by them," and this is as much as to imply that "He who first gave names to things did so with sure knowledge of the nature of the things"; he maintains in so many words that this first giver of names (Skr. *nāmadhāḥ*) must have been "a power more than human" and that the names thus given in the beginning are necessarily their "true names." The names themselves are dualistic, implying either motion or rest, and are thus descriptive of acts, rather than of the things that act; Socrates admits that the discovery of real existence, apart from denotations, may be "beyond you and me."

It is likewise the Indian doctrine (BD 1.27 ff., *Nirukta* 1.1 and 12, etc.) that "Names are all derived from actions"; insofar as they denote a course of action, names are verbs, and insofar as someone or something is taken to be the doer of the action, they are nouns. It must not be overlooked that Skr. *nāma* is not merely "name," but "form," "idea," and "eternal reason."[8] Sound and meaning (*śabdārtha*) are inseparably associated, so that we find this expression employed as an image of a perfect union, such as that of Śiva-śakti, essence and nature, act and potentiality *in divinis*. Names are the cause of existence; one may say that in any composite essence (*sattva*, *nāmarūpa*), the "name" (*nāma*) is the form of the "phenomenon" (*rūpa*) in the same sense that one says that "the soul is the form of the body." In the state of nonbeing (*asat*) or darkness (*tamas*), the names of individual principles are unuttered or "hidden" (*nāmāni guhyā*, *apīcyā*, etc.; RV *passim*);[9] to be named is to proceed from death to life. The Eternal Avatar himself, proceeding as a child (*kumāra*) from the unfriendly Father, demands a name, because it is "by name that one strikes away evil" (*pāpmānam apahanti*, ŚB vi.1.3.9); all beings on their way dread most of all to be robbed of their names by the powers of

[8] See Coomaraswamy, "Vedic Exemplarism," [in the present volume—ED.]. Also René Guénon, "Le Symbolisme du théâtre," *Le Voile d'Isis*, XXXVII (1932), 69.

[9] "When names were not, nor any sign of existence endowed with name" (Rūmī, *Dīvan*, Ode xvii).

Death, who lies in wait to thieve (*krivir nāmāni pravaṇe muṣayati*, RV v.44.4). "It is by his deathless name (*amartyena nāmnā*) that Indra overliveth human generations" (RV vi.18.7). So long as an individual principle remains in act, it has a name; the world of "names" is the world of "life." "When a man dies, what does not go out of him is 'name,' that is 'without end,' and since what is 'without end' is the Several Angels, thereby he wins the 'world without end'" (BU iii.2.12).

It is by the enunciation of names that a "more than human power" not merely designates existing things correctly but endows them with their being, and the All-maker can do this because He is omniscient of the hidden or titanic names of things that are not yet in themselves; it is by the foreknown names of mediate causes that He does all that must be done, including the creation of all separated beings. For example, RV i.155.6, "He by the names of the Four [Seasons] has set in motion the rounded wheel [of the Year] that is furnished with ninety steeds"; x.54.4, "Thy titan names, all these, O Maghavan, thou surely knowest, whereby thou hast performed thy mighty deeds"; viii.41.5, "Varuṇa knoweth the hidden names remote, many a locution maketh he to blossom (*kāvyā purū . . . puṣyati*), even as the light of heaven (*dyauḥ*, here the Sun, *pūṣan*, *savitṛ*, as in v.81.2) bringeth into blossom all kind (*puṣyati . . . rūpam*)." It is by the same token that all words of power are efficacious—for example, PB vi.9.5 and vi.10.3, "By the word 'born' (*jātam*) he 'brings to birth' (*jījanat*). . . . In saying 'lives' he enlivens them that 'live.'"

It is thus by a divine providence that all things are brought forth in their variety: "Varuṇa knows all things speculatively" (*viśvaṃ sa veda varuṇo yathā dhiyā*, RV x.11.1). "All-maker, supernal seer-at-one-glance (*saṃdṛk*), of whom they speak as 'One beyond the Seven Prophets,' who is the only one Denominator of the Angels (*yo devānāṃ nāmadhā eka eva*), to him all other things turn for information (*sampraśnam*)," RV x.82.2–3,[10] should be read in connection with i.72.3, where the Angels, by their sacrificial service, "obtained their names of worship, contrived

[10] It is quite right for *us* to think of "names as the *consequences* of things" (Aristotle, as quoted by Dante in the *Vita nuova*), because our knowledge of things is not essential, but accidental; aspiring to essential knowledge, names are for us a means to knowledge and not to be confused with knowledge itself. But let us not forget that from the point of view of the Creator, Plato's "more than human power" which was the First Denominator, names (ideas) *preceded* things, which He *knew* before they *were*. Already possessed of essential knowledge, for Him to *name* is the same as to *create*; from the point of view of the First Mind, "things are the consequences of names."

their high-born bodies"; to be named—to get a name, in other words—is to be born, to be alive. This denominative creation is a dual act: on the part of the One Denominator, the utterance is as single as himself; on the part of the individual principles, this single meaning that is pregnant with all meanings is verbally divided, "by their wordings they conceived him manifold who is but One" (RV x.114.5). And inasmuch as such a sacrificial partition is a contraction and identification into variety, it must be realized that to be named, while indispensable to wayfaring, is not the goal: "Speech (*vāc*) is the rope, and names the knot whereby all things are bound" (AĀ II.1.6). The end is formally the same as the beginning; it is as one "no longer fed by form or aspect (*nāmarūpād-vimuktaḥ*) that the Comprehensor reaches the heavenly Person beyond the yon, knowing the Brahman becomes the Brahman" (Muṇḍ. Up. III.2.8–9). "As these flowing rivers tend towards the sea, their name and aspect are shattered, it is only spoken of as 'sea'" (Praśna Up. VI.5). "The fastidious soul," as Eckhart says, "can rest on nothing that has name"; "On merging into the Godhead all definition is lost," and this is also why he says, "Lord, my welfare lies in thy never calling me to mind"; for all of these quotations innumerable parallels could be cited from other Christian as well as from Sūfī and additional Indian sources.

One thus begins to glimpse a theory of expression in which ideation, denomination, and individual existence are inseparable aspects, conceptually distinguishable when objectively considered, but coincident in the subject. What this amounts to is the conception of a single living language, not knowable in its entirety by any individual principle but in itself the sum of all imaginable articulations, and in the same way corresponding to all imaginable acts of being: the "Spoken Word" of God is precisely this "sum of all language" (*vācikaṃ sarvaṇmayam*; *Abhinaya Darpaṇa* 1). All existing languages are partially remembered and more or less fragmented echoes of this universal tongue, just as all modes of vision are more or less obscure refractions of the world-picture (*jagac-citra; Svātmanirūpaṇa* 95) or eternal mirror (*speculum aeternum*; Augustine, *De civitate Dei* XII.29) which, if one knew and saw in their entirety and simultaneity, would be to be omniscient. The original and inexhaustible (*akṣara*) affirmation (OṂ) is pregnant with all possible meaning; or, thought of not as sound but as "omniform light" (*jyotir-viśvarūpam*, VS V.35), is the exemplary form of very different things, and either way is precisely "that one thing by which when it is known, all things are known" (Muṇḍ. Up. 1.3, BU 1.4.5). The paternal comprehension and the mother tongue which are, thus, in their identity the first principle of knowledge are evidently inaccessible to empirical observation;[11] as long as an individual consciousness can be distinguished as such, an omniscience is inconceivable, and one can only "turn to the One Denominator for instruction" (RV x.82.3)—namely, to Plato's "more than human power," to recover lost potentialities by acts of recollection, raising our level of reference by all available dispositive means. The metaphysical doctrine of universal language is, thus, by no means to be thought of as asserting that a universal language was ever actually spoken by any people under the sun; the metaphysical concept of a universal speech is, in fact, the conception of a single sound, not that of groups of sounds to be uttered in succession, which is what we mean when we speak of "a spoken language," where in default of an *a priori* knowledge of the thought to be expressed, it may be "difficult to tell whether it is the thought which is defective or the language which has failed to express it" (Keith, AĀ, p. 54).

The assumption more immediately underlying the traditional science of hermeneutics (*nirukta*) is that there remains in spoken languages a trace of universality, and particularly of natural *mimesis* (by which, of course, we do not mean a merely onomatopoetic likeness but one of true anal-

[11] And thus, as a modern scholar would say, "meaningless to us and should not be described as knowledge" (A. B. Keith's edition of the *Aitareya Āranyaka*, Oxford, 1909, p. 42), where, however, it should be borne in mind that the kind of knowledge intended corresponds to Skr. *avidyā*, as being a relative knowledge or opinion, as distinguished from an ascertainment. [Augustine, *Confessions* xi.4, "Scientia nostra scientiae tua ecomparata ignorantia est . . . Ignorantia divisiva est erratium."] It is not, as Macdonell pretends, because the theory of an adequate symbolism of sound is devoid of philosophical (or, rather, metaphysical) interest, but because the modern scholar is not interested in principles but only in "facts," not in truth but only in statistical prediction, that "the [Pūrva Mīmāṃsā] system has not as yet much occupied the attention of European scholars." The same might be said with respect to any other traditional science.

All tradition proposes means dispositive to absolute experience. Whoever does not care to employ these means is in no position to deny that the proposed procedure can lead, as asserted, to a principle that is precisely *aniruktam*, no thing and no where, at the same time that it is the source of all things everywhere. What is most repugnant to the nominalist is the fact that, granted a possibility of absolute experience, no rational demonstration could be offered in a classroom, no "experimental control" is possible, very much as *cogito ergo sum* is to every individual an adequate proof of his own conscious existence, of which, however, no demonstrative proof could be offered to the solipsist because he cannot directly experience the consciousness of another who also claims to be a "person."

ogy); that even in languages considerably modified by art and by convention, there still survives a considerable part of a naturally adequate symbolism. It is assumed, in other words, that certain assonances, which may or may not correspond to the actual pedigrees of words, are nevertheless indications of their affinities and meanings, just as we recognize family likeness, both of appearance and of character, apart from the line of direct inheritance. All of which is anything but a matter of "folk etymology"; it is not a matter of etymology at all in the narrowest sense of the word, but rather of significant assonance,[12] and in any case the "folk" tradition is a matter of the "folk" only in respect to its transmission, not its origin; "folklore" and Philosophia Perennis spring from a common source.

To neglect the *nirukta* is, indeed, to impose upon oneself a needless handicap in the exegesis of doctrinal content. Compare in this connection the more intelligent procedure of "Omikron": "A further decision led me constantly to consult such ancient lexika and fragments of lexika as were obtainable; for I believed that in these original dictionaries of the Hellenes, the ancient scholars would have given apposite meanings, as well as clues to symbolic and allegoric expression. I paid particular attention to the strange *Hermēneia* of the old grammarians, supposing that they had good reasons for it, and even for giving, usually, more than one *Hermēneia* for the same word."[13]

From an empirical point of view, it can hardly be claimed that the connection of sounds with meanings has been seriously investigated in modern times; we have the word of Macdonell that "the system has not much occupied the attention of European scholars." Even if such investigations had been made, with indefinite or negative results, it would still hold that *hermeneia* (*nirukta*) as actually employed by ancient authors presents us with an invaluable aid to the understanding of what was actually intended by the verbal symbols that are thus elucidated. The words of Scripture are for the most part highly technical and pregnant with many meanings on various levels of reference, so that even the nominalist should feel himself indebted to the hermeneutist from a semantic point of view.

[12] "For example, we do not mean to imply that as between the words *Agnus* and *Ignis* (Latin equivalent of *Agni*) there is anything more than one of those phonetic similarities to which we referred above, which very likely do not correspond to a line of linguistic descent, but are not therefore to be regarded as purely accidental" (René Guénon, *L'Esotérisme de Dante*, Paris, 1925, p. 92, n. 2).

[13] Omikron, *Letters from Paulos* (New York, 1920), Introduction.

Nirukta = Hermeneia: addendum

In the preceding article, I described the Oṃkāra as the "sum of all language" (*vācikaṃ sarvaṇmayam*), and "that one thing by which when it is known, all things are known." There is a remarkable text exactly to this effect in CU II.23.3, "As all the leaves [of a book] are pinned together by a spike (*śaṅkunā*), so all speech (*sarvā vāc*) is pinned together by the Oṃkāra; verily, the Oṃkāra is all this, the Oṃkāra verily [is] all this"; and for this, too, there is a striking parallel in Dante (*Paradiso* XXXIII.85–92): "Within its depths I saw ingathered, bound by love in one volume, the scattered leaves of all the universe . . . after such fashion that what I tell of is one simple flame. The universal form of this complex I think that I beheld." The parallel is all the closer because in the first case the universal form is that of the eternal sound, in the other, that of the eternal light; for light and sound are coincident *in divinis* (cf. *svar* and *svara*), and just as Dante speaks of "these singing suns" (*Paradiso* X.76; cf. XVIII.76, "So within the lights the flying sacred creatures sang"), so JUB III.33 has "The Sun is sound, therefore they say of this Sun 'It is as sound that He proceeds' (*svara eti*)," and in CU I.5.1, "The Sun is OṂ, for he is ever sounding forth 'OṂ.' "

Incidentally, the *Chāndogya* passage cited above, "As all the leaves are pinned together by a spike (*yathā śaṅkunā sarvāṇi parṇani samtṛṇṇani*)," affords very strong evidence for the contemporaneity of writing with the redaction of this Upaniṣad, for everyone who has seen a South Indian palm leaf manuscript of many leaves held together by a spike passed through one of the string-holes will recognize the aptness of the simile.

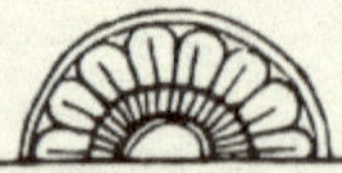

Some Pāli Words

"For an accurate understanding of the original meaning of most of the technical terms of Buddhism, a knowledge of their Sanskrit form is indispensable."

Max Müller, SBE, Vol. 10, liv.[1]

In the following article certain Pāli words are discussed, with particular reference to their treatment in the PTS Dictionary and to their translation in the now completed Nikāya volumes of the PTS. References are to the corresponding editions, by volume and page. The discussions of *Attha* (*artha*), *Rasa*, *Vyañjana*, and *Sahājanetta* amount to a first essay in the study of Buddhist rhetoric, and should be read together.

[This paper was first published in the *Harvard Journal of Asiatic Studies*, IV (1939). Thanks are due I. B. Horner, president of the Pali Text Society, for reviewing the text prior to this publication.—ED.]

[1] To this I would add that Buddhist doctrine is very largely addressed directly to learned Brahman hearers, already familiar with almost all of the technical terms in their Sanskrit forms and with the Indian rather than the specifically Buddhist content of the words: it follows that the more we can approach the texts from the same point of view, the better we shall be able to grasp them. Buddhism presupposes the Brahmanical position, and for the most part is only in conflict with actual or supposed perversions of this position.

Insofar as Buddhism is an argument addressed to a learned audience, it is an argument that presupposes a knowledge of the Vedas and Upaniṣads; if we are not equipped with a similar knowledge, we can hardly expect to understand more of the Dhamma that is "deep, deep in meaning, transcendental and coupled with negation (*te ye suttantā gambhīrā gambhīratthā lokuttarā suññatā-paṭisaññutā*, A 1.72, S 1.267, etc.)" than is directly addressed to the "untaught many-folk" (*assuta puthujjana*, "the man in the street").

In connection with the Buddhist commentaries, it may be remarked here that Buddhaghosa did not know Sanskrit or the history of Sanskrit terms, and in at least some cases interprets Pāli words in a fashion dependent on special usages in his own period; his treatment of *unhīsa* is a case in point. Hence, what a Brahman auditor face-to-face with the Buddha may be supposed to have understood by a given term may often represent its real value in "original Buddhism" better than the interpretation of a later Buddhist commentator.

akaniṭṭha. The Dictionary misses the full meaning of this word in its context, S v.237, J III.487, etc. It is not "'not the smaller,' i.e., the greatest, highest," but "amongst whom there is none younger (or lesser) than another." The Devas in question can only be the Maruts, of whom "None is come forth superior or inferior, or is waxen of medium glory" (*te ajyeṣṭhā akaniṣṭhāsa udbhido*[2] *madhyamāso mahasā vi vavṛdhuḥ*, RV v.59.6), but "as brothers have waxen together," RV v.60.5. As Vāyu is metaphysically the "Gale of the Spirit," so are these Storm winds "Blasts of the Spirit." It will not be overlooked that in MU II.1 Bṛhadratha (of the Īkṣvākuvaṃśa, also the Buddha's), who is about to become an *ātmajñaḥ* (Pāli *attaññū*) and *kṛtakṛtyaḥ* (Pāli *katakicco, kataṃ karaṇīyam*), is reputed a Marut, and *ibid.* VI.30, where he is actually *kṛtakṛtyaḥ* ("all in act") and enters through the Sundoor into the Brahmaloka, he is no longer referred to by a personal or family name, but only as "Marut." The Buddhist phrase *akaniṭṭhāgāmin*, which occurs with *parinibbāyin* in a list of designations of "Never-returners" in several contexts (D III.237, etc.), implies accordingly the attainment of the Brahmaloka and of companionship on equal terms with the highest Devas, the Blasts of the Spirit, amongst whom there is no distinction of superior or inferior or of early or late comers-in. Quite analogous to this is the position of the Comprehensor, of whom it is often said, e.g., S I.12, that he does not think of himself as "equal, or better than, or inferior to others."

G. P. Malalasekera, in his *Dictionary of Pāli Proper Names* (London, 1937), cites from DA II.480, Buddhaghosa's explanation of *akaniṭṭhā devā.* In this citation, *sabbeh'eva* should be *sabbe h'eva*. Moreover, B. does not give two different explanations of the name, but only one: the *akaniṭṭha* deities are so called because none amongst them is junior in attainment and virtues.[3]

akāliko. In S I.11–13, a Yakkhī asks of the Buddha what is meant by the designation of the Dhamma as "intemporal" (*akāliko*), i.e., "eternal." The Buddha answers that it is only by the understanding of what-can-be-told that eternal life can be attained: "Those who heed only what can be told

[2] *Udbhidaḥ* in the sense of MU VI.30, *sauraṃ dvāraṃ bhitvā* = *ūrdhvam. . . yo bhitvā sūryamaṇḍalam*, again with reference to a Marut.

[3] The implications of *akaniṭṭha* are similar to those of the well-known Parable of the Vineyard, Matt. 20:1–16. Cf. "for all shall know Him, from the least even unto the greatest of them" (Jer. 31:34), and Augustine's discussion in *De spiritu et littera* 41.

(*akkheyyam*, i.e., the tale itself, *ākhyānam*), who rest on what can be told, who do not fully comprehend what can be told, these come under the yoke of Death: but one who fully comprehends what can be told, makes no debate about the teller (*akkhātāraṃ na maññati*, the reference of *akkhātāro* being to the Buddha himself, as in Sn 167), reflecting (*iti*) 'It is not "*his*"' (*taṃ hi tassa na hoti*), and so makes no mistake (*yena naṃ vajjā na tassa atthi*)." The Yakkhī does not understand and asks the Buddha "to explain in detail the meaning of what has been said in brief" (*saṃkhittena bhāsitassa vitthārena atthaṃ jāneyyam*). The Buddha then more explicitly states the doctrine of *ākimcañña* by means of which he has already answered at one and the same time the Yakkhī's mistaken reference to the Buddha as "surrounded by other mighty Devatās" and her actual question as to the meaning of "timeless" (*akāliko*): "He is contrarious (*vivadetha*, with reference to the preceding *vajjā tassa*) who thinks in terms of 'equal, better or worse,'" i.e., who thinks of the Buddha as "someone." Still she does not understand (as before). More explicitly the Buddha says, "He that has done with 'number,' *him* neither gods nor men, whether here below or there beyond, can reach" (*pahāsi saṇkhaṃ . . . taṃ . . . nājjhagāmuṃ devā manussā idha vā huraṃ vā*). At last she understands the Buddha's meaning (*attham*): "timeless" can only apply to a doctrine that has not been taught by "some one"; the *dhamma* is *akāliko* as being, not the "dated" "view" of So-and-so (whether man or personal deity is irrelevant), but Truth itself. Neither the Buddha nor the Dhamma is "in time," but only their manifestations, which must not be taken absolutely, but must be penetrated and seen through. The designation of Dhamma as "timeless" is the Buddhist form of the well-known Indian doctrine of the "eternity of the Veda," for which there are good Christian equivalents, e.g., St. Augustine, *De lib. arb.* 1.6, *Lex, quae summa ratio nominatur, non potest cuipiam intelligenti non incommutabilis aeternaque videri*; *Sum. Theol.* I-II.91.1, *divina ratio nihil concipit ex tempore*, etc. "Dhamma" could hardly be rendered in Latin better than by *Lex, quae summa ratio nominatur . . . aeterna . . . divina ratio.* The modern scholar's objection to the doctrine of the eternity of the Word, Law, or Dhamma is based on a misunderstanding of what is meant; as remarked by St. Thomas Aquinas, *ibid.*, "the Divine Word and the writing of the Book of Life (which corresponds to the *vidyā* implied in "Jātavedas" and to "Providence") are eternal. But the promulgation cannot be from eternity on the part of the creature that hears or reads." The doctrine of the eternity of the *summa ratio* itself is the same as the

Platonic doctrine of ideas; that of its temporal promulgation corresponding to the appearance of the shadows on the wall of the cave. In the Buddhist texts in the same way we find the Dhamma described in one breath as *sandiṭṭhiko*, manifest, and *akāliko*, not in time. For, to borrow the words of Augustine, "This wisdom is not made; but it is at this present, as it hath ever been, and so shall ever be" (*Confessions* IX.10). There are many other texts in which the Buddha identifies himself, the Dhamma, and Brahma; the Dhamma is accordingly temporal and intemporal, just as the Brahman, single essence with two natures, is *kāla* and *akāla* (MU VI.15, etc.), "time and timeless," and therewith also *sakala* and *akala*, "with and without parts." Otherwise expressed, Brahman is on the one hand the audible *brahman* = *mantram*, and on the other silent: *śabda* and *aśabda*, "vocal and silent."

akiriyavāda. Just as in Brahmanism (e.g., TB III.12.9.7–8; JUB I.5.1–2; CU VIII.4.4; BU IV.4.23; KU II.14; Kauṣ. Up. I.4; MU VI.18, 35; BG V.15, etc.) and in Christianity (I John 3:9; II Cor. 3:17; Gal. V:18; *Sum. Theol.* I-II.93.6 *ad* 1 and II-II.180.2), ethical values are in the last analysis to be rejected and all responsibility ceases, so in Pāli Buddhism (M I.135, 160; M II.36–39; Dh 39, 267, 412; Sn 715, etc.); it follows, indeed, as a matter of course that when the whole burden of *kamma* (the operation of mediate causes, or "fate") is laid down forever, the relative factors of this burden (what ought to have been done and was not done, and what ought not to have been done but was done) are likewise discarded; this abandonment of ethical values inevitably accompanying the abandonment of the psycho-physical "self" (Pāli *appātumo, pāpa attā, anattā*), an abandonment that is styled in Brahmanism "self-sacrifice" or "self-conquest" (*ātma-yajña, ātma-jaya*), in Christianity "self-naughting" (Eckhart's "the soul must put itself to death," Christ's "hating one's own soul," and St. Paul's "dividing asunder of soul from spirit"), in Buddhism "self-conquest" (*atta-jaya*), "self-dompting" (*atta-damatha*), "self-allaying" (*atta-samatha*), "self-extinction" (*atta-parinibbāpana*), or more explicitly and technically, the attainment of the "station of not being anyone" (*ākiṃcaññāyatana*).

It will be seen that the ultimate negation of all responsibility is a purely metaphysical and contemplative position: it can have no applicable meaning for anyone who still is "someone," still "active" or, in other words, still "alive." To argue that "I," So-and-so, am not a responsible agent would be a ridiculous confusion of thought: it is only the I that is *not* a So-and-so that is free of the burden of responsibility, only one born of God, and in the spirit, that cannot sin. To pretend that this can apply to "me" (So-and-so) is to interpret the doctrine of filiation and theosis in the Satanic sense of the paranoiac. There have nevertheless been some modern scholars who have pretended to see in the "That art thou" of the Upaniṣads just such a deification as this; and have been "shocked" accordingly: and some others, the Amaurians for example, who were charged with maintaining that "as every human act is the act of God, there is no distinction between good and evil, and hence Nature should not be refused anything."[4] We are concerned here only with the latter sort of heretics, those whose heresy or "false view" (*micchā diṭṭhi*) is termed in Pāli Buddhism *akiriyavāda*, the proposition viz. that inasmuch as deeds are done without a doer,[5] it does not matter what "I" do, whether good or evil (D I.53): as against this position, the Buddha proclaims himself a *kiriyavādī, and* an *akiriyavādī* inasmuch as he teaches both what ought-to-be-done and ought-not-to-be-done (Vin I.233 ff., and A I.62); but a *kiriyavādī only* in the sense of "one who teaches that there is an ought-to-be-done" in opposition to the *akiriyavādī*, whose teaching is that there is no "ought-to-be-done" (D I.115); these distinctions depending on a word division *akiriya-vādī* (teacher of an ought-not-to-be-done) and *a-kiriya-vādī* (not the teacher of an ought-to-be-done).[6]

In A II.232, Gotama is accused of *a-kiriyavāda*, the accuser maintaining that he "teaches that there is no ought-to-be-done with respect to any acts" (*sabbakammānam akiriyaṃ paññāpeti*), and it is of interest that in the course of the refutation the Buddha points out that *akiriya* (the word might be rendered by "laissez-faire" in this context) amounts to an an-

[4] Maurice de Wulf, *History of Mediaeval Philosophy*, 3rd ed. (London, 1935), p. 235.

[5] See *ahaṃkāra*.

[6] There are actually three different ways in which the *akiriyavādī* claims irresponsibility (cf. J V.228). In A I.173, the translation of *akiriya* by "inaction" is mistaken; for inaction we should require *akamma* corresponding to *akarma* in BG IV.16. As a false "view," *akiriya* means "no *ought* to be done": as a "right view," that there is "an *ought not* to be done." The three grounds on which an irresponsibility is based are (1) fatalism, actions being the effect of past acts over which we have no control, (2) actions are not our acts but those of the Lord (*issara*), and (3) actions are uncaused and unmotivated (*ahetu, appacaya*): as against all these the Buddha maintains that "this should be done, should not be done (*idam vā karaṇīyam idaṃ vā akaraṇīyam*)," and it is in this sense also that he calls himself both *kiriyavādī* and *akiriyavādī*, as above.

nihilation of the world (*ucchedaṃ . . . lokassa*), "of which the very subsistence consists in the verity, i.e., causal efficacy, of action" (*kammasacca*, to be understood as in A II.197–98 with respect to any bodily, vocal, or mental activity, *kāya-, vācī-* and *mano-samārambha*), an argument reminiscent of BG III.8, *śarīra-yātrāpi ca te na prasidhyed akarmaṇaḥ* and III.24, *utsīdeyur ime lokā na kuryāṃ karma ced aham.*[7] It is indeed for this very reason that the Buddha sets the Wheel in motion in response to the desire of all the Devas, voiced by Brahmā, who exclaims that otherwise "the world is lost!" *nassati . . . , vinassati* (J I.81, S I.136 ff., M I.168, etc.). It is expressly stated too that the Buddha "practices what he preaches" (*yathāvādī tathākārī*, A II.24, reminiscent of RV IV.33.6, *satyam ūcur nara eva hi cakruḥ*, and IX.113.5, *satya-vadam-t-satya-karman*): it is as the Arhat, *passim*, that he has "done what was to be done"[8] (*katakicco, kataṃ karaṇīyam*, corresponding to the Brahmanical *kṛtakṛtyaḥ*).[9]

We can see now easily, then, how it can be that while in Ud 70 the notion that "I am the doer" is scouted (see *ahaṃkāra*), in Ud 45 the man "who even when he acts yet says 'I am not the agent'" (*yo cāpi katvā na karomīti cāha*) is likewise condemned. As in Christian doctrine, the moral virtues do not belong to the contemplative life essentially, but only dispositively, while they do belong to the active life essentially.

attā. (1) *Attā* can be equated with *kāya* only in the reflexive sense. For example, in D I.34, *añño attā dibbo rūpī manomayo* corresponds to D I.77, *aññaṃ kāyaṃ . . . rūpiṃ manomayam* (also in M II.17). This does not imply that *attā* can be translated by "body," meaning simply the flesh: on the contrary, "body" is used to mean the whole psycho-physical personality, just as in English we speak of "somebody," or as in "gin a body meet a body," and also make use of "soul" in the same way in such

[7] The Buddha's doctrine was evidently as much misunderstood or wrongly reported by some in his own day, as it has been misunderstood by some modern scholars (notably those who saw in *nibbāna* "annihilation"). In M I.140, for example, we find him accused of teaching the "cutting off, destruction and becoming naught of existent entities (*sato-satassa ucchedaṃ vināsaṃ vibhavam*)." He protests that the accusation is "naughtily, vainly, falsely made and contrary to what is fact (*asatā tucchā musā abhūtena*)," for "this is just what I do *not* teach."

[8] Not simply, of course, in the sense of "duty done," but that of "having done what was to be done," i.e., "having reduced all potentiality to act" and being therefore "all in act."

[9] Note the dramatic distinction of *kṛtakṛtyah*, "doer of evil," "worker of witchcraft," in AV IV.17.4.

expressions as "not a soul was to be seen." *Añño attā* and *añño kāyo* are much rather what we mean by "another man," a "new being," than either "spirit" or "body" in the stricter sense of these words. *Kāya* is found again in the general sense of "person" (*quisque*) in M I.206, where three young men are leading the higher life in one company: one of them says "I live in obedience to the will of these venerable (comrades), surrendering my private will (*sakaṃ cittam*); we, Sir, are many men (*nānā . . . kāyā*, several 'bodies'), but most assuredly one will" (*ekaṃ cittam*). In A I.168 (cf. II.68, D III.61) we find both *attā* and (instead of *kāya*) *sarīra* employed in the same sense of *quis* or *quisque* = *kaścit*: the objection is raised that this is the perfecting of only one person (*ekam attānaṃ . . . parinibbāpeti*), that this is an acquisition of merit affecting only "somebody" (*ekasarīrikaṃ puññapaṭipadaṃ paṭipanno hoti*); the Buddha shows that the monk's abandonment of the world affects not only himself, but is "everybody-ish" (*anekasarīrikā*).

The Dictionary notes the meaning *quis* or *quisque* only s.v. *tuma* (= *attā* = Skr. *tman* = *ātman*).

(2) One of the most remarkable examples of what C.A.F. Rhys Davids would call a "left in" in late Pāli literature occurs in J VI.252, where *kāyo te ratha-saññāto . . . attā va sārathi* corresponds to KU III.3, *ātmānaṃ rathinaṃ viddhi, śarīraṃ ratham eva tu*. The text is of utmost importance in connection with the "Chariot Parable" elsewhere, notably in S I.135 and Mil XXVI ff.[10] In the latter passage, so well known, it is shown that just as there is no "chariot" apart from the sum of the component parts to which the name of "chariot" is conventionally given, so there is no "Nāgasena" apart from the psycho-physical components of the variable phenomenon to which the name of "Nāgasena" is conventionally given; the psycho-physical composite is *anattā*, here and throughout our texts; there is nothing but a phenomenon (*rūpa*) to which a name (*nāma*) can be given.

Observe now, that just as the repeated analyses of the psycho-physical constitution of the so-called individual end invariably with the words

[10] We do not overlook that Milinda himself is referred to as the rider, but this is merely to introduce the subject of the parable. If Nāgasena had gone on to apply the parable not only to himself but also to Milinda, it is the psycho-physical personality by name "Milinda" that would have been analyzed, and Nāgasena might well have said to him, *na vo so attā*, "all that is not your essence," still without touching upon the nature of an essence thus defined by elimination, that spiritual essence to which we here, in accordance with J VI.252, refer to as the "rider" or "charioteer."

na me so attā, "*that* is not my 'self,' or 'spiritual essence,'" so Nāgasena shows that in all that can be named, whether "chariot" or "Nāgasena," no self-subsistent being or persistent substance can be found. Nāgasena no more denies that there may be a charioteer distinct from the chariot, or a principle distinct from all that can be called "Nāgasena," than the words *na me so attā* can be made to mean "there is no *attā*." He leaves out the rider altogether, only because his immediate purpose, like the Buddha's in so many texts, is to break down the belief in a "self" that is either physical or psychic. He has nothing to say, therefore, about a rider to whom no name can be given, that other "self" (*ātman*) of KU II.18 that "hath never become anyone" (*na babhūva kaścit*), a self that can only be defined by the elimination of all that it is not, but which is assuredly the substance of all those Buddhist saints who, like the Buddha himself, had realized that all phenomena are *anattā*, and had attained to the "Station of Not-being-Anyone" (*ākiñcaññāyatana*). And we can well say with Ud 80 that "if there were not this Unborn, Unbecome, Non-effected, Incomposite, there would be no way to escape from this world of birth, becoming, effection, and composition."

If the Buddha himself is the "most luminous and foremost charioteer" (*sārathi*, Sn 83), if Dhamma is the charioteer (S I.33), Attā the charioteer (J VI.252), and the chariot conversely "enspirited" (*attaniya*,[11] S V.6), all these are equivalent formulae: the Buddha is the Spirit, and it is only when He holds the reins, only when the Great Self (*mahattā*, A I.249) is in control, that the contemplative therewith "drives off and away from this world" in what is called the Brahma-vehicle or Dhamma-vehicle (S V.6).[12]

attha (= *artha*). In A I.151, the qualifications of the teacher and the hearer of Dhamma (the Doctrine as taught, *desitam*, *akkhyātam*, etc.) are that each separately and both together must be able to receive (*paṭi-*

[11] Certainly not here with any pejorative value! In the many contexts in which *attā* and *attaniya*, "self and self-ish" or "essence and essential" are denied (e.g., M I.297), the reference is to the composite vehicle itself, the soul-and-body that are "not my very-Self (*na me so attā*)" but the pseudo- or "petty self" (*appātumo*, A I.249). All our texts maintain that there is no entity of the chariot itself, but only the name and the appearance thereof; none of them affirms that there is no rider.

In S V.6, Woodward's rendering of *attaniyam bhūtam* as "built by self" betrays the meaning: *attaniyaṃ* is "enspirited," *bhūtam* is *geworden*; it is in a vehicle of which *attā* is in control that the contemplatives "drive away."

[12] *Brahmayānam anuttaraṃ niyyanti dhīrā lokamhā.*

saṃvedetī)[13] both the *attha* and the *dhamma*.[14] Woodward [translator of *Anguttara Nikāya* in the PTS edition] renders "must be able to penetrate both the letter and the spirit thereof" and adds in a footnote that "*Attha* is the primary, or surface meaning: *dhamma* the applied meaning."[15] He does not realize that his word "thereof" implies that there is a *dhamma* of a *dhamma*. There can be no doubt that what is intended is "must be able to receive both the application and the substance" of the teaching.

In the section immediately following, it is said that the same qualifications are prerequisite if the discourse (*kathā*) is to be effective (*pavattanī*, rendered by Woodward "profitable" here and in the similar context A I.125), i.e., are to *move* the hearer so that action results.

Before going further, let us observe that Skr. *artha* is the purpose, reason, use, value, application, and function, as well as the meaning, of whatever it may be that is referred to:[16] and that whereas in "primitive" thought function and meaning coincide, we who no longer think in terms of adequate symbols are unable to deal with function and meaning by a single act of the mind. This has a marked effect upon our theories of art,

[13] In *paṭisaṃvedeti*, *prati* is *secundum* and *sam* corresponds to *co* (= *cum*) in *cognoscere*: *pratisaṃvid* is *cognoscere secundum rem*. An *adaequatio rei et intellectus* is implied.

[14] Cf. Sn, prose preceding verse 1124, where we find that to every question an answer can be given in terms of *attha* or of *dhamma* accordingly. Dh 362, 363, *attham dhammaṃ ca dīpeti . . . tam āhu bhikkhum*. Cf. M I.37, A V.329, etc., *attha-veda* and *dhamma-veda*, as knowledge of or devotion to both *attha* and *dhamma*, "the law and the prophets."

[15] "Letter and spirit" is used in two senses, neither of which is that of "surface meaning and applied meaning." The two senses are (1) the most familiar, and that was developed by Origen (*De principiis*, Bk. 4, cc. 8–20), viz. that the literal meaning is no more than the symbol of the intended meaning, a figure of speech to be interpreted, as for example when it is said that of *samudda* the *adhivacanam* is *nibbāna*; and (2) that emphasized by St. Augustine in *De spiritu et littera*, in which "letter" refers to the moral law; this is the "letter that kills" inasmuch as it is by this law that the offender is condemned; while, on the other hand, the "spirit" is the Holy Ghost at work within the soul, imparting the knowledge of God by which those who are dead unto sin but live in Christ are liberated from the Law. *Attha* and *dhamma* could be rendered by "letter and spirit" in Augustine's sense, *attha* being the "applied meaning" and *dhamma* the "ultimate meaning": the distinction is that of *karmakāṇḍa* from *jñānakāṇḍa*, and it may be in this sense that the PTS Dictionary rightly distinguishes, s.v. Veda, *attha* from *dhamma* as the letter from the spirit of the Buddha's teaching, though Woodward's note, which gives for *dhamma* the meaning that belongs to *attha*, shows that he is *not* using "letter and spirit" in their original, Pauline sense.

[16] For example, in S I.34 (also Vin XI.147) *sampussam attham attano* is rendered "seeing his own good," but could also be translated "seeing the meaning of 'self' (*attā*)."

whether literary or plastic. It must be realized that from the Indian, as from the Scholastic point of view, it cannot be said that the meaning of a phrase has been conveyed otherwise than to the extent that the hearer acts upon what he is supposed to have understood.[17] In other words, the Dhamma cannot be understood apart from its application.

In A II.7 we find accordingly that the man who has learnt but little understands either the application (*attha*) or the substance of the Law (*dhamma*), and so by his audition (*sutena*) is "unborn" (*anuppanno*, an expression that vividly recalls JUB III.14.8, "Verily is a man unborn insofar as he does not sacrifice"). Woodward's version is "knows not the letter (*attham*), knows not the meaning (*dhammam*)," the very reverse of what is intended. In Ud 70, however, where we have "The blind, the unseeing, know neither the meaning nor what is not the meaning (*attham, anattham*, i.e., how to apply and how not to apply), nor the text itself nor what is not the text" (*dhammam, adhammam*, i.e., do not know when the doctrine has been correctly and when incorrectly stated), Woodward's version "know not the profitable (*attham*) . . . know not *dhamma*" is much nearer the mark. In Ud 6, "He is pure, he is a Brahman, in whom are Truth and Doctrine (*saccaṃ ca dhammo ca*)," *saccam* (= *satyam*) takes the place of *attham*, and amounts to *vera sentenzia*.

The foregoing interpretations of *attha* and *dhamma* are confirmed by two Jātaka texts. In J VI.389 we find the Bodhisattva instructing a king, Cowell and Rouse translating *atthaṃ ca dhammaṃ ca anusāsati* by "used to instruct the king in things temporal and spiritual";[18] the reference is unmistakably to Arthaśāstra and Dharmaśāstra, a meaning quite in agreement with the relative values found for *attha* and *dhamma* above. Finally we have J VI.251–52, where the king requests the Bodhisattva to teach him *atthaṃ ca dhammaṃ ca*, "policy and doctrine" (Cowell and Rouse misrender by "the sacred text and its meaning," reversing the sense of the terms). The Bodhisattva accordingly teaches him how to act; he is to protect Brāhmaṇas and Samaṇas; to feed the hungry; he should not put to labor the aged

[17] It is for this reason that the traditional Indian scholar feels that the deliberately objective and detached methods of modern scholarship (adopted, as Jung has said, "partly because of the *misérable vanité des savants* which fears and rejects with horror any sign of living sympathy, and partly because an understanding that reaches the feelings might allow contact with the foreign spirit to become a serious experience") can never lead to more than a superficial grasp of any doctrine. It is only when we ourselves participate in the quest and are hunters ourselves that we can understand the terms of venery, not as disinterested lookers-on.

[18] The same words occur in J VI.131, where they are rightly translated in the same way.

man, or ox, or horse, but give to each their due, since they served him when they were strong; in short, he is to avoid unrighteousness and follow righteousness. Then "the Great Person, having discoursed to him concerning liberality and morals (*dāna* and *sīla*) . . . proceeded to instruct him in the Law (*dhamma*) by means of the parable of the chariot that grants all wishes." This parable of the chariot begins, "Thy body is called the chariot," and concludes "The Spirit is the charioteer" (*kāyo te ratha-saññāto . . . attā va sārathi*, almost verbally identical with KU III.3; see above, s.v. *attā* [2]). We have here an actual example of what was implied by *attha* and what by *dhamma*.[19]

The foregoing analysis will be essential to the discussions of *rasa* and *vyañjana* below; see also *sahājanetta*.

attham (= *asta*). Pāli *attha* is not only Skr. *artha*, meaning, purpose, etc. (see *vyañjana*), but sometimes Skr. *astam*, "home." In this sense the word occurs in Sn 1074–76: the Muni, gone out as a flame is blown out by the wind, and released from denomination and embodiment, "goes home (*attham paleti*)[20] and is not reborn" (*na upeti saṅkhaṃ*, see *saṅkha*); it is asked, In the case of one thus "gone home" (*atthaṃ gato*), whether or not he "is" and whether he is forever well; the answer being that "for one 'gone home' there is no gauge, there is nothing by which he can be referred to,[21] when all qualities have been swept up, all wordways[22] too are swept up." The expression "gone home" derives from

[19] It need hardly be emphasized that in the present article we are dealing entirely with *attha* as contrasted with *dhamma* (or *vyañjana*), not with *attha* in the very frequent and simple sense of "meaning" for which the example of A v.194, etc., "Here in the world, it is by means of a parable that such men as are of ready wit understand the meaning of what has been said (*upamdyam idh'ekacce viññū purisā bhāsitassa attham ājānanti*)" will suffice.

[20] Max Müller's version in SBE is very defective and far too free. To have "gone home" in this anagogical sense is certainly to have "disappeared" from the field of objective perception, whether human or angelic, but we are not therefore justified in translating *attham gato* by "disappeared": it is always important to retain the literal meaning on which all other meanings depend. Nor is Max Müller's alternative, "Has he disappeared, or does he not exist?" the right one: the alternatives are posed with respect to one who *has* "gone home" (*atthaṃ-gato, so . . .*), about which "gone home" no question arises, the only question being as to what this "gone home" *implies*.

[21] As stated more fully in D XI.68, a *locus classicus*.

[22] *Vādapathā*: he has therefore entered into the silence of the unspoken word, *dharma* defined as in *Lalita Vistara*, text p. 423, "apart from any voice or sound of wordway, though the efficient cause of the voices of all beings (*sarva-ruta-ghoṣa vākpathānītaṃ . . . sarvasattva-ruta-racanam*)." "Nothing true can be said" of the

Brahmanical sources, where the Gale of the Spirit, the "One Whole Godhood" is the "home" to which the Sun himself and all separated essences return; for references see "*Svayamātṛṇṇā*: Janua Coeli," note 28 [in Vol. I of this edition—ED.].

anatam. The printed text of Ud 80 reads *duddassam anattaṃ nāma, na hi saccaṃ sudassanam*, but what is admittedly the best MS. (A), and also at least one commentary, read *anatam* for *anattam*, and though the commentator understands by *anatam* "unbent," hence "*nibbāna*" (cf. *Kindred Sayings*, I, 236, note 4) and Woodward's rendering "infinite," it is almost certain that the meaning of the whole is, "It is hard to discern what's false, nor easy to discern what's true," and that *anatam* here represents *anṛtam*, the regular antithesis of *satyam* in Sanskrit contexts. The reading *anattam* can be accounted for in two ways, either as an error on the part of the scribe, unfamiliar with the rare word *anatam* (not in PTS Dictionary, nor can I cite it elsewhere than as above)[23] or less probably by the fact that what is *anattam* is also *anatam* = *anṛtam*, as could easily be shown in sense from Pāli sources, e.g., A I.149, where of man's two selves, the "fair" (*kalyāṇa*) is true (*saccam*), the "foul" (*pāpa*) false (*musā*), M I.135, where the psycho-physical ego is "unreal" (*asat*), and similarly Dh 368; or literally from Brahmanical sources, particularly VS I.5 and ŚB I.9.3.23, cf. AB VII.24, and ŚB III.9.4.2 ("The Devas are the truth and men untruth").

ahaṃkāra. Ud 70, "Those who give ear to the notion 'I am the doer' (*ahaṃkāra*), or are captivated by the notion 'Another is the doer' (*paraṃkāra*), do not understand this matter, they have not seen the point": in A III.337, *attakāra* replaces *ahaṃkāra* and means the notion that "a self, or oneself, is the doer"; in S II.252 and parallel passages, it is a question of realizing that "there is no 'I' that does, no 'mine' that is the doer, no latent 'I am' (*ahaṃkāra-mamaṃkāra-[asmi-]mānānusayā na honti*),"

---

dharmakāya, but only of *sambhogakāya* or *nirmāṇakāya*. In the same way the *dhamma* is *akāliko*, "not *ex tempore*," but like the *akāla* Brahman of MU VI.15, "without parts," and like the *amūrta* Brahman of BU II.3.1, "immortal."

[23] The contrast of true and false in Pāli is usually *saccam musam*, as in A II.25, an interesting context in which the relativity of "true and false," in the factual sense, is emphasized; the Tathāgata is not circumscribed by these systematic fences (*saṃvutesu* = *saṃvṛtteṣu*); Buddhas are not interested in "facts." In this connection it may be observed that "fact" and "fiction" are both equally what we "make of" our "experience."

whether subjective or objective. The sense makes it clear that *ahaṃkāra* is really a "Karmadhāraya" compound, and not literally the "ego-factor" or "I-maker," but the notion that "I am the doer." Nor can there be much doubt that the same applies in Brahmanical contexts where, just as in many other traditions, the notion that "I am the doer" (*kartā'ham iti*, BG III.27, where it is inasmuch as he so thinks that the self of the man is "deluded by *ahaṃkāra*") is scouted, cf. BG v.8, JUB I.5.2, etc. It may be observed that a verification of "not being the doer" can only be made by one who has attained the "station of not being anyone" (*ākiṃcaññāyatanam*). This "I am not the doer" is a metaphysical position, not a moral one, and must not be confused with the *akiriyavāda* heresy, that of the man who in Ud 45 "even whilst acting says that 'It is not I that am agent' (*yo c'āpi katvā na koromī'ti c'āha*)," and as in D I.53 that it is therefore a matter of indifference whether one does good or evil: so long as "I am who I am," "this man," I cannot lay down the burden of my responsibility so easily, but only at the end of the road, at world's end, and as one "born of God," and no longer "myself," am I "not under the law" (Gal. 5:18).

ahetuvāda: A *micchā diṭṭhi*, in A II.31, S III.73, M III.78, grouped with *akiriyavāda* and *natthikavāda*. Also in M I.408; and synonymous with *ahetukavāda* in S III.210. The denial of causality, i.e., *kamma* as the operation of mediate causes, cf. A I.173 ff., *pubbe katahetu* "by the effect of what was formerly done," is a denial of the very core of Buddhist doctrine expressed in the so-called confession *ye dhammā hetupabhavā* . . . , Vin I.405, and in countless inscriptions; a refusal to see things *yathā-bhūtam*, i.e., as effects only. The opposite (*hetuvāda* in M I.409 = *kammavāda* in A I.187), the Buddha is a "causalist" (*kammavādi*), that is to say a "determinist" or "fatalist" (in the Christian sense, where "fate lies in the created causes themselves" and "is the very disposition or series, i.e., order, of second causes," *Sum. Theol.* I.116.2; cf. Boethius, *De consolatione philosophiae* v.6), as regards all things that are *anattā*, i.e., the psycho-physical self composite of the five *khandhas*. It is traditional doctrine that "nothing in the world happens by chance" (Augustine, *De diversis quaestionibus* LXXXIII.34, approved by St. Thomas, *Sum. Theol.* I.116.1 *ad* 2); it is only the little-witted (*alpabuddhayaḥ*) who maintain that the world is not produced in any ordered sequence (*a-paraspara-bhūtam*, opposite of *yathā-bhūtam*), but is as it is only as the result of an exercise of free will (*kim anyat kāmahaitukam*), and this view is tantamount to a destruction of the world (*kṣayāya jagataḥ*, BG xvi.9). It may be pointed out that it is only on the basis of a world order (*κόσμος, ṛta*) that the notions of an omniscience and omniscient "Providence" (*prajñā* as in Ait. Up. v.3, and *passim*) are intelligible; if "nothing happens by chance" the *possibility* of a Providence necessarily follows. In other words, it is only from the *hetuvāda, kammavāda* point of view that we can understand AĀ ii.3.2, where the *avijñāna paśavaḥ* (= Buddhist *puthujjana*) are said to "become such as they are, they verily are born in accordance with Providence" (*etāvantī bhavanti, yathā prajñaṃ hi bhavanti*); BU iv.4.2, where the *savijñānam* (*śarīram*) is "taken hold of by knowledge and works, and antecedent Providence" (*taṃ vidya-karmaṇī samanvārabhete, pūrva-prajñā ca*); and BG xviii.14, where beyond the four mediate causes (*hetu*) of whatever it may be that a man undertakes there is reckoned as a fifth the "Divine" (*daivyam*, sc. *prajñānam*, and admirably rendered by Barnett as "Providence"). Our principal object in this section has been to bring out the consistency and interdependence of the Buddhist doctrines of *kamma* on the one hand and *sabbaññā* on the other.

akoṭita. In S ii.281, *ākoṭitāni paccākoṭitāni cīvarāni*, the most correct translation would be, I think, "garments of material *calendered* on both sides."

āsivisa. "Derivation uncertain" according to the PTS Dictionary. In any case, the occurrence of the word is an interesting survival, as is that of *ahi*, both words occurring together in the *Mahāvagga*, Vin i.24–25, where the *ahi-nāga* overcome by the Buddha in the Jaṭila fire-temple is described as *nāgarājā iddhimā āsiviso ghoraviso . . . makkham asahamāno*. The word occurs in AB vi.1, where the *sarparṣi* and *mantrakṛt* Arbuda is an *āśiviṣaḥ*, "basilisk"; and in Avestan as *azhi-visha* in Azhi-vishapa. In S iv.172, the *āsivisā* are the four great families of snakes, and represent the Four Great Elements. *Visha* is certainly "poison"; *āsi* is probably Skr. *āśi* or *āśis* (perhaps from *āśi* to "sharpen"), in the sense of "fang." *Āsivisa* would then mean "poison-fanged," either as adjective qualifying *ahi*, or as noun = snake.

itthattā. The expression *nāparam itthattāya*, constantly concluding the series *khīna jāti, vusitaṃ brahmacariyaṃ, kataṃ karaṇīyam* descriptive of the Arahat, is usually rendered either by "after this present world there is no beyond" or "there is no hereafter for him." These versions do not convey the meaning and, on the contrary, state what is precisely the *natthika* heresy, which consists in the denial of a beyond (see *natthika*). The meaning is that "there is no more such and suchness for him henceforth": it is not that there is "no beyond," but that it is improper (*akallam*) to make any affirmation or denial about the state of the Arahat hereafter, it may not even be said that he does not see or know (D II.68)[24]; his mode is modeless, we cannot say what he is because he is not any *what.* Far better is the rendering of *nāparam itthattāya* in M I.184 by "there is no more of what I have been"; this, which is true of every death and rebirth, is preeminently true of the thoroughly dead, *parinibbuto.*

Itthattā may be noted in A II.82, with reference to change of occupation: "Dying thence, he is born to this" (*tato cuto itthattam āgacchati*): in the same way D III.146, with reference to the Buddha's descent from the Tusita heaven, "dying thence he entered into this condition of things (*tato cuto itthattam āgato*)": *itthatta* as "thisness" being the finite aspect of *tathatta* "thatness," i.e., *nibbāna*; just as one "comes to *this*" state of affairs, so one "goes on one's way to *that*" (*tathattāya paṭipajjati*, D I.175 and S II.199).

Itthatta is thus synonymous with *bhavābhava* (becoming in a given way, or not becoming in a given way), but not with *bhavaṃ ca vibhavaṃ ca* (becoming and not becoming, i.e., existence and nonexistence). Thus in A II.10, *iti-bhavābhava . . . taṇhā* (thirst for becoming thus, or not becoming so)[25] is a hindrance, the variant *ittha-bhāvaññathābhāvam* = *saṃsāra* occurring in the verses: in Sn 752 it is precisely from this "being in this way or not being in some other way" that the nonreturner is unloosed (*nissito . . . ittha-bhāvaññathābhāvam saṃsāraṃ nātivattati*). *Itthatta* is then the condition characteristic of the world, of being in some given way and not being in some other way: one could not wish for a better definition of "things as they are in themselves."

uṭṭhāna. Literally "uprising." In M I.354, where it is late at night and the Buddha lies down to sleep in the lion-posture, we have *uṭṭhānasaññaṃ*

[24] In A I.148, the same craving is called "unseemly" (*na-paṭirūpam*, literally "informal," i.e., ugly).

[25] For example, being warm, or not being cold. *Abhava* does not imply any privation of existence but, like *saṃkhāya-vimutto*, implies a not being in any determined manner. *Vibhava* (in Pāli) is "privation of existence," but in Sanskrit "omnipresence"; *vibhū* corresponding to *vikrama*, cf. also *vibhūti* as "power." The two meanings are by no means so contrary as might appear; since only that which is not any thing amongst others can be omnipresent.

manasikaritvā, to be rendered by some such phrase as "intent upon the thought of rising (in the morning)." Where the same phrase occurs in Ud 84, the Buddha has lain down in the same posture on his death bed. In both cases he is fully conscious and aware. In both cases, insofar as he is "some one" by personal and family name, there is a death of one consciousness and the arising of another, in accordance with S I.135 (cited, s.v. *natthika*), yet there is this difference that in our second case, the "uprising" which the Buddha expects is not to be in the body; and this leads us to call attention to the parallel use of *utthāna* in PB XXV.10.19–21, where it means the cessation of a ritual operation and primarily that cessation which is in order when the sacrificers on their countercurrent (see *samudda*) journey have reached their goal. Similarly in ŚB IV.6.9.7, *sattrotthāna*. Here, of course, *utthāna* as a "standing up" contrasts with *sattra* as sacrificial "session." Now life itself is traditionally a sacrificial session (CU III.17). It is from this session that the Buddha looks forward to a "rising"; he is *not* expecting to "get up again" in the temporal and common sense of the words, but to leave the bodily operation forever. He will, in fact, enjoy the "final reward" (*uṭṭhāna-phalam*) of the *ugghaṭitaññu*; *uṭṭhāna* in this context (A XI.135) corresponding very closely to the *utthāna* of PB cited above.

udda. The PTS Dictionary expresses doubt whether *udda* may not be "beaver" rather than "otter." "Otter" is presumably the etymological equivalent. That *udda* is "otter" is placed beyond doubt by the *Dabbhapuppha Jātaka*, where *uddā* catch and eat fish; and by the Bhārhut relief (Alexander Cunningham, *The Stûpa of Bharhut*, London, 1879, pl. 46, fig. 2), inscribed Uda Jātaka, in which two animals, more like otters than beavers, are represented. Beavers are strict vegetarians and neither catch nor eat fish.

Uddāraka in J V.416 is also "otter."

uyyoga. Dh 235–237 is addressed to the man at death's door, for whom the messengers of Yama have come, and who is now come near to Yama. The words "Thou standest at the door of disjunction (*uyyoga-mukhe*), nor hast thou any provisions-for-the-way (*pātheyyam*, 'fare')" are surely reminiscent of KU II.9, where Naciketas stands at Death's (Mṛtyu, Yama) door unfed. *Uyyoga* (*udyoga*) is primarily and literally any severance of connections such as takes place at a departure, and so implies departure: thus in DhA XI.252, *uyyojesi* is simply "departed" (similarly *udyuj* in ŚB

IV.1.5.7, and the "Udyoga" Parvan of Mbh); although more specifically, when it is a question of death, *udyoga* is the opposite of that *saṃyoga* (BG XIII.26) by which the Knower of the Field and the Field itself are connected during life. *Udyuga* in AV V.22.11 may be simply "mortal sickness" in the same sense of "departure";[26] *udyuje* in AV VI.70.2, obscure to Whitney, is simply "walks off with," the sense in full being "as the elephant walks away with its mate, keeping close step (*padena padam udyuje*)," or quite literally, "separating (his) foot with her (*hastinyāḥ*) foot," i.e., striding side by side: *udyuj* with *padam* as object corresponding to *chid* in *pādacchida*.

kalyāṇa. The Dictionary fails to note the very important context, A I.149, in which the "Lovely Self (*kalyāṇam attānam*)" is distinguished from the "foul self (*pāpam attānam*)"; a distinction parallel to that of A I.249 between the "Great Self (*mahattā*)" and the "little self (*appātumo*)."

In "Friendship with the Lovely (*kalyāṇa-mittatā*)" and "Lovely Friend (*kalyāṇa mitto*)," I am tempted to see not merely a reference to environment and human relations, but at least an ultimate reference to the "Lovely Self" of A I.149, with which "Self" one can also be "unfriendly" (S I.57, *amitten-eva-attanā*; cf. BG VI.5–6, *bandhur ātmaiva ripur ātmanaḥ*). Of what other "friendship" could it have been said that "friendship, companionship, intimacy with the lovely" is not the half, but the whole of *Brahmacariya* (S V.2), or that such friendship is "a single condition (*ekadhammam*)" whereby the Aryan Eightfold Path can arise, or if arisen can be perfected (S V.37); or what other "lovely friend" could have been described as the chief external factor in the development of the seven "limbs of wisdom" (S V.101–102)?

It is certainly also the *kalyāṇattā, mahattā*—not the *pāpattā, appātumo*—that is meant by *attā* in S I.75 (= Ud 47) which, following BU II.4, IV.5, and IV.3.21 (*ātmakāma*), praises the *attakāmo*, a term that can be rendered by "self-lover" only if it be understood that all that "is not myself (*na me so attā*)" has been excluded. It is in this sense also that "a man, out of charity, ought to love himself more than he loves any other person . . . more than his neighbor" (*Sum. Theol.* II-II.26.4); and similarly Hermes, *Lib.* IV.6b, "love thyself, if thou wouldst have wisdom"; cf. Aristotle, *Nicomachean Ethics* IX.8, on the two meanings of "self-love." As Scott remarks (Hermes, II.145), "The man whom the Hermetist de-

[26] We speak of a dying man as "nearly gone" or in slang as a "goner."

scribes as 'loving himself' corresponds to Aristotle's σπουδαῖος, who . . . shows himself to be φίλαυτος in the sense that he seeks τὸ καλόν (= *kalyāṇam*) for himself . . . (and) develops that which is best and highest in himself by religious meditation" (i.e., *jhāna*).

kāmakāra. "To do what one will does not pertain to the common herd (*na kāmakāro hi puthujjanānam*, Sn 351)." This denial of free will to the natural man is paralleled in Vin I.13, and S III.66–67, where the proposition, that body, feeling, willing, etc. are *anattā*, not I, nor mine, nor myself (*na me so attā*), is proved by the consideration that were they myself or mine I should be able to say, "Let my body (or feeling, willing, etc.) be thus, or not thus," and it would be so, since nothing can be called I or mine absolutely unless I have full power over it. Sn 351 implies, of course, that a Tathāgata is *kāmakāro*, can do what he will; and that this is so is elsewhere made explicit in the lists of *iddhis*, beginning with the formula *aham bhikkhave yāvadeva ākaṇkhāmi*, "I, almsmen, whatever I will . . . ," S II.212, etc. The word does not occur in Brahmanical texts before the Epics, but is the same in effect as *kāmācārin*, "mover-at-will," recognizable in RV IX.113.9 *anukāmaṃ caraṇam*, and thereafter throughout the literature, e.g., JUB III.28.3, CU VIII.5.4, TU III.5.

kūṭa (as a weapon). *Kūṭa* in Mil 38 is not so much the ridge-pole of a house, but rather synonymous with its roof-plate (*kaṇṇikā*) to which all the rafters converge. This roof-plate, as we have often shown, represents in the cosmic architectural symbolism for which we have so many data in Indian literature, the Sun; and in microcosmic symbolism the *brahma-randhra*, or scapular foramen, whence the spirit departs when the dying man "gives up the ghost."[27] *Kūṭa* is then, like *kaṇṇikā*, a likeness

[27] For further references and detailed analysis see Coomaraswamy, "The Symbolism of the Dome" and "*Svayamātṛṇṇā*: Janua Coeli" [both in Volume I of this edition—ED.]. In connection with "The Symbolism of the Dome," in which I identified the Ṛbhus with the three dimensions of space, I should like to add that this interpretation is virtually proved by RV IV.33.5 where, of the three brothers, the eldest proposes to make of Tvaṣṭṛ's vessel two, the second three, and the youngest four (one dimension makes of a single point *two* points separated by a line, a second creates a plane or field of *tri*angulation, a third creates a real space that can be thought of as *four*-cornered). I ought not, however, to have said that Tvaṣṭṛ disliked what had been done: on the contrary, he approves (*panayat*, Sāyaṇa *astaut*, *angīcakāra*) and likes (*avenat*, Sāyaṇa *akāmayat, angīcakāra*) the fourfold arrangement. If the Ṛbhus are also the best friends of the solar Indra, it is likewise because in the beginning he is desirous of a space within which he and his followers may fulfill their purposes.

of the Sun, and it may be assumed that like the *kaṇṇikā*, the *kūṭa* may be a perforated form. We understand accordingly that when the Yakkha of J I.146 "holds a metal *kūṭa*, a mighty sun, of the size of a roof-plate" (*kaṇṇika-mattaṃ mahantam ādittam ayakūṭaṃ gahetvā*), he is wielding what may be a discus, but is more probably a mace in the familiar shape of a discoid head and provided with a handle passing through its central opening, just as the Axis Mundi passes through the Sundoor, and as the central axis of a house or smoke from the central hearth passes through the eye of its dome, or luffer. The same is to be understood in JB I.49.9, where a Season, an agent of the Sun, is represented as descending on a ray of light, "armed with a mace (*kūṭa-hastaḥ*)"; and in ŚB III.8.1.15, where "they do not strike the victim with a mace (*na kūṭena praghnanti*)."[28] On the other hand, in JB I.49.2 where "one should strike the victim on the *kūṭa* (*kūṭe hanyāt*)," it is the top of the head that is referred to, in accordance with the microcosmic analogy mentioned above.

gadha (for *gaḍha*?). In S V.41 the factors of the Eightfold Path are said to "plunge into the Deathless (*amato-gadha*), have their beyond in the Deathless (*amata-parāyana*), to have their last-end in the Deathless

[28] Eggeling mistranslates as though the reading had been *kūṭe*. Sāyana's comment, "seizing it by the horn" does not support Eggeling's, nor does it conflict with our own interpretation: one holds the victim by the horn in order to strike it with the mace.

In Oertel's discussion of *kūṭa* (JAOS, XIX, 1898, 114) he renders by "hammer," quite satisfactorily in the ŚB context and JB I.49.9, and only finds *kūṭe* in JB I.49.2 difficult because he forgets that *kūṭa* is the head or top of anything. *Kūṭa*, from *kuṭ*, to be bent or curved, is peak or top because the top of anything such as a mountain, house, or skull is either an angle or a dome, just as *kuṭi* or *kuṭī* as "cottage" is evidently so called because of its pointed or bent roof (*kuṭaṅka*): as the peak of the roof, *kūṭa* coincides with *kaṇṇikā*: and becomes a mace or hammer by analogy because the top of the roof, the aforesaid roof-plate, is actually a perforated disc through which the axis of the house passes (as the Axis Mundi passes through the Sun), the handle of the hammer corresponding to this axis. It follows, in the last analysis, that the mace or hammer as a weapon "derives," like other weapons, from the primordial *vajra*. The mace or hammer is appropriately held by the "Season" of JB I.49.9 because the Seasons are the "doorkeepers" of the Sun, JB I.18.2. It is in the same way that Indra's *vajra* becomes a *hammer* in the hands of Thor.

In connection with the equation *kūṭa* = *kaṇṇikā*, it may be remarked that the meanings of *kaṇṇikā* as "earring" and "pericarp of a lotus" are secondary, the primary sense, depending on the etymological connection of *karṇa* with *śṛṅga* and *aśri* (and Ger. *Ecke*), being that of "projection" or "corner" (as in J VI.330). Both *kūṭa* and *kaṇṇikā* are, then, as "point" of the roof, equivalents of *angulus* and *γωνία*, "cornerstone" as interpreted in my "Eckstein" in *Speculum*, XIV (1939).

(*amata-pariyosāna*)." The Dictionary does not have *gadha* (from Skr. *gāh*, to dive or plunge into), and treats *amatogadha* here and elsewhere as *amat'ogadha*, i.e., *-avagāḍha*. The metaphor is closely related to that of rivers reaching the Sea = Nibbāna (see *samudda*): and corresponds to Eckhart's "Plunge in: this is the drowning" ("in the bottomless sea of the Godhead"). The distinction of a drowning in the Upper Waters from a drowning in the Nether Waters is, of course, well known; the latter corresponds to the shipwreck en route in S IV.179–80.

gavakkha. Not in PTS Dictionary. In *Eastern Art*, III (1931), 195, I supposed that no reference for a Pāli *gavakkha*, corresponding to Skr. *gavākṣa* (e.g., at Mhv II.36) and Prakrit *gavekkha*, "bull's-eye window," could be cited. The word occurs, however, in Mhv IX.15, 17.

cetiya. The PTS Dictionary omits to mention that *cetiya* is by no means necessarily a *thūpa*, but in fact more often a sacred tree. The definition of the three classes of *cetiyas* in the *Kālingabodhi Jātaka* (J IV.228) should have been cited. Cf. Coomaraswamy, *Elements of Buddhist Iconography*, 1935, and "The Nature of Buddhist Art" [in Vol. I of this edition—ED.]; B. C. Law, "Cetiya in the Buddhist Literature" in *Studia Indo-Iranica* (1931), pp. 42–48; and V.R.R. Dikshita, "The Origin and Early History of Caityas" in *Indian Historical Quarterly*, XIV (1938), 440–51. The suggestion that root *cit*, to consider, as well as root *ci*, to build up, enters into the meaning of the word *caitya*, *cetiya*, has been made independently by Dikshita and myself, on the basis of such texts as RV VI.1.5, where Agni is *cetyaḥ* (from *cit*), and ŚB VI.2.3.9, where the courses of the Fire-Altar are "*citayaḥ*" (from *ci*) because they were foreknown in accordance with the injunction "*cetaya-dhvam*" (from *cit*), and the fact that it was *cetayamānā* (from *cit*) that the builders foreknew the courses, and because the *cetiya* is not always in fact a thing "built up," but is always a support of contemplation (*caitya*, as if from *cit*).

jhāna, *samādhi*. *Jhāna* is always "contemplation," *jhāyin* (like *dhīra*) always "contemplative." C.A.F. Rhys Davids' and F. L. Woodward's usual rendering by "musing" or "quiet musing" enormously weakens the proper values of these terms.[29] Even less appropriate (and it may be added, rather

[29] It is regrettable that C.A.F. Rhys Davids has not consistently maintained the position so well expressed in *Kindred Sayings*, I.68, n. 2, where she explains *bhāvana* as "constructive work (in contemplation, of course) . . . contemplation

"early Victorian") is Lord Chalmers' rendering of *jhāyino* by "those who woo Reverie" and of *jhāyī* by "Reverie" (Sn 719, 638). Contemplation, a word of precise meaning in the corresponding European contexts, is anything but "day-dreaming." *Jhāna* tends towards and reaches its end in *samādhi*.[30]

Samādhi is etymologically and quite literally "synthesis," and is generally best translated thus in both Buddist and Sanskrit contexts: *dharaṇa*, *dhyāna*, and *samādhi* corresponding to the *consideratio*, *contemplatio*, and *excessus* or *raptus* of Richard of St. Victor and other Christian contemplatives; *excessus* and *raptus* imply in the one case a "going out of oneself" and a being "taken out of oneself," and in either case a consequent "being in the spirit" and thus one's real "Self," but of these two terms the latter is unsuited to the Indian contexts, *yoga* being an "active" rather than a "passive" or "mystic" discipline.

In *samādhi* there is no longer any object of contemplation; in *avitakka samādhi* one is what one knows; one knows indeed, but it is not a second thing, other than oneself, that one knows; there is *adaequatio rei et intellectus*, as *in divinis*.[31] The synthetic values implied in the common expression *ajjhataṃ* (*adhyātmaṃ*) *susamāhito*, "completely Self-centred,"[32] are clearly brought out in A II.29 (and corresponding AĀ III.2.1), where all the powers of the soul (the *kusalā dhammā*) are referred to as converging to one point, in which they are unified, just as the rafters of a dome converge towards and are at-oned in the roof-plate. It is upon *jhāna* and *samādhi* that the possession of *iddhis*, which are strictly speaking "powers" of the Spirit and not of the individual self, altogether depends.

---

means both elimination . . . and . . . creation." I am appalled by Rhys Davids' "Dhyāna was not meditation; it was the making attention a *tabula rasa* for psychic communication. It was the later monk who converted this into mental hypnosis," etc. (*New Indian Antiquary*, II, 1939, 46).

[30] In S I.48 a Deva suggests that "He is wake who 'awakens' contemplation (*yo jhānam abuddhi buddho*)"; the Buddha assents, with the reservation "Yes, if they be perfectly synthesized, or unified (*sammā te susamāhitā*)."

[31] Cf. A V.7, where in *avitakka samādhi* the Comprehensor is not aware of anything, and yet not without awareness (*asaññī*). This is the position so fully stated in BU IV.3; although, curiously enough, D III.127 pours contempt on the saying *passam na passati*, the very words of BU IV.3.23, *na paśyati paśyan*. D III.127 is a bad example of the tendency of the Pāli texts to pervert the meanings of Sanskrit logoi in order to gain the victory over a straw man.

[32] In the sense that "God is in all things self-intent," "sees only himself," and that the divine manner of knowing is "not by means of any object external to the knower."

Tathāgata. In support of the view that the reference of this word is to the Buddha's advent (cf. my note in *BSOS* IX) may be cited A II.23 where the Buddha is "Tathāgata" by virtue of his omniscience, infallibility, and because "as he teaches, so he does" (*yathā-vādī . . . tathā-kārī*, as also in Sn 357): in Sn 430 and Itiv, p. 122, the Buddha is *tathā-vādī*. *Tathā-kāri* and *tathā-vādi* are parallel to *tathāgata*; *tathāgata*, then, from this point of view, would be "He who came thus saying and thus doing." Sn 957 has *buddhaṃ . . . tādim . . . āgatam*, "Buddha come hither in such a fashion." S IV.195, *yathāgatamaggo* = Ariyan Eightfold Path, is suggestive. DhA III.226, *tusitā . . . āgato*, is another sense in which he is "thus-come." *Lalita vistara*, ch. 26 (Lefmann, p. 423), has *dharmacakraṃ pravartitaṃ*, *yasya pravartanāt*, *tathàgata ity ucyate*, "It is because of his turning of the Wheel of the Law (or Principial Wheel) that he is called 'Tathāgata' "; and this is confirmatory of the *tathā-vādī tathā-kārī* explanation, since it is precisely the Dhamma that he teaches and the Dhamma that he "does." The text is no doubt an echo of D III.135 (= A II.24), where all that the Buddha has said, from the time of his Awakening to that of his Decease, "all that is just so and not otherwise, and therefore is he called Tathāgata. For, O Cunda, what the Tathāgata says, he does, and what he does is what he says (*sabbaṃ taṃ tath'eva hoti, no aññathā. Tasmā tathāgato'ti vuccati. Yathāvādī, Cunda, tathākārī, yathākārī tathāvādī*)."[33] So much for *tathā*. *Āgata* occurs so often in connection with the Buddha's coming, as to make the word division *tathā-gata* very implausible; that *āgata* is likewise often found in connection with Agni affords additional evidence (*āgamana* is precisely "advent"). The *Tathāgata* is the "Thus-come" with reference to any or all of the "ways" of his coming, but especially with reference to his advent as one who "practiced what he preached." Cf. *sāgatam* (*su-āgatam*), "Welcome," in *sāgataṃ bhante bhagavato*, D I.179 = M I.481; not to be confused with *sugata*, "well-faring" or "well-fared," a common epithet of the Buddha.

tejanam. I have long had in mind to compile a vocabulary of the Sanskrit and Pāli terminology of archery. The two most difficult words are *kulmala* and *tejana*. Pāli contexts make the meaning of the latter word

[33] The concept is Vedic, cf. RV IV.33.6, where (with reference to the Ṛbhus) *satyam ūcur nara evā hi cakruḥ*. The perfect correspondence of thought, word, and act is the Tathāgata's integrity.

The Buddhist "Go thou and do likewise" may be cited from J II.130, "Those who do what the Buddha has enjoined, follow the path of fortune (*ye ca kāhanti . . . buddhena desitaṃ, sotthiṃ pāram gamissanti = nibbānaṃ gacchanti*)."

sufficiently clear. The PTS Dictionary emphasizes the sense of *tij* "to be sharp" and makes ***tejanam*** the point or shaft of an arrow or the arrow itself: we shall see, however, that it is always a "heating" that is directly referred to and a "straightening" that is implied. We first consider the Sanskrit contexts. ***Tejanam*** is a factor in the make-up of an arrow, but not any concrete part of the arrow. In RV IX.111.22 the fletcher (here simply *karmāra*, "wright") plies his trade equipped with "dry reeds, feathers of birds, stones,[34] and fire" *dyubhiḥ*, i.e., literally, "with flames," and as Sāyaṇa comments *tejanārthābhiḥ*, "for the purpose of heating" (hence as in RV I.53.4 etc., and in Grassmann's sense 15 for *div*). These four requisites correspond to the four factors of an arrow in AB I.25, where Soma is the shaft (*śalya*), Varuṇa the feathers, Agni the point (*anīka*), and Viṣṇu the ***tejanam*** (as he is also in TS VI.2.3.1).[35] In AB III.26, where the arrow is resolved into its equivalents, the ***tejanam*** becomes the blindworm (*andhāhi*). AV VI.57.1 is a protection from the arrow "of a single firing and a hundred shafts (*ekatejanāṃ śataśalyām*)," by which we understand a flight of however many arrows proceeding from any one source (as many rays proceed from one sun), and more especially a protection from sunstroke. In AV VI.49.1, where "the ape devours the *tejanam*" (whatever may be meant), there is not necessarily any reference to an arrow.[36] In AV V.18.8, the teeth are metaphorically arrows and are *tapasābhidigdhāḥ*, literally "well smeared by heating," and *ibid.* 15, *iṣur iva digdhā . . . sā brāhmaṇasyeṣur ghorā*, "and like the arrow smeared, so is that arrow of the Brahman terrible." It has generally been presumed that *digdha* in this and similar contexts (BD V.133, explaining RV VI.75.15 *ālākta . . . iṣvai*; ŚB XIV.9.4.8; R II.30.23, etc.) means "smeared with poison," and this is no doubt correct in some cases; in M I.429, *sallena . . . savisena gālhapalepanena* is certainly "with an arrow heavily

[34] Taken together, reference to stone arrowheads here, and to arrowheads of bronze in RV VI.75.15, implies a "chalcolithic" culture.

[35] In ŚB III.4.4.14–15, where it is a question of the making of the *vajra* (incidentally, the archetypal weapon, from which the sword, hammer or mace, and arrow are all "derived"), Viṣṇu is (1) *kulmala*, and (2) that which lies "between" Agni and Soma as between day and night. Without discussing *kulmala* at length, I will only say that the equation *kulmala* = *sandhi* implied here agrees with the meaning of "fastening" (of point to shaft) which I find for *kulmala* as a factor in the makeup of an arrow, and with the gloss on AV III.25.2, rendered by Whitney "thing to fasten (*saṃśleṣa-*) tip to shaft,"—not, however, "like a ferrule," but either a cement or glue, or as in AB III.26 a binding with "sinews" (*snāvāni*), as also in M I.429 *nahāru*.

[36] (Vṛṣā-) kapi, perhaps a prototype of Hanuman, hence = Vāyu, into whom the Fire (and all other "half-deities") returns when it goes out, being thus swallowed up.

smeared with poison," but it will be seen that there are other ways and for other reasons that an arrow can be "smeared."

We can now take up the Pāli contexts. In M II.105 and Dh 80 and 145, "Irrigators lead the water, fletchers straighten their shafts (*usukārā namayanti tejanam*), carpenters shape (*namayanti*) the wood, the learned train themselves (*attānaṃ damayanti paṇḍitā*)." It will be observed that *nam* is not here literally to "bend," but to "sway" in the sense of "control" or "manage," and give the proper form to any material.[37] "Fletchers straighten their shafts" is a legitimate but not a literal translation of what is really "fletchers control their fire"; and this is in some respects a better rendering from the Buddhist point of view, according to which it is precisely by the proper control of the fire of life that the "self" is rectified. What is important in the present connection, however, is the connection of a word implying heat with a metaphor that has all to do with a putting straight, an ordering of things in the way they should go, that is to say, straight to their end.

We can now conclude with the text of J VI.66 and the corresponding representation of the fletcher at work, at Bharhut (Cunningham, pl. 44, fig. 2). The "moral" is one of single-mindedness; the fletcher sees better with one eye closed, sighting along the arrow to see whether it is straight, and disregarding what might be simultaneously seen by the other eye, were it open. The text reads, *tasmin samaye usukāro aṅgārakapalle usuṃ tāpetvā kañjikena temetvā ekaṃ akkhiṃ nimīletvā eken'olokento ujuṃ karoti*, "Just then a fletcher, heating an arrow over a fire-pan, and moistening it with paste, had one eye closed and looking with the other was straightening the arrow." It should now be clear how it is that a heating (*tejanam* or *tapas*) is essential to the make-up of an arrow, but not a concrete part of an arrow. It appears also that an arrow may be smeared with a view to temporary softening and not with poison: the expressions *tapasābhidigdhā* and *digdhā* in AV V.18.8, 15 imply, then, rather a straightening than a poisoning of the Brahman's verbal shafts, which are "terrible," not as being venomous, but inasmuch as they fly "straight to the point." There is no evidence that *tejanam* ever refers to the sharpening of an arrow.[38] It is often possible to render *tejanam* literally by "heat" or "fire." A rendering by shaft or arrow is possible if we assume the series

[37] *Nam* is found already in AV III.25.2, where *śalyām . . . tām susaṃnatāṃ kṛtvā* is rendered by Whitney "having made that arrow well-straightened."

[38] An arrow is "whetted" literally or metaphorically by an incantation (*brahmasaṃśitā*, RV VI.75.16) or by "worship" (*upāsanisitam*, Muṇḍ. Up. II.2.4); just as a sword is "whetted" by an invocation of the Gale, ŚB I.2.4.5–7.

of associated ideas, heat straightening, straight, and straight-going (*ṛjīta*, RV VI.75.12; *ṛju-ga*, cited from a lexikon as a kenning for "arrow"): it is, in fact, in this way that in RV I.110.5, *tejanena* (in spite of Sāyaṇa's *tikṣaṇena śastreṇa*) must mean "with a (straight) rod," a rod compared to an arrow or "shaft" of light, *manus tejanena* here corresponding to *raśminā . . . mame* in RV VIII.25.18; that *tejanam* in AV I.2.4 (where it is the Axis Mundi, *diva-skambha*) is "fiery *pillar*"; and the *tejanam* in M II.105 = *śalyām*, "arrow," in AV III.25.2, as can be clearly seen from the use of root *nam* in both contexts.

thūpa. The original meaning of *stūpa*, top, peak, head, dome, etc., may be noted in D III.117, where Nāthaputta having died, the Nigaṇṭha doctrine and discipline are "broken-headed and without protection" (*bhinna-thūpe appaṭisaraṇe*). In J VI.117, a *vimāna*, palace, is described as *pañca-thūpa*, "five-domed," a meaning and reference found in the Dictionary, s.v. *thūpika*. But it makes no reference to *thūpikā* of Mhv XXXI.13, which here appears to be a noun meaning "dome"—the dome, or spire, of a *pāsāda*, palace. The Dictionary knows of *thūpa* only as "tomb" and "tope" (*dhātu-gabbha*). The Buddhist tomb is *dhātu-gabbha* by function, and *thūpa* by its domed form, which corresponds to that of the cranium.

Dikkhita. The purpose of the present article is to inquire whether or not the regular Buddhist ordination can be equated with initiation (*dīkṣā*).[39] The root occurs in Pāli only very rarely, in *dikkhita* = *dīkṣita*. In S I.226, a prophet (*isi* = *ṛṣi*; the word is also used of the Buddha and of Buddhist monks) is *cira-dikkhita*, "long initiated," explained by the Commentator as *cira-pabbajita*,[40] "long ordained as a Pilgrim." *Cira-*

[39] It should be needless to say that "ordination" as such must be distinguished from "initiation" as such: the former, however significant, is merely the conferring of a specific "character" and comparable to the imposition of a new "form" on already "formed" material; the latter is always a second birth, the birth of another and new man, not a *re*formation of but a *trans*formation of the man that was before. It does not follow that what has been called an ordination (in translation) may not in fact have been an initiation. In any case the Buddhist ordination is not the imposition of a "priestly" character; the monk is not a "priest." For a discussion of Buddhist ordination see *Psalms of the Brethren*, index, s.v. [cf. Theragāthā —ED.].

[40] The root meaning of *pabbajati* is to "go forth," "go into exile," and of the causative *pabbājeti*, to "be exiled" or "banished," hence technically to abandon the indoor and household life and adopt that of the "unroofed" Pilgrim. The Pilgrim carries his own roof (umbrella) about with himself.

pabbajita contrasts, of course, with *navo acira-pabbajita*, "recently ordained a Pilgrim," in other contexts, both terms being of common occurrence. J v.138–39, reading *cira-dakkhita*, refers to "prophets" (*isayo*) in the following of the Bodhisattva Sarabhanga-Jotipāla, who is unquestionably a solar principle; and this spelling is of interest because it preserves the form of the root *dakṣ*, "to be able," the basic value of *dīkṣita*, "initiated," being precisely "enabled."

Taking now for granted the reader's knowledge of the significance of initiation in India and elsewhere,[41] we shall argue that *pabbajita* has really the value *dīkṣita*, and *a fortiori* that *upasampadā* has that of a more advanced initiation. The first ordinations were necessarily made by the Buddha himself, who used the significant words "Come, mendicant monk (*ehi-bhikkhu*)," reminiscent of the welcome, "Come (*ehi*)" addressed by the Sun to the would-be entrant who has rightly answered the question "Who art thou?" (JUB III.14.5, cf. Rūmī, *Mathnawī* I.3602–3). If designations such as "Kinsman of the Sun" (*ādicca-bandhu*) are to be taken literally, as they must be for all those who are not misled by the "historical" form of the "Buddha legend," this is sufficient to show that such ordinations were really initiations and invitations, in the etymological senses of the words: the historical Buddha is surely an euhemerisation of the Vedic Agni,[42] who is likewise "awakened" at dawn (*uṣar-budh*) and is the "deity of the initiate" (*agni vai dīkṣitasya devatā*, *TS* III.1.3). Nor is anything changed in principle by the delegation of the power of ordination or initiation to others (who are constantly referred to as "Sons of the Buddha," e.g., S I.192), such a transmission being equally necessary and regular in the most unquestionably orthodox conditions, and indeed inevitable if there is to be a transmission of a veritable gnosis from generation to generation.

The original ordinations had conferred *pabbajjā* (the status of "Pilgrim") and *upasampadā* ("full attainment," and almost literally the state of being an "Adept") simultaneously. After the delegation of power we find that both are still conferred together, but by a quorum of the mendi-

[41] See the comprehensive series of articles on "Initiation" published by René Guénon in recent volumes of *Études traditionelles* [see René Guénon, *Aperçus sur l'initiation*, 2nd ed. (Paris, 1953), in which the articles cited by Coomaraswamy are collected—ED.]. We hope to publish on some future occasion some of the principal Indian texts in which the subject is treated.

[42] Cf. Émile Sénart, *La Légende du Bouddha* (Paris, 1875), p. 425: "[le] trône du Bouddha substitue à l'ancien autel brahmanique; [le Bouddha] perpétue sous une forme nouvelle la présence du feu sacré."

cant monks, upon those who having been tonsured and robed, repeated thrice the formula of "Taking Refuge." We find then that *upasampadā* can only be conferred on the recommendation of a teacher, upon some younger monk who has come to him as a pupil. The teacher is called *upajjhāya*, literally "one who is gone up near to," the pupil a *saddhivihārika*, literally "associate resident," i.e., who lives with the teacher in daily intimacy. The relation is formally paternal; the pupil renders the teacher personal service. Before a teacher can receive any monk as pupil, he must himself have been fully ordained, must have been an "Adept," for at least ten years. Under these conditions he may, when he sees fit, propose the pupil as a candidate for *upasampadā* to the monastic assembly; the pupil, for his part, formally requesting the assembly to "extract me" (*ullumpatu*[43] *mam*), suggestive of the Brāhmaṇa formula "as a snake (*ahi*) might be freed from (*nirmucyeta*) its slough, or as one might draw (*vivṛhet*) an arrow from a reed (*muñjāt*), so is he liberated (*nirmucyate*) from all evil" (JB II.134, etc.).[44] A monk thus fully ordained or initiated might after ten years himself receive pupils. The succession of such Vinaya teachers from Upāli to Mahinda is given in the *Dīpavaṃsa*. All this has the appearance of the regular system of transmission from spiritual father to spiritual son (*guru-paramparā*) in generation after generation, but with a specific adaptation to the more communal character of the Buddhist order of

[43] ŚB III.1.4.1 describes *dīkṣā* as an *audgrabhaṇa* or "lifting up" (from this world to that of the gods), and it is to this expression that the Buddhist designation of ordination as an *ullumpana* seems to correspond. A. Préau calls my attention to the fourteenth stanza of the *Paramārtha-sāra* of Abhinavagupta, where it is said that it is the function of the mantras, "by their conducive nature (*anugraha-svabhāvāt*) to extricate animal-men (*paśūn uddhartum*)."

[44] This well-known series of similes recurs in M II.17 (and D I.77, cf. I.34), "I have shown my disciples the means (*paṭipannā*, with reference to contemplative practices already listed) whereby they can create (*abhinimminanti*, *abhi-* implying a super- or transformation, where the simple *nimminanti* would mean only a formation) out of this body (the aforesaid *kāyo rūpī cātummahābhūtiko*, the formal body based on the four elements) another formal body of intellectual substance (*aññam kāyaṃ . . . rūpiṃ manomayam* = D I.34 *añño attā dibbo rūpī manomayo*), complete with all its limbs and members, and with transcendental faculties (*abhin-indriycam*, but in D I.34 and I.77 *ahīnindriyo*, not deprived of any faculty). It is just as if a man should draw out (*pabbāheyya* = *pravṛhet*) an arrow (*isīkam*) from a reed (*muñjamhā*), or a sword from its scabbard, or a snake (*ahim*) from its slough. He is aware that arrow and reed are two different things, that sword and scabbard are different things, that snake and slough are different things; he is aware that the arrow is just what has been extracted from (*pabbāḷhoprabṛdha*) the reed, etc." With this body of intellectual substance he enjoys omniscience (*abhiñña*) and is a Mover-at-will as far as the Brahma-heavens (*yāva brahmalokā pi kāyena vasaṃ vattenti*).

"Pilgrims (*pabbajita*)," who from the earliest times were thought of as a "congregation" (*saṃgha*) rather than as solitaries.

There are also internal evidences. Ordination involved the abandonment of one's own and of one's family name (*nāma-gotta*)—"just as when rivers reach the sea, they abandon their name and descent (*pajahanti nāma-gottāni*) . . . ," the Pilgrim now becoming a "Son of Buddha" (*sakya puttiya*, Ud 55). Ordination is, in fact, a second birth: we find together with *yato jāto*, "from the time I was born," such expressions as *yato ariyāya jātiyā jāto*, "from the time I was born of the Aryan kin" (*Majjhima Nikāya*, II.103), i.e., as a *sakya puttiya*, a "Buddha-son," and even more explicit the passage in which Kassapa speaks of his perfect mastery and calls himself a "natural son of the Blessed One, born of his mouth, born of the Dhamma, fashioned by the Dhamma, and an heir of the Dhamma (S II.221).[45]

[45] In the *Aggañña Sutta* (D III.84), where these formulae recur, it is explained that they are applicable only to those whose faith (*saddhā*) in the Buddha is settled, radical, well-grounded, and such that they cannot be robbed of it. The Sutta as a whole is an admirable description of the Fall and Regeneration of man, though at D III.81–82 it affords a good example of the childish level to which the Pāli texts can descend for controversial purposes; here the Brahman claim to be "Natural sons of Brahmā, born of his mouth, etc." is ridiculed, and refuted(!) by the argument that Brahmans, like other men, are visibly born of woman, despite the identification of Buddha with Brahmā (or Brahman) at III.84. The intention of the Pāli text is evidently to distinguish the Brahman by human birth from the Brahma = Arhat who becomes a son of God by adoption; but in order to make this distinction the real significance of RV x.90 is perverted. Equally childish is the argument of the *Tevijja Sutta* (D I.235 ff.) that the Vedas are futile because of the different "paths" that are taught in their schools; the Brahman protagonist rightly maintains that all alike are straight roads to Brahmā (i.e., Prajāpati), but the Buddha is made to say that this is ridiculous, because the Brahmans themselves do not claim to have seen Brahmā or to know where he is—an argument of really astonishing puerility. In the same way S I.61–62, where it is well said that "World's end is within you," but it is pretended that the Rohita of AB VII.15 did not know this and had thought that World's End could be reached by an actual locomotion. Or again D III.127, where the meaning of *passaṃ na passati* (= BU IV.3.23 *na paśyati paśyan vai*) is distorted. Passages such as these show clearly enough that the Pāli canon includes much that is of purely human, and all-too-human origin. It is in spite of such passages that a fairly thorough study of the Pāli texts has led us to believe that the early Buddhist *dhamma* is essentially orthodox and only superficially heterodox. We believe that the Buddha meant what he said when he affirmed that he "had found the ancient path and followed it" (ŚB II.106, reflecting BU IV.4.8), viz. that "ancient" (path) which the Brahmans of old are said to have remembered (S IV.117) but which others have forgotten (D III.81–82), the "primordial walk with Brahman" of D III.40. We believe that the Buddha came "not to destroy but to fulfill the law."

Nor is it by any means anyone or everyone that can be ordained. As an example of intellectual qualification there can be cited the case of the "Long-haired Fire-men" (*aggikā jaṭilā*, i.e., Brahman ascetics whose deity was Agni) who could be given *upasampadā* immediately, without the usual four months' probation (*parivāsa*) because they were already *kammavādino* and *kiriyavādino*,[46] i.e., believed in the "causal origination" of all phenomena whatever, and at the same time that there is an "ought to be done," to be contrasted with an "ought not to be done," or "savoir-faire" to be contrasted with a "laissez-faire" (the opposites of these positions are well known "heresies" from the Buddhist point of view). We need not cite here from the *Cullavagga* the long list of disqualifications, but only say that these may be moral, intellectual, or physical, the physical disqualifications including a great variety of deformities and diseases.[47]

Where, as in Burma, it is the rule for everyone to become a monk for a limited time, or when a Buddhist king is temporarily ordained,[48] it would appear that this temporary retreat from the world corresponds

[46] The opposites of these positions are well-known "heresies" (*miccha-diṭṭhi*) from the Buddhist point of view, as they must be from that of any orthodox teaching. Expressed in Christian terms, *kammavāda* is the doctrine that all "accidents" are causally originated, nothing whatever happening by chance or because of any direct divine intervention; *kiriyavāda* that there is an "ought-to-be-done" and an "ought-not-to-be-done (*akiriya*)." It should be noted, however, that *akiriyavāda* as a heretical doctrine implies that there is "not-an-ought-to-be-done" and corresponds to the "amoralism" with which the Amaurians were charged in the Middle Ages. In the same connection it should be observed that while the moral values are, if anything, overemphasized in Buddhism (a fact closely connected with its especially Kṣatriya character), it is not pretended that right conduct is of more than a necessary dispositive value in relation to the final attainment: as is clearly shown in the Parable of the Raft (M 1.135), where conduct is a "boat" to be abandoned when the "Farther Shore" has been reached, and in Dh 267, where those who have rejected virtue and vice alike (*yo ca puññañ ca pāpaṃ bāhetvā*) can rightly be called "walkers with God in this world" and "mendicant-monks."

[47] *Nāgas* (serpents of partly human character but retaining ophidian characteristics) are disqualified, even though they may be moved by the best intentions. To this corresponds the "folklore" principle, that mermaids cannot as such acquire a "soul," but must be "married" to a human being, at the same time losing their scaly tails, which are changed into feet, so that no trace of their ophidian origin remains. In reality, of course, it is always a Solar Hero that "marries" the mermaid (*nāginī*), and to this situation (that of Apālā in relation to Indra) can be applied the words of Donne, "Nor ever chaste unless Thou ravish me."

[48] For the cases of Asoka and of the Chinese Emperor Wu-ti, both of whom took orders without effective abdication, see Vincent Smith, *Early History of India* (Oxford, 1924), p. 168.

exactly to that of the Vedic Sacrificer (*yaja-māna*)[49] who devotes ***himself*** and, being initiated (*dīkṣita*), is during the operation no longer himself, no longer "this man," ***un tel***, until when the operation is relinquished he returns to himself, from the Truth to the Falsehood, and becomes once more "who he really is" in the worldly sense, So-and-so by name and lineage.

Buddhist ordination, we conclude, has not only the appearance but also the significance of an initiation. The only possible alternative would be to regard it as a pseudo- or even counter-initiation. The latter alternative is manifestly out of the question:[50] nor can the former be entertained by anyone who accepts the texts in their entirety, in which the Buddha is described as more than man and as of Agni's and solar lineage.

natthika. Literally a "There-is-not-ist," or a little more freely, "Nothing-morist," the term is used in Sanskrit and Pāli alike to mean approximately what is meant by our "skeptic," "materialist," "pragmatist," or "atheist." The man who maintains "there is no other world (***natthi paro loko***)"[51] despite the fact that "there is assuredly another world" (***santaṃ***

[49] In this connection it is worthy of note that *yajamāna* is a form that may be either reflexive or passive, and thus means both "Sacrificer" and "Sacrificed." That the Sacrificer who is also a Comprehensor of the ritual is really a "sacrificer of himself (*ātma-yajñī*)" is repeatedly affirmed (e.g., ŚB x.2.6.13–14), and this is also true of the Christian sacrifice (the Mass).

[50] The Purāṇas, in which the Buddha is reckoned an *avatar* of Viṣṇu, consider that he was born as a deceiver in order to lead astray the enemies of the Devas. We are more inclined to think that (as in Mark 4:11–12) the Buddhist *dhamma* is presented in a form that could easily be misunderstood (cf., for example, D III.40, where it is described as "hard to be understood by you who are of different views, another tolerance, other tastes, other allegiance, and other training"), and that it could have enlightened some ("to whom it is given to know the mystery of the kingdom of God") and deluded others ("them that are without, lest at any time they be converted, and their sins should be forgiven them"). I have known a modern scholar to admit that "temperament and training" alike prevented his acceptance of traditional points of view. The Indian paṇḍit rarely attempts to correct the European scholar who may entertain what he knows is a false view: one has to ask the right question before one gets the right answer. The Buddhist *dhamma,* in the same way, like many other "secret doctrines," protects its own "secret." What is in any case highly significant is the synthesis of Śaiva and Bauddha cults that is so conspicuous in the Indian Middle Ages.

[51] Cf. J v.228, where the *ucchedavādī* ("annihilationist," "materialist") is defined as one who maintains that "there is no such thing as going from this world to another; this world is cut off" (*ito paraloko-gata nāma natthi, ayaṃ loko ucchijjati*). In J vi.225 the same heresy is supported by the argument "for who has ever come

yeva, kho pana paraṃ lokam)[52] and as against "Arhats versed in the other world" (*paraloka-viduno*) is "a bad-liver, a man of false view (heretic), a denier" (*dussīlo . . . micchā-diṭṭhi natthikavādo*, M I.403, cf. A II.31 and S III.73). *Natthika* in S I.96 does not mean "empty of hand" or "one who refuses alms"(!) but a "denier" as above: we cannot understand the translator's comment "we find no parallel to this term." In S II.17 *natthitā*, "Not-ism," and *atthitā*, "Is-ism," are the two extreme views of denial and affirmation which are popularly maintained with respect to what may be called the question of the reality or persistent identity of the world or of the individual, in which connection it is further debated whether it is the same individual who in this life or in another both acts and reaps the reward of acts, or whether one acts and another reaps. The Buddha teaches a Middle Way[53] of "Causal Origination" (*paṭiccasamuppāda*), according to which "things" are to be regarded without any "in themselves"[54] and only as phenomena (*rūpa*) that have arisen in such and such a way (*yathā-bhūtam*, "as-become"), viz. in an ordered causal sequence. The gist of this doctrine (stated again very clearly in M I.421) has been admirably summarized by the translator in *Kindred Sayings* [= S]

back thence?" (*ko tato hi idhāgato*), an appeal to the common experience that the dead do not return (as stated also in D II.226 and J II.242 and in accordance with the normal doctrine of the Brāhmaṇas and Upaniṣads, ŚB II.6.1.6, XIII.8.4.12, etc., and CU VIII.2.3).

[52] Cf. Ud 80, *atthi ajātam abhūtam akatam asaṃkhatam*, "There *is* an Unborn, Unbecome, Not-made, Without-composition."

[53] Boethius, *Contra Evtychen* 7, maintains that faith holds a middle course between contrary heresies. Fact and fiction alike are "what we *make* of" our observations; neither is an absolute, or more than a useful *façon de parler*, neither are any but statistical proofs available for the recognition of fact or fiction. Truth itself is transcendent with respect to fact and fiction alike, as is Goodness with respect to virtue and vice, and Beauty with respect to lovely and unlovely.

[54] No Buddhist would deny that appearances appear. If our apprehension of these appearances can be corrected by closer observation, it may serve practical ends, but the better observation is still only the actual or theoretical registration of an appearance (shape), and so on *ad infinitum*. This will apply even if "things" are reduced to mathematical formulae, which are still "shapes." The question, "Is there a thing in itself?" is meaningless: we can only ask, "Is there a form corresponding to the matter (dimension or number)?" The traditional answer assumes the existence of such a form or idea of the thing, as its eternal reason; this is a "reality," but observe that we are now no longer dealing with a self-subsistent thing "in itself," but with the thing "in intellect" and consubstantial with this intellect. It is in this sense that the metaphysician is a "realist": popular and scientific "realism" (= philosophical "nominalism") coincides with "aestheticism" and "sentimentality."

II.22, note: "The subject of the resulting experience is himself the result of the causal experience, as much and as little identical as is, say, the tree with the seedling" (or the child with the man). For us today, whose view is animistic and whose interests are psychic rather than spiritual, and who think accordingly of a sentient identity as persisting through life or even after death,[55] this would be an "Is-ist" solution.[56] But for the Buddhist (as for Plato, *Symposium* 207DE; cf. Plutarch, *Moralia* 392[57]) this does not follow: the persistence of an identity even from day to day is not a "fact" but a merely "conventional truth"; the fact is that, as in the monkey parable of S II.95, "will, mind, knowledge (*cittam, mano, viññāṇam*, i.e., the whole mental personality), this every day and every night arises (*uppajjati*) as one thing and is destroyed (*nirujjhati*) as another," and as in the parable of the chariot,[58] S I.135, where the name of "essence" (*satta*) is said to be given only conventionally (*sammuccā*) to what is not really a simple substance, but an aggregate. In the same way at death "the soul and body that were in a previous becoming is destroyed without residue and another steps forward (*purimabhave nāma-rūpam asesaṃ niruddham, aññam uppannam*, Vis 413)," and it is a heresy to maintain that "*this* consciousness (*idaṃ viññāṇam*) concurs and migrates (*saṃdhāvati saṃsa-*

[55] Few if any materialists have attempted to disprove the immortality of the "soul" by adducing its manifest mutability, or by the argument that whatever has had a beginning in time must also end in time. That the scientist would rather disprove the spiritualist's "phenomena" than disprove the latter's interpretations of them is significant of the former's real position. For the metaphysician the phenomena, however well attested, are of no more interest than any other phenomena; but his interpretation of them is very different from the spiritualist's (cf. René Guénon, *L'Erreur spirite*, Paris, 1930). The attitude of orthodox religion (essentially one of indifference) is also very "correct"; in any case only the "intellectual virtues" survive, and these are certainly not those that the "dear departed" are said to display. How far the Buddhist is from the spiritualistic position appears not only in the whole treatment of "individuality" (liberation being precisely from the "personality" for the survival of which the spiritualist adduces "proofs"), but conspicuously in Sn 774, where the question "What shall we come to be after death" (*kim su bhavissāma ito cutāse*) is one that can only be asked by ignorant worldlings.

[56] The doctrine of "Causal Origination" is expressly described as "profound" and "hard to be understood" by those of an altogether different temperament and training (S II.92 and II.267, D III.40, etc.).

[57] Plutarch, *Moralia* 392D: "Dead is the man of yesterday, for he is passed into the man of today; and the man of today is dying as he passes into the man of tomorrow. Nobody remains one person, nor is one person. . . . Our senses, through ignorance of reality, falsely tell us that what appears to be, is."

[58] The "chariot" in Indian scripture generally is the psycho-physical vehicle, itself an aggregate, in which the simple substance of the Spirit "rides."

rati) without loss of identity (*anaññam*, M 1.256);[59] and yet it cannot be said that death is an automatic release from evil and from works (Mil 72) because "beings (*sattā*) are the heirs of acts (*kamma-dāyādā*)."[60] It must *never* be overlooked that traditional doctrine makes no distinction in principle between our daily deaths and births and death and birth "when the time comes": this together with an understanding of what is meant by the two selves[61] (in Buddhism the great or fair and little or foul selves) are essential to a grasp of any Indian scripture. As to the survival of personality, whether from day to day or life to life, the Buddha teaches a Middle Way of understanding—that of continuity without identity.

It remains only to add that the corresponding Skr. *nāstika* and *nāstikya* = *natthitā* are found in Brahmanical contexts. In MU II.5, *nāstikyam* is grouped with fear, hunger, anger, ignorance, etc., in a long list of *tāmasa* qualities; BG II.42 gives the sense of Pāli *natthika*, but not the word itself, thus, "Flowery words are uttered by the stolid, whose delight is in the literal sense of the Vedas, saying 'There is nothing more' (*nānyad astīti vādinaḥ*)." In the same way KU II.6, although not mentioning the term *nāstika*, actually defines the "nothing-morist" in words identical with those of M 1.403 and J v.228 cited above, viz. as one "who holds that 'there is no other world but this' (*ayaṃ loko nāsti para iti mānī*)," i.e., who denies that there are possibilities other than possibilities of manifestation. For Manu *nāstikya* is an *ahetuvāda* and effectively an *ucchedavāda*: we find in III.65 that "by the denial of causality, families are soon destroyed (*nāstikyena ca karmāṇāṃ kulāny āśu vinaśyanti*)," which we understand to mean that to deny the inheritance of the father's karmic character by the son is is to deny the reality of filiation, and thus to "destroy the family," as traditionally understood: for from this point of view, where there is no hereditary transmission of a vocation and a character, there is no family line. In the same way Manu VIII.22, a kingdom infested by *nāstikas* is destroyed; in II.11, and III.150, *nāstikas* are grouped with

[59] Cf. in M 1.366, *alam . . . aññathattāya*, "Have you had enough of otherness?" i.e., "of the vicissitudes" of life.

[60] For inheritance in this sense, see BU 1.5.17 and Kauṣ. Up. II.15 (*pitāputrīyaṃ sampratti* or *sampradānam*) and JB 1.18.10, *tasya putrā dāyam upayanti*.

[61] The one an essence (spiritual or intellectual), the other an existence (psychophysical and sensitive). In Christianity, the soul to be saved and soul to be lost in Luke 17:33, or hated, Luke 14:26, the spirit as sundered from soul in Heb. 4:12: the soul to be "hated" being precisely the *psyche* of the "psychologist." So also for Rūmī, "the soul (*nafs*) is hell" (*Mathnawī* 1.1375): cf. JUB IV.26, *mano narakaḥ*, etc.

thieves, belittlers of the Veda, outcasts, śūdras, etc., and in IV.163 and XI.67 *nāstikya* is coupled with belittling the Veda and with murder.[62]

We conclude that the *nāstika* is a nominalist, a denier especially of any but empirical truths: and that the word can best be rendered by "skeptic," a word that has the further advantage of corresponding in value to Pāli *diṭṭhika*, generally in the bad sense of one who entertains *false* opinions.

nāga. While in the vast majority of cases *nāga* as type or epithet of the Buddha or other Arhat is "elephant," there is a text of special interest, the *Vammīka* (*Valmīki*) *Sutta*, M I.142–145, in which the *khīṇāsava bhikkhu*, i.e., Arahat, is typified by a *nāga* that is unquestionably a cobra. A certain Deva appears to the elder Kumāra Kassapa and says, "almsman, almsman, this is an ant-hill that flames by day and smokes by night." The Brahman answers, "take a spade, Sumedha, and dig it up."[63] The Deva accordingly digs, and unearths a variety of objects, which he is told to

[62] That from an Indian point of view the lineage ceases as soon as the characteristic habit of the family is neglected is clearly seen in the *Makhādeva Sutta* (M II.75–83); it is the "lovely custom" (*kalyāṇa vaṭṭa*) of this royal line that when the barber finds the first gray hair in the king's head, the king adopts the religious life and hands over the kingdom to his son; this tradition is maintained for 84,000 years, but broken at last, the Buddha remarking "When on the part of one of two successive persons there is a breaking down of such a lovely custom, the former of them is the last (of the line)," *so tesam antimapuriso hoti*. In the same way the carpenter whose son should become a shopkeeper would certainly be considered the last of his line. A memory of the same point of view survives in the attitude of the parent whose son or daughter has committed some heinous offense and who says "you are no child of mine," or even simply "disinherits" the child. The extension of a lineage is literally the repeated rebirth of fathers in sons; each of whom is thought of as taking his father's place in the world. This is the principle of hereditary vocation, and it underlies all the resistance that is offered to the breakdown of the caste system in accordance with which one's function is determined by heredity and not by personal choice. It would hardly be possible to deny that in modern times and before our eyes "civilization" (in this sense, that of the Indian "family and kingdom") has been destroyed by skepticism (materialism), individualism (involving free choice of occupation) and the "rise" (to power) of the proletariat (śūdra). In a dictatorship there is government by a single śūdra, in a soviet government by a few śūdras, and in a democracy government by many śūdras; none of these conditions corresponds to Indian conceptions of civilization or order; what the modern terms progress is for the traditionalist disintegration.

[63] Chalmers' version confuses the speakers; it is quite clear from the sequence of the text that "Brahman" refers to Kassapa, and "Sumedha" to the Deva. From DhA III.146, we learn that the Deva had been a monk in the time of the Buddha Kassapa and had arisen in the Brahmā-world as a nonreturner but not yet fully perfected.

reject, and to dig further. At last he comes to a cobra (*nāga*), and says, "a cobra, your reverence (*bhadante*)." The Brahman answers, "let it be, harm it not, pay it honor."

At this point something is missing; it must be understood that the Deva asks fifteen questions about what has been found, and that Kassapa cannot answer them. The Deva then tells Kassapa to put the questions to the Buddha, whose answer will be convincing. He does so, and the Buddha explains that the interpretation (*adhivacanam*) of the ant-hill is "the body," of the fire "acts," of the smoke "thoughts," of the Brahman "the Tathāgata, the Arahat, the Fully-awakened"; of Sumedha an "almsman still a pupil," of the spade the "Aryan insight," of the digging "heroic effort,"[64] of the various objects "bonds, etc. to be rejected," and of the cobra (*nāga*)[65] "the almsman freed of the foul issues (*khīṇāsava bhikkhu*): Let him be, harm him not, do him honor." We learn from J I.148 and DhA III.147 that as a result of these interpretations Kassapa became an Arahat.

In one other context (S v.47, cf. v.63), the attainment of maturity by almsmen is compared to the development of young snakes (or eels)[66] who are born in the hills and go down to the sea by way of the lakes and rivers, only attaining their full development in the sea, which is here an equivalent of *nibbāna*, *amata* (see "*samudda*").

It is thus firmly established that *nāga* in the ophidian sense may be the symbol of an Arahat or Buddha. Further evidence is afforded by Dh 179,

[64] Digging for buried treasure, in a spiritual sense, appears several times in RV.

[65] In the chapter immediately following, two Arahats are described (M I.151) as "two great *nāgas*," and it is probable that in this case also it is *nāga* as "snake" rather than *nāga* as "elephant" that is meant. In Vin I.24–25, where the Buddha overcomes Ahi-nāga in the Jaṭila fire-temple, he is referred to as *manussa-nāga* and here *nāga* has certainly its ophidian sense; that the Buddha "fights fire with fire" (*tejasā tejam*) corresponds to TS v.2.4.1, where the kindled Agni and "the Agni that was before *hate one another*." In many other contexts the value of *nāga* is uncertain.

[66] The word is *nāga*, but the description suggestive rather of an imperfect knowledge of the life-history of eels than of snakes. If eels were regarded as "snakes," this may in part account for the characteristic association of *nāgas* with the Waters, but does not affect the symbolic values.

Nāga is probably also "snake" in M I.386 *nāgassa pantasenassa khīnasamyo-janassa*. Elsewhere *nāga*, as a symbol or epithet of the perfected Buddha or Arahat, is usually "elephant," and always, of course, where the symbol of the *hatthi-pada* is involved, *nāga* = *hatthi*, *gaja*. It is from a different point of view, of course, that the elephant's track *can* be followed up, as for example in Mil 346, *yathā pi gajarājassa padaṃ disvāna*, and similar texts corresponding to the doctrine of the *vestigium pedis* in Brahmanical contexts and in Christianity.

"That Buddha whose 'pasture' is infinite (*ananta-gocaram*), being without feet (*apadam*, a kenning for 'snake,' and implying also 'leaving no track'), by what track can you track him down? (*kena padena nessatha*)." This text is closely affiliated to BU III.8.8, where the Brahman is *acakṣuḥ-śrotraṃ tad apāṇy apādam . . . anantaram*, and Muṇḍ. Up. I.1.6, where the Brahman is *adṛśyam agrāhyam agotram avarṇam acakṣuḥśrotraṃ tad apāṇy apādam*, etc., and, it may be added with Shams-i-Tabrīz, "the last step, to fare without feet" and "in me is no 'I' and no 'We,' I am naught, without head, without feet" (Rūmī, *Dīvān*, pp. 137, 295).

At the same time we have wished to point out the parallel in Greek mythology, where not only may Zeus (= Dyaus Pitṛ = Varuṇa = *apara* Brahman = Buddha *parinibbuto*) be represented as a snake, but the Hero entombed is also a snake: Jane Harrison, *Prolegomena to the Study of Greek Religion* (3rd ed., Cambridge, 1922), fig. 96 (the snake is assuredly *within* the tomb) is the very picture of an Indian *thūpa* such as is erected for the Buddha (*passim*), or any *parinibbuto bhikkhu* (Ud 8). Without pursuing the subject further we shall only remark that if the snake is the symbol both of an imperfect nature to be abandoned and of a perfected nature to be realized, this corresponds to the double value of "nonbeing" (1) as a natural evil to be escaped from and (2) as a supernatural good to be attained, and to the polarity that is proper to all "negative" symbols, which imply on the one hand a privation and on the other a freedom from any limiting affirmation.

niccakappam. At M I.249, where, after delivering a discourse, the Buddha says that he composes and settles his heart, focuses it and synthesizes it (*cittaṃ saṇṭhāpemi sannisādemi ekodi-karomi samādahāmi*), and that this is in conformity with the former *samādhi*, "in which *niccakappaṃ nicca-kappaṃ viharāmi*," the translator renders by "in which I always dwell." This is to confuse *niccakappam* with *niccakālam*: the meaning is "which I enjoy, or in which I rest, *whenever I will*." "Always," indeed, contradicts both the sense of the present context, in which the Buddha speaks of himself as entering into this *samādhi* at a certain time, and that of such passages as M I.482, in which the Buddha's knowledge as a man, as "Gotama, now waking and now sleeping," differs from his knowledge in contemplation.

nibbāyati, *nibbāna*. It is familiar that *nibbāna* = *nirvāṇa* implies the extinction of a flame. *Nirvāṇa* is literally "not-blowing," or more technically, "despiration": *nibbutam* = *nirvātam* thus corresponding to *avātam* in RV x.129.2, *tad ekam ānīd avātam* being the exact equivalent of Eckhart's *Dā diu zwei apgründe in einer glicheit sweben gegeistet und engeistet* ("equally spirated, despirated"), *dā ist ein hōhez wesen* (Pfeiffer ed., p. 517). The PTS Dictionary, s.v. *nibbāna*, starts, however, with the erroneous statement that *nir-vā* means to "blow," ignoring the regularly privative value of *nis*. Insofar as *nibbāna* depends upon *nirvā*, then, it implies an extinction or death by ceasing to blow, i.e., ceasing to breathe, and not an extinction by blowing "which latter process," as the Dictionary remarks with unconscious pertinence to the history of the idea, "rather tends to incite the fire than to extinguish it": Agni being in fact very often referred to as "quickened" (*jūtaḥ*) or "churned" (*mathitaḥ*) by the Gale (of the Spirit),[67] Vāta, Vāyu, Mātariśvan, with whom he can also be identified, in accordance with the principle that both Agni and Vāyu are "self-kindled" (RV i.12.6; AB ii.34). Furthermore, the earlier references in the Dictionary are "to the fire going out, rather than to the fire being put out," for which there are excellent metaphysical reasons as well as those "ethical" reasons to which the Dictionary refers. The question of a being "blown out" does not, in fact, arise at any time in connection with the history of *nirvā*. The Dictionary, s.v. *nibbāpeti* (causative of *nibbāyati*), has, indeed, "to make cool by blowing" (this repeats the error noted above) and cites RV x.16.13 *nirvāpaya*, addressed to Agni, who is, as a matter of fact, besought to cool the ground that he has burnt, the still smoldering pyre; but here *nirvāpaya* (causative imperative) is by no means "make cool by blowing," but "make cease to breathe," or "cease to blow," and in this way extinguish his own flames. To "cool," though not by a "*blowing*" (which would not cool, but only fan the flame) is thus a proper sense of *nirvā*, causative; it occurs thus in J iii.157 *sabbaṃ nibbāpaye daram*, "cool all my fever," and survives in Brajabuli, e.g., *nā nibhāy hiyāra āguni*, "It cannot quench the flame at my heart" (S. Sen, *History of Brajabuli Literature*, Calcutta, 1935, p. 406). I cannot believe that *nibbāyati* or *nibbāna* has anything to do with any root (*vṛ*) meaning to "cover"; for example J vi.196 *jāla . . . nibbāyati* is simply "the fire ceases to draw," and so "goes out."

We can now proceed to notice some of the Pāli and Sanskrit contexts in which *nibbāyati*, or its equivalents, distinctly mean a "going out" of the fire, which is a death in the same sense that we speak of the fire as

[67] For Agni's despiration, because of which he would go out, and contrasted with his being kept ablaze by fanning or a supply of fuel, cf. ŚB ii.8.3.7.

"dying down." The sense in which the fire "goes out" is almost always, in fact, parabolical, the reference being to the extinction of the flame of life. In M I.487 the fire is "gone out for want of fuel" (*anāhāro nibbuto*),[68] that food or fuel, of course, by which the empirical consciousness is supported throughout "life": S I.159 refers to the "going out of a flame" (*pajjotassa nibbānam*): Sn 19 has "My roof yawns wide, my fire's gone out" (*vivaṭā kuṭi, nibbuto gini*). Needless to say, too, that there are many kinds of "fire," and that in many cases it is specifically the fire of anger (*kodha*, A IV.96), or more often the fires of passion, delusion, and defect (*rāga moha dosa*, S IV.261) that are extinguished. In Sanskrit contexts *vā, nirvā* are usually found with direct reference to spiration, e.g., KB VII.9, where it is a question of the "breaths" (*prāṇāḥ*), and these "though blowing (*vāntaḥ*) in various directions do not blow out" (*na nirvānti*; Keith's version).[69] When it is specifically a question of the going out of a fire, which no longer "draws" (air) the usual verb is *udan*,[70] in which the meanings of "aspire" and "expire" are combined: thus in CU IV.3.1, *yadā agnir udvāyati vāyum apyeti*, "when the Fire gives up its breathing (dies out), it enters the Gale," echoing ŚB X.3.3.8, "when the Fire goes out (*yadā agnir anugacchati*) it is into the Gale that it then blows out (*vāyuṃ tarhi anūdvāti*), wherefore they say 'It has expired' (*udavāsīt*)." In the same way for the Sun, Moon, and Quarters "established in the Gale, they are born again of the Gale, forsooth" (*vāyor . . . punar jāyante*, are "born of the Spirit"). "And the Comprehensor thereof, when he departs from this world . . . enters into the Gale with his life-breath, and being in and of it (*etanmaya eva bhūtvā*) he becomes whichever of these divinities he will, and moves at will" (*ilayati*, Sāyaṇa *saṃcarati, ceṣṭati*).[71] In the same way, Praśna Up. III.9, "For those whose fiery-energy has expired,

[68] Just as in MU VI.34, "As fire, of fuel destitute, is quenched in its own source, so the will (*cittam*) by the destruction of its versions is quenched (*upaśāmyate*) in its own source." The hermeneutic interpretation of *nibbāna* as *nir-vana*, "without wood," "without fuel," is based on this aspect of the decease of the fire of life. *Anāhāra* = *anābhoga* as interpreted by Paul Mus in the sense "not deriving nourishment from any external source."

[69] Cf. JUB I.2.5–6.

[70] Note that *udāna* in the sense of a "spontaneous utterance" is much rather an "aspiration" (actually, not in the sense of "ambition") than an "inspiration." It is a product of the speaker's own elevation. So C.A.F. Rhys Davids rightly translates *Udāna* (the book so called) by "Verses of Uplift" (ignoring, of course, the vernacular and social meaning of "uplift").

[71] Motion at will being a necessary consequence of consubstantiality with the Gale of the Spirit, which "bloweth where it listeth" (John 3:8), and "as it will" (*yathā vaśam*, RV X.168.4).

so that their fiery-energies are quenched (*tejo ha vā udānas tasmād upaśāntatejāḥ*) there is a regeneration (*punar bhavam*), by way of the consistence of the powers-of-the-soul in the intellect." There can be no question but that the Buddhist *nibbāyati* preserves the values which are contained in the older texts on despiration.

Our principal purpose in this note, however, is to emphasize that *nibbāna*, and a fortiori *parinibbāna*, is always a death or transformation, and to make it clear in what sense the death is a *summum bonum*, and coincident with a regeneration and the power of resurrection. *Parinibbāna* is, in fact, synonymous with the *parimara* of AB VIII.28, ŚA IV.12–13, and Kauṣ. Up. II.12,[72] where "entering into the Gale, and being dead, yet they do not die, because they rise again," with application alike to the divinities and to oneself. *Pari-* is not so much "round about" as (1) "thoroughly," in the sense that "the kingdom of God is for none but the thoroughly dead"; and (2) "towards" or "in," as when we speak of "dying *in* the Lord": who in these contexts as in those cited above is Brahman identified with "He who blows (*vāti*) here," i.e., Vāyu, who does not blow yonder (ŚB VIII.7.3.9), but as *tad ekam*, "That One," "bloweth *and* is still" (*anīd avātam*, RV X.129.2), nor ever "goeth home," being himself the "home" (*astam*) to which all others return (JUB III.1.1–3; BU I.5.22), not excepting the Muni freed from mental and physical both (*nāmakāyā vimutto = nāmarūpayā vimutto*), who "as a spark that is sped by the force of the wind 'goes home' and no count can be kept of him" (Sn 1074); they are "gone with the wind"; and, as we know, this expression (*vāyogataḥ*)[73] is the same as "unified" (*eko bhūtvā*), both of these being common ways in Indian literature of saying "dead."

It must be realized, however, that there are many deaths, of which that death in due course after which one is laid on the pyre is only one

[72] *Praviṣya vāyau mṛtvā n na mṛcchanti, tasmād eva punar adīranti*: one of the finest of the Indian texts on death and regeneration. The regeneration of the Comprehensor (*evaṃvit*) at death, when he is "born again" of the fire (and "Except a man be born again, he cannot see the kingdom of God," John 3:3), is prefigured in the ritual, where, for example, inasmuch as the priest repeats the whole of the hymns, "he brings to birth (*pra janayati*) the sacrificer, who is now an embryo, from the Sacrifice as womb," AB VI.9, the Sacrifice itself being identified with the Gale, *ibid.*, V.33.

[73] *Vāyogatah*, accordingly, presumes the fulfillment of the wish so poignantly expressed in the Vedic requiems X.14.8 and 16.3, *hityāvadyam punar astam ehi, saṃ gacchasva tanvā suvarcā . . . gacchatu vātam ātmā*, "All the accursed (evil) struck away, go home again, be constituted in a body of glory. . . . Fare thy spirit to the Gale."

amongst many others. All change is a dying, and at the same time involves the birth of a new man (who may be better or worse than the old, but in our contexts which are concerned with true Wayfarers, is always a better man),[74] as is explicit in S II.95, where "will, thought, discrimination (*citta*, *mana*, *viññāṇa*), all this arises as one and is destroyed as another, every night and every day," and A II.82, where with reference to a change of occupation and status, a man is said to "die to the one and be born to such another" (*tato cuto itthattam āgacchati*)."[75] It is from the same point of view that the application of *nibbuto* and *parinibbuto* to still-living human beings must be understood. The Mahāsambodhi as a *nibbāna* is the death of the Bodhisattva, and the birth of a Buddha, the Wake,[76] and similarly in the case of others spoken of as *nibbuto* or even *parinibbuto*[77] here and now.

Parinibbāyati thus implies not merely the death of a self, but like all deaths whatever, the bringing to birth[78] or making-become (*bhāvanā*) of

[74] M I.388–90, however, deals with the case of the man who "goes to the dogs."

[75] Cf. Augustine, *Contra Max.*, "all change is a kind of death." What is cited above from S and A is stated in almost identical terms by Plato in the Symposium, and by Eckhart, "The soul's progression is matter, wherein she puts on new forms and puts off old ones: the one she doffs she dies to, and the one she dons she lives in" (Pfeiffer ed., p. 530), like BG II.22 and BU IV.4.4, but no more than either of these a doctrine of "reincarnation."

The formula expressing change of occupation is identical with that in which the Buddha's descent from the Tusita heaven is stated, D III.146, *so tato cuto itthattam āgato* (where it may be further remarked that *itthattam āgato* is tantamount to *tathāgata*); and it is in the same terms that a series of rebirths is described, e.g., DhA IV.51 *tato cutā seṭṭhikule nibrattā.*

[76] In the same way ordination, in many respects analogous to initiation, is a "birth" (therefore also a "death" of the layman as such), as in M II.103, where we have (1) *yato . . . jāto,* "from the day I was born" and (2) *yato . . . ariyāya jātiyā jāto,* "from the day of my birth in the Noble Race," i.e., as a Sakyaputta, a "Buddha's son," birth in this sense being a filiation. To be awakened is the same as to come into being, RV *passim*, especially in connection with Agni (*uṣar-budh*). "Wake" in the sense "to be born" may be noted in *Widsith*, line 5, and we can still speak of "waking to the light of day" in this sense [see *Widsith*, ed. Kemp Malone, London, 1936—ED.].

[77] E.g., A II.155, which distinguishes those who are *parinibbuto* "here and now, before our very eyes" (*diṭṭh'eva dhamme*) and those who are *parinibbuto* only "at death" (*kāyassa bhedā*). These two *parinibbānas* are again subdivided according to whether they are attained "with means" (*sasaṅkhāra = sasaṃskarana*) or without, this depending on whether the pupil's powers (*sekha-balāni*) are "dull" (*muduttā*) or "superabundantly manifested" (*adhimattāni pātubhavanti*).

[78] This sense of *bhū* (causative) is explicit in AĀ II.5 *kumāram . . . bhāvayati.* In many other contexts *bhū* (causative) has the creative significance of *mā*, and similarly where it means to "evoke" a mental image.

another self. Every step on the Way uses a "dead self," now seen to be "not mine, not I," as a rung or stepping stone, and it is thus that the Wayfarer's very Self would come into being (*bhūṣṇur-ātmā*, AB vii.15), and is more and more clearly revealed (*āvistarām-ātmā*, AĀ ii.3.2): the final product, "when all has been done that was to be done" (*katakicco, kataṃ karaṇīyam, passim*; *kṛtakṛtyaḥ* in AĀ ii.5 and MU vi.30),[79] being the Spirit all-in-being, a finished and perfected Self (*bhāvitattā, passim*; *kṛtātman* as in CU viii.13).[80] *Parinibbāyati* in this sense of "bringing to perfection" occurs repeatedly in the striking text M i.446, where the word is used in connection with each of the ten stages of the training of a noble stallion (and it should not be overlooked that the Almsman whose lower self has been brought under complete control [*attā sudanto*] is often compared to a well-trained steed). What we have wished to bring out, then, is that *parinibbuto* in the sense of "dead" has not the limiting value that is commonly attached to this word,[81] but also implies "regenerate." *Parinibbuto* has both of the values that inhere in the word "finished," which can mean either "dead" (as in the expression, "that was his finish") or "brought to perfection" (in the sense that we speak of a "finished prod-

[79] AĀ ii.5 *ātmā kṛtakṛtyo vāyogataḥ praiti . . . prayann eva punar jāyate*, "the spirit, all in act, enters in to the Gale and departs, and departing, is regenerated": MU vi.30 *kṛtakṛtyo . . . sauraṃ dvāram bhitvā*, etc., "all in act, he breaks through the Sundoor, and follows the path of that one of the solar rays that pierces through the Orb and continues beyond the Brahma world, whereby men attain the highest goal."

[80] *Kṛtātmā brahmalokam abhisambhavāmi*, the "answer" to Sn 508, *ken' attanā gacchati brahmalokam*.

[81] A limiting value that can only be attached to the event of death by those who see *anattani attānam*, "their self in what is not their self." These must fear death and must grieve, both for their own loss, and for the deceased, who "is no more." It is precisely the same kind of grief that is felt by the profane when a religious "leaves the world" or is initiated, which events are also deaths, cf. JUB iii.8.1. On the other hand, funeral rites in a traditional society are occasions, not of grief, but of rejoicing: cf. D ii.161, where at the Buddha's decease he is honored as kings are honored "with dancing, singing, and instrumental music." Z. L. C. was at one time living near the Burning Ghat in Benares; she saw many funeral processions and observed that the "mourners'" faces were radiant. Only once she saw an old man weeping bitterly as he followed the corpse. On pointing this out to her old woman servant, the latter replied with scorn, "*He* is only an ignorant peasant" (or as the Buddhist would have expressed it, an *assuta puthujjana*: it is the "worldly-minded" Devas alone that weep at the Buddha's death, D ii.139). The traditional position assumes that the deceased, as *kṛtakṛtyaḥ*, etc., is *vāyogataḥ, punar bhutvā, udita, amṛta*; the traditional way of life presupposing this as its normal conclusion, death being "the ablution at the conclusion of life's ritual," as in CU iii.17.5.

uct").[82] We need hardly say that all perfection and all peace imply in this way the death of whatever had been imperfect or not at peace;[83] all motion ends when it attains the goal to which it was directed; Death is the "Ender" (*antaka*), but also the solar Eros, the Great Spirit (*mahātman*) who welcomes the perfected at World's End. *Parinibbuto*, literally "despirated," is thus "finished" in both senses of the word; and it is only if we realize this that we can fully understand why the faithful Buddhist, when he sees the Buddha's tomb (*thūpa*), is moved not by sorrow, but with the "thrill" (*saṃvejana*) of understanding, and exclaims triumphantly, "Here the Tathāgata was altogether finished (*parinibbuto*) with that attainment of despiration (*nibbāna*) that is without residuum of assumption."

nettiyā. *Bhava-nettiyā* is not, as it has been rendered at least once, "the Eye of Existence," but conduits of existence (or becoming, birth). Just as in M II.105, etc., *udakaṃ hi nayanti nettikā*, "irrigators (makers of channels, or 'leads' for the water) conduct the water." *Bhava-netti* is correctly explained in the Dictionary as "leader to renewed existence." But at ŚA II.336, cf. DA 127, etc., it is explained as *rajju*, "cord": *bhava-rajju* being the cord that ties one to becoming or renewed existence. Similarly at AĀ III.2, where it is explicitly stated that this *rajju* = *netti* is the cord "by which beings like cattle tied by the neck, are led to such and such an existence." The Tathāgata is the cutter of this *netti*, D I.46, which is the thirst for existence (DA 128), and so the cord that leads to it until cut.

[82] "Finished" in these two senses provides us with the reason (*ratio*) of the well-known superstition of the "evil eye." For only that which is imperfect, unfinished (*aparinibbuto*) is still "alive": to recognize that a thing is perfect is as much as to say that it is a finished product, no longer viable because already *geworden was er ist*, already come to its "end." For this reason (of which he may be quite unaware) the craftsman often leaves in his work some small defect, and for this reason that the possessor of a beautiful object does not like to hear it unduly praised, and will even give it away to the thoughtless admirer; or if it can not be given away, takes steps to "avert" the evil eye. We can also see why the "evil eye" does not necessarily imply an evil intention; the evil consequence is the result of what is usually an inadvertent imputation of "finish" in the sinister sense. And as usual, the superstition or "standover" is only really such when its reason has been forgotten: the superstition of the evil eye corresponds to what may have been a matter of fact in a society more sensitive than ours to the direct effects of mental acts, whether expressed or not expressed in words.

[83] *Santa*, "at peace," Skr. *śānti*, "peace," from *śam*, always in sacrificial contexts "to give the quietus," to slake, to kill. It should not be overlooked that the victim in these contexts is always, in the last analysis, the sacrificer himself, whose ritual death prefigures his final "rest."

Cf. Itiv, p. 94, *netticchinna bhikkhu*, he who has cut the *netti*, and for whom there is no renewed existence, thirst, or craving, *taṇhā*, being got rid of, UdA 272. We never meet with the expression *bhava-cakkhu* (only *maṃsa-cakkhu*); and the Pali *netta* = *netra* is more often "that which leads," e.g., "reins" (*nettāni*, S I.26), than literally "eye," which in any case is a secondary and not a primary meaning of the word.

pacchi. In *kilañja-pacchi*, J VI.370, rush-*baskets*," not, as translated by Cowell and Rouse, "rolls of matting." The baskets of J VI.370, with their lids, are clearly shown at Bharhut, Cunningham pl. 25, fig. 3. The Dictionary thinks the etymology "doubtful," but the root is surely *pracchad*, to cover, envelop, conceal.

pādavāra and *pādacchida*. DhA III.216 describes the Buddha's ascent to the Heaven of the Thirty-three, from Sāvatthi. "He lifted up his right foot and set it down on the summit of Mt. Yugandhara, then he lifted up his left foot and set it down on the summit of Mt. Sineru (Meru), and thus in just three stands (*tayo va pādavārā*) and two strides (*dve pādacchidāni*), he traversed sixty-eight hundred thousand leagues," and there seated himself on Indra's golden throne. Burlingame's version, "in three strides, setting foot on earth but twice," reverses the proper meanings of the two words in question, and is at the same time unintelligible. *Pādavāra* is the pause in walking, when both feet are brought together; there are three such "stands," first at Sāvatthi, second on Yugandhara, and third on Sineru. *Pādacchida* is, as the word itself implies, the "separation of the feet" in striding: the word corresponds to *padacchedana*, *padabhājana*, and *padavibhāga*, denoting the analysis of verse to form a *pada* text, the converse of *padasaṃsagga*, *padasaṃdhi* implying the conjunction of the words and corresponding to *pādavāra*. Not only does the corrected rendering make sense, but it enables us to recognize the correspondence of the Buddha's two with the first two of Viṣṇu's three strides; the summit reached by the Buddha on this occasion is solar, like that which he assumes on Mt. Gṛdrakūṭa, not supra-solar, the Heaven of the Thirty-three over which the solar Indra presides being neither a Brahmaloka nor an aspect of Nibbāna.

Pādavāra and *padavāra* occur also in J I.213 and 506: in the latter context it is especially clear that a pause is implied, the description being of a deliberate walk "as though at every step (*padavāre padavāre*) he were putting down a bag of a thousand pieces of gold"—which could not be done without pausing. It may be pointed out that it is, in fact, always with one foot that a stride is taken, the other being left behind during motion. In the Bhārhut relief (Cunningham, pl. 17, center) representing the subsequent descent at Saṃkassa, we therefore see on the topmost rung of the ladder one foot, and on its lowest rung the other: the descent is made in a single stride; we have the actual picture of a *pādacchida*. It is in the same way that the Sun has regularly "one foot" or ray with which he walks and thus reaches every creature upon whom he bestows its being, RV etc., *passim*, but the feet of Death (who is also the Sun), thought of as *planted* in the heart (*hṛdaye pādāv atihatau*, ŚB x.5.2.13) are *two*, "and when he separates them, he departs (*āchidyotkrāmati*)": where *āchidya* is rather "separating" than Eggeling's "cuts off," since it is actually a *pādacchida* that takes place at death, when the spirit "strides away (*utkrāmati*)," or as in BU iv.4.3, where "this spirit, striking down the body and dismissing ignorance, striding another stride (*anyam ākramam ākramya*), draws itself together," i.e., enters into its source, returns to itself, *ākramya* again implying a *pādacchida*.

The ŚB text continues, "and when he (Death, the Person in the solar Orb) ascends (*utkrāmati*), this person (in the right eye) dies. Hence they call the former (*etad*) the 'departed' (*pretam*), and say of the latter (*asya*) 'It has been cut off' (*āchedi*)."[84] The *preta* is the immanent *ātman*, the "ghost" that the man "gives up" when he "expires," "that *other* self of his" that having done its work "departs" or "proceeds" (*praiti*) when the time comes (AĀ ii.5), while the psycho-physical manifestation is left behind, just as one foot is left behind in striding.[85]

It should be noted that *pāduka* in Pāli is always "slipper," and is not

[84] Eggeling's version is insufficiently literal, ignoring the distinction of "former" and "latter."

[85] It is in just the same way that in the introductory sacrifice (*prāyaṇīya*), the sacrificer (who has just undergone the ritual death of initiation) "proceeds (*praiti*, AB i.7)" to the world of heaven—leaving behind him, of course, the human self to which he will only return (as from the truth to what is false) when the operation is abandoned, and he formally desecrates himself (ŚB i.9.3.23 with VS i.5, AB vii.24, cf. ŚB iii.9.4.2), the human self that he sacrifices in the rite (as *ātmayajñī*) so as to be "emptied" of self (ŚB iii.8.1.2). What is thus "left" behind is an *ahi* in the sense of JB iii.77 (*yad ahīyata tad ahīnām ahitvam*); cf. PB xii.11.11, where Kalyāṇa is "left behind, for he had told a lie" (as men do, but the gods do not, *passim*) and becomes a *śvitra*, i.e., *ahi*.

Preta is then, at least originally and properly, the immanent deity, the "ghost," i.e., Sanctus Spiritus, that a man "gives up" when he "expires (*apānati*, *ucchvāsati*, etc.)." If *preta* (and especially Buddhist *peta*) comes to mean also "ghost" in a much lower sense, it is in the same way that Yakṣa, originally = Brahman, Ātman, Daimon can become also "demon," and that "spirit" can refer to such all-too-human entities as those with which the "spiritualist" concerns himself.

a proper term to be applied to the footprints as represented in art. We find in the literature only *pada* or *pāda* for "footprint" as well as for "foot"; for example, in M I.175 ff. and S I.86, *tathāgatapada* and *hatthi-pada* are "Buddha's footprint" and "elephant's footprint." The expression *pada-valañja* occurs in DhA III.194, and the "foot-trace" left by the Buddha is referred to as a *pada-cetiya*; this last is clearly the term that should be used in iconographic descriptions.

pabbāhati. In the Dictionary, s.v. *pabāhati*, Skr. *prabarh*, *pravṛh*, as in KU II.13, *pravṛhya* (*aṇum*). *Pabbāheyya* and *pabbāḷhā* (v.l., *pavāḷha*) occur in M II.17, meaning "might draw forth" and "drawn forth." The Dictionary reference of *pavāḷha* to *pravṛh* is certainly correct, for the Pāli *muñjaṃhā isīkam pabbāheyya* corresponds exactly to *muñjād isīkāṃ vivṛhet* in JB II.134 and similar contexts. The metaphor is repeated in D I.77. The Pāli versions show clearly that the real meaning is not so much "might draw the reed from its sheath" as "draw the arrow from the reed"; if the *isīkā* had not been thought of as "arrow," there would have been no point in the words *añño muñjo aññā isīkā*. It is plain that when the fletcher goes to the *muñja* marshes to gather shafts, he pulls them from the plants which are left in place, and that what he pulls out is for him the "arrow" and what is left the "plant." The metaphor applies in the Pāli contexts to the drawing out of a supernatural body from this mortal body;[86] cf. ŚB IV.3.3.16.

pāsa. In J III.282, Francis and Neil misrender *pāse vijjhitvā* by "which pierced dice"; the Bodhisatta, however, is the subject of *vijjhitvā*, and *sūcim* its object; the meaning is "perforated with an eye." *Supāsiyam* and *supāsam* below mean "having a well-made eye."

That *pāsa* (Skr. *pāśa*) can mean "needle's eye" is of double interest. In the first place, *pāśa* is essentially "loop," and as such "noose," etc. The application of a word meaning "loop" to the eye of a needle suggests a period when the first metal needles were made of wire with one end bent over to form a "loop" or "eye." And in the second place, because the "eye of the needle" (and such a needle in particular as the Bodhisatta makes in the *Jātaka*, "it cannot be told how, but only that the purposes of the Buddhas succeed [*ijjhanti*]") is a recognized aspect of the Janua Coeli,

[86] In these contexts *isīkā* is no more "reed" (the plant) than *asi* (sword) is *kosi* (scabbard), or *ahi* (snake) is *karaṇḍa* (slough).

Sundoor and "narrow gate," and *pāśa* being also "noose" (in the hands of Mṛtyu, Yama, and Varuṇa), we realize that the loop of Death's lasso is still another aspect of the Gate, and that to slip through the noose without its tightening upon you is the same as to have passed through the jaws of Death without their closing upon you, just as the "threading of the needle" is the passage of the Sundoor in the symbolism of embroidery.

So far, of course, with reference to the "last death of the soul," in which the "threading of the needle" is the passage of the Sundoor. To pass through the needle's eye (cf. Dante, *Purgatorio* x.16) or to evade the noose can also be used with reference to any passage, all passages implying change, and all change a dying (to what was before). We are concerned here only with the general symbolic equivalence of the eye of the needle and loop of the noose.

piṇḍika. In J vi.376 it must be the globular termination or finial of the handle of the umbrella, *piṇḍa* being a lump, ball. This is supported by the facts that Skr. *piṇḍaka* is cited from a lexikon as "nave of a wheel," and also as a "round swelling or protuberance," and that in the *Aupapātika Sūtra*, §16, *piṇḍiya* corresponds to *uṣṇīṣa* in its later sense of "cranial protuberance." Cf. *sākhā*.

beluva (*-paṇḍu-vīṇā*). The Dictionary has "flute" (twice), but this is only a misprint for "lute." S.v. *vīṇā*, the Dictionary has "lute, mandoline . . . lyre." The *vīṇā* of the text is, however, a postless harp. For this and the Pāli names for other parts and appurtenances of the harp, see Coomaraswamy, "The Parts of a *vīṇā*" in JAOS, LVII (1937), with further references. The Dictionary in particular misrenders *koṇa*, which is not "bow" but "plectrum."

bhū. The following discussion is by no means to be taken as an argument against the general position taken by C.A.F. Rhys Davids in *To Become or Not To Become* (London, 1937); I am in agreement with this position. The discussion is solely with reference to the meaning of the future form *bhavissati* in A ii.37, where the Brahman Doṇa finds the Buddha's wheel-marked footprints and, as he looks at them, says to himself, "It cannot be that these are the footprints of a human being." It is not denied that *na bhavissati*, although future in form, has here the conjectural value "cannot be," with reference to the present fact, and not to any future becoming; that the footprints *are* surely not those of a man is the point. Before going further it may be remarked that there is no dispute that the future form of *bhū* can have this gnomic value in Pāli; of countless examples, not to mention those given by Rhys Davids herself, I cite only J vi.364, "your name must be Amarā (*tvam amarā nāma bhavissati*)," certainly with reference to present fact; and J vi.365, *udakaṃ na laddham bhavissati*, "It must *be* that you did not get water," i.e., at the time when it *was* needed for the crops. We find the same usage in Sanskrit already in RV i.164.39, *kiṃ ṛcā kariṣyati*, "What will he do with the verse?" i.e., what use *is* it to him.

So far so good. But in the following context of A ii.38, F. L. Woodward and Rhys Davids (*To Become or Not To Become*, p. 99) have insisted upon rendering *manusso . . . bhavissati* by "will become a human being?" and *na . . . manusso bhavissāmi* by "I shall not become a human being," with specific reference to the future. This is insisted upon in spite of the fact that the Buddha concludes his remarks by saying that all those conditions according to which he might have been a man (or *deva, gandhabba, yakkha*, etc.) have been killed, "so that I *am* the Wake (*tasmā buddho'smi*)." It is in just the same way that at Mil 346 we find *bhavissati* and *atthi* used synonymously in one and the same connection, and both meaning "must surely be" or "assuredly is." It may also be observed that in J v.317, where a similar question is put to Nanda, he replies that he is, or literally "has become," a man (*manussa-bhūto*).

In our disputed context we have, first, a future with an admittedly present conjectural value; then a series of futures with disputed value; and finally a pronouncement definitely in the present, with respect to the questions and answers that intervene. We cannot but think that our authors force the future sense only because of their extreme unwillingness to allow the Buddha to say of himself, "I *am* not a man, or god, or eros, or daimon." It is true that in innumerable contexts of the Nikāyas it is explicit that a Buddha or Arhat is emancipated from being in *any* given way, is nameless, cannot be reached or understood, and so forth; but all these our authors would reject as interpolations or developments. To me the texts appear to be self-consistent; for me the "higher criticism" of these texts amounts to a dangerous reading out of them whatever does not seem to *us* suitable or true. I take the texts as they stand. But it would seem to be far better to call our passage an interpolation than to translate it in plain contradiction of the syntax. The Buddha is asked "What are thou?" and answers "I am not any what," that is, essentially, as in Sn 455–56 *koci no'mhi . . . ākiṃcano . . . carāmi loke . . . akalla maṃ . . . pucchi gotta-pañham.*

rasa. We shall see that *vyañjana* is distinguished from *attha* very much as flavor is distinguished from food. In one *Nikāya* text the word *rasa* actually takes the place which is usually taken by *vyañjana*: this is A 1.36, where "those who get the flavor of the meaning" is *attha-rasassa . . . lābhino*, and here we can hardly fail to remark that *rasa* is used essentially as it is in the later rhetoric. The earlier history of the word *rasa* needs fuller treatment in a separate article, but we do wish to suggest that even in other than, and older than, *Alaṃkāra* contexts, and even when the reference is to Deity (*so vai rasa*), the word should be rendered in most cases by "flavor" rather than by "essence." The word "essence" is needed in its proper sense for such terms as *bhūtatā* ("being," in principle; for *atthitā* we should prefer to say "existence," distinguishing *esse* from *essentia vel quidditas*, i.e., "being in itself" from *iti-bhavābhava*, *τὸ ὄν* from *τὸ φαινομενόν*). On the other hand, to speak of the "flavor" of knowledge, or of "digesting an idea" (or "assimilation" = *adaequatio rei et intellectus*), or even of "tasting God" ("O taste and see that the Lord is good") is by no means foreign to the genius of European languages, Latin *sapientia* being etymologically a "tastiness," and as St. Thomas Aquinas expresses it, "Quasi sapida scientia, seu scientia cum sapore (Pāli *savyañjanam*!), id est cognitio cum amore (Pāli *pīti*!)," *Sum. Theol.*, I.43.5, and II-II.45.2–3 with further references.[87]

The *attha-rasassa lābhī* of our text will be, of course, the "Great Self," not the "little self" of A 1.249, the "Fair Self" and not the "foul self" of A 1.149: just as in AV x.8.44 it is the "Immortal, Contemplative Self," the Spirit that is, that is "delighted by the flavor" (*rasena tṛptaḥ*). The flavor, in other words, is the "immortal" part of the meaning: and just as in the later rhetoric (*Sāhitya Darpaṇa* III.2–3) the "tasting of the flavor" (*ra-*

[87] Cf. Ibn al-'Arabī, *Tarjumān al-Ashwāq* (ed. R. A. Nicholson, London, 1911) xxv.4, and his own commentary, where "the saliva in which I tasted white honey" stands for the "sciences of communion and converse and speech which leave a delicious taste in the heart."

The mention of honey here reflects the traditional symbolism of bees and honey, where "honey" is the knowledge of things *sub specie aeternitatis*, and in fact that "nectar" (*amṛta*) of which the gods partake and in virtue of which they are "Immortals" (*amṛtāsaḥ*).

sāsvādana) is called the cognate of the "tasting of Brahman" (*brahmāsvādana*), so here it can be said with Augustine that "even we ourselves as mentally *tasting* something eternal, are not in this world" (*De Trinitate* IV.20).

lekhaṇī. Pencil, crayon, brush,[88] or any pointed tool used in carving wood or ivory; never "stencil," as also given in the PTS Dictionary. In A II.200, where the making of a dug-out canoe from a tree is described, the *lekhaṇī* is the most delicate of the three tools used before the polishing is done. The log is "hewn with axes," or perhaps "adzes" (*kuṭhārīhi tacchetvā*), "cut with chisels (*vāsīhi tacchetvā*)," "graven with the 'spear-point' (*lekhaṇiyā likhitvā*)," and finally "smoothed with a round pebble (*pāsānaguḷena dhopetvā*)." We render *lekhaṇī* by "spear-point," the technical name of a certain wood-turner's tool, bearing in mind that one of the meanings of *likh* is to "turn" (wood or ivory),[89] and because in the present case, although there is no question of turning, something like a wood-engraver's pointed tool must be meant; and *likhitvā* by "graven" in the sense of "graven" image. *Lekhaṇiyā likhitvā* might also mean "carved" in the sense of decorated, but this seems unlikely in the present context, where the "graving" is preparatory to smoothing. It is probable that metal tools are implied at this period, but the process described must have come down from prehistoric times, when the same or similar terms could have denoted stone tools. There remains a further and perhaps even more plausible alternative, according to which *lekhaṇiyā likhitvā* would mean "painted with a paintbrush": that a polishing with an "agate burnisher" should follow this would be quite intelligible.

vatra. "Vṛtra": J V.153 *indo vatrabhū . . . sakko*: S I.47, *vatra-bhū.*

vaḍḍhamāna. I accept Dr. Johnson's argument (*JRAS*, 1932, pp. 392–98, and 1933, p. 690) to the effect that the three-pointed symbol sometimes called *triśūla* or *triratna* in early Buddhist art has properly been referred to as the "*vardhamāna.*" It is perhaps only by chance that we do not find any reference to the symbol in Pāli literature, and hence no occurrence of the word *vaḍḍhamāna* with reference to a symbol. The word occurs in early Jaina literature as the name of a symbol. As regards the word in

[88] For these senses at a later period see *Technical Studies*, III (1934), 71, 74. *Likh* occurs in Pāli in the senses of draw, write, carve, turn; *lekhaṇī* as pencil or brush in Mhv.

[89] Cf. JAOS, XLVIII, 263–64.

other senses, and primarily those of the root meaning ("increase"), it is curious that the Dictionary, s.v., equates *vaḍḍhamāna* in Dpv XI.33 with *vaḍḍhana* in Mhv XXIII.33, overlooking that *vaḍḍhamāna* itself occurs in the very next verse of the text in a sense explained in the Dictionary, s.v. *vaḍḍhati*. The word occurs also in Mhv XI.30, where *vaḍḍhamānaṃ kumārikam* is "a girl in the bloom of her youth" (Geiger, or as I should prefer to say, "a still growing girl"). There is also a Pāli *vaḍḍhanika* meaning a dish from which food is served, and this explains the later Jaina *vaddhamānaga* in the sense of "auspicious vessel" (distinct from *puṇṇa-ghaṭa*).

vitaṃsa. I fail to see why the proposed etymology (*vi tan*) is "not clear": the meaning is "snare" (for birds): it is proverbially "in vain that the net is spread in the sight of any bird"; the Old Testament abounds in references to the *spreading* of nets and snares; and for illustrations of *outspread* snares, see *MFA Bulletin*, No. 210, pp. 50–53.

vyañjana (contrasted with *attha*). Before we discuss these terms in the Pāli contexts, we must assume the meaning of *attha* in relation to *dhamma* discussed above, s.v. *attha* = *artha*. It will also be advisable to consider the meaning of *vyañjana* in pre- and post-Pāli contexts in order to put the question (of considerable interest from the point of view of the history of Indian rhetoric) whether or not Pāli *vyañjana* has really a meaning contradictory of its meaning in these pre- and post-Pāli contexts. The primary sense of the root (*vyañj*) is to "anoint," and hence to "adorn," "flavor" (drink, food), and "illustrate" or "manifest." For the first three of these values in RV, cf. Grassmann's *Wörterbuch*, s.v. *añj*. *Vyañjana* (n.) is "adornment" in RV VIII.78.2. In the later rhetoric, three kinds of meaning (*artha*) of a proposition (*vācakam*) are distinguished, viz. *abhidhā, lakṣaṇā*, and *vyañjanā*, respectively literal, figurative, and parabolical (*Sāhitya Darpaṇa*, II.3 etc.), the latter coinciding with what is called the "flavor (*rasa*)" of a poetical text defined as a "statement (having the letter for its body and) flavor as its informing spirit (*kāvyaṃ rasātmakaṃ vākyam*)."

On the other hand, the PTS Dictionary has under *Vyañjana*, "Letter (of a word) as opposed to *attha* (meaning, sense, spirit)," and under *Savyañjana* only "with the letters."[90] Most of the translators render, ac-

[90] It would be difficult to reconcile this with S II.51, where it is asked, "Have you declared Arahatta (*tayā aññā vyākatā*), viz. *khīṇā jāti . . . nāparam itthattāya*?"

cordingly, *attha* as "spirit" and *vyañjana* as "letter."[91] If this could be justified we should be faced with the curious phenomenon of a temporary reversal of the basic meanings of the word *vyañjana*. We have shown, s.v. *attha*, that the meaning of *attha* is anything but "spirit."

We propose to discuss the word in its Pāli contexts, beginning with the simplest and leading up to the more difficult. In J vi.366, Amarā Devī is preparing a rice pudding with milk, and "adds suitable flavoring" (*tadanurūpaṃ vyañjanaṃ sampādetvā*). When the Bodhisatta closes his teeth on her "flavored pudding" (*savyañjanaṃ yāgum adāsi*), his sense of taste is thrilled (*rasa-haraṇiyo*).

In Vin i.40 an inquirer asks, "What does the Master teach?" The disciple answers, "I am not able to set forth the doctrine to you at length (*vitthārena dhammaṃ desetum*), but I can tell you its purport briefly (*saṃkhittena atthaṃ vakkhāmi*)." The questioner replies, "Whether you say little or much, tell me in any case the purport (*atthaṃ yeva me brūhi*) —in accordance with its intention, I mean (*atthen'eva me attho*)—why should you make a great elaboration (*kiṃ kāhasi vyañjanaṃ bahum*)?" The answer is the following "doctrinal formula (*dhamma-pariyāyam*)": "Of all things that are of causal origin, the Tathāgata has told the cause, and so too has the Great Monk proclaimed their suppression" (the well-known "Buddhist confession" which is found as an inscription on so many examples of Buddhist art, as if this were the essence of their message). There is no question of "spirit and letter" here: what the inquirer

---

The answer is that this meaning (*attha*) was not stated "In these very words (*etehi padehi*) or with these very trappings (*etehi vyañjanehi*)." The Buddha responds by saying that by whatever "alternative formula (*pariyāya*, paraphrase, circumlocution)" *aññā* has been declared, one must take it as having been declared.

It may be noted incidentally that Pāli *vyatta* = Skr. *vyakta* (pp. of *vyañj*), and its opposite *avyatta* are applied to persons, not to statements, as if one should speak of an "explicit, or inexplicit speaker" rather than of "explicit, or inexplicit speech"; that *vyañjayati* (to "characterize," etc.) occurs only in Commentaries; and that the quite different word *vyākaroti* is rather to "state or propound" than to "explain."

[91] So, I think always, in the PTS translations by C.A.F. Rhys Davids and F. L. Woodward. The SBE version of the *Mahāvagga* by T. W. Rhys Davids and H. Oldenberg is inconsistent: at Vin i.40–41 (Mhv i.23.4–9), *attha* is rendered by "spirit" and *vyañjana* by "letter," but i.358 (x.6.2) *attha* is rendered by "letter" and *vyañjana* by "spirit."

In the last context (text) for *atthupetā ca vyañjanupetā ca* read *atthupetāvyañjanupetā*, i.e., *atthupetā-avyañjanupetā*: the contrast is with *atthupetā ca vyañjanupetā ca*.

really wants to know is "what he must *do* to be saved." In terms of the preceding reference, he is hungry and wants primarily food, not caring whether it be "seasoned" or "elaborated." *Attham* is here the application, or immediate bearing of the doctrine; *vyañjanam* its "flavor," and the same as that *attha-rasa* that is tasted only by the few (A I.36).[92]

In A II.160 where we have, "when the analytical factors of the meaning (*attha-paṭisambhidā*)[93] have been verified (*sacchikatvā*)[94] both as regards

[92] Even briefer is the Buddha's enunciation of *kammavāda* in the two words *paṭisamuppannaṃ dukkham*, with respect to which Ānanda exclaims, "It is marvelous, how this whole matter has been stated in a single phrase (*ekena padena*)! Had it been set forth at length, it would have been seen to be deep (*gambhīro*) in fact as well as in seeming!"

[93] For the four *paṭisambhidā* see the PTS Dictionary, s.v. The four are *attha, dhamma, nirutti* (= hermeneia), *paṭibhāna* ("illumination," a meaning given in the Dictionary (cf. S I.187 and *Kindred Sayings* [= S], Vol. I, p. 237), in connection with which it may be noted that *pratibhā* in the sense to "flash upon the mind" is hardly "late" Skr., since it occurs in the Upaniṣads). The four meanings would seem to be moral, literal, hermeneutic, and anagogic or parabolical. They are often mentioned in connection with and as if necessary to the attainment of Arahattā, in the formula *saha paṭisambhidāhi arahattam pāpuṇati*, Mil 18, etc. Cf. Dh 352, *nirutti-pada-kovido, akkharānam sannipātaṃ jaññā pubbāparāni ca, sa ve antimasarīro, mahāpañño, mahāpuriso ti vuccati.* Here there is an unmistakable recognition of the spiritual value of semantic and grammatical scholarship; but it must be remembered that these sciences cannot be exactly identified with their modern "equivalents," *nirukta* being much rather "hermeneia" than "etymology" in our sense.

The students will find it profitable to compare with this the four meanings, literal, moral, allegorical, and parabolical, in Scholastic Christian exegesis, as defined, e.g., in St. Thomas Aquinas, *Sum. Theol.* I.I.10. Most important and of universal application is the proposition that "the parabolical meaning is contained in the literal." For this reason it is very necessary not only to have understood the precise meaning of the Pāli symbols, but also to translate them literally (*ipsae res significatae per voces etiam significant aliquid*).

[94] We suggest the use of "verify" for Pāli *sacchikaroti* and "verification" for *sacchikiriya* (the so-called "Act of Truth"). Cf. our expression, "to make a thing come true." It should be noted, however, that from the Indian point of view, the possibility of this depends upon truth in the agent, cf. J I.214 *bodhisatto . . . saccasabhāvam ārabbha saccakiriyaṃ karonto.* In other contexts we find that "realization" is expressed by the phrase *yoniso manasikāra*, "an original act of intellect."

The use of *sacchikaroti* in the full sense of the words "hear and understand" may be noted in D I.150, where the Buddha, "as being one who has verified it by his own extra-generic gnosis (*sayam abhiññā sacchikatvā*) promulgates the Law and preaches it, lovely in its beginning, in its middle and in its end, both in its moral and in its spiritual significance (*sāttham savyañjanam*)": and DhA III.361, where *sakkaccan na suṇanti* is literally "do not hear with verification," i.e., hear but do not learn.

The same is expected of others: "Whatever Monk or Brahman here and now,

what is laid down (*odhiso*) and what is elaborated (*vyañjanaso*), I then explain them by many alternative formulae, teach and illuminate them, make them comprehensible, open them up, dissect and spread them out (*aneka-pariyāyena ācikkhāmi, desemi, pakāsemi, paññāpemi, vivarāmi, vibhajāmi, uttānī-karomi*)."[95] *Odhiso* here can only refer to the immediate meaning of the text: *odhi* deriving from *odahati*, Skr. *avadhā*, to "set down," analogous to *abhidhā*, the "literal power" of an expression, or "denotation." It is just in this sense, indeed, that the text itself is a "footprint (*pada*)," a trace set down and that can be followed up, in the sense of RV x.71.3 *vācaḥ padavīyam āyan*, and of the "*hatthi-pada*" in Pāli, *passim*. *Odhi* is thus also, like its Sanskrit equivalent *avadhi*, the object to which the mind is directed, and being thus equivalent to the primary meaning of the text, *vyañjanam* can only be the expanded meaning implied by the phrases concluding with *uttāni-karomi*. *Odhi* referring to the actual wording corresponds to *desanam*, "promulgation"; *vacanam*, "utterance"; *akhyānam*, "narrative"; *kathitam*, "relation"; *padam*, "verse," etc. *Odhi* refers to the "aesthetic surface" of the doctrine, and in this connection it may be pointed out that what is said in words differs in no way in principle from what is represented in plastic art, the interpretation of which from either a strictly aesthetic or a merely anecdotal point of view being equally superficial and insufficient: as *Lankāvatāra Sūtra* II.118–19 expresses it, "the real picture is not in the colors, the principle evades the letter."

We meet with the "four meanings" again in A II.139 in connection with the definition of four sorts of orators (*vādī*), of whom the best is the speaker "who is not brought to a standstill either as regards the practical purport (*atthato*) or the developed meaning (*vyañjanato*): it is impossible for one fully possessed of the four analytical powers (*paṭisambhidā*) to be brought to a standstill in either of these respects."

In A II.148 the first of four ways that conduce to the preservation of the "True Law (*saddhamma*)" is that condition which exists when the Almsman is in full possession of a text "with well-put verses and flavorings (*sunikkhittehi pada-vyañjanehi*): for, Almsmen, if the verses and their

---

by his own extra-generic gnosis has verified the meaning of monasticism and Brahmahood, he has 'arrived' (*sāmaññatthañ ca brahmaññatthañ ca diṭṭheva dhamme sayam abhiññā sacchikatvā, upasampajja viharanti*, S II.46)."

[95] Similarly, S II.28 *svākhyāto . . . mayā dhammo uttāno vivaṭo pakasito chinnapilotiko*, "Doctrine well taught by me, spread out, opened up, illuminated, divested of wrapping."

flavoring are well put, the practical meaning is likewise easy to follow (*attho pi sunnayo hoti*)." We hark back in this version to the notion of cooking: considering that *pada* corresponds to the rice, and *vyañjana* to the sauce, and that if these are suitably combined, the intellectual nourishment will be readily assimilated.

In D III.127–28, it is said that Almsmen are to meet together and talk over Doctrine, not contumaciously but "comparing moral (or literal) sense with moral (or literal) sense (*atthena attham*) and implicit meaning with implicit meaning (*vyañjanena vyañjanam*)," the discussion taking such a form as "to such and such a moral sense (*imassa . . . atthassa*) do these, or these other implicit meanings (*imāni vā vyañjanāni etāni vā vyañjanāni*) correspond most closely?" and conversely. Here it may be noted how the genitives imply that the moral or literal and the spiritual or implicit meanings are reciprocal and inseparable; it is never a question of arbitrary explanations but only of an adequate symbolism, in which there is a contrast but never an opposition of "letter and spirit" (Islamic *es-shariyaḥ* and *el-haqīqaḥ*). In S IV.281 and 296, *nānatthā nānavyañjanā* is clearly "different in denotation and in connotation," *ekatthā* in the same context meaning "alike in denotation."

In S V.430, a specifically moral theme, that of *dukkha*, "ill" or "sorrow," is effectively the "moral meaning" with reference to which the Buddha says that "there are definitely various phases and illustrations thereof (*aparimāṇā vaṇṇā aparimāṇā vyañjanā aparimāṇā saṃkāsanā*), and here *vyañjana* is certainly something like "coloring," "disguise," "shade of meaning," a sense quite in accordance with the root meaning of *vyañj*, "to smear on." Similarly in A II.182, where the Buddha says that "he has taught that such and such a proposition is right (*idaṃ kusalaṃ . . . mayā paññattam*), in countless verses (*aparimāṇā padā*), with countless colorings (*aparimāṇā vyañjanā*) and countless enunciations of the spiritual-meaning (*aparimāṇā dhamma-desanā*)."

The most difficult text is that of Mil 18, where the Buddha's word (*buddha-vacanam*) is learnt by heart at one hearing, is mastered in three months *vyañjanato*, and in another three months *atthato*. We should have expected the reverse order of words. We cannot, however, allow the apparent meaning of this isolated text to override that of so many others, and must conclude that the fully developed meaning is thought of here as having been grasped before the application of it was made.

As we have remarked, in nearly all of the foregoing contexts the translators render *attha* by "spirit" and *vyañjana* by "letter." It is by no means our intention to suggest that the very words "letter and spirit" are out of place in these contexts, but we do say that if these words are used, it is in precisely the opposite sense, *attha* being the "letter" and *vyañjana* the "spiritual" meaning. For we cannot employ the English words "letter and spirit" vaguely but only in one of two ways, either with reference to "literal meaning" and "inner meaning" (a relation expressed in Pāli by saying that "B is the *adhivacanam*, i.e., interpretation, of A"),[96] or in that way in which the words "letter and spirit" (or their equivalents) were used by St. Paul (II Cor. 3:6), from whom our use of the words descends. Whoever has any doubt as to the meaning of the words of St. Paul should consider Augustine's treatise, *De spiritu et littera*. St. Paul is not referring to figurative expressions but to the distinction between the moral law and spiritual understanding, the former essential to the active and the latter essential to the contemplative life. It is precisely in the same way that *attha* (as we have seen) refers to things to be done, and *vyañjana* to things to be understood: it would be true to say that in our contexts *attha* and *vyañjana* correspond to what are called *karma-kāṇḍa* and *jñāna kāṇḍa* in Sanskrit. In Vin I.40, it is the fact that an injunction to walk in a certain Way is implicit in the formula that makes it *attha* and not *vyañjana*. We can see also why it is that precedence is given to *attha*: it is just as it is for the hungry man, for whom food is the first consideration and flavoring the second; the flavor is better than the food, but not for the hungry man, who is still in need of food, without which he cannot "keep on going"; it is not this "little self," the so-called *attā* or *appattā*, but only the "great self," *mahattā*, "the immortal contemplative self, without desire" of AV x.8.44, that is "satisfied by flavor" only (*rasena tṛptaḥ*). It is from the same point of view that the Buddha so often refuses to discuss ultimates (such as "is or is not" after death) because they do not pertain or conduce to Wayfaring (*maggana*). Virtue is only a means, indeed; it is dispositive, but not essential to the end. But "while we are on the way, we are not there"; virtue is essential to the Way. *Attha* is thus prior to *vyañjana* in practice, but inferior in hierarchy since when the end of the road has been reached there is no more Wayfaring to be done.

[96] It is in this connection that we find the Buddhist parallel of St. Paul's "the letter killeth," viz. in S I.II, where "Men aware only of what can be told (*akkheyya*, the *akkhānam*, narrative or parable taken historically and literally) live under the yoke of death." This will apply, of course, as much to the understanding of the carved or painted parable as to the spoken symbol.

We have so far discussed *vyañjana* in what may be called its "good" sense, that sense in which the four *paṭisambhidā* are said to be essential to Arahatta. There are also some contexts in which *vyañjana* as "ornament" is disparaged, for example PugA 223, where *padaparamo*, "whose ultimate is the verse itself," is explained by *vyañjanapadam eva paramam assa*, "he for whom the verbal ornament only is the prime consideration." That the reference is disparaging is clear also from A II.135, where the final reward (*uṭṭhāna-phalam*) is contingent upon the nature of the mental effort put forth; there are four classes of hearers, "those who understand immediately (*ugghaṭitaññū*), those who understand upon reflection (*vipacittaññū*), those who must be led (*neyyo*, e-*duc*-ated, the Yakkhī of S I.11–12 being a good example), and those whose ultimate is the text itself" (*padaparamo*, the stupid king of J VI.131 being an example). *Padaparamo* is then either "literalist" (as condemned in S I.11, where indeed "the letter kills"), or in accordance with PugA, the man who cares more about the art of the text than its meaning, and may be compared to the man who in terms of our first citation (J VI.366) might be more particular about the taste of the food than about its nourishing essence. Our immediate concern is with the disparaged *vyañjanapadam* of PugA, where the reference is plainly to artistry considered as the final end of oratory: cf. A I.72, III.107 and S II.267, where a *suttanta* characterized by fine sounds rather than fine thoughts is called *cittakkhara* (cf. the later *citrakāvya*), and S I.38, where the syllables themselves (*akkharāni*, thought of as sounds rather than as written letters)[97] are called the "sauce or flavor" (*vyañjana*)[98] of poetry. In S II.267 and parallel passages, "the sermons (*suttantā*) preached by the Tathāgata are profound (*gambhīrā*), of profound moral significance (*gambhīratthā*), dealing with the other world (*lokuttarā*) and bound up with the emptiness of this world (*suññata-paṭisaṃyutta*); but a time will come when they will no longer be regarded as things to be studied and mastered; on the contrary, those sermons that are made by poets in the poetical style (*te suttantā kavikatā kāveyyā*), with embellished sounds (*cittakkharā*), overlaid with ornament (*citta-vyañjanā*), and spoken by profane auditors (*bāhirakā sāvaka-bhāsitā*), will be considered worthy of study, and the others will disappear."

[97] The reader will not forget that *akṣara* is primarily a sounded syllable, and only secondarily a written sign. Indian rhetoric, at least in its beginnings, has therefore more to do with oratory than with "literature" as we think of it.

[98] This is the Dictionary meaning, s.v. *akkhara*.

We see nothing in all this that is particularly monastic or puritanical, but only something serious; the repudiation of an art for art's sake and of sophistry and of aestheticism. The Buddhist is the same as the Platonic, Aristotelian, and Scholastic view of rhetoric as the art of giving effectiveness to truth. As Augustine says, "I am not now speaking of how to please: I am speaking of how they are to be taught who desire instruction." *Cittakkhara, citta-vyañjana* are "sophistic" in the sense of Augustine's definition, "A speech seeking verbal ornament beyond the bounds of responsibility to its burden (*gravitas*) is called 'sophistic.'" In the same way, "No matter in what connection, when Buddhas preach the Law, it is upon the Law that they lay weight (*gāravam*, etymologically and semantically the equivalent of Augustine's *gravitas*); they speak as though bringing down from heaven the Aerial River" (*ākāsagaṅgam otārento viya*, DhA III.360).[99] That the preaching of the Law "pierces the skin and flesh[100] and penetrates to the marrow of the bones" (DhA III.361) recalls St. Paul's "the word of God is quick and powerful, and sharper than any two-edged sword, piercing even unto . . ." (Heb. 4:12),[101] and St. Augustine's "O Eloquence, so much the more terrible as it is so unadorned; and as it is so genuine, so much the more powerful: O truly an axe hewing the rock!"[102]

On the other hand, it must not be inferred that the art of oratory, rightly used, is in any way disparaged. We find, for example, Mahā Kaccāna praised as the "chief of those who dissect at length the meaning of what has been briefly said (*saṃkhittena bhāsitassa vitthārena atthaṃ vibhajantānam aggam*)," Kumāra Kassapa as the "chief of flowery speakers (*citta-kathikānam aggam*),"[103] and Mahā Koṭṭhita as the "chief of the

[99] It seems to have been overlooked that this is an allusion to the "Descent of the Ganges," well known in the Epic. The simile is far more tremendous to Indian than it could be to European ears: "speaking as if with the roar of Niagara" would be a weak analogy.

[100] The full sequence frequently occurs: *chavi, camma, maṃsa, nahāru, aṭṭhi, aṭṭhi-miñja*, "scarf-skin, skin, flesh, sinews, bones and marrow" (*chavi* is generally "complexion," "bloom," and can only be rendered here by "scarf-skin"). At Vin I.83, the whole formula is applied to the love of a son.

[101] The completion of the text, "piercing even unto the dividing asunder of soul and spirit" corresponds exactly to the often repeated theme of Buddhist teaching, *na me so attā, sabbe dhammā anattā, suññam idam attena*, etc., and makes the parallel particularly poignant.

[102] The quotations from Augustine are from the *De doctrina christiana*, 4. Cf. the fuller references in *Art Bulletin*, XX (March 1938), 72–77.

[103] At Mil I, Nāgasena's discourse (*kathā*) is described as "adorned with parables and types (*citrā opammehi nayehi ca*)."

Masters of the Four Meanings" (*paṭisambhidappattānam aggam*)," A I.23–24. We find the Buddha praising an Almsman who "in his doctrinal discourse was demonstrating to the brethren, making the Law acceptable to them, setting them afire, gladdening them with urbane words, well enunciated without hoarseness, with exposition of the meaning, pertinent and unbiased" (S II.280, cf. I.189). The same expressions recur in D II.109, where the Buddha explains that he adapts his teaching to his audience ("Whatever may be their sort, I make myself of the like sort, whatever their language, I speak that language"—i.e., becoming as we are that we may be as he is), "But they knew me not when I spoke, and would ask 'Who may this be that speaks thus, a man or a god?' Whereupon I demonstrated the Law, made it acceptable to them, set them on fire (*samuttejetvā*), gladdened them, etc." The argument is always *ad hominem*: for as *Laṅkāvatāra Sūtra* II.122 expresses it, "Whatever is not adapted to such and such persons as are to be taught, cannot be called teaching." It is thus that "He preaches the lovely Law, with its moral and spiritual meanings (*dhammaṃ deseti . . . kalyāṇam sāttham savyañjanam*, D I.250).

It will not be inappropriate to conclude the present article with: "At the close of my discourse I compose and settle my heart, focus and synthesize it (*cittaṃ saṇṭhāpemi sannisādemi ekodikaromi samādahāmi*), in accordance with the former fashion of my interior synthesis (*samādhi*), in which assuredly I abide when and whenever I will (*niccakappaṃ niccakappaṃ viharāmi*, M I.249)."

The net result of the foregoing discussion, and that of *rasa*, is to indicate that Pāli *vyañjana* and *rasa* are often very nearly the same thing, a quality that may be regarded either as the most intimate flavor or color of the text, or from another point of view as an overlay of ornament, and thus "too much of a good thing." In any case, *vyañjana* is never "syllable," as it has been rendered at A II.182.

sākhā and *sākha*. Like the Skr. equivalent *śākhā*, the word occurs in Pāli in the primary sense of "branch" (of a tree), but also in Sn 688 as "rib" of an umbrella, and it is probable that this was also a meaning of the word in Skr. The word in this sense is of interest because of the coincident (axial) symbolism of "umbrella" and "tree"; the ribs surround the handle (*daṇḍa*, also "stem of a tree") "as branches surround the trunk of the tree (*vṛkṣasya skandhaḥ parita iva śākkhāḥ*, AV X.7.38)," forming a "circle (*maṇḍala*)." Cf. *piṇḍika*.

saṇkha. The primary meaning is "number," hence *saṇkhaṃ gam*, to "be reckoned" or "accounted," as in Ud 55, "they are accounted (*saṇkhaṃ gacchanti*) 'Sons of the Buddha'" (*sakyaputtiya*).[104] In this sense *saṇkhaṃ gam* is to "be called," to "get a name." It follows that in a more general way to be "numbered" is to exist in the quantitative and dimensioned (*nimitta*) universe, *saṇkha* from this point of view being equivalent to *mātrā* ("measure," and etymologically "matter," that which is known in terms of "form and phenomenon," *nāma-rūpa*), in which sense *saṇkha* is almost the exact equivalent of "number" as characteristic of "species" in Scholastic philosophy. To come into being, take birth, and be "named" is a good from some points of view, but never a final good, and therefore from another point of view, that of the man who is seeking to become "no one" (*akiṃcana*), an evil. So in Sn 1074 it is said of the Muni, sped like a flame blown out by the wind, and liberated from name and body (*nāmakāyā* = *nāmarūpayā*), that he "gets him home (*attham paleti*), he does not get a number (*na upeti saṇkham*),"[105] i.e., he is not cognizable: in the same way it is said of the Arhat, who is past finding out by gods or men in heaven or on earth, that he "has done with number (*pahāsi saṇkham*, S i.12)"; it is just such as these of whom Brahmā says, in fact, that he "cannot give any true accounting (*saṇkhātuṃ no pi sakkomi*, etc., D ii.218)"; and conversely in S iii.35, "Whatever it be that a man takes to bed, it is by that that he gets his number" (*yaṃ . . . anuseti tena saṇkhaṃ gacchati*), i.e., his unaccomplished purpose determines his birth[106] (as in MU ii.6d).

[104] It is in this sense that, in RV ix.61.7, Soma is "reckoned with the Ādityas (*saṃ ādityebhir akhyata*)."

[105] *Na upeti saṇkham*, like MU vi.20 *nirātmakatvāt asaṇkhyaḥ*, "out of count, because without a self": Sn 1076, *na pamāṇam atthi*. S iv.376–77 is explicit: the Tathāgata is "free of any reckoning" (*saṃkhāya-vimutto*) in terms of any one of the five *khandhas*, *rūpa*, *vedana*, etc., i.e., has no psycho-physical "number." "Number, if taken as a species of quantity, denotes an accident added to being" (*Sum. Theol.* i.30.3): "quia designatio individui respectu speciei est per materiam determinatum dimensionibus" (*De ente et essentia* iii.1), i.e., inasmuch as all things are *nimittāni*, "measured out."

It will be seen from what follows that like all other negative symbols, to be without number (the same as to be nameless) can have either a "good" or a "bad" meaning; *asaṇkhyaḥ* corresponding to *amātra*, and *ajāta*, etc. In the same way there is an *asat* (nonbeing) that is "naughty" (because of privation of being) and an *asat* (nonbeing) that is also a plenum (*pūrṇam*) because not limited by a being in any way (*iti-bhāva*).

[106] The idiom corresponds to that of "as one makes one's bed, so must one lie upon it." The corresponding word *anusaya* denotes the condition in which a man is naturally found, and from which he is summoned to arouse himself; and it is no doubt in the same sense that the New Testament "Arise, take up thy

There is, however, another use of the word, or rather of the corresponding verb, of no less interest, occurring in Sn 351, "To do what one will does not pertain to the common herd; it pertains to Tathāgatas to do what is correct," or more literally, "calculated" (*na kāmakāro*[107] *hi puthujjanānaṃ, saṇkheyyakāro ca tathāgatānam*). *Saṇkheyya* here can only be understood as equivalent to *prameya* in the sense of "correct" (an absolute *pramāṇa* is, in fact, attributed to the Buddha; all that the Buddha says or does is said or done well). The converse of the text is also, of course, implied: what is done by the untaught many-folk is informal, *apaṭirūpa*, *asaṇkheyya*,[108] the Buddhas do what they will. In the same sense, *saṇkha* must mean what is "right," one might even say "mathematically right" since it is precisely a question of "number," in Dh 267, where "he who has ousted good and evil, the walker-with-Brahma, whose course in the world is 'calculated (*saṇkhāya loke carati*),' he is rightly called an 'Almsman' ": or conversely, "wrong" when "calculating (*saṇkhāya*)" implies "with ulterior motives," as in A II.143. The use of *saṇkheyya* and *saṇkhāya* in the good sense corresponds to that of *saṇkhyānam* and *asaṇkhyānam* in JB II.69 and 73, where in opposing rites what is done by Prajāpati in good form overcomes what is done by Death informally, and what is "in order (*saṃkhyānam*)" being immortal (*amṛtam*) and what is "inordinate (*asaṃkhyānam*)" mortal (*martyam*)—a distinction corresponding to that of *satyam* from *anṛtam*. It is in the same sense that in an unidentified sūtra (A. F. Rudolf Hoernle, *MS. Remains of Buddhist Literature from E. Turkestan*, Oxford, 1916, I, 98–100), *saṃkhyām gacchati* is "reaches fullness."

samala. This word is cited for the sake of the light it throws on Skr. *śāmulya*, *śāmūla*. The Dictionary omits to note the immediate Skr. equivalent, *śamala*, but gives the meaning, "impure, contaminated, Vin I.5." We have also *sandhi-samala-saṃkaṭīra*, with the general sense of "garbage

---

bed, and walk" should be understood. *Saṇkha* is, in fact, virtually synonymous with *anusaya*, Skr. *anuśaya*, as "bed," *karmic* consequence, and finally "repentance" inasmuch as it is from this predestined condition that one uprises. Similarly *āśaya*: see *karmāśaya* as used by Patañjali, *Yogasūtra* [*The Yoga-System of Patañjali*, tr. J. H. Woods, Cambridge, Mass., 1914, HOS 17] II.12 ff. (rendered by Woods "latent deposit of karma"), and the discussion by Jaideva Singh in *Review of Philosophy and Religion*, VIII (1939).

107 *Na kāmakāro*, as in CU VIII.1.6, *ihātmānam ananuvidya . . . sarveṣu lokeṣv akāmacāro bhavanti*, "not having known the Spiritual-Self in this life, do not become 'Movers-at-will' in any world."

108 In very many contexts, of course, *asaṃkheyya* is simply "incalculable," i.e., of indefinite (not infinite, however) extent: for example, where *asaṃkheyya* = *kappa*.

heap" in S II.270, M I.334 and D II.160; and *dhammo asuddho samalehi cintito,* "an unclean doctrine conceived by foul minds" in Vin I.5, S I.137. It seems impossible to doubt that in RV X.85.29 *śāmulyam* is not (as commonly rendered) "woolen," but "filthy,"[109] the reference being in fact to the "snake-skin" that Kṛtyā must be thought of as shedding when she "has gotten feet" (*padvatī bhūtvī*), all in accordance with the well-known formula for procession from ophidian potentiality to human actuality; or that in JUB I.38.4, *śāmūla-parṇabhyām* is not, as rendered by Oertel, "with a woolen shirt(?) and a leaf," but "(clad) in dirty leaves."

samudda (as *adhivacanam* of *nibbāna*). In Buddhism, as in Brahmanism, the Pilgrim's "Way" considered as a voyage (*yāna*, in this sense) may be related in three different ways to the flowing river of life and death. The journey is either upstream to the waters' source; or over the waters to a farther shore; or downstream to the sea. This use of symbolisms which are contrary in their literal but unanimous in their spiritual sense very well illustrates the nature of metaphysics itself, which is not, like a "philosophy," systematic, but is always consistent. All that we have to be careful of here (as in any work of art) is to make use of our symbols consistently: it is only, for example, in the second case, that of "crossing over," that the symbol of the "bridge" can also be employed; it would be incongruous to speak of the "bridge" in connection with a going up or down stream.[110]

In the first case, the symbol is of a procedure against the stream, and the Buddhist Wayfarer is accordingly referred to as an "Upstreamer" (*paṭisoto* or *uddhaṃsoto*, with *anusotagāmī*, "drifting with the current" as opposite). Without going into the history of the underlying thought at great length, we may observe that in RV X.28.4, *pratīpaṃ śāpaṃ nadyo vahanti* ("the rivers carry the foam against the current"), is already a paradox to be explained. Whatever this may mean, the text of TS VII.5.7.4, "The heavenly world is counter-current (*pratikūlam*) hence" is explicit: and it is precisely in this sense that in PB XXV.10.12–16 the Sacrificers, going "counter-current" or "upstream" (*pratīpam*) along the whole course of the Sarasvatī (the River of Life), reach the heavenly world (it is clear

[109] The Vedic and Brāhmaṇa associations of "wool" are regularly with purity and purification. Sāyaṇa appears to be perfectly correct in his gloss *śāmulyam* = *śāmulam* = *śarīram malam, śarīrāvacchannasya malasya dhārakaṃ vastram*, "foul body, or garment reeking of the foulness of the body that was covered by it."

[110] Or only if we see in the river itself the "bridge" and Axis Mundi.

from verse 11 that the Sarasvatī is coincident with the Axis Mundi):[111] it is impossible to reach the goal "downstream." The symbolism here is one of return to the river's source, the Fons Vitae, Varuṇa's abiding place *sindhūnām upodaye* (RV VIII.41.2), the "Well of Honey in Viṣṇu's highest place (*viṣṇoḥ pade parame madhva utsaḥ*, RV I.154.5)," the Perennial Spring of Plotinus, *Enneads* III.8.10, etc. Among the Christian parallels may be noted Ruysbroeck, "a perpetual striving after the unattainable —this is 'striving against the stream'" (*Sparkling Stone*, ch. 9; cf. JB I.85, *pratikūlam udyan . . . samaṣṭyā*); Dante, *Purgatorio* I.40, "Against the dark stream fled the eternal prison"; Blake, "Jesus died . . . he strove against the current of this wheel."

More familiar is the symbolism of the "Farther Shore," to be reached in various ways, whether by raft, ship, bridge, or ford, and in connection with which we meet with a great variety of terms such as *tara*, *taraṇa*, *tārā*, *tīran*, *tīrtha*,[112] *trātṛ*, etc., deriving from *tṛ*, to "cross over." In this case the Waters to be crossed are specifically the River of Death (M I.225–27; DhA II.275, etc.), or as more fully explained in S IV.174–75, the Great Flood of Water (*mahā udakaṇṇavo*) is the flood of will, birth, opinion, and ignorance (*kāma*, *bhava*, *diṭṭhi*, *avijjā*), the Hither Shore represents "embodiment" (*sakkāya*), the Farther Shore *nibbāna*, and the "Brahman who has crossed and reached the farther side and stands on solid ground (*tiṇṇo pāraṃgato thale tiṭṭhati brāhmaṇo*)" is the Arahat. The formula of crossing over to a farther shore or haven of safety occurs so repeatedly in Buddhist and Brahmanical contexts alike that no further examples need be cited here. The metaphor of the saving "ship" (Pāli and Skr. *nāvā*) is preserved in our "nave" (of a church).[113]

[111] Coincident, then, with the Shaft of Light, the Bolt and Sacrificial Post that strikes downwards from the zenith to the nadir of the universe, and which must be reversed by those who would ascend. The digging out and setting upright of the Post in AB II.1–2, etc., has the same spiritual significance as the words "countercurrent," etc., discussed above; cf. Coomaraswamy, "Inverted Tree" [in Vol. 1 of this edition; the symbols discussed in this entry are also treated in "The Sea," Vol. I of this edition.—ED.].

[112] *Tīrtha* is "crossing place"; *tīrthakara* virtually synonymous with "pontifex," "pontiff." Tārā is "Savioress," and also "star," cf. the Virgin as Stella Maris. *Trātṛ* is ferryman or savior. *Tarana* is crossing; hence *avatarana*, "crossing back," i.e., the "descent" of a Savior. *Tīran* is "crossing" in S V.24 (where we have "few are they of mortal men who have reached the Farther Shore"). Our "term," Lat. *terminus*, is cognate.

[113] As in the well-known Parable of the Raft (M I.135), the crossing over is here by means of a raft, for which there is no more use when the Farther Shore has been reached, and as in Revelation 21:1, "there was no more sea." The

Less familiar, though by no means rare in Buddhist contexts, is the metaphor of a gliding downstream to a *nibbāna* represented by the Sea, not here as a mass of waters to be crossed, but itself the last end. This value of *samudda* (Sea) is overlooked in the PTS Dictionary. In S v.39–40, we find "just as rivers lean, tend, and gravitate towards the sea (*samudda-ninnā, -poṇā, -pabbhārā*),"[114] just so the Almsman who cultivates the Aryan Eightfold Path "leans, tends, and gravitates towards Nibbāna"; similarly S v.134. In the same way in the parable of the Log, S iv.179–80, floating downstream on the Ganges is gliding towards Nibbāna; the dangers are of stranding on either shore, being taken by those (men or gods) who dwell on these shores,[115] stranding on a shoal (*thale ussīdissati*),[116] sinking in mid-stream (*majjhe saṃsīdissati*),[117] or of rotting within, and if all these dangers are avoided, then "shall ye lean, tend, and gravitate towards Nibbāna." It is clear that the stream is here no longer Māra's, as in M i.226 (*mārassa sota*), but rather the Flood of Merit (*puññassa dhārā*) of A ii.56. In S v.47, cf. 63, young followers of the Eightfold Path are compared to the young Nāgas (snakes, or rather eels; see *nāga*) born in the Himālayas and who, as they grow bigger, make their way down to the Sea and there attain their full dimensions, the Commentary equating *nāga* with *yogāvacara* and *samudda* with *nibbāna*. In DhA iii.230 ff.,

---

Waters to be crossed are represented in the Gospels (John 6, etc.) by the Sea of Galilee; cf. W. Norman Brown, *Walking on the Water*, London, 1928, pp. 20 ff.

[114] The words *-ninnā, -poṇā, -pabbhārā* or their equivalents, *mutatis mutandis*, occur elsewhere, notably in the well-known metaphor of the rafters that converge towards and rest in the roof-plate of the dome, and it is thus that the powers of the soul converge towards and come to rest in *samādhi* (ŚA viii.8, M i.322–23, Mil 38, etc.).

[115] The interpretation (*adhivacanam*) of "this shore" is *ajjhattikānam āyatanānam* and of "that shore" *bāhirānam āyatanānam*, i.e., these internal (microcosmic) and those external (macrocosmic) conditions. This provides us with good evidence for what can be inferred in many other contexts, viz. that *ajjhattikam . . . bāhiram* correspond to *adhyātmam . . . adhidevatam* as, e.g., in JUB iii.33, where the two words have precisely the implication of "subjective" and "objective" that is fundamental to Pāli *ajjhattikam* and *bāhiram*, as in M i.421, where the five elements as they are within you (i.e., microcosmically) are contrasted with the same as they are outside you (i.e., macrocosmically).

[116] Observe that *thale* ("aground") here has the exactly opposite spiritual meaning of *thale* ("safe ashore") in S iv.174–75 cited above. In this connection cf. René Guénon, "Du Double Sens des symboles," in *Études traditionelles*, XLII (1937).

[117] "Drowning in the nether waters"; here the symbolism coincides with that of crossing over, and if one falls from the ship or bridge or if one sinks while "walking on the water," he may be drowned.

the significance of the downstream voyage, here in a boat, is the same, but the value of *nāga* is reversed;[118] because of a sin by which the voyage is interrupted the novice is reborn as the Nāga Erakapatta.

Finally, the foregoing texts in which *samudda* = *nibbāna*, and even more literally Ud 55, "Just as rivers lose their former names and clan names (*purimāni nāma-gottāni*)[119] when they reach the sea, and it is accounted only 'The Great Sea,'" correspond exactly to the better known "Just as these flowing rivers that tend towards the sea, when they reach the sea are gone home, and their name and aspect (*nāma-rūpa*) are broken up, and only 'the Sea' (*samudram iti*) is spoken of" (Praśna Up. vi.5, etc.), as well as to the almost identical images employed by Dante, Eckhart and Ruysbroeck.[120]

It may be added that where symbolism of a going downstream to the Sea is employed as above, a return to the source would be equivalent to "backsliding (*apāya*)," and that we actually find the expressions "counter-current" and "back-flowing" used accordingly in AV x.1.7, where the evil powers are enjoined to return "upstream counter-current" (*pratikūlam udāyyam*), and AV iv.17.2, where *punaḥsara* = apotropaic.

sahājanetta. Sn 1096: two MSS. read *sahajanetta*. We should render "possessed of the innate eye," i.e., as the Commentator implies, "of spontaneous omniscience." We do not agree with the Dictionary's "lit. 'coinciding eye,'" but take *sahaja* in its usual sense of "connatural," "inborn," and hence as in the later rhetoric, not acquired (*ahāryā*) or learnt (*au-*

[118] The two values of "*nāga*" are the same as those of JB iii.77 and PB xxv.15.4, where a distinction is made between those snakes (*ahi*) that are "left behind" (*ahīyata*) and the others (*sarpa*) who, inasmuch as they "creep on farther" (*atisarpanti*), vanquish death and become Ādityas (like the Buddha, *ādicca-bandhu*).

[119] Cf. JB i.18.5–6, *Taṃ hāgatam pṛcchati, kas tvam asi. Sa yo ha nāmnā vā gotreṇa vā prabrūte . . . taṃ ṛtavas . . . padgṛhītam*—i.e., if in answer to the question "Who art thou?" he answers by his own or his clan-name, he is dragged away by the representatives of time. For many other parallels see "*Ākiṃcañña*: Self-naughting" [in this volume—ED.].

[120] Cited in Coomaraswamy, *A New Approach to the Vedas*, 1933, pp. 45, 46. It may be added that in JB i.173–75, where the Sacrificers are on their way to heaven and ask, "Who shall be able today to swim away out of the open jaws of the crocodile?" with reference to the "crocodile standing in the one and only way, against the current, with open maw" (*ekāyane siṃśumārī pratīpaṃ vyādāya tiṣṭhati*), it is clear that the motion of the sacrificers themselves, on the one way, is downstream to the sea; the crocodile (*siṃśumārin* = *makara* = *mṛtyu* = *sūrya*) is the keeper of the Gate, which is in this case the "mouth" of the river (as we should say, although it is rather the mouth of the sea into which the river pours).

padeśikā) but "natural (*sahajā*)" illumination (*pratibhā*). That is the terminology of the *Kāvyamīmāṃsa*, ch. 2, where also *sahaja* is equated with *sārasvata*, tantamount to "communicated by Sophia." The parallel as regards *pratibhā* is fully justified by M I.240, "There flashed upon me spontaneously three parables unheard ere now (*tisso upamā paṭibhaṃsu anacchariyā pubbe assutapubbā*)." This is, of course, a quite different thing from the ability of the charioteer, well versed and expert in his art, to answer any question on the subject "on the spot (*ṭhānaso*)," without "taking counsel (*cetaso parivitakkam*)"; though this facility born of application and practice provides an analogy for the Buddha's ability to "answer on the spot (*ṭhānaso . . . paṭibhāti*)" as he can because "he has fully penetrated the realm of the Law (*dhammadhātu . . . suppaṭividdhā*, M I.396)," or as elsewhere stated because he *is* the Law (S III.120 *yo dhammam passati mam passati*, cf. D III.84). There are other ways in which the Buddha's power of immediate response is expressed, for example S II.105, " 'Origination, origination': so saying, there arose in me, brethren, a vision in matters of the Law unheard ere now (*pubbe ananussutesu dhammesu cakkhum udapādi*), gnosis, prescience, science, light arose (*ñāṇaṃ, paññā, vijjā, āloko udapāde*)." Observe that "unheard before," while implying literally "not to be found in *śruti*, and therefore to be regarded as *smṛti*," does not imply "original" in our individualistic sense, which conceives of a property in ideas, but an exegesis suited to the present conditions and audience, and authoritative precisely because "original (*yoniso*)" in the true sense of the word, that of "deriving from the source"; it is not a question of what we call "inspiration" but rather of infallibility,[121] comparable to that of the Christ when he says, "as my Father hath taught me, I speak" (John 8:28), or that of St. Paul when he says, "I have the mind (νοῦς) of Christ" (I Cor. 2:16).

Sahajanetta can also be explained in agreement with what has been said above, s.v. *nettiyā*, but as having a more explicit reference to the epithet *cakkhuṃ loke*, "Eye in the World,"[122] so often applied to the

[121] D III.127, nothing is to be added to or taken away from the promulgated Dhamma; D III.135, all that the Tathāgata has said, from the night of the Awakening to that of the Total Despiration, "all that is just so and infallible" (*sabbaṃ taṃ tath'eva hoti, no aññathā*).

[122] *Cakkhum loke* is not noted in the PTS Dictionary. It occurs in D II.159, Sn 599, etc. Cf. S I.138, *buddhacakkhunā lokam volokento*; S I.134, *sabbam passati cakkhunā*. Out of countless Brahmanical texts I cite only AB I.6, "The Eye is the Truth deposited among men" (with reference to Agni), and RV VII.61.1, *cakṣur . . . sūryas . . . abhi yo viśvā bhuvanāni caṣṭe*. With *sahajanetta, cakkhuṃ loke*, etc., cf. *cakkhubhūto ñāṇa-bhūto* in M I.111, S II.255, etc.

Buddha in other contexts, an epithet that in pre- and non-Buddhist contexts would be applicable only to the Sun or Agni; in this case *sahajanetta* would be more literally "born as the Eye," or "Eye by Nature" than "possessed of the innate eye." The distinction is hardly material.

suññatā. "Emptiness" (*suññatā*) in Pāli contexts is not the metaphysical Zero (Nonbeing as the principle of Being, Infinite Possibility as distinguished from Indefinite Actuality), but a characteristic of this world, as in S IV.295–96, where it has been explained that when the Almsman returns from a deathlike Contemplation in which consciousness and feeling have been arrested, "three touches touch him," "emptiness (*suññato-*)," "formlessness (*animitto-*)" and "making no plans (*appaṇihito-phasso*)," and he discriminates (*viveka*) accordingly; and the meaning of "emptiness" is explained at M I.29, "emancipation of the Will by Emptiness (*suññatā ceto-vimutti*) being consequent upon the realization that 'this world is empty of spirit or anything spiritual' (*suññam idam attena vā attaniyena vā*)"; *suññatā* is synonymous with *anattā*, of which it really only paraphrases and isolates the privative *an*. It is no doubt in the same sense that in A I.72, "the texts are coupled with 'emptiness' (*suttantā . . . suññatā-paṭisaññutā*)"; there is, in fact, nothing more characteristic of Buddhist teaching that its constant resort to negatives (above all in the sense of the word *anattā*), which even some contemporary hearers found perplexing. The denial of spirituality to contingent things in particular is a denial of any real essence to these things in themselves, and thus forms the basis of the more sweeping *śūnyavāda* doctrine which in the Mahāyāna denies not any "value" but any essence to even the Buddha's appearance and to the promulgation of the Dhamma itself. If such a doctrine disturbs us, it may be found more palatably expressed in the *Vajracchedika Sūtra* thus, "Those who see me in the body (*rūpeṇa*) and think of me in sounds (*ghosaiḥ*), their way of thinking is false, they do not see me at all. . . . The Buddha cannot be rightly understood (*ṛju boddhum*) by any means (*upāyena*)."[123] Not that "means" are not dispositive to a right understanding,[124] but that if regarded as ends, even the most adequate means are a hindrance. In such a radical iconoclasm as this all traditional teachings are finally agreed. What is true of ethics is also true of the supports of contemplation: as in the well-known Parable of the Raft, the means are of no more use when the goal has been reached.

[123] A. F. Rudolf Hoernle, *MS. Remains*, I, p. 270.

[124] Cf. Muṇḍ. Up. III.2–4, *etair upāyair yatate yastu vidvān . . . viśate brahmadhāma.*

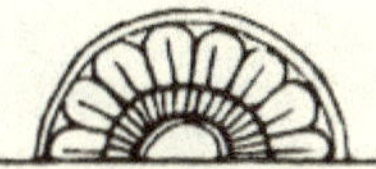

UNPUBLISHED WORKS

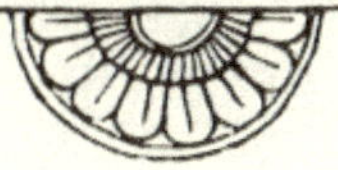

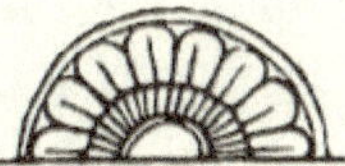

On the Indian and Traditional Psychology, or Rather Pneumatology

Ecce quomodo in cognitione sensitiva continatur occulte divina sapientia, et quam mira est contemplatio quinque sensuum spiritualium secundum conformitatem ad sensus corporales.[1]

St. Bonaventura, *De reductione artium ad theologiam* 10

Ὅστις αὖ σῶμα θεραπεύει, τὰ ἑαυτοῦ ἀλλ' οὐχ' αὐτόν θεραπεύει[2]

Plato, *I Alcibiades* 131B.

As Jadunath Sinha, in the only extensive work on Indian psychology (*bhūta-vidyā*), remarks, "There is no empirical psychology in India. Indian psychology is based on metaphysics."[3] The explanation of this is that

[Apparently written in 1943, this essay was rejected because of its length from the scholarly Festschrift to which it was contributed. Coomaraswamy seems to have made no further effort to publish this summary and extension of his late thought.—ED.]

[1] "Behold how the Divine Wisdom is secretly enclosed in sensitive perception, and how marvelous is the contemplation of the five spiritual senses in their conformity to the bodily senses." *Continatur occulte = guhā nihitam; sensus spirituales = jñānendriyani; sensus corporales = karmendriyaṇi.*

[2] "One who serves the body, serves what is his, not what he is." In the same way, "One who only knows the body, knows what is the man's, but not the man himself" (*ibid.*, A).

[3] Jadunath Sinha, *Indian Psychology: Perception* (London, 1934), p. 16. See also C.A.F. Rhys Davids, *Buddhist Psychology* (London, 1914); T. Stcherbatsky, *The Central Conception of Buddhism, and the Meaning of the Word "Dharma"* (London, 1923); and R. N. Dandekar, *Der vedische Mensch* (Heidelberg, 1938) (esp. pp. 21–24). Rhys Davids' book is very informative, but must be read with some caution, having been written "in ignorance of the stock of current nomenclature of which the Nikāyas made use" (p. 18). For this reason, perhaps, the author sees a contradiction between the Upaniṣad doctrine of the *Ātman* as "only seer," etc., and the Buddhist pronouncement that the question "Who sees?" cannot properly be asked; not realizing that the question is improper just because the "only seer"

"all Indian systems of philosophy are at the same time doctrines of salvation."[4] In other words, Indian philosophers are not interested in the facts, or rather statistical probabilities, for their own sake, but primarily in a liberating truth.[5] The traditional and sacred psychology takes for granted that life (*bhava*, γένεσις) is a means to an end beyond itself, not to be lived at all costs. The traditional psychology is not, in fact, based on observation; it is a science of subjective experience. Its truth is not of the kind that is susceptible of statistical demonstration; it is one that can only be verified by the expert contemplative.[6] In other words, its truth can only be verified by those who adopt the procedure prescribed by its proponents, and that is called a "Way." In this respect it resembles the truth of facts, but with this difference, that the Way must be followed by every individual for himself; there can be no public "proof." By verification we mean, of course, an ascertainment and experience, and not such a persuasion as may result from a merely logical understanding. Hence there can be no "propaganda" on behalf of the sacred science. Our only endeavor in the present article will be to expound it. Essentially, the sacred science is one of qualities, and the profane a science of quantities. Between these sciences there can be no conflict but only a difference, however great. We can hardly describe this difference better than in Plato's words cited above, or than in those of Kauṣ. Up. III.8, "Action (*karma*) is not what one should try to understand, what one should know is the Agent. Pleasure and pain are not what one should try to understand, what one should know is their Discriminant," and so on for the other factors of experience. We are careful not to say "of *our* experience," for it cannot by any means

---

never becomes anyone and is not any "who" or what. Seen in this light, the opposition of Brahmanical "realism" to Buddhist "nominalism" loses all its force (cf. n. 51).

[4] T. Stcherbatsky, *Buddhist Logic* (Leningrad, 1932), p. 195. In the same way, Plato's is a moral philosophy—*Bildung* rather than *Wissenschaft*, no "mere" theory, but also a way of life (cf. *Phaedo* 64 ff.), a *mārga* = ἴχνευσις, as, e.g., in *Phaedrus* 253A.

[5] Cf. Franklin Edgerton, "The Upaniṣads: What Do They Seek and Why?" *JAOS*, XLIX (1929), 102.

[6] Cf. Plato, *Phaedo* 65BC: "the Soul attains to Truth . . . best when none of these things, neither hearing nor seeing, nor pain nor any pleasure troubles it, and it is, as far as possible, all alone by itself (αὐτὴ καθ' αὑτὴν γίγνηται)." Note that "all alone by oneself" is not a phrase to be taken lightly, whether in English or Greek; it implies the distinction of the two selves, and the companioning of self with Self, that "other who never absconds" and to whom if one resorts he is "never alone" (BU II.1.11); cf. Manu, VI.49, *ātmanaiva sahāyena*; and A V.90, *kalyāna . . . sahāya*.

be assumed with safety that *we* are the Agent and Discriminant, nor safely argued *cogito ergo sum*.

It may be objected that the application of both the empirical and the metaphysical psychologies is to a salvation; and this can be granted, in view of the fact that *salv*ation imports a kind of health. But it does not follow that we must, on this ground alone, choose between them as a means to that end; for the simple reason that "salvation" means different things in the different contexts. The health envisaged by the empirical psychotherapy is a freedom from particular pathological conditions; that envisaged by the other is a freedom from all conditions and predicaments, a freedom from the infection of mortality and to be as, when and where we will (TU III.10.5; John 10:9, etc.). Furthermore, the pursuit of the greater freedom necessarily involves the attainment of the lesser; psychophysical health being a manifestation and consequence of spiritual well-being (Śvet. Up. II.12, 13). So whereas the empirical science is only concerned with the man himself "in search of a soul,"[7] the metaphysical science is concerned with this self's immortal Self, the Soul of the soul. This Self or Person is not a personality, and can never become an object of knowledge,[8] but is always its substance; it is the living, spirant principle in every psycho-hylic individuality "down to the ants" (AĀ I.3.8) and, in fact, the "only transmigrant"[9] in all transmigrations and evolutions. Hence we call the traditional psychology a pneumatology rather than a science of the "soul." And because its Self "never became anyone" (KU II.18), the metaphysical science is fundamentally one of "self-naughting"; as in Mark 8:34, *si quis vult post me sequi, denegat seipsum*.[10] In what follows we shall take for granted the distinction of "soul" (*ψυχή*, *nephesh*,

[7] C. G. Jung, *Modern Man in Search of a Soul* (London, 1933). Jung frankly admits, "I restrict myself to what can be psychically experienced, and repudiate the metaphysical" (R. Wilhelm and C. G. Jung, *The Secret of the Golden Flower*, New York, 1931, p. 135). Such a "restricted" approach becomes a "Taoism without Tao" (cf. André Préau, *La Fleur d'or et le taoïsme sans Tao*, Paris, 1931) or Brahmavāda without Brahma, and cannot be taken seriously as a scientific account of any traditional psychology.

[8] "Whereby (*kena*, by what, as whom) might one discriminate the Discriminator?" (BU II.4.14, IV.5.15).

[9] Śaṅkarācārya, BrSBh I.1.5, *neśvarād anyah samsārī*; i.e., Plato's Soul that "is coextended (*συντεταγμένη*, cf. n. 75) now with one body, now with another" (*Laws* 903D), as in Śvet. Up. V.10, "whatever body he assumes, therewith is he united (*yujyate*)," and BG XIII.26, "whatsoever is born is from the conjunction (*samyogāt*) of the Knower of the Field with the Field."

[10] Cf. Coomaraswamy, "*Ākimcaññā*; Self-naughting" [in this volume—ED.]

śarīra ātman) from "spirit" (*πνεῦμα, ψυχῆς ψυχή, ruah, aśarīra ātman*) implied in the customary printing of "self" with a small "s" and "Self" with the capital.

Our human self is an association (*sambhūtiḥ, συγγένεια, συνουσία, κοινωνία*) of breaths or spirations (*prāṇāḥ, αἰσθήσεις*, JUB IV.7.4, cf. II.4.5), or troop-of-elemental-beings (*bhūtagaṇa*); and as such an "elemental-self" (*bhūtātman*) to be distinguished logically but not really from "its immortal Self and Duke" (*netṛ*[11] = *ἡγεμών*), immanent Agent (*kartṛ*) and Giver-of-being (*prabhūḥ*, MU III.2, 3, IV.2, 3, VI.7), the "Inner Man of these elemental-beings" (*bhūtānām antaḥ puruṣaḥ*, AĀ III.2.4); these two selves being the passible and impassible natures of a single essence. The "elemental beings" (*bhūtāḥ, bhūtāni*) are so called with reference to the Being or Great Being (*mahābhūtaḥ*), Brahma, Self (*ātman*), Person (*puruṣaḥ*), or Breath (*prāṇaḥ*), Prajāpati, Agni or Indra, etc.,[12] from whom or which all these "our" powers of expression, perception, thought, and action[13] have come forth as spirations or "breaths" (*prāṇaḥ*) or "rays" = "reins" (*raśmayaḥ*), BU II.1.20, II.4.12, IV.5.11; MU VI.32, etc. The designation "Being" (*bhūtaḥ*, more literally "has-become")[14] is "because-of-the-coming-forth" (*udbhūtatvāt*) of the One who makes himself many (MU

[11] From *nī*, to lead. *Prāṇaḥ* is properly from *pra-an*, to breathe forth, but is also connected hermeneutically with *pra-ṇī*, to lead forth, in a metaphor closely connected with irrigation, as in RV II.12.7, where Indra is *apāṃ netṛ*, and in JUB I.58.4.

[12] The names of God are given, as repeatedly stated in Indian texts from RV onwards (as also in other theologies), according to the aspect under which he is considered, or power that he exerts; and because of his omniformity (as Viśvarūpaḥ) and universal creativity (as Viśvakarmā) there can be no end to the names. From RV onwards the procedure from aspect to aspect and function to function is a "becoming" (√ *bhū*); for example, "Thou, Agni, art Varuṇa in being born, and when kindled [born], becomest (*bhavasi*) Mitra," RV V.3.1. We retain the various names in their contexts; but the reader, from the present point of view, need only think of these names as those of "God" as the First Principle of all things.

[13] One, two, three, five, seven, nine, ten, or indefinitely numerous (cf. JUB II.6, etc.).

[14] This is the true sense of "I am" in Exod. 3:14, where *ehyé* = *bhavāmi* (cf. D. B. Macdonald, *The Hebrew Philosophical Genius*, Princeton, 1934, p. 18); similarly Egyptian *ḳhefr*. However, Macdonald (like C.A.F. Rhys Davids in *To Become or Not To Become*, London, 1937) does not see that becoming is not a contradiction of being but the epiphany of being, or that what can "become" represents only a part of the possibility inherent in the Being that "becomes." God becomes *what* he becomes "to mortal worshippers" (RV V.3.2), but in himself is "what?" (*ḳaḥ*), i.e., not any "what," and "where?" i.e., not "anywhere."

v.2).[15] The powers of the soul thus extended by the Prabhūḥ and Vibhūḥ are accordingly called "distributive essences (*vibhūtayaḥ*)."[16] The operation of these powers in us is what we call our consciousness (*caitanyam, saṃjñānam, vijñānam*), i.e., conscious life in terms of subject and object. This consciousness, with which all ethical responsibility is bound up, arises at our birth and ceases when "we" die (BU IV.4.12–14, Eccl. 9:5); but this consciousness and its correlated responsibility are only particular modes of being, not ends in themselves, but means to an end beyond themselves.[17] Our life, with all its powers, is a gift (AV II.17) or loan (*Mathnawī* I.245).

So "He who giveth-selfhood (*ya ātmadā* = *prabhū*)[18] becometh sole king of the moving-world . . . becometh overlord of elemental-beings (*bhūtānām adhipatir babhūva*);[19] and when he takes up his stand

[15] *Udbhū*, to come forth, i.e., be manifested, is the opposite of *nirbhū*, to abscond, disappear; as *pravṛt*, to extrovert (intrans.), is the contrary of *nivṛt*, to introvert. *Udbhutatva* = *prapadana* is precisely, in the theological sense, "procession."

It is important to bear in mind that *bhūta* is not primarily (but sometimes by analogy) any such "being" as ourselves, who are not one being or power, but a composite of cooperative beings or powers, rather to be regarded as "Intelligencies" or "Angels" than as human beings. God is the "*only* seer, hearer, thinker, etc." in us (BU III.8.23, etc.); it is He that takes birth in every womb and that "indwelling the secret cave [of the 'heart'] looks round about through these elemental beings (*guhām praviśya bhūtebhir vyapaśyata*, KU IV.6)," of which "we" are a "troop"; we are his "lookouts." Our "being" is not our own, and not in fact a being, but a becoming (*bhava*, γένεσις), as is admirably stated in strictly traditional terms by Plutarch, *Moralia* 392 (*guhām praviśya* = *occulte immanens*) and Plato, *Symposium* 207DE.

[16] In AĀ II.1.7 and BG X.40, described as "powers"; and in RV I.166.11, what amounts to the same thing (as will later appear), Maruts, *vibhvo vibhūtayaḥ*.

It is by this distributive becoming (*vibhutva, vibhūti-yoga*) that the Self is omnipresent (*sarvagataḥ*, Śvet. Up. III.21, cf. Praśna Up. III.12, Īśā Up. IV) and by the same token omniscient (MU VI.7) or synoptic (*vimanā . . . samdṛk*, RV X.82.2; cf. *Nirukta* X.26), and providential (*prajñaḥ*) in that its whole experience is *ex tempore*, no more dated than it is placed. All this is the basis of the Indian and Platonic doctrines of Recollection and Providence, and inseparable from that of the Only Transmigrant.

[17] Cf. Coomaraswamy, *Hinduism and Buddhism*, 1943, n. 249.

[18] "One as he is there, and many as he is in his children here" (ŚB X.5.2.16; cf. BG XIII.27, 30 and Plotinus, *Enneads* IV.4.2), i.e., "rays"; cf. n.25.

On the gift of selfhood see Coomaraswamy, "The Sunkiss," 1940, esp. p. 47, citing ŚB VII.3.2.12 (where it is because the Sun, Prajāpati, "kisses," i.e., breathes down upon, his children that each can say: "I am." So Dante, *Paradiso* XXIX.13–15, "perchè suo splendore potesse, risplendendo, dir: Subsisto"; and Rūmī, *Mathnawī* I.2197, "For this 'I-hood' comes to me from Him moment by moment.").

[19] The usual gnomic aorist; "has become" = "is become," *bhūtam*. The psychology that we called a *bhūta-vidyā* is the understanding of things, in the Buddhist phrase *yathā-bhutām*, "as become" (M I.260, etc.).

(*atiṣṭhantam*),[20] all [these gods] equip (*abhūṣan*) him; putting on the kingdom-the-power-and-the-glory (*śriyaṃ vasānaḥ*), he proceeds (*carati*), self-illuminate. . . . Unto him, the great [Brahma-] Daimon (*yakṣam*)[21] in the midst of the world-of-being, the supports-of-the-realm bring tribute (*baliṃ rāṣṭrabhṛto bharanti*).[22] . . . And even as his retainers attend upon a king when he arrives, even so all these elemental-beings (*sarvāṇi bhūtāni*) prepare for him, crying, 'Here comes Brahma!' and just as men surround a king when he is setting out on a journey, so, when the time has come, all these breaths (*prāṇāḥ*) gather about the Self (*ātmānam . . . abhisamayanti*) when This-one [Brahma] aspires"[23] (RV x.121.2; AV iv.2.1, 2; AV iv.8.1, 3; AV x.8.15; BU iv.3.37, 38).

The nature of this divine procession in Person,[24] the relation of the

[20] "Takes up his stand here" (*ā-sthā, adhi-sthā*), is the regular expression for the "mounting" of the bodily vehicle by its spiritual passenger (CU viii.12.1; Śvet. Up. iv.11; BG xv.9, etc.). When he takes up a stand here he is no longer *svasthaḥ* but now with a "support" (*pratiṣṭha, adhiṣṭhāna*), until he returns to himself.

[21] The Brahma-Yakṣa, proceeding as Person (Puruṣa), who lies (*śete*) in the heart as the Overlord of Beings (*bhūtādhipati*), and "to whom, as he lies (*śayānāye*), these deities bring tribute" (*balim haranti*, JUB iv.20.11–23.7 ff., with BU iv.4.22). See also Coomaraswamy, "The Yakṣa of the Vedas and Upaniṣads," 1938.

Puruṣa is interpreted by *pur* = πόλις combined with *śī* = κεῖμαι (√ *kei*, also in *castra* and *civis*), and denotes, accordingly, "the Citizen in every city" (BU ii.5.18; cf. AV x.2.28, 30, ŚB xiii.6.2.1). Our heart is the true "city of God" (*brahma-pura*, CU viii.1.1–5), which is the same as to say that "the kingdom of God is within you." This is essentially the Platonic doctrine of man as a city or body-politic (*Republic*, and *passim*), and Philo's, whose μόνος κυρίως ὁ θεὸς πολίτης ἐστί (*De cherubim* 121), is virtually a translation of *sa vā ayam puruṣaḥ sarvāsu pūrṣu puruṣayaḥ* (BU ii.5.18, as above); cf. Philo, *De opificio mundi* 142, where Adam (not "this man" but the Man) is called "the only citizen of the world" (μόνος κοσμοπολίτης). It is only on such a basis as this that a salutary *civ*ilization can be established or any sound *poli*tical economy founded. "The city can never otherwise be happy unless it is drawn by those painters who follow the divine original" (*Republic* 500e).

[22] The delegated powers are, precisely, his "attributes" (*ābharaṇāni*) and "ornaments" (*bhūṣaṇāni*), the original sense of both words being that of "equipment"; cf. Coomaraswamy, "Ornament" (in Vol. 1 of this edition—ed.). The king's retainers (*bhūtāh, vibhūtayah, prāṇāh*, etc.) are his "adornment" (*bhuṣanam*, √ *bhū*), and that quite literally, not only a "wall" but also a "crown," namely of "glory," as we shall see in connection with the word *śrī*—the glory that he "wears" (*śriyam vasānaḥ*), "he upon whose head the Aeons are a crown, darting forth rays" (ἀκτῖνες, *Coptic Gnostic Treatise* XI), "who wears the cosmos as his crown" (Hermes, *Lib.* xiv.7; cf. n. 52).

[23] I.e., when "the Spirit returns to God who gave it" (Eccl. 12:7) and we "give up the ghost," the Holy Ghost.

[24] AĀ ii.2.1, *lokam abhyārcat puruṣa-rūpeṇa . . . prāṇāḥ*; JUB iv.24.1, *puruṣam eva prapadanāya' vṛṇita*. Cf. n. 21.

One to the Many,[25] and the origination of our consciousness and mobility are nowhere more clearly formulated than in MU II.6 ff. Here the intelligizing Person (*manomayaḥ puruṣaḥ*,[26] cf. Muṇḍ. Up. II.2.7), Prajāpati, the Progenitor (the Breath, AV XI.4.11), awakening as if from sleep, divides himself fivefold,[27] to awaken (*pratibodhanāya*) his lifeless offspring. "He, having still unattained ends (*akṛtārthaḥ*),[28] from within

[25] "One as he is there, and many as he is in his children here" (ŚB X.5.2.16, cf. BG XIII.27, 30 and Plotinus, *Enneads* IV.4.2), i.e., "rays," for the Sun's rays are his sons (JUB II.9.10). Thus he is "bodiless in bodies" (KU II.22), "undivided in his divisions . . . in elemental beings" (BG XVIII.20, XIII.16): Ὁ ἀσώματος, οὗτος ὁ πολυσώματος, μᾶλλον δὲ παντοσώματος (Hermes, *Lib.* V.10A).

[26] One and the same Person may be considered ontologically from more than one point of view or level of reference. In a threefold arrangement he is, (1) the Person in the eye, or heart, (2) the Person in the Sun, and (3) the Person in Lightning; these Persons assuming the "sheaths," respectively vegetative (*anna-maya*), intellectual (*manomaya*), and beatific (*ānanda-maya*), in accordance with which the personal Brahma is "existent-intelligent-beatific (*sac-cid-ānanda*)" and logically differentiated from the impersonal, "nonexistent (*asat*)" Brahma, though no real distinctions can be made in the Supreme Identity of "That One (*tad ekam*)" that is both "existent and nonexistent (*sad-asat*)." These two are Meister Eckhart's "God" and "Godhead," and, as he says, "you must know what God and Godhead are"; he uses the expression, "free as the Godhead in its nonexistence," and says that "where these two abysms hang, equally spirated, despirated, there is the Supreme Essence." It will be understood that our affirmative psychology (pneumatology) as such, like the affirmative theology with which it really coincides, is with reference to "God" as Being (*ens simpliciter*), while the negative psychology, which proceeds by way of remotion (*neti, neti*; *na me so attā*) to a residual but ineffable Self, is not thus limited as to its end but extends to the absolute unity (*ekatvam*) or aloneness (*kevalatvam*) that transcends the distinction of natures (KU III.11; MU IV.6, VI.21; BG XV.16, 17; etc.).

[27] There are many ways in which the division is fivefold (cf. AĀ I.3.8; Śvet. Up. I.5 ff.), among which the five senses or powers are here primarily intended; cf. BU IV.4.17, Praśna Up. III.12. The Ātmavādins (autologists) maintain that the "Five Races" (*pañca-janāḥ*) are those of speech, hearing, sight, mind, and breath (of the nostrils) (BD VII.67), as must be the case in RV III.37.9, where Indra's powers (*indriyāṇi*) are "in the Five Races" (cf. RV I.176.5, V.32.11, V.35.2). But this is not the only meaning of the terms, and speaking more generally, God divides himself indefinitely (BU II.5.19, MU V.2) to fill these worlds, "with only a part of himself, as it were" (MU VI.26, BG XV.7): part "*as it were*," because the Spirit remains a total presence "undivided in the divided beings" (*avibhaktam ca bhūteṣu . . . vibhaktesu*, BG XIII.16, XVIII.20); "no part of what is divine is cut off or separated, but only extends itself" (*ἐκτείνεται* [= *uttanute*], Philo, *Deterius* 90).

[28] It will be seen that unrealized potentialities are the occasion of the Self's embodiment and apparent bondage; when Prajāpati has entered into his children fondly, he cannot extricate himself without their help (TS V.5.2.1; ŚB I.6.3.35, 36)—a conception with this profound implication, that "our" liberation is also and more truly *his* liberation. With the state of the "bird in the net, or cage," self-fettered by its own desires (MU III.2, S I.44; *Phaedo* 83A; *Mathnawī* I.1541), is to

the heart considered, 'Let me eat[29] of sense objects (*arthān aśnāni*).' Thereupon breaking through these apertures (*khānimāni bhitvā*)[30] and

---

be contrasted the liberty of the Self "whose ends have been attained" (*kṛtārthaḥ*, Śvet. Up. II.14)—this is the state of the Marut, Bṛhadratha, who, "having done what there was to do" (*kṛtakṛtyaḥ*, MU VI.30, AĀ II.5; equivalent to *karma kṛtvā* in TS I.8.3.1, and to *katakaraṇiyam* in the Buddhist Arhant formula), "goes home" (*astaṃ praiti*, TS I.8.3.1); his state whose desires are attained, who has no desire (*akāmaḥ*) and is self-sufficient (BU IV.4.6.7, IV.3.21, etc.), for whom there are no longer any ends to be attained by action (*naiva tasya kṛtenārthaḥ*, BG III.18) and who can say, "there is nothing I needs must do" (BG III.22), and is thus liberated from all *necessitas coactionis, conditionata, ex fine*.

In all these contexts the "work to be done" (*kṛtya, kārya, karaṇīya*) is always, of course, in some sense sacrificial (*karma kṛ = operare = sacra facere*).

29 "Food" (*anna, bhoga, āhāra*) must not be understood in any restricted sense, but is whatever nourishes any contingent existence; food is life's fuel, whether physical or mental (cf. MU VI.11, M I.260, and *Phaedrus* 246E ff.). Our life is a combustion. The Sun "rises up on food (*annena ati rohati*, RV X.90.2)," i.e., "comes eating and drinking" (Matt. 11:19), and it is the same solar Fire that "eats food in the heart," within you (MU VI.1), by means of his "rays" (MU VI.12), so that "whoever eats (lives), it is by *his* ray that he eats" (JUB I.29.6). Of the two selves or natures, "one eats the sweet fruit of the tree" (*pippalaṃ svādu atti*, RV I.164.20; Muṇḍ. Up. III.1, Śvet. Up. IV.6), like Eve and Adam in Genesis, and suffers accordingly. In other words, of the conjoint pair (*sayujā sakhāyā*), so often represented in the iconography as one bird with two heads, one eats "poison" (*viṣam*), the other "ambrosia" (*amṛtam*, cf. the *Pañcatantra*, HOS, Vol. 11, p. 127, and Anton Schiefner, tr., *Tibetan Tales*, London, 1924). In this connection it is significant that √ *viṣ*, to "set," "work," "serve," gives rise equally to *viṣam*, poison, and *viṣaya*, object of sense perception. On these considerations depends the theory of continence (again, in no restricted sense of the word); the withholding of their fuel from life's fires (MU VI.34.1, with its Buddhist equivalents, and as in Philo, *De specialibus legibus* IV.118, ὑφαιρῶν, καθάπερ ὕλην πυρός, σβέσιν τῆς ἐπιθυμίας ἀπεργάζεται) being in order to conquer hunger (TS II.4.12.5), i.e., death (BU I.2.1), by fasting.

In this broader sense of the words, which includes, for example, "the love of fine colors and sounds" (*Republic* 476), the majority, even of those who lay claim to "culture," really "lives to eat," not realizing that, as was so well said by Eric Gill, "a good taste is a mortified taste"—not an appetite for all sorts of food. The kinds must be chosen according to the part of our soul that we propose to nourish most; cf. *Phaedrus* 246E.

30 *Khāni*, the "doors of the senses" (*dvārāṇi*, BG VIII.12) = τὸ τῶν αἰσθήσεων στόμα (Philo, *Deterius* 100) = πύλαι, of which νοῦς is the πυλωρός (Hermes, *Lib.* I.22, cf. V.6). *Khāni*, pl. of *kha* (also *khā*), are such openings as connect one "space" with another, hence passages that lead from the within to the without, and collectively one *khā* is "Varuṇa's Fount of Order" (*khām ṛtasya*, RV II.28.5). From *kha* derive *sukha* and *duḥkha*, weal and woe. *Ṛta* (cf. "rite") is κόσμος as Order: the Rivers pour out Order (*ṛtam arṣanti sindhavaḥ*, RV I.105.2) and are of the nature of Order, and acquainted with Order (*arṣanti ṛtavārī*, RV IV.18.6, *ṛtajñāḥ*, IV.19.7; cf. *Enneads* III.8.10, "Imagine a spring that has no source outside itself; it gives itself to all the rivers, yet is never exhausted by what they take, but itself remains integrally what it always was; the tides that proceed from it are at one

going forth, with five rays (*raśmibhiḥ*)[31] he eats of sense objects (*viṣayān atti*): these cognitive powers (*buddhindriyāṇi* = *prajñāni*, *prajña-mātrā*, *tan-mātrā*, intelligences) are his 'rays,' the organs of action (*karmendriyāṇi*) are his steeds,[32] the body is his chariot, mind (*manas* = νοῦς) is their Governor (*niyantṛ*),[33] his nature (*prakṛti* = φύσις)[34] the whip; impelled by him as its only energizer, this body spins like the potter's wheel,[35] impelled by him alone is this body set up in a state-of-conscious-

---

within it before they run their several ways, yet all, in some sense, know beforehand down what channels they will pour their streams").

[31] These "rays," which are also the "reins" by which the steeds are yoked to the Mind, are those of St. Bonaventura's *lumen cognitionis sensitivae*, which acts in combination with the five corresponding elements, sight, hearing, smell, taste, and touch in ourselves (*De reductione artium ad theologiam* 3, based on St. Augustine, *De genesi ad litteram*, c. 4, n. 6), the distinction of *lux*, *lumen*, and *color* (as percipient, means, and object of perception) being taken for granted: "ipsa divina veritas est lux, et ipsius expressiones respecter rerum sunt quasi luminosae irradiationes, licet intrinsicae, qua determinata educunt et dirigunt in ad quod exprimitur" (St. Bonaventura, *De scientia Dei* 3c). Cf. Rūmī, *Mathnawī* I.3268, 3273, 3275, "Through *my* beams *thou* hast come to life for a day or two. . . . The beams of the Spirit are speech and eye and ear. . . . The heart . . . has pulled the reins of the five senses"; Hermes, *Lib.* X.22B, θεοῦ καθάπερ ἀκτῖνες αἱ ἐνέργειαι; and Plotinus, *Enneads* VI.4.3, where οἷον βολάς (ἡλιοῦ) = καθάπερ ἀκτῖνες θεοῦ. Cf. n. 59.

[32] "Yoked are his thousand steeds" (RV VI.47.18), Indra's ten thousand steeds, rays of the Sun (JUB I.44.1–5); tens of thousands consubstantial with their source (BU II.5.19), who is at once the knower, means of knowing, and the known.

[33] Mind is the prism by which the Light of lights (RV I.113.1, etc.) is refracted, and in which, conversely, its spectra are reunited. The Mind is twofold, pure or impure according to whether or not it is affected by its perceptions, whence the necessity of a *katharsis* (*śuddha karaṇa*) if we are to know the truth, as distinguished from opinion; on the two minds, and the sense of μετάνοια, see Coomaraswamy, "On Being in One's Right Mind," 1942.

Mind is the *niyantṛ* (coachman, √*yam*, as in ἡνία), but is itself curbed by the ultimate Controller (*antaryāmin*, BU III.7; *niyantṛ*, MU VI.19, 30, cf. KU III.9). The Mind that has ends in view may be unable or unwilling to control the horses, which may or may not be unruly.

The ultimate Controller (*antaryāmin*), immanent deity, synteresis and "conscience," is the Socratic Daimon "that always holds me back from what 'I' want to do" (Plato, *Apology* 31D): Socrates thinks it "very fine to be opposed thus," but the man whom his desires constrain is only "angered by the voice from the Acropolis that says 'Thou shalt not' " (*Republic* 440B, with *Timaeus* 70A); resents, in other words, his "inhibitions," and "kicks against the pricks."

[34] *Prakṛti* as the stimulant (not the "inspirer") of action, BG III.27, 33.

[35] *Sūryasya cakram*, RV V.29.10; *deva-cakram*, AB IV.15; *brahma-cakram*, Śvet. Up. I.6; *saṃsāra-cakram*, MU VI.28; Pāli Buddhist *bhava-cakkam* = ὁ τροκός τῆς γενέσεως, James 3:6 (the last more likely of Orphic than Indian origin).

> Nichts ist, das dich bewegt, du selber bist das Rad,
> Das aus sich selben läuft, und keine Ruhe hat.
>
> Angelus Silesius, *Cherubinische Wandersmann* I.37.

ness (*cetanavat*), he only is its mover."[36] As a spectator (*prekṣakaḥ*, play-goer, on-looker) and as he is in himself (*svasthaḥ* = ἀπαθής, αὐτὸς, ἐν ἑαυτῷ ἑστώς, Hermes, *Lib.* II.12A), he transmigrates (*carati*)[37] wholly unaffected (*alepyaḥ*)[38] by the fates in which his vehicles, whether aughty or naughty, are involved; but insofar as he thinks of himself as this man, So-and-so, insofar as he identifies himself with his experiences and passions, "he fetters himself by himself, like a bird in the net," and as "elemental-self (*bhūtātman*)" is overcome by causality, good and evil, and all the

[36] Ψυχὴ μὲν ἐστιν ἡ περιάγουσα ἡμῶν πάντα (Plato, *Laws* 898c); "questi nei cor mortali è permotore" (Dante, *Paradiso* I.116); "Sanctus Spiritus qui est principaliter movens . . . homines qui sunt quaedam organa ejus" (*Sum. Theol.* I-II 68.4 *ad* 1).

[37] As in AV IV.8.1; "multifariously born" (*carati bahudhā jāyamānah*, Muṇḍ. Up. II.2.6; *carati garbhe antar adṛsyamāno bahudhā vi jāyate*, AV X.8.13)—for, indeed, "this Breath (=Prajāpati, Ātman) hath entered into manifold wombs" (JUB III.2.13). Elsewhere, often *samscarati* = *saṃsarati*, "transmigrates."

[38] *Alepyaḥ*, "not adherent," not moistened, as the smooth surface of a lotus leaf is not moistened by the drops of water that may fall upon it; √ *lip*, to smear, etc., whence *lepam*, plaster, lime, bird-lime, glue. The "clean" Self, master of its own powers, and by no means their servant, is not contaminated as it acts (*kurvan na lipyate*, BG V.7); as the Sun is unaffected by evils under the sun, so our Inner Man is unaffected (*na lipyate*) by worldly evils, and remains aloof (KU V.11); the true Brahman is not (like a fly in honey) captivated by his desires (*na lippati kāmesu*, Dh 401, cf. Sn 71, 547, 1042, etc.). We need hardly say that Rawson's objections to these notions (in *Kaṭha Upanishad*, Oxford, 1934, p. 180) are Patripassian and Monophysite, and it is interesting to observe that in combatting an Indian doctrine he is forced to adopt a Christian heresy!

In the Indian and traditional psychology, all sense perception depends on contact (*sparśa*, cf. ἀντέρεισις, *Timaeus* 45C). He who does not touch (*na spṛśati*) sense objects is the true ascetic (MU VI.10). "All experiences are contact-born (*ye hi samsparsaja bhogaḥ*). . . . One whose Self is unattached (*asakta*, √ *saj*, to stick to, cf. "sticky" = sentimental) enjoys a happiness incorruptible" (BG V.21, 22). In fact, the powers of perception and action both "grasp" and are grasped by their objects as "super-graspers" (*atigraha*, BU III.2); and this is dramatized in the widely distributed "Stickfast" stories, of which S V.148–49, where the "monkey" (mind, consciousness, cf. S II.94) is held fast (*bajjhati*) by the "glue" (*lepam*) it "impinges upon," may be called an archetype; in a remarkable Spanish version the captive has baited his own trap (see W. Norman Brown, "The Stickfast Motif in the Tar-Baby Story," in *Twenty-fifth Anniversary Studies; Philadelphia Anthropological Society*, 1937, p. 4, and A. M. Espinosa in the *Journal of American Folklore*, LVI, 1943, 36).

The same impassibility is implied by the word *prekṣaka* (θεωρητικός), "looker-on," as if at a play, and the corresponding *upekṣā*, *uppekkhā*, "impartiality" analogous to the Sun's, who "shines alike upon the just and the unjust." The Spectator is not affected by or involved in the fates of his psychophysical vehicles; the passible nature only is involved for so long as it does not "know its Self," who it is; cf. *Enneads* IV.7.9 ff.

"pairs" of contradictories.[39] The cure for this elemental Self is to be found in the dissipation of its "ignorance" (*avidyā*) by the recognition of "its own immortal Self and Duke," of which it is said elsewhere, in the most famous of the Aupaniṣada λόγοι, that "That art thou."

Thus the immanent deity is the sole Fructuary (*bhoktṛ*, √*bhrij*, to eat, use, enjoy, experience as, e.g., in JUB II.10) within the world and in individuals. "Self with sense-power yoked they term the 'Fructuary'" (KU III.4); "this Person within you is the only Fructuary and Nature is his usufruct (*bhojyam*, MU VI.10)," "taking up his stand on ear, eye, touch, taste, and smell, he is concerned with sense-objects (*viṣayān upasevate*)"; "enjoyments contact-born" (BG XV.7–9, V.22). That is, of course, in his passible nature, in which he literally sym-pathizes with "us," as experient (*bhoktṛ*) of both pleasures and pains (BG XIII.20, 22), the real and the unreal (MU VII.11.8) of which "our" life and development are the product (AĀ II.3.6), a mixture[40] of corruptible and incorruptible, seen and unseen (Śvet. Up. I.8). In "us," however, just because of its fruitional-nature (*bhoktṛtvāt*) the self is bound and lordless and cannot be released from all its limitations (*sarva-pāśaiḥ*) or from its births in aughty or naughty wombs until it recognizes its own divine essence (Śvet. Up. I.7, 8; MU III.2 ff.; BG XIII.21); until, that is, "we" know who we are,[41] and become what we are, God in God and wide awake (*brahma-bhūtā*, *buddhā*).[42] To that

[39] It is precisely from the "pairs" of contraries that the Freedman (*muktah*, √*muc* = λύω, ἐλευθερόω, *liberare*) is freed (*dvandvair vimuktaḥ*, BG XV.5, cf. V.3), in other words "from name-and-aspect" (*nāma-rūpāt*, Muṇḍ. Up. III.2.3), from the tyranny of all things definable in terms of what they are-and-are-not, such as big and small, pleasure and pain, good and evil and other "values." The coincidence of contraries—for example, of past and future, near and far—can only be in a now without duration ("other than past and future," KU II.14) and in a space that cannot be traversed. Hence the symbolism of the "strait gate," Wunderthor and Symplegades, met with all over the world from India to Alaska. Thus, "the Paradise in which God dwells is girt about with the coincidence of contraries, and that is its wall, of which the gate is guarded by the highest spirit of reason and cannot be passed until he is overcome; nor canst Thou be seen on the hither side of this coincidence of contraries, but only beyond them" (Nicholas of Cusa, *De visione Dei* IX), where as Meister Eckhart says, "neither vice nor virtue ever entered in." For the history of the "contraries" (ἐναντία) in Greek metaphysics, see E. R. Goodenough, "A Neo-Pythagorean Source in Philo Judaeus," *Yale Classical Studies*, III (1932).

[40] Philo's σύγκριμα and φύραμα.

[41] "Iam scio," inquit [Philosophia], "morbi tui aliam uel maximum causam; quid ipse sis, nosse desisti" (Boethius, *De consolatione philosophiae* I.6). "Quod autem de scientia magis necessarium est scire, hoc est ut [homo] sciat se ipsum" (Avencebrol, *Fons vitae* I.2). γνῶθι σεαυτόν: not τὰ αὐτοῦ, but αὐτόν.

[42] S III.83, with many parallels.

end there is a Way and Royal Road[43] and a Rule dispositive to the eradication of all "otherness,"[44] means that are often called a medicine; it is literally for the "patient" (for such are all whose "ruling passions," good or evil, are their masters) to decide whether or not to follow the prescribed regimen, or if the end does not attract him, to go on "eating and drinking and being merry" with the *οἱ πολλοὶ νομίζοντες ἑαυτῶν πάντα κτήματα.*[45]

In the Vedic angelology (*devavidyā*), the Intelligences which are the constituents of our psychic personality, and of which we have spoken mainly as "elemental-beings," are called by many other names; we shall consider them accordingly as "Breaths" (*prāṇāḥ*), "Glories" (*śriyaḥ*), "Fires" (*agnayaḥ*), Faculties (*indriyāṇi*), Seers or Prophets (*ṛṣayaḥ*), "Storms" or "Gales" (*marutaḥ*), and as Gods or Angels (*devāḥ, devatāḥ*).

The immanent deity, solar Ātman, Brahma, Prajāpati, Agni, Indra, Vāyu, is continually called the "Breath" (*prāṇaḥ, spiration*),[46] and his

[43] The Way is that of the Philosophia Perennis, both in theory and practice: a metaphysics that must not be confused with the empirical and systematic "philosophy" (*τὰ ἐγκύκλια φιλοσοφήματα, De caelo* 279a.30 = *τὰ ἐξωτέρικα*, and not at all the same as the "primary philosophy" or "theology" *περὶ τοῦ ὄντος ᾗ ὄν, Metaphysics* 1026a.22 ff.) that is now usually taught in our universities, or with the "philosophies" of individual "thinkers." The distinction of the traditional from modern "philosophies" is of fundamental importance, but cannot be further considered here. We do wish, however, to point out that a like distinction (which is really that of realism from nominalism) must be made in our interpretation of the word "naturalist" (*ψυσικός*) which, as applied to the early Ionian philosophers, and notably Thales, is much more nearly *φιλόμυθος* than to be equated with the modern "physicist"; cf. Philo, *De posteritate Caini* 7, where it is taken for granted that theirs was an "allegorical way." *Φύσις*, indeed, as *Natura naturans, Creatrix universalis*, is *Deus ordinans naturae omnium* (cf. AV VIII.10; Philo, *De sacrificiis* 75, 98), and in this sense "natural history" coincides with theology. We need hardly point out that this "Mother Nature" is another than the natured world of which we ourselves are part.

[44] Nicholas of Cusa's *ablatio omnis alteritatis et diversitatis*, essential to *theosis*, St. Bernard's *a se tota deliquescere*, St. Paul's *divisio animae et spiritus*, Christ's *denegat se ipsum*, Islamic *fanā al-fanā*, etc.: "All scripture cries aloud for freedom from self" (Eckhart).

[45] "The rabble that imagines that all possessions are its 'own,'" those who talk of an "I and mine," the Buddhist "untaught manyfolk" who take their own inconstant and composite personality to be an essence, and all those who hold with Descartes, *cogito ergo sum*. These are also Aristotle's *οἱ πολλοί, les hommes moyens sensuels*, whose "good" is the life of pleasure (*Nichomachaean Ethics* 1.5.1).

[46] Breath (*prāṇaḥ*, often rendered by "Life") has two senses, (1) as Spirit, Self, and Essence, and (2) as the breath-of-life (in the nostrils, and so, as one of the senses, smell). In the first sense, the Breath, stationed in the breath-of-life as its body, to which it is unknown, is your Self (Ātman), the Inner Controller, the

divisions and extensions are accordingly the "Breaths" (*prāṇāḥ*). All these Breaths are the activities or workings (*karmāṇi*, ἐνέργειαι) of vision, audition, etc., that Prajāpati unleashes; severally mortal, it is only of the median Breath that Death could not take possession; it is after him as their chief

---

Immortal (BU III.7.16, cf. KU V.5); as for Philo, πνεῦμά ἐστιν ἡ ψυχῆς οὐσία (*Deterius* 81, *De specialibus legibus* IV.123). Accordingly, "Breath moves with breath, Breath giveth breath (*prāṇah prāṇena yāti, prāṇah, prāṇam dadāti*, CU VII.15.1)" corresponds exactly to "breathed into his nostrils the breath of life" (Gen. 2:7); as "in whose nostrils was the breath of life" (Gen. 7:22) does to Skr. *prāṇinah, prāṇabhṛtaḥ*, "breathing things," i.e., living beings. *In divinis* the Breath is the Gale (*vāyu*), and it is evident that, as an immanent principle (TS II.1.11.3, ŚB I.8.3.12, etc.), this "Air" corresponds to the ἐντὸς ἀήρ which Theophrastus describes as "the real agent of perception, being a tiny fragment of God within you" (*De sensibus* 42).

This whole doctrine as enunciated in the cited passages (cf. TU II.3, *prāṇo hi bhūtānam āyus*; Kauṣ. Up. III.2) might be described as that of the traditional animism or vitalism. It is not, however, a "theory of the origin of life" in any temporal sense, or as if life might have reached this planet from some other place; for the Self or Spirit or Breath does not merely initiate life, but as its principle, maintains it, and it "has not come from anywhere" (KU II.18; John 3:8). The doctrine is also exclusive of any theory of an origin of life "by a fortuitous concourse of atoms (!)," since it is a fundamental axiom of the Philosophia Perennis that "nothing in the world happens by chance" (St. Augustine, *De diversis quaestionibus* LXXXIII, q.24; Boethius, *De consolatione philosophiae* I.6 and IV.6; Plutarch, *Moralia* 369); in Buddhism, the notion of an origination by chance is the *ahetuvāda* heresy, the true doctrine being, "this being that becomes, and this not being that does not become." Sanskrit has no word importing "chance" in the modern, "random," connotation of the word and, in fact, "chance" itself, together with all the corresponding and equivalent words in other languages, imports no more than simply "what takes place," without any implied denial of causation.

One fundamental distinction between the metaphysical and the empirical approach to the problem of origins may be noted. The latter considers only mediate causes, all belonging to one and the same realm of compossibles; while for the former the problem is one of a first cause that would not be a *first* cause if it could be included in the category of any of its effects. Metaphysics, therefore, while not denying that life transmits life, can only consider an origin of life or being from what is neither "alive" nor "being" (τὸ δὲ ὑπὲρ τὴν ζωὴν αἴτιον ζωῆς, *Enneads* III.8.10); will predicate, in other words, a production *ex nihilo*.

All generation (origination, production) is from contraries (*Sum. Theol.* I.46.1 *ad* 3). The Supreme Identity (*tad ekam*, RV) is a syzygy (*principium conjunctum*) of being and nonbeing, spiration and despiration, etc., one essence of two natures (RV X.129.2, MU VII.11.8). When these two natures are considered apart and as interacting, being takes birth from nonbeing, life from what is not alive, as from a father and a mother (RV X.72.2, *asatah sad ajāyata*; JUB IV.18.8, *yat prāṇena na prāṇiti yena prāṇaḥ prāṇīyate*; Muṇḍ. Up. II.1.2,3, *aprāṇo . . . tasmāj jāyate prāṇaḥ*). The doctrine is expressed also by Philo, ὁ ἀγένητος φθάνει πᾶσαν γένεσιν, *De sacrificiis* 66, cf. 98; and by Plotinus, *Enneads* VI.7.17, "Form is in the shaped, the shaper is formless." It is in this sense that the world *ex nihilo fit* (*Sum. Theol.* I.45.1, *emanatio totius esse est ex non ente, quod est nihil*).

(*śreṣṭhaḥ*; literally, most glorious)[47] that the others are called "Breaths" (BU I.5.21); they are not "our" powers, but only the names of his (Brahma's) activities (BU I.4.7). In us these Breaths are so many unwhole "selves" (those of the seeing, hearing, thinking man, etc.), but they act unanimously for the Breath (or Life) whose "own" (*svāḥ*, etc.) they are, and whom they serve as his retainers serve a king (BU I.4.7; Kauṣ. Up. III.2, IV.20)[48]; to whom, accordingly, they "bring tribute" (*balim haranti, bharanti, prayacchanti*, AV X.7.37, X.8.15, XI.4.19; JUB IV.24.9; Kauṣ. Up. II.I, etc.) and "resort" or "incline" (*śrayanti*, ŚB VI.I.I.4, etc.), and by whom they are in turn protected (AV X.2.27; BU IV.3.12). The operation of the Breaths is unanimous,[49] for the Mind (*manas* = νοῦς), to which they are "yoked," and by which they are directed, is their immediate dominant (TS IV.I.I, VI.I.4.5; ŚB X.5.7.I). The Mind cognizes what the other senses only report (BU I.5.3); as *sensus communis* it "partakes of and enjoys their several ranges and pastures" (M I.295).

At the same time, amongst all these powers, in which the Mind as "practical intellect" is included, the outstanding superiority of the Breath itself is emphasized in very many recensions of the myth of the contests of the Breaths amongst themselves: it proves invariably that the Breath is the best and only essential power, for the organism can survive if deprived of any of the others, but only the Breath can erect the body, which falls down when it departs (AĀ II.I.4; BU I.5.21, VI.I.I–4; Kauṣ. Up. II.14, III.12, etc.). It is, in fact, the Breath that departs when we "give up the ghost"; and, in leaving, it tears up the Breaths by the roots and carries them away with it, in what is at once their death and ours (BU IV.4.2, VI.I.13; BG XV.8, etc.). Nothing of "us" remains when "we, who before our birth did not exist and who, in our combination with the body, are mixtures and have qualities, shall be no more, but shall be brought into the rebirth [παλιγγενεσία, resurrection] by which, becoming united to immaterial things, we shall become unmixed and without qualities" (Philo, *De cherubim* 114, 115).[50]

[47] Cf. *śreṣṭhin* as the "head of a guild"; the guild being a *śreni*, group, series, and both words from √*śri*, as to which see below. The organization of a guild, like that of any other traditional society (*sāhitya*), "imitates" the cosmic order.

[48] All in the same sense that for Plato, Philo, and Hermes, *passim*, we are God's "possessions" (κτήματα) and "ministers" or "servants" (ὑπηρέται).

[49] They indeed, in their feeding, "conspire" (*samananti* AĀ II.I.2), and having thus conspired, aspire (*samānyo'dānan*, JUB IV.22.6).

[50] Philo's *palingenesis* is the "third birth" or resurrection of the "other self" that takes place at our death, the human personality of "this self" having already been

In the above account of the Breaths, the equally Indian and Platonic symbolism of the chariot (*ratha*, *ἅρμα*) is assumed. Self is the passenger to whom the vehicle belongs and who knows its destination, and Mind the driver (*saṃgrahitṛ, niyantṛ*) that holds the ray-reins (*raśmayaḥ*, *ἀκτῖνες*; *ἡνία*, √*yam*) by which the sensitive steeds are curbed and guided. The horses may or may not have been well trained; while the Mind itself, because of its twofold quality, human and divine, clean and unclean, may either allow the horses to stray from the highway (*mārga*) into pagan (*deśi*) fields, or may direct them on behalf of the Spirit.[51]

---

reborn in the man's descendants, by whom his functions will be carried on (AĀ II.5, cf. AV XI.8.33, ŚB XI.2.1.1–3, and JUB III.11.1–4). In the whole tradition that we are considering, there is no doctrine of the survival or "reincarnation" of personalities, but only of the Person, the only transmigrator; recognition of the composite and inconstant nature of the human personality and its consequent corruptibility leads to the whole problem of mortality, expressed in the questions, "In whom, when I depart, shall I be departing?" (Praśna Up. VI.3), and "By which self is the Brahma-world attainable?" (Sn 508), myself or the Self? The Christian and orthodox answer is, of course, that "No man hath ascended up to heaven, save he which came down from heaven, even the Son of Man, which is in heaven" (John 3:13), and therefore, "If any man would follow me, let him deny himself" (*ἀπαρνησάσθω ἑαυτόν*, Matt. 14:24). In the last citation, *ἀπαρνέομαι* is very strong, and might better have been rendered by "disown" or "utterly reject"; it is by no means a merely ethical "self-denial" that is intended, but a denial like St. Peter's of Christ (in which connection the same verb is used) and such as is implied by Meister Eckhart's "the soul must put itself to death." See further Coomaraswamy, *Hinduism and Buddhism*, 1943, p. 57.

The problem of immortality—to be or not to be, after death—obviously hinges upon the psychological analysis, in the sense that the answer must depend upon our view of what we are now, mortal or immortal; for, evidently, nothing composite or that has had a beginning can by any means become immortal. The Indian resurrection (*punar janma, abhisambhava*, etc.), sacrificially prefigured (AB II.3, etc.), and actually consequent upon the consummation of the last sacrifice in which the body is offered up on the funeral pyre (ŚA VII.7, JUB III.11.17, AV VIII.2.8, BU VI.2.14, ŚB II.2.4.8, RV X.14.8, etc.), is, indeed, "from ashes" (*Sum. Theol.* III.Supp.78.2, cf. ŚB VIII.1.1.9) and in a "whole and complete body," but it is not delayed, and is not a reconstitution of *this* body or personality, but of our "other Self," this self's "immortal Self," in an immortal body of "gold" (light, glory), wanting in nothing but wholly immaterial. The distinction of "saved" from "lost" is similarly immediate; the saved are those who have known their Self (St. Paul's *jam non ego, sed Christus in me*), the lost are those who have not known themselves and of whom, therefore, there is nothing to survive when the vehicle disintegrates and the Self departs.

[51] Typically in *Phaedrus* 246 ff., and in KU III.3 ff., but throughout both traditions, e.g., Philo, *De agricultura* 72 ff. In Buddhism, the chariot is the typical *exemplum* of the Ego fallacy: there was no chariot before it was constructed nor will there be when it finally falls to pieces, and so for the "soul"; both are conventional ex-

To the Self, as we said, as to their "chief" (*śreṣṭhaḥ*) or "none more glorious" (*niḥśreyasaḥ*), the Breaths "resort" or "incline" (*śrayanti*). In this sense they are at once its beams and glories (*śriyāḥ*) and, collectively, its "glory" (*śrī*), it being the "head" (*śiras*, L. *caput*) to which they tend and on which they rest (*śritāḥ*) as their resort or shelter (*śarman, śaraṇam*); inasmuch as the Breaths are his tributaries, Brahma is "surrounded by glory" (*śriyā parivṛdham*) which is both a wall and a crown.[52] This is a description at once of the cosmic and microcosmic household (*gṛha*, with its *gṛhāḥ* and *gṛhapati*) and of the domed house (*gṛha*, *dama*, δόμος) itself (this earthly body, in which "the two selves" dwell together); of which house the "beams" (in both senses of the word) or rafters both surround and support and are supported by the capital of its axial kingpost (*sthūṇa-rājā*, *śāla-vaṃśa*), just as in the cosmic home of which the roof is sup-

pressions for what is not an essence but only a causally determined process. This is the so-called Buddhist "nominalism": but it should be clear that to deny the reality of a pseudo universal is by no means to deny the reality of universals. For the equivalent picture, again Platonic and Indian, of man as an articulated puppet pulled this way and that by his passions, if not rectified by the "single golden cord" by which (in accordance with the "thread-spirit" doctrine) he is suspended from above, see Coomaraswamy, *Līlā* and "Play and Seriousness" [both in this volume—ED.]. See also Saṇkara on BU III.4I (the body and its functions are operated like a wooden puppet by the Self).

[52] ŚB VI.I.I.4, 7; JUB IV.24.II; AĀ II.I.4. Cf. RV I.59.9; IV.5.I; X.I8.I2. All the Skr. words in the sentence above are from √*śri*, to tend towards, lean against, enter into, join with, of which √*śrī*, to shine or glow, is only a variant. With *śri* in the first sense may be compared ἁρμόζω, to join, and other forms of ἄρω, e.g., Lat. *ars*, and Skr. *ṛ* in *sam-ṛ*, to join together, infix (pp. *samarpita*); ἁρμονία as the peak or keystone of a roof (Pausanias IX.38.3, cf. Hermes, *Lib.* I.I4) may be specially noted.

We rendered *śrī*, above, p. 338, by "the kingdom-the-power-and-the-glory," for as a feminine "personification" Śrī is all these things (ŚB XI.4.3.I ff., etc.), i.e., the characteristic Fortune or Success (τυχή) that accompanies the successful hero or protects a city, without which—or rather whom—the hero would be helpless or the city lost. The identification of Śrī with Virāj (lit. radiance, √*raj*, to shine, and so to rule, cf. ŚB VIII.5.I.5, XI.4.3.I0)—"governance," "administration," "supply" as an attribute of, or mythologically the "wife" of the Ruler (and esp. of the solar Viṣṇu)—will be easily understood. And also, just as the Ruler's "glories" considered together are his crowning "Glory," so in the case of Indra (king of the gods, *in divinis* and within you), his faculties (*indriyāṇi*) considered together are his "wife" Indrāṇī, and his abilities (*śaciḥ*, √*śak*, to be able, as in Śakra = Indra) are his "wife" Śacī; it is in just this sense that a king "espouses" his realm, "the lady of the land," and that the soul is the "bride" of the spirit. In the same way for Philo, the relation of αἴσθησις to νοῦς (i.e. *vāc* to *manas*) is that of Eve to Adam, the "woman" to the "man."

ported by the (invisible) Axis Mundi.[53] In the closely related symbolism of the Wheel and Circle (*cakra*, *κύκλος*, *circus*, cycle),[54] the Breaths, our selves, and all things are fixed-together-in (*samarpitāḥ*) and supported by (*pratiṣṭhitāḥ*) the central Self and "Person to-be-known," as are the spokes in the hub of a wheel of radii in the center of a circle, from which they radiate to its circumference.[55]

It is in connection with the architectural symbolism that there can be found the explanation of the important term and concept *samādhi* (√ *sam-ā-dhā*, to put together, mend, heal, literally and etymologically "synthesis"), of which the opposite is *vyādhi* (√ *vi-ā-dhā*, to divide up, disintegrate), "analysis," a term that is only, and significantly, met with in the medical sense of "disorder."[56] For "just as all other beams are united (*samāhitāḥ*,

[53] RV I.10.1, *tvā . . . ud vaṁśam iva yemire*. See Coomaraswamy, "Pali *kaṇṇikā* = Circular Roof-Plate" and "The Symbolism of the Dome" [both in Vol. I of this edition—ED.]; "Eckstein," 1939; "The Sunkiss," 1940, n. 30. Cf. also "Vedic Exemplarism" [in this volume—ED.].

[54] Not unrelated to the notion of a "Cyclopean" architecture.

[55] RV I.33.15, I.149.19; AV X.8.34; TS VII.4.11.2; AB IV.15; BU II.5.15; CU VII.15.1; Kauṣ. Up. III.8; Praśna Up. VI.6: Plotinus, *Enneads* VI.5.5, VI.8.18. The symbolisms of the round house and the wheel are very closely related; for a man is a moving house, and in the same way Skr. *ratha* and *vimāna* are equally "vehicle" and "building," while to "walk" is to "roll" (*vṛt*).

The construction of a wheel corresponds to that of a domed roof, or that of an umbrella (a moving roof); cf. Coomaraswamy, "Uṣṇīṣa and Chatra," 1938.

It will be noticed that our metaphysics makes continual use of analogies drawn from art. Such a procedure is intelligible in a traditional culture in which the arts are applications of first principles to contingent problems, i.e., "art imitates Nature in her manner of operation"; and where also, inasmuch as the artist is not a special kind of man, but every man a special kind of artist, the jargon of art is familiar. The technical terms of traditional thought are those of construction (*ἁρμονία*, carpentry, as a working in a "wood," ὕλη, analogous to that in which He worked "through whom all things were made"; cf. *Timaeus* 41B). Under such conditions "manu-facture" provides for the needs of the soul and body at once, and accordingly every artifact can be used not only for immediate ends but also as a support of contemplation. Therefore, St. Bonaventura could rightly say, "The light of a mechanical art is the path to the illumination of scripture. There is nothing therein which does not bespeak true wisdom, and for this reason Holy Scripture makes constant use of such similes" (*De reductione artium ad theologiam* 14). And although this procedure is strange to us whose education is more in words than in things (a natural consequence of our nominalism), a student of the traditional philosophy must learn to think in its own terms. For example, the background of Classical Greek philosophy is better and more fully preserved in the forms of "geometric art" than it is in the literary "fragments."

[56] Inasmuch as it is in the "heart" (identified with Brahma, BU IV.1.7, and elsewhere) that man's various selves are unified (*samāhitāḥ*, *ekadhā bhavanti*), it will be seen that our words schizo*phren*ia and *fren*zy are highly appropriate designations

pp. pl. of *sam-ā-dhā*) in the kingpost of the house, so are all the Powers in the Breath" (AĀ III.2.1); and just as all the rafters converge towards and are thus united in the roof-plate or peak of the house, so all virtues or skills (*kusalā dhammā*) converge and tend towards their synthesis in the state of *samādhi* (Mil 38).[57]

Herein also is to be found the explanation of the term *hitāḥ* (pp. of *dhā*, and literally "things put," *posita*, with the secondary sense of "aids"), applied in the Upaniṣads[58] to the flowing Breaths and equivocally to their channels, vectors, or courses (*nāḍyaḥ*)[59] which are similarly unified in

---

of what takes place in a state of "alienation," or estrangement from our Self.

On the other hand *vi-dhā*, to distribute, apportion, has no specifically pejorative connotation other than is implied in the very notion of "division." The constituents of the world are "distributed" in the primordial sacrifice, where it is asked, "how-many-fold (*katidhā*) did they divide up (*vy adadhuḥ*) the Person?"—in effect, "into how many *hitāḥ*"? These divisions are alluded to in RV I.164.15, *vihitāni dhāmasah*; and are, in fact, of the primordial Waters (*āpo vy adadhāt*, AV X.2.11), i.e., their release. The answer to *katidhā* is, of course, the *bahudhā* of many other contexts, cf. n. 37.

[57] *Samādhi* in its best known sense is, of course, the consummation of *yoga*, of which the three stages, *dharana* (consideration), *dhyāna* (contemplation), and *samādhi* (synthesis) correspond to the *consideratio*, and *raptus* or *excessus* (ἔκστασις) of Western contemplatives.

[58] For a collation of the references see the concordance published by G. Haas in Robert Ernst Hume, *Thirteen Principal Upaniṣads*, 2nd ed. 1934, p. 521, and cf. n. 59.

[59] *Nāḍi* is a "tube" or "pipe," like that of a flute (RV X.135.7). Plato's special word στενωπός (*Timaeus* 70B) implies the extreme tenuity of these ducts, which is emphasized in the Upaniṣads by comparison to a hair. As was rightly observed by Haas, in *Thirteen Principal Upaniṣads*, p. 159, the *suṣumnā* (MU VI.21) by which the Spirit ascends from the heart—by way of the bregmatic fontanelle—to the Sun, is not a vein or artery. This is not a physiology but a psychology, and it would be futile to seek any of these ducts in the body (as futile as it would be to seek the soul by a dissection of the body), for only their analogies, our nerves and veins, can be seen.

All the Powers of the Soul are "extensions" (τεταμένα, *Republic* 462E, cf. Philo, *Legum allegoriae* I.30, 37) of an *invisible* principle; when it abandons any inveterated body, then just as a goldsmith "draws out for himself (*tanute*)" from the gold another shape (*rūpam*), so the Self (of all beings, not our 'self,' but the Only Transmigrant) "makes for itself" (*kurute*) another shape (*rūpam* = *tanus*, BU IV.4, cf. BG II.22). Our Breaths are the "threads" (*tantu, tantri, sūtra*) of which the solar Spider (KB XIX.3), our Self (RV I.115.1), spins his web (BU II.1.20) of seven rays (RV I.105.9), the "tissue" of the Universe; and in the last analysis, "one thread" (Brahma Up. 1) on which all this universe is "strung" (BG VII.7, "on Me, like rows of gems on a thread"; Dhyāna Up. VIII, "all these elemental beings on the Self, as on a jewel thread," cf. BG II.17, IX.4, 11, etc.). Accordingly, to know the extended thread (*sūtram . . . vitatam*) on which these offspring are woven, to know the "thread of the thread," is to know God (AV X.8.37). To the same pattern belong the life-lines spun by the Greek Fates, and by the Norns, and the life-ray and life-the Brahma-heart from which they proceed and to which they return; for he is both "fontal and unflowing" (*kṣaraścākṣaraḥ*), fontal (*kṣaraḥ*) as "all elemental-beings," and "unflowing" (*akṣaraḥ*) in his eminence (*kūṭa-sthaḥ*, BG xv.16);[60] it is because the Winds and Waters ever return upon themselves that they flow without the possibility of exhaustion (JUB I.2.5 ff.). The *hitāḥ*, then, are just those Breaths which, as we have seen, are *sam-ā-hitāḥ* at the center of their circling. As the several "members" (*aṅgāni*) of the Breath they are "externally divided up" (*parastāt prati-vi-hitāḥ*), and their relation to that Breath is that of *upa-hitāḥ* to *hitāḥ* (Kauṣ. Up. III.5; ŚB VI.1.2.14, 15). The immanent deity—Agni, Ātman, Prajāpati—is himself "deposited" (*nihitaḥ*,[61] RV III.1.20; KU II.20; MU

threads of RV I.109.3 (*raśmi*) and II.28.5b (*tantu*).

We said "extensions" above with explicit reference to Skr. *tan,* to which the foregoing words beginning with "t" are referable. The basic senses of the root are those of tension, tenuity, and tone, all highly appropriate to the Breaths; and it is also noteworthy that Skr. *tan*, to "extend," and *stan*, to "sound, thunder," are as closely related as are τείνω and στένω, the latter present in Plato's στενωπός. The "paths" of the Powers of the Soul are thus much rather "directions" than concrete channels; and in fact, as a group of five, the microcosmic Breaths are precisely what the "five visible directions" (four quarters and zenith) are macrocosmically (ŚB XI.8.3.6, AĀ II.2.3, etc.).

The whole conception is a part of the well-known "thread-spirit" (*sūtrātman*) doctrine and of the symbolism of weaving and sewing (cf. Coomaraswamy, "Primitive Mentality," [in Vol. I of this edition—ED.]), according to which the Sun connects all things to himself by means of pneumatic "threads" which are "rays" that he extends. For some of the references, see "Primitive Mentality," "Literary Symbolism" [also in Vol. I], and W. B. Henning, "An Astronomical Chapter of the *Bandahishn*," JRAS, 1942, p. 232, n. 6, referring to "these indivisible and indestructible connecting lines . . . [or] pipe-lines, Coptic *lihme*." The pneumatic "threads" or "rays" are likewise the "wind-cords" of MU I.4 (cf. BU III.7.2) and Rūmī's "cords of causation" (*Mathnawī* I.849). The *hitāḥ* and *nāḍyaḥ* with which they coincide are essentially what we should now call "forces" and "lines of force." Cf. notes 31, 51, 67, 75.

[60] *Kūṭa-sthaḥ* is rendered by "eminent" because the expression reverts to the architectural symbolism explained above, *kūṭa* being the ridge, peak, or "angle" of a building and equivalent to *kaṇṇikā* (see Coomaraswamy, "Pāli *kaṇṇikā*: Circular Roof-plate" [in Vol. I of this edition—ED.]).

That "all things flow" (as the ῥέοντες maintained) and that "the whole is stationary" (as the στασιῶται maintained) no more involves a contradiction than are time and eternity contradictories, one true, the other false (cf. *Theaetetus* 181 ff.). Where all things turn about one center, one and the same whole moves and does not move; the mover (trans. or intrans.) remains unmoved—"One unstirring outgoes others running, though standing still," and is neither diminished by what it gives or increased by what it takes (Īśā Up. 4; BU IV.4.23, V.1; *Enneads* IV.8.2).

[61] Pp. of *ni-dhā*, to set down, implant, deposit, bury. This en-graving or housing is at the same time a bondage from which the Person cannot easily disentangle himself, whence the prayer "Release us that are bound," as it were in a net (*nidhā* = *pāśāḥ*, snares, AB III.19).

II.6c) in the "cave" (*guhā*)[62] of the heart, and so therefore are the Mind and the Breaths "deposits" (*nihitam*, *nihitāḥ*, RV I.24.7; AV X.2.19; Muṇḍ. Up. II.1.8). Agni, again, is "sent forth" or "put forth" (*prahitaḥ*) as a messenger (ἄγγελος) (AV XVIII.4.65)—it is one of his commonest epithets; and so are the powers of the soul, which are "Measures of Fire,"[63] put forth (*prahitāḥ*, AĀ II.1.5) and to be equated, as we shall see, with the Seven Ṛṣis, our body-guard,[64] and with the Maruts who are similarly

[62] *Guhā*, "cave," with respect to the "mountain (*giriḥ* √ *gṛ*, swallow) of Brahma," our elemental soul, composite of eye, ear, mind, speech, and smell, in which Brahma is "swallowed up" (AĀ II.1.4). This conception is the same as that of the "entombment" of the soul in the body (*Phaedrus* 250c; *Enneads* IV.8.3; Philo, *De opificio mundi* 108, etc.), or macrocosmically in the "heart" of the world-mountain; in either sense the "cave" is the same as Plato's (*Republic*, ch. 7). The image of the "cave," moreover, in which the deity is "seated" or "deposited" (*niṣīdan, nihitam*), and that he inhabits (*praviśya*) as his mansion (*brahma-sālā*), underlies the symbolism of buried treasure (*nidhi*) and that of mineral "deposits" (*dhātu*), delving, and mining (MU VI.28). Cf. René Guénon, "La Montagne et la caverne," *Études traditionelles,* XLIII (1938). Again, because of the correspondence of "center" with "summit," there is an analogous interpretation of mountain climbing; the radiating powers of the soul are so many paths converging to the mountain top (*ad eminentiam mentis,* in the words of St. Bonaventura, who likewise assimilates *mons* to *mens*), by which paths the Comprehensor can reach their source (JUB I.30.1)—climbing the "slope" (*ucchrāyam*, √ *ud-śri*, JUB I.5.7; cf. *ucchrāyī*, a sloping plank, side of a triangle or pyramid) that corresponds to the Platonic and Hermetic ἀνόδος. Of all the ways that lead to the summit of the mountain, those of the active life are on its outward slopes, and that of the contemplative is an inward and vertical ascent, while the point at which all meet is one and the same.

[63] See Coomaraswamy, "Measures of Fire" [in this volume—ED.]. The psychic faculties are "fires" (*prāṇāgnayaḥ*, Praśna Up. IV.3; *indriyāgnayaḥ*, BG IV.26); the Breaths "kindle" (*samindhate*, √ *idh*, as in αἰθήρ) everything here (AB II.4), i.e. quicken, awaken all things to life. Agni himself is the Breath (*passim*), and "in that they bear him apart in many places, that is his form as the Universal Gods" (*viśve-devāḥ*, AB III.4), i.e., Breaths (TS V.6.4.1), speech, sight, hearing, mind, and all else (ŚB X.3.3) that this Great Being (*mahābhūta*) suspires (BU IV.5.11). *Noster Deus ignis consumens* (Heb. 12:29) is "the principle of every life" (Jacob Boehme, *Signatura rerum* XIV.29) and Heracleitus' "ever-living Fire, in measures being kindled and in measures dying out" (Fr. XX).

[64] The Seven Ṛṣis are said to "guard" (*rakṣanti*) the body, VS *loc. cit.* This guardian function is also that of the Maruts in relation to Indra, whom they support in battle, and that of the Breaths to the Breath, as whose *svāḥ*, *svāpayaḥ*, φίλοι, etc., they are a sort of regiment of the "King's Own," whose duty is to him and to the "house" in which all dwell together. This is just as it is also in the Greek sources, where the powers of perception and action (αἰσθήσεις) are the Janissaries (δορυφόροι) in attendance upon the Great King, Mind, or rational Soul, of which they are the allies (σύμμαχοι) and friends (φίλοι, Philo, *De specialibus legibus,* IV.122; *Deterius* 33) they "escort" (δορυφορέω) the Royal Reason to the perception of sense objects, which it would not otherwise have apprehended as such (*De opificio mundi* 139); and the

"sent forth" (*prahitāḥ*, VS xxxiv.55) and "placed" (*hitāḥ*, RV i.166.3). The deity himself, Viśvakarman (All-Worker; Indra, Agni) is at once Positor and Dispositor (*dhātṛ, vidhātṛ*, RV x.82.2, 3, where he is called "the one above the Seven Ṛṣis"). That Vāyu "puts the in and out breaths" (*prāṇāpānau dadhāti*) into man (TS ii.-1.1.3, cf. ŚB i.8.3.12), i.e., "the deities, sight, hearing, mind, and speech" (AĀ ii.3.3), or that Brahma "put" (*adadhāt*) these Breaths (AV x.2.13) *ipso facto* makes these Breaths *hitāḥ*:[65] In all these "dispositions," indeed, the Spirit is at the same time Agent and Subject, Sacrificer and Sacrifice, Divider and Dividend.

In their identification with their excavated channels (*nāḍyaḥ = niṣkhātāḥ panthāḥ*, JUB iv.24.9; cf. AV x.7.15, CU viii.6), the Breaths are thought of as streams or rivers (*nadyaḥ, sindhavaḥ*) of light, sound, and life.[66] They are, in fact, the very waters and rivers that are released when Vṛtra is slain, and are called *nadyaḥ* "because they sounded (*anadata*)" as they went their way (AV iii.13.1; TS v.6.1.2); and in the same way "the Breath is a noise (*prāṇo vai nadaḥ*)," and when it sounds, all else resounds (*saṃnadati*, AĀ i.3.8).[67] Speech is a flowing (*kulyā*), originating in the pool (*hraḍa*)

---

heart is the "guard room" (δορυφορικὴ οἴκησις) of these sensitive powers, whence they take their orders (Plato, *Timaeus* 70B). The Royal Breath himself is the Guardian Angel of the whole organism, and in this guardianship his powers are his comrades. It is only when they, in the pursuit of their own private pleasures, neglect their duty or even lead their master astray, that "we" go wrong.

[65] Cf. Philo's explanation of αἴσθησις as εἰσ-θέσις, "a putting in" (*Immut.* 42). If, on the other hand, we connect αἴσθησις with ἀίω (Skr. *av*; *avere*), to "perceive," then it will be significant that ἀίω (*Iliad* xv.252) also means to "breathe."

[66] Collectively, these are the flood or torrents of the qualities, etc. (*guṇ'oghāḥ*) by which the elemental self is swept away (MU ii.2), the Buddhist "flood so hard to cross" (S i.53), though Indra "stands upon these flowing streams at will" (AV iii.13.4), cf. Coomaraswamy, *Hinduism and Buddhism*, 1943, n. 269, and W. N. Brown, *Indian and Christian Miracles of Walking on the Water* (Chicago, 1928). This River of Life in which we may be swept away and drowned is Plato's "river" (ποταμός) of the six irrational motions of the senses (αἰσθήσεις), in which the soul is rolled along and tossed about (*Timaeus* 43), Philo's "river of the sense perceptions" (ὁ τῶν αἰσθητῶν ποταμός, *Legum allegoriae* iii.18, cf. *Deterius* 100), and Hermes' "flood of ignorance that sweeps along with it the soul imprisoned in the body" (*Lib.* vii.11B). This is the sea that separates "this" from "yonder" shore, and that can only be crossed by the "Bridge" or in the "Ship," or on the Wings of a Bird, or by one who can "walk on the Water" as if it were dry land.

[67] That the Breaths "sound" in their "pipes" (*nāḍī = nāḷī*, flute, RV x.135.7) involves the symbolism of the body compared to an organ, as enunciated in Jacob Boehme, *Signatura rerum* xvi.3-7, "as an organ of divers and various sounds or notes is moved with only one air, so that each note, yea, every pipe, has its peculiar tune . . . and yet are only one in the divine, eternal speaking word, sound, or voice

of the Mind (JUB I.58.1), and the Seven Rays of the Sun by which we see[68] and hear, etc., are also Seven Rivers (JUB I.29.8, 9). The faculties (*indriyāṇi*), together with all else that the Person emanates, are "flowing streams" (*nadyaḥ syandamānāḥ*), parts of him who is the Sea in which, when they go home, their distinctive names and aspects are lost (Praśna Up. VI.4, 5).[69] It is in just the same way that in the Greek sources, vision, speech, and other powers of the soul are "streams" (*ῥέος*, *νᾶμα*, *Timaeus* 45B, 75E, etc.), as also in Chinese, vision is a "stream" (*yenpo*, 13,219 + 2336); and, indeed, we can still speak of eloquence as "fluency."

With this conception of the Breaths, and indeed of all manifested things, as streams or rivers, we can revert to the contexts in which the doors of the senses are opened, through which as if through sluices they rush forth, singing (BU I.3). We saw that the Person, Svayambhū (*αὐτογενής*), pierced, or breached these openings (*khāni vyatṛṇat khāni bhitvā*) and so looks out, etc., through them. Indra, Puruṣa, Svayambhū, Brahma, are, or rather is, the answer to the question of AV X.2.6.11, "Who pierced the seven apertures (*sapta khāni vi tatarda*, $\sqrt{}$ *tṛ* as in *vyatṛṇat*) in the head, these ears, the nostrils, eyes and mouth . . . who divided up the Waters (*āpo vy-adadhāt*) for the flowing of the rivers (*sindhu-sṛtyāya*)

---

of God; for one only spirit rules them; each angelical prince is a property out of the voice of God, and bears the great name of God" (in which sense, also, as we shall see, the Breaths are Devas); and in Plutarch, *Moralia* 404, where the soul is God's organ. In a closely related image, the body is compared to a harp (*vīṇā*, AĀ III.2.5, ŚA VIII.9.10; cf. *Phaedo* 84E ff.), which must be kept in tune if it is to be made to speak well. In Praśna Up. II.2, the body, indwelt by the deities (*devāḥ*), is referred to as a *bāṇa* or *vāṇa*, either *vīṇā* as in AV XI.4, or flute, as in RV I.85.10.

[68] "Whoever sees, it is by his ray that he sees," JUB I.28.8; "in me there is another, by whom these eyes sparkle," Rūmī, *Dīvān*, Ode XXXVI. It is because he looks outward from within us that we do not see him; to see him who is the "only seer, himself unseen" (BU III.7.23), our eye must be turned round (*āvṛtta cakṣus*, KU IV.1). In other words, it is not with the eye of sense, but that of heart or mind that one must look for him. Rawson's attempt (KU, 1924, p. 149) to show that Plato held an opposite view is ridiculous; see *Symposium* 219, *Phaedo* 83B, and especially *Republic* 526E, where, in order to facilitate an apprehension of the Good, we should pursue "those studies that force the soul to turn its vision round to the region wherein dwells the most eudaimonic part of the Real, which I must needs see," and *Philebus* 61E, where vision is either of transitory things *or* of the immutable. Conversion (*μεταστροφή*, *āvṛtti*, turning round) is, in fact, "a philosophical term which Plato invented in order to describe the turning of the soul from the world of opinion and error to the principle of true being" (Werner Jaeger, *Humanism and Theology*, Milwaukee, 1943, notes 55, 58).

[69] Parallels abound in all traditions; cf. Coomaraswamy, "The 'E' at Delphi," n. 2 [in this volume—ED.], and Angelus Silesius, *Cherubinischer Wandersmann* II.25,

Wenn du das Tröpflein wist im grossen Meere nennen,
Den wist du meine Seel'im grossen Gott erkennen.

in this man?" (AV x.2.6.11).[70] "What Ṛṣi put man together? (*samadadhāt*, AV xi.8.14)." The answer is that Indra "with his bolt pierced the sluices of the streams" (*vajreṇa khāni vyatṛnat nadīnām*, RV ii.15.3) and so let loose the "Seven Rivers" (RV *passim*) by which "we" see, hear, think, etc. (JUB i.28, 29). This opening up of the *Fons vitae* (*utsam akṣitam*, RV i.64.6, viii.7.16, *utsa madhvas*, i.154.5, etc.) that had been restrained by the Vedic Dragon, Vṛtra, Varuṇa, the Vedic "Pharaoh,"[71] is the primordial and incessant act of creation and animation that is repeated in every generation and in every awakening from sleep. In "Grail"

[70] This is, almost word for word, Hermes, *Lib.* v.6, "Who is it that has traced the circles of the eyes, who pierced the openings of the nostrils and the ears, who opened up the mouth?" More shortly, "Who hath made man's mouth?" (Exod. 4:11).

There are no peculiarly Indian doctrines; all can be found elsewhere, and stated as nearly as possible in the same words, often in the same idioms. Compare, for instance, D ii.144, "How, then, can this be possible—whereas anything whatever born, brought into being, and organized, contains within itself the inherent necessity of dissolution—that such an existence should not be dissolved? No such situation exists," with *Phaedo* 78c, "Is not that which is compounded and composite naturally liable to be decomposed, in the same way in which it was compounded?"; or BG ii.22, "Even as a man, casting off worn-out garments, puts on other new ones, so the body-dweller (*dehin*, Inner Man, Self), doffing worn-out bodies, puts on other new ones," with *Phaedo* 87d, "Each soul wears out many bodies, especially if the man lives many years. For if the body is constantly changing and being destroyed while the man still lives, and the soul is always weaving anew that which wears out, then when the soul is released (*ἀπολλύοιτο*, *pratīyate*, "ab-solved"), it must needs have been wearing its last garment," and with Meister Eckhart's "Aught is suspended from the divine essence; its progression is matter, wherein the soul puts on new forms and puts off her old ones. The change from one into the other is her death, and the ones she dons she lives in" (Pfeiffer ed., p. 530). This is the true doctrine of "reincarnation," as it characterizes this present or any other contingent existence, of which the notion of the return of an "individual" to this earth after death is only a popular perversion.

In connection with all these parallels, which could be singly of relatively slight significance, but taken together and recognized as the parts of a consistent pattern are very impressive, let us say once and for all that it is by no means our intention to suggest any borrowings or influences, but rather a remote and common inheritance, just as in comparing Greek and Sanskrit words with common roots, it would not be meant that the former are of Sanskrit origin, but only that these are cognates. The parallels are etymological, idiomatic, and doctrinal, but the most that can be said is that if Greeks and Indians met in Alexandria, they could have understood one another very well, and far better than we, from our nominalist and empirical point of view, can understand either. The much argued question of Indian influence on Plotinus is beside the point; what we have to consider is the likeness of the whole Platonic to the whole Indian tradition, and what this means. It is more than a simple problem of literary history, and much rather one of a remote prehistory.

[71] "Pharaoh, king of Egypt, the great dragon that lieth in the midst of the waters, which hath said, my river is my own, and I have made it for myself" (Ezek. 29:3).

terms, the worlds-to-be are as yet unirrigated, unpeopled, and infertile, and Indra is the Great Hero (*mahāvīra*), or as the Breath the "Only Hero (*ekavīra*, JUB II.5.1)," by whom their life is renewed and the Waste Land refreshed. When he "smote Ahi, sent forth the Seven Rivers, opened the doors that had been closed (*ahann ahim, ariṇāt sapta-sindhūn, apa avṛṇot apihitāni khāni*, RV IV.28.1)," then "he filled-full the waste-lands, and the thirsty fields (*dhanvāni ajrān apṛṇak tṛṣāṇān*, RV IV.19.7)," i.e., "peopled" (*apṛṇat*, $\sqrt{pl} = pṛ$, in "folk," "people," "plenty," etc.) these worlds. The Breaths, as we have already seen, are also the Ṛṣis ($\sqrt{}$*ṛṣ*, rush, flow, shine cf. *ṛṣabha*, "bull," and ἄρσην), Seers, Sages or Prophets (*vates*), and Sacrificers, usually referred to in a standard group (*gaṇa*) of seven. These Seers, expressly identified with the Breaths,[72] are notably "co-born" (*sajātāḥ, sākaṃjātāḥ*), modalities (*vikṛtayaḥ*) or "members (*aṅgāni*) of one and the same [sevenfold] Person entered into many places," composers of incantations (*mantrakṛt*) and "being-makers" (*bhūta-kṛt*), sacrificers and lovers of sacrifice (*priya-medhinaḥ*), "born here again for the keeping of the Vedas"; they attend on "One beyond the Seven Ṛṣis" (Viśvakarman, solar Indra, Agni, Self, and "Only Ṛṣi") whom they importune by labor, ardor, and sacrifice to reveal the *Janua Coeli*; they are visibly the seven lights of Ursa Major in the center of the sky and invisibly the powers of vision, hearing, breathing, and speaking in the head.[73] Implanted in the body (*śarīre prahitāḥ*), they protect it, and are these seven Breaths, the six

[72] ŚB VI.1.1.1, VIII.4.1.5 and 3.6, IX.1.1.21, IX.2.1.13; Sāyaṇa on RV X.82.2 and AV II.35.4; Uvvata and Mahīdhara on VS XXXIV.55; *Nirukta* X.26, *sapta-ṛṣīṇānindriyāṇi, ebhyaḥ para ātmā, tāni asminn ekaṃ bhavanti*; cf. also Śaṅkara on BU II.2.3. As Keith on AĀ II.2.1 points out, "the names of the seers of RV can be deduced from *prāṇa's* actions." Whitney, on AV X.8.9 = BU II.2.4, calls the identification of the Ṛṣis with the Breaths "extremely implausible," but if there is one scholar whose opinions on any but purely grammatical questions are negligible, it is he. To me the identification is "extremely plausible," but instead of merely saying so, I cite the authority of several texts and the five greatest of Indian Commentators.

[73] RV I.164.15, X.73.1, X.82.2; TS V.7.4.3; AV X.8.5.9, XI.12.19, XIX.41.1; ŚB II.1.2.4, VI.1.1.1 ff.; JUB I.45, I.46.1, 2, I.48.3, IV.14.5, 6, IV.26.2; BU II.2.4.

In JUB I.46.6, *guptyai* corresponds to AV X.8.9, *gopāḥ*. In JUB IV.14.6, *ava rurudhire* ("they beset") corresponds to RV X.73.11, *upa seduḥ*, and AV XIX.41.1, *upa-ni-ṣeduḥ*, being desirous of the Good (*bhadram*, *ibid.*)—that of finding the Janua Coeli, or of entering-into (*apitvam*, AV X.8.5 = *apāyam*, AĀ II.2.3) Indra. These contexts throw light on the nature of the sacrificial sessions (*sattra*) in which all participate on their own behalf, and the reward is not a fee but the Self (*ātman*); "Upaniṣad" as a doctrine or mystery deriving from *upa-ni-ṣad* (*upa-sad*), in the sense of *avarudh*, "to lay siege to" the teacher as one who knows the Self, and as it were by pressure to make him reveal it. In the psychology of Indian education it is not so much the teacher that is expected to hand out the truth, as it is the pupil who is expected to get it from him.

indriyāṇi and *manas* (VS xxxiv.55 and Commentary). The formulation in BU ii.2.3, 4 (cf. AV x.8.9; AĀ i.5.2)[74] is sufficiently explicit; the Seven Ṛṣis are the powers of hearing, seeing, breathing (smell), and eating, of which the seven openings are in the head; they surround the median Breath, and are the Breaths. This "median Breath" is, of course, the "One beyond the Seven Ṛṣis" of RV x.82.2, the "ultimate Self," as Sāyaṇa says, and the "single-born" of RV i.164.15. To put this all in Philo's words, "God extends (τείναντος) the power that proceeds from himself through the median Breath" (*Legum allegoriae* i.37),[75] of which the seven most essential factors are set in the head, where are the seven apertures through which we see, hear, smell, and eat (*De opificio mundi* 119), while the "one beyond the Seven Ṛṣis" he speaks of astrologically as "a supercelestial Star, the fountain of the perceptible stars" (*De opificio mundi* 31). More generally, "our soul is divided into seven parts, five senses, speech, and generation, to say nothing of their invisible Duke" (ἡγεμονικός, *De opificio mundi* 117), a listing of the powers of the soul that often recurs in the Indian texts.

Philo's astrological allusion brings us back to the identification of the Seven Ṛṣis with the stars of Ursa Major and to the "One beyond," Indra, "the mover of the Ṛṣis" (*ṛṣi-codanaḥ*, RV viii.51.3; cf. i.23.24, *indro . . . saha ṛṣibhiḥ*). Eisler cites *Testamentum Ruben*, c. 2, to the effect that "Seven spirits (πνεύματα) were given [to man] at the creation to do all his works . . . spirits of life, sight, hearing, smell, speech, taste, and generation, and as eighth the Spirit of Sleep," and remarks that these are the "seven parts of the soul which, according to Stoic teaching, flow from the heart or the ἡγεμονικόν of the soul as air currents toward the appropriate intellectual functions, these seven parts consisting of the five senses, the power of generation and the ability to speak."[76] However, I

[74] In AĀ i.5.2, the seven Breaths are "placed" (√*dhā*) in the head by a repetition of the seven verses of RV i.11. The Voice is separately mentioned and "not associated" (*an-anuṣaktā*) with the other Breaths. The logical reason for this is the well-known fact that while one can see, hear, smell, and breathe or eat at the same time, one cannot simultaneously speak and breathe, a fact that is often insisted upon (Kauṣ. Up. ii.5, ŚA iv.5, etc.; cf. Coomaraswamy, "The Sunkiss," 1940, p. 63), while the practical reason is to avoid the stuttering that would result if one tried to talk and breathe at once.

[75] Forming what Plato called "the community (of powers) extended (τεταμένη) throughout the body to the Soul for their single integration with its ruling part" (*Republic* 462E).

[76] "*Orphisch-Dionysische Mysteriengedanken in der christlichen Antike*," *Vorträge der Bibliothek Warburg*, II (1922–1923), 87. Gk. ὕπνος = Skr. *svapna*, hermeneutically a "coming into one's own," or "one's Self" (*svam-apitvam*). The "Spirit

cannot but suspect that this most Indian psychology is of older than Stoic formulation, Ionian, and indirectly Babylonian. A remarkable parallel appears in the Iranian *Bundahishn*,[77] where Haftōreng (the Great Bear) is the General of the North, and Mēχ-ī Gāh (Polaris), called also *Meχ-ī miyān āsmān* (the peg in the center of the sky), is the "General of Generals," and, further, "A tether [*rag, band*] ties each of the seven continents [= Skr. *sapta dvīpa* or *dhāma*] to the Great Bear, for the purpose of managing the continents during the period of the Mixture. That is why the Great Bear is called Haftōreng [*haft rag*]." Henning remarks in a note, "These seven tethers constitute the 'light' counterpart to the seven ties which connect the seven planets with the lower regions, and through which the planets exercise their influence upon terrestrial events." All these "ties" are what in Indian texts are called the cosmic "wind-cords" (*vāta-rajjuḥ*), mentioned in MU I.4 in connection with the Pole Star (*dhruvaḥ*; cf. *dhruti*, necessity, RV VII.86.6). But I do not know why Henning speaks of "planets," since he remarks elsewhere that the planets are "unknown" to his text, "with its nearly prehistoric views." The mention of "planets," however, introduces us to the fact that in some earlier (ŚB VI.7.1.17, VIII.7.3.10 and BU III.7.2, where it is to the Sun, and not the Pole Star, that all things are tied by pneumatic threads) and some later texts (Hermes Trismegistos, and the traditional astrology generally), it is by the Planets which are themselves governed by the Sun and not by the Bears that terrestrial events are influenced. All this can best be explained by a transposition of symbols[78] to be connected with early migrations: the Axis Mundi from a "northern" point of view naturally extending from the North Pole to the Pole Star, but from an "equatorial" point of view from the "center of the earth," established sacrificially anywhere, to the Sun in the

---

of Sleep" thus corresponds to the Breath, or Self, into which the powers of the soul re-enter (*api-i*) in sleep or death. Man's *yea* is the gods' *nay* (AB I.16, etc.), and in this case what men call waking is for the gods a being asleep, and what men call sleep (or death) is for the gods a waking (cf. BG II.61; Phaedo 71c): a point of view that can be traced throughout the whole tradition, in which our all-too-human values are transvalued.

[77] See W. B. Henning, "Astronomical Chapter," pp. 229 ff.; our citations from pp. 230–34. In the same connection see also J. Pryzluski, "Les Sept Puissances divines dans l'Inde et l'Iran," *Revue d'histoire et de philosophie religieuses*, XVI (1936), 500–507, and L. D. Barnett, "The Genius: a Study in Indo-European Psychology," JRAS, 1929, pp. 731–48 (*Fravashi* = *Puruṣa*; the *Amesha Spentas* correspond to the *Ṛṣis*).

[78] Cf. René Guénon, "Les Portes solsticiales," *Études traditionelles*, XLIII (1938), 180 ff.

zenith; so that in the one case the Polaris and in the other the noonday Sun is taken to be the "captain" of our soul, our "Indra."[79] The significance of all this will only appear when we come to a discussion of our "Fate" and its mastery.

One of the most remarkable accounts of the Ṛṣis is to be found in ŚB VI.1.1.1 ff. In the beginning, they were "this non-existent" (*asat*). Men ask, "Who were those Ṛṣis?" They were, indeed, the Breaths. The median Breath is Indra; he by his power (*indriya*) kindled those Breaths from the center, and they originated the "seven several Persons"; these they made into One Person (*puruṣa*), concentering their virtue in his head, and that was the "sevenfold Person" of Prajāpati, the world's Progenitor. The emanation of the worlds is his disintegration, and the building up of the Fire (-altar) is at once his reintegration and the sacrificer's.

This is, as nearly as possible, also the story as told by Hermes, *Lib.* 1.9 ff. There the "second Mind made out of fire and water Seven Governors (*διοικήτορες*), i.e., the Seven Planets, and set agoing their revolutions. Man (*ἄνθρωπος* = *puruṣa*), the Son of God, having in himself the working (*ἐνέργεια*) of these Seven Governors and knowing their essence, looked down through the (solar) roofplate (*ἁρμονία*), broke through the cranium (*κύτος*)[80], and loved and wedded the downward-tending Nature, who then gave birth to "seven men according to the natures of the Seven Governors," and of elemental constitution; in them the Man, from being Life and Light, became soul and mind, subjected to mortality and destiny because of the body, but still immortal in his essential form (*οὐσιώδης* = *svarūpa*); so "let the man endowed with Mind recognize that he is immortal, and that the cause of death is carnal love." The text goes on to show how the Man in us can return by the way he came.

[79] A Sun that never really rises nor sets for the Comprehensor, for whom it is evermore high noon (CU III.11.1–3, cf. AB III.44; *Enneads* IV.4.7). So Meister Eckhart, "alse daz götlich licht der sêle unde des engels licht sich sliezent in daz götlich licht, daz heizet er den mitentac" (Pfeiffer ed., p. 123). Hence the various "miracles" in which the Sun "stands still" in the zenith for the Hero. The "Hero"—for, as Meister Eckhart says, "a perpendicular sun on one's head is a thing that few can survive" (Evans ed., I, 183).

[80] Κύτος, I think, as in *Timaeus* 45A, *τὸ τῆς κεφαλῆς κύτος*, "the bowl of the head," and here with special reference to its top, since the entry is from above; as in AĀ II.4.3, where the One Self, "cleaving the hair-parting, entered by that door," i.e., by the bregmatic fontanelle, which corresponds to the macrocosmic Sundoor, the capstone (Hermes' *ἁρμονία*) of the Universe, through which the Spirit enters into and departs from it.

The Maruts, Vedic "Storm Gods" and, *entre nous*, our "stormy passions," are expressly identified with the Breaths (AB III.16, *prāṇā vai marutaḥ, svāpayaḥ prāṇāḥ*) or are the source of our Breaths (ŚB IX.3.1.7, *prāṇā vai mārutaḥ*). As Rudras they are the offspring of Rudra (Agni) and Pṛṣṇi (Earth), but win their "sacrificial names" by their cooperation with and "shouting around" Indra at the sacrifice of Vṛtra, and thus "free-willed (*svadhām anu*)[81] obtained the rebirth" (RV I.6.4, *punar garbhatvam erire*, with V.29.1 and VIII.53.5, 6), i.e., are regenerated from the sacrificial operation as gods (RV X.56.7, *karmaṇaḥ . . . mahna . . . udajāyanta devāḥ*).[82] It need hardly be said that the gods, *in their plurality*, were originally mortal, and only obtained their immortality by "worth" (RV X.63.4; cf. ŚB II.2.2.8, XI.1.2.12, XI.2.3.6), or that for this very reason the sacrificial Breaths are "Perfectible Gods" (RV X.90.16, *sādhyāḥ santi devāḥ*, with reference to those first sacrificers whom Sāyaṇa rightly calls "Prajāpati's Breath-forms," *prajāpati-prāṇa-rūpā*;[83] ŚB X.2.2.3, *prāṇā vai sādhyāḥ devāḥ*, "the 'Perfectible Gods' are, indeed, the Breaths"). Indra ("impeller of the Ṛṣis," RV VIII.51.3) is "the Ṛṣi of the Maruts" (RV V.29.1); and they are notably "household sacrificers" (*gṛhamedhinaḥ*, ŚB II.5.3.4) and participate in the sacrificial session (*sattra*)[84] as fellow initiates

[81] As *vi-dhā* (cf. n. 56) implies a dispersion of power, so *sva-dhā* is self-determination, self-placement (cf. *svasthaḥ*, αὐτόθετος), authenticity, and in effect "free will (*kāmacāra, yathā vaśaṃ caraṇa*)," like that of the Gale that "bloweth as it listeth (*yathā vaśaṃ carati*)."

[82] For "insofar as he does not sacrifice, one is still unborn" (JUB III.14.8; cf. JB I.17, born of the flesh, but not of the Spirit): the Man, himSelf, is born of the Sacrifice, the Fire in which "this man" sacrifices himself (ŚB III.9.4.23, VII.2.1.6, XII.9.1.1; KB XV.3), and so is redeemed from death (ŚB III.6.2.16); which sacrificial rebirth is the second birth (in the sense of John 3:6, 7), and prefigures the third birth or resurrection after death "when the time comes."

[83] Being only the names of his acts, the "forms" (*rūpāṇi*) that he assumes in his sacrificial operation (*karma*, BU I.4.7, I.5.21, 22); or in Indra's words addressed to the Ṛṣi Viśvāmitra, "I am the Breath, that art thou, that all elemental-beings (*bhūtāni*), and he that shines yonder (the Sun); it is in this form (*rūpa*) that I pervade all the airts (*sarvā diśo viṣṭo'smi*), thereof is my food" (AĀ II.2.3)—"my food," for "all the airts bring him tribute" (CU II.21.4), and it is thus that "he rises up on food" (*yad annena atirohati*, RV X.90.2).

[84] A sacrificial "session" (*sattra*), notably as performed by the *gṛhamedhinaḥ* and *gṛhapati* of the human "household," i.e., mentally and meta-physically (*manasa, parokṣam*), is conducted by priestly initiates on their own behalf; there is no patron (*yajamāna*) and therefore no pecuniary "reward" (*dakṣinā*), "only the Self is their reward, and it is because they obtain the Self as their reward that they reach heaven" (TS VII.4.9.1; cf. TS VII.2.10.2; KB XV.1; ŚB IX.5.2.12–16; cf. Coomaraswamy, "*Ātmayajña*" [in this volume—ED.] and *Hinduism and Buddhism*, 1943, p. 21).

of their Gṛhapati (Indra, Prajāpati, Agni, PB x.3.5,6, xiv.14.9)—the "house" being, of course, that of this body in which we live. It is in their capacity as sacrificers that the Maruts agree most of all with the Breaths, for "the gods, mind-born, mind-yoked, are the Breaths, in them one sacrifices immaterially" (*teṣu parokṣaṃ juhoti*, TS vi.1.4.4), and with a view to immortality, since it is only with incorporeal offerings that immortality can be won (AB ii.14).

It will not surprise us to find that nearly everything that is said of the Breaths is also predicated of the Maruts. They are "Powers" (*vibhūtayaḥ*) and "appointees" (*hitāḥ*), besought to guard (*rakṣatā*) the sacrificer (RV i.166.3, 8, 11), and "ward the mortal" (*pānti martyam*, RV v.52.4); they are "fires" (*agnayaḥ*, RV iii.26.4), "rays" (*raśmayaḥ*, PB xiv.12.9; ŚB ix.3.1.25), mingled with "glory" (*śriyā*, RV vii.56.6, cf. v.55.3); and like the Breaths they are compared to the spokes of a wheel (RV v.58.5, x.78.4). They are notably "co-born" (*sākaṃ jātāḥ*, RV v.55.3 = *sākam-ukṣ*, vii.58.1), brothers of whom none is older or younger (v.59.5, 6. v.60.5).[85] As rain-gods they are very closely associated with (RV) and even identified with the Waters (AB vi.30), and it is either as winds or waters that they make the mountains "roar" (*nadayanta*, RV i.1665), while, like the Seven Rivers, they are "acquainted with Order" (*ṛtajñaḥ*, RV v.58.8). Like the elemental-beings (MU vi.10.35), they are identified with Soma-stalks[86] (RV i.166.3; Sāyaṇa, *prāṇādi rūpeṇa śarīre sthitaḥ*; TS vi.4.4.4, *prāṇā vai aṇśavaḥ*). They are, like the Ṛṣis and Breaths, a troop (*gaṇa*), or troops of seven or sevens (ŚB ii.5.1.13, v.4.3.17,[87] ix.3.1.1–25;[88] TS v.4.7.7, etc.), whose troop-leader (*gaṇānāṃ gaṇapati*,[89] RV ii.23.1, x.112.9; *sagaṇa*,

[85] See *akaniṭṭha* in Coomaraswamy, "Some Pāli Words" [in this volume—ED.]. The equality of the Maruts who, like the Breaths, are compared to the spokes of a wheel, of which spokes none is first or last in order, is like that of clansmen or guildsmen and gives its proper meaning to the phrase, "all men are born equal."

[86] For the implications of this, see "*Ātmayajña*," p. 239 ff.

[87] An analysis of the "chariot" (cf. AĀ ii.3.8; KU iii.3; J vi.252) with its wooden body, four horses, driver, and royal passenger, "seven in all," like the "sevenfold Person" of ŚB vi.1.1.1 ff.

[88] Verses 4–6, beginning "and these worlds are the same as this head," correspond very closely to the description of the cosmic "head" in *Timaeus* 44D, 45B, 81D.

[89] The Maruts being also Rudras, their father, Rudra, is also called the "leader of hosts" (*gaṇānām gaṇapati*, VS xvi.17; ŚB ix.1.1.18). In the "later" mythology, in which Śiva (Rudra) is attended by troops (*gaṇa*) of spirits (*bhūta*), this leadership is exercised by his sons, intellectually by Gaṇapati (Gaṇeśa, the elephant-headed deity) and in the military sense by Kārttikeya (Senāpati), these two representing the Sacerdotium and the Regnum and corresponding to the Vedic Agni-Bṛhaspati and Indra.

III.47.4) is Brahmaṇaspati (the Sacerdotium)[90] or Indra (the Regnum)—Indra, "the impeller of the Ṛṣis" (RV VIII.51.3), "is their Ṛṣi" (V.29.1). In other words, they are the subjects, liegemen, yeomen, and militia of the dual government of Indrābṛhaspatī,[91] and the pattern of the "Commons" of the body politic, whether of the state or the human being, of which the health depends upon their loyalty to their head; as is explicit in TS V.4.7.7 and VI.1.5.2, 3, where the unanimity and loyalty of earthly peoples is a consequence of the attachment of the Maruts to the Regnum *in divinis*.

It is chiefly here, in their relation to Agni and Indra, to whom, indeed, the Maruts may be disloyal (RV I.165, VIII.7.30, 31, etc.) but whom they normally serve as allies in the battle with Vṛtra and the winning of the Rivers with which they are so closely connected, that their significance for our psychology mainly centers. Throughout the Vedic literature we find that in the battle with Vṛtra, "overweening (*abhimāti*)" Indra is forsaken by the terrified gods and fights alone, or rather with no other aid but that of his "good allies" (RV VIII.53.5, 6) the Maruts or Breaths, who by their participation in this sacrificial operation attain their divinity (RV I.87.5, VIII.96.7; AB III.16, 20, etc.).[92] It is as their leader, not when they are pursuing their own ends, that he is victorious; he is the Regnum, and the whole science of government is one of self-control (*Arthaśāstra* I.6).

We have already seen, incidentally, that the powers of the soul, whether as Breaths or otherwise designated, are referred to as "gods" (*deva*, *devatā*), although it might be more intelligible here, inasmuch as these powers are the subjects of God and sent forth by him on His errands, to render by "angels"; for these are not the "many gods" of a "polytheism" (if such a thing ever or anywhere existed), but the delegations and extensions

[90] *Saptagu*, RV X.47.6 i.e., "seven-rayed"; cf. Grassmann, s.v. *gu* in senses 7, 8: as is explicit for Agni-Bṛhaspati in RV I.146.1 and VI.44.14.

[91] For the theory, see Coomaraswamy, *Spiritual Authority and Temporal Power in the Indian Theory of Government*, 1942. The application of the whole of this theory is as much with respect to self-control as with respect to the government of a State: this is, in other words, a psychology of government.

[92] In the Buddhist version of the same story, the Bodhisatta is in the same way deserted by the gods and left "alone"; but the cardinal virtues or powers that are "as it were his henchmen" (*parijana*, cf. *paribṛhan* in AB VI.28, and *śrijā parivṛaham* in JUB IV.24.11) do not desert him and, using them as his shield, he overcomes Māra's (Namuci's, Vṛtra's) army (J I.72 ff.). What this implies, equally for Indra and the Bodhisatta, is that they are victorious inasmuch as they are recollected, have collected themselves, are "in *samādhi*": for "he is 'deserted by the gods' who knows them otherwise than in himself" (BU IV.5.7).

of the power of one God. With this reservation, however, we shall continue to employ the usual rendering of *deva* and *devatā* by "god" or "divinity." By now we should be in a position to understand the statement of AV xi.8.18b, "having made him their mortal house, the gods [angels] inhabited man" (*gṛhaṃ kṛtvā martyam devāḥ puruṣam āviśan*), and that of JUB i.14.2, "all these gods are in me," and ŚB ix.2.1.15 (cf. VS xvii.14), where they are neither in the sky nor on earth but in animated beings (*prāṇinaḥ*).[93] These gods as they are within you (*adhyātmam*) are voice, sight, mind, hearing, but *in divinis* (*adhidevatam*) manifestly Fire, Sun, Moon, and the Quarters. "Whatever they give me not is not in my power" (AĀ ii.1.5; cf. VS xvii.15). The latter enter into man according to their stations (*yathāyatanam* = *yathākarma*, BU i.5.21), at the command of the Self: Fire becoming Voice enters into the mouth; the Quarters becoming hearing enter the ears; the Sun the eyes; Plants becoming hairs, the skin; the Moon becoming mind in the heart; the Waters becoming seed, the penis. Hunger and thirst are apportioned to all these deities, as partners, sharing in all that they obtain (AĀ ii.4.2).[94] It is precisely this hunger and thirst that distinguish the animal judgment (*abhijñāna*)[95] from that of the Person endowed with prescience (*prajñāna*), the former knowing only today, and the latter tomorrow (AĀ ii.3.2):[96] contacts with the quantitative (*mātrā-sparśāḥ*) are the source of pleasure and pain (*sukha-duḥkha*), and only the Person whom these do not distract (*na vy-athayanti*, do not "burn apart," obsolete √*ath*), one who remains the

[93] The words *yadā tvaṣṭā vyatṛnat* in the first line of the verse show that this empsychosis or anima-tion is predicated as taking place when the doors of the senses are pierced, here by the divine Artifex (Tvaṣṭṛ = δημιουργός); the following verses show that these deities that enter into us at birth are the totality of all our powers, whether for good or evil.

[94] Hunger and thirst are at once the origin and the disease of our contingent existence, and a definition of our mortality. The natural man is insatiable (AĀ ii.3.3): "Wer viel begehrt und will, der gibet zu verstehn, dass ihm noch mangelt viel" (Angelus Silesius, *Cherubinischer Wandersmann* v.156). All eating is a changing, and "all change is a dying." To satisfy our hunger is impossible; the enemy can be overcome only by fasting. Those who choose "hunger and thirst" for the sake of the corresponding pleasures are rejecting the true Life of the spirit (Plato, *Philebus* 54, 55): our very Self is "the Self that sur-passes (*atyeti*) hunger and thirst, distress and delusion, old age and death" (BU iii.5).

[95] The use of *abhijñāna* here for "estimative knowledge" is sarcastic, as Plato is when he speaks of those who are governed by pleasure and pain as ἀκολασίᾳ σώφρων (*Phaedo* 68E).

[96] The definition of the very Person of a man in AĀ ii.4.2 is very striking, and should be read in connection with the classic European definition of "Person" in Boethius, *Contra Evtychen*.

"same" under both conditions, is fitted to participate in immortality (*amṛtattvāya*, BG II.31 = *ἀθανίζειν*, Aristotle, *Nichomachean Ethics* X.7.1077b.31 = the *s'eternar* of Dante, *Inferno* XV.85), the goal to which the whole of our traditional psychology points and which is, therefore, as has been so well said, "the supreme aim of human education."[97]

Thus the instinctive life of the "gods within you," veritably fallen angels, is the passion of the Self for so long as it desires and pursues; and the purpose of Initiation or Consecration, *dīkṣā*, being precisely the destruction of ignorance and the recovery of the knowledge of the Self, we can readily understand the necessity for an initiatory[98] regeneration of the powers of the soul, if they are to be set free from their mortality. It will be clear that only he "is really initiated whose 'gods within him' are initiated," namely, mind, speech, breathing, sight, and hearing (collectively "man's constitution," *manuṣyasya sambhūti*), each by its own equivocal principle (KB VII.4; cf. ŚB III.1.3.18–22 and XIII.1.7), so that we by "setting free the Hearing of hearing, the Mind of the mind—that is, indeed, the Breath of breathing—and the Seeing of sight, may, when we leave this world, leave it as immortals" (JUB IV.18.2 = Kena Up. 1.2).[99] For whether we are saved

[97] Jaeger, *Humanism and Theology*, pp. 34–35 and notes 34–36.

[98] Initiation, or a being born again, is—no less from an Indian than a Platonic and Neoplatonic point of view—indispensable to ultimate liberation. Needless to say that Initiation implies a Master (*guru*) through whom the spiritual power is transmitted and by whose mediation the disciple is born again of God as father and of Sophia = Sāvitrī as mother. We cannot go into this at length here but only refer, for Plato, to *Phaedo* 69CD, where Socrates maintains that "whoever goes uninitiated and unperfected to the other world will lie in the mire, but he who arrives there cleansed and perfected will dwell with the gods," adding that the Bacchoi are the true philosophers and that he has ever striven to be one of them; and to *Theatetus* 155E, where the "uninitiated" are described as "those who think that nothing is other than what they can grasp firmly with their hands, and who deny the existence of actions (*πράξεις* = *karma*) and of becomings (*γενέσεις* = *bhava*), and of all that is invisible"; and for Neoplatonism to Hermes Trismegistos, *Lib.* XIII.

Where all instruction is encyclical and there are no "mysteries," the traditional psychology can only be taught as a curiosity or, at best, can effect an intellectual preparation which may dispose the student to work out his own salvation, but cannot do it for him. Yet to have accepted, even in theory, that "I" and "mine" are baseless concepts, to have consented to "deny ourself" even though we have not been able to do so, is already a partial release and deliverance from the dominion of pleasure and pain.

[99] For some discussion of this, see Coomaraswamy, "*Prāṇā-citi*," 1943, p. 108. Cf. Aristotle, *Metaphysics* XII.9.4, "Thinking cannot be the highest good. Therefore Mind (*νοῦς* = *manas*), if it be the Master Mind that we are speaking of, thinks nothing but itself, and its thinking is the 'Thinking of thinking' "; similarly Witelo, *Liber de intelligentiis* XXIV, XXVII, "Intelligentia semper intelligit . . . [sed] se ipsam

or lost depends entirely upon whether we have "known ourselves," Who we really are, and on the answer to the pregnant question, "In whom, when we depart, shall we be going forth?" (BU IV.4.13, 14, Praśna Up. VI.3), i.e., in our mortal selves or in the "self's immortal Self," the "Soul of the soul."[100]

This whole problem can as well be stated in terms of the mastery of Fate and the transcending of Necessity. Here we must revert to what was said above concerning the Seven Ṛṣis; for the conception of our constitution and consequent Destiny that was there implied is by no means uniquely Indian but, for example, identical with the Platonic doctrine set forth by Hermes Trismegistus (*Lib.* I.9.16, XVI.13 ff., *Excerpt* XII, and elsewhere). Here the creative (δημιουργός) solar Mind "made out of Fire and Spirit Seven Governors, who encompass in their orbits the sensible universe, and their Government (διοίκησις, literally housekeeping, economy) is called 'Destiny' (εἱμαρμένη)." These Governors are the Seven Planets (ἀστέρα, stars, lights) and they act upon us, or rather in us, through the corresponding Daimons[101] who take charge of us at birth, entering into the two irra-

cognoscendo non cognoscit alia" (Commentary, *per receptionem non intelligit, sicut anima*); BU IV.3.28 and IV.5.15, "For where there is a duality, as it were, there one thinks of another. But where everything has become just one's own Self (*yatra svasya sarvam ātmaivābhūt*), then how and of what would one 'think'?" So far is this, indeed, from *cogito ergo sum*, that that which "thinks" is precisely "not my Self"!

[100] The hoped-for answer to the question of Praśna Up. VI.3 is, of course, that of AĀ II.6, "departing hence with the Prescient Self (*prajñenātmanā*), he is reborn (*samabhavat*) immortal." In general, it is assumed that a full life here, sacramentally understood, must imply the full life there; and for this reason death is traditionally an occasion for rejoicing rather than for sorrow. For those who know their Self, there can be no fear of death (AV x.8.44). The display of grief at an Indian funeral (cremation) is exceptional; when such a display takes place, even a peasant will say, "poor man, he knows no better."

[101] Our speaking of the Indian psychology as a *bhūta-vidyā* was, in fact, as much as to say a "demonology." We must, of course, divest ourselves of the pejorative connotations with which Christianity has invested the word "*daimon*," which, like its Indian equivalent, *yakṣa* and *bhūta*, refers to God or to beings of divine origin, though they may be either good (obedient) or evil (disobedient). The traditional demonology is at once an angelology and a psychology. We nowadays look back on all these things as "superstitions," and such indeed they are, in the literal sense of "survivals"; but that we now call the demons within us "instincts" changes nothing in the nature of the "ruling passions" to which we are subjected until we have learned to master them and use them for ourselves. An instinct is an impulse (*instinguere*, instigation) and we still rightly speak of our instincts as "*ten*dencies" (because they pull us) and of wishful thinking as *ten*dentious. Psychology is fundamentally a pathology, as

tional parts of the soul and pervading the body, wherein, being seated in its vessels[102] they pull us to and fro towards themselves (*ἀνθέλκουσι . . . εἰς ἑαυτούς*), thus governing our earthly life, using our bodies as their instruments. Most of us are led and driven by these Daimons because of our enjoyment of the activities in which, as Hermes says, their being consists. But "neither the gods [the aforesaid Seven Planetary Governors] nor the Daimons have any power against the One Light-Ray that is of God,"[103] and "there are some few[104] in the Reasonable Part[105] of whose soul there shines this Ray that comes from God by way of the Sun [the aforesaid Creative Mind]," and in these the working of the Daimons

Plato's *πάθη ἐν ἡμῖν* announces, and "every passion is an epileptic seizure" (*ἐπίληπτον*, being captivated, caught), Philo, *Legum allegoriae* IV.79. To "behave" according to our likes and dislikes is not a liberty, nor an act, but a subjection and a passion. The soul's sickness is its own self-will. By whatever name we call the "horses," the problem remains the same, to drive or to be driven by them.

We cannot discuss the etymology of "*daimon*" here, but would connect it with Skr. √ *day* or *dā* and with *daitya* and *dānava*; and it is probably significant that Indra is said to overcome the Daityas and Dānavas in seven groups of seven in their respective stations (*yathāsthānam*, BD VII.51, 52), which seems to refer to a "victory over the powers of perception and action," such as in *Arthaśāstra* I.6 is called "the whole science of government."

[102] The aforesaid *nāḍyaḥ*, *στενωποί*, etc. (see n. 59), and to be thought of as the "lines of force" by which our being is penetrated.

[103] Plato's "golden chain" (*Laws* 645) and Dante's "raggio dell'alta luce, che da sè è vera" (*Paradiso* XXXIII.53).

[104] "For, as they say with reference to the mysteries, 'Many are the thyrsus-bearers, but few the Bacchoi'; and these, I hold, are the only true philosophers" (*Phaedo* 69CD). "To you it has been given to know the secrets of the kingdom of heaven, but to them it has not been given. . . . Seeing they do see, and hearing they do not hear, nor do they understand . . . lest they should perceive . . . and hear . . . and understand . . . and turn for me to heal them," Matt. 13:11–15. The last thing that the "modern man in search of a soul" desires is to be healed—"In the last days men shall be lovers of their own selves," II Tim. 3:1, 2.

[105] Although it is almost unavoidable to render *λόγος*, *λογισμός*, *λογιστικός* by "Reason" and "reasonable," the notion of an infallible Calculus is what is really implied, and it must be clearly understood that the Platonic "Reason" is by no means our "rationality," but much rather Aristotle's "Mind of the mind," the Mind that is "always right" (*De anima* III.10, 33a.27), and the Scholastic *Synteresis, Intellectus vel Spiritus*, than it is our "mind" or "reasoning power" that forms opinions and acts accordingly. Already for Boethius, reason is a mortal faculty, and when he calls himself a "reasoning and mortal animal," Philosophia rejoins that he has forgotten Who he is. The greater part of what is nowadays called "knowledge" is based on nothing better than statistics, and its "facts" are only what we "make" of these; the greater part of modern education, therefore has little or nothing to do with man's last end, *s'eternar*.

(i.e., the pulls of the sensitive powers pursuing their natural objects) comes to naught. And so God rules the gods, and they the Daimons, their representatives in us; he works through both, and so makes all things for himself; and all things are members (μόρια)[106] of himself.

This profound psychology is all derived directly from Plato,[107] mainly from *Laws* 644E, 645A. Plato's doctrine of the irrational and mortal soul (with its better and worse parts) and its distinction from the rational and immortal Soul is, of course, identical with the Indian distinction of our passible self from "its immortal Self and Duke." These two dwell together in the house or city of the body, or ride in one and the same bodily vehicle, and the question arises as to which shall control it. In the figure of the puppet[108] Plato speaks of man as literally dis-tracted by his passions. He says that these affects in us (ταῦτα τὰ πάθη ἐν ἡμῖν) pull us to and fro (ἀνθέλκουσι), and being contrary to one another (ἀλλήλαις ἐναντίαι, as in Aristotle, *De anima* III.10.433b.5) do so in contrary directions, either to good or evil as the case may be.[109] But there is "one holy golden leading

[106] Closely related to μοῖρα, "share," and so "fate," as discussed below.

[107] Scott [cf. Hermes—ED.] calls the notion of εἱμαρμένη "Stoic," but it was Platonic before Stoic: cf. *Phaedo* 115A and *Gorgias* 512A. Equally Platonic is the doctrine of the Gods and Daimons, of whom Plato says that they are "our allies in battle, and we their properties" (*Laws* 906, cf. *Phaedo* 62B and Philo, *De specialibus legibus* IV.122). All these things are "myths" of the Philosophia Perennis, and there is no more reason to stop short with the Stoics, or even to suppose that Plato invented them, than there is to suppose that they are of Indian origin in their Greek setting.

[108] For which there are many Indian parallels, Hindu and Buddhist. See Coomaraswamy, *Līlā* and "Play and Seriousness" [both in this volume—ED.]. A puppet is a "wonder" (θαῦμα) and, as Plato also says, "Wonder is the beginning of philosophy" (*Theatetus* 155D). We need hardly say that the *gravamen* of all traditional "jugglery" is metaphysical.

[109] Contrary directions, whether ethical or aesthetic. It is precisely in a liberation from these alternatives, these "pairs of opposites," that freedom consists. The freeman's *act*ive con-duct (cf. συνάγω, ἀγωγή, Skr. *samaj*, *samāja*, √ *aj*, ἄγω, Lat. *ago*, whence "act") is anything but an instinctive and passive behavior; (by one of the "coincidences" of Skr. etymology, *a-ja* means "unborn": and the Mover of all things is *aja* in both senses) to conduct oneself is to "be in act," to behave is to "be *in potentia*"; conduct is con-*sider*ed, behavior inconsiderate—the former, that is to say, in agreement with the orderly motion of the stars, behavior eccentric. The distinction parallels that of σύννοια from παράνοια, and that of Skr. *svarāj* (autonomy) from *anyarāj* (heteronomy) as drawn in CU VII.25.2, cf. VIII.1.5, 6.

In connection with "being in act," it is significant that Vedic *aja* (agent, agile, and hence also "goat") is a characteristic Vedic epithet of the Sun, Rudra, or Indra (troop leader of the Maruts), while the *ajāsah* (pl.) who "bring tribute" (*balim . . . jabruh*) to Indra (RV VII.18.19) are almost certainly the Maruts.

string of Reason, viz. the common Law of the body politic,[110] and this we should always hold on to and cooperate with, so that the golden kind within us may overcome the other kinds." Aristotle's doctrine is the same, although he does not use the "myth" of the puppet: motion always implies a choice of some kind, but the choice may be made either in accordance with the Reason (λογισμός) or determined by the Passions (ἐπιθυμία), in which last case (that of Plato's ἥττω ἑαυτοῦ, *Republic* 431B, 440B, etc.) the resulting motion will be irrational. The Mind (of the mind) is always right; but appetite and mental images (φαντασία, = *saṃkalpa* or *rūpa*) may be either right or wrong (*De anima* III.10. 433a.22 ff.).[111]

These summaries of the Platonic and Neoplatonic psychology introduce the problem of Fate and Free Will, fundamental in the present context, in which we are considering a science dispositive to Freedom in the fullest and every sense of the word. There is hardly any doctrine of the Philosophia Perennis that has been more misunderstood, and therefore more resented, than that of Fate; resented, because it has been supposed that Fate (implied in the notion of Providence) is, as it were, an arbitrary decree imposed upon us by an all-too-personal deity—nowadays also referred to by the new name of "economic determination." The traditional and orthodox doctrine is a recognition of the causal chain by which all events are linked in a phenomenal succession,[112] but of their intrinsic and not extrinsic operation. It can be stated in the words of St. Thomas Aquinas, "Fate lies in the created [i.e., mediate] causes themselves" (*Sum. Theol.* I.116.2), or those of Rūmī, "Endeavor is not a struggle with Destiny, because Destiny itself has laid this endeavor upon us" (*Mathnawī* I.976); "Necessitarianism is to sleep amongst highwaymen" (*Mathnawī* I.943); "You have feet; why do you make yourself out to be lame?"

[110] We cannot refrain from calling attention here to a serious error in R. G. Bury's version, Loeb Library edition, p. 69; the "golden chain" is not "the public law of the State" but "the common law of the (individual) body politic": "common law" (κοινὸς νόμος) because our own psychophysical constitution is a κοινωνία (*Republic* 462C), we are an "aggregate animal" (κοινὸν ζῷον, *Timaeus* 89D). It would have been against Plato's whole position to make an absolute of the law of any State; he is talking of a Law (Skr. *dharma*) on which all other laws are to be based.

[111] Cf. Philo, *De opificio mundi* 117 (where he reverts to the myth of the puppet); *Legum allegoriae* 30; *Quod Deus* 43.

[112] Buddhist *hetupaccaya*, "causal sequence"; St. Augustine's "series of causes" (*De civitate Dei* V.8). For Plato's mediate, or more literally "ministerial causes" (αἰτίαι ὑπηρετοῦσαι), called also sons of God, young gods and gods of gods (θεοὶ θεῶν, cf. VS XVII.13, 14 and ŚB IX.2.1.14, 15, *devā devānām* = *prāṇāh*, a remarkable parallel), see *Timaeus* 41, 42, 68, 69, 70; *Republic* 617E; *Laws* 904.

(*Mathnawī* I.930). Similarly in Buddhism, where the infallible operation of causes is insisted upon at least as strongly as it is by St. Thomas ("non-causation" [*ahetuvāda*] being a heresy), it is no less forcibly taught that there is an "ought-to-be-done" (*kiriya*) and that to plead a causal necessity by no means absolves a man from the responsibility of making a choice between the ought-to-be-done and the ought-not-to-be-done; and the fact that such a choice can be made is a predication of Free Will. The traditional doctrine is one of Fate and Free Will, and must be so, just because there are "two in us," one fatally determined and the other free. Of these two, to have become what we are is to have risen above our fate. The chain of fate can never be broken, but we can break away from it to become its spectator, no longer its victim.

The traditional conception of Fate involves no concept whatever of a possible injustice. Εἱμαρμένη or μοῖρα is literally an "allotment": the essential meaning of √ *mer*, present in Latin *mereo* and English "merit," is simply to "receive one's portion, with the collateral notion of being one's due" (H. G. Liddell and R. Scott, *A Greek-English Lexicon*, 8th ed., Oxford, 1897). Μοῖρα is sometimes simply "inheritance," and to be ἄμοιρος is to be deprived of one's due share, usually of something good, and in this case of "life"; κατὰ μοῖραν is the same as κατὰ φύσιν, "naturally" or "duly": to quarrel with our fate is to quarrel with our own nature, and to wish we had never been born. For how otherwise could we have been born than at a given time and place, and with given possibilities or "gifts"? Our Fate is only "what is coming to us," and "what we ask for"; "there are no special doors for calamity and happiness; they come as men themselves summon them" (*Thai-Shang*, SBE, XL, 235). "Nothing, whether good or bad, that has to do with the body, can happen apart from Destiny (εἱμαρμένη). It is moreover 'destined' that he who has done evil shall suffer evil; yea to this end he does it, that he may suffer the penalty of having done it. . . . And all men undergo what Destiny has appointed for them, but rational men (those of whom I said that they are led by Mind) do not suffer it in the same way as the irrational. . . . For the Mind there is nothing impossible, neither to exalt the soul of man over Destiny, nor, if the soul, as sometimes happens, give no heed, to subject it to Destiny" (Hermes, *Lib.* XII.1.5, cf. X.19, as well as Plato, *Phaedo* 83A, and MU III.2).

The traditional doctrine predicates a First Cause which is directly the cause of our Being (by participation), but only indirectly, through the working of the second or mediate causes, with which it never interferes, the cause of our being what we are. We, in our idiosyncracy, are, therefore, precisely the *heirs*[113] of things done (*karma*). This "unseen" (*adṛṣṭa*) force of "our *karma*," although a weird that must be dreed, is nothing imposed upon us, but the law of our own nature. God, from the Indian point of view, is not an arbitrary appointer of fates, but simply the "overseer of *karma*." In other words, as Plato also says, all that is done by the cosmic Draughts Player, and that "is a wondrous easy task," is "to shift the character that grows better to a superior place, and the worse to a worse, according to what belongs to each of them, thus apportioning an appropriate fate (*μοῖρα*). . . . For according to the trend of our desires, and the nature of our souls, each one of us usually becomes of like character[114] . . . the divinely virtuous being transported by a holy road to another and better place" (*Laws* 903, 904). So in Christian doctrine, similarly, "Fate is the ordering of second causes to effects foreseen by God" (*Sum. Theol.* I.116.4), "without which the world would have been deprived of the perfection of causality" (*Sum. Theol.* I.103.7 *ad* 2).

We are, then, at the mercy of our own characteristic willing; when the sensitive powers are given free rein, whenever we are doing what we like or thinking wishfully, insofar as our whole behavior—whatever good or evil—is unprincipled, we are not free agents, but passive subjects of what are rightly called our "passions." This is the only orthodox doctrine, namely, that man as he is in himself, "this man" who does not know what is true but only what he likes to think, who does not know what is right but only what he wants to do, and who knows nothing of art but only what he likes, is not a free man and makes no choices, but is pulled and driven by forces that are not his own because he has not mastered them. So St. Augustine asks, "Why, then, should miserable men venture to pride themselves on their 'freewill' before they are set free?" (*De spiritu et littera* 52); Boethius explains that "Everything is by so much the freer from Fate by how much it draweth nigh to the Pivot (*cardo*).[115] And if it

[113] References in Coomaraswamy, *Hinduism and Buddhism*, 1943, notes 211, 218, 221, 225.

[114] Cf. BU IV.4.5; MU VI.34.3c.

[115] *Cardo*, √ *krad* as in Καρδία, Skr. *hṛd*, "heart." Meanings of *cardo* include pivot, pole (North Pole), and especially "hinge" (originally pivot) of a door. Cf. Meister Eckhart, "the door goes to and fro upon its hinge. Now I liken the swinging door itself to the Outer Man, and the hinge (*angel*, pole, pivot, hinge) to the Inner Man [*is qui intusest*, II Cor. 4:16; *antah puruṣaḥ* MU III.3; *antar-ātman*, KU VI.17, MU VI.1, BG VI.47]. As the door opens and shuts it swings out and in, but the hinge remains unmoved in one and the same place and never changes" (Pfeiffer ed., p. 489). *Cardo* as "Pole" = Skr. *skambha, sthūṇa, vamsa*, and Islamic *quṭb*, the "cardinal" principle on which all things "hinge."

sticketh to the stability of the Supreme Mind, it transcends the necessity of Fate" (*De consolatione philosophiae* IV.6); and St. Thomas Aquinas says, "The will is free insofar as it obeys reason, not when we are doing 'what we like'" (*Sum. Theol.* I.26.1). "The spirit is willing, but the flesh is weak" (Matt. 26:41); i.e., in terms of the classic symbols, the horses are untrained.

Thus Free Will is not ours by nature, but only potentially; our self-will is only a wanting, a hunger and a thirst, and anything but a Free Will. Yet there is a Free Will *in* us, which can be ours if we know Who we are, and can say to that Self, "Thy will be done"; but only by that consent can it be won, for "whoso hath not escaped from (self-)will, no (free-)will hath he" (Rūmī, *Dīvān*, Ode XIII); nothing but the perfect practice of Islam ("resignation") is perfect freedom.[116] Man is free only when the victory over pleasure has been won (*Laws* 840C); only "where the Spirit of the Lord is, there is liberty" (II Cor. 3:17); "if you are led by the Spirit, you are not under the Law" (Gal. 5:18). "Other than that single, all-inclusive Life, all other life is darkness, petty, dim and poor" (Plotinus VI.7.15); "That (Brahma) is your Self; other than That all else is misery" (BU III.4.2). In other words, our Inner Man is in the world but not of it, in us but not of us, our Outer Man both in the world and of it, and must suffer accordingly.

The problem is one of internal conflict and its resolution, one of war and peace[117]: internal conflict because, as our whole tradition is agreed, there are "two in us," soul and spirit, king and priest, female and male,

[116] On *jabar* (necessity) and *qadar* (freewill), see Nicholson's notes on *Mathnawī* I.470–73, 617–41.

[117] The private and public problems are inseparable, political wars being a projection of the civil war within us, and our "peace where there is no peace" such as it is because "everyone from the least even unto the greatest is given to covetousness" (Jer. 8:10, 11). "All wars arise for the sake of gaining money to serve the body, in which service we are slaves" (*Phaedo* 66C); "those who care for their bodies more than anything else . . . draw to them the produce of every region of the globe. . . . All these people are war-makers . . . to gain advantages pertaining to the body and outward things. But for the sake of culture and virtue, the 'goods' of the discriminating mind, the ruling part of us, no war whether foreign or civil has ever yet broken out" (Philo, *De posteritate caini* 116 ff.; cf. *Deterius* 34, "enjoying the privileges of subject peoples"). In its application to what Hesiod called "the best thing of all for a man," viz. to be always at peace with himself, the traditional psychology proposes the one and only means of escape from the state of perpetual economic or political warfare in which civilization nowadays moves. No remedy can be effective but a change of heart. In this connection, cf. Aldous Huxley, *Ends and Means* (London, 1937).

mortal and immortal,[118] and it is, as Plato says, a question "which shall rule, the better or the worse" (*Republic* 431ABC, *Laws* 644E, etc.).

This is the problem of self-mastery, for the sake of which the traditional psychology is taught, and to which Plato so often reverts. When the inward government is of the better by the worse part of the soul, i.e., of mind by the mob of the passions, then we say that a man is "subject to himself" (*ἥττω αὑτοῦ*) and so censure him, but when, conversely, the inward government is of the worse part by the better, then we say that he is "master of himself" (*κρείττω αὑτοῦ*), by way of praise; and the same applies to the right government of States (*Republic* 431; *Laws* 645B, 841C; *Protagoras* 358, etc.). In other words, "this man and wife, the reason and the flesh . . . are engaged in strife and altercation day and night" (Rūmī, *Mathnawī* I.2617); "Self is at once self's only friend and only foe: Self is the friend of self in his case whose self has been vanquished by Self, but wages war as the foe of not-Self" (BG VI.5, 6). This is, mythically, the battle of the Gods and Titans, Devas and Asuras within you, where alone the Dragon can be killed, and ethically the psychomachy of the Virtues and the Vices.[119] The issue is literally one of victory or death, for, as our whole tradition assumes, there is a real division of the saved from the lost.[120]

How is the Victory to be won in this *jihād*? Our self, in its ignorance of and opposition to its immortal Self, is the enemy to be convinced. The Way is one of intellectual preparation, sacrifice, and contemplation, always presuming at the same time a guidance by forerunners. In other words, there is both a theory and a corresponding way of living which cannot be divided if either is to be effective. The intellectual preparation is philo-

[118] *Sum. Theol.* II-II.26.4, *Duo sunt in homine*, etc.; Meister Eckhart, "Know then, that . . . there are in everyone two men," Evans ed., I, 344; cf. *Republic* 604B, and Philo, *Deterius* 82.

[119] On the Psychomachy, cf. Emile Mâle, *Religious Art in France of the Thirteenth Century* (New York, 1913 [1956]), p. 98 ff.; and the Buddhist *Māradharṣaṇa*.

[120] "When death comes to a man, his mortal part, it seems, dies, but the immortal part departs, unhurt and undestroyed" (*Phaedo* 106E), and the question is, "in whom [viz. in my mortal self, or in its immortal Self] shall I be departing, when I depart hence?" (Praśna Up. VI.3). "He whose Self has been found, whose Self is awake . . . , the (other-)world is his, indeed, he is that world. That Self may be found even here and now; if you have not found it, great is the destruction" (BU IV.4.13, 14). I do not know whether the empirical psychology has ever attempted to deal with man's natural fear of death; the traditional philosophy affirms that one who has known his own, immortal, and never-aging Self, cannot fear (AV X.8.44).

sophical, as "philosophy" was understood by the ancients. The proper object of this philosophy is stated in the words of the Delphic Oracle, "Know thy Self" (*γνῶθι σεαυτόν*). That means also, of course, to distinguish Self from what is not-Self, the primary form of ignorance being a confusion of Self with what is not-Self.

The battle will have been won, in the Indian sense and Christian wording, when we can say with St. Paul, "I live, yet not I, but Christ in me" (Gal. 2:20); when, that is to say, "I" am dead, and there is none to depart, when body and soul disintegrate, but the immanent God. Philosophy is, then, the art of dying. "The true philosophers are practitioners of dying, and death is less terrible to them than to any other men . . . and being always very eager to release the Soul, the release and separation of the soul from the body is their main care" (*Phaedo* 67DE). Hence the injunction "Die before you die" (*Mathnawī* VI.723 ff., and Angelus Silesius, IV.77). For we must be "born again"; and a birth not preceded by a death is inconceivable (*Phaedo* 77C; BG II.27, etc.). This dying is to self. It is a matter both of a will, and of a method.

As regards the will, an intellectual preparation is all-important—*intellige ut credas*; and here we revert to our psychology. The whole force of this science is directed towards a destructive analysis of the animistic delusion that this man, So-and-so, who speaks of himself as "I," is an entity at all. The situation is nowhere better or more briefly stated than by Plutarch when he says, "Nobody remains one person, or is one person" (*Moralia* 392D). The argument can be followed in the European tradition from Heracleitus onwards: our "life" is a succession of instants of consciousness, everyone different from the last and from the next, and it is altogether illogical to say of anything that never stops to be, that it "is"; a thing can only be, if it never changes (*Symposium* 207D, *Phaedo* 78D ff., etc.). Our existence is not a being, but a becoming. The systematic demonstration is typically Buddhist: the personality is analyzed, generally as a composite of body, feeling, cognition, complexes, and discriminating awareness, and it is shown successively that each of these factors of the so-called "self" is inconstant, and that neither of any one nor of all together can it be said that "that is my Self." The traditional psychology is not "in search of a soul," but a demonstration of the unreality of all that "soul," "self" and "I" ordinarily mean. We cannot, indeed, know what we are, but we can become what we are by knowing what we are not; for what we *are* is the immanent God, and he himself cannot know *what* he is, because he is not any what, nor ever became anyone.[121] Our end will have been attained when we are no longer anyone. That must not, of course, be confused with an annihilation; the end of all becoming is in *being*, or rather, the source of being, richer than any being. "The word 'I,' *ego*, is proper to none but God in his sameness" (Meister Eckhart, Pfeiffer ed., p. 261). The notion of an ego of "ours" is an infatuation or opination (*abhimāna*, *οἴησις*, *οἴημα*) based on sensitive experience (MU VI.10; Philo, *ut infra*); as we have seen, it has no rational foundation—"Our senses, through ignorance of reality, falsely tell us that what appears to be, actually is" (Plutarch, *Moralia* 392D). And since the notion that "I am the doer" (*ahaṃkāra*, *karto'ham iti*) is both the primary form of our ignorance and the cause of all suffering felt or inflicted, the whole complex of "I and mine" (*ahaṃ ca mama ca*) and the notion of an "I" than can survive the dissolution of the psycho-physical vehicle, are under constant attack. To think that it is our own mind that works is a "pierced and cloven doctrine"; nothing is more shameful than to suppose that "I think" or that "I perceive" (Philo, *Legum allegoriae* I.47, II.68, III.33). To infer from the accidents of my existence that "I am" (*upādāya asmi*) is ridiculous, because of the inconstancy of all experience (S III.105). "Were it not for the shackle, who would say 'I am I'?" (*Mathnawī* I.2449); *Εἴθε, ὦ τέκνον, καὶ σὺ σεαυτὸν διεξεληλύθεις* (Hermes, *Lib.* XIII.4). There can be no greater sorrow that the truly wise man can feel than to reflect that "he" still is "someone" (*Cloud of Unknowing*, ch. 44).

To have felt this sorrow (a very different thing from wishing one had never been born, or from any thought of suicide) completes the intellectual preparation. The time has come for action. Once convinced that the Ego is "not my Self" we shall be ready to look for our Self, and to make the sacrifices that the quest demands. We cannot take up the operation in its ritual aspect here (except, in passing, to stress the value of ritual), but only in its application to daily life, every part of which can be transformed and transubstantiated. Assuming that we are now "true philosophers," we shall inevitably begin to make a practice of dying. In other words, we shall mortify our tastes, "using the powers of the soul in our outward man no more than the five senses really need it" (Meister Eckhart, Pfeiffer ed.,

[121] Our self can be known, but not our Self: for "by what might one understand him by whom one understands?" (BU II.4.14). "How, then, do we ourselves come to be speaking of it? seeing that we cannot know it and may not grasp it. . . . We can and do state what it is not, while we are silent as to what it is; we are, indeed, speaking of it only in the light of its consequences; but although we are unable to define it, we can nevertheless possess it" (*Enneads* V.3.14).

p. 488); becoming less and less sentimental ("sticky"), and ever more and more fastidious; detaching ourselves from one thing after another. We shall feed the sensitive powers chiefly on those foods that nourish the Inner Man;[122] a process of "reducing" strictly analogous to the reduction of fleshly obesity, since in this philosophy it is precisely "weight" that drags our Self down, a notion that survives in the use of the word "gross" = sensual. Whoever would *s'eternar, transumanar*, must be "light-hearted."[123]

At the same time, if we are to act in agreement with our altered thinking (*Laws* 803C), our whole activity must be purified of all self-reference. We must—like Christ—"do nothing of ourselves"; must act without any personal motive, selfish or unselfish. For this is more than any simple "altruism," and harder; in Plato's phrasing, we are to become God's "toys" and "instruments," unmoved by any inclinations of our own, whether to evil or good. This is the Chinese Wu Wei, "do nothing, and all things will be done." That "inaction" is often, and often willfully, misunderstood by a generation whose only conception of leisure is that of a "leisure state" of idleness. The renunciation of works (*saṃnyāsa karmāṇām*, BG v.1), however, bears no such connotation; it means their assignment to another than ourselves (*brahmaṇy ādhāya karmāṇi*, BG v.10, cf. JUB 1.5.1–3); the harnessed man should think, "I am doing nothing," whatever it is that he may be doing (BG v.8). This "abandonment" and "yoking" (*yoga*) are one and the same, and neither is a doing nothing, but much rather "skillful operation" (BG vi.2, ii.50). "'Inaction' is not attained by undertaking nothing" (BG iii.4): almost in these very words Philo says that "Moses does not give the name of 'rest' (*ἀνάπαυσις*) to a merely doing nothing (*ἀπραξία, De cherubim* 87)," and he adds, "The cause of all things is naturally active. . . . God's 'rest' is [not a doing nothing, but] rather a working with absolute ease, without toil or suffering. . . . A being free from weakness, even though he be making everything [as Viśvakarman], will never cease through all eternity to be 'at rest.'"

[122] Cf. *Timaeus* 90BC; *Phaedrus* 246E ff.; *Phaedo* 64 ff., etc.; BG xvii.7–xviii.39.

[123] In the Egyptian psychostasis, the heart of the deceased is weighed against a feather, representing the goddess Truth (Maat). See further Coomaraswamy, *Hinduism and Buddhism*, n. 269, on levitation.

We have not attempted to deal with the Egyptian psychology, but would say in passing that the whole conception of the Breath and Breaths, or Power from Above and "powers of the soul," is paralleled in that of the Egyptian *ka* and its attendant *kau*, the powers of life which the divine power "yokes." For details see A. Moret, *The Nile and Egyptian Civilization* (London, 1927), pp. 181–83 and 358–59; and H. Kees, *Totenglauben und Jenseitsvorstellungen der alten Ägypter* (Leipzig, 1926). There can be no doubt of the equation, *ka* = Ātman, Prāṇa.

So the injunction not to cease from working is categorical, and according to vocation. In the case of the soldier, he is told, "Surrendering all works to Me, do thou fight" (BG III.20); and more generally, "Even as the ignorant are busy because of their attachment to activity, so also should the Comprehensor work, but without attachment, with a view to the guarding of the world (*loka-saṃgraha*, BG III.25)." This is, precisely, the doctrine of guardianship enunciated in the Seventh Book of the *Republic*: the philosopher who has made the steep ascent and seen the light, though he may naturally wish to stand aloof, will not be governed by his inclinations, but will return to the Cave "to care for and to guard the other citizens," so that the city may be governed by "waking minds" and that those may hold office who are least eager to do so (*Republic* 519D ff.). This κατάβασις corresponds to the Indian *avataraṇa* and *avasthāna* of the All-worker, who is in the world but not of it. In Kṛṣṇa's words, "There is nothing in this whole universe that I needs must do, nothing attainable that I have not attained, nevertheless I am in act, for were I not, these worlds would be unsettled and I should be an agent of confusion of functions and a slayer of my children" (BG III.23, 24). We must not confuse this point of view with that of the philanthropist or "servant of society"; the Comprehensor is a servant of God, not of society. He is naturally impartial, not an adherent of any party or interest, and is never the passive subject of righteous indignation; knowing *Who* he is, he loves no one but himSelf, the Self of all others, none of whom he loves or hates as they are in themselves. It is not *what* he does, whatever it may be, but his *presence*—even in a monastery, which is as much a proper part of an ordered world as any farm or factory—that "cares for and protects" the other citizens.

The true ascetic (*saṃnyāsī*), then, is, as the words ἀσκητής and its Skr. equivalent *śramaṇa*[124] alike imply, a "worker" but, unlike the ignorant laborer, one who "takes no thought for the morrow" (Matt. 6:34)[125]; "thy concern is with the action only [that it be correct], not

[124] The semantic development of the words ἀσκητής and *śramaṇa* is the same: both are primarily "laborer," and secondarily in the modern religious sense "ascetic" and "wayfarer" or "hermit." In exactly the same way, σοφία and *kauśalyā* are primarily technical knowledge and skill, and secondarily "wisdom" and "virtue."

[125] These words, so easily misunderstood from the modern point of view, must not be understood to imply a commendation of any irrational aimlessness on the worker's part; that the work should be at the same time *pulcher et aptus* (as our whole tradition maintains) involves its utility, and this implies that very foresight that distinguishes a person from an animal (*puruṣa* from *paśu*). The phrase μὴ

with its fruits" (BG II.47). Thus the traditional psychology, however practical, is anything but pragmatic; the judgment is not of ends, but of the means. The results are beyond our control and therefore no responsibility of ours. One result, however, and that the best, follows inevitably on the use of the right means, and that is the worker's own perfecting. Man perfects himself by his devotion to his own tasks, determined by his own nature (BG XVIII.45, 47): and this is also Justice, τὸ ἑαυτοῦ πράττειν, κατὰ φύσιν (Plato, *Republic* 433). At the same time, "mentally renouncing all his activities, the ruling Body-dweller [Inner Man], rests happily in the nine-doored city of the body, neither acting nor compelling action" (BG V.13). In other words, "You must know that the outer man's employment can be such that all the time the Inner Man remains unaffected and unmoved" (Meister Eckhart, Pfeiffer ed., p. 489).

Such are the immediate fruits of the traditional psychology, understood and practiced. But at the same time that such a man is freed from the domination of his hopes and fears—and this is what it means to be the "master of one's fate"—he is becoming Who he is; and when he departs, and a successor takes his place, which is provided for in traditional societies by the inheritance and formal transmission of the ministerial functions, then, "having done what there was to be done," the psycho-physical personality will fall like a ripe fruit from the branch, to enter into other combinations, and this self's other and immortal Self will have been set free. And these are the two ends that the traditional psychology proposes for whoever will put its doctrine into practice: to be at peace with oneself whatever one may be doing, and to become the Spectator of all time and of all things.

Our primary purpose has been to describe the traditional psychology, as a contribution to the history of science. In doing so we have had in view both European and Indian, professional and lay, readers. We have wished, among other things, to show that it will be of the greatest possible advantage in all philosophical studies to consider the Greek and Sanskrit

---

μεριμνήσητε means "not being anxious about," "not distracted by hopes or fears for" the consequences of whatever has been done correctly. The Comprehensor is neither to be elated by success nor disappointed by failure, but always the same. The meaning "not to be anxious about" is well brought out by Terence's words, "*curae quae* meam animam divorse trahunt" (*The Lady of Andros* [LCL], I.5.25), a reminiscence of Plato's puppet, pulled in opposite directions by its contrary passions (*Laws* 644E).

sources simultaneously, and also, of course, if one's competence admits, as mine does not, such other sources as the Arabic and Chinese. We have wished to emphasize that the doctrine of the Philosophia Perennis, in which our psychology is included, is stated in different areas and at different times not only in cognate words, but often in the same idioms and in terms of the same symbolism, e.g., that of the puppet or that of the chariot; the greater part of these symbols are of prehistoric, at any rate neolithic, if not greater antiquity. We have sometimes dwelt on etymologies with a view to showing that the doctrines referred to are implicit in the very structure of the sacred languages in which they are stated; and to remind the reader that the idioms, even of modern English, preserve the primary assumptions of the perennial philosophy, however little we may be conscious of, for instance, the doctrine *duo sunt in homine* when we speak of an "internal conflict" or of being "at peace with oneself," or aware of the metaphysics of light and generation when we "argue" with a view to "clarifying" our "concepts." In conclusion, let us emphasize again that the perennial psychology is not a science for its own sake, and can be of no use to anybody who will not practice it. The popular conception of the philosopher as one who "takes life philosophically" is perfectly correct; the philosopher of our tradition is one who not only has the habit of first principles, but also one who approaches all contingent problems in the light of these principles. And finally, that the philosopher is not a victim of his desires is as much as to say that his whole concern is with "the things that make for peace"; one who is at peace with himself will have no occasion to wage war on others. For him, power and the balance of power are matters of no interest whatever.

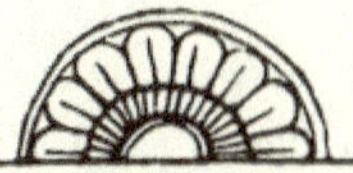

Mahā Puruṣa: "Supreme Identity"

That the word *puruṣa*, of uncertain derivation, but probably from *pṛ*, "to fill," (cf. *puru*, "many") is properly rendered by and corresponds to "person" can be readily established by a confrontation of texts. In AĀ II.2.2–3, "the more clearly one knows the Essence (*ātman*), the more one is fully in being." Consciousness of the Essence is wanting in minerals, perceptible in plants and trees, more evident in animated things (*prāṇabhṛt*), and "though there are sundry in whom no intelligence is apparent, [it is] most evident in a 'person' (*puruṣa*). For a 'person' is most endowed with understanding (*prajñā*), he speaks of what has been discriminated (*vijñāta*), he perceives distinctions (*vijñātam paśyati*), he comprehends (*veda*) the future, he comprehends what is and what is not mundane (*lokālokau*),[1] and is so endowed that by the mortal he seeks the immortal.[2] But as for the sundry, mere animals (*paśu*),[3] theirs is an estimative understanding (*abhivijñāna*) merely according to hunger and thirst, they do not speak what has been discriminated. . . . Their becoming is only so far, they have being (*sambhavāḥ* = *habent esse*) only in the measure of their understanding (*yathā prajñaṃ hi*). The

[Coomaraswamy's translation of *ātman* as Essence indicates that this paper was written ca. 1935; the "experimental translation," as he called it, was proposed in "Two Vedāntic Hymns from the *Siddhāntamuktāvalī*," BSOS, VIII (1935), 91–99, and withdrawn in "Vedic Exemplarism," 1936 (see pp. 188–189 in this volume).]

[1] Worldly and superworldly, i.e., what is in time and space, and what is apart from time and space.

[2] That is, he sees contingent things eternalwise, for him the world is a theophany, he can employ the *via analogia*, and can follow the *vestigium pedis, padaṃ na gorapagūḷham*, RV IV.5.3.

[3] *Paśu*, in the same sense of "human being that is no better than an animal," occurs in BU I.4.10, where he who worships any angel otherwise than as his own Essence (*ātman*) is called a "mere animal," and in *Siddhāntamuktāvalī*, verse XXXVI, where the author in the same way designates as "mere animals" those who refrain from the Essence that is man's last end (*puruṣārtha*). The distinction of *puruṣa* from *paśūn* (pl.) is like that between a "proper man," German *Mensch*, and "the herd."

'person' thus defined (*sa eṣa puruṣaḥ*) is the sea, and transcends the whole universe (*sarvaṃ lokam ati*)."[4]

The use of "person" in the sense proper to *puruṣa*, above, can be cited in Boethius, *Contra Evtychen* II, "There is no person of a horse or ox or any other of the animals which, dumb and unreasoning, live a life of sense alone, but we say there is a person of a man, of God, or an Angel," as well as in his better known definition, *ibid.* III, "Person is an individual substance of a rational nature," and in St. Thomas, *Sum. Theol.* I.39.1c, where Person is defined as referring to the divine Essence when regarded as subject, i.e., "concretely" and in relation to the world as object. St. Thomas also wrote, *Sum. Theol.* I.29.3 and *ad* 2, "Person signifies what is most perfect in all nature—that is, a subsistent individual of a rational nature. Hence . . . forasmuch as His Essence contains every perfection, this name 'person' is fittingly applied to God; not, however, as it is applied to creatures, but in a more excellent way . . . the dignity of the divine nature excels every other dignity; and thus the name 'person' preeminently belongs to God."

It is thus clear that the words *puruṣa* and "person" are as nearly as possible synonymous in reference. In the last passage, "more excellent" and "preeminently" exactly correspond to the designation *Mahā Puruṣa*, "Great Person," in AĀ III.2.3, where four *puruṣas* are distinguished as follows: (1) the corporeal (*śarīra-*), which is the "embodied essence" (*dehika ātmā*) and of which the principle (*rasa*) is the "comprehending Essence" (*prajñātmā*); (2) the aggregate of syllables of which the principle is "A" (cf. II.3.6, "A is the whole Word"); (3) that by which one comprehends (*veda*) the Four Vedas, and of which the principle is the Brahman priest as being filled with the spiritual power (*brahman*); and (4) the *Mahā Puruṣa*, the Year (*saṃvatsara*), which "distinguishes some things and unifies others.[5] And be it known that the incorporeal comprehending Essence and the Sun are one and the same, and thus it comes about that the Sun is present to every 'person' (*puruṣaṃ puru-*

[4] *Ati*, as denoting transcendence, is discussed below. The "sea" is of infinite possibility, cf. RV X.5.1 *ekah samudro dharuno rāyinām* (Agni), VIII.41.8 *samudro apicyaḥ* (Varuṇa), and for the idea, St. John Damascene, *De Fide Orthodoxa* I, "HE WHO IS (= *asti* in KU VI.12) is the principal of all names applied to God; for comprehending all in itself, it contains existence itself as an infinite and indeterminate sea of substance."

[5] I.e., brings life to some and death to others, and is thus the author of the being of all beings, cf. X.121.2 (Hiraṇyagarbha, Prajāpati) *yasya chāyā amṛtaṃ, yasya mṛtyuḥ*, "Whose overshadowing is of life, and likewise of death."

ṣaṃ pratyāditya)."[6] The *Aitareya Āraṇyaka*, continuing, cites RV I.115.1, "The bright face of the Angels has arisen (*ud agāt*), the eye of Mitra, Varuṇa, and Agni. It hath filled (*āprā*, from √ *pṛ*) Heaven, Earth, and Midgard. The Sun is the Essence (*ātman*) of all that is motionless or mobile (*jagataḥ tasthuṣaḥ*)."

This evidently, and sentence for sentence, corresponds to RV x.90.4, where "With three-fourths the *Puruṣa* went upwards (*ūrdhva ud ait*).[7] One-fourth of Him became recurrent (*abhavat punaḥ*) here.[8] Thence He proceeded universally (*viśvaṃ vy akramat*) unto what eats and does not eat (*sāśanāśane*)."[9]

[6] The identity of the "person in the heart" with the "Golden Person in the Sun," is, of course, a fundamental doctrine in the Upaniṣads, e.g., MU VI.1, "He bears Himself twofold, as the breath of life (*prāṇa*) here, and as yonder Āditya . . . Yonder Āditya is verily the outer-Essence (*bahir-ātmā*), the breath of life the inner-Essence (*antar-ātmā*)." The form *pratyāditya* in *Aitareya Āraṇyaka* corresponds to *pratyagātman*, *passim*. *Pratyagātman* is almost literally "hypostasis," *ātman* is never "body."

[7] As remarked by W. Norman Brown, "the verb *ud i* is almost exclusively a Sūrya word."

[8] That is, as Agni Vaiśvānara, "Universal Man," and/or Soma, etc., who as the fire (or water) of life in the worlds takes on death (*nirṛtim ā viveśa*, RV I.164.32), is subject to inveteration (*jujurvān*, II.4.5), and is born again and again (*muhur . . . ā bhūta, ibid.; janman janman nihitaḥ*, III.1.20: *bhūrijanmā*, x.5.1; *jāyate punaḥ . . . navo navo bhavati jayamāna*, x.85.18–19); or as the Sun, the eighth Āditya, whom Aditi "bore hitherward unto repeated life and death" (*prajāyai mṛtyave punaḥ*, x.72.9), cf. II.5.2, "Agni, eighth in place." In the same way, Prajāpati is "stupified by eld" (*jīryyā mūra*, PB xxv.17.3), Agni, Soma, and Varuṇa "sink down" (*cyavante*, x.124.4), Cyavana's youth and potency are lost, and must be renewed (RV, *passim*). Agni's mortalities and resurrections are both daily and aeviternal. It is with reference to the indefinite duration of aeviternity that Agni is commonly called "undying amongst those that die" (*amartyam marteṣu*, IV.1.1, etc.), that he is said to bestow upon the Angels their aeviternity (VI.7.4, cf. IV.54.2), and that the latter are themselves referred to as "aeviternal" (*amṛta, passim*). It does not appear that the *Ṛg Veda* anywhere attributes an absolute immortality to any manifested aspect of deity, but rather assumes that "God comes and goes, God passes away" (Eckhart). But expressions such as *amṛtattva uttama*, I.31.1, may refer to what Śaṅkara calls "absolute immortality" (*ātyantika amṛtattva*) conceived of as an end attainable by men or angels, and in any case the *Ṛg Veda*, in stressing the doctrine of resurrection, assumes an eternal principle underlying all its formal manifestations. That, for example, which surveys the past and future at once, cannot be thought of as itself belonging to the past or future; He who looks through the Sun, is not himself the Sun.

[9] Adopting Sāyaṇa's perfectly intelligible explanation of *sa-aśana* and *an-aśana* as designating respectively "the intelligent animated and generated, that partakes of food," and "the motionless and unintelligent, such as a mountain"; which corresponds exactly to *jagataḥ tasthuṣaḥ* (motionless and moving), in RV I.115.1. In view of Sāyaṇa's explanation (Monier Williams also gives "not eating" as the meaning of *anaśana*), I do not see how *sāśanānaśane* can have come to be called "obscure." W. Norman Brown does not think it worthwhile even to mention Sāyaṇa in the

The *Puruṣasūkta* affirms the transcendance of the *Puruṣa* in terms that can be closely paralleled in other hymns, as well as in the Brāhmaṇas and Upaniṣads. That one-fourth of Him which, as we have seen, is the "Person in the Sun," "is all existences" (*viśva bhūtāni*), "this entire world (*evaṃ sarvam*) both past and future (*bhūtaṃ yac ca bhavyam*)." The latter expression corresponds to "what has been done and shall be done" (*kṛtāni yā ca kṛtvā*) in I.25.11: here Varuṇa is described as operating *ab extra*, in the Sun, as the expressions "far-seeing (*uru-cakṣasa*)," "diffusing a golden garb, wearing a glistening-robe (*vibhṛd drāpiṃ hiraṇyaṃ . . . vasta nirṇijam*),"[10] "enthroned for universal empire (*ni sasāda . . . saṃrajyāya*)," clearly show; and being seated thus, *ibid.* 11,[11] "thence He who knows all hidden things (*viśvā adbhutā cikitvān*)[12] surveys what has been done and shall be done (*ābhi paśyati kṛtāni yā ca kṛtvā*)." In X.88.13–14, this "ancient star, the Yakṣa's outlook, Agni Vaiśvānara," is said to have "exceeded Heaven and Earth in power (*mahimnā pari babhūva urvī*)," and called "an Angel here below and there beyond (*uta avastāt uta deva parastāt*)." Neglecting many other parallels that could be cited, this takes us back to the *Puruṣasūkta*, where in verses 2 and 3, we have "Great as is the power (*mahimā*) of the Lord of Aeviternity (*amṛtasya īśānaḥ*, the Sun) when he rises up with food (*annena-ati rohati*), still more (*jyāyaś ca*) is the Person," as also in verses 1 and 5, it is said that He "transcends the ten-finger-space (*aty atiṣṭhad daśaṇgulam*),"[13] and "surpasses Earth (*aty aricyata . . . bhūmim*)," where, as usual, "Earth" means the whole "ground" of existence. AĀ II.3.3, where the *Puruṣa* transcends

---

present connection. Not that Sāyaṇa is always right, but he is always worth considering, and here the confrontation of texts proves him right beyond doubt.

[10] *Nirṇija* implies "washed white." Cf. RV VIII.41.10, where Varuṇa, manifested as the Sun, is said to have "made, by his operation, the blacks to be glistening white (*śvetān adhi nirṇijaḥ cakre kṛṣṇān*)."

[11] In verse 6, the dual *venantā* implies Mitrāvaruṇa; calling them in effect, the "dual solar being," *ven* being typically a "sun word."

[12] *Adbhuta*, equivalent to *adṛṣṭa*, "invisible," as in IV.2.12, where Agni is said to behold both what is evident and what is hidden (*dṛśyān agne etān . . . paśye adbhutān*). *Adbhuta* is often rendered by "marvelous," but the things past and future are here thought of as marvelous, not as being miraculous in themselves, but as being mysterious, unknown, and inaccessible to observation.

[13] *Daśāngulam* has been much discussed. Here I merely adduce VI.44.24 *daśayantram utsam*, X.51.3 *daśantaruṣyāt*, and PB XXV.15.1, "the Year consists of tens and tens," to suggest that "ten" may have reference to the directions of space. [Also see Coomaraswamy, "RV X.90.1 *āty atiṣṭhad daśāngulam*," 1946—ED.].

the whole universe (*sarvaṃ lokam-ati*), cited above, evidently depends on the foregoing texts, nor is there anything that the Upaniṣadic statements, though more detailed, can be said to add to this.

At this point a digression will be necessary, in order to speak of the two different ways in which a knowledge of the divine nature has been sought. The Upaniṣads employ these two ways, those of the *via analogia* (the technique of symbolism) and the *via remotionis* (the technique of abstraction) in precisely the same way as Christianity, which inherited the positive (*καταφατιχή*) and negative (*ἀποφατιχή*) methods from Neoplatonism through pseudo-Dionysius, who employed them in the *De divinis nominibus*. The positive method consists in the attribution to God, in a superlative and absolute manner, of all the perfections and beauties conceivable in existing things; these absolute perfections in Him, although distinguishable logically, are regarded as inexplicable in Him and as identical with His essence. Each of these attributions constitutes an "essential name," such essential names being as many as the perfections that can be enumerated. Examples of this method may be cited in the designation of God as Light, Love, Wisdom, Being, etc., and in the Brāhmaṇas' *sac-cid-ānanda*. On the other hand, the negative method proceeds to the definition of the divine nature by the way of abstraction and the assertion of transcendence with respect to antitheses. From this point of view, the highest understanding that we can have of God is expressed by a denial in Him of any of those attributes the notion of which is derived from things external to His superessential unity. According to this method, God may be spoken of as Nonbeing, No-thing, or Darkness, or as in the Upaniṣads by the famous expression *neti, neti*, "No, no," or as That "from which words turn back, together with the intellect, not finding Him" (TU II.4), and "where high fantasy falls short of power" (Dante, *Paradiso* XXXIII.142). Eckhart follows this method when he says that "Nothing true can be said of God." Such examples could be multiplied indefinitely from all kinds of sources, Christian, Sūfī, Hindu, Taoist, and others. In Upaniṣadic metaphysics, no less than in Christian theology, "C'est la voie négative qui a la primauté sur l'autre, Dieu n'est pas un objet. Il est par delà tout ce qui est, donc par delà le connaissable, puisque la connaissance a l'être pour limite. A ce point de vue suréminent, Dieu n'est pas seulement au-dessus d'affirmations et de négations contradictoires, mais sa nature supersubstantielle est enveloppée de ténèbres"

(M. de Wulf, *Histoire de la philosophie médiévale*, 6th ed., Paris, 1934, p. 107). "He does not know what He Himself is, because He is not any thing. . . . Wherefore it is said that God is Essence, but more truly that He is not Essence" ("Deus itaque nescit se quid est, quia non est quid. . . . Essentia ergo dicitur Deus, sed proprie essentia non est"), Erigena, *De div. naturae*, II.13 and I.14; or putting this into Indian terms, "The Brahman is called *ātman*, but more properly *anātmya*." These reflections may prepare us to consider the nature of the *Puruṣa* in greater detail according to the Vedic and Upaniṣadic formulations, which seem strange only to those who are unfamiliar with the methodology of theology and metaphysics universally. The main point to be realized is that if, indeed, His nature transcends all logical antitheses, He cannot be found as He is in Himself by the seeker who regards only His being, that is, His "Face" or "Light," but only by the Comprehensor who sees also His "Back" or "Darkness." He is not only Love and Life but also Dread and Death, the omnipresent (*vyāpaka*) and uncharacterized (*aliṅga*) Person (*puruṣa*), "by knowing Whom a man is liberated and attains eternity (*amṛtatvam*)."[14]

The similar list of concepts in KU III.10–13 interpolates "beyond the sense are their values or meanings (*arthā*),"[15] substitutes *buddhi* for "pure

[14] Here evidently not "aeviternity," but as also in KU IV.1, *ātyantikam amṛtatvam*, "eternity."

[15] R. E. Hume and J. N. Rawson render *arthā* by "sense objects," and the latter naturally finds a lesion in the logical sequence of thought—a characteristic result of want of "trust" (*śrāddhā*) in the scriptural text. *Artha* means the value or significance that is attached to the sense-perceptions. From our empirical point of view, such values are introduced *post factum* and cannot be thought of as causal principles: but ontologically, *artha* as last end in this sense is the same as the *raison d'être* of the thing in its inception; cf. the Scholastic view that "the ultimate end of the work is ever the same as the real intention of the work's first cause" (Eckhart, Evans ed., I, 252), and similarly AĀ III.2.6, "What is the inception, that indeed is the fulfilment (*yo hy eva prabhavah sa eva āpya yah*)."

We say, moreover, with Abelard that *nomen est vox significativa*, with BD II.117 that "the word which designates a thing is derived from its significance (*arthāt padam svābhidheyam . . . -jam*)," with Nirukta II.1 that "names have their basis in subsistence (*sattva-pradhānāni nāmāni*)," and scarcely need to demonstrate that from the Vedic point of view, "names" are the immediate causes of the coming into being of things, viz. in virtue of their being the ideas or forms of things. It is the knower who projects the known beyond himself; and where *esse est percipi*, the significance of the thing is thus the formal cause of its becoming, as well as the final cause of its existence. Cf. Erigena, "Finis enim totius motus est principium sui" (*De div. naturae* V.3, c. 866). In this way, then, significance is logically prior to perception.

being of the intellect (*manasaḥ sattvam uttamam*)," affirms that there is "nothing whatever beyond the Person," and employs the expression "Essence at rest (*śānta ātman*)"[16] as another designation of the superessential Person.

The series in TU II.6 begins with vegetative (*anna-maya*) essence (equivalent to "senses" above); beyond this is the pneumatic (*prāṇa-maya*) essence which is our life (*āyus*) and All-life (*sarvāyuṣa*); beyond this the *manō-maya* essence, consisting of the Vedas and exegesis; beyond this the discriminating (*vijñāna-maya*) essence, identified with Eternal Law (*ṛta*) and Power or Glory (*mahas*), and corresponding to *buddhi* in KU III.10; beyond this the beatific (*ānanda-maya*) essence (the last four modalities of essence are said to be in the similitude of "person" [*puruṣa-vidhaḥ*],[17] as in AĀ III.2.3); and this is supported by the Brahman, whether as nonbeing (*asat*) or as being (*sat*).

An over-anxious scholarship seems to have made a needless mystery out of these only slightly varied formulations. That the vegetative manifestation of the sense-life depends immediately upon "food" is obvious. The pneumatic, or sometimes "fiery" (*tejo-maya*), essence is evidently represented in Agni Vaiśvānara, Universal Man (RV I.35.6 *ekāyus*, IV.28.2 *viśvāyus*, IV.58.11 *antaḥ ayuṣi*). The practical intellect (*manas*) and the pure or possible intellect (*manasaḥ sattvam*, *buddhi*, *vijñāna-maya*) are distinguished, the latter being identified with the Great (*mahat*, etc.) and consequently with the Sun (TU I.5.2, "Mahas, the Sun; the worlds are all empowered [*mahīyante*] by the Sun"). This is of particular importance for the understanding of KU VI.8, where "beyond the un-

[16] The "end" of any motion is defined as that in which this motion is brought to rest; cf. AĀ I.5.3, "rest is full-support" (*śāntir vai pratiṣṭhā*), or as rendered inversely by Keith, "atonement is rest." Cf. Eckhart, "There no work is done at all."

[17] It may appear strange to speak of "form" (*vidha*, *svarūpa*, etc.) in connection with the superessential and unmanifested Essence. But cf. Boethius, *De Trinitate* II.21, "Omne namque esse ex forma est," "All being is formal." The form that is predicated of the superessential Essence is not a form, but the principle of form, altogether simple and immutable in Itself, although the form of all things; cf. Boethius again, "esse ipsum, forma essendi," "Being in itself is the form of being," and Thierry of Chartres (*Der kommentar des Clarenbaldus von Arras zu Boethius De Trinitate*, ed. Wilhelm Jansen [attributed to Clarenbaldus of Arras, but more probably by Thierry of Chartres], Breslau, 1926, p. 108), "divinitas singulis rebus forma essendi est," "Godhood is the (exemplary) form of the being that is in singular things." This "Sovereign Form" (*rupamaiśvaram*) of the Most-Personal (*puruṣottama*) can only be apprehended in its multiplicity (*pravibhaktam anekadhā*), though one in Itself (*ekastham*), hence the nature of Arjuna's vision in BG XI (the terms cited are from verses 3 and 13).

shown" (*avyakta*)[18] requires as logical antecedent "beyond the shown" (*vyakta*): for it is precisely the Great, the Person in the Sun, that as the light and eye of the divine understanding is the divine manifestation of all that can be manifested (*vyakta*). What the *Kaṭha Upaniṣad*, then, affirms is that the uncharacterized Person is "beyond" both the shown and the unshown, transcending their distinction, not to be thought of merely as one or the other, but rather as *vyaktāvyakta*, "shown-unshown"; and thus interpreted, the Person "beyond whom there is naught whatever" coincides in reference with the Upaniṣadic superessential Essence (*paramātman*) and the Brahman as transcending the distinction of *satasat*, being and nonbeing alike.

[18] That Rawson, KU, p. 21, renders *avyakta* by "matter" shows that he has in mind the customary renderings of the Sāmkhyan *puruṣa* and *prakṛti* by "spirit and matter." But "spirit and matter" represents an antithesis unknown to Indian thought, which rather distinguishes essence from nature or substance, or act from potentiality, in the Supreme Identity. Indian *avyakta*, like the "unshown" of pure metaphysics in general, cannot be identified with Christian "primary matter," which is a "potentiality only with respect to the reception of natural forms" (*Sum. Theol.* 1.7.2 *ad* 3); *avyakta* embraces all possibilities, not only those of being, but also those which are not in any sense possibilities of manifestation. This metaphysically infinite possibility (*aditi*, *mūla-prakṛti*, etc.), as being the divine nature (*svabhāva*) and the matrix (*yoni*) of the divine essence, becomes the means whereby (*śakti*, *māyā*, *svadhā*, etc.) the latter operates, the distinction of essence from nature arising simultaneously with the divine act which presupposes it.

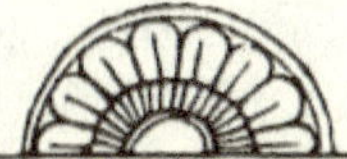

Bhakta Aspects of the Ātman Doctrine

But when the sun has set . . . moon has set . . . fire gone out, and speech hushed, what light does a person here have?
Bṛhadāraṇyaka Upaniṣad IV.3.6

A sharp distinction is often drawn between the Way of Gnosis (*jñāna-mārga*) on the one hand and the Way of Dedication (*bhakti-mārga*) or Way of Love (*prema-mārga*) on the other, this distinction corresponding at the same time to that of the Contemplative Life (*sāṃkhya yoga* and *saṃnyāsa* of BG) from the Active Life (*karma yoga* of BG). The distinction, which is made as if the operations of the intellect and will could be isolated as clearly in the subject as they can be in logic, is one in any case of procedure and, under certain conditions, also one of ends; and such a distinction is certainly not without meaning insofar as it corresponds to one of mysticism from gnosticism, that is, of devotional faith and religious exercises from initiatory teaching and metaphysical practice, of a "deification" in the sense of assimilation with a perfect consent of will from a "deification" in which the distinction of knower from known is past.

On the other hand, whatever may be the facts about the devotional works generally attributed to Śrī Śaṇkarācārya, there can be no doubt that Indians whose thought and mode of being is traditional have never found any difficulty in thinking of this greatest and most intellectual exponent of nondualistic (*advaita*) metaphysics as having been at one and the same time a *bhakta* and a *jñānī*. Consider in this connection also the markedly devotional phraseology of certain hymns included in V. P. Bhaṭṭa's *Siddhāntamuktāvalī* (J. R. Ballantyne, tr., Calcutta, 1851), where, for example, we find, addressed to the spirit (*ātman*), "Now that

[Internal evidence points only to a date after 1936 for the composition of this paper —ED.]

I have gotten Thee, I shall never let Thee go" (*idānīṃ tvām ahaṃ prāpto na tyajāmi kadācana*); it is only the academic scholar to whom such an expression of feeling on the part of a Vedantist can seem incongruous. The *Bhagavad Gītā*, v.2–4, indeed, plainly affirms that for one perfected (*āsthitaḥ samyak*) in either Way, one and the same fruition (*ekaṃ . . . phalam*) and *summum bonum* (*niḥśreyasa*) results, nor can this *summum bonum* intended be any other than the "despiration in Brahman" (*brahma-nirvāṇam*) of BG v.24–25, *nirvāṇam* here corresponding to *anātyam* in TU II.7. BG VIII.22 is equally explicit: "That supernal Person is to be gotten by an exclusive self-dedication" (*puruṣaḥ sa paraḥ . . . bhaktyā labhyas tu ananyayā*), that is to say, by an undivided or "pure" love as defined by St. Bernard.

"Perfected" (*samyak*) in the passage just cited implies an important reservation, since it is not to be supposed that the reward (*phala*) of one who has followed either path halfway will be the same as that of one who reaches its end.[1] One who goes but halfway, whether by a move-

[1] "According as men approach me, so do I deal unto them" (BG IV.11), i.e., I give them whatever they seek, whether it be mundane welfare, or "salvation," or "liberation": "Whatever desire he has, that is bestowed upon him," i.e., by the Sun (ŚB I.9.3.16). How the wayfarer's attainment is thus self-determined is admirably stated in the *Abhidharmakośa*, VI.45d: "Whatever desire is bound up with a given Way, cannot be eradicated by that Way"; the exoteric Christian Way, for example, cannot lead to anything but a "personal immortality," cannot lead beyond "salvation" to "liberation." No Way can be thought of as extending beyond the goal to which it is actually directed.

It may be remarked that although deliverance (*mokṣa, nirvāṇa*) involves a cessation (*nirodha*) of intellection (*vijñāna, citta*, cf. *viññānassa nirodha = ceto vimutti*, D I.223), a sharp distinction of *citta, mana, viññāna*, from *atta* is maintained: "This (*citta, mano, viññāna*) is not 'mine' this is not 'I,' this is not my Spirit (*atta*)," S II.94–95. Cf. also *mano nidoddhavyam hṛdi*, MU VI.34; *ātmasaṃstham manaḥ kṛtvā na kiṃcid api cintayet*, BG VI.25; and "The mind must be de-mented" (Eckhart, Evans ed., I, 243). Such a cessation can be of two sorts, (1) a state of real unconsciousness (*asaṃjñi*), or (2) a state of peace (*śānti*) and sameness or perfect simplicity (*samtatā*). The former is expressly described (*Abhidharmakośa* 42–64) as a mistaken conception of deliverance (*niḥsaraṇa*) entertained by certain of the profane (*pṛthagjana*), who may indeed attain to such a condition, but will reawaken to contingent being (cf. Īśā Up. 12, where those who are attached to an ideal of non-entity, *asambhūta*, go to realms of darkness no less than those who are attached to the concept of entity, *sambhūta*); while others of the profane shrink from the idea of "deliverance" just because they understand that by deliverance is meant "annihilation." The quoted passages and whole context show that it is not a destruction of the intellect that is implied by *amanībhāva*, but rather that when the intellect no longer intelligizes, i.e., when there is no longer any distinction of knower and known, of being and knowledge, but only knowledge as being and being as knowledge (in our text, *yet cittas tan mayo bhavati*), "One *is* what he thinks" and is no longer one who

ment of the will as in mysticism, or by means of an intellectual contemplation as in theology, guided only by "faith," may indeed attain to the highest level of contingent human being and to the vision of the Face of God, but has not yet reached the Supreme Identity (*tad ekam*), and is still in multiplicity.

The Christ as such, as *a* Person, is not the final goal, but rather the Path itself.[2] The Christ is the Axis of the Universe, Agni "columnar [*skambhaḥ* = σταυρός] in the nest of proximate life,[3] standing in His ground at the parting of the ways" (*pathāṃ visarge*, RV x.5.6), the Sun (*savitā satyadharmendraḥ*) to Whom all paths converge (*samare pathīnam*, VS xii.66), and by the same token the Gate of the World, the way out into time and way back into eternity. "I am the door, by Me if any man enter in, he shall be saved, and shall go in and out and find pasture. . . .[4] I am the Way, the Truth, and the Life: no man cometh to the Father but by Me" (John 10:9 and 14:6). Similarly, in the Vedic tradition the supernal Sun, the "Truth" (*satyam*), is the Portal of the Universe and Heaven's only Opening (Cleft, *loka-dvāra, divās-chidra*), as it were the "Hub of the Chariot Wheel" (*rathasya kha*) passing through which (*ādityaṃ samaye*, "through the midst of the Sun") the Comprehensor (*vidvān*) is "wholly liberated" (*atimucyate*) (JUB i.3, 5, and iii.33, CU viii.6.5, Īśā Up. 15, 16, etc.). "There is no approach by a side path here in the world" (MU vi.30).[5]

---

thinks *of* anything; that is Gnosis. Cf. Indra in CU viii.11, with Kauṣ. Up. iv.20 and Eckhart's, "What the tyro fears is the expert's delight; the kingdom of God is for none but the thoroughly dead" (Evans ed., i, 419). On the other hand, by a dementation in the second sense is implied that form of beatitude to which the Transmundane or Aryan Path is ordered; cf. BG ii.71, "The man who rejects all desires and proceeds apart, absolved from 'I and mine,' he reaches Peace" (*śāntim gacchati*), and BG vi.15, *śāntim nirvāṇam aparamāṃ matsaṃsthām adhigacchati*; *matsaṃsthām* = *ātmasaṃsthām*, cf. BG x.20, *ahamātmā*).

[2] See Coomaraswamy, *A New Approach to the Vedas*, 1933, p. 43.

[3] "Nest," the sacrificial fire-altar; the seat of the Sacrifice accomplished in the beginning and perpetuated in the ritual. "Columnar": Vedic *skambha*, coincident with the trunk of the Tree of Life and axle-tree of the Chariot of Light, corresponds to the Gnostic σταυρός by which Heaven and Earth are at the same time parted and connected, and to the vertical of the Cross as well as (in the present connection especially) to the Pillar of Fire by night and Pillar of Smoke by day.

[4] "Shall . . . pasture," as in CU viii.5.4; when the knowers of the Spirit are possessed of the Brahma world, it is said that "theirs is a movement at will in every world" (*sarveṣu lokeṣu kāmacāraḥ*), i.e., independent of local motion; cf. TU iii.10.5, etc., quoted in Coomaraswamy, *A New Approach to the Vedas*, p. 113.

[5] There is an apparent contradiction in ŚB xi.4.1, where six "doors" of access to Brahman are described. But of these, the first five lead only to an acquisition of great possessions; it is only by means of what is "perfect in the Sacrifice" (*yajñasya sam-*

The "Cleft" or "Hub" is enveloped by Rays of Light (*raśmibhis saṃchannaṃ dṛsyate*, JUB I.3), which must be withdrawn before the Orb (*maṇḍala*) can be clearly seen (Īśā Up. 16 *vyūha raśmīn*, JUB I.6 *raśmīn . . . vyūha-*

---

pannam) that the sacrificer "enters the Sundoor of Brahman" (*āditya ha sa brahmaṇo dvāreṇa pratipadyate*) and becomes a "Fellow of the World of Heavenly-light (*svargalokaḥ*)"; cf. BG VII.22, 23. The foregoing is one of many passages in which it is clear that *svarga* does not necessarily mean an inferior heaven on the hither side of the Sun, but may denote the Empyrean.

In Kauṣ. Up. I.2, it is the Moon that is the Door of the World of Heavenly-light which admits some and returns others. The question is evidently put, "Who art thou?" but the abbreviated text has only, according to various readings, either (1) "One who answers Him, obtains Him completely" (*taṃ yaḥ pratyāha tam atisṛjate*), taking *atisṛj* as in KU I.11 (cf. *sṛj* in the sense "receive" [interest] in Manu VIII.140, and *atisṛṣṭi* in BU I.4.6), or (2) with the same reading, "One who answers Him, him He sets free," taking *tām atisṛjate* as repeated at the end of Kauṣ. Up. I.2, probably with the Moon as subject, or (3) "One who answers Him, saying 'Thou,' He liberates" (*tam yaḥ pratyāha tvam iti sṛjate*), where we adopt the variant *iti sṛjate* and make the emendation obviously needed in this case, of *tvam* for *tam*. In any case translators, ignoring the parallel with JUB III.14 and JB I.18, have missed the point. "But one who does not answer thus" (*ya enaṃ na pratyāha*), or much less plausibly "does not answer" (*atha yo na pratyāha*), "descends with the rains to birth in this world as animal or person (*puruṣa*) according to his works and his wisdom" (*pratyājāyate yathā karma yathā vidyam*, cf. AĀ II.3.2, *yathā prajñam hi sambhavāḥ*; the list of animals in Kauṣ. Up. corresponds to *itareṣam paśūnām* in AĀ, and is to be taken in a purely symbolic sense, distinction being made of animal men from those *puruṣaḥ* in whom the form of Humanity is actually realized). Kauṣ. Up. now twice cites the question assumed above, "Who art thou?" (*ko'si*), and to this two answers are given: (1) one which is evidently that of the man destined to be reborn includes the words, addressed to the Seasons (who in JUB III.14, "drag him away caught by the foot on the verge of success"), "Send ye me forth in man as a doer (*mā puṃsi kartary irayadhvam*), through a man as agent inseminate me in a mother," this answer being appropriate for those of whom it is said that they who go to the Moon in the dark fortnight "He makes to be born" (*prajanayanti*); and (2) "I am Thou" (*tvam asmīti*), corresponding to the *tvam iti* assumed above, and appropriate to the Comprehensor who actually makes this answer (*enam . . . pratyāha*), as cited above, and accordingly "obtains the Moon," or "whom the Moon sets free (*tam atisṛjate*)." The Path is often formulated as leading to the Sun, thence to the Moon, and thence into the Lightning (e.g., CU IV.11–12 and V.10.2) or Fire (MU VI.38), i.e., Agni Vaidyuta, the Lightning; notwithstanding that the Sun and Moon are Heaven and Earth, OṂ and Vāc, the world of the divinities and world of men respectively (JUB III.13 and BU III.8.9). It is explained in MU VI.38 that "in the midst of the Sun is the Moon, in the midst of the Moon, Fire," and in any case it must be remembered that unification of the Sun and Moon is a concomitant of death (*candramā ivāditya dṛśyate*, AĀ III.2.4). There must be borne in mind the "*Liebesgeschichte des Himmels*": it is a constant theme throughout our sources that the Sun and Moon, Heaven and Earth, were "once" united, are separated in the beginning when time and space come into being, and are reunited at the End of the Worlds, End of the Heaven, End of the Year, where Heaven and

tī;[6] cf. BU v.5.2, where it is a prognostication of death when "he sees that orb quite clear, those rays no longer reach him," *śuddham evaitan maṇḍalaṃ paśyati nainam ete raśmayaḥ pratyāyayanti*).[7] One sees the "Golden Disk" (*hiraṇya patra*, Īśā Up. xv) that is represented in the cosmic rite by a golden disk (*rukma*), which is analogically the Sun (*āditya*), the Truth (*satya*), and is provided with twenty-one peripheral knobs, which represent the solar Rays extended to the thrice seven "worlds" (ŚB III, and *passim*). The Golden Disk, the Orb itself, is an operculum by which the Mouth or Inlet (*mukha*, Īśā Up. 15, JUB III.33.8, cf. BG XI.25, *mukhāni*, cf.

Earth embrace; cf. *Zohar*, *Shelah Lecha* section: "When the light of the Sun arrives, the Moon is embraced in it; but the Sun and Moon cannot shine together; the Moon cannot shine till the Sun is gathered in." When the Sun and Moon are unified, the worlds are as it were closed up, the "middle space" (*antarikṣa, rajas*) is closed up; for one who sees them thus there is no more place for any "world." And so it is said that one "climbs the Tree, conjoining these two Divinities pairwise" (*ete dve-dve devate saṃdhāye*, JUB I.3.2), and it is indeed at the Treetop that "the Eagle-pair of conjoint lovers are embraced together" (*dvā suparṇā sayujā sakhāyā samānaṃ vṛkṣaṃ pari ṣvajāte*, RV I.164.20; cf. VS XXXVIII.25 and TS VII.4.19p), who are at once the Sun and Moon, Mitra and Varuṇa, Heaven and Earth, and as in BU IV.3.19 and 21, the Spirit of God and self-same Spirit in Man (*prajñenātmanā sampariṣvaktaḥ*, *ibid.*), which Foreknowing Spirit, even though embodied Itself, is bodiless and consubstantial with the Sun (*yas cāyaṃ aśarīraḥ prajñātmā yas cāsav āditya ekam*, AĀ III.2.3 and 4 which, as remarked by Keith, is "the most common doctrine in the Upanishads").

[6] Misunderstood alike by Oertel ("parts his rays") and by Hume ("Spread forth thy rays"). Sāyaṇa's *vyūha* = *vigamaya* is correct; *vyūh* is here indeed to "scatter," but in the sense "dispel," "remove," "withdraw."

The formulation in AĀ III.2.4 is foolproof: "The Sun's rays are no longer manifest" (*na rasmayah prādur bhavanti*). The Sun's rays are extended and withdrawn in accordance with the "spider" symbolism explained in Coomaraswamy, "Angel and Titan," 1935.

[7] The Rays are often spoken of as the "feet" of the Sun, who is thus (1) *ekapāda* with respect to the single Life-ray by which each being is immediately connected with him, and which is that individual's "Way" (*devapatha*), and in the case of the Eternal Avatar as manifested at the Navel of the Earth (*nābhir pṛthviyā*) is the *skambha*, or Axis of the Universe; and (2) *sahasrapāda* if we consider all the Rays that reach all beings severally. That those Rays "no longer reach him" who is dying can then be otherwise expressed by saying that the feet of Death, the person in the solar Orb, which during life are "deeply planted in the heart" (*hṛdaye padau atihatau āditasya raśmaya . . . nāḍīṣu sṛptā*, sc. *hṛdayasya*, CU VIII.6.2), are cut off, and when He thus departs, the person dies (ŚB x.5.2.13); cf. AĀ III.2.4, where it is a sign of death when the rays of the Sun are no longer seen (*na raśmayaḥ prādur bhavanti*). He then who could not gaze upon the sun in life but only sees his rays (speaking now in terms of the physical analogy), at death no longer sees the rays, but only the well-defined orb.

anīka)[8] is covered up (*apihitam*).[9] That is, the Intelligible Truth conceals what God is in Himself, "The Immortal veiled by Truth": the Immortal, i.e., Spiration (*praṇa* = *ātman*); Truth, i.e., Form and Aspect (*nāmarūpa*) in Him as forms or ideas or eternal reasons or "hidden names" (*nāmāni guhyāni*), which are ontologically speaking the causes of the being of things as they are in themselves. In this there is no contradiction, inasmuch as the knowledge of God by which He "creates" cannot be distinguished from His essence; "It knew only Itself, that 'I am Brahman,' thereby It became the All," BU I.4.9–10. We are thus brought back to the ultimate problem of "distinction in identity," and it would appear that "things as they are in God," in their "own form" which is also His form, are at the same time "themselves" as being capable of a distinct manifestation and of specific pleasures (TU III.10.5, like John 10:9, and in our text cited here), although this is neither a local motion nor a physical experience, since "He circles there (*sa tara paryēti*) taking his pleasure (*ramamaṇaḥ*), regardless of any appended body to which the breath of Life (*prāṇa*) may be yoked," and "When He, the Spirit, proposes to be aware of this or that, Intellect (*manas*) is His Divine Eye, it is therewith that He recognizes and takes his pleasure in loves" (*kāmān apaśyan ramate*), CU VIII.12, 3 and 5). "To know God as He is, we must be absolutely free from knowledge" (Meister Eckhart, Evans ed., I, 365), that is, from any "knowledge-of" Him, any theodicy whatever. Accordingly, the Comprehensor prays, or rather being himself of a like nature with the Sun, demands of the Sun to "gather in His brilliance" (*samūha tejo*), that is, to contract it to a central point without dimension, "That I may see Thy fairest form" (*rūpaṃ kalyāṇatamam*), and exclaims triumphantly, "He that is yonder, yonder Person in the Sun, That am I," Īśā Up. 15, 16.

This Person in the Sun, who is in fact the "Truth of Truth" (*satyasya satyam*), is otherwise called Death (*mṛtyu*, sometimes *yama*): "Death is the Person in the Orb (*maṇḍale*); the Light that shines (*arcir dīpyate*)

[8] Literally "mouth," but here, as commonly also in architectural terminology, "way in," just as we say "mouth of a tunnel." This is, of course, like the "door" of John 10:9, both a way in and a way out, and in the latter sense the "gateway of his emanation." What the Comprehensor seeks is to be swallowed up. *Mukha* is also "face," (Meister Eckhart, Evans ed., I, 364), "His countenance whereto He admits no creature and whereinto no creature can get," without, that is, abandoning its creaturehood.

[9] TU I.4.1 addressed to the omniform (*viśvarūpa*) Indra (as the Sun): "Thou art the sheath (*kośa*) of Brahman, shut in by wisdom (*medhayā apihitam*)." Also cf. *brahmāvarta* as the land of the Devas, Manu II.17. The distinction of *āvarta* from *patha* is doubtless intentional; *āvarta* also implies *samsarana*.

is what does not die (*amṛtam*). Accordingly, Death does not die, forasmuch as He is within (*na mriyate hy antaḥ*), nor is He seen (*na dṛśyate*), being within what does not die" (ŚB x.5.2.3), viz. the Light of the Unconquerable Sun, who really "neither rises nor sets, but only inverts Himself" (AB III.44). It is precisely with this Death, Privation (*mṛtyu, aśanāya*) that the Comprehensor is unified, and so forever escapes contingent death (BU I.2.7), though He dogs the Wayfarer's steps until he reaches the Treetop and escapes through the midst of the Sun (JUB I.3).

What lies beyond, within, is a "Divine Darkness," blinding to all human faculties by its excess of light, and "hidden from all knowledge" (Dionysius, *Epist. ad Caium monachum*; cf. Vedic *guhā nihitam*, etc.), the "Darkness where God was" of Exodus 20:21, "the City [that] had no need of the Sun, neither of the Moon, to shine in it" (Rev. 21:23 ff.); "There the Sun does not shine" (KU v.15, Muṇḍ. Up. II.2.10, etc.), "neither Sun, nor Moon, nor Fire" (BG xv.6). "What the soul grasps in the light, she loses in the darkness. Yet she makes for the cloud, deeming His darkness better than her light" (Meister Eckhart, Evans ed., I, 364).

Here in the empyrean (*parama vyoman, brahma-loka*, etc.), corresponding to the "third Heaven" of St. Paul, "there is no more any guidance robed in human likeness (*puruṣo'mānavaḥ*[10] *sa enaṃ brahma gamayateṣa devapatho brahmapathaḥ*), nor do those who enter there any more return to this human wayfaring" (*etena pratipadyamānā imaṃ mānavam āvartam navārtante*), CU IV.15.5-6, cf. V.10.2; *paramāṃ gatiṃ, yaṃ prāpya na nivartante*, BG VIII.21.

The interior and exterior operations, respectively hidden and revealed (*guhya, āvis*), infinite and finite (*aditi, diti*), inexplicit and explicit (*anirukta, nirukta*, etc.), are divided by an opaque screen[11] ("veiled by my Māyā," BG), penetrable (*nirvedhya*) only through the Sun. Divinity, if we think of it objectively as far away, is there beyond, or if we think of it as very near is here within us (*antarbhūtasya khe, hṛdayākāśe guhā nihitam*, etc.). But these two natures, of God as He is in Himself, and as He is in us, are really one, and as explained in JUB III.33 (and less clearly in AĀ II.1.5), he only really attains to the Persons who know them both ways, as transcendent and as immanent (*adhidevatam, adhyātman*)

[10] Cf. Muṇḍ. Up. II.1.2 *puruṣaḥ . . . aprāṇo hy amānāḥ*; in JB I.50, *na manuṣyaḥ* = *devānām ekaḥ*; cf. BU I.2.7 = Agni Vaidyuta, the Lightning, and see Kena Up. 29.

[11] Islamic "murity" (*jidāriyyā*); Eckhart's "boundary line between united and separated creatures" (Meister Eckhart, Evans ed., I, 464).

in identity (*ekadhā*); "he knows the Spirit (or very self), he knows Brahman, the Gate or Face (cf. *anīka*) accepts him, he getteth all and overcometh all, his every desire is fulfilled" (*sa ātmānaṃ veda, sa brahma veda . . . mukha ādhatte*,[12] *tasya sarvam āptaṃ bhavati, sarvaṃ jitaṃ*; *na hāsya kaścana kāmo'nāpto bhavati*; cf. BU IV.3.21). And whereby or wherein these Persons "become one" (*ekaṃ bhavanti*) is called a "superhuman wayfaring" (*brahmaṇa āvarta*), evidently identical with the *devapatha* or *brahmapatha* of CU IV.15.6[13] and *devayāna* of Kauṣ. Up. I.3.[14] In the same way, in AV XIII.4.20, "All the Devas become simplex in Him" (*ekavṛto bhavanti*), and similarly in AĀ II.3.8 (*ekaṃ bhavanti*), and AĀ V.12, where a "becoming onefold" is equated with "attainment of the highest" (*ekadhā bhūyaṃ bhūtvā paramatāṃ gacchataḥ*). Such a "becoming one" implies a "dying to oneself" (*suum et proprium = aham ca mama*, cf. MU VI.17), and in fact "to be unified" acquires the specific meaning "to die" (they say of the dying man in BU IV.4.2, *ekī bhavati*), in the same way that to effect the unification of any creature is to "kill" (AĀ III.2.3, where the Year is said to "separate some things and unify

[12] The whole passage reads *sa yo ha eva vidvān prāṇena prāṇya apānena apānya manasā, etā ubhayīr devatā ātmany etya, mukha adhatte*, etc. (the arrangement as a *pada* text and the punctuation are mine). Oertel's rendering (JAOS, XVI, 1894, 193) is imperfect: the conspiration, or return of the breath of life (*prāṇa, spiraculum vitae*) to its source is to be effected "intellectually" (*manasā*), cf. KU IV.11, "This is only to be gotten intellectually" (*manasaivedam āptavyam*); *i* takes the accusative of the goal, and this is "these divinities under both aspects" (*eta ubhayīr devatā*), *ātmani* being "in the Spirit"; cf. Rev. 4:2, "immediately I was in the Spirit, and behold," etc. *Mukha*, as in Īśā Up. 15, is the Sun or Face of God, hidden from human vision by the "golden disk" of manifested Truth (*satyam*); Oertel translates as if the reading were *mukhe*. That the manifested truth is in the last analysis a veil explains the designation of the "nonproceeding" or "inexhaustible" (*akṣara*) Brahman within as the "Truth of Truth" (*satyasya satyam*, AĀ II.3.8 = *veritas veritatis*).

[13] Merely to pass through the Sun is not then forthwith to have reached that end in which all progress ends: as pointed out by Sāyaṇa, there is still to be accomplished that union which is implied by the words "being Brahman one attains to Brahman." The stations of the unseen path that leads beyond the "Door of the world of Heavenly-light, to the throne of Brahmā," (Kauṣ. Up. I.3) are described symbolically.

[14] *Devapatha*, in BU V.5.2 *devayānah pathah*; cf. Kauṣ. Up. I.3, "Having entered upon this *devayāna* he comes . . . to the Brahma world." The "two paths" are those of RV X.88.15, repeated in BU VI.2.2. The *devapatha* is also the same as the *sāmapatha* of JUB I.6. These two paths are further analyzed in BG VIII.23–27 (distinction of yogis who are "returners" and "Nonreturners." Also in AĀ II.1.5, *etaddha tat* corresponds to *akadhā bhavanti*). The same idea is expressed in JUB I.3 in a simpler form; here one ascends the worlds "uniting these divinities pairwise" (Sun and Moon, etc.).

[*aikyā bhāvayan* | others," i.e., to bring into being some and to bring about the death of others).[15]

Two Ways or Cycles (*āvarta*)[16] are thus distinguished, a "human" and a "superhuman" Way, *manavārta* and *brahmapatha*, one of return (*pitṛyāna*) and one of nonreturn (*devayāna*); corresponding exactly to what is called in Mahāyāna Buddhism[17] respectively, the "Mundane" or "Taught" (*laukika*, *śaikṣa*) and "Transmundane," "Untaught," "Pure," or "Aryan" (*lokottara*, *aśaikṣa*,[18] *anāsrava*, *ārya*) Paths, of which the former leads the Wayfarer to the "Summit of Contingent Being" (*bhavā gra*), which is the highest ground attainable by a Bodhisattva as such, whence he proceeds by the latter to omniscience and Buddhahood. It is not to be inferred that having reached the Summit of Contingent Being one there abandons the Mundane and enters the Transmundane Path. On the contrary, although the Mundane Path alone is available in the lowest of the "Three Worlds," or rather "States of Contingent Being" (*kāmadhātu*, *rūpadhātu*, *ārūpyadhātu*), beyond this level of reference the Paths run side by side, but end at different points—"Only the Transmundane or Aryan Path can destroy the passions that remain at the Summit of Contingent Being" (*Abhidharmakośa* VI.47). Nor must the "Worlds," although the sphere of transmigration, be conceived of only in a spatial or temporal sense (the *Ārūpyadhātu* in particular is "placeless," *asthāna*); they are rather, at least in the present connection, states of being by which the whole of time and space are permeated, and are distinguishable somewhat as one distinguishes the "Life of Pleasure" from the "Active Life" and "Contemplative Life," or the "Householder's" from the "Homeless" life. The Buddha, for example, is considered to have attained the *bhavāgra* when he took his seat beneath the Tree, and to have attained to omniscient Buddhahood then and there, in virtue of the Aryan Path that had been previously trodden.

These two sharply distinguished Paths correspond, on the one hand, to the exoteric, religious, and passively mystical means of approach to

[15] As also formulated in MU VI.15, "From the Year indeed are they engendered . . . and in the Year they go home" (*astam yanti*, "go to their rest," "die").

[16] *Āvarta* is "Way" in the sense of course or cycle, or even eddy, with an implication of turning or spiral motion; both the centrifugal and centripetal motions of consciousness with respect to its center are, in fact, of this sort; cf. René Guénon, "La Double Spirale," *Études traditionnelles*, XLI (1936).

[17] *Abhidharmakośa*, II.12 and 42–44, VI.45, 47, etc., VIII.5, etc. (see the summarized account of the Way, Poussin ed., Vol. IV, *avant-propos*).

[18] Cf. Kena Up. I.3, *yathāitad anuśiṣyāt*, "How would one teach it?"

God and, on the other, to the esoteric, initiatory, and metaphysical means of access to the Supreme Identity. But it would be begging the question to assume that they are to be identified with mutually exclusive paths of dedication (*bhakti*) and of Gnosis (*jñāna*); the question is rather whether these two Paths are not inseparably connected, if not in their beginning then in any case in their development. Can we imagine a perfected ardor apart from understanding, or a perfected understanding without ardor? Can any qualitative distinction be drawn between a consummated union of lover and beloved and a consummated union of knower and known? It is precisely a consideration of the *ātman* doctrine that may lead us to a conclusion in agreement with the negative answer that had already been foreshadowed. It is not by any means to be supposed that such a negative answer implies that there can be any transcendence of or liberation from human substantiality, both physical and psychic, apart from initiation (*dīkṣā*) and gnosis (*jñāna*); what is implied is, rather, that a perfected Gnosis necessarily involves a Beatification (*anirdeśyaṃ paramaṃ sukham*, KU v.14; *paramo hy eṣa ānandaḥ*, ŚB x.5.2.11; *sukham uttamam upaiti . . . brahmabhūtam*, BG vi.27; Dante's *piacere eterno, Paradiso*, xviii.16).

The *bhavāgra* may be more fully explained. Broadly speaking, this "Summit of Contingent Being" corresponds to the Christian concept of Heaven, where there is a direct vision of God, but by no means necessarily a "mystic union." But, as Eckhart expresses it, "As this is not the summit of divine union, so it is not the soul's abiding place" (Evans ed., I, 276), and this is in perfect agreement with the words of SP v.74, "That is a resting-place (*viśrāma*), not an involution" (*nivṛti*)—not, that is, what Eckhart means by the "Drowning."

Those who reach the Summit of Contingent Being are, strictly speaking, "saved," since their essence (*ātmabhāva*,[19] individual substance considered as a "naturing of the Spirit" or as a "state of selfhood") is indestructible (*Abhidharmakośa* ii.45b), though they may or may not be reborn when their term of being on the plane is completed, those who still have "connections" (*saṃyojanāni*) being "returners" and those who have not, "Nonreturners." A Bodhisattva, for example, "returns" to the lower worlds of contingent being, being drawn thereunto by the force of his messianic vows, while a Buddha does not return at the end of time, but is "wholly despirated" (*parinirvṛta*).

[19] *Bhūtātman* as distinct logically but not really from *ātman* in MU ii.7 and iii.1.

The Summit of Contingent Being corresponds to the station otherwise called the "Treetop" (*vṛkṣāgra*): "Those who ascend to the Top of the Great Tree, how do they fare thereafter? Those who have wings fly away, those without wings fall down" (JUB III.13). The latter correspond to the "fallen from *yoga*" (*yogabraṣṭaḥ*) of BG VI.41 ff., i.e., those whose vision of the Truth is obscured by an imperfect fixation (stabilization) of the Intellect in *yoga* (*yogāc calita mānasaḥ*) by which they have fallen short of perfection (*saṃsiddham*); consider in Buddhism the six kinds of *Arhats*, of whom only the "Immovable" (*akupya-dharman*) cannot fall, while the deliverance of the others is temporal (*Abhidharmakośa* VI.56 ff.), a "going and coming" as in BG IX.21.

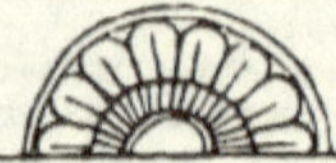

The Flood in Hindu Tradition

The primary object of the present note is to present the Indian flood legend[1] as a special case of the Patriarchal Voyage (*pitṛyāna*), and at the same time in coherent and intelligible relation with other fundamental conceptions of Vedic cosmology and eschatology. Some analogies with other traditional aspects of the flood legend are incidentally noted. Whatever grounds may or may not exist for belief in an historical flood, the doctrine of *manvantaras* is, like that of *kalpas*, an essential part of Hindu tradition, and can no more be explained by any historical event than can the Vedic angels be explained by the deification of heroes. Further, the Flood legend clearly belongs to a tradition older than any existing Indian redaction or reference, older than the Vedas in their present form; these Indian redactions must be thought of as having, with the Sumerian, Semitic, and perhaps also Eddaic versions, a common source, the correspondences being ascribable not to "influence" but to transmission by inheritance from the common source.

"Floods" are a normal and recurrent feature of the cosmic cycle, i.e., the period (*para*) of a Brahmā's life, amounting to 36,000 *kalpas*, or "days" of Angelic time. In particular, the *nāimittikapralaya* at the end of every *kalpa* (close of a "day" of Angelic time, and equivalent to the Christian "Last Judgment"), and *prākṛtikapralaya* at the end of the lifetime of a Brahmā (close of a "day" of Supernal Time) are essentially resolutions of manifested existences into their undetermined potentiality, the Waters; and each renewed cycle of manifestation is a bringing forth on the next "day" of forms latent as potentiality in the floods of reservoir of being. In each case the seeds, ideas, or images of the future manifestation persist during the interval or inter-Time of resolution on a higher plane of existence, unaffected by the destruction of manifested forms.

As to this, it will be understood, of course, that the chronological sym-

[This essay appears to have been written in the mid-1940s.—ED.]

[1] For the principal texts see Adam Hohenberger, *Die indische Flutsage und das Matsyapurāṇa* (Leipzig, 1930).

bolism, inevitable from the empirical point of view, cannot be thought of as really characterizing the timeless actuality of all the possibilties of existence in the indivisible present of the Absolute, for Whom all multiplicity is mirrored in a single image. As, then, there can be no destruction of things as they are in the Self, but only of things as they are in themselves, the eternity, or rather timelessness, of ideas is a metaphysical necessity. Hence, indeed, the conception of another type of transformation, an *atyantika pralaya*, ultimate or absolute resolution, to be accomplished by the individual, when or wherever he may be, as Realization: when, in fact, by self-naughting a man effects for himself the transformation of things as they are in themselves, and knows them only as they are in the Self, he becomes immortal—not relatively, as are the Devas, enduring merely to the end of Time—but absolutely, as independent of time and of every other contingency. It should be noted that the ideas (images, types) in question are not exactly Platonic ideas, but ideas or types of activity, the knowledge and being of the Self consisting in pure act; in the chronological symbolism their creative efficacy is expressed in terms of *adrśya* or *apūrva karma*, "unseen" or "latent consequence."

While the creation of a cosmos (Brahmāṇḍa) at the commencement of a *para*, and the recreation of resolved elements of the cosmos at the commencement of every *kalpa*, are the work of Brahmā (Prajāpati), the All-Father, the more proximate genesis and guidance of humanity in each *kalpa* and *manvantara* is brought about by a Patriarch (*pitṛ*) of angelic ancestry, and designated Manu or Manus. In each *kalpa* there are fourteen *manvantaras*, each presided over by an individual Manu as progenitor and lawgiver; so also the *ṛsis*, and Indra and other (*karma-*) *devas*, are individual to each *manvantara*. The first Manu of the present *kalpa* was Svāyambhuva, "child of Svayambhū"; the seventh and present Manu, Vāivasvata, "child of the Sun." Each Manu is a determined and conscious survivor from the previous *manvantara*, and through him the sacred tradition is preserved and transmitted. The particular Manu intended is not always stated in the texts, and in such cases it is generally to be understood that the reference is to the present (Vāivasvata) Manu. It is not expressly stated that a flood arises at the conclusion of each *manvantara*, but this may be assumed on the analogy of "the" flood connected with Vāivasvata Manu (ŚB 1.8.1–10), and the analogy of the greater "flood" that marks the conclusion of a *kalpa*; but whereas in the latter case the principle of continuity is provided by the creative Hypostasis, floating recumbent asleep on the surface of the waters, supported by the Nāga

"Eternity" (Ananta), in the case of the partial resolution or submergence of manifested forms which takes place at the close of a *manvantara*, the connecting link is provided by the voyage of a Manu in an ark or ship. It may be observed that this is essentially a voyage up and down the slope (*pravat*) of heaven rather than a voyage to and fro, and quite other than the voyage of the *devayāna*, which is continuously upwards and towards a shore whence there is no return.

We are not informed of the chronological duration of the flood and Manu's voyage. From the analogy of the greater *pralayas*, a duration equal to that of the preceding *manvantara* might be inferred, but a more plausible analogy is perhaps to be found in the "twilights" of the *yugas*, and this would suggest a relatively much shorter period of submergence. As to the depth of the flood, we have better information. In the first place it is evident that the resolution of manifested forms at the close of a *manvantara* will be less in cosmic extent than that, namely of the "three Worlds," which takes place at the close of a *kalpa*, and this will mean necessarily that of the "three Worlds," *svar* (the "Olympian" heavens) at least, and perhaps also *bhuvar* (the "atmospheric" spheres) are exempt from submergence; we know in any case that Dhruva (the Pole Star) remains unaffected throughout the *kalpa*. The earth (*bhur*) is submerged completely. Now the voyage of a Manu, typically a Patriarch (*pitṛ*), is a special case of the Patriarchal Voyage (*pitṛyāna*), and this as we know is a voyage to and from the "Moon," those regularly traveling by this route being the Patriarchs (usually spoken of collectively as *pitaras*), and the Prophets (*ṛṣayaḥ*) "desirous of descendants" (*prajā-kāmaḥ*, Praśna Up. 1.9). The flood, therefore, on which Manu's ship is borne upwards, must rise at least to the level of the sphere of the Moon, though it is not necessary to suppose that the Moon itself is submerged.

While it is out of the question that the flood waters should extend to the Empyrean heavens, Mahar-loka or therebeyond, there is good reason to suppose that in rising to the level of the Moon they must also touch the shores of the Olympian heavens (Indra-loka, deva-loka). For, notwithstanding that Indra- or deva-loka is regarded as a station, not of the Patriarchal, but of the Angelic Voyage, it is undeniable that Indra-loka is continually thought of as a place of reward of the worthy[2] dead, warriors in particular, who reside there enjoying the society of *apsarasas* and other pleasures until in due course the time comes for their return to

[2] "Worthy," i.e., due to receive the reward of *kāmya* Works, though not qualified by Understanding for either gradual or immediate Enfranchisement (*mukti*).

human conditions. And while it is said that the latent effect of Works remains effective in the last analysis throughout a *kalpa* (*Viṣṇu Purāṇa* II.8), it would appear from the fact that the occupancy of Indra's office lasts only during the period of a *manvantara*[3] (hence a *kalpa* may as well be called a period of fourteen Indras as a period of fourteen Manus)[4] that reward in Indra-loka generally must be of the same duration; therefore at the commencement of any *manvantara* a general descent from the Angelic World must be initiated, no less than from the Patriarchal. It is clear that the two Worlds, Indra- or deva-loka and the Moon as pitṛ-loka, are psychologically equivalent, both being stations of the reward of *kāmya* Works; in fact, the Patriarchs are constantly spoken of as enjoying Soma in company with the Angels, and it is specifically stated in *Vālakhilya* IV.1 that Manu drank Soma in company with Indra. One might express the situation by saying that whereas the Moon is naturally pitṛ-loka from the (*Brāhmaṇa*) point of view, as the posthumous abode of "those who in the village reverence a belief in sacrifice, merit, and alms-giving" (CU V.10.3), Indra- or deva-loka is naturally the home of the dead from the (*Kṣatriya*) point of view of the warrior. And if Indra-loka is listed *only* as a station of the *devayāna*, this is because it represents actually a station from which there is not only the necessity of return for those who have performed Works only, but also the possibility of a passing on by way of the Sun to the Empyrean heavens in the course of *Krama mukti* and without return, in the case of those "who understand this and in the forest truly worship" (BU VI.2.15). When it is said in RV

[3] Those who, as individuals, are particular to a given *manvantara* are the presiding Angels (*devāḥ*), Prophets (*rsayah*), and Manu and his descendants, i.e., kings and other men. The Angels in question cannot, of course, be thought of as any of those of the *ājānaja* ("by birth," e.g., Kāmadeva) order, but will be of the *karma* class, holding positions to which a qualification by Works has entitled them; and of these *karma-devāh* or Work Angels the chief is Indra. Hence it is constantly assumed that an individual duly preparing himself here and now may become the Indra (or for that matter even the Brahmā) of a future age; and jealousy is often attributed to the Angels with respect to those who will thus succeed them in office.

There is some inconsistency of detail, though not of principle, as between *Viṣṇu Purāna* II.8, where it is said that the "immortality" of the Angels means a survival without change of state until the end of the *kalpa*, and *ibid.*, III.1, where the lifetime of an Indra and other (*karma*) Angels is restricted to the *manvantara*.

In any case, the Hindu view of the nature of angelic offices is identical with that of orthodox Christian theology, cf. St. Gregory and St. Augustine, *Angelus nomen est officii, non naturae*; for which, and the rendering of *deva* by "Angel," see Coomaraswamy, "On Translation: *Māyā, Deva, Tapas*," 1933.

[4] Cf. *Viṣṇu Purāṇa* III.1, and *Mārkandeya Purāna* C.44.

x.14.17 that the two kings whom the dead meet on reaching "heaven" are not Indra and Yama, but Varuṇa and Yama, that is, Varuṇa in the case of the Angelic Voyage (since he who has reached the level of the heavenly waters is confronted with the possibility of future being only under heavenly conditions), and Yama in the case of the Patriarchal Voyage, it may be supposed that Indra (-loka) is omitted as being only a stage on the way to Varuṇa.

Now with respect to Yama, as he is the brother of Manu (Vāivasvata) at the present time, it must be understood that "Yama" implies always the Yama of a given *manvantara*. Yama and Manu, both designated Patriarchs (*pitṛ*), are contrasted in this respect, that whereas Yama, being the first man to die, was also the first to find out the way to the other world, in other words to map out the outward passage on the *pitṛyāna*, and thereby, as first settler, became king and ruler of all those who followed him, Manu is at once the last and only survivor of the previous *manvantara* and progenitor and lawgiver in the present. Hillebrandt's view (*Vedische Mythologie*, I, 394; II, 368, etc.) of Yama as original ruler of the sphere of the Moon, perhaps at one time simply the Moon-god, his realm or paradise being specifically that of the dead, is naturally acceptable. In any case, in one way or another. Yama and the Moon are regarded as dividers out of the dead, appointing their course (*yāna*) according as they are qualified by Works or by Understanding. This "judgment" is expressed exceptionally in Kauṣ. Up. 1.2 as a selection effected by the Moon itself, qua door of the heavenly world.[5] More characteristically, the dividing out is accomplished by the two dogs of Yama, Śabala and Śyāma ("Iridescent" and "Dark"), who correspond to the Sun and Moon, as argued by Bloomfield (JAOS, XV, 171) with reference to RV x.14.10; and this is supported by Praśna Up. 1.9 and 10 (and Śaṇkarācārya's Commentary), where the Sun, considered as a station on the *devayāna*, is not merely in a passive sense impassible by those devoid of Understanding, but actually and actively a barrier (*nirodha*) restraining those unqualified from passing on to a paradise (*amṛtam āyatanam*) whence there is no returning. Incidentally, this also enables us to establish the correspondence of the Hebraic Angel with the Flaming Sword with the Vedic Sun qua *nirodha*; the "Flaming Sword" being the Angel's natural weapon, in

[5] Cf. BU III.1.6, where the Moon, reached through the efficacy of the Brāhmaṇa priest, now identified with the Intellect, is in turn identified with Intellect, Brahman, "complete release."

virtue of his solar character. The analogy of the *pitṛyāna* with Jacob's ladder may also be noted.

While the partial Understanding which constitutes the Wayfarer's ship on the Angelic Voyage absolves him from the necessity of return to human corporeal conditions, the latent effect of Works necessitates a return course of the Patriarchal Voyage. In other words, the *pitṛyāna* is a symbolic representation of what is now called the doctrine of reincarnation, and is bound up with the notion of latent (*adṛṣṭa* or *apūrva*) causality. The purely symbolic character of the whole conception is made all the more apparent when we reflect that from the standpoint of very Truth, and in the absolute Present, there can be no distinctions made of cause and effect; and that what is often spoken of as the "destruction of *karma*," or more correctly as a destruction of the latent effects of Works, effected by Understanding and implied with *mukti*, is not really a destruction of valid causes (as though it were possible to make that which has been not to have been, or to conceive of any potentiality of being unrealized in the Self), but simply a Realization of the identity of "cause" and "effect." It must be similarly understood with reference to the designation of states of being in spatial terms, for example as "the Sun" or "the Moon," that these are no more to be taken literally with respect to visible luminaries than are the analogous designations of states of being as time phases, for example, those of the light or dark fortnight, cf. Praśna Up. 1.12. It does not appear, in fact, that the Vedic tradition really propounds any doctrine of reincarnation in the highly individual and literal Buddhist, Jāina, and modern sense, nor in any case an individual return to identical conditions,[6] such as those of any one *manvantara*, but merely a return to analogous conditions in another age, *manvantara* or *kalpa* as the case may be. Divested thus of a too literal interpretation, the Vedic (Upaniṣadic) doctrine of "reincarnation" bears a certain resemblance to modern conceptions of "heredity": we too speak of the continuity of "germ-plasm," of relatively everlasting "genes," and the possibility that the characteristics of a remote ancestor may recur in any descendant; we know only too well that "Man is born like a garden

[6] An exact repetition of any past experience would be inconceivable metaphysically, since any two identical experiences, regarded from the standpoint of the absolute present, in which all potentialities of being are simultaneously realized, must be one and the same experience. Metaphysics asserts the unique character of every monad, and it is precisely this uniqueness which makes the individual unknowable as he is in himself, though intelligible as he is in and of the Self.

ready planted and sown," and few of us can always discard the conviction that "a man gets what is coming to him."

One further point of importance in this connection: while the Vedic point of view necessarily presumes an immortality, that is to say timelessness, of all potentialities of being typally subsistent in the Self (and this may be thought of from the standpoint of the Self as an eternal existence in the world picture not merely of every individual, but of every act of every individual on whatsoever plane of being), an immortality of this kind is in no way to be thought of as an immortality from the standpoint of any individual consciousness. It is clearly enough brought out that both the relative immortality of the Angels, and the absolute immortality of Realization are conditions which are altogether dependent on individual effort; or, as it is expressed from a more limited point of view in the Christian tradition, every individual must work out his own salvation. There can be no "immortality" for the individual monad who has not, so to speak, either acquired a "soul" by the due performance of Works, or realized the Self either partially as a Wayfarer or wholly as a Comprehensor. As to the infrahuman beings, "the small, continually returning creatures" of whom it is said "Be born, and die," theirs is a "third state"; their course is ephemeral, and neither by the *devayāna* nor the *pitṛyāna*, though the possibility is not excluded that even an animal, under special circumstances, could develop a consciousness with survival value. And as to those beings human in form but so little *menschlich* in nature that they do not achieve even any virtuosity (*kāuśalya*) in Works, their Psyche is said to be reborn in animal wombs, or alternatively to be lost. Hence (of course only from the human point of view, there being no superiority of one state over another in the eyes of the Self) the primary importance of birth in human form; for here and now it is determined whether or no the individual shall inherit Eternal Life, or at least a renewed possibility of winning Eternal Life. Furthermore, Veda is the body of Truth in which is set forth the way of life; and this Truth, eternal in the consciousness of the Self (without distinction of "knowledge" from "being"), is transmitted as it has been "heard," by a succession of Prophets (*ṛṣayaḥ*) from *manvantara* to *manvantara*.[7]

While the *pitṛyāna* is thus manifested in the succession of *manvantaras*, the *devayāna* is primarily a course whereon the individual is removed ever farther and farther from the "storm of the world-flow" (Meister Eck-

[7] In some other versions of the flood legend, the continuity of tradition is more mechanically explained.

hart, Evans ed., I, 192), those who journey by the ship of Knowledge normally "never returning" (*punar na avartante*). The only exception to this is in the case of an *avatara*, whose return or descent is indeed inevitable, like that of the Patriarchs, but with this difference, that in this case the necessity arises from a purely voluntary self-commitment (as is brought out so clearly in the case of the Bodhisattvas, whose appearance as a Buddha is a consequence of previous *praṇidhāna*), and with this further distinction that in such cases the descent is not so much an actual embodiment or helpless subjection to human conditions, as a manifestation (*nirmāṇa*) not infringing the centering of consciousness in the higher state of being from which the *avataraṇa* takes place.[8] In the case of an *avataraṇa* of the Supreme Lord, this has to be thought of as an immediate act of will or grace;[9] and here *a fortiori* the doctrine of *nirmāṇa* or that of merely partial (*aṃśa*) incarnation must be invoked.[10]

We have seen that every procedure from one state of being to another, though formally "death again" (*punar mṛtyu*), is envisaged from the Vedic point of view as a passing from one station to another of a voyage on the sea of life. This sea can only be thought of as having a horizontal surface for so long as our attention is confined to any one and the same state of being; whenever a change of state is involved, as in the Angelic or Patriarchal Voyages, the surface of the sea of life is necessarily conceived of as a slope[11] or limiting form of a succession of degrees, leading upwards or downwards as the case may be, and as though from a valley to a height and *vice versa*. The slope, steep, or height is designated *pravat*, contrasted with *nivat*, descent or depth. *Pravat* is met with frequently in the *Ṛg Veda* and *Atharva Veda*. Here it will suffice to note AV vi.28.3, where it is said that Yama was the first to achieve the scarp (*pravat*), spying out the way for many; AV x.10.2, where the steeps are said to be seven in number, evidently with reference to the seven planes of being, that is to say the

[8] For an explanation of *avatarana* with reference to the Vedic Apāntaratamas and others, reference should be made to Śaṇkarācārya's Commentary on the *Vedānta Sutras* iii.3.30–31. The *nirmāna* doctrine corresponds to the Docetic Heresy in Christianity, and has its equivalent in Manichaeism.

[9] As in BG, *passim*.

[10] Just as from the Christian point of view it is not supposed that the whole being of the Son was by the fact of Incarnation imprisoned in Mary's womb.

[11] A general consideration of traditional symbolism would lead us to identify this "slope" with the pitch of a spiral having for its center the vertical axis of the universe; or as that of the phyllotaxy of the Tree of Life.

"three Worlds" and four Empyrean heavens, Mahar, Janas, Tapas, and Satyam; and AV xviii.4.7, where the crossing of the fords (*tīrtha*) of the great steeps is said to be by means of the sacrificial Works of the worthy. All this is consistent with the Angelic Voyage of the enlightened in the ship of Understanding, and the Patriarchal Voyage of those whose ship is Works.

The conception of the sea of life as an ocean and of its "surface" as a slope further explains much of the terminology of the posthumous voyages, and that of a Manu. For example, the attainment of the level of any state of being, a port of call on the voyage, is thought of as a tying up in harbor: hence in AV xix.39.7, where there is an incidental allusion to the Angelic Voyage, the sky-faring vessel is provided with a golden hawser (*bandhana*), and corresponding notions are found in ŚB i.8.1.6 in the injunction to Manu, *vṛkṣe nāvaṃ pratibandhīṣvataṃ*, "tie up the ship to a tree"; in Mbh iii.187.48, "tie up the ship to the summit of Himālaya"; and iii.187.50 *nāu-bandhana*, "ship-tying," denoting the summit of Himālaya, where Manu's ship made land as the Flood subsided. In the same way the conception of a slope or "up" contrasted with a "down" explains the constant use of the verbal prefix *ava-*, "down," whenever a descent on the sea of life is envisaged, as in AV xix.39.8, where it is said that for those (wayfarers on the *devayāna*) who "see immortality" there is "no gliding down," *na'avaprabhraṃśana*,[12] and ŚB i.8.1.6, where the descent of Manu's ark is spoken of as *avasarpaṇa*, with the same sense of "downward gliding."

The general parallel with Biblical tradition is very close; the account of creation in Genesis corresponding to the creation at the commencement of the present *kalpa*, that of the Flood and Noah to that of the Flood and Manu Vāivasvata. Manu, however, is not thought of as taking with him into the ark a wife and pairs of creatures after their kind; in other words, the apparatus of the Hebraic version in this respect is more mechanical. Manu is a progenitor of mankind in the sense that all men are of the seed of Manu; and as the reincarnation of the Patriarchs is not all at once, but day by day in the natural course of events, it must be understood not that they descended in Manu's ark literally, but by the *pitryāna* in its general connotation, their genealogy from Manu being,

[12] This word, divided *nāva-prabhramśana,* was at one time interpreted as equivalent to *nāu-bandhana*, but this has been rightly rejected on grammatical and other grounds. The AV passage does not refer to the descent of Manu's ark, but is an incidental reference to a voyage upwards on the *devayāna*.

as it were, implicit and by seminal virtue. Their actual birth from day to day is somewhat obscurely described in various accounts of return on the Patriarchal Voyage as a descent of *rasa* with the rain, and a subsequent evolution.

The Eddaic Götterdämmerung and subsequent restoration of the world may also represent the original tradition of a flood at the close of a world period: in *Völuspa*, such expressions as *vepr oll válynd, ragna rok, verold steypesk, skelfr Yggdrasels, snysk jormongandr, himenn klofnar*, followed by *Sér upp koma opro sinne jorth ór aegre ipjagroena . . . sás á fjalle fiske veiper*, and the assembly of the Aesir calling to mind the *fornar rúnar*, all closely parallel Indian descriptions of the end of a world age and subsequent restoration. The finding of the *gollnar toflor paers í árdaga átta hofpo* recalls the Berosus version of the flood legend (Isaac Preston Cory, *Ancient Fragments*, London, 1832, pp. 26 ff.), where a history of the beginning, procedure, and conclusion of all things (a veritable *Purāṇa*!) is buried at Sippara before the submergence of the earth, and found again after the subsidence of the flood, and then again made known to mankind.

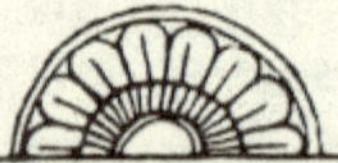

Does "Socrates Is Old" Imply That "Socrates Is"?

> The flower and fruit of speech is meaning.
>
> Yâska, *Nirukta* 1.19

> The flower and fruit of speech is truth.
>
> *Aitareya Āranyaka* 11.3.6

> A real art of speaking, says the Laconian, which does not lay hold of the truth does not and never will exist.
>
> Plato, *Phaedrus* 260E[1]

Bertrand Russell says that in such a sentence as "Socrates is old," "the tendency of language is to assume" that the word "is," connecting "Socrates" with an attributed quality, presumes in him a more or less persistent being; and argues that what we "ought" to say is that the series of events or phenomena to which we refer by the label "Socrates" has already continued for many years.[2] I agree that that is what we ought to mean; it is, in other words, what I do mean by such a statement. At the same

[Evidence in this essay suggests that it could not have been written before late 1944.—ED.]

[1] With these statements compare Wilbur Marshall Urban's: "In the ultimate metaphysical context truth and intelligibility are one," and "The metaphysical idiom is the only language that is really intelligible" (*Language and Reality*, London, 1939, pp. 716, 729, and *The Intelligible World*, New York, 1929, p. 471). Whatever has no meaning is not language, but only a noise.

As Philo says: "Spoken words contain the symbols of things apprehended by the understanding only" (*De Abrahamo* 119). Here the word "contain" is proper, because the real symbols are the concrete things to which the words refer by first intention. At the same time, it must always be remembered that the verbal symbols are a species rather than the genus of language, and that the connotations of things can be as well (or sometimes even better) communicated by visual symbols. Semantics, though now restricted to the study of the significations of words, is really the study of their iconography, and is in principle the same thing as the study of the intentions of visual symbols.

[2] Bertrand Russell, "Logical Atomism," in *Contemporary British Philosophy*, First Series, cited and discussed by Wilbur Marshall Urban in *Language and Reality*, pp. 285 ff.

time, I think we have a right to make use of such elliptical expressions for practical purposes, without incurring any charge of bad faith, even though we know that our full or real meaning will only be understood by a hearer who is not only aware that a real "being" of anything that can be named or tagged can be very seriously questioned, but is also aware that we do not, in fact, attribute a persistent "being" to any composite or variable, subject to change and decay. Such a hearer will recognize that I am not "lying," but only speaking "common current English" in order to avoid a language of such complication as would tend to paralyze all communication about everyday affairs. It is true that another hearer who assumes that "Socrates" must have a being may assume that I agree with him; but it is more likely that he does not consider the ultimate meaning at all. In such contexts all that is needed is a communication of the empirical or surface meaning; it may be supposed that the hearer is in search of "Socrates," the man, and only wants to know what sort of man to be on the look out for; it is only if he raises the question of the implications of my words that it will be needful for me to interpret them.

Before going further, I must ask, What can Bertrand Russell mean by his personification of language? It is, surely, only human beings that can have "tendencies to assume" anything whatever. If the proposition "Socrates is old" implies that "Socrates is," it must be the human assumption that has determined the form of the expression, and not the language itself that leads us to suppose that Socrates is simple. Language can never be misunderstood: it is human beings who can misunderstand one another, which happens when what is voiced is actually a mere noise, or seems to be a mere noise because the hearer hears but does not understand. No doubt it has been more or less generally assumed that I and others "are" persistent beings; and it is this *suppositio* that can alone explain a universe of discourse in which it is both meant and understood that Socrates is. At the same time, we must be very careful not to confuse this personalism[3] with the metaphysical animism that refers the acts of the so-called beings to the presence in (or to) them of a Power that moves them —*questi nei cor mortali è permotore*—the pervasive Power of another than "themselves," and apart from which they could no more "run" than any other engine without "power." In this universe of discourse, that "Socrates is old" will not imply that Socrates is, but much rather that "he" is not.

[3] By "personalism" (Philo's *οἴησις*, Indian *ahaṃkāra*), I mean an identification of the *persona* (mask), personality, or personification with the very Person of any agent: in other words, any confusion of the disguise with the actor.

Thus the meaning of the words "Socrates is old" will depend in part upon the universe of discourse in which they are spoken. To the philosopher in any traditional sense they will not mean that Socrates "is." For it is no new discovery of modern positivism that *I* "is merely a name for a series of atomic events"; this is a traditional doctrine, integral to the Philosophia Perennis, and of unknown antiquity. In Plato's words: "Although a man is called 'himself,' still he is never at all such that he retains the selfsame properties in 'himself'; he is forever becoming a new man . . . not only in his body but in his soul, nothing of his moral disposition (*τὰ ἤθη*), opinions, desires, pleasures, pains, or fears ever remaining the same in any individual (*ἑκάστῳ*) . . . nor are we ever the same selves as regards the content of our knowledge" (*Symposium* 207DE, 208A); and so, he says also, "it naturally belongs to whatever is compounded (*σύνθετος*) to suffer a corresponding dissolution," and it is only to a real and immutable being that it belongs to be and ever remain itself; so that things that are named, such as men, horse, or garments, although the naming seems to imply that they "are," are not really essences, and never the same; this applies to everything sensibly perceptible, and it is only the invisible and simple substances of which it can properly be said that they "are" (*Phaedo* 78C–79A). Similarly for Plutarch: "Nobody remains one person, nor is one person . . . and if he is not the same person, he has no permanent being, but changes his very nature as one personality in him succeeds to another. Our senses, through ignorance of reality (*τὸ ὄν*, what 'is'), falsely tell us that what appears to be, is" (*Moralia* 392DE, cf. Philo, *De cherubim* 113 ff.). And so "the fastidious soul can rest her understanding on nothing that has name. . . . We must have symbols (*gelīchnüsse*) . . . [but] our understanding of them is totally unlike the thing as it is in itself and as it is in God. . . . I have always before my mind this little word, *quasi*, 'like'; children at school call it an 'adjective' (*bīwort*)" (Eckhart, Pfeiffer ed., pp. 552, 331–332, 271). Language, in fact (and however "scientific"), is essentially conditioned by "the philosophy of 'As if' "; and this is only overlooked by fundamentalists and a majority of scientists, for whom all communication is only of literal facts, the "bread alone" of conversation.[4]

[4] Hence the supposed conflict of science and religion; cf. Coomaraswamy, "Gradation and Evolution: I," *Isis*, XXXV (1944), 15–16; and "Gradation and Evolution: II," *Isis*, XXXVIII (1947), 87–94.

The "bread alone" of discourse suffices for all "practical purposes" in our modern world of "impoverished reality," but is not sufficient for the expression or communication of the whole of human experience, of which only a part is recognized by "science."

In India it has been consistently maintained that our true Self can only be described by a negation of whatever qualities (relations) can be predicated of it. This *via remotionis* represented by the *neti neti*[5] of the Upaniṣads and by the axiom that birth and death are inseparable correlatives is strongly developed in Buddhism, where we meet with a repeated analysis of "personality" (*atta-bhāva*) in terms of its five psycho-physical components, to each of which, because of its impermanence (*anicca*), the words "that is not my Self" (*na me so attā*) apply (*Nikāyas, passim*), and it is emphasized that "whatever has been born, has come to be (*bhūtam*), and is compounded, is a naturally corruptible thing" (*paloka-dhamma*, D II.118). Whoever, then, understands things "as-become" (*yathā-bhūtam*), i.e., in the natural sequence of causes and effects, will not ask: What 'was' *I*, What 'am' *I*, or What shall *I* 'be'? (S II.26, 27). This is the familiar doctrine of *anattā*, that there is no "self" recognized in the constituents of personality, which are nothing but a chain of causally determined factors. At the same time, the Buddhist adept (Arhat), no less than the Wake aware that " 'I' am naught of an anyone anywhere" (A II.177), "neither 'brahman,' 'prince,' nor 'farmer,' nor anyone at all" (Sn 455), is allowed to say "I" for convenience—even as a Bertrand Russell might, even though he knows that "he" is nothing but a series of events that had a starting point in time and will come to an end; the Buddhist master may possibly be misunderstood by an untaught personalist, but there is little danger that he will be misunderstood within the community of discourse[6] to which he belongs, that of the monastic order, or even by instructed laymen.

Alike in Indian, Islamic, and Christian contexts we meet with the thought that God alone *is* and that He alone can properly say "I"; as Meister Eckhart puts it, "*Ego*, the word 'I,' is proper to none but God in his sameness" (Pfeiffer ed., p. 261), although, indeed, "we have no means for considering what God is, but rather how he is not" (St. Thomas

[5] I.e., to whatever can be predicated of the Self, as distinguished from its accidents, the answer is "No, no." *Neti* is "no" in quotes.

[6] Community, or universe of discourse: Skr. *saṃdhāya-saṃbhāṣā*, *sāhitya* or *saṃgha*, all etymologically cognate with syn-thesis. The nature of a universe of discourse is well illustrated by a gloss cited by Meister Eckhart (Evans ed., II, 65): "No one can understand or teach the Pauline writings unless he be of the same mind in which Paul spoke and wrote," or William Law's "Would you know the truths of Jacob Behmen you must stand where he stood." This has an important bearing on the problem of translation, for which a knowledge of grammar alone, however scholarly, is an inadequate qualification. Real translation is only possible when the translator has himself already experienced (*erlebt*) something of that which his author is communicating.

Aquinas, *Sum. Theol.* 1.3.1).[7] In other words, this is a point of view that has been almost universally entertained; and so it can be said that it is perhaps only to the modern and untaught "man in the street" that the proposition "Socrates is old" will really imply that "Socrates is." To anyone who has been taught, it will appear that the proposition, on the contrary, denies to "Socrates" a being; for he will be aware that whatever is now old, must have been young, and will be older, and that in our experience, exclusively of past and future, there is no "now" in which we would pin him down, to say that he *is* this or that. This man, Socrates, is nowhere to be found.

We have seen that there is an ambiguity of meaning in the predication, which may be differently understood on the one hand by a personalist and on the other hand by a positivist or any traditional philosopher.[8] So far I agree with Professor Urban; but I cannot agree with his analysis of the nature of the ambiguity.[9] He says that Socrates is not a persistent being in the practical, physiological sense, but is so in his moral and po-

[7] This is as much as to say that it is only the *how* of phenomena that can be described; their *what* eludes us. All language not merely indicative must be metaphysical or symbolic; or if not, must resort to negations. I agree with Professor Urban that whatever cannot be expressed literally is not therefore unreal, but simply neither true nor false; no relative terms, such as young or old, or good or evil, can communicate its essence; the relatives are only the names of its modalities, and not *its* name. God, as Nicholas of Cusa says, is hidden from us by these pairs of contraries; and these are the "Clashing Rocks" of the great tradition, between which none can pass without being docked of a characteristic appendage, to wit, his outer man; this contingent "self" being, in fact, his "sop to Cerberus."

[8] So far—viz. as to the mutability and consequent unreality of all that can be perceived, measured, and named—modern positivism and the traditional philosophy agree; the existence of "things" is what they do. But whereas for the positivist there are no realities whatever, the realist, who is also a nominalist with respect to phenomena, affirms the reality of which the things that can be named are the phenomena, and employs their names as adequate symbols without which no discourse about their reality would be possible. Positivism is a "nothing-morist" (*nāstika, natthika*) doctrine, and as such, as Professor Urban says, "would eliminate whole areas of human discourse as meaningless and unintelligible," adding that the taking up of such a stand may be "a symptom of a decaying culture and a prelude to a scientific barbarism and a cultural nihilism"; cf. René Guénon, *Le Règne de la quantité et les signes des temps*, Paris, 1944 [English tr., London 1953—ED.], and Iredell Jenkins, "The Postulate of an Impoverished Reality," *Journal of Philosophy*, XXXIX (1942).

[9] William Marshall Urban, *Language and Reality*, p. 286. Since I am at variance with him on this one point I should like to say that I am in full agreement with nearly everything else in his book, and notably with the conclusion that "the metaphysical idiom of the Great Tradition is the only language that is really intelligible."

litical aspect. But, assuredly, it is not only our physical, but also our moral and political nature that is changeable; is not the soul subject to persuasion? In the traditional philosophy at least, the soul is as much as the body a thing that becomes, according to the food that it assimilates (cf. *Phaedrus* 246c); τὰ ἤθη, as Plato says, are never constant in any individual, while the Buddhist holds that it is even more dangerous to identify the soul with our Self than the body. That "Socrates is old" cannot, in any superior universe of discourse, mean that Socrates "is," but, on the contrary, implicitly denies that he "is."

It will be only if we predicate in "Socrates" an authentically constant property, some "absolute," that "is" will imply a veritable essence. In this case, however, we shall have to ask, What do we *now* mean by "Socrates"? we cannot be referring to this man, So-and-so, subject to inveteration. If we say that "Socrates is infallible," then we *are* attributing a being to "Socrates," because infallibility is not a more-or-less attribute but, like "perfection," without degree, and therefore immutable. This will be even more obvious, perhaps, if we say that "Socrates is immortal"; for this is as much as to say "eternal, immortal, and selfsame" (ὡσαύτως, *Phaedo* 79D), and will necessarily mean that we are referring to a "Socrates" that has never been born. Both propositions are like Aristotle's "νοῦς is never wrong" (*De anima* III.10.433a).

The notion of an infallibility attributed to any individual properly offends us; the notion is irrational. For, indeed, as this man, Socrates, says himself: "It is the Truth that you cannot gainsay; Socrates you easily may" (*Symposium* 201C, cf. *Apology* 23A). When, then, is "Socrates" infallible? When it is not "himself" that speaks, but the "voice from the Acropolis" (*Timaeus* 70); the voice, that is to say, of Socrates' and everyman's immanent Daimon, "who cares for nothing but the truth" and is "a very near relative of mine, living in the same house with me" (*Hippias major* 288D, 304D); in other words, our soul's immortal and divine part (*Timaeus* 73D, 90A) and our real Self (*Laws* 959AB), Philo's "Soul of the soul" (*Heres* 55), St. Paul's πνεῦμα as distinguished from the ψυχή (Heb. 4:12), and the Indian "self's immortal Self and Leader" (MU VI.7). When, then, we say that Socrates is infallible, "Socrates" is no longer a label for the man that was once young, and is ever getting older, but a symbol standing for that man's very Self, the Self of all men, that "never becomes anyone." It is the same when we speak of the Pope's infallibility, viz. when he speaks oracularly (*ex cathedra*), and the reference is not to this or that Pope, Pius or Gregory, but to the Sanctus Spiritus, whose *cathedra* is in heaven and who teaches from within the heart (St. Augustine, *In ep. Joannis ad Parthos*). What can the Pope as a man *know* about the Truth? he can only believe; for "Omne verum, a quocumque dicatur, est a Spiritu Sancto" (St. Ambrose on 1 Cor. 12:3). "Pope," as being "infallible," is an office, not a name, and as such a symbol that stands for another than "this man." "Not *I*, the I that I am, knows these things, but God in me" (Jacob Boehme).

Now, if Bertrand Russell asserts that the Holy Ghost does not exist,[10] and that, therefore, my sentences are meaningless, I shall agree with the first part of his proposition, since God is properly called nothing, i.e., no thing amongst others; it will not, in fact, be overlooked that in propositions that do attribute a real being to their subject, the form of predication is typically negative, the negation implying an absence of any or all of those qualities of which there can be more or less. I shall not agree with his second part, but only say that if my sentences are meaningless to him, that is because his universe of discourse is not identical with mine; his is a universe of discourse only about things that are never the same.[11] It may be worthwhile to observe here that a Hindu, even in the vernacular, does not say that "I am cold," but that "Cold adheres to me" (*haṃ ko ṭhaṇḍā lagtā*); the *suppositio* being that I, my Self, remain to be discovered by a process of remotion from all those accidents by which my being is veiled and from which I must es-cape if I would be authentically what I *am*.

[10] Existence is necessarily in terms of space and time, from which the language of *meta*-physical discourse, concerned with the nature of reality in an unextended here and now, as necessarily abstracts. Therefore, it constantly resorts to paradoxes or negations such as "motion without locomotion." But merely because of this enigmatic phraseology we must not overlook (unless we are willing to throw away "the baby with the bath") that, as Professor Urban says (p. 708), "these idioms are an expression of authentic experiences which can be communicated, and which are confirmed or authenticated precisely in these processes of communication." When, for example, we say that "my mind was elsewhere," our reference is actually to a motion without locomotion and to a possible omnipresence. On the other hand, if on looking at an excellent portrait we say "that's me," we are literally talking nonsense, just as we are if we say that "Socrates *is* old." Not even our everyday language is literally intelligible; even the "language" of mathematics cannot be explained in terms of experience, because it deals with only a fraction of human experience, of which the most valuable part is immeasurable. The language of metaphysics applies to the whole of reality; its universals are not ex- but in-clusive.

[11] "Things that are never the same" is, of course, a tautology. Such is the nature of "things."

To sum up, it appears that a real ambiguity lies in the verb to "be" which, as an English word, can mean either to "become" or to "be";[12] which of these meanings is to be understood in a given proposition depending on the nature of the quality or property attributed to the subject of the proposition; a variable quality or property implies a variable subject, and conversely. In German one could better distinguish *ist geworden alt* from *ist unfehlbar*, in Greek *πρέσβυς ἐγένετο* from *ἐστίν ἀθανατός*, or in Sanskrit *jīrṇo babhūva* from *amṛto'sti*; the first terms implying processes, and the latter simple aspects of being. That modern English has not (except in the rare expression, "Woe worth") preserved the Anglo-Saxon *weorthan* (G. *werden*, Lat. *vertere*, Skr. *vṛt*) represents a real loss of expressive power. In many other cases, in the "common current English" of today, words or phrases (or in the same way visual or enacted symbols)[13] have lost their primary intentions and retain only their indicative values.[14] To the extent that we forget that "illustrate" and

[12] See, on this subject, the discussion by C.A.F. Rhys Davids, *To Become or Not to Become* (London, 1937), rightly dedicated to "fellow-translators." Note especially the contrast presented in A II.37–39 where, in reply to questions, the Buddha answers: "No, I shall not *become* a Deva, Gandharva, or Yakṣa," and concludes with "I *am* Buddha." This "am" corresponds to the "That art thou" of the Upaniṣads, where it is a question of the absolute *being* of the immanent and immortal Self, and the verb to "be" is required, because it would be nonsense to imply that what is mortal could *become* immortal. "Becoming" can only have to do with the *process* of remembering and realizing what we are or who we are (*Γνῶθι σεαυτόν*), not with this what itself. Rhys David's book is of the highest value in its bearing on the problems of translation, but it is vitiated throughout by her own phobia of the notion of an absolute *being*, to which she would prefer an endless *progress*.

[13] What were originally rites, for example, survive only as ceremonies, i.e., merely in their utilitarian or decorative aspects. This applies to all the arts, of which the techniques themselves, e.g., of sculpture or weaving, are naturally symbolic. In sculpture, for example, one either imposes a form upon the clay (*via affirmativa*) or discovers a form in the wood or stone (the more that one removes, the nearer one comes to the formless source in which the forms inhere), and this is the metaphysic of the impropriety of modeling in clay a form that is to be copied, not in metal, but in stone. In weaving, the warp threads are the "rays" of the Intelligible Sun (in many primitive looms they still proceed from a single point), and the woof is the Primary Matter of the cosmic "tissue." When these things have been altogether forgotten, in a world of "impoverished reality," then the work, which originally served the needs of body and soul together, becomes either a mechanical task or a pastime.

[14] When the "virtue" has gone out of any word, this is not merely a semantic fact, but an indication that a similar virtue has gone out of the activity to which the word directly refers. In metaphysical discourse it is very often necessary to use current words in their archaic or obsolete senses, i.e., more exactly than in the shop-worn speech of commerce or the emotive speech of politics. "Every term that

"argument" imply to "throw light upon" and to "clarify," or that *métier* is etymologically *ministerium*,[15] or that the original meaning of such words as "nature" (originally of things, but now denoting an aggregate of the things themselves), "art" (now used for "works of art"), or "inspiration" (now very commonly used to mean "external stimulant") has been actually materialized, these expressions have become clichés or superstitions for us, who use them only for indicative purposes.[16] In fact, as I have said elsewhere, "if we exclude from our theological and metaphysical thinking all those symbols, images, and theories that have come down to us from the Stone Age, our means of communication would be almost wholly limited to the field of empirical observation and the statistical predictions (laws of science) that are based on these observations; the world would have lost its meaning."[17] The original symbols, as a well known archaeologist has said, "were anchored in the highest, not the lowest"; there subsisted in them "a polar balance of physical and

---

becomes an empty slogan as the result of fashion or repetition is born at some time from a definite concept, and its significance must be interpreted from that point of view" (Paul Kristeller, *The Philosophy of Marsilio Ficino*, New York, 1943, p. 286); and what is true of the verbal is equally true of visual symbols, which always had their reasons long before they became mere "art forms."

[15] It is partly because we no longer realize (verify) that a vocation, or trade (= *way* of life, Skr. *ācārya*) is properly a ministry (in both the political and sacerdotal senses of the word) that we cannot "understand" a caste system, i.e., cannot imagine what a social order could be like in which the notions of honor and hereditary function coincide. Any such loss of a capacity to understand represents a constriction of our "world"; and, in fact, whatever we cannot understand we try to eliminate from the world, usually by "giving the dog a bad name." Our way of saying "no" to anything is, logically enough, to call it naught-y. In this word "naughty" (Skr. *asat*, in this sense) the *suppositio* is that *ens et bonum convertuntur*; and, similarly, in the case of German *Unthat* (Skr. *akṛtam*, in this sense), literally "undeed," and hence "sin," the sinner himself being "not in act," and as such, as St. Thomas Aquinas says, really non-existent. If we ignore the *suppositio*, the words themselves have little more than an exclamatory value and hardly any real meaning.

[16] In the same way phrases such as "our better self," "be yourself," "came to himself" and "self-government" and "self-control" (i.e., of self by Self, *le moi* by *le soi*) are not understood (*erlebt*) if we overlook their *suppositio*, equally Platonic, Scholastic, Islamic, Indian, and Chinese, that *Duo sunt in homine*. It is precisely when we have not really understood the implications of such a term as "self-government" that we are most liable to make a fetish of it. It has often been asserted by rationalists that religion has been "the opium of the people"; however that may be, it is quite certain that the modern shibboleths of "race," "equality," "democracy," and notably, "progress," are the people's drugs, and that they are deliberately administered as such by politicians and advertisers.

[17] *Speculum*, XIX (1944), 123.

metaphysical" (denotation and implication, use and meaning), but they have been "more and more emptied on their way down to us."[18]

Moreover, to the extent that we have "overspecialized," and do not understand one another, we are "idiots"—etymologically "peculiar individuals," and *so* peculiar as to be excluded from whole continents of the normally human universe of discourse. Scientist and theologian, maker and consumer, philosopher and folk no longer understand one another; and we talk of the "mysterious East" in a way that would have been impossible in the Middle Ages. It sometimes seems that the more our means of communication are improved and multiplied, the less are we really able to understand one another, and that the more we know of less and less, the more impossible it becomes to understand our own past. It would be difficult to imagine a culture more provincial than is that of the average educated man of today.[19]

So our discussion leads us back to the "miracle of language."[20] The very facts that we can communicate with one another, that we can translate from another, even an ancient, language into our own, and that the human and noninstinctive universe of discourse is so much more really universal than is often supposed, call for an explanation.[21] Communication implies a communicator and a communicant; if the latter under-

[18] Walter Andrae, *Die ionische Säule: Bauform oder Symbol* (Berlin, 1933), p. 65 [cf. review of this book in Vol. I of this edition—ED.].

[19] There was a time when all civilizations were so much alike that a traveller could feel at home wherever he went; Plato was better understood by Philo and Plotinus, Marsilio Ficino, and Peter Sterry than he can be by any modern nominalist, however learned; and "the greater the ignorance of modern times, the deeper grows the darkness of the Middle Ages." Archaeological discoveries and anthropological investigations have done but little to widen our horizons, mainly because our eyes have been blinded to their meaning by our own belief in "progress" (i.e., by the application of evolutionary concepts to culture) and by the pathetic fallacy (which attributes to primitive man our own aestheticism).

[20] An expression used by Professor Urban. Cf. also R. A. Wilson, *The Birth of Language* (London, 1937); and E. Dacqué, *Das verlorene Paradies* (Munich, 1938).

[21] The different human cultures being, as Alfred Jeremias said, the dialects of one and the same spiritual language. Its idioms are recognizable everywhere, alike in folklore and in the classical literatures. Without knowledge of these idioms, a history of literature is impossible; without it we cannot distinguish between an individual poet's inventions and universal formulae, between *le symbolisme qui cherche* and *le symbolisme qui sait.* In words we must "distinguish at least the subjective symbol of psychological association from the objective symbol of precise intellectual meaning. The latter implies some knowledge of the doctrine of analogy" (Walter Shewring in *Weekly Review*, August 17, 1944), which Philo calls "the laws of allegory." Without a knowledge of the meaning of verbal or visual symbols a real history of ideas is inconceivable.

stands the former, although in his own way, this implies the existence of a something in common, and *a priori* with respect to the particular communication. "I love you" will be meaningless if we have *no* prior conception of what it might be "to be loved"; in other words, experience (*Erlebnis*, Skr. *anubhava*) must have preceded recognition. It is true that the content of "I love you" may range from the lowest levels of desire to the highest of identity; but language is capable of conveying also shades of meaning, and, for example, when Rūmī says: "What is love? Thou shalt know when thou becomest me," it is obvious that he is not speaking of love as desire.

But the difficulty of understanding one another, or of understanding our own past, is greater now than it has ever been; our "science" knows of "love" only as a chemical reaction, and the "quest of immortality, the effort of men and women to master matter by spirit, is the chief intellectual preoccupation of the men and women *outside* the sphere of 'civilization' today."[22] Our universe of discourse has long been undergoing a process of contraction, mainly by an elimination of values from the symbols that once implied both facts and values; and it is precisely this elimination of values from our minds that prevents us from understanding the normal cultures in which the notion of value predominates. We can only communicate with what remains of traditional civilizations on the level of a *lowest* common denominator, for which the vocabulary of "basic" English will probably suffice. There is little or nothing in a modern American education to qualify a man for converse with a Tibetan or Indian peasant—not to mention a scholar; all we *can* do together is "eat, drink, and be merry."

It is, however, the fact that a mutual understanding is *possible*, the fact that even the most despatialized and detemporalized experiences, insofar as they can be referred to by adequate symbols in any language, can also be referred to in any other, the fact that there can never be laid a valid claim to any property in ideas, that remains to be explained. The excesses of evolutionism are past; the philologist no longer maintains that a non-instinctive language capable of expressing ideas can have been developed from the cries of animals; there is an art of speaking, and the crying of babies and the gambolling of lambs is not an art, but instinctive.

What is the "mutuality of minds," or the "common good," that makes

[22] K. N. Chadwick, *Poetry and Prophecy* (Cambridge, 1942), p. 94 (italics mine). With the general thesis of this book, cf. Paul Radin, *Primitive Man as Philosopher* (New York, 1927).

their "contact" possible? Some kind of transcendental, metempirical explanation of the "common denominator" is inevitable. If a common experience can be shared by two "individual" minds, if both can "recognize" the same object or idea, this can only mean that the minds in question, say those of a Chinese and an American, are not so individually and empirically distinct from one another as might have been inferred from the fact of the spatial distinction of the Chinese and American bodies, "in which" we think of them as functioning. If a mutual understanding has been only partial, we can speak of a like-mindedness; but to the extent that a complete understanding subsists, the notion of a kind of unanimity, or *one*-mindedness, is forced upon us. In more than one sense, mind transcends both space and time. Another way of putting this would be to say that truth is universal, and that only misunderstandings of truths, or what amounts to the same, only untruths, are peculiar to individuals.

The word "denominator" (in the expression "common denominator") is itself significant in this connection; for naming implies understanding, and the primary meaning of the word "denominator" is that of a "giver of names." To speak of the "common denominator" is, then, as much as to say that it is "Adam," the Man in us, and not this man So-and-so, that recognizes and understands. In the Old Testament story we are told that Adam named the animals; and it is obvious that the latter had not then, and have not since, named themselves. The giving of names endows the factors of the passing show with a permanent existence in our mental world; and our total experience is therefore one of "name *and* appearance" (Skr. *nāma-rūpa*), not alone of sensation. The fact that names have a permanent meaning enables us to understand not only our contemporaries, but also those of our ancestors, whose words have been transmitted, whether orally or in writing.[23] It is because our speech,

[23] As Floryan Znaniecki has remarked, "the golden period of Greek philosophy is thus characterized with respect to this problem by an assumption of the community of the essential, conceptual part of contents and the community of the rational perfect meanings corresponding to it and determined by it, while the varying individual meanings of objects were assumed to be determined by the individually differentiated, unessential, sensual part of contents" (*Cultural Reality*, Chicago, 1919, p. 88). This is as much as to say that meanings are objective and intrinsic for those who know, but subjective and arbitrary for those "independent" thinkers who construct their own philosophies. Any misuse of words or visual symbols reflects an ignorance of their proper meanings and is useless for purposes of communication. And so, as Plato asks: Why consider the inferior philosophers? That words have a permanent meaning, however evanescent their enunciation, or the

as the *Ṛg Veda* says, retains the signatures (*lakṣmīḥ*) of the contemplative "denominators" who first wedded speech to mind (*manasā vācam akrata*, RV x.71.2), without which speech is a mere babbling (ŚB iii.2.4.11). So, as Jacob Boehme says, it is the Spirit that manifests and reveals itself in the sound with the voice; to hear and to understand are two different things; we only understand one another when signatures and images are entertained in common; and "by this we know that all human properties proceed from One; that they have only one root and mother; otherwise one man could not understand another in the sound . . . the inward manifests itself in the sound of the word, for that is the mind's natural knowledge of itself" (*Signatura rerum* i.1–6).

In speaking, then, of a common denominator as the basis of all mutual understanding and possibility of argument or clarification, we are referring not to a lowest but to a *highest* common denominator; and, in fact, not to "ourselves" but to our common Self, the Self of all beings, the omniscient fount of memory (MU vi.7, CU vii.26.1), and only seer, hearer, thinker, speaker, and knower in us (BU iii.7.23 and 8.11). The "common denominator" is that one *qui intus corda docet* and *ex quo omne verum, a quocumque dicatur* proceeds; a merely family likeness of minds, presumed to be as distinct from one another as our bodies are, does not suffice for unanimity. The possibility of mutual understanding presupposes a common experience, and more than any single mind can ever have experienced in a single lifetime. In other words, the fact of linguistic communication, the possibility of what we call "learning," presupposes the Platonic and Indian concept of Recollection,[24] that there is a better part of us that knows already whatever we seem to learn, but of which we are in reality only reminded by the spoken word.

Common universes of discourse will correspond to those areas of this latent knowledge of which the parties involved are already conscious, and under these circumstances discourse can be readily conducted even when the language employed is very technical or reduced to almost algebraic terms; theologian and theologian, or physicist and physicist, for example,

material on which they are recorded, underlies the Indian, Islamic, and Christian doctrine of the "eternity of Scripture," in which doctrine the date of promulgation is, of course, to be distinguished from the timelessness of the embodied meaning. It is a form of the doctrine of immutable ideas.

[24] See my "Recollection, Indian and Platonic," and "On the One and Only Transmigrant" [in this volume—ED.].

can understand each other, though the layman overhearing may not have understood a word that was said, and may go so far as to call the, to him, "foreign" language a gibberish. In other cases, typically that of master and student, the purpose is to *create* a common universe of discourse by *reminding* the pupil of an area of knowledge that he possesses only potentially and can only with effort, and the help of some external "midwifery" (as Socrates used to put it), bring to life. It would be theoretically possible for all men to understand one another perfectly, and to be able to make themselves understood by anyone; actually, however, I think I have made it clear that it is, for me, only in the most superficial sense that individuals can be said to understand one another; it is an almost trite observation to remark that the more individual men are, the less they have in common. When, then, we do understand (or love) one another, it is not so much these men, you and I, distinguished by their "accidents," that understand (or love) one another as it is the Man in us that understands (and loves) himself.

Professor Urban (p. 84) maintains that "the entire marvel of intelligible communication can be *understood* only on the basis of transcendental presuppositions." Explicitly, however, he does not mean by this to claim for the Philosophia Perennis the status of a divine revelation; this traditional philosophy and the preeminently intelligible language in which it is expressed, notwithstanding that "there is that in it which is timeless and, in principle, irrefutable," he calls a product of human thought (p. 728).

There is not so much divergence here as might appear; so much depends upon what we mean by "human" and what by "thought." I think he would agree that it is not the sensitive outer man who hears the sounds, but our intellectual or spiritual Inner Man that understands; and only might not agree that this Inner Man is the Person of an immanent deity whose throne is in heaven. I need not quarrel with him if he replies that the kingdom of heaven is within you, but should only add, within *and* without.

What is important for the student of the history of language and the interpreter of literature is his proposition that the implications of language are metaphysical; which will mean that the forms of words, like the iconography of the other traditional arts, have not been arbitrarily determined, but rather "well-found" than "well-made." If this is true at all, it must have been true from the beginning.

We can, then, ask: By which men, amongst the others of a primitive community learning to speak intelligibly, were the adequate symbols "found"? The *Ṛg Veda* (x.71.1, cf. AV vii.1.1), comparing them to men who winnow corn, calls them "contemplatives" (*dhīrāḥ*, sometimes more loosely rendered by "wisemen"). In other words, the mantic "culture heroes" or "medicine men," by whom the arts were given to men in general, "saw" their useful inventions, and the meanings of these inventions, at one and the same time. One can no more imagine that men invented wheels and then attributed meanings to them than that they invented rituals and afterwards deduced from them the myths of which the rituals are an enactment. That is only to say that in any creative art, content (form, idea) and shape, intuition and expression, theory and practice are inseparable; and that if it is otherwise in any mere labor, such as that of a galley slave or factory hand, this only means that the theory has been forgotten by the laborer. And just as an industry without art, such as is known only to "civilized" men, is brutality, so are the modern materializations of word meanings and the reduction of visual symbols (of which the references were originally at the same time physical and metaphysical) to the level of art forms to be appreciated only as aesthetic and otherwise meaningless surfaces, symptomatic of a deviation from that human nature of which the intelligible languages are a natural function. It is not without good reason that both Plato and Mencius asserted that the misuse of words is the outward sign of a sickness of the soul.

If, indeed, the implications of language are metaphysical, the traces of this should appear in language itself. There are, in fact, many languages, notably those of a hieratic quality, such as Greek or Sanskrit, that seem to have been made expressly with a view to the clear expression of metaphysical ideas; nor can even the terms of "common current English" be properly understood apart from their metaphysical presuppositions, our word "naught-y" and Skr. *asat* in this sense, for example, implying the assumption, ***ens et bonum convertuntur***. It is not at all so sure that primitive man, the creator of language, did not live more by his ideas than by facts; at any rate, it was by an application of his myth to the facts that he expected to "control" them, and there can be no doubt that he thought of names as evocations of the things named. An important example of the metaphysical bias inherent in language itself can be cited in the fact that in many of the oldest vocabularies (and with survivals in modern languages, where, however, the tendency is to give an exclusively good or bad meaning to such words as "reward," which are properly neutral) a single root so often embodies opposite meanings; for example, in Egyptian the sign "strong-weak" must be qualified by determinants if we are to know which is meant, while in Sanskrit the same word can mean either zero or plenum; one infers that the movement of primitive logic is not abstractive from an observed multiplicity but deductive from an axiomatic unity.[25]

Again, modern scientific and proletarian dialects tend to restrict the meanings of words to their merely denotative powers, while the more expressive languages (which we only call more picturesque) can employ the most ordinary terms with extraordinary significance; a large part of the technical language of theology, for example, is supported by the arts. It is only, in fact, when the polar balance of physical and metaphysical is preserved in a language that the whole man, who does not live by "bread alone," can communicate more than a fraction of his experience. We can still say that a girl "angled for" a man and "hooks" him, but this is for us only a rather cynical metaphor. We have forgotten that every technique had once also a spiritual significance; as we can observe if we consider in this case Meister Eckhart's "for love is like unto the fisherman's hook," and realize that he is using here, not a mere simile but the idiom of a tradition that can be recognized as well in Marsilio Ficino, in the Gospels ("fishers of men," Matt. 4:19, Mark 1:17, Luke 5:10), and in the words of Hāfiz: "Fishlike in the sea behold me swimming, till He with His hook my rescue maketh." This will be all the more apparent if we reflect that "swimming in the sea" has also its technical significance, and that in this language the fisherman's "line" stands for the "thread-spirit" or chain on which all things are strung, and by which the solar Deity "draws" all things unto himself, a concept that can be

[25] On the subject of verbal roots embracing contrary meanings, see Carl Abel, *Über den Gegensinn der Urworte* (Leipzig, 1884) (also in his *Sprachwissenschaftlichen Abhandlungen*, Leipzig, 1885); B. Heimann, "Deutung und Bedeutung indischer Terminologie," *XIX Congr. Internaz. di Orientalisti*; "Plurality, Polarity and Unity in Hindu Thought," BSOS, IX, 1015–1021; and "The Polarity of the Indefinite," JISOA, V (1937), 91–96; M. Fowler, "Polarity in the Rig-veda," *Review of Religion*, VII (1943), 115–123. As St. Thomas Aquinas says, "everything composed of contraries is necessarily corruptible," but "the principles of contraries are not themselves contrary," "our knowledge of contraries is a single knowledge," and "therefore our intellectual Self must be incorruptible" (*Sum. Theol.* 1.14.8, 1.75.6, and 1.80.1). Hence the concept that the Wall of Paradise is made of contraries (Nicholas of Cusa, *De visione Dei* IX), that of a liberation from the pairs of opposites (*Bhagavad Gītā*), and the worldwide symbols (verbal and visual) of the Symplegades, or Jaws of Death, between which the traveller to the world of immortality must pass.

traced in European literature (not to mention Babylonian, Islamic, Indian, and Chinese) from Homer to Blake.[26] In the same way, the Christian can speak of the soul as following the "spoor" of her quarry, Christ, and in so saying is employing the hunting idiom that Plato uses when he speaks of being "on the tracks of truth" and that underlies the Sanskrit *mārga*, "Way" (in the highest sense), from *mṛg*, to "track." One other illustration: our words "beam" (of wood, German *Baum*, tree) and "beam" (shaft of light) are etymologically identical, while Pali *rukkha*, tree, is a derivative of *ruc*, to shine, and related to *lux*, light, as is *lux* itself to *lucus*, grove; and it will be seen that here are implications that reappear in the concept of a *Branstock*, *Rubus Igneus* and Burning Bush. Linguistic studies have often been employed for ethnographical purposes; it is, for example, inferred from existing vocabularies that a people who spoke a proto-Indo-Aryan language must have lived where the birch grows. But through an investigation of the iconographies of words we can go much further than this to discover their fullest and, generally speaking, oldest content; for these words and phrases are a key not alone to the material culture but to the vision or thinking of the people who invented them. We must also remember that words themselves are only the images of things and acts, and that it is the latter that are the real bearers of the connotations that the words communicate; so that when we can no longer trace the words "tree of life" in a preliterate culture, but meet in prehistoric art, or "superstanding" in a folk art, only with visual representations, these are fully as valid as the written word would have been, and we can properly translate the visual symbol into "our own words." As Edmund Pottier says, "à l'origine toute représentation graphique répond à une pensée concrète et précise: c'est véritablement une écriture," and we ought never to forget that the history of literature begins long before letters.

Our point is, then, that we are denying in advance all real possibility of an understanding of the "history of literature" if we fail to read back into superstanding words and phrases (that we are disposed to think of as the fancies or inventions of individual poets but are really so much more than "one man deep") their full and original meanings. As I see it, our teaching of literary history is a farce because we do not know what it is "all about" and treat the universal figures of thought as if they were only invented figures of speech; so that if precise English is for the great

[26] Most of the references will be found in Coomaraswamy, "The Iconography of Dürer's 'Knots' and Leonardo's 'Concatenation,'" 1944.

majority of our "literate" proletariat a dead language, it may be as much because of as in spite of their "literacy." In the present connection, I say that nothing but a familiarity with the supremely intelligible language of the traditional philosophy, of which the various cultures are the dialects, will make it clear that in such sentences as have been discussed above, the meaning of the copulative "is" will depend entirely on *what* it is that is predicated of the subject: there is one Socrates that ages, and another Self of Socrates that is immortal, one that becomes and another that is. Paraphrasing Sophocles (*Oedipus Tyrannos* 870), "A God in him is great, *he* does not age." "As he is in himself," Socrates is a phenomenon. "As he is in God," he is an essence. Within these two sentences, "is" has different meanings: in the first case that of "becoming," in the second that of "being."

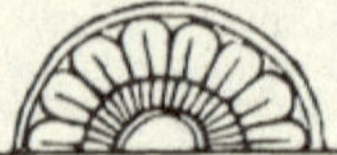

The Meaning of Death

Ez ist nieman gotes rîche wan der ze grunde tôt ist.
Meister Eckhart (Pfeiffer ed., p. 600)

The meaning of death is inseparably bound up with the meaning of life. Our animal experience is only of today, but our reason takes account also of tomorrow; hence, insofar as our life is intellectual, and not merely sensational, we are inevitably interested in the question, What becomes of "us" on the morrow of death. That is, eidently, a question that can only be answered in terms of what or who "we" are now, mortal or immortal: a question of the validity that we attach on the one hand to our conviction of being "this man, So-and-so" and on the other to our conviction of being unconditionally.

The whole tradition of the Philosophia Perennis, Eastern and Western, ancient and modern, makes a clear distinction of existence from essence, becoming from being. The existence of this man So-and-so, who speaks of himself as "I," is a succession of instants of consciousness, of which no two are the same; in other words, this man is never the same man from one moment to the next. We know only past and future, never a now, and so there is never any moment with reference to which we can say of our self, or of any other presentation, that it "is"; as soon as we ask what it is, it has "become" something else; and it is only because the changes that take place in any brief period are usually small that we mistake the incessant process for an actual being.

This holds good as much of the soul as of the body. Our consciousness is a stream, everything flows, and "you can never dip your feet twice in the same waters." Moreover, considered individually, every stream of consciousness has had a beginning, and must therefore have an end. Even

[Features of the manuscript and the absence of footnotes indicate that this essay, composed in the late 1930s or 1940s, was originally either a lecture or a formal letter intended for publication.—ED.]

if we assume that an individual continuity of consciousness can survive the dissolution of the body (as would not be inconceivable if we suppose the existence of a variety of substantial supports not all so gross as, but rather more subtle than, the "matter" that our senses normally report), it is evident that such a "survival of personality," still involving a duration, affords no proof that such an existence must last forever. The universe, however many different "worlds" (i.e., loci of compossibles) it may be thought of as embracing, cannot be thought of apart from time; we cannot, for instance, ask What was God doing before he created the world? or What will he be doing when it comes to an end? because the world and time are concomitant and cannot be thought of apart. If we suppose that the universe has had a beginning, we also suppose that it will come to an end when time and space are no more; and that will mean that whatever exists in time and space must come to an end sooner or later. We emphasize this point because it is important to realize that the spiritualist "proofs" of the survival of personality, even if we should grant their validity, are not proofs of immortality, but only of a prolongation of personal existence. To presume a survival of personality is only to postpone the problem of the meaning of death.

The whole tradition of which I am speaking assumes, then, and in this respect agrees with the "materialist's" or "nothing-morist's" opinion, that for this man So-and-so, having such and such a name, appearance, and qualities, there is no possibility of an immortality; his existence under any conditions is an ever-changing one, and "all change is a dying." It is held, alike on grounds of authority and reason, that "this man" is mortal, and that there is "no consciousness after death." Whatever has been born must die, whatever is composite must break down, and it would be idle to grieve over what is inherent in the very nature of things.

But the matter does not end here. It is true that nothing by nature mortal can become immortal, however long or short a time it may endure. The tradition, however, insists that we should "know our self," what and Who we are. In confusing our intuition-of-being with our consciousness-of-being-So-and-so, we may have forgotten ourselves. The case is, in fact, one of amnesia and mistaken identity. Let us recall that a "person" is primarily a mask and assumed disguise, that "all the world's a stage," and that it may have been a rather childish delusion to have assumed that the *dramatis personae* were the "very persons" of the actors themselves. From the point of view of our tradition, the Cartesian *cogito ergo sum* is an absolute *non sequitur* and argument in a circle. For I cannot say *cogito* truly, but only *cogitatur*. "I" neither think nor see, but there is Another who alone sees, hears, thinks in me and acts through me; an Essence, Fire, Spirit, or Life that is no more or less "mine" than "yours," but that never itself becomes anyone; a principle that informs and enlivens one body after another, and than which there is no other that transmigrates from one body to another, one that is never born and never dies, though president at every birth and death ("not a sparrow falls to the ground . . ."). This is a Life that is lived *dove s'appunta ogni ubi ed ogni quando*, a place without dimensions, and a now without duration, of which empirical experience is impossible, and that can only be known im-mediately. This Life is the "Ghost" that we "give up" when this man dies and the spirit returns to its source and the dust to the dust.

Our whole tradition everywhere affirms that "there are two in us"; the Platonic mortal and immortal "souls," Hebrew and Islamic *nefesh* (*nafs*) and *ruaḥ* (*ruḥ*), Philo's "soul" and "Soul of the soul," Egyptian Pharaoh and his Ka, Chinese Outer and Inner Sage, Christian Outer and Inner Man, Psyche and Pneuma, and Vedantic "self" (*ātman*) and "self's Immortal Self" (*asya amṛta ātman, antaḥ puruṣa*)—one the soul, self, or life that Christ requires of us to "hate" and "deny," if we would follow him, and that other soul or self that can be saved. On the one hand we are commanded, "Know thy self," and on the other told, "That (self's Immortal Self) art thou." The question then arises, In whom, when I go hence, shall I be going forth? In my self, or its Immortal Self?

On the answer to this question depends the answer to the question, What happens to man after death? It is evident, however, from what has been said, that this is an ambiguous question. With reference to whom is it asked, this man or the Man? In the case of this man, we can only answer by asking, What is there of him that could survive otherwise than as an inheritance to his descendants? and in the case of the Immortal, only by asking, What is there of him to die? If in this life—and "once out of time, your chance is gone"—we have remembered our Self, then "That art thou," but if not, then "great is the destruction."

If we have known that Man, we can say with St. Paul, "I live, yet not I, but Christ in me." Whoever can say that, or its equivalent in any other dialect *der einen Geistessprache*, is what is called in India a *jīvan-mukta*, a "free man here and now." This man, Paul, announced his own death; the words "Behold a dead man walking" might have been said of him. What of him remained to survive when the body ceased to breathe, but

Christ?—that Christ who said, "No man hath ascended into heaven save he which came down from heaven, even the Son of Man, which is in heaven"!

"The kingdom of God is for none but the thoroughly dead" (Meister Eckhart, Evans ed., I, 419). So, in the same Master's words, "the soul must put itself to death." For what else does it mean to "hate" and "deny" ourselves? Is it not true that "*all* Scripture cries aloud for freedom from self"?

Come l'uomo s'eterna? The traditional answer can be given in the words of Jalālu'd-Dīn Rūmī and Angelus Silesius: "Die before you die." Only the dead can know what it means to be dead.

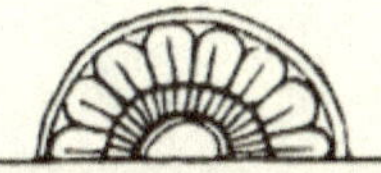

THE SEVENTIETH BIRTHDAY ADDRESS

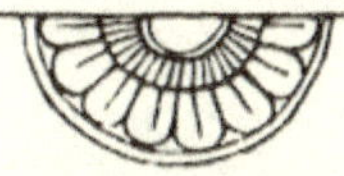

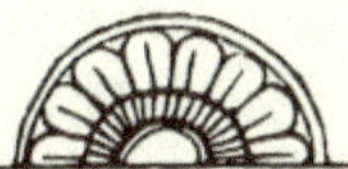

The Seventieth Birthday Address

I am more than honored—somewhat, indeed, overcome—by your kindness in being here tonight, by the messages that have been read, and by the presentation of Mr. Bharatha Iyer's *Festschrift*.[1] I should like to recall the names of four men who might have been present had they been living: Dr. Denman W. Ross, Dr. John Lodge, Dr. Lucien Scherman, and Professor James Woods, to all of whom I am indebted. The formation of the Indian collections in the Museum of Fine Arts was almost wholly due to the initiative of Dr. Denman Ross; Dr. Lodge, who wrote little, will be remembered for his work in Boston and Washington, and also perhaps for his aphorism, "From the Stone Age until now, *quelle dégringolade*"; I still hope to complete a work on reincarnation with which Dr. Scherman charged me not long before his death; and Professor Woods was one of those teachers who can never be replaced.

More than half of my active life has been spent in Boston. I want to express my gratitude in the first place to the directors and trustees of the Museum of Fine Arts, who have always left me entirely free to carry on research not only in the field of Indian art but, at the same time, in the wider field of the whole traditional theory of art and of the relation of man to his work, and in the fields of comparative religion and metaphysics to which the problems of iconography are a natural introduction. I am grateful also to the American Oriental Society, whose editors, however much they differed from me "by temperament and training," as Professor Norman Brown once said, have always felt that I had a "right to be heard," and have allowed me to be heard. And all this despite the fact that such studies as I have made necessarily led me back to an enunciation of relatively unpopular sociological doctrines. For, as a student of human manu-

[This address was published in the *Journal of the Indian Society of Oriental Art*, XV (1947).—ED.]

[1] [AKC saw only galley proofs of the volume edited by K. Bharatha Iyer, which was soon after published under the title *Art and Thought: A Volume in Honour of the Late Dr. Ananda K. Coomaraswamy* (London, 1947).—ED.]

factures, aware that all making is *per artem*, I could not but see that, as Ruskin said, "Industry without art is brutality," and that men can never be really happy unless they bear an individual responsibility not only for what they do but for the kind and the quality of whatever they make. I could not fail to see that such happiness is forever denied to the majority under the conditions of making that are imposed upon them by what is euphemistically called "free enterprise," that is to say, under the condition of production for profit rather than for use; and no less denied in those totalitarian forms of society in which the folk is just as much as in a capitalistic regime reduced to the level of a proletariat. Looking at the works of art that are considered worthy of preservation in our museums, and that were once the common objects of the market place, I could not but realize that a society can only be considered truly civilized when it is possible for every man to earn his living by the very work he would rather be doing than anything else in the world—a condition that has only been attained in social orders integrated on the basis of vocation, *svadharma*.

At the same time, I should like to emphasize that I have never built up a philosophy of my own or wished to establish a new school of thought. Perhaps the greatest thing I have learned is never to think for myself; I fully agree with André Gide that "toutes choses sont dites déjà," and what I have sought is to understand what has been said, while taking no account of the "inferior philosophers." Holding with Heracleitus that the Word is common to all, and that Wisdom is to know the Will whereby all things are steered, I am convinced with Jeremias that the human cultures in all their apparent diversity are but the dialects of one and the same language of the spirit, that there is a "common universe of discourse" transcending the differences of tongues.

This is my seventieth birthday, and my opportunity to say farewell. For this is our plan, mine and my wife's, to retire and return to India next year; thinking of this as an *astaṃ gamana*, "going home." . . .[2] We mean to remain in India, now a free country, for the rest of our lives.

I have not remained untouched by the religious philosophies I have studied and to which I was led by way of the history of art. *Intellige ut credas*! In my case, at least, understanding has involved belief; and for me the time has come to exchange the active for a more contemplative way of life in which it would be my hope to experience more immediately,

[2] [Some brief personal references, of no relevance to the theme, are deleted at this point.—ED.]

more fully, at least a part of the truth of which my understanding has been so far predominantly logical. And so, though I may be here for another year, I ask you also to say "good-by"—equally in the etymological sense of the word and in that of the Sanskrit *Svagā*, a salutation that expresses the wish "May you come into your own," that is, may I know and become what I am, no longer this man So-and-so, but the Self that is also the Being of all beings, my Self and your Self.

General Index

Index of Greek Terms

Index of Sanskrit and Pāli Terms

Note: This index, compiled by Kenneth J. Storey in consultation with Roger Lipsey, is arranged according to the Devanagari alphabet. Translations are those of Coomaraswamy when these are given in the text, and standard modern translations elsewhere. In the case of Sanskrit and Pāli cognates, the Sanskrit form appears first and the Pāli second.

GPSR Authorized Representative: Easy Access System Europe - Mustamäe tee 50, 10621 Tallinn, Estonia, gpsr.requests@easproject.com

www.ingramcontent.com/pod-product-compliance
Lightning Source LLC
LaVergne TN
LVHW050954080826
845145LV00006B/1492
* 9 7 8 0 6 9 1 2 7 7 5 3 0 *